*Deep Knowledge*

# AFRICANA RELIGIONS

*Edited by*
Sylvester A. Johnson, *Virginia Tech*

ADVISORY BOARD:
Afe Adogame, *Princeton Theological Seminary*
Sylviane Diouf, *Historian of the African Diaspora*
Paul C. Johnson, *University of Michigan*
Elizabeth Pérez, *University of California, Santa Barbara*
Elisha P. Renne, *University of Michigan*
Judith Weisenfeld, *Princeton University*

Adopting a global vision for the study of Black religions, the Africana Religions book series explores the rich diversity of religious history and life among African and African-descended people. It publishes research on African-derived religions of Orisha devotion, Christianity, Islam, and other religious traditions that are part of the Africana world. The series emphasizes the translocal nature of Africana religions across national, regional, and hemispheric boundaries.

# Deep Knowledge

*Ways of Knowing in Sufism and Ifa,
Two West African Intellectual Traditions*

OLUDAMINI OGUNNAIKE

The Pennsylvania State University Press
University Park, Pennsylvania

This book is freely available in an open access edition with the generous support of The Pennsylvania State University Libraries. Digital copies are available for download through the Pennsylvania State University Press website.

Library of Congress Cataloging-in-Publication Data

Names: Ogunnaike, Oludamini, author.
Title: Deep knowledge : ways of knowing in Sufism and Ifa, two west African intellectual traditions / Oludamini Ogunnaike.
Other titles: Africana religions.
Description: University Park, Pennsylvania : The Pennsylvania State University Press, [2020] | Series: Africana religions | Includes bibliographical references and index.
Summary: "Studies the epistemologies of two of the most influential intellectual/spiritual traditions of West Africa: Tijani Sufism and Ifa"—Provided by publisher.
Identifiers: LCCN 2020036971 | ISBN 9780271086903 (hardback)
Subjects: LCSH: Tijānīyah—Africa, West. | Ifa (Religion)—Africa, West. | Knowledge, Theory of (Religion)
Classification: LCC BP189.7.T5 O47 2020 | DDC 297.40966—dc23
LC record available at https://lccn.loc.gov/2020036971

Copyright © 2020 Oludamini Ogunnaike
All rights reserved
Printed in the United States of America
Published by The Pennsylvania State University Press,
University Park, PA 16802–1003

The Pennsylvania State University Press is a member of the Association of University Presses.

It is the policy of The Pennsylvania State University Press to use acid-free paper. Publications on uncoated stock satisfy the minimum requirements of American National Standard for Information Sciences—Permanence of Paper for Printed Library Material, ANSI Z39.48–1992.

FOR MY GRANDFATHER, ADEṢIJIBOMI OGUNDẸRỌ OGUNNAIKE,
AND ALL THOSE WHO CAME BEFORE.

FOR MY SON, JIBRIL OLUWAṢANUMI OGUNNAIKE,
AND ALL THOSE COMING AFTER.

# Contents

List of Illustrations  *viii*

Acknowledgments  *ix*

Introduction: African Philosophy?  *1*

### PART 1: WAYS OF KNOWING IN TIJANI SUFISM

1 | What Is Tijani Sufism?  *31*

2 | What Is *Ma'rifa*?  *56*

3 | How Is *Ma'rifa* Acquired?  *108*

4 | How Does *Tarbiya* Work?  *159*

### PART 2: WAYS OF KNOWING IN IFA

5 | What Is Ifa?  *195*

6 | Knowledge in Ifa  *231*

7 | How Is Knowledge Acquired in Ifa?  *251*

8 | How Is Knowledge Verified in Ifa?  *305*

### PART 3: COMPARING IFA AND TIJANI SUFISM

9 | Comparing Ifa and Tijani Sufism  *323*

10 | Comparative Conclusions  *351*

Notes  *397*

Index  *439*

# Illustrations

1. *Fayḍ* in macrocosm  49
2. *Fayḍ* in microcosm  50
3. Diagram of the Yoruba cosmos  211
4. Order of markings  216
5. Ranking of Odus  216
6. *Ọpẹlẹ* in the position of Odu Ika-Iwori  217
7. The sixteen primary Odu (in order of seniority)  261
8. Ọpọn cosmogram  293
9. The Ifẹ numbering of the sixteen basic figures  293

# Acknowledgments

الحمدلله

First and foremost, I wish to thank my parents, Dr. Babatunde and Anna Ogunnaike, for their love, support, example, and for teaching me to love knowledge. Neither this work nor any other achievement would be possible without them.

Next, I would like to thank my wife, Mrs. Naseemah Mohamed Ogunnaike, for her understanding, unflagging support, humor, care, and patience, and for her efforts in helping me edit this work. Thanks also to our son, Jibril, for distractions both welcome and unwelcome, and for helping me keep things in perspective.

Next, I would like to thank my brothers, Ayọdeji and Olumakinde Ogunnaike, who have supported this project from its inception in every conceivable way. Even though they are both younger than I am, I look up to them in many ways, and words cannot express the gratitude I feel for their generosity, ideas, encouragement, edits, selfless help, and inspiring conversations. Deji has also forgotten more about Ifa than I will ever know, and his advice on this project has been invaluable.

I am also deeply grateful to my adviser, professor Jacob Olupọna, for his tireless support of me and my work, for his inspiring example, and for giving me the freedom to explore my ideas with confidence. He has blazed the trail on which so many of us now walk.

I would also like to extend my deepest gratitude to professor Ousmane Kane and the entire Kane family, Sidi Ben Omar Kane, Sidi Mohamed Kane, Shaykha Maryam Niasse, and especially Zeynabou Kane, for their incredible hospitality, generosity, kindness, and friendship, as well as their insights on, and interest in, this project. The knowledge and experiences they shared with me, not to mention the doors they opened, are what have made this project possible.

Thanks are also due to Professor Agboola, Fajimi Faniyi, and especially the Araba of Modakẹkẹ, Chief Ifarinwale Ogundiran, for sharing their wisdom, time, knowledge, and for their patience and instruction. I would also like to extend my appreciation to my friend Wale Bambigboye for his selfless support and friendship during my stays in Nigeria, and I must also thank professors Ṣola Ajibade and David Ogungbile for their hospitality and insights and help during my research there. I am grateful as well to my Uncle Ṣeun, Aunty Bimbọ, and the rest of my family in Nigeria for going out of their way to take care of and host their "Fulani Man" on his travels.

Furthermore, I thank professor Khlaed el-Rouayheb for his consistent help, numerous discussions and correspondence, and impeccable scholarly example. I would also like to acknowledge professor David Carrasco for his every-ready encouragement and wisdom, and professor Barry Hallen for his support and interest in my work. I am also profoundly appreciative of the care, attention, and encouragement of professor James Morris, whose classes and seminars on Ibn ʿArabi and the Islamic humanities have deeply enriched my life and thinking. Moreover, I am grateful to the late professor Francis Abiola Irele for his support, professor John Mugane for his encouragement, friendship, and humor, and professor Biodun Jeyifo for his example.

I would also like to express my gratitude to Shaykh Māḥī Niasse, Pape Makkī, Pape Mahdi, Shaykh Māḥī Cissé, Shaykh Tijānī ʿAlī Cissé, and especially Sidi Inaya Niang and the late Ustadh Barham Diop, for generously sharing their precious time, knowledge, and profound insights with me.

For their encouragement, guidance, support, and inspiration, I am also sincerely grateful to Zachary Wright, Rudolph Ware, Andrea Brigaglia, and Rüdiger Seesemann.

Many heartfelt thanks go out as well to my friends—Abubakar Sadiq Abdulkadir, Shaykh Moustapha Niang, Sega Diagne, Mohammed "Momo" Diallo, Benoit Schirmer, Thierno Athie, Mehdi Boutayeb, Yousef Casewit, Alison Cohen, Nana Menya Ayensu, Olakunle Oladehin, Sangu Delle, Shankar Nair, Nariman Aavani, Nicholas Boylston, Munjed Murad, Nworah Ayogu, Nourhan Shaaban, Mafaz al-Suwaidan, Alex Angelov, and Brandon Terry—who have all supported me and my work over the years. I also thank Elliot Ikheloa, Gallaudet Howard, and Noor Sullivan for reading portions of the manuscript.

I am also grateful to the editors of this series, Sylvester Johnson and Edward Curtis, and to Patrick Alexander and Alex Vose of Penn State University Press for their patience, guidance, and flexibility in helping me to publish my first book. Many thanks are due to Nicholas Taylor for his diligent copyediting—any remaining errors are entirely my own. I would also like to thank the anonymous reviewers of the work who provided many helpful comments and suggestions.

Special thanks to Bob LaPointe of Harvard University, Robert Crews and Burcak Keskin-Kozat of Stanford's Abbasi Center for Islamic Studies, and Deans John Donahue and Kate Conley of the Faculty of Arts and Sciences at the College William and Mary for their assistance and financial support of this work, without which it could not have come to fruition.

I would also like to offer my gratitude to the Awan and Moneeb families for their hospitality and support during this project.

And last, but certainly not least, I must thank Gholamreza Aavani and especially Seyyed Hossein Nasr for introducing me to the living presence of philosophy and showing me what it means to truly love wisdom.

# Introduction
*African Philosophy?*

> Are those who know equal with those who know not?
> But only those of understanding will remember.
> —QUR'AN 39:9

> So ask the people of remembrance, if you do not know.
> —QUR'AN 16:43

> *Odo to ba gbagbe orisun, o ma gbę ni.*
> The spring that forgets its origin will run dry.
> —YORUBA PROVERB

While browsing through a bookstore during my first year of college, I saw the title of a book that got me so excited that I almost shouted out loud. The book was called *African Philosophy*, an anthology edited by Emmanuel Eze. I bought the book on the spot and almost ran into a few trees and lampposts on my way home because I could not take my eyes off it. But the more I read, the more my excitement cooled into disappointment. Aside from one or two articles, the book's title seemed to me to be false advertisement. I felt as if I had bought an album labeled *The Royal Drummers of Burundi*, but when I played the music it was Taylor Swift—enjoyable in its own right, but not what I was looking for.

A little bit of context will help explain why I felt this way. At the time, I had been reading, spellbound, a translation of al-Ghazālī's *Deliverance from Error* while borrowing the books and handouts from my roommate's Indian philosophy course, most of which were translations of mind-blowing primary texts by Buddhist philosophers such as Nagarjuna (d. 250 CE) and Dignaga (d. 540 CE) and the Vedantin philosophers Adi Shankara (d. ca. 820 CE) and Sri Harṣa (d. 1180 CE). In middle school and high school (besides the books on Greek and Norse mythology that my brothers and I wore the spines off), my favorite book was another anthology, *Classics of Philosophy* edited by Louis Pojman, which contained the equally mind-blowing (at least to me at the time) excerpts of the writings of some of the most influential figures in Western philosophy from the pre-Socratics to Wittgenstein, along with short introductions designed to contextualize the readings and make them more accessible. So, when I saw Eze's anthology, I was excited to have my mind blown again, but this time by the thinkers and traditions of Africa! I was expecting to be introduced to radically new ways of seeing the world (as Indian philosophy had done), to have my assumptions exposed and challenged (as both Indian and Western philosophy did), and to find the concepts and words for, and origins of, some of the ideas I already had half-formed in my head.

Instead, I found a group of academic articles, almost exclusively by Western-trained scholars, about what should count as African philosophy, and about the philosophy of race, gender, slavery, colonialism, and so forth. Almost all of the articles in the book seemed to be writing around the things I wanted to read about,[1] and virtually all of them seemed written from a perspective with which I had become familiar through years of schooling, but in which I never fully felt at home. With the exception of an article by the seventeenth-century Ethiopian philosopher Zera Yacob, I felt more at home in the works of al-Ghazālī, Nagarjuna, Plotinus, St. Augustine, and even Kierkegaard, Hume, Spinoza, and Wittgenstein, than I did in the articles of the *African Philosophy* anthology. I remember asking myself the following questions: If this was African philosophy, and I'm African, should I just suck it up and learn to love it, like I do with my great-aunt's *moin-moin* (bean cakes)? Is there no African equivalent to Greek, European, Indian, and Islamic philosophy? Does it matter if there is or is not? Should it matter?

I now have a bit of perspective on this important experience of disappointment. Part of the problem, I think, was that I was looking for the wrong thing. I was looking for an *African version* of the works of philosophy with which I already had some familiarity—that is, I was looking for a treatise with clearly stated premises, standard logical arguments, refutations of other known positions, and relatively clear conclusions that defined the author's position on a certain topic. I already knew what I was looking for and was just hoping to find a new flavor or style that perhaps had some resonances with my ancestry and upbringing. What I have since concluded is that while the works of many African intellectuals do fit this description (such as those of the neo-Platonic, North and Northeast African Christian, and the even more voluminous Islamic traditions of the continent), part of what makes the indigenous philosophies or intellectual traditions of the continent so interesting and worthy of study are the ways in which they *do not* fit this description. Practitioners of African traditions such as Ifa pursue knowledge and truth and engage in critical debates with one another, but they do so in very different ways, which I may not have recognized as philosophy back in the bookstore in 2003 during my first year of college.

Because of this, not only was I not looking for the right thing, I was also not looking in the right place. I began to realize this while reading Amadou Hampâté Bâ, the seminal Malian Africanist, belle-lettrist, activist, and scholar of traditional West African culture, orature, and religion. A Tijani Sufi himself, Bâ quotes his master Tierno Bokar's observation, "Writing is one thing and knowledge is another. Writing is the photographing of knowledge, but it is not knowledge itself. Knowledge is a light which is within man. It is the heritage all the ancestors knew and have transmitted to us as seed, just as the mature baobab is contained in its seed."[2] Or more succinctly, in the words of Shaykh Ibrahim Niasse (one of the focal points of this study), "Secrets are in the chests [*ṣudūr*] of the spiritual heroes [*rijāl*], not in the bellies of books."[3] Thus I came to realize that in order to find what I was looking for back in the bookstore, I would have change my ideas about what philosophy looks like and where I could find it.

The present work is the result of this effort to learn about, learn from, learn with, and present two "ways of knowing" popular in West Africa: Tijani Sufism and Ifa. The term "ways of knowing" has two meanings: (1) the process or manner in which something is known; and (2) a program, a path, a way of life characterized by knowledge. In this book, I present an account of the "ways of knowing" (first meaning) that are used in Tijani Sufism and Ifa, which are themselves "ways of knowing" (second meaning).

Ifa and the West African branches of Tijani Sufism are perhaps the most widespread and influential of African religious traditions, claiming millions of adherents throughout the continent as well as in Europe, North America, East Asia, and the Middle East (Sufism), and Europe, the Americas, and the Caribbean (Ifa). Texts and spiritual leaders of West African origin have wide influence and authority in these traditions, both of which have their geographic centers in the region: Ile-Ifẹ, Nigeria, for Ifa; and Medina Baye, Senegal, for the most widespread branch of Tijani order, the Fayḍa, founded by Shaykh Ibrahim Niasse (d. 1975). While issues of "African" authenticity are largely outside the scope of this project, both traditions had a significant presence in precolonial West Africa. Moreover, the practices and opinions of communities in Senegal and Nigeria are regarded as authoritative and normative by many adherents worldwide, and people come from around the globe to study with babalawo (priests of Ifa) in Nigeria and shaykhs (Sufi masters) in Senegal. There is a modest but growing secondary literature on these traditions in European languages, which attests to the intellectual sophistication and wide appeal of both traditions. Thus Tijani Sufism and

Ifa represent two different African worldviews and ways of knowing, similar in transnational appeal and profound influence.

After providing a brief introduction to each tradition (chapters 1 and 5), I discuss how each tradition defines knowledge, how these forms of knowledge are acquired, and how they are verified (chapters 2, 3, 4, 6, 7, and 8). Finally, I conclude with a comparison of these two traditions to each other and to contemporary academic perspectives (chapters 9 and 10, respectively). Chapters 1 and 5 can serve as stand-alone introductions to Tijani Sufism and Ifa, respectively; alternatively, chapters 2 through 4 can serve as a detailed study of Tijani epistemology, while chapters 6 through 8 can serve as a completely separate in-depth study of epistemology in Ifa. The two traditions are neither compared nor addressed together before the ninth chapter.

But before moving on to these discussions, it is important to consider the reasons I did not find what I was looking for in the bookstore all those years ago. Why did the anthology (with a few exceptions) not have the kind of African philosophy, the "photographs of knowledge," I sought? And why was I looking for that kind of philosophy in the first place? To answer these questions, we must first understand a bit of the history of philosophy itself, and how I (and most of the rest of the Western-educated world) came to have the particular conception of it that I did back in 2003.

## CLEARING THE GROUND: AFRICA, RELIGION, PHILOSOPHY, AND RATIONALITY

**A Brief History of the Conception of Philosophy in the West**

Although it is now a professional academic discipline and subject of study like mathematics, physics, economics, or history, philosophy started out as something rather different. The first person to call himself a "philosopher" (*philosophos*, which means "friend or lover of wisdom") was probably Pythagoras (d. 495 BCE),[4] whom we all know for his theorem about triangles. But just as Pythagoras's geometry was about much more than shapes and angles, his school of philosophy, which we today would probably call a religion, cult, or monastic order, was concerned with achieving a divine mode of life. Through initiation, strict moral discipline, secret lessons on the esoteric symbolism of numbers and forms, the study of the world through this numeric symbolism, and other ritual exercises, including listening to music, Pythagoras's school sought to mold the characters of its members into this divine ideal. This school is believed to have profoundly influenced Plato (d. 348 BCE) and his Academy, which was but one of many such philosophical schools that operated in Greek and Roman antiquity.

These schools or brotherhoods of philosophers differed greatly on some points, but all of them were concerned with using argument and reason (as well as other rituals) as "spiritual exercises" in order to cultivate an ideal way of life. As Pierre Hadot writes:

> Philosophy thus took on the form of an exercise of the thought, will, and the totality of one's being, the goal of which was to achieve a state practically inaccessible to mankind: wisdom. Philosophy was a method of spiritual progress which demanded a radical conversion and transformation of the individual's way of being. Thus, philosophy was a way of life, both in its exercise and effort to achieve wisdom, and in its goal, wisdom itself. For real wisdom does not merely cause us to know: it makes us "be" in a different way.... First and foremost, philosophy presented itself as a therapeutic, intended to cure mankind's anguish.[5]

Thus the idea of the "philosopher" and "philosophy" of the ancient Greek, Hellenistic, and Roman eras was something very different from the contemporary idea and practice of academic philosophy, although something of the older notion still resonates in today's popular imagination.

The coming of Christianity eventually eclipsed these philosophical schools, but many of their texts, practices, ideas, and terminology (including that of "philosophy" itself) were assimilated (and transformed) by Christian thinkers to the extent that many Christian intellectuals interpreted and presented Christianity itself, especially the monastic life, *as philosophy*.[6] The texts, doctrines, and exercises of the Greek and Roman philosophical schools did not only find a receptive home in Christianity, they were also taken up with great enthusiasm and creativity in Islamic civilization (by Muslims, Christians, and Jews living under Islamic rule) from the ninth century onward, as well as by some pre-Islamic Jewish intellectuals, such as Philo of Alexandria (d. 50 CE).

What many today call Islamic philosophy took the form of many distinct traditions that engaged with Greek and Roman philosophical traditions in various ways. The discipline or science known in Arabic as *falsafa* or *ḥikma* creatively engaged with Pythagorean, Aristotelian, neo-Platonic, Stoic, and other traditions and sought to wed them with, and interpret them in the light of, Islamic prophecy and spirituality. To a large extent, this discipline maintained the goal of cultivating an ideal mode of life that characterized Greek and Roman philosophy. The most important and influential philosopher of this tradition was Ibn Sīnā (d. 1037), known as Avicenna in the medieval West. However, his influence in the West was eclipsed by that of Ibn Rushd (Averroës) (d. 1198), who, ironically, never had much influence in the Islamic world as a philosopher, being better known as a first-rate jurist of the Mālikī school of jurisprudence (*fiqh*). As he was the last Muslim philosopher to have a significant impact on Western thought, some Western scholars (and their Muslim students) declared Islamic philosophy dead after Ibn Rushd, but the fact is that the traditions of *falsafa* and *ḥikma* have continued to thrive and produce remarkable works and thinkers such as Suhrawardī (d. 1191), Naṣīr al-Dīn Ṭūsī (d. 1275), Quṭb al-Dīn al-Shīrāzī (d. 1311), Mullā Ṣadrā (d. 1640), Sabzawārī (d. 1873), ʿAllāma Ṭabāṭabāʾī (d. 1981), and Seyyed Hossein Nasr (b. 1933).

Since the twelfth century CE, however, the discipline of *falsafa/ḥikma* began to become more integrated with the disciplines of *kalām* (theology) and *taṣawwuf* (Sufism, a tradition of Islamic mysticism or spirituality). The discipline of *kalām* was primarily concerned with the dialectic exposition, proof, and defense of Islamic doctrines about God, man, and the cosmos, and its various schools engaged in highly sophisticated arguments with one another and with schools of *falsafa* and Sufism that would be considered philosophical by any measure.[7] The work of al-Ghazālī (d. 1111), the most celebrated Islamic theologian (*mutakallim*) of the Ashʿarī school, shows the increasing convergence between Sufism, theology, and *falsafa* in Islamic philosophical thought. Sufism will be introduced more fully in the next chapter, but for the purposes of the current discussion, it designates an important tradition of Islamic spirituality and thought that posited and sought a direct, experiential knowledge of God (*maʿrifa*) through an intensive regimen of spiritual exercises. The Sufis articulated this knowledge in various forms, often borrowing from, debating, and engaging with the traditions of theology and *falsafa*, to the extent that it became difficult to distinguish the three disciplines in the works of many figures from the twelfth century (the sixth Islamic century) onward. Prominent examples of such syntheses that came to dominate Islamic intellectual life include Suhrawardī's "Philosophy of Illumination" (*ḥikmat al-ishrāq*) and the Andalusian Sufi Ibn ʿArabi's (d. 1240) school, both of which were integrated into Mullā Ṣadrā's school of "Transcendent Philosophy" (*al-ḥikma al-mutaʿāliya*). In the Western lands of the Islamic world, even the most popular texts of theology, such as the *Umm al-Barāhīn* (*Source of Proofs*) of al-Sanūsī (d. 1486), which was and still is widely used in North and West Africa, comprise a synthesis of ideas and terminology from Avicennan philosophy (*falsafa*), Ashʿarī theology (*kalām*), and Sufism (*taṣawwuf*).

Overall, the tradition of Islamic philosophy was and is characterized by a synthesis of reason, mystical intuition, and revelation, and an abiding interest in cultivating an ideal way of life, just as it was for the philosophers of Greek and Roman antiquity.[8] For the Islamic philosophers, righteous living, logical thinking, ritual practice, and spiritual realization supported and reinforced one another.[9]

However, Islamic philosophy's sister tradition of Christian philosophy/theology was to go in a very different direction, especially during the Renaissance and Enlightenment. In Western Europe, from the thirteenth century onward, philosophy and theology began to drift apart—philosophy being reduced to its technical and discursive aspects and made the "handmaiden of theology"—until the two disciplines became completely separate and even antagonistic with the arrival of Descartes. The gradual hardening of the Catholic Church's dogmatic Aristotelianism combined with the new availability of Greek and Roman texts led to the decline of scholasticism and the rise of new forms of philosophy and new relationships between philosophy and Christianity.[10] Most significant, however, was the gradual collapsing of the classical triad of noetic faculties: intellect (Latin: *intellectus*; Greek: *nous*), reason (Latin: *ratio*; Greek: *dianoia*), and the senses (Latin: *sensus*; Greek: *aisthesis*) into just reason and sense. In Platonic, neo-Platonic, and many Christian schools of philosophy and theology, the intellect was a faculty that allowed one to directly perceive truths of a metaphysical nature and, in some cases, was even described as being mysteriously united with God or the Holy Spirit. Hadot illustrates the distinction between reason and intellect in Plotinus's philosophy by explaining that his philosophy was not meant "to be a discourse about objects, be they even the highest, but it wishes actually to lead the soul to a living, concrete union with the Intellect and the Good. . . . Reason, by theological methods, can raise itself to the *notion* of the Good, but only life according to Intellect can lead to the *reality* of the Good."[11]

In the late Renaissance and early modern period, philosophers gradually abandoned this distinction between intellect and reason, rejecting or reducing the former to the latter, and reading this rationalist tendency back into the Greek, Latin, and Arabic texts they translated. Thus, the only valid sources of knowledge became reason and the senses. As a result, the "wisdom" that was philosophy's goal became more mental and practical and less existential and divine. In this way, the conception of philosophy gradually shifted away from "a way of life" to a mode of rational discourse, or as Hadot says, from "philosophy" to "philosophical discourse."[12]

With this gradual disappearance of the intellect from Western philosophical discourse in the early modern period (fifteenth–eighteenth century), philosophy also became more distant from theology and mysticism. Furthermore, as the senses and reason came to be regarded as the only sources of knowledge, "the immaterial became immaterial," and the elaborate metaphysical cosmologies of medieval Europe gradually faded from mainstream intellectual life and thought. Moreover, reason replaced intellect as the *imago Dei*, the divine trace that marked man as being made in God's image, and rationality rather than spirituality or conformity to the Divine through the intellect became the measure of humanity. But as God was no longer directly perceived by the *intellectus*, but abstracted from sensory data and the rational faculty, His role in Western intellectual thought became more and more vague and distant, culminating in the nineteenth-century view of the divine as a creation of the mind of man—a god made in man's own image.[13]

While the possible reasons for these related shifts are many and complex,[14] the early modern thinkers seemed to want to create a space for themselves to think outside the theological dominion of the church. From its inception, the Enlightenment project of the modern period was concerned with creating and defining itself *against* its past through categories based on the newly enthroned reason. For example, the post-classical, pre-Renaissance period became known as the "medieval" period, or Middle Ages, or "Dark Ages" based on the early modern notion that this period marked a lapse in Europe's history between two glorious ages of reason: the Greco-Roman classical period, and its "rebirth" in the Renaissance. And so modern philosophy emerged as a privileged category of difference, to define "reborn" or "enlightened" Western Europe against and elevate it above its ancestral past and other civilizations.

Relatedly, the new philosophy of the Enlightenment (as opposed to the religious theology of the Middle Ages) emerged as one of a number of new categories created to define modern Europe against and above its "other," what it considered itself not to be. For example, the medieval category "mystical" (*Mustikos*) was used to refer to three closely linked elements: a method of allegorical biblical interpretation (such as Dante's anagogical), liturgical mysteries (such as the Eucharist), and the contemplative or experiential knowledge of God.[15] However, the Enlightenment philosophers, especially Kant, took up the task of oppositional definition and defined the new, rational "philosophy" against "mysticism," which was in turn defined against rationality and characterized as subjective as opposed to objective, emotive as opposed to intellectual, private as opposed to public, irrational as opposed to rational, and so forth. Mystical worldviews were dismissed as backward and prerational, mystical experiences became subjective psychological states (usually described as the result of some kind of disorder), mystical practices and rituals were dismissed as "superstition" and "magic," and mystical modes of interpretation such as allegory were largely relegated to secular literary criticism and poetry.[16] This deeply affected modern readings of classical and medieval thinkers, as the seemingly "rational" elements, texts, and figures were emphasized and the seemingly "mystical" elements, texts, and figures were excised and devalued. For modern thinkers such as Kant, "the mystical" was the death of philosophy, in part because the modern conception of "philosophy" was given life through its definition against "the mystical."

As the work of Emmanuel Eze and Peter K. J. Park has demonstrated,[17] this dynamic had profound significance for Enlightenment Europe's understanding of itself in relation to other civilizations and peoples. With the disappearance of the *intellectus/nous*, and the noetic realms of reality perceivable only by it (the divine and angelic realms or world of Platonic Forms), Western man found himself in the curious position of being at the top of the "great chain of being," the neo-Platonic and medieval hierarchy of the cosmos.[18] To be sure, God and heaven still lurked in the background or up in the clouds somewhere; but in terms of the knowable, perceivable universe of philosophers and scientists, Western, rational man was at the summit, with his newly defined rationality as the mark of his superiority. Whereas in the Middle Ages humanity was judged by participation in or proximity to a transcendent, divine ideal (Christ or God), the secularization process of the Enlightenment resulted in humanity being judged by proximity to the immanent ideal of rational, enlightened European man.[19]

In the nineteenth century, Hegel explicitly enunciated this doctrine, declaring Western Europe "the land of the elevation of the particular to the universal";[20] and eighteenth-century English dissident philosopher James Beattie wrote, "That every practice and sentiment is barbarous which is not according to the usages of Modern Europe seems to be a fundamental maxim with many of our critics and philosophers."[21] The particular mode of reasoning that came to characterize Enlightenment thought was elevated to the level of "universal reason," the mark and determiner of humanity. This allowed Enlightenment thinkers, and their descendants, to "speak from nowhere and for everyone." Just as the Enlightenment thinkers defined themselves against their "dark," "mystical," and "irrational" past, they also defined themselves against their "dark," "mystical," and "irrational" neighbors. Thus, membership in this elite class of humanity—"rational Europeans" (what later became "whiteness")—emerged as the transcendence of "race," which was seen as a privation of full humanity, an impediment to participation in that which makes one human: rationality.

Kant and Hegel also contributed to the development of a temporalization of this "great chain of being," creating a narrative in which the rational faculty was responsible for man's progress from "primitive" to "civilized." In his works on geography, on which he lectured more than any other subject, Kant argued that "lower" human beings exist for the sake and use of those at a "higher level of humanity"—of greater rationality—just as plants exist for the sake of animals.[22] Similarly, Hegel's evolutionary theory established a temporal continuum with evil, ignorance, darkness, the past, the "primitive" and the nonwhite races of humanity on one end; and good, knowledge, light, the future, "civilization," progress, and the white race on the other. In his *Lectures on the Philosophy of World History*, Hegel combined this teleology with environmental determinism to argue for the right and duty of the conquest, subjugation, and even elimination of the dark side of the continuum by the light.[23]

This is the philosophy at the foundations of modern notions of progress and development. Socially and politically, the markers of "full humanity" have shifted from "rationality" to "scientific and technological innovation," "liberal democracy," and "human rights,"[24] but the basic architecture and the complexion of the people at the top of the hierarchy generally remain the same. Thus, philosophy became more than just a means of rational inquiry; by exemplifying the functioning of rationality, it became an important criterion for "civilized humanity," and provided the rationale to "civilize," often with great force, those segments of humanity deemed lacking in it. So as imperial Europe came into contact with the intellectual traditions of other civilizations, it compared them to the "mystical" thought of the European medieval period, categorized them as "irrational," and generally considered none of them to "rise to the level of philosophy."[25]

This has begun to change in recent years due to the careful study by Western-trained scholars of Islamic as well as South and East Asian texts and thinkers whose sophisticated logic, dialectics, critical acumen, and well-developed theories made it difficult for scholars to categorize these traditions as "irrational." As Jay Garfield writes, illustrating this new approach and broader understanding of "philosophy":

> Ignoring the philosophical traditions of other cultures in fact, whether we like it or not, continues the colonial project of subordinating those cultures to our own. That project was "justified" by the white man's burden of bringing civilization to the benighted heathen, a burden of which we can only make sense if we deny their manifestly existent intellectual traditions the epistemic status we grant ours. Giving the Western philosophical tradition pride of place as "philosophy" while marginalizing in our departments or in our individual life all other traditions . . . hence implicates us directly in institutional racism. Recognizing that we are so implicated and refraining from changing our individual practice and from working to change our institutional practice constitutes, however passive it may be, individual racism. It also constitutes a profound epistemic vice, that of willfully ignoring sources of knowledge we know to be relevant to our own activities.[26]

But what of those traditions that do not so closely resemble modern European philosophy, and are thus not so easily recognized? What of the intellectual traditions of the Amerindians, of the Polynesians and Aboriginal Australians, and what of those of Africans, the ultimate racial other of the Enlightenment?

**African Philosophy?**

Most of the contemporary debates about what should and should not be called African philosophy appear to boil down to arguments over the worth or status of the tradition in question, and thus whether it is worthy of the privileged category of "philosophy," or debates about the authenticity of the tradition, and thus if it is worthy of the appellation "African."[27] Because such concerns are foreign to the traditions I have studied (most babalawo and Sufis do not care whether people call them "African philosophers"), this issue is not urgent for my work; however, were I to suggest a definition of philosophy, it would be the original Socratic or Pythagorean sense of the term, "the love of wisdom," the love and pursuit of that *sophia* (Greek), *sapientia* (Latin), *ḥikma* (Arabic) that is at once knowledge and an ideal mode of being. Defining the "African" half of "African philosophy" is more difficult (not least of all because the adjective "African" is a largely peripheral and foreign category to these traditions that divide the world up in different ways),[28] but I would reserve it for those continuous indigenous (itself a problematic term), Christian, and Islamic traditions that have shaped and been shaped by people living on the continent for several generations. So, for example, a Russian man initiated into Ifa and practicing in England would qualify as a member of an African philosophical tradition, while a Yoruba woman living in Lagos who is a student of Buddhist Madhyamika philosophy would not.[29] The work of Africans on the continent and in the diaspora in various traditions of Western philosophy may be insightful, incisive, and interesting philosophical discourse, but in this definition, it would not qualify as what I would call "traditional African philosophy."

The following contrasting historical examples should help to clarify this point. Anton Wilhem Amo (ca. 1703–ca. 1759) was an Akan man from the Axim region of present-day Ghana who was brought to Germany as a child, where he was raised as a member of the family of the Duke of Brunswick-Wolfenbüttel. He studied at the Universities of Helmstedt, Halle, and Wittenberg, and received his doctorate in philosophy from the University of Wittenberg in 1734 for his dissertation, an argument against Cartesian dualism titled "On the Absence of Sensation in the Human Mind and Its Presence in Our Organic and Living Body." He lectured at the Universities of Halle and Jena, but after his patron, the duke, died, life in Germany became more difficult for him. In 1747, Amo returned to Ghana, and little is known about his life thereafter, save that he died around 1759.[30]

Susanne Wenger (1915–2009) was an Austrian artist who married the German scholar Ulli Beier and moved with him to Nigeria in 1949, when the latter accepted a post at the University of Ibadan, Nigeria. She was attracted to the traditional Yoruba religious ceremonies she heard going on down the street and, after a bout with tuberculosis, was initiated by the priest Ajagemọ into the mysteries of the Oriṣa Ọbatala (a Yoruba deity). She became a respected and important priestess, and eventually settled in the town of Oṣogbo, where she revived the worship at the town's Sacred Grove of Ọṣun (the Yoruba goddess of beauty and magic), building shrines for the Oriṣa (Yoruba deities) and fostering a whole "school" of traditional worshippers and artists. In large part thanks to her efforts, the Sacred Grove was declared a UNESCO World Heritage Site in 2005. Upon her death in 2009, one of her students offered the following tribute:

"Her internment completes Susan Wenger's transformation into a spirit, as devotees will henceforth make supplications to her, too."[31] In this definition, Susanne Wenger (and any who have followed in her footsteps) could be considered as a traditional African philosopher, whereas Anton Amo (and those who have followed in his footsteps) would not.

This is what I think I was looking for all those years ago in the bookshop, and why the piece by the seventeenth-century Ethiopian philosopher Zera Yacob was the one that spoke to me the most out of all of the articles in Eze's anthology. Now, as with any definition, this suggested one becomes fuzzier the more one investigates it. It is possible and increasingly common for someone to be a member of, and have training in, several different intellectual traditions, both traditional African and modern Western ones. Moreover, given the strong influence some of these traditions still exert on the general cultures of their societies (such as those of the Yoruba- or Dogon-speaking peoples among others), it is often difficult to say who belongs to a tradition and who does not. However, these traditions often draw their own boundaries through rites of initiation. Nevertheless, this provisional definition differs most strongly from those discussed above, not by the way it defines "African," but by the way it defines "philosophy," distinguishing "philosophical discourse" from "philosophy itself," which is envisioned as a way of life, a love and pursuit of wisdom. Within this definition, some African philosophers may engage in written philosophical discourse, some (like Socrates) may engage in oral philosophical discourse, and others may not engage in philosophical discourse at all. It is not the discourse, but rather the practice of philosophy, as in Plato's definition from the *Phaedo*, as a "preparation for death," that is of greatest significance. The critiques that these traditions should not be called philosophical because they are not "critical" or "written" or "discursive" would thus be irrelevant. It would be like arguing that Genghis Khan should not be called a "world conqueror" because he did not play the video game of the same name—the two definitions of philosophy deal with different domains.

There is something of an inferiority complex that drives many scholars on the African continent and in the major centers of learning abroad to beg for the recognition and acceptance of these traditions (and/or their own work) into the privileged category of philosophy by trying to emphasize their similarities with contemporary academic philosophical theories. This has not been terribly successful, and with good reason, since what should be of interest is not the mere fact that precolonial Africans learned Aristotelian logic, but the distinct ideas, theories, perspectives, and modes of life developed by these African thinkers (e.g., why they learned, and what they did with Aristotelian logic). Musicians do not go to West Africa to hear local symphonies play Beethoven and Bartók; they go to appreciate, learn from, and be inspired by the region's many incredible indigenous musical traditions.[32] Moreover, these musical traditions do not rely on Western approval for their continued relevance, popularity, and success, and neither do traditional African intellectual traditions. While traditional African philosophies may be of interest to non-Africans and Africans alike for the alternative perspectives they offer to recently dominant ways of life and knowing, I argue that, like traditional African musical traditions, they should be of interest, not because they are African, but because they are good—because their accounts of reality, the self, virtue, knowledge, and so forth, and the ways of life they exemplify, are compelling.

The facts, as I see them, are these:

1. The African continent has been and currently is home to a number of intellectual traditions, including some of the earliest to bear the name "philosophy" (North African Pythagoreanism, Platonism, neo-Platonism, etc.).
2. Some of these traditions are relatively recent importations from modern Europe, take place primarily in European languages, are taught in modern universities, and are primarily based on modern Western European worldviews, philosophies, and pedagogies.
3. Some of these traditions have a longer history on the continent, primarily take place in non-European languages, and are based on traditional worldviews, philosophies, and pedagogies that are distinct from those of modern, Western Europe.
4. Many of these traditions have long written traditions of discursive, rational argument (in Greek, Latin, Ge'ez, Arabic, Swahili, etc.) in addition to their oral traditions, while others, while still critical and dynamic, are "unlettered."[33]
5. Virtually all of these older, traditional, non-Europhone traditions are categorized as "religious" and bear a family resemblance to the ancient Greco-Roman schools of philosophy in terms of methods and goals: ritual practices and exercises leading to the cultivation of "wisdom," an ideal mode of life. On the other hand, virtually all of the newer, modern, Europhone traditions do not share in this family resemblance, and focus instead on philosophical, academic, or modern scientific discourse.
6. The members of these older, non-Europhone traditions have done and are doing sophisticated, compelling, and profound intellectual work that is worthy of academic attention.
7. Virtually all of these traditional, non-Europhone traditions exist quite independently of the modern academic traditions, have their own names for their traditions and categories of thought, and many of their members are largely

unconcerned with whether what they are doing is called "philosophy" by those outside the tradition.

Given these facts, the question now becomes, how does one engage with these traditional, primarily non-Europhone traditions?

Valentin Mudimbe's *Invention of Africa*[34] convincingly demonstrates many of the dangers and pitfalls involved in trying to represent "Africa" in Western discourses. His basic argument is that discourse about Africa, even by Africans, takes place firmly within dominant Western discourses and philosophies, and thus tells us more about the Western training of the author than it does about anything "African." Mudimbe asserts that the vast imbalance in political and epistemic power between Western discourse about Africa and the reality of Africa itself prevents "Africa" from becoming anything more than a product of Western theory and imagination. He labels this secret "knowledge" that experts claim to represent in their books and articles about Africa as "gnosis."

As this discussion illustrates, academia has inherited a tradition of ignorance and arrogance when it comes to other intellectual traditions, especially those of Africa. This has provoked the problematic reactions of *négritude*, Afrocentrism, and certain new age movements, which (like other colonized nationalisms—e.g., Arab, Turkish, Persian, and Hindu) accept the basic categories of the "oppressive" discourse (such as "racial essence," "rational," "mystical," "philosophical," and "civilization") they seek to counter in their representations of Africa. In their many forms, these reactionary movements describe an imaginary Manichean dichotomy in which the "African" is natural, intuitive, and spiritual in contrast to the artificial, rational and material West. While such reactions are understandable, they are limited by their acceptance of these colonial categories.

Similarly, as Mudimbe, Paulin Hountondji, and others have demonstrated, Western attempts to understand and engage with traditional African worldviews and philosophies are fraught with the difficulties inherent in trying to learn and then represent a particular tradition from the perspective, and in the language, of another tradition. *Traduttori traditori*, the Italian saying goes—"Translators, traitors." And yet, translation, or at least something like it, does happen.

Following other postmodern thinkers, one of the main contentions of Mudimbe's work seems to be that the representation of "Africa" will never be the thing itself, and will thus always be the product of Western imagination, a mental construction of Western discourse. To use a linguistic analogy, when writing a translation of an Arabic text in English, I have to obey the conventions and rules of English prose, punctuation, and capitalization (which are not shared by Arabic), and when reading (especially if I am a nonnative speaker), I bring my own categories of thought, deeply shaped by my own mother tongue, to bear on the text. Similarly, when presenting African traditions in Western academic discourse one must follow the academic conventions of logic, argument, genre, and even theory that are often not shared by the "translated" tradition. Moreover, one often brings one's own theoretical assumptions, often unshared by the tradition, to bear on the study of it.

For Mudimbe, as for many poststructuralist and postmodern theorists, the task of representation and translation seems to be an impossible one. What one produces is a work "inspired" by the object of inquiry, but not an "accurate" representation. Some accounts may be better than others, but this superiority can only be relative, since one can never access the truth or reality of the original, which is located "outside of the text," the discourse, and the self. This account of representation is based on something akin to the Kantian distinction between the noumenal and phenomenal, "things as they really are" and "things as they appear to us." Ironically, this distinction is not universally held, and is certainly not absolute in many traditions I would classify as "African philosophies." For example, in Sufism and some traditions of Islamic philosophy (and other neo-Platonic philosophies), the intellect (*al-'aql*), especially in its highest form (the Universal Intellect [*al-'aql al-kullī*] or the Divine Intellect [*al-'aql al-rabbānī*]), can know things directly, "as they are," because it is identical with their ontological root. The resulting knowledge, coincidentally, is also known as "gnosis." Thus Mudimbe's "problem of translation" derives from the very fact that he situates himself within a particular Western (primarily Foucauldian) epistemology in which such "gnosis" is not a real possibility.[35]

Returning to the metaphor of translation, in his essay the "The Task of the Translator" Walter Benjamin quotes a passage by the German philosopher Rudolf Pannwitz that I believe both elegantly describes and points the way out of this impasse:

> Our translations, even the best ones, proceed from a mistaken premise. They want to turn Hindi, Greek, English into German instead of turning German into Hindi, Greek, English. Our translators have a far greater reverence for the usage of their own language than for the spirit of the foreign works.... The basic error of the translator is that he preserves the state in which his own language happens to be instead of allowing his language to be powerfully affected by the foreign tongue. Particularly when translating from a language very remote from his own, he must go back to the primal elements of language itself and penetrate to the point where work, image, and tone converge. He must expand and deepen his language by means of the foreign language.... However, this last is true only if one takes language seriously enough, not if one takes it lightly.[36]

Similarly, I would argue that many, if not most attempts at engaging with, describing, or performing African philosophies (and other, traditional intellectual traditions from around the world) have tried to turn them into contemporary Western philosophies and theories. Especially when dealing with intellectual traditions that differ greatly from those of the (post)modern West, it behooves scholars to go back into the historical and philosophical origins of their own discourses to examine where categories such as "reason," "mysticism," "religion," "practice," and "theory" converge and emerge.

Western-educated scholars who wish to understand African thought would do well to revisit the premodern philosophical traditions of Greco-Roman antiquity (especially Platonism and neo-Platonism) as well as medieval and Eastern Orthodox Christian theology. By this I do not mean the caricatures of this thought that have emerged after the Enlightenment. Any scholar familiar with the Pythagoreans, the Orphic mysteries, Socrates's *daimon*, Plato's mythology, the theurgy of the neo-Platonists,[37] the spiritual exercises of the early church fathers, the syntheses of critical reason, revelation, and mystical experience and exegesis found in medieval Catholic and Orthodox theologians, philosophers, and mystics, would instantly recognize parallels with traditional African rituals, modes of expression, and thought, and would be in a much better position to understand these diverse African traditions, and their similarities to and differences from various Western traditions. The spiritual and mystical dimensions of these philosophical traditions can no more be excised from their "rational" elements than the racist dimensions of Enlightenment thinkers such as Kant and Hegel can be excised from their more "rational" elements. My point here is not that these Enlightenment thinkers are wrong because they are racist, but rather that they are racist because they are wrong about knowledge, its conditions, and the universality of their theories.

Moreover, just as Pannwitz suggested that the translated language should "powerfully affect" and "expand and deepen" the language into which it is translated, African traditions can and should "powerfully affect," expand, and deepen Western conceptions of philosophy and theory, and transform its discourses, but this can only happen if they are approached with reverence and taken seriously. To give a concrete linguistic example, this expansion and reshaping can be seen in the influence of Arabic on languages as diverse as Wolof, Swahili, Persian, and Malay, many of whose speakers have learned Arabic, and many more of whom interact with the Arabic language through daily religious rites—all of which has had a deep and lasting influence on the vocabulary, categories, and in some cases even the grammatical structures of these languages. Or, to give an example a bit closer to home, in describing Wọle Ṣoyinka's "Big English" (*Igilango Gẹẹsi*), Biọdun Jeyifo remarked, "When you use language in the *Igilango Gẹẹsi* manner, you are transforming the English language, you are doing things with it and in it that the owners of the language themselves had not thought imaginable."[38] I argue that we should do the same with Western theories and the philosophies behind them.[39]

## APPROACHING AFRICAN INTELLECTUAL TRADITIONS ON THEIR OWN TERMS

In light of the difficulties highlighted in the above discussion, prominent scholars from a wide range of disciplines, including Latin American studies, South Asian studies, sociology, anthropology, religious studies, Islamic studies, history, and African studies have proposed the development of a "theory from the South" or "indigenous theory." For example, the scholar of Yoruba art Babatunde Lawal writes, "Unfortunately, some scholars have become so obsessed with theories which attempt to relate the 'particular' to the 'universal' that their conclusions often reflect the Eurocentric bias of the theories *per se* rather than the traditions of the culture they purport to analyze. Moreover, the search for paradigms often results in intellectual fantasies that mystify rather than clarify the subject being studied. A number of scholars . . . have called for a new critical approach that will allow African traditions to be studied on their own terms, instead of being viewed through Eurocentric lenses."[40]

This dynamic is particularly troublesome when the theories and the theorized differ in power, place, and culture, but is especially so when they differ radically in their worldviews and philosophies that define "power, place, and culture." It's hard enough for an American university student to understand an English-language article about colonial history written by a West African academic, but it can be an even more complicated task to get the same student to understand an Arabic poem by a West African Sufi, because the worldviews expressed therein are even more different. However, from another perspective (perhaps that of the Sufi poet), the poem could be easier to understand than the article, because it addresses universal matters of the heart (or at least more so than does the academic work). These dynamics illustrate the inescapable effects of perspective and theory and highlight the importance of this call for new methods that allow cultures and traditions to "speak for themselves."

However, such methods are not necessarily "new," as demonstrated by the seminal works of Ananda Coomaraswamy on Asian art and philosophy, Toshihiko Izutsu on East Asian and Islamic philosophy, Seyyed Hossein Nasr and William Chittick on Islamic philosophy and Sufism, and Jacob Olupọna and Rowland Abiọdun on Yoruba religion and art (to name but a few). What all of these figures have in common is a strong grasp of Western philosophy and a remarkably profound understanding not only of the languages of the traditions they study, but also of the metaphysics and epistemologies of these traditions, with which they have a great affinity, and even identity. Moreover, their works are largely presented from the perspective, and in the terms of, the traditions studied, and so one frequently finds Arabic, Persian, Chinese, Sanskrit, and Yoruba terms—not "sprinkled in for flavoring," but as the fundamental categories of thought and analysis. Additionally, they all emphasize the relevance of the works and figures they study not merely for an academic understanding of the intellectual, artistic, or political history of a particular sector of humanity, but also for the merits of their arguments and their relevance to the art of being human, a position very much in line with the traditions themselves. Thus, at times, these works can seem to stretch the contemporary conventions of academic language and genre, although never abandoning scholarly rigor in the process.

The present work is inspired by Toshihiko Izutsu's groundbreaking *Sufism and Taoism*, which demonstrates the power of taking seriously two non-Western thinkers and their arguments on their own terms (much as academics would with figures like Spinoza or Descartes) and the profound insights that can emerge from such a comparison.[41] William Chittick's books on the Sufi thinkers Ibn 'Arabi and Rumi (d. 1273) have also been particularly useful in demonstrating how to let texts and traditions "speak for themselves."[42] These books mostly consist of original translations from the primary texts of these two figures. However, through careful arrangement, discussion, and contextualizations of these texts, what emerges is much more than a straightforward translation; rather, it is a masterful exposition of the oeuvres of thinkers, almost entirely in their own words, and seemingly from their own perspectives. I have tried to follow suit in this work, allowing the texts and members of the tradition to speak for themselves as much as possible, and I beg the reader's indulgence and patience with the resulting long quotations from interviews and translations of texts, which I deemed necessary in order to preserve the unique voices of each tradition.[43] Valerie Hoffman's *Sufism, Mystics, and Saints in Modern Egypt* also provided an important model for combining the study of classical texts and contemporary representatives of a tradition.[44]

**Ibn 'Arabi as a Theorist**

However, the primary theoretical inspiration and model for the present work comes from the work of the thirteenth-century Andalusian Sufi, Ibn 'Arabi. Another one of Chittick's works, *Imaginal Worlds*, invites us to consider Ibn 'Arabi, known as the Shaykh al-Akbar, "the greatest master," as a theorist of religion. Chittick writes:

> The bewildering diversity of religion's historical actuality is accentuated by the great variety of methodological approaches that are employed by specialists to study religion. Each of these approaches makes important contributions to our understanding of religion ... but most are firmly rooted in the experience of modernity undergone by the West.... Ibn al-'Arabi's perspective on religion differs profoundly from that of contemporary Western methodologies in its assumptions about the role and function of human beings in the cosmos. Of course, most scholars of

religion do not voice their assumptions on such matters, but it is precisely the unspoken assumptions that provide the greatest commonality among them. These assumptions are perhaps easier to express in negative than positive terms. For example, modern scholarship—in contrast to traditional Islamic scholarship—does not presuppose an ultimate reality that unifies all of existence, a clear purpose to human life, a moral dimension to both human activity and the natural world, the divine origin of religion, or the truth of scripture.[45]

For the purposes of the present study, Ibn ʿArabi can serve as a theorist since he is by far the most influential theorist of the Sufi tradition itself, and his works are frequently cited in the Tijani tradition. Moreover, the Shaykh al-Akbar's work is uniquely suited to this task not only because of its subtlety, depth, and dizzying breadth, but also because of its unique understanding of different perspectives on or theories of the Real (*al-Ḥaqq*, one of the ninety-nine Names of God in Islam). For Ibn ʿArabi, the Islamic declaration of unity (*tawḥīd*)—that "there is no god but God" (*lā ilāha illā Llāh*)—therefore also means that "there is no reality but the Reality."

This "Ultimate Reality," by virtue of its nature, is also all-powerful ("there is no power but God"), all-living ("there is no life but God"), and all-knowing ("there is no knower but God"). By virtue of being all-knowing, this Ultimate Reality must know Itself both in and of Itself, and as another—or if you like, both perfectly and imperfectly. Thus, creation comes into being as means for this Reality to know Itself both in Itself and as another. Thus, Ibn ʿArabi often describes the cosmos as a "mirror of nonbeing" or a "dream" of the Real, in which it can contemplate Itself as not-Itself. While everything in a dream is distinct, but also nothing other than the dreamer, the characters through which the dreamer experiences the dream are somehow different. Because the dreamer (the Real) "sees through their eyes" they are more directly connected to him, and therefore to everything else in the dream. In Ibn ʿArabi's account, these "dreamers in the dream" are human beings, and their diverse and unique perspectives on and beliefs about reality are described as so many "self-portraits" of the Real (Ibn ʿArabi calls them "gods created in belief"). Because they are just representations, they are not and should not be confused with the Real itself, but because there is no other reality save the Real, they are also identical with the Real, like images in so many mirrors.

Ibn ʿArabi describes all these different approaches ("religious" or not) to reality as "knots" in the fabric of reality, because they represent so many limitations of the Real. To mix metaphors, as "dreamers in the dream," human beings are only truly themselves, and therefore truly happy, when they "wake up inside the dream" or "untie all of their knots," fulfilling their function of knowing the Real. Ibn ʿArabi calls this "knot-free" state, the "station of no station" or the "perspective of no perspective"—the perspective the Real has on Itself. Because the Real wants to be known, or because God is merciful, concerned with human felicity, He helps guide people toward felicity, toward knowledge of the Real. That is, He helps them untie their knots (or from another perspective, He unties the knots in Himself). This is usually accomplished through the forms of revelations/religions, which as particular limited self-portraits of the Real are knots in themselves. However, they have the distinction of being knots that undo other knots, including themselves. These "not-knots" and the process of untying they involve require the use of both reason and imagination.

The function of reason is analytic, to distinguish between the Real and its manifestations, the dreamer and the dream. The function of imagination is synthetic, to connect the manifestations to the Real, to see the dreamer in the dream. Because the purpose of these religious traditions is to connect human beings back to the Real, religious forms often emphasize imagination through poetic language and ritual symbolism. However, when taken too far, imagination leads to confusing and conflating the dream and the dreamer; while if reason is taken too far, it destroys the imaginal coherence of the religion, and makes the dreamer (the Real) seem out of reach, if not out of the picture altogether. Thus, according to Ibn 'Arabi, people must learn to "see with two eyes"—reason and imagination—in order to untie their knots.

But what does all of this have to do with theories and methodologies of religion? Chittick explains:

> Any methodology can be nothing but a knot in terms of which reality is construed. In the name of objectivity or other norms, certain assumptions are made about experienced reality. Modern methodologies are often considered to have achieved a superior view of things because of their critical approach, but the belief that one's approach is "critical" already represents a particularly intractable knot. As the Shaykh would point out, the gods of critical belief have no privileged place in the pantheon. God is also the Critic, no doubt, but God as the Guide has a far greater claim to human loyalty.[46]

He then sketches an outline of an Akbarī (i.e., an Ibn 'Arabi–based) approach to the study of religion:

> Ibn al-'Arabi's approach provides a predisposition toward the study of religion that is also a knot, no doubt. Nevertheless, by recognizing the existence of knots and appreciating their value, and by acknowledging the position (perhaps never attainable) of untying all knots, this approach may provide certain insights unavailable

to other points of view. By taking up the Shaykh's standpoint, one is predisposed to deal with religious diversity as follows: Religion appears among human beings because the Real as Guide desires to bring about human wholeness and felicity. But manifestations of the Guide can never embrace the total truth of the Real as such, which lies beyond expression and form. Hence each religion has its own specific mode of expression that is necessarily different from other modes of expression. . . . The specific imaginal forms that guidance assumes in a given religion will be determined by the cultural and linguistic receptacles as much as by the specific self-disclosure of the Guide—the prophet, avatara, buddha, sage—who initiates the religion. In the last analysis, these two sides of reality are inseparable: The cultural and linguistic receptacles, like the revelations, are self-disclosures of the Real. "The water assumes the color of its cup," but the cup is nothing but frozen water.[47]

Thus, Ibn 'Arabi's unique appreciation of the diverse and differing perspectives (self-portraits of the Real) on reality, his understanding and use of both of rational and imaginal modes of discourse and thought, and his sensitive appreciation of sociohistorical context without becoming reductionist all make him a compelling theorist. Moreover, as a result of the "theory" outlined above, Ibn 'Arabi takes each of these "knots" or perspectives seriously "on their own terms," since each is a divine self-portrait that reveals aspects of the Real not explicitly contained in any other. Thus he writes, "Beware of becoming delimited by a specific knotting and disbelieving in everything else, lest great good escape you. . . . Be in yourself a matter [*hyle*] for the forms of all beliefs, for God is wider and more tremendous than that He should be constricted by one knotting rather than another."[48] And elsewhere advises, "He who counsels his own soul should investigate, during his life in this world, all doctrines concerning God. He should learn from whence each possessor of a doctrine affirms the validity of his doctrine. Once its validity has been affirmed for him in the specific mode in which it is correct for him who holds it, then he should support it in the case of him who believes in it."[49]

For this reason, in his writings, Ibn 'Arabi constantly shifts between different perspectives, always evaluating the topic at hand from multiple points of view, in a manner that contemporary theorists would call "perspectivist" or "polyvocal."[50] Ibn 'Arabi's peculiarly flexible style of arguing from and for multiple different positions (while still remaining mysteriously coherent) is such that even if you do not agree with him or all of his arguments, his undeniable acumen forces you to see the issue at hand from new perspectives, and always illuminates the issues at stake in these various discussions. Ibn 'Arabi gave answers (many, many different answers) to many questions similar to those we would ask of a contemporary theorist of religion: What is the relationship between practice and doctrine? What is the purpose of prayer? What is knowledge? What is truth? Who has the authority to answer these questions, and why?

Thus, Ibn 'Arabi is well suited to serve as a model and a theorist for approaching religious traditions, particularly those that appear to have much in common with his plural metaphysics. Nevertheless, while I use Ibn 'Arabi a great deal in presenting Tijani Sufism, when presenting Ifa, a non-Islamic tradition of at least equally staggering profundity, breadth, subtlety, and insight, I try to use the terms, categories, and theories of the tradition itself. From time to time, in explaining Ifa, I also contrast and compare Ifa to other traditions in order to clear up confusions and false analogies that I anticipate may arise in the mind of the reader. As Abrahamic traditions, Christianity and Islam share a great deal of intellectual history and conceptual categories, and thus the categories of Sufism typically require less of an explanation for Western-educated readers (whatever their religious affiliation) than do those of Ifa.

**Comparative Philosophy**

In this book, I also draw on Barry Hallen's work in comparing Yoruba and Western epistemologies. One of Hallen's most important insights is that when moving back and forth between different traditions, discourses, or languages, one has to be careful to understand the role that each term plays in its own context before constructing equivalencies and translations. His masterful analysis of the categories of "witchcraft" in English versus *ajẹ* in Yoruba and of "knowledge" and "belief" in ordinary language and Anglophone philosophical discourse and *imọ* and *igbagbọ* in the discourse of Yoruba ritual specialists (*onisẹgun*) inspired my own methods in comparing forms of "knowledge" in Ifa and Tijani Sufism.

Ibn 'Arabi's kaleidoscopic method of shifting perspectives also deeply influenced the way I conduct and present these comparisons: examining Tijani Sufism from the perspective of Ifa, examining Ifa from the perspective of Tijani Sufism, and then examining certain topics from various positions within each of these traditions and those of Ibn 'Arabi's work.

This structure is also related to the main motivation for the comparative nature of this project. Comparing these traditions in this way allows us to experience how they can operate as theoretical perspectives in and of themselves and understand that they are more than just "data" to be theorized about from other perspectives. The exercise of adopting the perspective of each of these traditions to analyze the other also makes us more aware of the limitations and specificity of academic theoretical perspectives derived from Western intellectual traditions.

## Sources

This study is based on textual and oral sources, as well as my own observations during extended periods of research in Ile-Ifẹ and Modakẹkẹ, Nigeria (June–August 2011 and September–December 2013), and in Dakar and Medina Baye, Senegal (January–February 2012 and January–May 2014). The oral sources from Senegal come primarily from formal interviews with Tijani shaykhs conducted in Arabic and French, as well as formal interviews with disciples conducted primarily in French, but also in Arabic and English. A few group discussions and interviews in which I participated (through the kind translation of friends) took place in Wolof (the most common language of Dakar), but the lack of Wolof oral sources is a major gap in the source material. My primary access to the community was through the incredible generosity of the Kane family, the sons and grandchildren of Shaykha Maryam Niasse, the daughter of Shaykh Ibrahim Niasse. Through their mediation I was able to interview shaykhs from several different branches of the family and spiritual lineage of Shaykh Ibrahim Niasse, and interact with a wide variety of disciples. Disciple interviews in Dakar primarily came from the time I spent in the zawiyas of Baba Lamine, Shaykh Mamour Insa, Shaykh Babacar N'Diaye, the home of Shaykha Maryam Niasse, and "Keur Baye" in Dakar. As for textual sources, I made frequent reference to the Tijani sourcebooks *Jawāhir al-Ma'ānī*[51] and the collection *Aḥzāb wa Awrād*,[52] as well as the prose works of Shaykh Ibrahim, particularly his collection of letters, *Jawāhir al-rasā'il*;[53] his Qur'anic commentary, *Fī Riyāḍ al-Tafsīr*;[54] his *Kāshif al-Ilbās* (translated as *The Removal of Confusion*);[55] and Maigari's edition of his *al-Sirr al-Akbar*.[56] Shaykh Ibrahim's published collections of poetry—*Dawāwīn al-Sitt*, *Jāmi' al-jawāmi' al-dawāwīn*, and *Sayr al-qalb*—were also frequently consulted, but seldom cited in the present work (the translations and analyses of these poems form part of another work).[57] I was a participant observer in many communal prayers as well as gatherings both formal and informal in Medina Baye and Dakar, but as a noninitiate there were strict limits to my participation in these rites and discussions. As a matter of methodological integrity, I shared the drafts of my chapters on Tijani Sufism with the Anglophone disciples and shaykhs I interviewed, and have tried to incorporate their suggestions into the present work.

In Nigeria, oral sources came primarily from interviews and conversations with babalawo, especially Chief Ifarinwale Ogundiran, the Araba of Modakẹkẹ, Professor A. F. Agboola of Ọbafẹmi Awolọwọ University, and Awo Fajimi Faniyi, which were primarily conducted in Yoruba with some English, as well as informal conversations with apprentices (ọmọ awo). I made video recordings of performances of a number of Ifa verses with the Araba of Modakẹkẹ, and Ayọdeji Ogunnaike's digital database of Odu Ifa was another important oral source.[58] I was an observer, but not a participant, in the Araba's daily practice of divination as well as several rites of worship and festivals. Textual collections of verses of Ifa such as William Bascom's *Ifa Divination*, Epega and Neimark's *The Sacred Ifa Oracle*, Wande Abimbọla's books, and verses recorded in the works of Rowland Abiọdun and Jacob Olupọna were also important textual sources. In addition, I shared several of my ideas and chapters with the babalawo whom I interviewed and have tried to incorporate their feedback.

**The Present Work**

The primary purpose of this book is to provide philosophical accounts of the "ways of knowing" of the branch of Tijani Sufi order founded by Shaykh Ibrahim Niasse, and that of Ifa. That is, taking Hadot's definition of philosophy as a "way of life," I propose to examine how each tradition defines, acquires, and verifies "knowledge" through various ritual and discursive means—or in Hadot's terms, through "spiritual exercises" and "philosophical discourse," which can itself be a spiritual exercise. These accounts, for the most part, will be developed in the categories of the traditions themselves, and will attempt to represent the intellectual dimensions of these "ways of knowing" as a rigorously as possible.[59] Basically, I ask the representatives of each tradition: "What do you know?," "How did you come to know it?" and "How do you know that you know it?" and critically investigate and "think with" or "think through"[60] their responses as well as those provided by the texts, orature, and practices of each tradition.

That is, I attempt to not only ask how each tradition defines different forms of knowledge in the ways that it does, but also why, intellectually, it does so. I endeavor to not only outline the means of acquiring knowledge, but ask how and why these means yield this knowledge, and I try to not only explain how these forms of knowledge are verified in each of these traditions, but also investigate the theories of verification in each tradition. Taking care to respect the plurality of voices and opinions, I construct a representation of the epistemology of *ma'rifa* among contemporary disciples of Shaykh Ibrahim Niasse (chapters 2, 3, and 4) and of the epistemology of *imọ ijinlẹ* (deep knowledge) of contemporary babalawo (priests of Ifa) (chapters 6, 7, and 8). While my goal is not to write an apology for or defense of either Ifa or Tijani Sufism, if I have done my job well and effectively communicated the ways in which these traditions "make sense" of and "make a case" for themselves, it may appear as such. This is because, following Ibn 'Arabi's lead, I make an effort to "learn from whence each possessor of a doctrine affirms the validity of his or her doctrine. Once its validity has been affirmed in the specific mode in which it is correct for he or she who holds it, then I attempt to support it in the case of he or she who believes in it."[61] I have generally not included critiques of the claims of the traditions in question, as I believe such critiques first require the positive work of understanding them, a task that takes up the entirety of the present volume.

The secondary purpose of this work is, on the basis of these characterizations, to construct a comparison of Ifa and Tijani Sufism. Although currently neighbors in Nigeria, Benin, and some places in the African diaspora, Ifa and Tijani Sufism appear to have developed in radically different spiritual, intellectual, and cultural contexts.[62] However, the primary purpose of this comparative exercise is to examine each tradition from the perspective of the other, demonstrating how each tradition can and does serve as a critical, theoretical perspective that can analyze other perspectives. Moreover, the epistemologies of both traditions appear to share certain structural traits that make comparison not only possible, but potentially fruitful. Namely, the epistemologies of both traditions seem to be based on a kind of self-knowledge, one in which the knowing subject is identical with the known object. As such, these modes of self-knowledge are cultivated through various ritual practices, especially the watershed rites of initiation, which are believed to transform the knowing subject, leading to a kind of identification with the founder of the tradition, who is conceived of as the perfect embodiment of knowledge. It should be noted that this structure is in no way unique to these two traditions, but seems to be found in other religious traditions and forms of philosophy around the world. Thus, I attempt to construct an academic dialogue between contemporary perspectives from Ifa and Tijani Sufism, to complement and perhaps enrich the limited but ongoing dialogues between the two traditions outside of the academy.

That being said, I try to guard against facile and superficial comparisons through both the structure and method of this comparison. Following Izutsu, I divide the work into three parts: the first is an exploration of the epistemology of *ma'rifa* (direct knowledge) in Tijani Sufism, the second is an exploration of knowledge (specifically *imọ ijinlẹ*, or deep knowledge) in Ifa, and only in the third section do I attempt a comparison of the two traditions. Furthermore, this third part is further subdivided into four parts: In the first part, I present the opinions of practitioners of Ifa on Tijani Sufism, and then conduct a comparison of the two traditions from the perspective of Ifa. In the second part, I present the opinions of representatives of the Tijani tradition on Ifa, and then conduct a comparison from the perspective of Tijani Sufism. In the third part, I attempt to compare, and use the two traditions and Ibn ʿArabi's work to "think through," certain topics that emerge from the descriptions of the traditions given in the first and second parts of the book. Finally, in the fourth and final section of the book, I take some of the points where Ifa and Tijani Sufism appear to converge and suggest ways in which their perspectives can expand conceptions of these topics among contemporary academics.

## Metaphysics and Epistemology

I decided to focus my research on epistemology or "ways of knowing" in these traditions because it links their metaphysical doctrines and the rituals and practices designed to realize or actualize them in the souls and bodies of their adepts. Without an understanding of the epistemology of these traditions, one can study the doctrines of Sufism and remain baffled by its rituals (What does the oneness of being have to do with sitting in a dark room and repeating an Arabic phrase?), or conversely learn all about the rituals of Ifa and remain mystified by its mythology (What do incantations and sacrifices have to do with the relationship between the Supreme God and other deities?). Moreover, as the site where doctrine meets practice, epistemology can provide important insights into both and their relationship to one another.

From a certain point of view, the metaphysics or ontology of a given philosophical system is the result of the application of a particular epistemology: it is a knowledge arrived at through certain means. However, this epistemology itself is dependent on a particular metaphysics or ontology, because this particular ontology will, in turn, determine a psychology or anthropology: the nature of the knowing subject. In order to know something, I have to put some practice of knowing into action. For example, I may come to the conclusion that electrons exist through the application of a certain epistemological process. However, this epistemological process is itself determined by a priori assumptions about the nature of reality and knowledge (i.e., messages from angels in dreams about superstring theory may not count as valid knowledge). I have chosen to focus on the epistemological pole of this philosophical loop, because it allows me to bracket some of the more difficult metaphysical disparities between these African traditions and contemporary Western academic worldviews and to explain how they arise.

### CONCLUSION

However, the point of all this research and theory and critical engagement with philosophy is to produce a work that would be able to speak to that seventeen-year-old back in the bookstore. Hopefully, the present project can add to the growing literature that provides introductions to the intellectual dimensions and philosophical discourse of non-Western worldviews and traditions. Such literature is important not only because it introduces alternative perspectives on reality, knowledge, ethics, and so forth into Western discourses, but because these perspectives can be compelling and transformative in their own right. At the very least, they can make us aware of unexamined assumptions and prejudices, and perhaps they can even help us "untie our knots," as Ibn 'Arabi suggests. But this can only happen if we allow ourselves to take these traditions not only as anthropological or historical data, but seriously as "philosophical" accounts of knowledge and knowing—if we take them "on their own terms"—much as we are trained to do with Western theorists and philosophers. Such serious consideration does not require that we embrace these traditions or blindly accept all their claims, but rather that we acknowledge the possibility that our difficulties in understanding them may have more to do with our history and training than with the particularities of the traditions themselves. As Amadou Hampâté Bâ writes, "To discover a new world, one must be able to forget one's own; otherwise one merely carries that along with one and does not 'keep one's ears open.' The Africa of the old initiates warns the young researcher, through the mouth of Tierno Bokar, the sage of Bandiagara: 'If you wish to know who I am, if you wish me to teach you what I know, cease for a while to be what you are, and forget what you know.'"[63] This is much more easily said than done, but I hope the following chapters can facilitate this kind of serious consideration and reflection. This is indeed a serious endeavor; for to take the epistemologies of Tijani Sufism and Ifa seriously on their own terms means to be open to possibilities that may seem foreign, strange, or uncomfortable, such as the possibility of a "deep knowledge" that is a discovery or remembrance of one's true self, at once one's origin and destiny.

PART 1

✧✧✧

# Ways of Knowing in Tijani Sufism

CHAPTER 1

# What Is Tijani Sufism?

> The light of Truth . . . is a darkness more
> brilliant than all other lights combined.
> —SHAYKH TIERNO BOKAR

Over the past two centuries, Tijani Sufism has become one of the most influential and popular religious movements in West Africa. But before exploring the history of Tijani Sufism, we must first explain *what* it is. The term "Tijani Sufism" has two components, "Tijani" and "Sufism," the former qualifying the latter. Sufism is an English term that roughly translates the Arabic word *taṣawwuf*. A term of uncertain origin,[1] *taṣawwuf* has been given thousands of definitions by its proponents,[2] including "a reality without a form,"[3] "the science of the Real," "the science of hearts," "acting upon knowledge," "good manners," "character," "excellence," "taste," "sincerity," "love," "certainty," and "seeing things as they really are." For the purposes of this chapter, we will take *taṣawwuf* to be the name of the most popular and influential tradition of Islamic esoterism, mysticism, and spirituality.[4] Here again we are confronted with a dichotomy: "Islamic" and "esoterism, mysticism, and spirituality." Sufism is Islamic because it is derived from and based on[5] the Islamic revelation, namely the Qur'an and the Sunna (the example of the Prophet Muḥammad). Sufism is esoteric in that it emphasizes the inward (*bāṭin*) aspects of the Qur'an and Sunna; it is mystical[6] in that it emphasizes an existential knowledge of the Divine or direct perception that transcends discursive description; it is spiritual in that its focus is the Divine, and that it privileges the meaning or spirit (*ma'nā*) over the outward form (*ṣūra*).

## WHAT IS SUFISM?

According to Sufis, the Sufi tradition begins with the Prophet Muḥammad, his close companions, and those whom they taught and instructed on the inner meaning of the Qur'an, ḥadīth (sayings of the Prophet), and Islamic rituals. Sufism during this time was famously described as "a reality without a name,"[7] since such distinctions in Islamic practice and piety had yet to formally arise. This previously unnamed reality took the name *taṣawwuf* during the period in which the other early disciplines of Islamic knowledge—such as the discipline of the transmission of ḥadīth (*ʿilm al-ḥadīth*), the science of jurisprudence (*ʿilm al-fiqh*), the science of Qur'anic commentary (*ʿilm al-tafsīr*)—also began to emerge.[8] These Islamic sciences or disciplines (including Sufism, *ʿilm al-taṣawwuf*) were (and are) defined, classified, and delimited according to their subject matter (*mawḍūʿ*).[9] For example, the subject matter of medicine (*ʿilm al-ṭibb*) is the human body in terms of health and disease, and the subject matter of mathematics is number in terms of quantity. The subject matter of Sufism, however, is nothing less than the Divine Essence, or Reality as such, and therefore the subject matter of Sufism has no limit. Sometimes Sufism was called the science of hearts (*ʿilm al-qulūb*) and its subject matter was defined as the states of the heart and the soul, but later Sufis equated these two definitions, citing the well-known Prophetic maxims "The heart of the believer is the throne of the All-Merciful," "Heaven and Earth do not contain me, but the heart of my believing servant contains me," and "He who knows himself, knows his Lord."[10]

This demonstrates why, although Sufism is described as the most inner aspect of Islam, it is also characterized as the most all-encompassing, dealing with questions of universal concern and interest. Very few people care what Islamic jurisprudence has to say about how Muslims should pray at the North Pole, whereas nearly everyone cares about the question of what is real and what is not. The Sufi tradition addresses questions such as "What is truth/reality?" "Where did we come from?" "How did we get here?" "Who are we?" "Where are we going?" and "How do we get there?" in a specific way. Its perspective is based on the Qur'an and Sunna, and secondarily on the experiences and insights previous Sufis acquired during their quest to mold their souls to the "beautiful model"[11] of the Prophet (whose wife ʿAisha equated his character with the Qur'an[12] and called him "the Qur'an walking on earth").[13]

However, this vast treasury of scripture, wisdom, meditations, and ideas is only the beginning. The tradition of Sufism seeks answers that come not from authority or tradition, but rather from direct realization and personal experience. As one of Sufism's most famous and influential figures, al-Ghazālī (d. 1111), writes, "How great a difference there is between *knowing* the definition and causes of health and satiety and your *being* healthy and sated, and how great a difference there is between your knowing the definition of drunkenness ... and your being drunk!"[14]

The Sufi is not satisfied with mere mental assent to the doctrines contained in the Qurʾan, ḥadīth, and traditions of Sufi masters; he or she seeks their confirmation in direct experiential knowledge (*maʿrifa*). Sufism is interested in realities, not concepts. As al-Ghazālī himself experienced, arguments from authority, historical authenticity, and even reason and sense data are all subject to doubt, but what Sufism seeks is certainty, the realization of the truths proclaimed by these sources. It is one thing to accept or agree with the verse of the Qurʾan "From God we come and to God we return" (2:156): it is quite another thing to confirm the same through personal experience (before death), as many Sufis claim to have done.[15] Accepting the historical validity of and believing in the tradition that "Prayer is the heavenly ascent of the believer" (*al-ṣalāt miʿrāj al-muʾmin*)[16] is a far cry from experiencing it as such. Thus, Sufism can be described as an empirical, verifiable tradition, but one whose findings cannot be fully contained in language, because they are existential rather than discursive.[17]

Ibn ʿArabi (d. 1240), the great Andalusian mystic whose influence is only rivaled by that of al-Ghazālī, likens the knowledge of Sufism to "the knowledge of the sweetness of honey, the bitterness of aloes, the pleasure of sexual intercourse, love, ecstasy, yearning, and similar knowledges. It is impossible for anyone to know any of these sciences without being qualified by them and tasting them."[18] In the same vein, the great poet and Sufi master Rumi (d. 1273) compared the discursive exposition of the existential realities of Sufism to explaining the pleasure of sex to a child by using the sweetness of candy as an analogy.[19]

But unlike a particular culinary tradition or the *Kama Sutra*, the content of the experience on which Sufism is based (often symbolically called *dhawq*, "taste," or *kashf*, "unveiling") is not merely sensory or emotional, but rather metaphysical and intellectual. It is important to distinguish this direct knowledge (*maʿrifa*) from the visions and other mystical experiences that sometimes accompany its "unveiling." These visions, dreams, and the like are considered but another form of sensory experience (albeit a potentially lofty one), which, on its own, does not constitute the certain knowledge that is the goal of the Sufi path.

The Whirling Dervishes do not spin around to make themselves dizzy, and the mystical states (*aḥwāl*) that sometimes overtake Sufis are not pursued for their own sake. The Sufi wants to see things as they are, not things that are not really there.[20] The knowledge and certainty that Sufis seek is not opposed to reason; rather, it is said to be above it. Those Sufis who also took part in discursive, rational philosophy claim that the suprarational mode of knowing that characterizes Sufism (*kashf*, *dhawq*, etc.) establishes the foundational axioms on which reason can build its philosophical edifices.²¹ This relationship between the discursive nature of rational philosophy and the suprarational nature of Sufism is perhaps best described in the legendary meeting between the great philosopher Ibn Sīnā and the Sufi master Abū Saʿīd Abū'l Khayr. As the story goes, when asked what he thought of Ibn Sīnā, the Sufi master said, "He knows what I see." When asked about Abū Saʿīd, the philosopher replied, "He sees what I know."

Thus, the vast corpus of Sufi theoretical and intellectual works (which covers abstract topics such as the nature of being and its relationship to knowledge, the relationship of time to eternity, and the problem of qualia) is not approached as rational speculation, nor poetic flight of fancy, but rather a record of verified and verifiable metaphysical truths and realties. The following statement from the introduction to ʿAbd al-Karīm Jīlī's (d. 1424) magnum opus of Sufi metaphysics, cosmology, and anthropology, *The Universal Human* (*al-Insān al-Kāmil*), is typical: "I will mention of all that only that which happened to me on my own journey to God; moreover, I recount nothing in this book, neither of myself nor of another, without having tested it at the time when I traveled in God by the path of intuition and direct vision."²²

SUFI DOCTRINES

But what exactly is this "direct vision" and how can it possibly meet the Sufi criterion of certainty that everything else seems to fall short of? A look at the tradition's conception of certainty (*yaqīn*) should help answer these questions. Works of Sufism commonly distinguish between three degrees of certainty: "the lore of certainty" (*ʿilm al-yaqīn*), "the eye of certainty" (*ʿayn al-yaqīn*), and "the truth of certainty" (*ḥaqq al-yaqīn*).²³ "The lore of certainty" is likened to hearing about a fire, "the eye of certainty" is compared to glimpsing the fire, while "the truth of certainty" is being consumed in its flames.²⁴ In this last degree, the knowledge of the object, the being of the knower, and that of the object are all identified. When the object of knowledge is God, this degree of certainty of spiritual attainment is known as annihilation in God (*fanāʾ fī Llāh*), a term derived from the verse of the Qurʾan (55:26), "All upon it is passing away" (*fānin*). This mysterious state of annihilation is celebrated and described in numerous Sufi treatises and poems, one of the most famous of which comes from the pen of the famous Sufi martyr Manṣūr al-Ḥallāj:

> I saw my Lord with the eye of my heart
> I asked him, "Who are You?"
> And He said, "You."²⁵

Another comes from Ibn 'Arabi:

> When my Beloved appears,
> with what eye do I see Him?
> With His eye not with mine;
> for no one sees Him except Himself.[26]

But this state of annihilation is not the end of the Sufi path: there remains the "annihilation of the annihilation" or *fanā' al-fanā'*, which the Sufis call subsistence (*baqā'*), a term derived from very next verse of the Qur'an (55:27), "And there subsists/abides [*yabqā*] the face of your Lord, the Possessor of Majesty and Magnanimity." If *fanā'* is seeing nothing but God,[27] then *baqā'* is seeing everything in God, doing everything in God, and knowing everything through God (or, rather, God knowing through one). For this reason, Sufi masters are often given the title *al-'ārif bi Llāh*, "The Knower by God," instead of "The Knower of God." These are the spiritual heights from which Sufi masters have articulated their visions of reality, their doctrines, all of which are said to be summarized, or symbolized, in the two testimonies of faith (*shahādatayn*): "There is no god but God" (*Lā ilāha illā Llāh*) and "Muḥammad is the Messenger of God" (*Muḥammadun Rasūlu Llāh*).

### The First Shahāda

As Titus Burckhardt writes, "In conformity with the Qur'an, the central idea of Sufism is Divine Unity."[28] The first shahāda, *Lā ilāha illā Llāh*, is the formulation par excellence of this doctrine of Divine Unity, *tawḥīd*. Although Sufis often quote the maxim *al-tawḥīd wāḥid*, meaning "The doctrine of Divine Unity is unique/singular," this doctrine has taken many forms and descriptions over the centuries. As with certainty, Sufi texts and masters often describe three degrees of *tawḥīd*, again with phrases drawn from the Qur'an. The first stage corresponds to the verse *Lā ilāha illā Huwa*, "There is no god but He" (2:255), in which God is described by the distant third-person pronoun. At this level, God is out there somewhere, and we believe there is only one of Him, but that is about as deep as it goes. This is called the shell of *tawḥīd*. However, as the Sufi novice progresses, he or she reaches the stage of *Lā ilāha illā Anta*, "There is no God but You" (21:87). At this level of *tawḥīd*, the Sufi stands before God as in the ritual prayer, where she says to Him, "You alone do we worship, on You alone we rely" (1:1). But in this stage, the Sufi addresses God like this all the time, not only in prayer. The Sufi relies only on God, and when she speaks, she speaks only to God, and when she listens, she hears only God. This is the kernel of *tawḥīd*. Then, if she continues, she arrives at annihilation in God and there is only *Lā ilāha illā Anā*, "There is no God but I" (21:27). The twentieth-century Tijani Shaykh Ibrahim Niasse (d. 1975) explains:

> It would be strange for a person to hear his brother saying "There is no God but I." He might think that this person is claiming divinity for himself, but it is only the speech of the Real [*al-Ḥaqq*] on his brother's tongue. And he likewise hears the speech coming from him, while he is not the speaker. God spoke like this to Moses on the tongue of a [burning] bush [in the Qur'an], *innī anā Llāh*, "Verily I am God" [20:14]. And if He can say, "Verily I am God" through a bush, then He can certainly say it through a person.[29]

This recalls the fatally famous saying of al-Ḥallāj, *Anā al-Ḥaqq*, "I am the Truth," and Maḥmūd Shabistarī's poetic commentary on it:

> If saying "I am the Truth" was permissible for the bush
> Why is it not in the mouth of a good man [Ḥallāj]?
> Every man whose heart is pure from doubt
> Knows for sure that there is no Being but One
> Only "the Truth" can say "I am."[30]

Similarly, Shaykh Aḥmad al-Tijānī is recorded as commenting that "the reality of *tawḥīd* [saying 'There is no god but God'] cannot be grasped, because so long as you are speaking, you exist and God exists, so there are two, and so where is the unity [*tawḥīd*]? There's no *tawḥīd* except that which is [said] by God, through God, and to God. The servant has no entrance to this, and no exit from it."[31]

Perhaps the most celebrated (and misunderstood/controversial) formulation of this doctrine comes from the school of Ibn 'Arabi, which became known in Arabic as *waḥdat al-wujūd*, or the "Oneness of Being" or "Unity of Existence." While Ibn 'Arabi gives many metaphors or symbols to describe this doctrine, one of the easiest to understand is the Qur'anic symbolism of light.[32] Just as pure light brings about perception but cannot be perceived, so God's Being (Pure Being) brings about existence but cannot be found in existence. Similarly, things can only be seen if they are not light, and then come into contact with light. Light by itself cannot be seen, and nothing can be seen in the dark. If we take light as a metaphor for being, and visibility for existence, then this means that everything that exists is a coming together of being and nonbeing. When we look at a thing, what we see is light, but it is not pure light. If we turned off the light, we wouldn't see anything, and if we were to turn on very powerful lights, all we would see is light, and if they got bright enough, we wouldn't see anything at all. So from one perspective, we can say that all we see is light (everything that exists is Pure Being—i.e., God), and from another point of view we can say that what we see is not light (the world is not God). So, according to Ibn ʿArabi, everything that exists is both being and nonbeing, both God and not-God.

Now, light has different gradations or intensities while still remaining the same reality. Similarly, being has different levels, while still remaining a single reality. These different levels of being were often called presences or ḥaḍarāt by Ibn ʿArabi and his students, who divided them up into five and sometimes six levels: (1) *Hahūt*, the level of the Divine Essence (being—i.e., light so bright you can't see it); (2) *Lahūt*, the level of the Divine Names and Qualities (existence—i.e., what we'd perceive as light so bright you can't see anything else); (3) *Jabarūt*, the level of the Divine Acts and pure intellects (brilliant light); (4) *Malakūt*, the subtle or imaginal level between the physical and the spiritual worlds (dimmer light); (5) *Nasūt* or *mulk*, the everyday, physical world (light so dim you can hardly see anything). Human beings are said to also exist on all of these levels—we have a physical body, emotions, and a soul/spirit with many levels, going all the way up to the highest—and so sometimes the human being is added as a sixth presence, encompassing all the others in a slightly different version of this schema.

A different school of *waḥdat al-wujūd* is associated in the West (North Africa) with Ibn Sabʿīn and his better-known (and liked) disciple, the poet Abūʾl-Ḥasan al-Shushtarī, who wrote the following famous poem:

> After extinction, I came out
> Eternal now am, though not as I
> And who am I, O I, but I?[33]

Similarly, in the East, it is associated with the trope of *Hama Ust* ("All is He") in Sufi writings and poetry from Persia and the Indian subcontinent. This "extreme" form of *tawḥīd* asserts that everything is God, whereas Ibn ʿArabi and his followers asserted that everything is simultaneously "God and not-God." The former school was (somewhat understandably) often confused with that of Ibn ʿArabi, as in the case of the famous *Treatise of Oneness* by Awḥad ad-Dīn Balyānī, which was often mistakenly attributed to Ibn ʿArabi. This treatise, which takes the doctrine of *tawḥīd* to the very limits of language and logic, begins as follows:

> Praise belongs to God, before whose Oneness there is no before, unless the before is He and after whose Singularity there is no after, unless the after is He! He was, and there was not with Him any before, nor after, nor above, nor below, nor closeness, nor distance, nor how, nor where, nor when, nor time, nor moment, nor

period, nor duration, nor manifested existence, nor place. "And He is now as He was." He is the One without oneness, the Singular without singularity. He is not composed of name and named: for His Name is He and His named is He and there is no name or named other than Him. . . .

Understand this so as not to fall into the error of those who believe in incarnation: because He is not in anything and no thing is in Him whether entering in or coming out. It is in this way that you should know Him and not through (theoretical) knowledge, reason, understanding, or conjecture, nor with the eye nor the external senses, nor even with interior sight or perception. No one sees Him, except Himself; no one reaches Him, except Himself; and no one knows Him except Himself. He knows Himself through Himself and He sees Himself by means of Himself. No one but He sees Him. His very Oneness is His veil since nothing veils Him other than He; His own Being veils Him. His Oneness is concealed by His Oneness without any condition. . . .

When this secret is revealed to you, you will know that you are not other than God but that you yourself are the object of your quest. You do not need to cease to be—you have not ceased and never will cease to be, without time and without moments, as we have already mentioned. You will see His attributes as your attributes, your exterior as His exterior, your interior as His interior, your first as His first and your last as His Last, without any doubt or uncertainty. You will see your attributes to be His attributes and your essence to be His essence, without your having to become Him and without His having to become you in the least degree.[34]

And yet, as lofty as this all sounds, this is only half the story.

**The Second Shahāda**

For Ibn ʿArabi and his students, Balyānī is right—there is no real existence but God, and this is confirmed by the experience of *fanā'* (annihilation in God)—and yet we also experience the world as being separate from God. Ibn ʿArabi explains that this is because human beings are an isthmus (*barzakh*) between the world and God. As Chittick explains, "Man[35] is an 'isthmus' (*barzakh*), i.e., something that stands between two other things, yet possesses the attributes of both. Hence man is 'all-comprehensive' (*jāmiʿ*), for there is nothing on either side—God and the world—that escapes him. Of course here we must distinguish between the Perfect Man (*al-insān al-kāmil*), who truly actualizes and lives this reality, and ordinary men, who have not realized their potentialities. Only the Perfect Man may truly be considered as the All-Comprehensive Isthmus (*barzakh*), who embraces within himself the realities of both God and the world."[36]

Louis Massignon called this doctrine of the Perfect or Universal Human (*al-insān al-kāmil*), "the privileged myth of Islam." This is what *Muḥammadun Rasūlu Llāh* ("Muhammad is the Messenger of God") means for Sufis; it is not just the mere fact that a particular man happened to receive a message from God; rather, it is a statement about the nature of the connection between God and humankind, a spiritual anthropology. The Universal Human connects all the levels of being discussed above, from God on down to the physical world, and contains them all within himself/herself. On the basis of the verses of the Qur'an "God taught Adam all the Names" (2:31) and "We have recounted all things in an evident prototype" (36:12), Sufis such as Ibn 'Arabi and Shaykh Aḥmad al-Tijānī explain that whereas the universe, the macrocosm, reflects all of God's Names and Attributes in a composite and indirect way—as if it were a cracked or clouded mirror—humans reflect all of these Divine Names and Attributes that are scattered throughout the cosmos within a single, unified being. Thus, the human being (*insān*) is a microcosm, a polished mirror (or the polish of the cosmic mirror) that contains everything in the universe in a clear and distinct miniature.[37]

Employing the same metaphor of the mirror, a Mauritanian Tijani shaykh explained to me that because human beings (*insān*) encompass all levels of reality, we combine the spiritual and the material, just as a mirror has a transparent/reflective side and an opaque side. In fact, it is because of this opaque side that a mirror can reflect. Whereas angels only occupy a single level of reality, and are thus like transparent glass, human beings encompass all levels of reality, from the physical to the Divine Essence, and can thus serve as a mirror in which God can contemplate Himself.[38]

Elsewhere Ibn 'Arabi cites the ḥadīth "God created Adam in His image" to make the same point and explain that man's theomorphism is the secret behind the Qur'an's anthropomorphic language—the Qur'an isn't just describing God in human terms, because these "human terms" are actually reflections or depictions of Divine Qualities and Attributes.[39] Thus, the Universal Human is the mirror in which God contemplates His Names and Qualities, and through which the world was created. Everything is in the Universal Human, and he or she is in everything.

Another way of explaining this reality is through the common metaphor of the world as a dream. If the world is a dream and God is the dreamer, then the Universal Human is the dreamer within the dream. Everything in the dream is or represents an aspect of the dreamer, but the persona of the dreamer within the dream represents him in a comprehensive manner, and therefore this persona also reflects or contains everything in the dream. Moreover, it is through this persona that the dreamer experiences the dream; if the dreamer within the dream were to disappear or die, the whole dream would collapse and disappear.[40] Ibn 'Arabi clarifies this relationship in other terms: "In relation to the Real [one of the Names of God], man is like the pupil in relation to the eye, through which vision occurs; one calls this the faculty of sight. For this reason he is called 'man' [the word for 'man' in Arabic, *insān*, also means pupil], and through him the Real looks upon His creation and shows mercy upon them."[41] This is the function of the Universal Human: he connects God (metacosm) and the world (macrocosm), and mirrors both within his own being (microcosm).

This "theoanthropocosmic" perspective, which bears some similarities to the neo-Platonic/Christian doctrine of the Logos and the doctrine of "Buddha nature" is identified with the *ḥaqīqat al-Muḥammadiyya*, or Muḥammadan reality, sometimes referred to as the *nūr Muḥammadī* or Muḥammadan light.[42] The Sufis say that this is the reality to which the Prophet referred in the ḥadīth "I was a prophet while Adam was betwixt water and clay." Like Ibn 'Arabi and many other Sufis before him, Shaykh Aḥmad al-Tijānī takes the following ḥadīths—"The first thing that God created was the Intellect" (*al-'aql*); "The first thing that God created was the spirit" (*rūḥ*); and "The first thing that God created was my Light"—to equate the Intellect with this reality; other Sufis also cite the verse of the Qur'an "He created you from one soul" (4:1, 7:189, 39:6) to demonstrate that the whole cosmos was created through this Muḥammadan reality, the primary and principle figure of creation.[43]

### *Fayḍ*

One of the main metaphors Ibn 'Arabi and later Sufis employ to describe this process of creation mediated by the Muḥammadan reality or other "divine presences" is that of *fayḍ*, which means effusion, outpouring, overflowing, or emanation. This was the term (in its plural form, *fuyūḍ*) used by the Islamic philosophers to translate the neo-Platonic concept of the emanations (*aporrhoiai*) through which the intellects, heavenly spheres, and the world come into existence. Within Ibn 'Arabi's (and later Sufi) cosmology, the *fuyūḍ* refer both to the outpourings that give existence and form to the things of the world, and also to the graces that give human beings, especially the prophets and the saints, knowledge of God.[44] The significance of the *fuyūḍ* having both ontological and epistemological dimensions will be explored further in the next chapter, but for now it is sufficient to note that in this schema, the Muḥammadan reality is the distributor of both existence and knowledge to all creation.

This Muḥammadan reality also has an inward dimension connected to spiritual realization. The Qur'an states that "the Prophet is closer to the believers than their own souls" (33:6), that "God comes between a man and his heart" (8:24), and "We [God] are closer to him than his jugular vein" (50:16). The Prophet is considered not only as an intermediary between God and man externally, but internally as well. If God is considered in terms of His name "The Inward" (*al-Bāṭin*) or as being contained in the "heart of his believing servant," as the ḥadīth says, then the Prophet's mediation can be understood as also existing between the believer and his innermost self with which he or she tries to connect through spiritual practice. Titus Burckhardt writes, "He [the Prophet] appears as an aspect which withdraws gradually as one approaches him, until his disappearance in Divine Unity. It is in this sense that one says that nobody will meet God before meeting the Prophet."[45] As the Universal Human and the Muḥammadan reality, the Prophet is considered the best of mankind, both as the most perfect of all and as the perfection within each.

## Walāya

The second shahāda also has profound implications on the related Sufi doctrine of sainthood called *wilāya* or *walāya*, literally, "alliance or friendship with God." Islamic thinkers throughout the ages have drawn different distinctions between messengers (*rusul*) and prophets (*anbiyāʾ*), one of the more common views being that all messengers are prophets, but not all prophets are messengers. Messengers are those prophets who, like Moses and Jesus, bring a revealed scripture, and sometimes a new sacred law (*risāla* and *sharīʿa*). Similarly, all prophets are saints/friends/allies (*awliyāʾ*), but not all saints are prophets. Prophets are those saints to whom God has sent to guide a sector of humanity and given a revelation that may or may not be in the form of a scripture (if it is a scripture, then the prophet would also be a messenger). Sufis, however, are primarily interested in the sainthood (*walāya*) of the prophets because the particularities of messengerhood and prophecy come to an end with the world, while sainthood exists in this world and the next.[46] The prophets are more revered for their exalted spiritual or inward status as the highest of saints, than for their specifically outward, prophetic functions.[47]

While the cycle of prophecy ended with Muḥammad, that of sainthood remained open. This initiatory power of sainthood, known as *wilāya* or *walāya*,[48] itself formed a whole branch of Sufi doctrine, to which Ḥakīm al-Tirmidhī and Ibn ʿArabi made significant contributions. These authors described an elaborate hierarchy of saints headed by the *quṭb* or "pole" under whom a whole pyramid of saints occupy different levels of sanctity and perform different functions. The saints (both male and female) holding positions in this vast hierarchy were called the "men of the unseen" (*rijāl al-ghayb*), and this concept, and its terms and titles, played and continues to play an important role in Sufi discourse.[49] For example, Shaykh Ibrahim Niasse defined the Knower by God (*ʿārif biLlāh*) as a special category of saint, writing "Every Knower by God is a saint [*walī*], but not every saint is a Knower."[50]

Another feature of this elaborate hagiology was the identification of different modes of sainthood with different prophets. The most perfect kind of sainthood was called

Muḥammadan sainthood, which was said to contain and be the source of all other types of sainthood, just as Muḥammad was said to contain and be the source of the attributes of all the other prophets. Just like prophecy, each type of sainthood had a "seal," a final, most perfect representative who is the source of that particular type of sainthood. The seal of Muḥammadan sainthood (*khatm al-walāya al-Muḥammadiyya*), often shortened to the "seal of the saints" (*khatm al-awliyāʾ*), therefore was described as the source of all sainthood.[51] This doctrine was a source of great controversy, and several prominent Sufis, including Ibn ʿArabi and Shaykh Aḥmad al-Tijānī, claimed to be the seal of Muḥammadan sainthood.[52]

This power of *walāya* is understood to originate with God (one of whose names is *al-Walī*, "The Friend/Protector") and to be transmitted by the Prophet to certain of his companions who, in turn, transmitted it to their disciples, and so on and so forth from master to disciple to the present day.[53] In this aspect, *walāya* can be understood as the power that makes spiritual progress possible—in other words, that which can turn an ordinary person into a "friend of God."

METHODS

For most Sufis in history, however, the process of becoming a "friend of God" was much more difficult than merely taking the hand of a Sufi master. Sufism has developed several techniques and practices designed to help the novice realize the doctrines outlined above, to embody the reality of the Universal Human (according to his or her capacity), to befriend God. These methods vary widely across history and geography, but there are some normative universals that can be discussed. The foundation of all "mainstream" Sufism is the *sharīʿa*. Echoing generations of Sufi masters, Shaykh Aḥmad al-Tijānī is recoded as saying "If you hear someone quoting me, place the statement on the scale of the noble *sharīʿa*; if it balances, take it, if it doesn't, leave it."[54] But the *sharīʿa* is only the beginning. As its name suggests (it literally means path or way), it is only the threshold to much more. This is outlined in one of the most famous and oft-cited *ḥadīth qudsī* (a ḥadīth in which the Prophet reports the speech of God): "The Messenger of God said, 'And the most beloved things with which My servant draws near to Me, is what I have enjoined upon him; and My servant does not cease drawing near to Me through supererogatory acts of worship until I love him. Then when I love him, I become his hearing with which he hears, and his sight with which he sees, and his hand with which he grips, and his leg with which he walks.'"[55] This ḥadīth outlines one of the most popular triads of Sufism: *sharīʿa*, *ṭarīqa*, and *ḥaqīqa*, or "the law," "the way," and "the reality." The acts "that have been enjoined" constitute the *sharīʿa*. The supererogatory acts of worship constitute the *ṭarīqa*, the Sufi path to God, and the state of divine union described at the end of the ḥadīth, the goal of the Sufi path, is the *ḥaqīqa*, the Divine Reality that overtakes the illusion of separation.

The supererogatory acts of worship constitute the practical backbone of the Sufi way, the *ṭarīqa*. Different Sufi traditions have developed different ways of carrying out these acts of worship, but they almost all revolve around *faqr*, *dhikr*, and *fikr*.[56] *Faqr* literally means poverty, but in the context of Sufism it means something more like emptiness or passivity toward the Divine. Sufism tends to place a high premium on good conduct/manners (*adab*) and service to others (*khidma*), as a means of cultivating virtues (*akhlāq*) and subduing one's carnal soul or ego (*nafs*). However, in Sufi ethics the virtues ultimately belong to God. Virtues are not something that one adds to one's character like a skill; they are innate qualities of the *fiṭra* (primordial human norm), which are revealed as one becomes empty or "poor" before God. The process of acquiring virtues is then the process of becoming transparent before God, or in a common image, of polishing the mirror of one's heart, so that the fullness of God's Qualities and Attributes, the source of all virtues, can be reflected therein.

But how is this polishing accomplished? According to a ḥadīth, "For everything there is a polish, and the polish for the hearts is *dhikr*."[57] *Dhikr* at once means mention, invocation, and remembrance, and is the central practice of Sufism. More than one Sufi author has argued that the point of all religion, of all the rites of all religion, is the remembrance of God (*dhikruLlāh*).[58] *Dhikr* can take many forms, including the recitation of the Qur'an or various prayers and litanies, but it most commonly takes the form of the repeated invocation of a name of God or revealed formula such as a prayer on the Prophet, or the shahāda (*Lā ilāha illā Llāh*, "There is no god but God").

Virtually all Sufism is based on *dhikr*, but as this kind of invocation requires a great deal of concentration, different Sufi traditions have developed forms of meditation or *fikr*, to help the mind transition from its everyday dispersion to the single-pointed focus of *dhikr*, and to remain focused on the invocation. *Fikr* (meditation or reflection) is a support for *dhikr* (invocation). While the practice of *dhikr* differs little from one Sufi tradition to the next, the variety of forms of *fikr* seems infinite.[59] Dance, music, parts of the body, geometric patterns, rhythm, poetry, colors, calligraphy, and the human face are all commonly used in different methods of *fikr*. The Qur'an encourages Muslims to meditate (*tafakkur*) on various aspects of the natural world, and these symbolic natural phenomena or signs (*ayāt*, such as the ocean, the sun, the wind, the moon, the desert, a tree, etc.) are also used by various Sufi traditions in their meditative practices.

The point of all of these practices is to remember God and become beloved. The *ḥadīth qudsī* cited above distinguishes between two phases: in the first, the servant travels the path through his or her own efforts in performing obligatory and supererogatory acts of worship. In the second, when he or she becomes beloved, it is God who "walks" the path with the servant's legs. These two stages on the spiritual path—one of individual effort, and the second of divine attraction—are called *sulūk* (wayfaring) and *jadhb* (rapture, attraction). While the path to realization can be characterized by one stage or another to a greater degree (those who proceed primarily by attraction are known as *majdhūb*, and those by wayfaring, *sālik*), the ideal espoused by most Sufi orders is some combination of the two.[60]

SUFI ORDERS

Around the sixth Islamic century, the structure of this kind of spiritual training changed dramatically with the emergence of new social institutions and traditions around Sufi masters. These traditions came to be known as *ṭarīqas* (Arabic plural *ṭuruq*) or Sufi orders. Before this time, the teaching and training of Sufism largely took place in the context of individual master-disciple relationships or in small circles, like the famous school of Baghdad, which formed around Junayd (d. 910). But this informal structure gradually gave way to the more formal structure of the *ṭarīqa*, from the twelfth/thirteenth Christian century onward,[61] as increasing numbers of disciples and changing social and spiritual conditions demanded a greater degree of organization.[62] The new Sufi orders served as organizations and structures designed to facilitate spiritual teaching, training, and a particular way of life. Typically a *ṭarīqa* would form around a great Sufi saint, whose disciples would organize and formalize his method of spiritual instruction and practice.

Sufi orders are typically run by a shaykh, or spiritual guide, who initiates and trains disciples according to a particular method. The shaykh will have had completed this process of spiritual training him- or herself, at the hands of another spiritual master, and so on back to the Prophet Muḥammad. This chain of transmission or spiritual lineage is called a *silsila*, and is seen as a sign of the orthodoxy and efficacy of the order. Disciples, often called *murīds* ("aspirants"), *fuqarāʾ* (singular: *faqīr*, "a poor person"), or the Persian equivalent, "dervishes," can join the *ṭarīqa* and attach themselves to its *silsila* through the process of initiation. Initiatory rites and practices vary greatly from order to order: sometimes initiation takes the form of the bestowal of a cloak (*khirqa*) from master to disciple; sometimes it takes the form of a pledge (*bayʿa*), in which the disciple grasps the shaykh's hand;[63] and sometimes it is just the mere repetition of a phrase. Sometimes shaykhs go out looking for disciples to initiate, and sometimes disciples have to undergo trials and tests of their sincerity and humility before initiation. Whatever the case may be, initiation connects the disciple to the initiatory chain of the *silsila*, and authorizes him or her to perform the rites of the Sufi order. These specific rites, usually called *awrād* (singular, *wird*) are typically daily litanies consisting of Qurʾanic passages and formulae to be recited a certain number of times, in both the morning and the evening. A typical example would be one hundred recitations of *astaghfiruL-lah*, "I beg forgiveness of God," followed by one hundred Ṣalāt ʿalāʾl-Nabī (prayers on the Prophet), and one hundred recitations of the shahāda, *La ilāha illā Llāh*, "There is no god but God." The *wird* may also be accompanied by invocations (*dhikr*, pl. *adhkār*) of various names of God or other formulae. Shaykhs sometimes prescribe *khalwas*, or spiritual retreats, in which the disciples remain isolated, devoting themselves only to a particular *dhikr* (invocation) or set of invocations for a set period of time (one week, forty days, one year) or until they have achieved the desired spiritual result.

The shaykh of an order will often have several *muqaddams* or representatives who can initiate disciples on his or her behalf and train them in the practices of the order. Some orders also appoint *khalīfas* (vicegerents or successors), who act as shaykhs in their own right, appointing *muqaddams* and initiating their own disciples, all the while remaining attached to the shaykh of the order. Sufi orders often also have group sessions of *dhikr*, called *ḥaḍras* or *majālis* (singular, *majlīs*), which sometimes involve drumming, singing, poetry, and dance.[64] The most famous, and one of the most elaborate, Sufi rituals of this kind is the *sema* (in Arabic, *samāʿ*) of Rumi's Mawlāwī (Mevlevi) order, from which comes their nickname, the "Whirling Dervishes." These activities usually take place in a Sufi center or mosque called a *zāwiya* (also called a *tekye*, *khanaqa*, or *darga*, in the Turkish and Persianate worlds, respectively, including India). A major order, like the Qādiriyya, founded by the famous shaykh ʿabd al-Qādir al-Jīlānī (d. 1166) will typically have a main or mother *zāwiya* and other *zāwiyas* in different cities around the world.

The Sufi orders are often likened to branches of a tree, and within the context of a particular order, an especially great master may inaugurate a new branch. For example, the predominantly North African Shādhilī order has spawned many branches, including the Shādhilī-Darqawī, founded by Shaykh Muḥammad al-Darqawī (d. 1823), which itself spawned a new branch, the Shādhilī-Darqawī-ʿAlāwī, founded by Aḥmad al-ʿAlāwī (d. 1934). Sometimes shaykhs who have been initiated into multiple orders can merge these different Sufi lineages into one order, such as the Qādirī-Rifāʿī order or the Khalwatī-Jerrahī order. Some Sufi orders—like the Chishtiyya of the Indian subcontinent (famous for its qawwali music and influence on classical Hindustani music), the Mūridiyya of Senegal, or the Ba ʿAlawī of Yemen of the Indian Ocean coastal region—are localized to a particular cultural or geographic zone, while others, like the Qādiriyya, have spread all over the world. Some *ṭarīqas* emphasize ecstatic experience, while others emphasize sobriety; some emphasize charity and service to society, while others emphasize contemplation and retreat from society; and these emphases can change over time or vary from zawiya to zawiya within the same order. In addition to those described above, the Naqshbandī, Niʿmatullahī, and Bektashī Sufi orders should also be mentioned as contemporary, popular Sufi orders. While Sufi initiation and practice still do take place outside the structure of Sufi orders, they have been and remain the most popular vehicles for the tradition of *taṣawwuf* for the past millennium.

## THE TIJĀNIYYA

One of the more recent Sufi orders to emerge is the Ṭarīqa Tijāniyya. Its name is derived from that of its founder, Aḥmad al-Tijānī, who was born in 1737 in Aïn Madi, an oasis in the southwestern desert of Algeria, and died in 1815 in the city of Fes, where his beautiful mausoleum is an important site of pilgrimage. Shaykh Tijānī traced his lineage to the legendary Mawlay Idrīs, whom many consider the founder of North African Sufism and Islam, and through him, to the Prophet of Islam. As a young man, Aḥmad al-Tijānī traveled to Fes to study religious sciences, where several of his teachers initiated him into different orders of Sufism, including branches of the Qādirī and Shādhilī orders. According to the hagiographical literature, one of his teachers predicted that the young Tijānī would attain the lofty spiritual rank of Shaykh Abū'l-Ḥasan al-Shādhilī (who was widely recognized in the Magbreb as the "pole" or *quṭb* of his age), but that this spiritual opening (*fatḥ*) would only come to him in the desert.[65]

Shaykh Tijānī then returned to the Algerian desert, teaching religious sciences while devoting himself to his spiritual exercises. On his way to perform the ḥajj in 1773, Tijānī was initiated into the Khalwatī order in Algiers. In Mecca and Medina, Shaykh Tijānī is said to have met with and learned from several great Sufi masters, and on his way back to the Maghreb he was made a muqaddam of the Khalwatī order by Maḥmūd al-Kurdī (d. 1780) in Egypt.

However, Shaykh Tijānī's affiliation with the Khalwatī order ended in extraordinary circumstances. According to the hagiographical sources, in 1784, in the oasis of Abū Samghūn, Tijānī had a waking vision of the Prophet, who told him to leave everything he had taken from other spiritual teachers and masters, since he (the Prophet) was now his spiritual guide. The Prophet gave him the basis of a new *wird* or litany, establishing a new spiritual way, which was to become known as the Ṭarīqa Tijāniyya.[66]

In 1798, Shaykh Tijānī settled in Fes, where he enjoyed the favor of the Alaouite sultan, Mawlay Sulaymān, establishing his zawiya in the center of the city. Before he died, Shaykh Tijānī's most famous muqaddams—Sīdī ʿAlī Tamāsīnī (d. 1844), Sīdī ʿAlī Harāzim al-Barrāda (d. 1856), Muḥammad al-Ḥāfiẓ (d. 1830), and Muḥammad Ghālī (d.

1829)—spread and established the Tijani order across North Africa and the Sahara, into Mauritania, and in the Ḥijāz. Sidi ʿAlī Harāzim's *Jawāhir al Maʿānī*[67] gives an account of Shaykh Aḥmad al-Tijānī's life, visions and mystical experiences, teachings, and aphorisms, and has become the most influential written source of Tijani doctrine.

Recent scholarship has linked the Tijani order with the rather nebulous concept of "neo-Sufism," and while I believe there is little "neo" about neo-Sufism, it should be noted that the order was founded in and shows the influence of the context of eighteenth-century Sufi reform movements that became popular and influential in North Africa, the Ḥijāz, and the Indian subcontinent.[68] This movement included Sufi masters such as Shah Walī Allāh (d. 1762) of Delhi in India; Aḥmad ibn Idrīs (d. 1837) and his disciples: Muḥammad al-Sanūsī (d. 1859), founder of the Sanūsiyya order,[69] Muḥammad al-Mirghānī (d. 1852), founder of the Khatmiyya order;[70] as well as Muṣṭafa Kamāl al-dīn al-Bakrī (d. 1749), the spiritual master of Shaykh Sammān (d. 1775)[71] and the spiritual grandfather of Shaykh Kurdī (who initiated Shaykh Aḥmad al-Tijānī). All of these figures and the traditions associated with them emphasized strict observance of the *sharīʿa* and often advocated for social reform through spiritual renewal among scholars and at the grassroots level. These various movements also continued a trend in Sufism that seems to have begun in the fifteenth century,[72] in which the role of the Prophet and prayers on him (*taṣliya*) in individual spiritual attainment was explicitly emphasized to a greater degree than before, and which saw a shift away from the extraordinary asceticism and seclusion that characterized much of early Sufi practice, instead emphasizing "being with God in the midst of people." Many of these trends can be seen in the written works and records of the Shādhilī Shaykhs Aḥmad Zarrūq (d. 1493), whom Tijani authors frequently quote, and his contemporary, Muḥammad al-Jazūlī (d. 1465), author of the popular *Dalāʾil al-Khayrāt*. Many of the orders associated with the eighteenth-century reform movements that embodied these trends took the name Ṭarīqa Muḥammadiyya including the Tijāniyya.

**Tijani Doctrine**

While the Tijāniyya shares many of the same doctrines and practices of other Sufi orders, especially the Shādhilī and Khalwatī, there are a few features that distinguish it from other *ṭuruq*. The most unique feature of the Tijāniyya is that its *silsila*, the chain of initiatory transmission, goes directly from Aḥmad al-Tijānī to the Prophet Muḥammad. Virtually all other Sufi orders, such as the Shādhiliyya or the Qādiriyya, have chains of transmission that go back to the founder of the order, and then from the founder back through various Sufi masters usually converging on ʿAlī ibn Abī Ṭālib, and then going back to the Prophet.

For Tijanis, this direct link to the Prophet was and is regarded as the source of the superiority of the order. Virtually all Sufi orders have traditions making some kind of claim for the superiority of the order and its founder,[73] but the Tijāniyya claims its founder as the seal of the saints (*khatm al-awliyā'*)—the hidden source of sainthood (*al-khatm al-maktūm*) for all the other saints of all Sufi orders of all times—just as the Prophet Muḥammad is understood to be the source of prophecy for all other prophets. Extending the analogy further, Tijanis sometimes describe the order as playing "in Islam the same role that Islam plays among the other religions"—that is, completing, perfecting and synthesizing them.[74] Many Tijanis also predict that all Sufi orders will eventually become incorporated into the Tijāniyya. For similar reasons, and on the basis of Shaykh Aḥmad al-Tijānī's explicit instructions, Tijanis are generally forbidden from taking other initiations and, upon entering the order, must abandon the litanies they may have been given by previous non-Tijani masters. Needless to say, these doctrines of Tijani supremacy have been the source of some controversy among members of other Sufi orders, but only seem to have contributed to, and not detracted from, the order's growth.[75]

But perhaps the most characteristic feature of Tijani doctrine is its emphasis on the related concepts of *fayḍ* and the *ḥaqīqa Muḥammadiyya*. On the latter, Shaykh Ibrahim Niasse writes, "In a *ḥadīth qudsī*, Allah says, 'If not for you (O Muḥammad), I would not have brought forth creation. I created you for Myself and I made the rest of creation for you.' The Prophet said, 'All Muslims are from my light, and my light is from the light of Allah.' All of creation—believers and non-believers, the heavens and the earth—came from his light and his light came from Allah."[76] For Tijanis (and Sufis in general), the Prophet is not a merely a historical figure, but rather a living reality through whom God continuously creates the world, and through whom He pours out His light, mercy, being, knowledge, and blessings on all of creation. This is the meaning of *fayḍ*, divine effusion or overflowing,[77] and one of the secrets behind the importance of the *Ṣalāt al-Fātiḥ*[78] and other prayers on the Prophet (several prayers on the Prophet from other orders use similar imagery and language of *fayḍ*)[79] is that they call forth the divine *fayḍ*, which is simultaneously being, knowledge, and light.[80] Shaykh Ibrahim Niasse writes, "Know that the intention behind the masters of spiritual training is to reach the Prophet, the highest of all intermediaries, through their mediation. 'Abd Allāh ould al-Ḥājj al-'Alawī once told me, 'The purpose of the recitations in the Tijāniyya is to get a whiff of the Muḥammadan reality.'"[81]

The basic structure of the concept of *fayḍ* as it operates in the Tijāniyya-Ibrāhīmiyya is perhaps most clearly explained in the following extended metaphor:

> There is a parable the Professor Ibrahim Mahmud Diop heard from Shaykh Ibrahim which helps to explain the concept of *fayḍa*. We are to picture five things. First

imagine a fathomless well—not an ordinary well, but a well that has no bottom. Next imagine a leather bucket that never needs repair. Next, imagine a tireless worker who continually draws water from that well. Fourthly, imagine a basin next to that well which eventually becomes full. Finally, imagine water so precious it cannot be thrown away and yet cannot be put back into the well already overflowing. The question arises, what should be done with the water after the basin is full? The answer: many basins will be constructed around the well to receive the precious water. In the parable, the well represents Allah, glorified and exalted is He, whose being is continuous without end. The water is Divine gnosis (*maʿrifa*) and experience (*dhawq*). The leather bucket is the Prophet. A saying among Sufis indicates, "Without an intermediary, one never reaches a goal," and the Prophet is the greatest intermediary between the creation and Allah. The worker in the parable is Shaykh Aḥmad al-Tijānī. The basin is an extraordinary spiritual adept who has received so much in the way of Divine gnosis that he must communicate this Gnosis to others or it will overflow. He is the owner of the *fayḍa* or flood.[82]

This schema can be pictured in two ways. First there is the macrocosmic model in which God sends down blessings and spiritual realization on the Prophet, who passes it along to Shaykh Aḥmad al-Tijānī, who passes it along to Shaykh Ibrahim Niasse, who passes it on to his disciples (see fig. 1). Remembering that Shaykh Tijānī is also the seal of sainthood, he also receives this outpouring of divine knowledge and blessings from the other prophets, and is the source for all the other saints.[83]

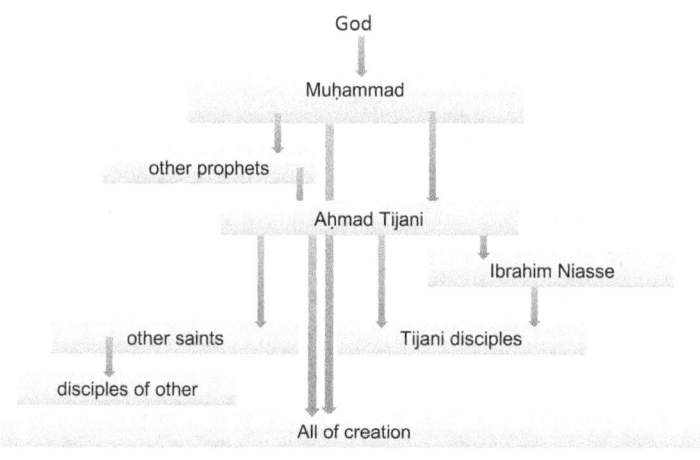

FIGURE 1 *Fayḍ* in macrocosm.

What Is Tijani Sufism? • 49

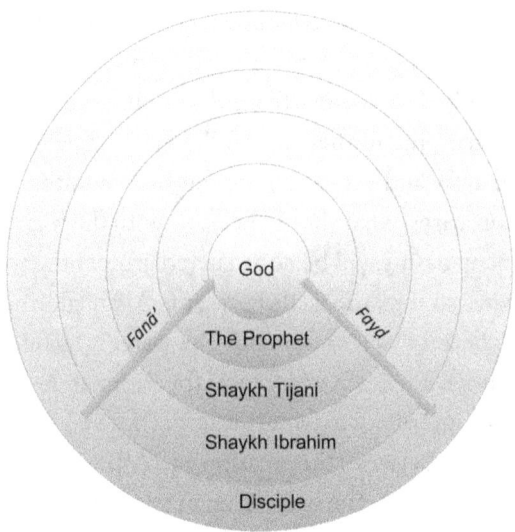

FIGURE 2 *Fayḍ* in microcosm.

The second schema is microcosmic and depicts the different levels of inner spiritual realization. From this perspective, the *fayḍ* is experienced as a fountain welling up from the deepest depths of the aspirant's soul, which are identified with God, the Prophet, and the shaykh (see fig. 2).

**Tijani Method**

The methods of the Tijāniyya do not differ significantly from those of other *ṭuruq*. They include the observance of the *sharīʿa*, including the observance of the five prayers (in congregation when possible), an obligatory *wird*[84] to be recited morning and evening, an additional litany called the *waẓīfa*[85] that can be recited either once or twice daily, and a weekly gathering for *dhikr* on Friday afternoons known as the *ḥaḍra* or *hailala*.[86] The *wird* and *waẓīfa* must be made up if missed, and strict adherence is a condition of being a disciple. Tijani disciples are also encouraged to recite the *Ṣalāt al-Fātiḥ* or, with permission, the shahāda and the divine name "Allāh," outside of these formal sessions. There are numerous optional litanies and invocations for particular spiritual purposes (largely consisting of prayers commonly recited by other Sufi *ṭuruq*), many of which can be found in printed collections, but these require the authorization, supervision, and initiation (*talqīn*) of a spiritual guide. The most important of these are the litanies used in the *tarbiya*[87] (*awrād al-tarbiya*) of Shaykh Ibrahim Niasse's branch of the order.

50 • Ways of Knowing in Tijani Sufism

The Tijani method in general is, however, distinguished by its general lack of *khalwa* (the practice of putting disciples into prolonged spiritual retreat),[88] its emphasis on the *Ṣalāt al-Fātiḥ* and *Jawharat al-Kamāl* and the particular practices surrounding the latter's recitation,[89] and its emphasis on *shukr* or gratitude toward God, rather than *zuhd* or asceticism.[90] In his *Rimāḥ*, Shaykh ʿUmar Tal explains that real *zuhd* is not defined by not possessing things, but in not being possessed by things, and that the Sufi path is concerned with "the journey of the hearts, not the journey of the bodies," meaning that ascetic practice is not an end in and of itself.[91]

In this sense, *shukr* means something more than ordinary gratitude, but represents the purest and most disinterested approach to worship. The Prophet was once asked why he continued to pray fervently even though God had forgiven all his past and future sins, to which he answered, "Should I not be a grateful servant?"[92] Similarly, Shaykh Ibrahim Niasse counseled his disciples not to worship God in expectation of receiving spiritual enlightenment, as this is just another form of horse-trading that props up the *nafs* (ego / carnal soul), but rather to worship God for His own sake, and ask God for God.[93]

Likewise, the earliest Tijani literature identifies the founder and the followers of this *ṭarīqa* as being among the Malāmiyya or "People of Blame."[94] This term originally named an early movement of Islamic piety whose adherents would actively court the blame and disapproval of religious authorities and the public as a means of combating hypocrisy and pride.[95] However, Ibn ʿArabi (and later Sufi authors, including the Tijanis) use this term to refer to the highest category of mystics who "know and are not known," those saints who are outwardly ordinary and inwardly extraordinary, who do not make a show of miracles or their high spiritual station, but remain hidden in plain sight.[96] Thus, Tijanis tend to have ordinary professions and "blend in" to their societies rather than standing apart or aloof from them.

Finally, the particular Tijani method that is the subject of this study is distinguished by the special mode of *tarbiya* established by Shaykh Ibrahim Niasse, which his disciples claim has produced a remarkable quality and quantity of realized Sufis in West Africa and around the world.

## A BRIEF HISTORY OF THE TIJĀNIYYA IN WEST AFRICA

Shaykh Tijānī was born and raised in the Sahara bordering West Africa. The desert is often compared to an ocean dotted with islands of oases and traversed by ships of caravans, and like an oceanic zone, the desert paradoxically increases cultural, economic, and intellectual exchange along its borders. This was very much true of the Sahara, where goods, books, ideas, and spiritual movements like the Ṭarīqa Tijāniyya spread from "coast" to "coast."⁹⁷ While today the Tijāniyya has spread to South Africa, Indonesia, Europe, and North America, the core of its membership is still found in western Africa, particularly in the Saharan and sub-Saharan countries between Mauritania, Nigeria, and Sudan.

During Shaykh Aḥmad al-Tijānī's life, one of his closest disciples and *khalīfas*, Muḥammad al-Ḥāfiẓ (d. 1830), spread the order in Mauritania, converting the scholarly Idaw ʿAlī tribe to the *ṭarīqa*. The Ḥāfiẓiyya branch of the *ṭarīqa* was known for its scholarship and respect for other *ṭuruq*. The influential Tijani manual of spiritual training, *Mīzāb al-Raḥma al-Rabbāniyya fī'l-Tarbiya bi'l-Ṭarīqa al-Tijāniyya*, was written by ibn Anbūja, a disciple of Muḥammad al-Ḥāfiẓ.⁹⁸ Muḥammad al-Ḥāfiẓ's close disciple, Mawlūd Fāl, spread the order among other tribes in Mauritania and along the Senegal River valley, making further inroads south of the Sahara, even as far as present-day Nigeria. Mawlūd Fāl's older brother, Aḥmad Ibn Baba, authored the *Munyāt al-Murīd* (*Goals of the Aspirant*), which became famous through the influential commentary *Bughyat al-mustafīd* by the Moroccan Tijani Shaykh Muḥammad al-ʿArabī ibn Sāʾiḥ (d. 1892), who founded the prominent Tijani zawiya of Rabat. This commentary has become one of the main sources of Tijani doctrine and illustrates the flow of knowledge and writing both north and south in western Africa. Members of the scholarly Idaw ʿAlī tribe played an important role in spreading the Tijāniyya throughout the region, but it was the appearance of the singular personality of al-Ḥājj ʿUmar Tal that firmly established the *ṭarīqa* south of the Sahara.

Al-Ḥājj ʿUmar Tal (d. 1864) was originally initiated by a disciple of Mawlūd Fal in Futa Tooro (northern Senegal), but it was Muḥammad al-Ghālī (d. 1829), a close disciple and *khalīfa* of Shaykh Aḥmad al-Tijānī, who appointed Tal as a *muqaddam* and *khalīfa* of the order after meeting him in Mecca and taking him as a disciple. Ghālī completed Tal's spiritual training over the course of three years and charged him with spreading the *ṭarīqa* in West Africa, and this he did, by the pen and the sword.⁹⁹ On his return from Mecca, al-Ḥājj ʿUmar spent time in the court of the Sokoto caliphate, befriending Muḥammad Bello, the son of ʿUthman dan Fodio, and further spreading the order there. Through a series of jihads (he fought the French, non-Muslim African, and other Muslim polities), Shaykh Tal established the extensive, but short-lived, Toucouleur Empire, and spread the Tijani order in what is today Mali, Guinea, and Senegal. Al-Ḥājj ʿUmar is also the author of the *Rimāḥ Ḥizb al-Raḥīm ʿalā Nuḥūr Ḥizb al-Rajīm* (*The Lances of the Party of the Compassionate against the Necks of the Party of the Accursed*), a veritable compendium of Tijani doctrine, history, rules for disciples, aphorisms, and quotations from other Sufi works on a variety of topics. The *Rimāḥ* is often printed in the margins of the *Jawāhir al-Maʿānī*, from which it quotes extensively.¹⁰⁰

Tal's nephew Alfa Hashim (d. 1931) left the Sokoto caliphate after its defeat at the hands of the British in 1902–3 and fled to the Ḥijāz, eventually settling in Medina, where he became one of the most prominent Tijani scholars in the region. Many West Africans sought and took initiation from him during pilgrimages to Mecca and Medina, spreading his lineage back in West Africa upon their return. Al-Ḥājj 'Umar Tal's grandson, Seydou Nourou Tal (d. 1980), whom the French nicknamed *le grand marabout*, and who was also the son-in-law and contested successor of al-Ḥājj Malik Sy (see below), was an important leader of his grandfather's branch of the order in Senegambia and Mali.

The Ḥamawwiya branch of the Tijāniyya, founded by Shaykh Ḥamāhallāh (d. 1943) in Nioro, Mali, emphasized mystical experience over formal learning, and despite persecution from the French colonial authorities and conflicts with other branches of the order, found success among merchants, former slaves, laypeople, and a few scholarly families in Mali, Mauritania, Burkina Faso, and Côte D'Ivoire, where Shaykh Yacouba Sylla established a sizeable following.[101] Tierno Bokar (d. 1939), himself a descendant of al-Ḥājj 'Umar Tal, and his disciple, the celebrated Africanist and belle-lettrist Amadou Hampâté Bâ (d. 1991), were both members of this branch of the Tijāniyya.[102]

Mention must also be made of al-Ḥājj Mālik Sy (d. 1922), founder of the largest Tijani lineage in Senegal. Sy's initiations linked him to both the Ḥāfiẓiyya and al-Ḥājj 'Umar Tal's branches of the order, and he spread the Tijāniyya and Islamic learning throughout Senegal, Gambia, and Mauritania at the turn of the century. A consummate teacher and savvy navigator of the tricky French colonial system, Mālik Sy established many schools throughout Senegal and authored a substantial body of doctrinal and didactic works in both prose and poetry deserving of further scholarly attention. He established his zawiya in Tivaouane, which has become one of the main centers of the order in Senegal.[103]

Although al-Ḥājj Mālik's close friend, 'Abdallāh Niasse (d. 1922), is better known as the father of Shaykh Ibrahim Niasse, he was an important scholar and shaykh in his own right. Like Mālik Sy, he corresponded frequently with the Tijani zawiyas of Mauritania, Aïn Madi, and Fes and was granted an *ijāza muṭlaqa* (unlimited authorization) by Shaykh Aḥmad Skīraj (d. 1944), the great Moroccan scholar, judge, and defender of the Tijāniyya, on a visit to the latter in Fes. In addition to his initiatory lineages (*asānid*) connecting him to al-Ḥājj 'Umar Tal and the Ḥāfiẓiyya, Shaykh 'Abdallāh also received an important chain of initiation connecting him to Shaykh Aḥmad al-Tijānī through the latter's successor, 'Alī Tamāsīnī.

However, it is through Niasse's son, Shaykh Ibrahim Niasse, that the Tijāniyya order became the most widespread and influential Sufi order in West Africa, and one of the largest Muslim organizations in the world. Shaykh Ibrahim instituted a special form of spiritual training, known as *tarbiya*, which is claimed to have led a great number of disciples, from all walks of life, to high spiritual stations more quickly than was common among other branches of the *ṭarīqa*, or even other *ṭuruq*. As a result, hundreds of thousands of people were initiated into the Tijāniyya by Shaykh Niasse and his *muqaddams*, establishing important zawiyas in Nigeria, Ghana, Senegal, and Sudan. This was widely interpreted as the fulfillment of a prophecy prevalent in Tijani sources of the coming of a *fayḍa*, or outpouring of mystical knowledge and spiritual realization.[104] Ibrahim Niasse authored two major works on Sufism, defending and explaining his methods, titled the *Kāshif al-Ilbās* (*The Removal of the Veils*) and *al-Sirr al-Akbar* (*The Greatest Secret*), in addition to several shorter works and *diwāns* of poetry. One of his popular oral *tafsīr* sessions has been transcribed and published as *Fī Riyāḍ al-Tafsīr lil-Qurʾān al-Karīm* (*In the Gardens of Tafsir of the Noble Qurʾan*), as has a collection of his short treatises, letters, and sermons (as *Jawāhir al-Rasāʾil*, or *Pearls of Letters*). Shaykh Ibrahim traveled widely throughout the West Africa, the Middle East, Europe, and even Asia, and his branch of the order, the Tijāniyya-Ibrāhīmiyya, commonly known among its members simply as the Fayḍa, is currently the most popular branch of the Tijāniyya, with zawiyas throughout the continent, the Middle East, Southeast Asia, and in North America and Europe.

In addition to continuing his legacy of *tarbiya*, some of Shaykh Ibrahim's most recent successors—Shaykh Ḥan Cissé (d. 2008) and his brothers, Shaykh Tijānī ʿAlī Cissé and Shaykh Māḥī Cissé—have been responsible for the spread of the Tijāniyya in the United States, Europe, and South Africa, and have overseen the publication and translation of many of Shaykh Ibrahim's works into English. Shaykh Aḥmad Tijānī ʿAlī Cissé was recently placed nineteenth on a list of the five hundred most influential Muslims by the Royal Islamic Strategic Studies Center of Jordan, which described him as "the Spiritual leader of around 100 million Tijani Muslims."[105] While the Tijāniyya began in the Sahara and the Maghreb, the remarkable legacy of Shaykh Ibrahim Niasse has transformed it into a global Sufi order centered in West Africa.

THE PRESENT STUDY

*Deep Knowledge* is a study of the epistemology and associated spiritual exercises, or ways of knowing, among contemporary members of the Tijāniyya-Ibrāhīmiyya in Dakar and Kaolack. Life in many neighborhoods in Senegal is accompanied by the soundtrack of the rites of Tijani and Mouride Sufis, broadcast over loudspeakers from mosques or chanted in the street. The pictures of Tijani shaykhs adorn taxis and shop stalls, and on Fridays prayer beads become a nearly universal accessory. If you were to examine any young person's cell phone, you would probably find pictures of hip-hop artists, football and wrestling stars, and Sufi shaykhs. The Sufi orders of Senegal have adapted themselves well to the increasingly globalized and digital world of contemporary Senegal, and seem to be in no danger of going anywhere. But as fascinating as these sociological dynamics are, this work is primarily concerned with the intellectual or philosophical dimensions of the tradition.

Sometimes, when participating in or listening to conversations about different Sufi masters or topics, I felt as if I were in a Socratic dialogue. Like the Pythagoreans, many Senegalese Sufis refuse to discuss the "mysteries" (*asrār*) of doctrine or method whenever an outsider is present. For example, Ibrāhīmī Tijanis sometimes ask, "Are there any clouds in the sky?" before speaking about the order's secrets, such as the process of *tarbiya*.[106] While many of the spiritual exercises of *tarbiya* are secret, and I have done my best to protect their integrity, I have tried to approach them as part of a larger philosophical praxis, taking Hadot's definition of philosophy as a "way of life." That is, I tried to approach and interpret contemporary Sufi practice, discourse, and discourse about practice, not as anthropological or historical data, but as a philosophical program of theory and praxis that can be analyzed and evaluated (to a certain extent) intellectually. In this chapter, I have attempted to provide a brief introduction to the various terms and concepts of Sufism in general and the Tijāniyya in particular, in order to contextualize and define the terms of the main arguments of this study. In the next chapters, I will attempt to describe the unique knowledge contemporary Tijanis claim to possess, how they acquired it, and how and why they describe this knowledge as being *ḥaqq al-yaqīn* or *'ayn al-yaqīn*, the very reality or essence of certainty.

CHAPTER 2

# What Is *Ma'rifa*?

> What is *ma'rifa*? That's hard to say because you live it.
> —M. D.

> Conceiving of the reality of knowledge is extremely difficult.
> —IBN ʿARABĪ

What is knowledge? Like "being" or "consciousness," "knowledge" is one of the most everyday, and yet mysterious, aspects of human life. What can we know? How is it that we know? How well can we know? How well can we know ourselves? How can we know that we know? These questions have inspired some of the greatest minds of civilizations around the world, from the earliest recorded history through the present day. In contemporary Africa, and in the Islamic world, some of the most dynamic and fascinating approaches to these questions can be found in the branch of the Tijani Sufi order founded by Shaykh Ibrahim Niasse. The community of Shaykh Ibrahim Niasse—known in Arabic as *al-Ṭarīqa al-Tijāniyya al-Ibrāhīmiyya*, in French as Niassènes, in Wolof as the Taalibe Baay, and among themselves as the Fayḍa—is a self-defined community of knowledge. Membership in this community is largely defined by having gone through the process of *tarbiya*, a process of spiritual transformation that is supposed to lead to the acquisition of *ma'rifa*, direct knowledge of God and of self.

This section of the book is an exposition of the epistemology of Ibrahim Niasse's branch of the Tijāniyya as articulated by the masters, disciples, and authoritative texts of the tradition. The present chapter examines various definitions and explanations of *ma'rifa* and its relationship to other kinds of knowledge; the following chapter discusses the means by which this special knowledge is acquired; and the final chapter of this section discusses the ways in which *ma'rifa* is verified. I begin with two long quotations from disciples that summarize and illustrate the main themes and arguments that will be explored throughout the rest of this section.

S. D. is a new father and philosophy instructor who moonlights as an English teacher for Senegalese students, and as a Wolof and French teacher for expats in Dakar. I met S. D. at his wife's family home in the neighborhood of Ouakam on the day after his son's *batème* (naming ceremony). S. D. took me to meet his shaykh, Babacar N'Diaye, who greeted us warmly and, after hearing a little bit about my research, assured me that I was in good hands with S. D., whom he described as an *'ārif biLlāh* (knower through God) and a leader of his disciples. While S. D. and I waited for my official interview with Shaykh N'Diaye, he told me how he first came to the *ṭarīqa*:

> I was out late one night with my friends. We were coming back from a club—in those days, I used to party and smoke cigarettes—and it was very late, and I heard the sound of a *gammu* [of Shaykh Ibrahim's branch of the Tijāniyya]. I liked the sound of the *zikrs*, they were different from what I had heard before.... Since that day, I started being interested in the *ṭarīqa*, in *tarbiya*, but I didn't go immediately. I think I waited two or three years later to decide, and I don't know what exactly made me join. But I know that since that day, I was clearly interested in that. Then one day, my elder brother, he is a *taalibe* [disciple] also, a *taalibe* of Shaykh Babacar N'Diaye, I asked him to bring me to the shaykh to introduce me to him. And that is what he did....
>
> I think I took the *wird*, and a week later I asked for *tarbiya*, because I always heard Niassènes [followers of Shaykh Ibrahim Niasse] say that we have to know God first when we want to practice His religion. And that idea made me curious. How can we know God? Who is God? If we can know God, where is God? Can I communicate with Him? So that made me curious, so I wanted to know, to discover if we can really know God. Also, they give a sentence from the Qur'an that says that God asks us to know Him first before practicing. I don't know exactly the passage, but I think it is in the Qur'an.[1] People have many interpretations of this sentence; for some people, it means that we have to know that He is the greatest, that He is the one that gives you life, food, et cetera, and that He is the One who has created the world, everything; but I, myself, I do not think this answer is very strong. So that made me curious to go further and understand if we can actually know God. And while I was doing my initiation [*tarbiya*], during the night while I was alone near the beach, I looked at the beach and then I said, probably something will come from the sea... [*laughs*] and tell me that He is God—but I said no, it's not

possible, because God is not limited. Whatever it is, no matter how awesome it is, it is still limited, so it can't be God. So days later, I still didn't know who God was. And one moment I said, hmmm, these Niassènes, they make people silly, to lose their sense, . . . but my shaykh, he gave me three or four words: *Awwalu* [the First], *Akhiru* [the Last], *Ẓāhiru* [the Outward], *Bāṭin* [the Inward]. That means that God is the First and the Last, and God is the Visible and the Invisible. So, for example, if I put my hand here, I can see this, but I can't see what is behind [it]. So I say that probably all things that we are seeing, all things that I can see, there is a visible and invisible side—the visible side is God and the side that I can't see is also God, and likewise with the First and the Last. So I asked myself, who was here to know that God was here first, or here last, I didn't understand that part. What I understood was that all things that we can see, if God really is unlimited, if God is everywhere, all things that we see can be God or are God, but I was not very sure. Because what disturbed me about that idea was, when I was going to the toilet, . . . is God in the toilet? In our religion, we have the habit of not pronouncing even the name of God when we are in the bathroom. I am seeing the dirty things inside—can I consider this, too, God?

So I was thinking that I was making a mistake. Then I was confused again. But, one day, while my *marabout* was giving a lesson for all the *taalibes*, he came back to those four words: *Awwalu, Akhiru, Ẓāhiru, Bāṭin* . . . and there is a proverb in Wolof that says, "All things that are not good are nothing." So, I asked myself, Who can show nothing? Who can identify nothing? He made us ponder that idea. Can we identify nothing? Can we put our finger on or point toward nothing? So what if all things that are not God are nothing? So that means everything is God. . . .

When I was in the terminal class of lycée, our philosophy teacher asked us a question: If God can do everything, if He is All-Powerful, can He create a stone that would be bigger than God? So now we would have to recognize that there is something bigger than God. If God cannot do it, we would have to limit God's power. When I studied Ibrahim Niasse's philosophy, I understood that he [the teacher] was ignorant, because there is no difference between the stone and God. That is why I appreciate [the initiation]; once you do the initiation, you are able to explain, or to understand, many things, even if you have never dealt with them before. In every situation you understand or you know how to proceed. . . .

My shaykh explained that in initiation we go through four levels, or *ḥaḍarāt*: *Ḥaḍrat al-Qudsi*—there is nothing, there is only one mystery here; *Ḥaḍra Aḥmadiya, Ḥaḍra Muḥammadiyya*, and *Ḥaḍra khutbu or Nasūt*. . . . After the initiation, once you know who God is, you are in what we call the *Ḥaḍrat al-Qudsi*, that *Ḥaḍra*, there is only One God, nothing except God, everything is God. . . . I don't believe that we can get all knowledge from the *muqaddams*; the *muqaddams* only give us the principles. The main things you need to discover yourself. My own initiation, it took two months and a half. I still went to work, but every day after praying, I would go around the streets with my prayer beads, and I went to the beach at night to do my prayers, but since I've finished, since I've gone through the four *ḥaḍarāt*, in my life I always practice it. . . .

I remember when I had just finished my initiation, I called myself God and everything God. My brother-in-law told me, "You are stupid." He asked me, "Can we see this furniture and call it God? That's God for you, but maybe I don't see it that way." Or "If you are God, you can make rain right now." That's what they used to say. Also I heard from a shaykh who was telling me the origin of things, and he said that everything—God Himself said that everything—will return to the way it was. . . . People, human beings, everyone is from their parents, all the way back to Adam and Eve—Eve is from Adam, Adam comes from the earth, the earth comes from the foam (of the ocean), and the foam comes from water and the heaven of the Prophet, and the heaven of the Prophet comes from the Prophet and the Prophet comes from God. So everything—the sofa, the wood, the trunk, the tree—has an origin, and everything will return to its origin, back to its primary material, back to the Prophet, back to God. So when we see that the sofa is God, that is justified because all of its materials are derived from God. It is not possible that God should create anything apart from nothing, because nothing is that which does not exist. Like Antoine Lavoisier said, "Nothing is created, nothing is lost, all is transformed." Everything is only transformation . . . if God created something from other than nothing then that thing would exist alongside Him—it would be a self-contradiction since God is the First and the Only. God cannot coexist with anything, so "creation" is the profane term—really "transformation" is the more correct term. . . .

Just after my initiation, I remember my shaykh asked me if it was good to drink beer as a Muslim. I said that beer and water are the same thing, because I was in the state of *Ḥaḍrat al-Qudsi* and everything was identical. But now, according to the shaykh, it is dangerous to let someone always live in *Ḥaḍrat al-Qudsi*, because he may create some problems with other people; he would misbehave and say that this is God. That is why after the initiation, immediately, you have to put him in the second step, the third step, so that he leaves the *Ḥaḍrat al-Qudsi* and goes back to the *Ḥaḍrat al-Nasūt*, to know that here you are God, but there you are not God. . . .

I said that this is like philosophy. In philosophy, for example, we put some rules, some main elements that are the foundation, axioms. . . . After the initiation, there are some elements, keys, they give you. Because what the shaykh has given you, it is a liberation, but not an absolute liberation. For example, they tell you that in everything you should see the four *ḥaḍras*, in everything you should see God, the Prophet, Shaykh [Tijani], and Shaykh Ibrahim....

It's like philosophy from Greek antiquity; they had what they called the public place, the agora, where the intellectuals met to discuss diverse questions. The same thing is reproduced during the *gammu* at Kaolack, when we are together and we ask each other questions. Each person has his own question that he thinks about and asks, often prompting a debate. I forget when, but I remember one debate we had all night, until dawn. Each person has his perspective and opinion—that is to say, there is no dogmatism, equally one can even swim against the current of the shaykh.... The shaykh may have more knowledge, more wisdom than us, especially regarding what is in religious books, so we follow what he says in these matters, but in the domain of social life, we are all initiated. Once you have been initiated you can see differently, you can see farther than another, so when it comes to *maʿrifa*, there is no absolute authority, no absolute truth. Each person can see from and present his own perspective and try to pose questions and arguments that follow from that position. It is like this that we develop our understanding and experiences.[2]

About a week later, I met with Abu Ibrahim, a French convert to Islam who had been a member of the Tijāniyya for five years. After meeting him at the zawiya of Baba Lamine, one of Shaykh Ibrahim's sons and a prominent shaykh in Dakar, Abu Ibrahim invited me over to his apartment to discuss his time in the *ṭarīqa* and *maʿrifa*. When I asked him about what he has learned in the *ṭarīqa*, he told me:

I've learned the inside knowledge, knowledge of oneself, knowledge of God, of life, of reality. It's changed the way I see things, the way I react to events, the way I plan things, just the way I live, I'm less affected by outside events, because you don't see life the same way you saw it before.... What happens, happens; it's like that. You accept destiny. All Muslims say they believe in destiny, but when something bad happens, it's like they don't believe in destiny anymore. If something bad happens, they say, ah, it shouldn't be like this. I tell you this and I feel this, but of course sometimes I get sad, I get angry, it's not like you totally just [*moves hands in a flat line*], but you get closer to that.... It's that inside knowledge, it's different reading and living it. It's something you feel and you're sure about it. It's difficult to express, it's something you live. It's like, you ask me, how does an apple taste? I can talk for hours and you'll still not gonna know how it tastes until you go and taste it yourself, and that knowledge is the same, so it's difficult to talk about it. I couldn't prove it, but I know myself, and that's enough....

[Question: How would you define *ma'rifa*? What are its conditions?]

To me, *ma'rifa* is knowledge of God, knowledge of reality, knowledge of inward things, like esoterism, that's what it is for me, that's how I see it.... I think that in order to have *ma'rifa*, the person should be correct. He should be pious, a very good Muslim, inwardly, outwardly. It should be like a reward, that's what I think it should be. But obviously it's not the case, you know? And even Shaykh Ibrahim, he said it's open to everyone. And it's like it's not even a reward; I've read that it's rather like a way to improve yourself, to do *tarbiya*. Sometimes, I see people, it's like they're not even good Muslims, and they do *tarbiya*. Like you don't even pray correctly, you don't make effort, and we give you *tarbiya*, we give you the secrets of the universe, the best thing you can get. To me, it should be like a reward. Like previous Sufis, it was only the elite who had this knowledge and these *awrāds* [litanies], but now it's given to everyone. Sometimes, I don't like that, but it seems Shaykh Ibrahim was not against that, that's what I've read, I don't know if it's true or not, 'cause it's getting so democratic, you know.... If you want to have *Iḥsān*, but you don't have good *Islām*, it's not worth doing it. That's what I think, but obviously, maybe Shaykh Ibrahim or other *shuyūkh* they see it differently. It's the most precious thing and they're just giving it away like that, but I guess that's the way God wants it. If I were a *muqaddam*, for example, if I see a girl who doesn't wear hijab, I'd never give her [*tarbiya*]. But you see people in the *ṭarīqa*, even disciples of Shaykh Ibrahim, you don't see Islam in them, but they've done *tarbiya*, you know. The problem is that after that, it can be dangerous. That's what I think.... Sometimes it can help the person be better, but sometimes the things you discover may also not make you want to make more effort, because with what you discover you may tend to say oh, so it's like this? Why would I want to make more effort then? But the rules of the Tijāniyya are very strict, you have to pray in groups, you have to do this, this, this.... If you respected this, you wouldn't give *tarbiya* or the Tijani *ṭarīqa* to anyone.

But, on the other hand, I've witnessed an excellent example of the opposite. I once heard of someone who was about to take *ṭarīqa* and do *tarbiya*. I thought it wasn't appropriate to give it to that person because of the behavior he had at the time. He did take the *ṭarīqa* and do *tarbiya*, though, and he very quickly changed his way of life and his habits, did a good *tarbiya*, and became a very good disciple!

When I asked Abu Ibrahim if people outside of his *ṭarīqa* could also have access to this *ma'rifa*, he told me:

Sometimes when we listen to atheists, or non-Muslims in general, we hear things that we got to know, and sometimes we think it's really close. The nonbeliever is really close to the believer, to some extent, you know? Sometimes, when an atheist speaks, you think he is a gnostic, an *'ārif*, you know? That's very strange. For example, some people say there's no God, there's nothing, it's just a game, and it's true, but it depends how you see it, but to some extent it's true, and at least it's his truth. Because he's sure of that, too, you know, he believes it, that's the way he sees the world. Sometimes, maybe I think they could be gnostics. Some Muslims say, no, God's religion is Islam, all the rest is false. But also Truth is everywhere, even in the false there is Truth. Allah is *al-Ḥaqq* [the Real / the Truth] so everything is truth, you know? When we say "He exists, He doesn't exist," the border between these two is so slight, so thin, so difficult to express. Because you say *lā ilāha*—there is no God—we start with this—except Allah. It's not so simple, eh? Of course, yeah, Islam is the religion of God, but as I said, an atheist, he can speak like a gnostic. That's very difficult to judge. . . .

[Question: Like philosophers, for example? Do they sound like gnostics? Could they be gnostics?]

. . . To me, philosophy is just speaking, it's like turning around. You talk, you talk, but you're not getting anywhere, like a mouse on a wheel. Sometimes though, philosophy is deep, philosophers can say deep things, but it's like they don't react to what they're saying, and they keep on speaking and speaking. Whereas Sufism is part of a practice, it's something practical. We could also say that it's also a philosophy, a spirituality, but it's also acts. *Awrāds* [litanies] you do, prayers you do, fasts you do, and you have a concrete result of your thoughts, of your philosophy, you know? It's not just speaking, it has to change you. Whereas I'm not sure philosophers become better people with what they say—do they become better people with what they say, with what they discover? That's how I see it.

When asked about some the technical terms of Sufism, Abu Ibrahim had this to say:

It's pretty strange, because I want to know more of God, you know, I'm still thirsty. But all of these things, the *ḥaḍarāt*, the *ṣifāt* [attributes], I'm not interested. But does it mean I know less than the ones who know this? Because these things, we can explain to you these things, but what I know, it can't be explained. But all the rest, you can read it, you can explain it, you can understand it, but the big knowledge, it's personal, you know? Sometimes you hear people, they speak about all these things, but are you sure they got the most important thing? Sometimes they speak well, it's like they know many things, but maybe they just repeat what they heard, and maybe they didn't feel what you feel. . . . When do you start *baqāʾ* [subsistence]? Because *fanāʾ* [annihilation], yeah [I get it], but should you always die more, or you only die once? That's very technical, and the problem is that the true shaykhs who can explain this to you and guide you well on this path are very few. The true ones are very few.

But also explaining it, what's the point of explaining it, you're supposed to discover it for yourself. I've been in some *dahiras* [Sufi circles/associations], it's like they give lessons. I'm not for that. It's things you have to discover. Like the *fatḥ* or the knowledge that everything is God, if you tell it to the person before he does [*tarbiya*] he will think he lived it, but he just understood a bit more maybe, or, yeah, maybe he feels he understands, but it's better not to speak about that, and if you start, try not to know or understand too much before you start. Because if you have all the answers, how will you know if you validated them yourself? That's a big problem. Also, knowing the five *ḥaḍarāt*, what's the point? What will it give me more? Will it make me sin less or become a better person? Or do this or that? Maybe it's good to know, because it's "just" knowledge—like historical knowledge, for example, you know, it's good, it's knowledge, but I'm not very interested in that.

In some way it's all interrelated [i.e., the different kinds of knowledge]. But also you can know some Islamic sciences and not be good at others. But *maʿrifa*, which is one of them, is also very specific, eh? And I would say, if you have this, you have everything. So sometimes, even, I don't feel like learning; it's not that I'm not interested, it's rather that I already have the most important knowledge. The point of all these other things is to get you to the Knowledge [*maʿrifa*], you know? The rest is "small" or "smaller" knowledge—it's important, yes for sure, but if you have the Knowledge, the Truth, then all the rest seems small. Still the best *shuyūkh* know everything, and even after their *fatḥ al-akbar*,³ they've got books everywhere, and they read all the time. So for sure, it's better for someone who's got *maʿrifa* to also know the rest.

I think *maʿrifa* is the opposite of rational knowledge, or sensory knowledge. I think it's not rational, it's even difficult to speak about, it's not like "this is white," or "this is black." It's so difficult to put words on it. And I told you, even if I speak for hours, you will still not know the thing. You can't really learn it. It's something you experience, it's different. . . . It's like scholars, they read, they learn. . . . It's like you read a guidebook about Paris, you learn the history of Paris, you see the pictures of Paris, but it's better to go there for two days, now you *know* Paris! But if you're just, you're outside Paris, you read about Paris for years, but you don't know Paris, the guy who's never read anything, but he's been to Paris, he knows

Paris better than you do. It's the same with God. Like some young guys here, they maybe don't know much of "conventional" knowledge, but they know God and that makes them "better" than imams and *shuyūkhs* who've studied for years but never experienced this knowledge. You see?

The best Sufis, they are also the most crazy. You don't know what they think deep inside of them. You see them, they're nice, they smile, they're like normal people, but they're not! You don't know what they think, live, and experience deep inside!... There are some things I think, I wouldn't even dare to share them with anyone, I am sure some things I think, if I said it in an assembly, they would say he's talking bullshit, because it goes almost the opposite of what I am hearing publicly. Well, even though it's opposite, they might well both be true, maybe both are correct.

When I asked him how the process of *tarbiya* works to bring about *ma'rifa*, Abu Ibrahim leaned back, shook his head, and said:

I don't know [how the *adhkār* work]. I do it, I know it works, but how? That's too mystical, that's too crazy for me. But also everything, why we do four *rak'ats* for *Zuhur*, why three for *Maghrib*, why thirty-three *subhan'Allāh*'s, everything! Why we have five fingers, two eyes, one nose, there has to be a reason, there has to be, but I don't know. And how *adhkār* changes you, your mind, if you're supposed to do one hundred but if you do one hundred and three, then it's not going to work, it's crazy, no? But it's like this.... Behind all this, everything is well-ordered, so perfectly, that if you do one more or one less, it's not going to work, that's crazy, huh? But so is all of creation.

I think this *tarbiya* of Shaykh Ibrahim, if you follow it, I think it's sure you're gonna access [God and/or *ma'rifa*]. I don't know anyone who did it, who didn't say he accessed. Well, I do know some, but they admit themselves that they didn't access because they don't follow the things correctly [being regular, making *adhkar* on time, etc.]. But also some people, they say they accessed, but you don't know what kind of access they are talking about. So some they say, yeah, I did *tarbiya* in one day, but also some they say *tarbiya* is never finished, so there's "*tarbiya*" and "*tarbiya*." But I haven't heard anyone say I've been doing *tarbiya* now for fifteen years and I didn't access—everyone, everyone who did *tarbiya* [correctly] accessed, from what I know. But I don't know what access, but at least everybody pretends they've accessed [*laughs*]. It's already a good thing, I think [*laughs*].... Anyway, it's all God's wish, it's so great and so precious, it's the ultimate knowledge he's giving us—there's nothing greater than that.[4]

While one could devote an entire chapter just to the analysis of these two accounts, for now it suffices to note that while representing two distinctly different descriptions of *ma'rifa*, both insist that it is the most important form of knowledge; emphasize its ineffable, existential, and transformative nature; and connect it to self-knowledge while contrasting it to modern philosophy and/or formal learning. These features were present to one degree or another in virtually every interview I conducted. But for now, I will postpone further discussion of these fascinating accounts in order to provide a background discussion of *ma'rifa* from various classical Sufi sources, before turning to the works of Shaykh Ibrahim and the words of his disciples.

I will begin with a summary of *ma'rifa*, as it is described within the broader Sufi tradition and contemporary scholarship on Sufism, before presenting descriptions from within the Tijani tradition of Shaykh Ibrahim and his followers. This will be followed by a discussion of how *ma'rifa* is acquired and verified, with reference to Shaykh Ibrahim's writings and interviews with contemporary disciples. Finally, I will conclude with a summary of these epistemological accounts, briefly highlighting important similarities and differences with contemporary theories of epistemology, in order to demonstrate how and why the category of *ma'rifa* does not neatly fit within contemporary academic frameworks of knowledge.

WHAT IS *MA'RIFA*?

### *Ma'rifa* in Early and Classical Sufism

Deriving from the Arabic root *'-r-f*, *ma'rifa* began to be distinguished from its close synonym *'ilm* in the third century AH / ninth century CE as Sufism and other Islamic sciences began to separate into distinct disciplines with their own specific, technical vocabulary. Before this differentiation, *'ilm* was the predominant term used to refer to knowledge of all types, whereas *ma'rifa* and its derivations featured less commonly in the Qur'an and ḥadīth literature, and usually had the connotation of "recognition"[5] or "acquaintance" (somewhat similar to the distinction between the French *connaissance* and *savoir*). In the newly differentiated discipline of Sufism, however, *ma'rifa* came to have a distinct and technical definition, referring to the direct, unmediated, experiential knowledge of God (in both senses of the phrase—God's knowledge and knowing God—at once).

For example, Ja'far al-Ṣādiq (d. 765 CE), regarded as one of the early authorities of Sufism, Islamic jurisprudence, and several other Islamic sciences (as well serving as the sixth imam of Shi'ism), famously wrote, "Surely he alone knows [*'arafa*] God who knows Him by means of God [*biLlāh*]. Therefore, whoso knows Him not by means of Him knows Him not."⁶ Similarly, the seminal Sufi Dhū'l-Nūn al-Miṣrī (d. 859), widely credited with developing the emphasis on *ma'rifa* that came to characterize later Sufism, defined this form of knowledge in the following formulation: "I knew my Lord by my Lord; without my Lord I would not have known my Lord."⁷

Abū'l Ḥasan 'Alī al-Hujwīrī's (d. 1077) famous and influential treatise *The Uncovering of the Veiled* (*Kashf al-Mahjūb*), which summarizes many of the theories and debates of early Sufism, contains this eloquent description of *ma'rifa* and its importance:

> Gnosis [*ma'rifa*] is the life of the heart through God, and the turning away of one's inmost thoughts from all that is not God. The worth of everyone is in proportion to gnosis, and he who is without gnosis is worth nothing.... According to the view of orthodox Moslems, soundness of reason and regard to evidences are a means (*sabab*) to gnosis, but not the cause (*'illat*) thereof: the sole cause is God's will and favour, for without His favour (*'inayat*) reason is blind. Reason does not even know itself: how, then, can it know another? Heretics of all sorts use the demonstrative method, but the majority of them do not know God.... In reality man's only guide and enlightener is God. Reason and the proofs adduced by reason are unable to direct anyone into the right way.... When the Commander of the Faithful, 'Ali, was asked concerning gnosis, he said: "I know God by God, and I know that which is not God by the light of God."⁸

Hujwīrī continues to contrast *ma'rifa* to rational demonstration, the favored tool of the philosophers (*falāsifa*) and theologians (*mutakallimūn*):

> The first step of demonstration is a turning away from God, because demonstration involves the consideration of some other thing, whereas gnosis [*ma'rifa*] is a turning away from all that is not God. Ordinary objects of search are found by means of demonstration, but knowledge of God is extraordinary....
>
> Accordingly, the miracle is not that reason should be led by the act to affirm the existence of the Agent,⁹ but that a saint should be led by the light of the Truth to deny his own existence.¹⁰ The knowledge gained is in the one case a matter of logic, in the other it becomes an inward experience. Let those who deem reason to be the cause of gnosis [*ma'rifa*], consider what reason affirms in their minds concerning the substance of gnosis, for gnosis involves the negation of whatever is affirmed by reason, i.e., whatever notion of God can be formed by reason, God is in reality something different. How, then, is there any room for reason to arrive at gnosis by means of demonstration?...

Therefore, when reason is gone as far as possible, and the souls of His lovers must needs search for Him, they rest helplessly without their faculties, and while they so rest, they grow restless and stretch their hands in supplication and seek a relief for their souls; and when they have exhausted every manner of search in their power, the power of God becomes theirs, i.e., they find the way from Him to Him, and are eased of the anguish of absence and set foot in the garden of intimacy and win to rest.... God causes man to know Him through Himself with a knowledge that is not linked to any faculty, a knowledge in which the existence of Man is merely metaphorical. Hence to the gnostic, egoism is utter perfidy; his remembrance of God is without forgetfulness, and his gnosis is not empty words but actual feeling.[11]

In a move that was to be repeated by countless Sufis throughout the ages, Hujwīrī takes his definition of *maʿrifa*, "the turning away of one's inmost thoughts from all that is not God," to its extreme limit, arguing that awareness of *maʿrifa*, or anything else other than God, veils one from true *maʿrifa*: "So long as there is room in the heart for aught except God, or the possibility of expressing aught except God, true gnosis has not been attained. The gnostic is not a gnostic until he turns aside from all that is not God. Abu Hafs Haddád[12] says: 'Since I have known God, neither truth nor falsehood has entered my heart.'"[13]

From these early Sufi texts up through contemporary usage by Sufi authors such as Shaykh Ibrahim, *maʿrifa* is usually contrasted with *ʿilm*, which is commonly used to refer to "ordinary" conceptual knowledge. However, due to the fact that *maʿrifa* is not used in the Qurʾan and ḥadīth to refer to God's knowledge (whereas *ʿilm* is),[14] *maʿrifa* is sometimes considered a special category of *ʿilm*,[15] while this latter term is also used to refer to various esoteric sciences associated with *maʿrifa* (such as the "science of letters," *ʿilm al-ḥurūf*). In the works of some Sufi writers, such as Ibn ʿArabi, the two terms are used almost interchangeably, the context determining the type of knowledge meant by either term. Despite these nuances of vocabulary, Sufi authors unanimously emphasized the distinction between conceptual knowledge that could be acquired through formal learning, and existential knowledge that could only be acquired through spiritual practice, direct experience, and/or "unveiling."

Early Sufi treatises often based their expositions of this second kind of knowledge on two oft-quoted ḥadīth and an early commentary on a verse of the Qurʾan, all three of which employ the root *ʿ-r-f* from which the word *maʿrifa* is derived. Later Sufi authors, including Shaykh Ibrahim Niasse, have followed suit, making these three traditions a kind of canonical foundation for Sufi discussions of *maʿrifa*.[16] The Qurʾanic verse in question reads, "I created man and jinn only to worship Me" (51:56), and the oft-cited commentary of Ibn ʿAbbās (d. 687) glosses "to worship Me" (*liya ʿbudūni*) as "to know Me" (*liya ʿrifūni*). Many Sufi authors, including Shaykh Ibrahim,[17] take this as proof of *maʿrifa*—knowing God in a direct, experiential manner—being man's raison d'être.

The two ḥadīth cited alongside this commentary have become such as staple of Islamic mystical literature that one would be hard-pressed to find a Sufi text that does not reference one or both.[18] In the first ḥadīth, God says (through the mouth of the Prophet), "I was a hidden treasure and I loved to be known [*uʿraf*], so I created the creatures that they might know me." This is often cited to identify *maʿrifa* as the reason for creation,[19] and to explain the intimate relationship between this kind of knowledge and love, which is the cause of the former. In this respect, this saying is often quoted alongside the *ḥadīth qudsī* "My servant does not cease drawing near to me through supererogatory acts of worship until I love him. Then when I love him, I become his hearing with which he hears, his seeing with which he sees, his hand with which he grasps, and his foot with which he walks." The state described in the second half of this ḥadīth, in which the God "becomes" the various faculties of the servant, is identified with *maʿrifa*, wherein God becomes the servant's noetic faculty, his knowledge, and that which is known.[20]

The other foundational ḥadīth cited in discussions of *maʿrifa* reads, "He who knows [*ʿarafa*] himself, knows his Lord," connecting *maʿrifa* with self-knowledge. Perhaps more than any other author, Ibn ʿArabi discusses this ḥadīth from a variety of perspectives. He writes:

> The root of the existence of knowledge of God is knowledge of self. So knowledge of God has the property of knowledge of self, which is the root. In the view of those who know the self, the self is an ocean without shore, so knowledge of it has no end. Such is the property of knowledge of the self. Hence knowledge of God, which is a branch of this root, joins with it in a property, so there is no end to knowledge of God. That is why in every state, the knower says, "My Lord increase me in knowledge!" (20:144). Then God increases him in knowledge of himself that he may increase in knowledge of his Lord. This is given by divine unveiling.[21]

Elsewhere, he further explores the nature of this self-knowledge, explaining that since God created human beings in His own image, and since they are actually identical with His Selfhood and Reality (apart from which there is nothing else), knowledge of the self is identical to knowledge of God. Moreover, this self-knowledge cannot be achieved through theological discussion or discursive reasoning, since the object of knowledge is identical with its subject, and so "whosoever seeks knowledge of it by way of mental reasoning does so in vain."[22]

## Ibn 'Arabi's Epistemology of *Ma'rifa*

In the 177th chapter of his magnum opus, the *Futūḥāt al-Makkiya* (*Meccan Openings*), the Andalusian sage expands on this description of *ma'rifa* and its relationship to other forms of knowledge. Before delving into the arguments for the necessity of *ma'rifa*, Ibn 'Arabi begins with a dense poem that connects *ma'rifa* to self-knowledge and the spiritual realization described in the ḥadīth in which God "becomes" the faculties of the aspirant, underscoring the importance of spiritual practice (particularly following the example of the Prophet) in acquiring this form of knowledge:

> Whoever climbs the degrees of *ma'rifa*
> Sees he who is in himself from his Attribute
> Because that [attribute] points to the One
> Because of the difference between *'ilm* and *ma'rifa*
> It [the self/soul] has being in the being of he who
> Was sent by the Real and what He required of him
> For he is the leader of the moment [*al-waqt*] in his state
> And the bystander [*wāqif*] longs to Know him
> His rulings proceed from wisdom
> In the exalted level of his vantage point

*Ma'rifa* is unique in its place and seeks nothing but the One, so *ma'rifa* according to the Folk [the Sufis] is a pathway, for it is only acquired through practice, mindfulness [*taqwa*], and spiritual wayfaring [*sulūk*], because it is [acquired] through verified unveiling [*kashf muḥaqqaq*], which is never subject to doubt, unlike [conceptual] knowledge [*'ilm*], which is acquired through speculative thought. So know that the only one who Knows [*'arafa*] correctly is he who knows things through himself. For everyone who knows a thing through something added [to himself] is a follower [*muqallid*] of that which is added [to himself] and what it gives him.[23]

Ibn 'Arabi continues this exploration of self-knowledge, explaining why all other forms of knowledge (even sensory and rational knowledge) are really just fallible forms of "following authority" or "blind imitation" (*taqlīd*), a powerful rhetorical move, as this often negatively charged term was the philosophers' and theologians' insult of choice for their opponents:

Nothing in existence knows things through itself other than the One. The knowledge of things and not-things possessed by everything other than the One is a following of authority [*taqlīd*]. Since it has been established that other-than-God cannot have knowledge of a thing without following authority, let us follow God's authority, especially in knowledge of Him.

Why do we say that nothing can be known by other-than-God except through authority? Because man knows nothing except through one of the faculties given to him by God: the senses and reason. Hence man has to follow the authority of his sensory perception in that which it gives, and sensory perception may be mistaken, or it may correspond to the situation as it is. Or man has to follow the authority of the rational faculty in that which it gives him, either in that which is a logical necessity [*ḍarūra*] or speculation. But reason follows the authority of thought [*fikr*], some of which is correct, and some of which is corrupt, so its knowledge of things is "hit-or-miss" [*bi'l-ittifāq*]. Hence there is nothing but following authority.[24]

Since there is no escape from following authority, and both reason and the senses can err, what authority can be reliably followed? Moreover, how can one know that this authority is reliable, given that even one's rational speculation can be suspect? Ibn 'Arabi's answer sheds light on the relationship between the spiritual practice and the acquisition of the certain knowledge of *ma'rifa*:

Since this is the situation, the intelligent man who wants to know God should follow His authority in the reports He has given about Himself in His scriptures and upon the tongues of His messengers. So if a person wants to truly know things as they really are, he cannot do so simply by what he is given by his [natural] faculties [of sense and reason]; instead he needs to expand [himself] through many acts of willing obedience until the Real becomes his hearing, and seeing, and all of his faculties [referring to the previously cited *ḥadīth qudsī*], then he will truly know all things through God and know God through God. In any case, there is no escape from following authority. But once you know God through God and all things through God, then you will not be visited in that by ignorance, obfuscations, doubts, or uncertainties. . . .

The rational thinkers from among the people of speculation imagine that they know what speculation, sensory perception, and reason have given them, but they are following the authority of these things. Every faculty is prone to a certain kind of mistake. Though they may know this fact, they seek to throw themselves into error, for they distinguish between that within which sensory perception, reason, and thought may be mistaken and that within which it is not mistaken. But how can they know? Perhaps that which they have declared to be a mistake is correct. Nothing can eliminate this incurable disease [of doubt], unless all of a person's knowledge is known through God, not through other than Him. God knows through His own Essence, not through anything added to it. Hence you will also come to know through that through which He knows, since you follow the authority of He who knows, who is not ignorant, and who follows the authority of no one. Anyone who follows the authority of other than God follows the authority of he who is visited by mistakes and is correct only accidentally.

Someone may object, "How do you know this? Perhaps you may be mistaken in these classifications without being aware of it. For in this, you follow the authority of that which can be mistaken: reason and thought."

We reply, you are correct. However, since we see nothing but following authority, we have preferred to follow the authority of he who is called "Messenger" and that which is called "The Speech of God." We followed their authority in knowledge until the Real was our hearing and our sight, so we came to know things through God and gained knowledge of these classifications through God. The fact that we were right to follow this authority was fortunate, since, as we have said, whenever reason or any of the faculties accords with something as it is in itself, this is by chance. We do not hold that it is mistaken in every situation. We only say that we do not know how to distinguish its being wrong from its being right. But when the Real is all a person's faculties and he knows things through God, then he knows the difference between the faculties' being right and their being mistaken. This is what we maintain, and no one can deny it, for he will find it in himself. "Since this is so, busy yourself with following what God ordered you to do, including the acts of willingly obeying Him, watching over your heart . . . until the Real becomes all of your faculties, and you have clear insight with regards to your situation . . . for the Messenger of God said that there is no way to truly know God except by truly knowing the self when he said, 'whoever knows himself, knows his lord.'"[25]

In this insightful passage, Ibn 'Arabi establishes the fallibility of the sensory and rational faculties, and posits that these limitations can only be overcome when God Himself replaces these faculties, as promised in the ḥadīth. However, before this transformation, he admits that, strictly speaking, one only has the fallible authority of the senses and reason by which to judge the promises and propositions of scripture, but he preferred to follow them, and claims to have verified their truth. Thus, he advises his readers to follow his example and focus on their spiritual practice and their hearts. Implicit in this passage is the notion that one is not truly oneself, or not truly aware of oneself, without spiritual practice and transformation. Based on the ḥadīth, Ibn 'Arabi asserts that the self-knowledge that results from this discipline is identical to the knowledge of God.

This passage continues by relating this ḥadīth to the Qurʾanic verse "We will show them our signs on the horizons and in themselves until it is clear to them that It/He is the Real" (41:53), explaining that God has directed us to acquire knowledge of Himself by reflecting on that which is within us and that which is without. After further explaining why self-knowledge is not subject to the same doubts as those forms of knowing acquired through reflection on the external world, Ibn ʿArabi concludes, "But everything is in ourselves, so if we examine and reflect upon what is in ourselves we will realize from our knowledge of the self what is acquired by the person who reflects upon the horizons. So the Prophet, since he knew that the self encompasses all the realities of the world, focused you on that self-knowing out of his solicitude for you.... So this [path of self-knowing] is the path of salvation [najāt], ... and it is the path which has been traveled by the elite among the true servants of God."[26]

As a whole, this passage contains several important points that outline the epistemological foundations of *maʿrifa* in classical and later Sufism. First and foremost, in this perspective, sure knowledge of the self, or things, or of God, is not possible for an ordinary, everyday human being merely *as he or she is*. The sensory and rational faculties can be right and they can be wrong, but without some other means of discrimination it is impossible to determine when they are right and when they are wrong, and so these faculties alone cannot guarantee us true knowledge. Thus, there is no escape from following fallible authority, at least initially. However, following the authority of that which people claim to come from "the Word of God" (the Qurʾan and other scriptures) and "His Messengers" (the Sunna and divine laws) can lead to a transformation whereby one becomes identified with the Real, allowing one to know It through self-knowledge. This in turn allows one to verify the authority of the Qurʾan and Sunna, discern correct rational speculation and sensory perception from that which errs, and dispense with external authority, since one now knows things through oneself, which is identical to the Real's self, in a certain respect.

Thus, the initial poem (quoted above) can now be understood as indicating that the spiritual adept comes to know the Real through the Real's faculties ("his Attribute"—the pronoun is intentionally ambiguous since these attributes or faculties are now shared by the Real and the adept), and sees the Real as being "in himself." Thus, through the Real's faculties ("his Attribute"), the adept realizes the true oneness of the Real, a unity that includes his own being. This is accomplished by following the Prophet ("he who / Was sent by the Real"), who is the archetypal example of this nexus of the Divine and the human. By following the Prophet's example, the adept can know the Real through this same self-knowledge of existential identification because the Prophet's, and now his, own faculties and attributes are the same as those of the Real. In fact, it is only by following the Prophet that the adept can become who he or she really is—the Real.

In the line "It [the self/soul] has being [*wujūd*] in the being of he who / Was sent by the Real," the word *wujūd* can also mean "finding" and "consciousness," and so it also means that the self finds itself in finding the Prophet / the Prophet's finding of the Real, or that the self's consciousness has its root in the consciousness of the Prophet / the Prophet's consciousness, which is identified with that of the Real.

Later in the same passage, Ibn ʿArabi writes, "When Junayd was asked about gnosis [*maʿrifa*] and the gnostic [*al-ʿārif*], he replied, 'The water takes on the color of its cup.' In other words, the gnostic assumes the character traits of God, to the point where it seems as if he is He. He is not he, yet he is He."[27] Because the Prophet is perpetually in this state of annihilation in God, because his attributes have been subsumed in the Divine Attributes, he can serve as this existential mold and model for others. This model is necessary due to the fact that ordinary knowledge cannot be sure without the foundation of the certainty of existential self-knowledge ("the difference between *ʿilm* and *maʿrifa*"). This existential knowledge requires an initial following of authority, and thus the novice who has yet to embark on this path ("the bystander" of the poem) longs to know the model by becoming him, by discovering the Prophet's being within himself, and in doing so, discovering the Real. The rulings that come from the Prophet (*sunna* and *sharīʿa*) cannot be understood unless they are put into practice—that is, unless one ascends to his level by following him through the ascending degrees of *maʿrifa*, of existential identification or oneness with the One, the Real.

**Limitations of *Maʿrifa***

Junayd's saying "The water takes on the color of its cup" is also cited to describe the individual limits of *maʿrifa*. Despite what poetic descriptions of annihilation may suggest, the knower (*ārif*) does not simply pop out of existence like a bubble or a drop falling into the ocean. The process of obtaining *maʿrifa* is perhaps better described as the whole ocean becoming contained in one drop, or as a drop of water, or a pearl or ruby becoming perfectly clear and being placed in a spot where the whole world seems reflected within it. In this regard, Sufis such as Ibn ʿArabi and Shaykh Ibrahim Niasse often quote the following verse of poetry:

> It is not difficult for God
> To gather the whole world in one [human][28]

Similarly, in his commentary on the previously cited Qurʾanic verse "We will show them our signs on the horizons and in themselves" (41:53), Shaykh Ibrahim writes, "There are some who say man is a small world (microcosm), but in reality, he is the large world (macrocosm) since all the worlds are contained in him."²⁹ But despite containing all the worlds *in potentia*, in actuality, individual human beings are still limited, especially when compared to God. Sidi Mohamed Kane, Shaykh Ibrahim Niasse's grandson, explained that "the Qur'an refers to God as *al-'Alīm* because it [His knowledge] is unrestricted, and not *al-'ārif*, because *ma'rifa* comes from the human side, and is therefore limited. It is true that it is absolute, but it is also limited." Commenting further, he related:

> Shaykh Ibrahim said, "God does not manifest Himself to the same person in the same way." God is infinite, the way He will manifest himself to you is different from the way He will manifest Himself to me or to Shaykh Ibrahim, because God is infinite. He will manifest Himself to you in a form that corresponds to you.... The way in which God manifests Himself is different, just as people are different. It's also like drunkenness, the Sufis also talk about drunkenness, and people get drunk differently: one person cries, another laughs, another does something else.... People do not become drunk in the same fashion, it somewhat depends on the quantity, on what, on how much they can handle. It's the same with *ma'rifa*.³⁰

In a similar vein, Ibn 'Arabi comments on Junayd's saying, comparing knowledge of God (*ma'rifa*) to water, and the knower (*'ārif*) to its container.

> Junayd was asked about knowledge (*ma'rifa*) and the knower (*'ārif*). He replied, "The water takes on the color of its cup." In other words, the container displays its effects in what it contains. Junayd said this to let you know that you will never judge your object of knowledge except by yourself, since you will never know anything but yourself. Whatever may be the color of the cup, water becomes manifest in that color. The person without knowledge judges that the water is like that, since sight gives that to him. Water discloses itself in the forms of all the cups in respect to their colors, but it does not become delimited in its essence. You only see it that way. In the same manner, the shapes of the containers in which water appears display their effects in it, but in all of them it is still water. If the container is square, the water becomes manifest as square....
> 
> He who sees the water only in the cup judges it by the property of the cup. But he who sees it simple and noncompound knows that the shapes and colors in which it becomes manifest are the effect of the containers. Water remains in its own definition and reality, whether in the cup or outside it. Hence it never loses the name "water."³¹

God's knowledge of Himself, like water, is formless and without color, but it necessarily takes on the appearance and form of the knower, while remaining completely itself. Ibn 'Arabi elaborates further:

> Since there are as many cups as drinkers at the Pool which will be found in the abode of the Hereafter [every person who has ever lived], and since the water in the cup takes the form of the cup in both shape and color, we know for certain that knowledge of God takes on the measure of your view, your preparedness, and what you are in yourself. No two people will ever come together in a single knowledge of God, since a single constitution is never found in two different people, nor can there be such a thing.... Hence no one ever knows anything of the Real except his own self.[32]

The knowledge of Himself that God bestows to each person is a formless divine self-disclosure or manifestation (*tajallī*) that takes on the person's form (and is thus a form of self-knowledge). But in this perspective, we must remember that each person, indeed, each thing, is itself a divine self-disclosure or manifestation. So it is as if water first forms several cups of ice, and then pours itself out into these containers, taking on their forms.

Ibn 'Arabi calls the forms of these ice cups "preparedness" and refers to them as "immutable entities"—what we are in God's knowledge of Himself. Thus God's self-knowledge of us, which is the root of our existence, is what determines our particular limitations, which in turn colors and shapes our knowledge of God. This can be summed up in the following way, revealing another meaning of the previously cited ḥadīth "He who knows himself, knows his lord," since "his lord," that which he worships, is nothing other than his own beliefs, which are the product of his own limited knowledge of God. Thus:

> God's knowledge of us in Himself = Our delimited form (self/*nafs*) =
> Our knowledge of God = The God we worship (lord/*rabb*)

Just as each of us has a unique self (*nafs*), we each have a unique lord (*rabb*), a limited conception of unlimited or ultimate reality. For Ibn 'Arabi, true knowledge (*ma'rifa*) is not discovering or coming up with all-embracing conception of reality, since this is impossible. Nor is true knowledge to be confused with the limitations it assumes in "filling our cups." Instead, true knowledge (*ma'rifa*) consists of recognizing these limitations and transcending them by recognizing God in all the various forms in which he reveals Himself—that is, recognizing the water in every container. This point is so important that Ibn ʿArabi concludes his most influential work, *The Ringstones of Wisdom*, with this passage:

> This is as we have said concerning the believer: he only praised the God who is in his belief and to whom he has tied himself. His [the god's] action all goes back to himself [the believer], so he praises only himself. For without doubt, he who praises the product, praises the maker, for its beauty or lack of beauty goes back to its maker. The God of the believer is made by him who observes Him, so this God is his artifact. Hence his praise of what he has made is his praise of himself. That is why he considers the belief of others blameworthy. But if he were fair, he would not do so. But, of course, the possessor of this specific object of worship is ignorant of that, since he objects to others in what they believe concerning God. If he knew what Junayd said—that the water takes on the color of the cup—he would let every believer have his own belief and he would recognize God in the form of every object of belief. But the believer has "an opinion," not knowledge. That is why God said, "I am with My servant's opinion of Me,"[33] that is, "I do not become manifest to him except in the form of his belief." If he likes, he declares Him nondelimited, and if he likes, he delimits [Him]. The God of beliefs assumes limitations. He is the God who is "embraced" by the heart of His servant.[34] But nothing embraces the Nondelimited God, since He is identical with the things and identical with Himself. It cannot be said that a thing embraced itself, nor that it does not embrace it. So understand! *God speaks the Truth and He guides on the way* (33:4).[35]

Earlier in the same work, Ibn ʿArabi writes, "Beware lest you bind yourself with a specific belief and reject others, for much good will escape you. Indeed, the knowledge of reality as it is will escape you. Be then, within yourself, a pure substance (*hyle*), for the forms of all belief, for God is too vast and too great to be confined to one belief to the exclusion of another, for indeed He says, *Wheresoever you turn, there is the face of God* (2:115)."[36]

The only way to get beyond mere "opinion" or the "god of belief" is to recognize both its limitations and its identity with our limited forms and God's formless Essence. To extend Junayd's metaphor, this means recognizing that our cups (we ourselves) are nothing but water (the inscrutable Divine Reality), in a sense making them translucent or "melting" them, and becoming like the water, like a pure substance (*hyle*), capable of accepting any form.[37] This is the work of the heart, and not reason, as Ibn ʿArabi explains:

> And since beliefs are various, and preparednesses are different, whenever God manifests Himself, anyone who has limited Him to the form of a particular description

denies Him in other than that form. Whereas whoever has disengaged Him from the limitation of one form other than another—like the Perfect Men and the gnostics ['urafā']—does not deny Him in any form of theophany [tajallī]. Rather, he glorifies Him as he should and performs the worship worthy of His station, for the theophanies of God possess no end at which the perfect gnostic and the understanding knower of God might stop.

"Wear the turban, or the dress, or the robe! By thy father, it will only increase my love!"

Do you not see that God "Every moment is in a state" (Quran LV, 29)? In the same way, the heart is constantly undergoing transformation in accordance with His transformations in the states of its consciousness. Therefore He said, "Surely in that," i.e., in the Quran, "there is a reminder to him who has a heart" (L, 37) which undergoes transformation according to different forms and attributes. He did not say, "who possesses a reason," because the reason becomes limited according to particular beliefs, so the Divine Reality—Who is infinite—becomes restricted in that which it perceives, in contrast to the heart ... since it undergoes transformation according to the forms of these theophanies, it remembers its forgotten existence before it appeared in this physical and elemental level, and it finds here what it had lost, as the Prophet said, "Wisdom is the believer's stray camel." So understand![38]

So here *ma'rifa* is identified as the recognition of God in every form of belief, in every aspect of creation, starting with one's self. The knowledge that one contains in one's self at any given moment cannot encompass the Real, since the Real is itself identical with both the knowledge and its container.[39]

In Ibn 'Arabi's epistemology, reason and its mental constructions are fixed and limited, and so cannot adequately comprehend reality and its perpetual and infinite transformations. The best reason can do is to endlessly chase after an impossible grand theory of everything. But the heart, on the other hand, can overcome its individual limitations through its limitless receptivity to the perpetual transformations of the Real itself.[40]

A cup can only show the true color of water if it itself is colorless like water—that is, if it is capable of taking on every single color. Similarly, by accepting every form in which the Real discloses itself, the heart becomes like the Real itself—allowing it to realize that it and everything else *is* nothing other than the Real itself. Thus, being and knowing coincide and the true Knower (*'ārif*) knows the Real not by her limited self, but by the Real, which is her true self. As Ibn 'Arabi writes, "Whosoever sees the Real from Him, in Him, by His Eye is a Knower [*ārif*]. Whosoever sees the Real from Him, in Him, by his own eye [i.e., those mystics still bound to a particular belief] is not a Knower. Whosoever does not see the Real from Him nor in Him, and waits to see Him with his own eye [i.e., those limited to rational speculation] is veiled and ignorant."[41] Ibn ʿArabi's most famous poem illustrates and summarizes these points, equating *maʿrifa* and love:

> My heart became capable of accepting any form
> A meadow for gazelles, a cloister for monks
> A temple for the idols, the Kaʿba for the circling pilgrim
> The tablets of the Torah, the scrolls of the Qurʾan
> My religion is the religion of Love
> Wherever its caravan turns
> Love is my religion
> And my faith

This, in summary, is one of the most influential classical Sufi epistemologies of *maʿrifa*. The careful reader will doubtless have noticed resonances between these descriptions of *maʿrifa*, and those given in the accounts at the opening of this chapter. While neither of the two disciples had ever read Ibn ʿArabi or other classical works of Sufism, through the texts and oral traditions of the Tijani order, especially those of Shaykh Ibrahim Niasse, this extensive classical tradition both formed and informed the oral and written discourses about *maʿrifa* in which these two disciples are embedded, not to mention the tradition of spiritual exercises through which they acquired *maʿrifa*. But before delving into the texts of the Tijāniyya and the oral accounts of contemporary Tijanis, a note about *maʿrifa* in contemporary scholarship—particularly those works that deal with Ibrahim Niasse's branch of the Tijāniyya—is in order.

### *Maʿrifa* in Contemporary Scholarship on the Tijāniyya

As can be seen in some of the translations cited above, *maʿrifa* has often been rendered into English as "gnosis." This translation is a felicitous one, drawing on the Indo-European root *k/g-n-o* from which words such as "knowledge," "ignorance," the German *kennen*, and even the Sanskrit *jnana* are derived. Moreover, "gnosis" is the term used in the Orthodox Christian tradition to designate a form of knowledge that appears to have much in common with *maʿrifa*. The main drawback, aside from connotations of the Gnosticism of late antiquity (which appear to bear little resemblance to Sufi conceptions of *maʿrifa*), is that there is no verbal form of the word in English to correspond to the commonly used Arabic verb *ʿarafa*. While "gnosis" may be used to translate *maʿrifa* in the technical usage of Sufism, it cannot be applied to the more everyday uses of *ma'rifa* (which are quite similar to the French *connaissance*). This is another shortcoming of the term "gnosis," as it makes *ma'rifa* seem like something so exotic and mystical that its important similarities to more commonplace forms of knowledge are obscured.

In his masterful study of the history of Ibrahim Niasse and his early community of disciples, Rüdiger Seesemann translates *ma'rifa* as "cognizance," which has the benefit of including the connotations of "awareness through experience," which the original Arabic term carries. However, this translation also suffers from the lack of a verbal and an agent form ("to cognize" and "a cognizant") and sounds too "cognitive," in contrast to the existential nature of *ma'rifa*. Another potential drawback of this translation, which Seesemann points out, is that cognizance implies a separation of subject and object, which technical Sufi use of *ma'rifa* does not.[42] In his recent, outstanding book situating the pedagogy of the community of Shaykh Ibrahim Niasse in the broader Islamic intellectual history of West Africa, Zachary Wright follows Seesemann in rendering *ma'rifa* as "cognizance" but writes that "*ma'rifa* thus means an experiential awareness of God achieved in the absence of deductive speculation, through the erasure of the individual ego in God."[43]

In his dissertation, an in-depth anthropological study of communities of disciples of Ibrahim Niasse, Joseph Hill uses "divine knowledge" to translate the Arabic/Wolof *ma'rifa/ma'rifat*,[44] which was the French term (*connaissance divine*) that I most regularly heard used in place of *ma'rifa* during the course of my research.

In the present work, I have chosen to either leave *ma'rifa* untranslated or render it as "Knowledge," *'ārif* as "Knower," et cetera, capitalized to highlight the distinction between this special form of knowledge and its more commonplace varieties. On the other hand, in other places I have tried rendering *ma'rifa* as "recognition," where it better reflects not only the Qur'anic sense of the term, but also its experiential dimensions and parallels with everyday experiences.[45] For example, like *ma'rifa*, the act of recognizing is a kind of perspective shift in which the same sense data are understood in a new way; similarly, "recognition" implies a prior knowledge that is remembered or recalled, as is the case for *ma'rifa* in the Sufi tradition and its close relationship to *dhikr* (invocation, remembrance, recollection). In any event, the meanings of *ma'rifa* will become clearer as we explore their descriptions in Tijani texts and the accounts of disciples.

## *Ma'rifa* in Tijani Texts and Contemporary Accounts

The *Jawāhir al-Ma'ānī* records Shaykh Aḥmad al-Tijānī's answer to the question this chapter poses, "What is *ma'rifa*?":

I asked the Shaykh about the reality of Knowledge by God [*ḥaqīqat al-maʿrifa biLlāh*] and he responded: Real Knowledge [*al-maʿrifa al-ḥaqīqiyya*] is that in which the servant is taken by God in such a way that he does not know its origin, or division, or cause, and he is not able to determine its particular means of operation. The awareness of his senses, his witnessing, his will, his desire, and even his disappearance do not remain for him. Rather, Knowledge comes from a divine self-disclosure [*tajallī*] that has no beginning and no end, nor limit. It effaces the servant such that no awareness of anything, even of the lack of his awareness, of his effacement, remains. He is not able to distinguish the root from its branches, nor vice versa. Rather, he only knows from the perspective of the Real, by the Real, in the Real, from the Real. And this is real Knowledge [*al-maʿrifa al-ḥaqīqiyya*]. Then an outpouring of the lights of His Holiness is poured out upon him, giving him perfect discernment and discrimination amongst the levels [of existence] and their particularities, and that which has been given to their realities in all their rulings, judgments, necessities, and the distinction between the Attributes and Names and levels of existence and their effects and their Knowledges and sciences. This discernment is called complete subsistence [*al-baqāʾ al-tāmm*] and perfect sobriety [*al-ṣaḥū*]. The primary origin [of Real Knowledge] is called complete annihilation [*al-fanāʾ al-tāmm*] and perfect effacement [*al-maḥū*]. This subsistence is only established with the annihilation of the first annihilation as its origin and foundation. So when the first is absent, so is the second.[46]

In this account, *maʿrifa* is identified with the complete and total annihilation of the consciousness of the Knower, in which only the Real is known by the Real. Then, the resulting annihilation of that annihilation brings a kind of sobriety and subsistence in which the Knower is granted discernment of the different levels of existence, but through the Real, not through his or her own faculties as before.

In reading Tijani texts such as the one quoted above (indeed most later Sufi texts), one is confronted by a dizzying array of terms related to spiritual experience and knowledge that all seem synonymous or somewhat related to *maʿrifa*. Often these terms seem to be used in lists of synonyms for rhetorical effect, but careful attention to their usages reveal nuances in their meanings, which often vary from author to author, and tradition to tradition. Within the Tijani tradition, the *Jawāhir al-Maʿānī* contains one of the clearest expositions of the relationship between these terms:

I asked him [Shaykh Aḥmad al-Tijānī] about the difference between knowlegdes/sciences [*ʿulūm*], secrets [*asrār*], lights [*anwār*], openings [*futūḥ*], outpourings [*fuyūḍ*], realities [*ḥaqāʾiq*], subtleties [*laṭāʾif*], divine self-disclosures [*tajāllīyāt*], witnessings [*mushāhadāt*], unveilings [*kashshāf*], Knowledges [*ma'ārif*], presences [*ḥaḍarāt*], stations [*maqāmāt*], stages [*manāzil*], inspirations [*wāridāt*], and states [*aḥwāl*]. He responded with the following statement:

Know that the opening [*al-fatḥ*] designates all of these things. The reality of the opening is what emerges from the unseen when the veils disappear from that which they hide. It encompasses all of the realities mentioned above, all that was veiled from him is opened for him in it [the opening], and this is the *fatḥ*, the opening. It also designates the lifting of the veils. The realties and meanings mentioned above that come after this are called *fayḍ*, outpouring, because it pours out after being blocked. Moreover, the outpouring encompasses the sciences and secrets and realities and Knowledges and lights. The secret [*sirr*] comes from the outpouring [*fayḍ*] and is that which God places directly in the heart of the servant in the way of understandings, among which are what God acquaints him with of His will in the disposal of things: why they are the way they are, substantially or accidentally, what He wants from them, and from which presence [*ḥaḍra*] they come.

Among the secrets are the outpourings of wisdom and their subtleties, and among these secrets is that which relieves the servant completely and takes him out of the circle of his senses while he is drowned in the ocean of the Divine Presence to the point where he has no awareness of himself or anything other than himself. Here he hears and witnesses what intelligences/rational faculties [*'uqūl*] do not have the capacity to understand—of his beginning and also the perception of his end. So by this secret which absorbs him, he perceives his beginning and end through witnessing and hearing and perception and tasting. And this is among the most exalted of secrets which is poured out upon the servant which can neither be conceived nor imagined let alone expressed nor come within the compass of allusion due to the splendor of its power and majesty and what they contain of benefits and perfections. These secrets have no limit. They can only be known by he who tastes them, and this suffices [as an explanation] for this point.

Knowledge [*ma'rifa*] is the lifting of the veils of the unseen realities of the Names and Attributes. Knowledge is inseparable and yet distinct from the opening [*fatḥ*]. For the reality of the opening is the lifting of the veils which come between the servant and the emergence of the realities of the Names and Attributes, accompanied by the disappearance of the forms of created things from the knowledge, senses, perception, understanding, and attachment of the servant until nothing remains for him—neither the existence of others nor otherness—except for the being of the Real by the Real, for the Real, in the Real, from the Real. Once this is realized, direct Knowledge [*ma'rifa*] emerges by necessity and the ocean of Universal Certainty [*al-yaqīn al-kullī*] is poured out upon the servant. But this is dependent upon annihilation [*fanā'*] and subsistence [*baqā'*]. And as for what precedes this of the witnessing of the hidden things and their appearance to the servant, this is called unveiling [*kashf*] and not called an opening [*fatḥ*] or Knowledge [*maʿrifa*].

As for inspiration [*wārid*], it is an expression for the appearance of what comes to the servant from God, from the presence of the Real to the servant in the form of Divine Power or Divine Beauty. It combines all the knowledges/sciences [*ʿulūm*], Knowledges [*maʿārif*], mysteries, states, certainty, and lights.

And as for state [*ḥāl*], it is an expression for the affair which comes from the presence of the Real in the form of Divine Power or Beauty transforming the servant into a form that corresponds to it. For example, it can be that a man who is capable of taking a hundred blows on the skin without crying out or turning pale, can cry out when hit by a single blow. In the first case, he was in a state of witnessing the Real, enshrouded in the perfection of love for the Essence of the Real and the perfection of its magnificence and glories which flow in its totality through that state, so it [this state] removes his sensation of pain when he is overcome by the sweetness of witnessing. So he doesn't feel the weight of the blows, and they don't hurt him. But as soon as the tablecloth of this state is folded up and he is no longer veiled from witnessing being hit with one blow, he cries out as a result of losing that state.

As for the lights, their realities are well known. They are brightness. As for the delicate points and subtleties, they are an expression for what is hidden/occult amongst the realities of knowledges/sciences [*ʿulūm*], and Knowledges [*maʿārif*], and mysteries.

As for the presences and stages and witnessings and haltings, they have been alluded to earlier in this work. All success relies on God! Here ends the dictation that the Shaykh (R. A.) gave us.[47]

In this passage, Knowledge depends on "the lifting of the veils," a common Sufi image referring to the purification of the soul (*tazkiyat al-nafs*) through spiritual exercises, and the resulting existential transformations of consciousness (annihilation [*fanā'*] and subsistence [*baqā'*]). This Knowledge is also connected to certainty, and compared to "taste" in its immediacy and ineffability. Moreover, as above, *maʿrifa* is described as being closely related, or even identical, to a divine outpouring (*fayḍ*), and, due to the single-pointed focus associated with it, can induce unusual psycho-physical states (*aḥwāl*).

Shaykh Ibrahim further clarifies the fine distinction between the opening or enlightenment (*fatḥ*) and Knowledge, writing that "every Knower [*ʿārif*] is open [has achieved the *fatḥ*/spiritual enlightenment], but the opposite is not true." Thus, the opening can be likened to the complete polishing of a mirror and Knowledge to what subsequently appears therein. One disciple described the opening (*fatḥ*) as "the removing of the veil between the human being and Allah, between the person and Knowledge of Allah [*maʿrifa*], the veils that cover your heart, seeing, hearing that separate them from Allah. . . . *Fatḥ* is the process of unveiling secrets . . . it's a process of getting into the real nature of things."[48] Furthermore, in Shaykh al-Tijānī's account, "the secret" of this Knowledge is equated with self-knowledge, and is described as being beyond the capacity of reason. Similarly, Shaykh Ibrahim Niasse is said to have treasured Shaykh Aḥmad al-Tijānī's poetic description of his own attainment of *maʿrifa*:

> I was pushed forward all at once from the Divine Presence.
> My beginning became my end, my end my beginning.
> My whole became my every part, and my every part became my whole.
> I became Him, and He, me,
> but as His becoming, and not as mine.
> At that moment, if I were asked a million questions,
> I would have given only one answer
> And so I became like the "lamp."[49]

Ibrahim Niasse himself defines a Knower by God (*ʿārif biLlāh*) as "one who turns toward God in all of his states . . . and there is nothing for him except God"[50] and "the Knower [*ʿārif*] among the Sufis is he who sees the other as the essential, that is, he witnesses the Real in the other."[51] This recalls and refers to Ibn ʿArabi's description of the Knower as one who can see and recognize the Real not only in his own form, but in its other forms as well. That is, he can recognize the water in cups other than his own. In the same work, Shaykh Ibrahim defines *maʿrifa* as "the spirit being deeply rooted and firmly established in the presence of direct witnessing [*mushāhada*] with complete annihilation [*fanāʾ*] and subsistence [*baqāʾ*] through God."[52]

Similarly, Shaykh Tijani ʿAli Cissé, one of Shaykh Ibrahim's grandsons, successors, and one of the most prominent and popular leaders of his disciples, described the Knower (*ʿārif*) to me in an interview:

> The spiritual wayfarer [*sālik*] is he who arrives by invocations [*adhkār*] to the presence of God, Most High. When he recognizes [*ʿarafa*] himself, he recognizes his Lord. When he recognizes himself as nonexistent, as nothing, he recognizes his Lord as Being [*wujūd*]. When he recognizes his meagerness, he recognizes his Lord's Majesty. And it is like this, you find that there is no god but God [*lā*

ilāha illā Llāh], there is no god but you [lā ilāha illā Anta], there is no god but I [lā ilāha illā Anā].⁵³

In my interviews with disciples in Dakar and Kaolack, the most common response to the question "What is *ma'rifa*?" was a shaking of the head, an exhalation of breath, and a raising of the hands in exasperation. Virtually all members of this community, from revered shaykhs who were direct disciples of Shaykh Ibrahim to young novices who had just completed their *tarbiya*, responded by insisting that *ma'rifa* was beyond anything that could be expressed in words. When they did attempt to define *ma'rifa* verbally, their responses tended to share certain common features. The disciples of Shaykh Ibrahim frequently described *ma'rifa* as "knowledge of God," "knowledge of self," "knowledge of reality," "knowledge that you are nothing and God is everything," "knowing who you really are," "knowing that everything is God," "knowing with God's knowledge," and "seeing God, seeing God in everything and everything in God." Some even described it in apophatic terms as "a kind of ignorance or bewilderment," "unlike any other kind of knowledge." The ineffable quality of *ma'rifa* was often linked to its experiential dimension in statements such as "It's something you have to experience, you can't describe it, it's very deep inside, very personal"; "It's something very personal, it's hard to describe, you have to experience it"; "I know it, I feel it, but I can't tell you how, it's like I smell something, you either smell it, too, or you don't"; "It's like if you ask me, 'How does an apple taste?' I can talk for hours and you'll still not gonna know how it tastes until you go and taste it yourself, and that knowledge is the same, so it's difficult to talk about it."

Disciples also frequently commented on the existential dimension of *ma'rifa*, noting that "it's something you live," "you have to live it, to be it." They also commented on its transformative nature with phrases such as "It is like waking up"; "It changes the way you view yourself, the world"; "It changes you, you're like a new person"; "When you get *ma'rifa*, you can't be the same as before, it changes the way you see things, the way you react to things, the way you behave, even the way you think, it's not like before"; "After you know God, you see the good things and the bad things clearly, so it's easier to avoid the bad things and to do the good"; "When you do *tarbiya*, you know God and the Prophet and the shaykh, and you love them, and you want to be like them so you won't do things that they don't like"; "After *tarbiya* I'm not so hard on myself because I know I'm weak, I'm only human, and of course we all still make mistakes, but we know God has forgiven us, and we are grateful, so we try to do good." Disciples also frequently described *ma'rifa* as being "the most important form of knowledge you can get," "the goal of life," "the reason for creation," "the most important thing," and "the most precious thing in the world." They also referred to it as being "certain" or "certainty" itself.

## Nuances and Levels of *Ma'rifa*

However, often in the same interviews, disciples also described *ma'rifa* as being qualified. Sidi Inaya Niang, the son of one of Shaykh Ibrahim's earliest and closest disciples, told me that "certainty is achieved when the adept (*al-sālik*) attains the Divine Presence (*ḥaḍrat al-Quds*), the sacrosanct spiritual station, by the Muḥammadan reality (*al-ḥaqīqa al-Muḥammadiyya*). But after this certainty, the Knower (*al-'ārif*) is in a state of uncertainty, and vice versa. It is the spiritual station of doubt or perplexity, the station of bewilderment (*maqām al-ḥayra*), or the negation, 'there is no God' (*la ilāha*), which precedes the affirmation 'but God' (*illā Llāh*). *Ma'rifa* also has its own dialectic."[54]

Echoing many other disciples, Sidi Inaya described *ma'rifa* as being "dynamic," "living knowledge" that "has no end, just as God has no end." Echoing Junayd's statement about the color of water, Sidi Inaya told me that "the *'ārif* [Knower] is the container, the Knowledge [*ma'rifa*] is the content, and the purpose of this Knowledge is the use of the content and its transmission to other containers." While many disciples described *ma'rifa* as the realization of the identity of the Knower, Known, and Knowledge with God, Sidi Mohamed Kane gave a more nuanced account (as quoted above):

> Shaykh Ibrahim said, "God does not manifest Himself to the same person in the same way." God is infinite, the way He will manifest himself to you is different from the way He will manifest Himself to me or to Shaykh Ibrahim, because God is infinite. He will manifest Himself to you in a form that corresponds to you. . . . The way in which God manifests Himself is different, just as people are different. It's also like drunkenness, the Sufis also talk about drunkenness, and people get drunk differently: one person cries, another laughs, another does something else. . . . People do not become drunk in the same fashion, it somewhat depends on the quantity, on what, on how much they can handle. It's the same with *ma'rifa*.[55]

While some disciples presented *ma'rifa* as an "all or nothing" affair, the more senior shaykhs and disciples described *ma'rifa* and *fanā'* (annihilation) as having different levels or intensities, describing some people as being more strongly annihilated in the Prophet than others and some surpassing others in *ma'rifa*. Many connected this to self-knowledge in that if someone is "deeper," he or she can handle "more" or "deeper" *ma'rifa*. In this way, the receptivity or preparedness of one's self determines the degree of the profundity of *ma'rifa* one can achieve.

Similarly, commenting on the ḥadīth "He who knows himself, knows his Lord," Sidi Inaya Niang explained, "If you want to know your Lord, you must go through knowledge of yourself or the realization of self. That is, the Names and Divine Attributes must first manifest themselves in you. The search for the Truth requires the discovery of the truth in yourself."[56]

K. S., a Senegalese disciple in his mid-twenties who is currently pursuing an undergraduate degree in economics in Paris, also described *ma'rifa* as a kind of self-knowledge that contains all other knowledge, using the role the brain plays in decision making as a metaphor for the individual self and what lies beyond it:

> What is *ma'rifa*? *Ma'rifat biLlāhi* [Knowledge by God] is gnosis. *Ma'rifa* is the most important knowledge a person can get. Because it is the box that contains the whole repository of knowledge, knowledge we know and what we don't know. Imagine your brain, if you do something like, for instance, I am raising my hand—it is a command I gave to my brain, and in my brain after that there is a stimulus or something like that and my hand is raised. That thing that tells your brain, it is something inside you, it is something you don't control, and in this state, the brain has a sort of *ma'rifa* [existential self-knowledge], but you have to know what your brain is exactly and exactly what your brain contains, or might contain, or could control, what is exactly the extent of your brain, what exactly it is. Do you command your brain, or does your brain command you? When you raise your hand, there is a basis for the decision to raise my hand, where does it come from exactly?
>
> *Ma'rifa* is the content [*contenu*]. *Ma'rifa* is something everybody can reach, but there are many conditions. The gnosis, what is important is not the gnosis itself, but the consequences of having the gnosis, of seeing the gnosis, of understanding the gnosis, what does it imply? This is what is important. And *ma'rifa* could be said to be like a key that opens all areas in your brain and displays exactly what each thing is.
>
> Of course, *ma'rifa* is very, very certain knowledge. If you see *ma'rifa*, it is like a door that opens onto something. As I said, the consequences of having *ma'rifa* are the most important thing of the *ma'rifa* itself. We all come from the main source, and truly what is inside you is inside other people, and there is a process of waking up. First you have to know you are asleep, recognize that state, and after, you must strongly have the will to wake up yourself, and start the process of waking up. Next you recognize that you are sleeping and that you have to wake up and put yourself in the path of deepening knowledge, of awakening what is inside. . . . All life is a process of getting knowledge, whatever happens, you always learn something, life is a process of getting knowledge. . . . The first *ayah* that God had Gabriel reveal to the Prophet was *Iqra'*! [Read/Recite!] *Iqra'* is the process of getting knowledge, "recite in the name of your Lord." Life is a process of getting knowledge, *ma'rifa*

and other kinds. What is important is to have a strong will for knowledge and to get yourself to that path.⁵⁷

Many of the members of Shaykh Ibrahim's community whom I interviewed had received extensive formal education in Arabic-language traditions of Islamic scholarship, both in West Africa and the Middle East, or had been educated in the French-language educational systems of Senegal and France. For example, Sidi Mohamed Kane received a traditional West African Qurʾanic and Islamic education in his youth at the hands of his mother (Shaykh Ibrahim's daughter, Seyyida Maryam Niasse), but went on to study in French-language schools in Senegal, where he developed an interest in Marxist philosophy, which he pursued during his university studies in Paris. However, after undergoing *tarbiya*, he lost interest in Marxism as his philosophical pursuits became more aligned with his spiritual practice and the works of his grandfather. Many other disciples had pursued higher degrees in Islamic studies or Arabic literature in Egypt at the universities of al-Azhar and ʿAyn Shams, while many more had graduated from, were currently enrolled in, or were hoping to attend the Francophone Cheikh Anta Diop University in Dakar, where they studied a variety of subjects from economics, to physics, to literature, to philosophy.

These disciples often contrasted *maʿrifa* to the forms of knowledge they acquired in these institutional settings, saying that *maʿrifa* is "beyond reason," "beyond what you can find in books," "not something you can learn in any class," "the realization of the things we used to talk about in philosophy class," "like philosophy, but the philosophers don't realize what they are saying"; Sidi Inaya even paraphrased Rabelais by describing *maʿrifa* as "the conscience of all forms of science [knowledge], for science [knowledge] without conscience is but the ruin of the soul."⁵⁸ In the same interview, he further contrasted *maʿrifa* to other forms of knowledge: "*Maʿrifa* is innate (*infuse*) knowledge, while the other forms of knowledge are diffuse. *Maʿrifa* is esoteric knowledge, while other forms of knowledge are exoteric. *Maʿrifa* is mystical knowledge, while the other forms of knowledge are rational. *Maʿrifa* is metaphysics (*la Métaphysique*), while the others are logical (*les sciences logiques*)."⁵⁹

**Relationship of *Maʿrifa* to Other Forms of Knowledge**

In a speech given for a *mawlid* (celebration of the Prophet's birthday) in Abidjan, Ivory Coast, in 2011, Shaykh Tijani ʿAli Cissé asserted the superiority of *maʿrifa* as "the most important of the religious obligations and the most sublime honor, as it is the foundation of faith and the goal of Islam. The Knowledge of God is the utmost goal in the perfection of the human condition, the highest rank of spiritual realization, and the most cherished ideal. . . . Mankind's Knowledge [*maʿrifa*] of God is above all other types of knowledge."⁶⁰ In the same speech he quoted the ḥadīth "The support of the house is its foundation. The support of the religion is the *maʿrifa* of Allah the Most High, certainty and the restrained mind"⁶¹ to assert the primacy of *maʿrifa* to all other forms of knowledge.

The late, illustrious Shaykh Barham Diop (d. 2014), who served as Shaykh Ibrahim Niasse's personal secretary for several decades until the latter's death in 1975, told me a story about Shaykh Ibrahim that eloquently captures the relationship between *maʿrifa* and other forms of knowledge:

> The people of his [Shaykh Ibrahim's] time in West Africa, the learned [*ʿulamāʾ*] and the legal scholars [*fuqahāʾ*], they were frozen in their thinking and rulings out of fear of making a mistake or deviating. But Shaykh Ibrahim's thought was dynamic and living, since he took it from God and the Prophet. For example, the issue of praying with one's hands folded over the chest [*qabḍ*] [as opposed to the standard Mālikī practice of praying with your hands at your sides]—when Shaykh Ibrahim started doing this, from the response, you would think he was calling people to infidelity [*kufr*]. People said all kinds of things. But Shaykh Ibrahim didn't say that you couldn't pray with your hands at your sides, he merely said that he and his followers could pray with their hands folded. He had this directly from the Prophet, in a vision, but he then gave proofs by going through the texts of Mālikī jurisprudence [*fiqh*] and showing its validity on this basis as well. He did this out of *adab* [good manners], so that others would be able to understand and not attack him and his disciples, and the *adab* of the Knowers is to give everyone and everything its due.⁶²

Shaykh Barham's description of Ibrahim Niasse's thought alludes to a famous saying of the early Sufi Abū Yazīd al-Bisṭāmī (d. 874), which Ibn ʿArabi quotes in the following passage:

> Abū Yazīd addressed the exoteric scholars with his words, "You take your knowledge from the dead, but we take our knowledge from the Alive [*al-Ḥayy*, one of the 99 Names of God] who does not die." The likes of ourselves say, "My heart told me of my Lord." You say, "so-and-so told me." Where is he? "Dead." "And he had it from so-and-so." Where is he? "Dead." When someone said to Shaykh Abu Madyan (d. 1198), "It is related from so and so, from so and so," he used to say, "We don't want to eat dried meat. Come on, bring me 'fresh flesh'!" Thereby he would lift up the aspirations of is companions. He meant: These are the words of so and so. What do you yourself say? What God-given knowledge has God singled out

for you? Speak from your Lord and forget about "so and so related form so and so." They ate fresh meat and God has not died. He is "nearer" to you "than the jugular vein" (50:16).[63]

Similarly, Shaykh Ibrahim's grandson, Sidi Mohamed Kane, told me that his grandfather said, "Knowledge [*connaissance*] that is dead comes from the dead, but knowledge that is living comes from the Living [*al-Ḥayy*]." "This latter knowledge," Sidi Mohamed continued, "is *ma'rifa*. Book knowledge you get from a book written by someone who is dead about someone else who is dead, but living knowledge comes from God."[64]

Shaykh Ibrahim's emphasis on this latter form of knowledge led him to take seriously the inspirations he received. In the previous quote, Shaykh Barham Diop refers to the controversy stirred up when Shaykh Ibrahim made a minor change in the way he said his daily prayers (with his hands folded over his chest, instead of hanging down at his sides) on the basis of a visionary experience of the Prophet. Niasse later published a short treatise defending this change in practice on the basis of the tradition of Islamic jurisprudence (specifically Mālikī *fiqh*), citing prior opinions from within the tradition and adducing arguments from the ḥadīth and the Qur'an, but without referencing his vision.[65] This work and the change in practice it defended were controversial, but what is of interest here is that although the inspiration for the change came from a form of unveiling, a visionary encounter with the Prophet, Shaykh Ibrahim did not cite his personal experience as definitive proof; instead, he followed the conventions of the discipline of *fiqh* in providing rational and transmitted proofs for his position. This example illustrates both the continuity that can exist between *ma'rifa* and the rational (*'aqlī*) and transmitted (*naqlī*) sciences, and the priority that *ma'rifa* was given over the latter.[66]

Shaykh Barham Diop described Shaykh Ibrahim's actions as being motivated by *adab*, a word that is notoriously difficult to render into English, but simultaneously carries the connotations of the state of being well-mannered, cultured, considerate, and of good character. *Adab*, in this context can perhaps best be described, paraphrasing Shaykh Barham Diop, as the acquired disposition of giving everything and everyone its due. In this case, Shaykh Ibrahim Niasse adduced proofs to clarify and defend his position to others, since they were not privy to his own visionary encounter; however, these proofs were for the sake of others, not for himself. In this instance, Shaykh Ibrahim's visionary experience, which was a result of his *ma'rifa*, guided his work in Islamic jurisprudence (*fiqh*).

However, Shaykh Ibrahim insisted that not every "mystical experience," dream, or vision was to be regarded as Knowledge; he drew a sharp distinction between *dhawq* (tasting, experience) and *dhawq sālim* (sound tasting, experience). Anyone could have a vision or a dream for any number of reasons, but the only guarantee of the veracity of this experience and its interpretation was to have already obtained complete *ma'rifa* by passing through annihilation to subsistence and coming to recognize and judge things by the Real itself. Before achieving this, one would have to submit such extraordinary experiences to the scrutiny of one who had done so.[67]

Moreover, just as the spiritual seeker doesn't just pop out of existence after attaining *ma'rifa*, but rather continues to walk and talk and eat, he or she also continues to think and engage in rational discussions, albeit from a different standpoint, with a different perspective. In a famous speech, which he gave in Nouakchott, Mauritania in 1944, Shaykh Ibrahim described the state of the Knower (*'ārif*):

> He knows there is nothing but God and he perceives things as they are, and he puts every created thing in its place, in which God placed it. And he knows that he is nothing. He exalts things, while not considering them existent; and he fears things, without considering them existent, and he loves things without considering them existent. And he acquires all good actions, he prays, and he fasts, and he makes ḥajj, and he tells the truth and he spends his money. And all of that is out of good manners [*adab*] to God, while he knows that there is nothing there.[68]

In this same speech, he gives an example of how *ma'rifa* can even influence the way one studies disciplines such as grammar: "I teach students in grammar lessons: the grammarians say 'In reality the subject of the verb [*al-fā'il*] is God.[69] Metaphorically, the one who gives existence to the action, and technically, the one on whom the action relies completely, all of these are God.'"[70]

In his earliest-known work, a poem titled *Rūḥ al-Adab* (*The Spirit of Good Manners*), Shaykh Ibrahim lists the forms of knowledge that a disciple must acquire:

> Obtain the knowledge of four things, O spiritual traveler, the first of which is the Knowledge ['*irfān*] of the Lord, the Master;
> The second is to know that on which the acts of worship depend, that you may realize/verify [them];
> Third is the Knowledge ['*irfān*] of the states of the soul: its deceptions, tricks, and schemes;
> The soul has its fault, the heart has its fault, and the spirit has its fault, of this, there is no doubt;
> And *Adab* [good manners], [knowledge of] *adab* is the fourth, O traveler, it is the door for every traveler.[71]

What is interesting here is that Knowledge of God (*'irfān/ma'rifa*) is listed first—it is not the end of the path, but rather its beginning. The other forms of knowledge are listed as being secondary and tertiary to the Knowledge of God, in line with the *ḥadīth qudsī* oft-cited by Shaykh Ibrahim and his disciples, "Search for knowledge of me before you worship Me. How will he who does not know Me worship me?" However, Knowledge of God is only obtained through the correct performance of rites such as prayer and invocation, so there must be some initial knowledge of these acts of worship, although their efficacy and meaning is "verified" through the acquisition of *maʿrifa*.

Similarly, the acquisition of the Knowledge of God depends on some initial form of self-control and *adab*, however these forms of knowledge find their completion and fulfillment in and through *maʿrifa*. Thus, as for Sufis before him such as Ibn ʿArabi and al-Ghazāli, *maʿrifa* for Shaykh Ibrahim was both the foundation and the crown of other forms of knowledge, revealing and verifying their inner meaning and significance. These other forms of knowledge—be they rational, like logic, or transmitted, like ḥadīth or the correct way to perform the prayers—may lead to *maʿrifa*, but *maʿrifa* leads to their perfection.

Thus, within this epistemology, *maʿrifa* is not separated from other forms of knowledge, and it can only be opposed to them apparently, since in reality it is their root and their perfection. This is why, on the basis of his *maʿrifa*, S. D. could resolve the version of the classic omnipotence paradox with which his philosophy teacher had presented him—"Can God make a rock too heavy for Him to lift?"—not by resorting to notions of logical impossibility as other thinkers have done, but by dissolving the question on the basis of his own experience of annihilation, in which there could be no stone that is not God. Other disciples told me that after having done *tarbiya* and acquiring *maʿrifa*, they would ace all of their philosophy exams without even reading or studying because it gave them a deeper insight and new perspectives on the metaphysical questions posed in their classes.[72]

Echoing al-Ghazālī, Shaykh Aḥmad al-Tijānī contrasts *maʿrifa* to the merely rational methods and arguments of theology and philosophy (*falsafa*) through a parable of two men: the first is healthy and has no knowledge of medicine, while the second suffers a variety of maladies and acquires knowledge of medicine in order to treat his illnesses. The second man disparages the first for his lack of medical knowledge; the first man points out that the point of such knowledge is to restore the sick to health, but since he is already healthy, he has no need of such knowledge.[73] In this analogy, the first man is the *ʿārif*, the Knower of God, unafflicted by the illnesses of ignorance or doubt, while the second man is the scholar who needs knowledge of the medicine of rational proofs in order to treat his doubts and uncertainties. Furthermore, the analogy suggests that just as health and knowledge of medicine belong to two different domains—the existential and the conceptual—so do *maʿrifa* and merely rational forms of knowledge.

Ibn 'Arabi further clarifies the distinctions between these different types of knowledge, writing:

> The sciences are of three levels. [The first] is the science of reason, which is every knowledge which is actualized for you by the fact that it is self-evident or after considering proof, on condition that the purport of the proof is discovered....
>
> The second science is the science of states (*aḥwāl*), which cannot be reached except through tasting. No man of reason can define the states, nor can any proof be adduced for knowing them, naturally enough. Take for example the sweetness of honey, the bitterness of aloes, the pleasure of sexual intercourse, love, ecstasy, yearning, and similar knowledges. It is impossible for anyone to know any of these sciences without being qualified by them and tasting them....
>
> The third knowledge is the sciences of the mysteries (*asrār*). It is the knowledge which is "beyond the stage of reason." It is the knowledge through the blowing (*nafth*) of the Holy Spirit (*ruḥ al-quddūs*) into the heart (*rū'*), and it is specific to the prophet or the friends of God. It is of two sorts:
>
> The first sort can be perceived by reason, just like the first of the kinds above. However, the person who knows it does not acquire it through consideration: rather the level of this knowledge grants it.
>
> The second sort is divided into two kinds. The first is connected to the second kind above [knowledge of states], but its state is more noble. The second kind is the science of reports (*akhbār*), and concerning them, one can say that they are true or false, unless the truthfulness of the report-giver and his inerrancy in what he says have been established for the one who receives the report. Such is the report given by the prophets from God, like their reporting about the Garden [heaven] and what is within it. Hence the words of the Prophet that there is a Garden is a science of reports. But his words that at the resurrection there is a pool sweeter than honey is a science of states, a science of tasting. And his words, "God is, and nothing is with Him," is one of the sciences of reason, perceived by consideration.
>
> The knower of this last kind—the science of mysteries (*asrār*)—knows and exhausts all sciences. The possessors of the other sciences are not like that. So there is no knowledge more noble than this all-encompassing knowledge, which comprises all objects of knowledge.[74]

In this schema, ordinary knowledge is divided up into that which can be acquired by reason (e.g., the sum of the interior angles of a triangle is 180°) and that which can be acquired by the senses (e.g., honey is sweet, sex feels good). The "knowledge of mysteries," which is identified with *ma'rifa* and described as being beyond reason, is itself divided into that which could be acquired by reason (e.g., God is, and there is nothing with Him) but is acquired through unveiling, and that which in no way could be acquired by reason alone (e.g., what heaven is like). This latter category of knowledge is subdivided into that which is like sensory knowledge (e.g., the Prophet's tasting of a heavenly pool sweeter than honey) and that which is like factual knowledge (e.g., the fact that there is a heaven). This "knowledge of mysteries" is described as "all-encompassing" and "comprising all objects of knowledge" since it concerns the divine principles of all created things, as well as the Real itself. It is important to note that this particularly exalted "knowledge of mysteries" is not opposed to sensory or rational knowledge, but is rather described as "encompassing" or "going beyond them," so that these more common forms of knowledge can and should conform to *ma'rifa*. Ibn 'Arabi further explains:

> The way of gaining knowledge is divided between reflection (*fikr*) and bestowal (*wahb*), which is the divine effusion (*fayḍ*). The latter is the way of our companions.... Hence it is said that the science of the prophets and the friends of God are "beyond the stage of reason" (*warā' ṭawr al-'aql*). Reason has no entrance into them through reflection, though it can accept them, especially in the case of him whose reason is "sound" (*salīm*), that is, he who is not overcome by any obfuscation deriving from imagination and reflection, an obfuscation which would corrupt his consideration....
>
> Two ways lead to knowledge of God. There is no third way. The person who declares God's Unity in some other way [merely] follows authority in his declaration. The first way is the way of unveiling [*kashf*]. It is an incontrovertible knowledge which is actualized through unveiling and which man finds in himself. He receives no obfuscations along with it and is not able to repel it. He knows no proof for it by which it is supported except what he finds in himself. One of the Sufis differs on this point, for he says, "He is given the proof and what is proven by the proof in his unveiling, since, when something cannot be known except through proof, its proof must also be unveiled." This was the view of our companion Abū 'Abdallāh [Muḥammad] ibn al-Kattānī in Fez. I heard that from him. He reported about his own state and he spoke the truth. However, he was mistaken in holding that the situation must be like that, for others find the knowledge in themselves through tasting without having its proof unveiled. This kind of knowledge may also be actualized through a divine self-disclosure given to its possessors, who are the messengers, the prophets, and some of the friends.
>
> The second way is the way of reflection and reasoning (*istidlāl*) through rational demonstration (*burhan 'aqlī*). This way is lower than the first way, since he who

bases his considerations upon proof can be visited by obfuscations which detract from his proof, and only with difficulty can he remove them.[75]

In this passage, while *ma'rifa* is still portrayed as being "beyond the stage of reason," Ibn 'Arabi describes a kind of continuity between reason and unveiling, with "sound" reason being capable of accepting, if not deriving, the truths and knowledge of *ma'rifa*. Moreover, he even states that these unveilings may also include their rational proofs, as was the case for his contemporary, al-Kattānī. The knowledge acquired through unveiling could thus potentially be acquired through rational demonstration; but this is a more difficult and arduous route, and even this "lower route" still depends on the "soundness" of the rational faculties, which can by no means be assumed.

When I interviewed K. S. about the limitations of reason and its relationship to *ma'rifa*, he offered a slightly different perspective:

What is your definition of reason? For me, reason itself is not limited, but it is the person who limits reason. If we have only one approach to understand, if we try to define a scheme in which we speak, it is a process in which we are limiting reason ourselves. But reflection (*tafakkur*) is a combination of many elements, and reason is one of them, they move forward together. Never can one element move forward in a stage and leave the others behind, or even if one element is leading, there is feedback, so the other elements know what is going on. So reason is not limited, but we have to discover all the elements and merge them in order to know exactly how to use perfectly our reason. For example, scientific thinking or scientific experimentation with observation, experimentation, trying to discover interactions, collaboration and comparison of theories, is something very valid for all kinds of thinking that we have. But sometimes what is problematic is the observation, there are many things you can't observe, but you shouldn't reject them or say that it doesn't exist, simply because you can't observe them. As for our reasoning, if it has a false basis, we will always be in a circle of flaws. For example, if I say one plus one equals two, or one plus one plus one equals three, it is simply a way of thinking which we have learned, which is very strong in us, and of course we have the certainty that it is true, and it would be very difficult to get out of that way of thinking, of that schema. But we have to have a plurality of ways of thinking, and understand exactly how to enlarge our reasoning.

Because reason is not limited, but it is something the human limits, himself. For example, take this pencil, it is one, one pencil, and if I break it, this way [*snaps pencil*]—OK, I have broken it—and for you, I have two parts. And if I join them, and for you, one plus one is two, and if I say to you, one plus one is one, this way [*holds the pieces of the pencil apart*] you will say it is not possible. For me, one plus one is one [*puts the pieces of the pencil together*], even though I broke it, and you can see the two parts are one, everything can be united. Mathematics, truly, mathematics is a process of uniting everything to one. Then a person will understand that everything, all mathematics leads to just one, one, one. . . . Why Allah gave us mathematics is just to understand that all the elements we see are just one, so we have to resolve not one plus one equals two, but one plus one equals one, like this [*puts the pieces of the pencil back together*]. And so we just have to consider very different ways of thinking and not just adopt a schema and generalize it to everyone, every person, every situation. But for me, reason is not limited, but we limit it, and we don't understand, and we can't make it function correctly because we don't know how to use, how to combine all the elements to do reflection. . . .

*Fatḥ* is the process of being conscious that you have no limits, and you can only keep discovering, and discovering, and finding out, and destroying walls and discovering the true interaction between things. You just keep moving forward and moving forward and moving forward, and that limit that you think you have in your reason is destroyed and you move forward by a combination of many elements in which you have reason, and all the elements that you have to combine in order to move forward. . . . Reason is a part and you have to combine reason and the other elements in order to form one element capable of knowing things, so if you consider only one element, for instance, only reason, you will fail. But you have to join reason and all elements in order to form one thing that will give you the strength to know, and those other elements include *fayḍa*, being hardworking, acting only for the sake of Allah, et cetera. . . . There is a way of thinking that says that reason and the heart are very different, and this is something distorted, because reason is exactly the heart and the heart is reason. And we will never be able to understand the different things without understanding that reason and heart are one entity, and to understand this we must be able to think from inside us and from outside, because to reach the Truth we need both, we need reason and we need the heart, it is very important to join them, to unite them in a single entity and unite the many other elements in a single entity in order to think, to see things properly.

[Question: So when you can synthesize these different elements into one, then you can know the truth? When you become one, then you can know the One, the Truth?]

K. S.: Yes, Yes. Because if the truth is just a point, you can come from here, from here, from here [*pointing from all different directions*], or you can come from just one direction. OK, so there are very different approaches, but the one coming just from one direction and getting to the point has many flaws, but the one coming from this direction, that direction, that direction, and reaching the point is more complete. He is more complete, so we have to be plural in our way of thinking and, after, try to unite all our different forms of knowledge and realize that there is only a single entity, and realize that the solid, the liquid, the gas is just one entity.[76]

In this account, reason is described as a part of a larger whole, a whole with a seemingly unlimited capacity for knowledge. Reason can be fallible or "unsound" when it is limited to a particular perspective or way of looking at things, but these limits can be overcome, and reasoning can be expanded through spiritual practice. This process of transformation unites the various cognitive and noetic elements of the knower into one, transcending individual limitations, allowing the knower to see everything as one. This is a clear allusion to the process described in the ḥadīth in which God becomes "his hearing with which he hears, his seeing with which he sees, his hand with which he grasps, and his foot with which he walks." In this ḥadīth and in K. S.'s account, the faculties are all united into one, and allow the knower to reason correctly and see things properly. K. S.'s concluding description of the necessity of having plural approaches to, and ways of thinking about, the truth recalls, in a different mode, Ibn ʿArabī's insistence that the truth cannot be encompassed by a single form of belief or doctrine. Overall, K. S.'s account stresses the continuity and unity of reason and unveiling, and insists on the necessity of both in order to "see things properly" to have a more complete and unlimited knowledge of the unlimited truth.

In a similar vein, Sidi Inaya Niang directed my attention to a passage of *Jawāhir al-Maʿānī* in which Shaykh Aḥmad al-Tijānī describes the different levels of the intellect (ʿaql) and their relationship to one another.[77] In many Sufi texts, the term ʿaql can often be glossed as "reason," with limitative and pejorative connotations, but in this passage Shaykh Tijānī describes ʿaql as a kind of continuum with various degrees and levels running the epistemological gamut, from the most sublime and complete form of *maʿrifa* to the most mundane forms of knowledge and cunning:

> The intellect here [ʿaql] is the Divine Intellect [al-ʿaql al-rabbānī] hidden in the presence of the unseen [ḥaḍrat al-ghayb], which was an attribute of the spirit at first, before it was combined with the body, being for the spirit what vision is for the eye. Just as by vision, the realities of apparent things are revealed in the eye, likewise by the Divine Intellect, the inward realities of hidden things are Known. By it [the Divine Intellect] the truth is Known as true, and the false as false in reality and by certain unveiling, without confusing things, and without becoming overwhelmed by the difficulties of trials. This is maintaining the just balance between

the two pans [of the scale]: the true and the false. By it [the Divine Intellect] is Known the means of weighing things and placing everything in the pan of truth or the pan of falsehood. By it is Known the way of distinguishing between things and their equivalents.

This Divine Intellect takes knowledge from God without an intermediary, without requiring the teaching of a teacher or the reports of a reporter, rather all that it desires of knowledge it takes directly from the Real. . . . The degrees of the intellect are three:

The first is the Divine Intellect, which is pure, Divine Light that is poured out in the inward reality of the spirit. It is the guide and it leads to the goal. None attains this intellect save the perfect Knower by God [al-'ārif biLlāh al-kāmil].

The second level of the intellect is the Universal Intellect [al-'aql al-kullī], which is covered by thin veils of darkness. It discovers the realities of existing things, the apparent and the hidden. The difference between it and the first intellect is that the first intellect reveals things outwardly and inwardly and discerns the secrets of the Holy Presence [ḥaḍrat al-Quds] while sitting on the footstool of magnificent power, and while governing all things as it wills—everything obeys it and nothing disobeys it. As for the second intellect, which is the Universal Intellect, it is veiled from the Divine Presence [ḥaḍrat al-Ilāhiya] by many veils, so it does not glimpse anything of the secrets of the Holy Presence, but it does discover the realities of existing things, the apparent and the hidden, but only by the Divine Light cast into it. It governs things as it wills, sometimes carrying out its wishes, sometimes with difficulty. It Knows the source of things and their origins from the apparent aspect of the cosmos, not from the hidden aspect of the Holy Presence. The Knowledge [ma'rifa], which is taken from the inward aspect of the Holy Presence, of the realities of the universe, outwardly and inwardly, and the knowledge which is taken from the apparent existents of the unseen and visible worlds—the distance between them is great.

The Universal Intellect, in this level, weighs things on the just scale. It Knows things and their outcomes and their ends to which they are returned. This is one of the greatest and most elevated matters. Even if the situation does not allow one to attain this level of the Divine Intellect, he or she can still greatly benefit from sciences and Knowledges [acquired by the lower level of the intellect], even if they only concern the external forms of the world.

This intellect is shared by both the believer and the unbeliever. This second intellect can be given to some unbelievers through their persistence in opposing the passions of their souls and their contemplation of the Divine Presence. Although this does not avail them against their lack of faith, they can attain some of the special qualities of the Universal Intellect in this world by discovering some aspects of the unseen. So they can have command of certain specialties and mysteries, and thus they can have a great deal to say on many different topics. But this lures them to their destruction in the afterlife. May God preserve us from this by His grace and generosity.

The third level of the intellect is the lowest, the most trivial, and it is the practical intellect [al-ʿaql al-maʿāshiyy] by which one organizes worldly affairs and its external aspects, out of one's own passions, penchants, and love of rest, and tenacity in pursuing one's whims and avoiding anything that opposes one's affairs. This intellect is shared by both men and beasts. The intellect that takes precedence is the greater Divine Intellect, which is beyond the scope of the Universal Intellect.[78]

This passage draws on the ḥadīth "Knowledge is a light that God casts into the heart of whomever He wills" and the long tradition of Islamic epistemology equating knowledge with light, as well as the Islamic philosophical tradition's adaptation of the Aristotelian/neo-Platonic concept of various levels or kinds of intellect. In this perspective,[79] the intellect is likened to varying degrees of light, which allow for various modes of perception and understanding. The most common, and lowest, form of intellect allows one to discern the helpful from the harmful, and obeys one's whims and desires. The next level of the intellect can only be achieved by those who master their passions and desires and direct their attention toward aspects of reality beyond one's own worldly affairs. This intellect can govern over the soul of its possessor, but it can also be opposed. Furthermore, it can "govern over" external things by understanding their origins and predicting their outcomes. But again, this knowledge and control is only partial, and proceeds from the appearances of things to their inner realities, whereas the highest level of the intellect knows both the apparent and hidden aspects of things from their divine origins. One imagines that some rationalist Islamic theologians and philosophers (as well as many contemporary academics) would be categorized as having this second kind of intellect. The highest level of intellect, the Divine Intellect, is described as being a kind of "eye of the spirit," and as being a faculty that derives knowledge directly from the Real, with neither intermediary nor doubt. It is the exclusive purview of the most perfect of Knowers who have passed through both *fanāʾ* (annihilation) and *baqāʾ* (subsistence), so that they know things both in and through God. It is the instrument of *maʿrifa*. Due to its immediate and certain nature, its spiritual requirements, and its identification with the Divine, it "governs over" both the soul of its possessor and external things in that its perceptions cannot be refuted and that it knows the apparent and hidden realities of things, both as they exist in the world and as they exist *in divinis*.

But by far the most common schema for relating *ma'rifa* to other forms of knowledge had to do not with the varying degrees of the intellect, but with those of certainty, as mentioned in the previous chapter. The popular Tijānī prayer book *Aḥzāb wa Awrād* (*Litanies and Prayers*) describes these levels in the following way: "Our knowledge of death is the knowledge of certainty [*'ilm al-yaqīn*], our seeing someone die is the eye of certainty [*'ayn al-yaqīn*], and death [itself] is the reality of certainty [*ḥaqq al-yaqīn*], because we have realized [*nataḥaqqaqu*] it."[80] The connection between knowledge and death here is significant, since the annihilation (*fanā'*) that leads to *ma'rifa* and certainty is often likened to death, and the Prophetic injunction to "die before you die" is often interpreted as referring to *fanā'*. The first level of certainty is identified with discursive knowledge, the second with perception, and the third with an existential transformation. At this highest degree of certainty, knowledge and being are united and inseparable.

Similarly, Shaykh Māḥī Niasse, one of Shaykh Ibrahim's sons and spiritual successors, told me that the knowledge of certainty (*'ilm al-yaqīn*) is like my knowing that Medina Baye exists but without knowing where it is; the eye of certainty (*'ayn al-yaqīn*) is like seeing the city, and the reality of certainty (*ḥaqq al-yaqīn*) is like entering the city and gaining a complete understanding of its residents and history.[81] This formulation was repeated, with minor variations, by virtually every shaykh I asked about certainty. As quoted above, the French disciple Abu Ibrahim used a similar metaphor of discursive description versus personal experience to characterize the difference between *ma'rifa* and other forms of knowledge:

> It's like scholars, they read, they learn.... It's like you read a guidebook about Paris, you learn the history of Paris, you see the pictures of Paris, but it's better to go there for two days, now you *know* Paris! But if you're just, you're outside Paris, you read about Paris for years, but you don't know Paris, the guy who's never read anything, but he's been to Paris, he knows Paris better than you do. It's the same with God. Like some young guys here, they maybe don't know much of "conventional" knowledge, but they know God and that makes them "better" than imams and *shuyūkhs* who've studied for years but never experienced this knowledge. You see?[82]

Before concluding, a note is in order about the "knowledge of mysteries" (*'ilm al-asrār*) that is associated with *ma'rifa*. In this worldview, God reveals or manifests Himself in three main domains or "books": the book of the cosmos, the book of the soul, and the book of scripture. These three books are intimately related to one another, and Knowledge of God necessarily grants profound knowledge of these three "books" and the relationships that exist among them. For example, K. S. described the relationship between spiritual realization and one's understanding of the Qur'an in the following terms: "When we read Quran and if you have *Fatḥ*, you could understand exactly without any doubt in the interpretation, what Allah wants to say.... It is very important to have *Fatḥ* because without that you won't be able to understand the interaction between what you see in the world, between many things, you won't be able to link them to each other and to Allah."[83]

These insights, which can only be obtained through spiritual realization (or by transmission orally or in writing from one who has had such realization), are often referred to as "secrets" or "mysteries" (*asrār*) and, as the name suggests, are jealously guarded by those who possess them. The most popular category of these occult sciences is called *'ilm al-ḥurūf*, or "the science of letters," which concerns the numeric, cosmological, and metaphysical symbolism of the letters of the Arabic alphabet, and the magical effects of reciting or writing certain combinations of them.

Shaykh Aḥmad Zarrūq's (d. 1493) statement on this branch of knowledge is characteristic of Shaykh Ibrahim Niasse's perspective regarding its dangers, merits, and the means by which it is acquired:

> Many dervishes of this time have become obsessed with gaining knowledge of secrets, experiential mysteries, and the subtle profundities of the Sufis, without taking care to live up to the requirements of proper worship and good etiquette with God. Thus they have strayed away from the true goal and disconnected themselves from the path to God's love. The result of this is that they are hindered while displaying the guise of righteousness. Some of them are delighted when they understand something that the Sufis say, and mistake this for actual experience of it, even going so far as to claim that they have realised this spiritual state, when in fact they have been barred from it. The sincere man ought to busy himself with perfecting his character, attachment and realization, and ignore all distractions. Ibn 'Aṭā' Allāh says in the Ḥikam, "To be curious about the flaws hidden within you is better than being curious about the mysteries hidden outside you." The Sufis have said, "If the disciple speaks about a station he has not yet reached, he will be barred from reaching it, since he will have become one of those people who merely know about it. After that, he will not be safe from being misguided by it or getting lost in one of its symbols—that is what happens when one tries to take these things from the words of other people."
>
> One of the prime examples of this is obsession with mysterious sciences such as the sciences of letters and names, and the like. Knowledge of these sciences is attained by a divine gift and opening, and its experts only speak about it at all by way of aiding those who have been given such an opening and benefitting those who have already been shown the reality of them....

Likewise, Shaykh Muḥyī al-Dīn [ibn 'Arabī] said, "The science of letters is a noble science learned by divine bestowal alone; actively seeking it is blameworthy for one's religion and worldly life."

In sum, the sciences of divine gift are all praiseworthy in themselves, but blameworthy to seek.... Avoid everything but invocation [*dhikr*], and you will be saved from evil. By God, we have fond all of the secrets in invocation; we have not found them in the esoteric study of Arabic words, nor of non-Arabic words.[84]

Shaykh Tijānī is supposed to have said that "revealing divine secrets among the veiled folk is worse, in the presence of God, than committing forbidden acts [*ḥarām*]."[85] As mentioned in the above quotation, the reasons for this prohibition are many, ranging from the fact that some secrets are considered to be dangerous, while others could constitute a substantial distraction (such as those secrets believed to bring wealth, power, visions, or other unusual experiences) for those whose hearts have not yet been cleansed of baser desires, to the inevitable misunderstanding, confusion, and discord that would result from revealing such secrets to those who do not have the capacity to understand them.[86] Many of the "discoveries" or "realizations" that disciples whom I interviewed came to during their spiritual journeys fall into this latter category, and so some disciples were reluctant to share them with me. Others told me about some of these "secrets" they had discovered but asked me to not share some of them with others, and not to tell anyone what they had told me. I have done my best to respect their wishes. In this regard, Shaykh Ibrahim quoted the following poem, employing the standard Sufi trope of the beloved Layla standing for the Divine:

> As for the one seeking information of Layla's secret
> I have sent him away in ignorance of her, with no certain knowledge
> They say, "inform us, for you are her custodian!"
> But if I were to inform them, I would not have been the custodian.[87]

But some secrets or aspects of *ma'rifa* are not only forbidden, but actually impossible to reveal to anyone else. In this regard, Shaykh Tijani 'Ali Cissé quoted the following poem to explain the futility of describing *ma'rifa*:

> Without tasting it, you won't understand it, and tasting it renders explanation irrelevant
> Whoever tastes the flavor of the drink of the people [the Sufis] knows it
> And whoever becomes aware of it tomorrow [on the Day of Resurrection] will give his soul for it.[88]

Similarly, in his *Three Stations of Religion*, Shaykh Ibrahim Niasse equates "the reality of *ma'rifa*" with the Qur'anic verse "There is nothing like unto Him" (42:11), drawing on the long tradition of Sufi commentaries on this verse that connect it to the ineffability of *ma'rifa*. For example, Ibn 'Arabi writes:

> The things—I mean everything other than God—have likes and similarities. Hence it is possible to establish technical terminology concerning them in order to make oneself understood to everyone who tastes their flavor, whatever kind of perception it may be, but as for the Author [God]—"Nothing is like Him" (42:11). Hence it is impossible for a technical term to tie him down since that which one individual witnesses of Him is not the same as what another witnesses in any respect. This is the manner in which He is known by the gnostics. Hence no gnostic is able to convey to another gnostic what he witnesses of his Lord, for each of the two gnostics witnesses Him who has no likeness, and conveying knowledge can only take place through likeness. If they shared a form in common . . . , they would establish a technical term as they willed. If one of them accepted that, then everyone could accept that.
>
> The gnostics among the folk of Allah know that "God never discloses Himself in a single form to two individuals, nor in a single form twice." Hence for them the situation does not become tied down, since each individual has a self-disclosure specific to himself, and man sees Him through himself. . . . Hence he cannot designate a technical term concerning this through which any positive knowledge would accrue to those who discuss it. So the gnostics know, but what they know cannot be communicated. It is not in the power of the possessors of this most delightful station, higher than which there is no station among the possible things, to coin a word which would denote what they know.[89]

This perhaps explains the "democratizing" nature of *ma'rifa* that many disciples mentioned, since each person's Knowledge of God is unique and distinct from everyone else's; each Knower, in fact, each person, has a unique perspective on God that is not shared by anyone else. This fact also explains why so much of the technical terminology of Sufism concerns the process of acquiring this ineffable form of knowledge, and the light it sheds on other domains of knowledge such as scriptural hermeneutics, psychology, cosmology, philosophy, and so forth.

**Conclusion**

In summary, since *ma'rifa* is "beyond the scope of discursive reason," it resists standard definition. However, in the various accounts of it presented in this chapter, *ma'rifa* was described as foundational, as certain or as certainty, as existential, as being linked to spiritual practice and the resulting radical transformations of *fanāʾ* and *baqāʾ*. It was described as being self-knowledge, and as simultaneously as being knowledge of God and God's knowledge. *Maʿrifa* could be said to be the way God knows Himself through a given individual, which is also the way this individual knows God. This knowledge is described as being dynamic, ever-changing, and unique to each Knower (*ʿārif*), such that the *maʿrifa* of each Knower is colored by the individual particularities of each Knower, as water is by its vessel. This knowledge is closely associated with and accompanied by the unveiling (*kashf*) of mysteries/secrets (*asrār*)—that is, the experience ("tasting"), direct witnessing (*mushāhada*), or realization of certain truths or realities that lie beyond the scope of one's ordinary sensory and rational faculties. However, *maʿrifa* is not opposed to these faculties, but rather is understood as the result of the integration and perfection of these various noetic faculties through the transformations of *fanāʾ* and *baqāʾ*. Thus *maʿrifa* is intimately related to other forms of knowledge, being, in a sense, their foundation and their perfection. So while *maʿrifa* is not necessary to become proficient in these other domains of knowledge, within the community of Shaykh Ibrahim Niasse it does determine the perspective from which one approaches these forms of knowledge, and serves as their implicit epistemic foundation and their ultimate goal.

For example, in explaining the relationship between *maʿrifa* and the intellect (*ʿaql*) Shaykh Ibrahim writes that "if there is intellect but no *maʿrifa*, that intellect is completely lost, and it is useless,"[90] positing *maʿrifa* as both the purpose of and necessary condition for the proper working of the intellect. Furthermore, in his discussion of reflection (*tafakkur*), which is often associated with the rational faculty, Shaykh Ibrahim connects it with the knowledge of God of the "elite":

> It has been narrated in a ḥadīth, "the reflection of an hour is better than the worship of a year." Reflection [*tafakkur*] is better than worship because worship is an action of the physical limbs while reflection is an action of the heart, and because worship is from the servant and reflection is from God. There are some people who worship God through reflection.... The reflection of the common people is that they reflect upon the creation of God so that by it they may draw conclusions about the Creator. The reflection of the elite is upon the Essence of God, whereas reflection upon the Essence of God is forbidden [*ḥarām*] for the common people because they do not have the ability to conceive of the Essence of God, which has no where nor how nor foot nor head nor hands. If a common man were to reflect upon that, he would simply conceive of our Lord like a watermelon and would thereby fall into that which is not to be praised. But as for the elite, they reflect upon the Essence of

God, and so for that reason it has been related "the reflection of an hour is better than the worship of a year."[91]

Reflection is described as an intellectual activity whose instrument is the heart. It is a form of worship that can lead to *ma'rifa*, but *ma'rifa* also leads to the perfection of reflection (*tafakkur*). Shaykh Ibrahim extends this paradigm further, defining different modes of intellectual activity in light of spiritual practice and realization:

> Meditation [*fikr*] is among the actions of the servant, it is the journey of his heart [*sayr qalbihi*], either [meditating] about his Lord or about his messenger or about his saint—that is, about God or His signs [*ayāt*] if we take the signs of God to be His prophets and saints—and as for [meditation] about his soul and its wretchedness, that returns to God and His signs also. And we have an answer for the question that came to us: Are thought [*khāṭir*], reflection [*fikra*], and insight [*'ibra*] synonyms or not? They are from one point of view, and are not from another. Thought [*khāṭir*] is what descends on the heart either with the acts of meditation [*fikr*] or not. The real thought [*al-khāṭir al-ḥaqīqī*] is the thought united with God when the servant ceases to exist and his being is annihilated so that nothing remains except the thought which roams, freed from its restrictions, wherever it wants....
> 
> Reflection [*fikra*] is among the actions of the slave, the journey of his heart either in his Lord or in himself, and both are sources of great benefit, because if you reflect upon God and upon the beauty of His Attributes and Actions, you will necessarily long for Him and draw near to him by the means of those actions of the limbs which bring you near to Him. And if you reflect upon your soul and its wretchedness, you will necessarily flee from it, and the flight from it is the flight to God by the means of those actions of the limbs which draw you near to Him. This is reflection. Insight [*'ibra*] is the benefit obtained by reflection, and it is that when something occurs to your vision [*baṣar*], large or small, of potential significance, you discover its meaning.... By this you know that thought [*khāṭir*] is what is from God to you, reflection [*fikra*] is what goes from you to God, and insight [*'ibra*] is the effect of both of them and their result. *And it is for God to show the way* [16:9].[92]

In this passage, "real thinking" only occurs in the absolute freedom of annihilation and both God and the thinker are active participants in these processes. "Insight" (*'ibra*), the result of these two activities, is the correct interpretation and discernment of whatever comes to one's mind. In this perspective, intellectual activity finds its perfection in spiritual realization.

*Maʿrifa* determines the approach to intellectual activity in general and the various branches of knowledge, for which it is foundational. In his *Removal of Confusion*, Shaykh Ibrahim writes, "There is no science that cannot be dispensed with occasionally except for the science of Sufism: one cannot do without it for a single moment. As for its relationship to the other sciences, it is comprehensive of all of them, as well as [being] their prerequisite, since there is no knowledge and no good deed without genuine dedication to Allah. . . . From the standpoint of the external, the religious sciences may exist superficially without Sufism, but they become defective and disreputable [without it]."[93] In the same work, Shaykh Ibrahim cites a letter that Ibn ʿArabi supposedly wrote to his contemporary Fakhr ad-Dīn al-Rāzī, the great theologian and polymath (who became something of a stock figure in later Sufi literature, representing the scholar who could not give up his book learning for divine Knowledge).[94] This version of the letter, as received by the Tijani tradition,[95] provides a nice summary of *maʿrifa* and its relationship to other forms of knowledge:

> Know my brother, may Allah assist us and you with His enabling grace, that a man does not attain perfection in the station of knowledge until he receives his knowledge directly from Allah the Exalted without intermediary, such as the transmitted report of a shaykh. If one's knowledge comes only from transmitted reports, one becomes obsessed with the study of temporal phenomena (*muḥadīthāt*). This is well known by the people of Allah. If someone devotes his life to the study of temporal phenomena and their detailed classification, this becomes his allotment with his Lord. Such a person becomes completely engrossed in temporal phenomena and fails to recognize their reality.
>
> O my brother, if you traveled (the path) with the help of a shaykh from among the people of Allah, you would be led to the presence of witnessing the Real. You would learn from Him knowledge of affairs through genuine inspiration, without difficulty, fatigue, or sleeplessness, just as Khiḍr learned it. There is no true knowledge except that which comes from unveiling (*kashf*) and witnessing (*shuhūd*), rather than speculation, thinking, supposition, and conjecture. The perfect Shaykh Abū Yazīd al-Bisṭāmī used to say to the scholars of his era: "You have taken your knowledge from the scholars of written texts like a dead man from a dead man. But we have received our knowledge from the Ever-Living who never dies."
>
> O my brother, it is incumbent on you to refrain from seeking any of the sciences except those by which your essential nature will be perfected, and which will travel with you wherever you go. This is only the knowledge of God (*al-ʿilm biLlāh*) the Exalted, by way of bestowal or witnessing. As for your knowledge of medicine, for example, you only need it for the world of sickness and disease. If you moved to

a world in which there is no sickness and no disease, whom would you treat with that knowledge?

So you have to come to know, my brother, that it is unnecessary for the intelligent person to acquire anything of the sciences except that which will travel with him between worlds. Otherwise (leave the sciences that) will part with you at the time of your move to the world of the hereafter. Only two forms of knowledge travel with a man to the hereafter. The first is the knowledge of Allah. The second is the knowledge of the regions (*mawāṭin*) of the hereafter, so he will not fail to recognize the manifestations that occur to him there. This is so he will not say to the Real when He manifests Himself to Him, "We take refuge with Allah from You!"[96] Therefore, my brother, you must discover these two forms of knowledge in this abode so you may reap the benefits of them in the next abode. You should refrain from carrying around anything from the sciences of this abode, except that for which there is a pressing need in your journey to Allah the Almighty and Glorious. And this is according to the consensus of the people of Allah the Exalted.

The two desired forms of knowledge can be discovered only by means of spiritual retreat (*khalwa*), spiritual discipline (*riyāḍa*) and effort (*mujāhada*), and rapture (*jadhb*) in the Divine. I had intended to describe for you the retreat and its prerequisites, and what will appear to you during it—one thing and the next in its proper sequence—but shortage of time has prevented me from that.

The habitual practice of one with no interest in the secrets of the sacred law is disputation. So they have refuted everything of which they are ignorant. They have become addicted to fanaticism and the love of appearance and leadership. They use religion to eat of the world, instead of yielding to the people of Allah and submitting to them.[97]

This knowledge that accompanies one after death is *maʿrifa*, the perfect and perfecting knowledge, which can only be attained through transformative spiritual practice and divine grace.

So what is *maʿrifa*? Although ineffable, according to the above accounts, *maʿrifa* is certain knowledge of God, of self, of reality, of things as they are. It is epistemologically prior to all other forms of knowledge, for which it serves as both a foundation and goal. It is existential, and not merely conceptual, and as such, its acquisition is achieved through the existential transformations of consciousness described as *fanāʾ* (annihilation) and *baqāʾ* (subsistence), in which the duality of knower and known is effaced, and even this effacement is effaced. *Maʿrifa* is thus a mode of knowing, seeing, and being radically different from our average, everyday modes of knowing and living, but in the Tijani and broader Sufi tradition it is *ma'rifa* that is normative, being the mode of being and knowing of the Prophet and the masters of the tradition.

As this chapter demonstrates, Shaykh Ibrahim and his disciples have creatively drawn on a long tradition of Sufi thought in their attempts to describe the ineffable and fundamental knowledge of *ma'rifa*. As one recent study of the community of Shaykh Ibrahim Niasse concluded, what is unique about the movement is its mass popularization of the search for and acquisition of *ma'rifa* such that "these philosophical ideas become reworked and embedded in practical situations by perhaps millions of non-specialists."[98] It is not the acquisition of *ma'rifa* that makes Shaykh Ibrahim and his movement unique, but rather its claim to make *ma'rifa* available to anyone and everyone who sincerely desires it in a relatively short period of time through the regimen of "mystical education" known as *tarbiya*. As Shaykh Ibrahim proclaimed in one of his poems:

> I have folded up [shortened] and made easy the path to the Real
> For everyone who aspires to union with the Real by the Real
> I have folded up [combined] the worship of all the worlds
> By love of the Messenger of God, Aḥmad, the virtuous
> I have folded up all of the knowledge of the Knowers
> By smelling the fragrance of the Chosen One [the Prophet], the sincere.[99]

The next chapter will explore various accounts of this extraordinary process of *tarbiya*, the primary means by which *ma'rifa* is acquired in this tradition.

CHAPTER 3

# How Is *Ma'rifa* Acquired?

Virtually all the Tijani disciples and shaykhs I interviewed told me that *ma'rifa* was usually acquired through the process of *tarbiya*. But what exactly is this process, and how does it work? The present chapter will examine several different accounts of *tarbiya*, while the next chapter will examine different theories and accounts as to how this process actually works to bring about *ma'rifa*, that special knowledge that, for Sufis, is the purpose of human existence. As in the previous chapter, we will begin with two long accounts from contemporary disciples before exploring in greater detail the points they raise.

In a Skype interview, K. S. provided me with his own account of *tarbiya* as a "drop merging with the ocean," using this image to flesh out the concepts of *fanā'*, *baqā'*, and *ma'rifa*:

> What is *tarbiya*? *Tarbiya* is something that consolidates your faith, your faith in Allah, and once you have taken *tarbiya*, there is no doubt possible in your faith, it is something that completes your faith. But you have to understand that *tarbiya* does not belong to a person, not Baye Niasse or Shaykh Aḥmad Tijānī; it is something that belongs to God....
>
> There are normal questions a person asks himself: Who am I? Why am I in the world? Why are there so many people? Why are there different people, white, black, Japanese? Existential questions. It is very natural for a person to try to understand the environment in which he or she is. The most important question in philosophy is "Who am I?" so people want to understand the world and themselves. And

mostly they want to know God: Who is God? Where does He come from? Why does God exist? Or simply, "Is there a God?" or "Is the world a creation of someone, or is it just something that happened by chance?" And *tarbiya* gives answers to all these questions. Let's go to the Qur'an; Allah says that "I created the human being in my image" [actually a ḥadīth]. And this implies something, in order to understand the world, in order to know God—it is something like a prism, when you have light that refracts—to know who you are or to know God, you first have to know first who you are, and after that you will know the environment around you and step by step you will reach God, or what we call God, but when you reach the highest step you will not be able to see differences between all the steps you went through—and what Allah said in the Qur'an is very important: I created human beings in my image. Before that, we know that Allah created first the Prophet Muḥammad, his light, and from the light of the Prophet Muḥammad, he created all the things we know: me, you, whatever. This is the chain of creation.

    I am going to talk about *ma'rifa*; *ma'rifa* will give you all the things you need to understand who you are, who is God, what is the environment, whatever you see in the world, whatever you can imagine. The process of knowing God from the beginning to the end is like you take a drop of water and you put it in the ocean. If you take a drop of water like this and it goes into the ocean, you won't be able to see that it is a drop of water, and you won't be able to differentiate between the ocean and the drop. But there is a process of merging between the drop of water and the ocean, it is something which can be very short or very long, the merging is not something immediate, it is a process, and *tarbiya* is the process of the drop of water becoming completely fused in the ocean. The ocean is God, an ocean of light, or an ocean of water. Let's say that Allah is an ocean of water and the only condition to know Allah is to be, yourself, of water, so that you can fuse with the ocean, but there is a process between the moment the drop of water falls and the complete fusion between the drop of water and the ocean. Then the drop of water will be the ocean and the ocean will be the drop of water. There won't be any difference. Let's suppose that we have five oceans—the Atlantic, Pacific, et cetera—and there are many places, many elements within these oceans, and you are the drop of water, and you just have reached the ocean. At the beginning, you are just at the surface, but after the complete fusion between the drop and all oceans, you will be yourself the oceans—the Pacific, Atlantic, Arctic—and you will be yourself, the elements, and you will have a complete knowledge of whatever is in the ocean because you are the ocean. This is the process.

    *Fanā'* [annihilation] is a state when you are not able to make any differences between yourself and all elements and anything else. *Fanā'* is a state when you think that you are the sky, all the planets; it is a state when you are not able to differentiate between yourself and whatever you see. *Fanā'* is a state of searching, in which you are not able to make any differences between yourself and the elements. There is a traditional way of thinking that people have where you think that Allah is everywhere, but it is not exactly true. Everywhere is in Allah, but Allah is not in everywhere, and *fanā'* is a state when you realize that Allah is not everywhere, but everywhere is in Allah, and you are trying to understand that, and that is why you are confused, because you are in a state that you are searching, you are trying to understand, you are searching. And it is a state where you don't have the notion of time, because time is something Allah gave us to guide us—it is very useful to know this, 10:00 p.m., 5:00 a.m., but Allah doesn't need that. Allah doesn't need time. *Fanā'* is a state where you are escaping time and, in that state, you understand that what is important is the present. Because past and future are illusions, the real time is the present. If you think about yesterday you are bringing it into the present; if you think about the future you are bringing it into the present, you are thinking about it all in the present. And if you think deeply, you understand that all is present. If you are able, if you can think about tomorrow, that's because you are in the present, and if you can think about yesterday it is because you are in the present and you are bringing all those notions in the present. So *fanā'* is a process of understanding what time is and what space is. And it is a very rich moment, a very rich state.

Let's go back to what I was talking about, the ocean. Now the drop of water is starting to merge with the ocean, with all oceans, and the drop itself is something very tiny, very minuscule... and it is a state of confusion, bewilderment, because it is a process of understanding. There is a moment when the process of merging is complete—in that moment, something happens and the person has reached something very important, something very deep, very grand. But no matter how deep, how grand, how important it is, the person can support it, can bear it, because in that state, the person reaches the highest of his capabilities, and we should not underestimate the capabilities of a person, the real capabilities of a person in the scale of creatures. Allah says that in all creatures, humans are the most variable.... When God said that humans are the most variable in the creation, that means that you were better than angels, better than anything, better than the ocean, the moon, the jinn. And even though you have many knowledges inside of you, many powerful things that are in you that you don't know exactly, but you know what could be the power of an angel, or the power of Satan, or the power of a jinn, but you don't know the power that is inside of you. But in order to know what is inside of you, in order to know your complete capabilities, you have to reach the complete fusion in the process between the ocean and the drop of water, but before reaching the complete fusion, you will understand many things, and will discover many secrets that are inside of you.

Have you ever noticed how God in the Qur'an uses "We" and "Us"? Once you reach the complete fusion, you become part of the "We" of the Qur'an. That is *baqā'* [subsistence]. It is a state of complete fusion.¹

In response to my query "How to you get *ma'rifa*?" M. D., a disciple in his early twenties who runs a hip-hop clothing store in a chic quarter of Dakar, asked me, "Have you read *Rūḥ al-Adab* [*The Spirit of Good Manners*]?² That's it, that's how you do it." M. D. also described his experience of *tarbiya* using creative and colorful metaphors, like decoding satellite channels, to describe the process of acquiring *ma'rifa* through the experience of *fanā'* and *baqā'*:

My friend brought me to Shaykh Mamour Insa [a popular Tijani shaykh] to ask him to pray for my *bac* [end of high school exam]. The shaykh said, "I won't pray for your *bac*, but I will pray for you to become part of the Divine Government." Do you know what that is? Alright, well I didn't, and said to myself, what the heck is this? Then I went back to my house to sleep and I saw the shaykh in my dream as clear as I see you now. I was surprised, so I went back to the shaykh and asked him who he was and what he was doing in my dream. I told him I wanted to take initiation from him, but he told me to finish studying for my *bac* and to come back and see him during Ramadan. I did—this was when I was eighteen—and I took *tarbiya* from him and I knew God. Since then, many of my friends have come to Shaykh Mamour Insa, to the *ṭarīqa*. . . .

It's a lot like philosophy. The philosophers say, "I think therefore I am," but do they know what this means? Philosophers say things, but they don't have certainty. You've studied philosophy, right? They say, "Philosophy is a preparation for death," no? In school, I think we learned that Plato said this. That's it, no? That's *tarbiya*, a preparation for death, dying before you die. . . .

It [*tarbiya*] fortifies your faith. For example, I was born as a Muslim, I was given the name Mohammed, I prayed because my father prayed, I fasted because he fasted, but I didn't know why I did these things because I was brought up in it. If you're born Muslim, everyone prays, so you pray. But afterward, you start asking questions: "When I prayed, was that prayer accepted or not?" It can get to a point that when you pray, you pray, you pray, and it's just like doing gymnastics [just physical motions]. But when you do this [*tarbiya*] you gain the knowledge of why you pray, you are ignorant of nothing; you know everything. When you know God, you know yourself, because it is God who owns everything, who is in everything, and who is everywhere. If you know God you know everything. It's the law of all-or-nothing. If you don't know it, you don't know anything. If you know God, you know everything. . . .

When I was young, I studied the Qur'an, I practiced the religion, but the *ṭarīqa* allowed me to cling to the religion, to practice the religion better. It's true that the *sharīʿa* is there, it forbids certain things, but I did them. But when I took the *wird*, it strengthened my faith because they told me, "Don't take the *wird*, because if you take the *wird* and you do these things, such and such will happen." With the *sharīʿa* it's like this, you shouldn't do things because it's a sin, if you do this, God will punish you, don't do that—but it's more immediate with the *wird* . . . when you start saying it you don't want to do those things anymore. . . .

It's true the Qur'an is there, but you always have need of someone to guide you, you need a *wasīla*, because without that, you think that you know but you don't really know. It's like if you have a plate of rice, what is the *wasīla*? It's the spoon. Because if the food is hot—let's say the food is Islam, the Qur'an—if you put your hand inside, you will burn it, but if you take the spoon, because the spoon can never burn, if you take the spoon, you will not burn yourself because the spoon cannot burn. That's the *wasīla*, that's what we are in need of. Anything you consider, there's someone who directs it. A country, there is a president. A car, there is someone who drives it, and the rest are passengers. In the bureaus and ministries there is a director, someone who directs it. The one who directs it, he is the *wasīla*. . . .

A person is a person, you can't be holy just like that. There is a Wolof proverb that says "Soap does not clean everything by itself." There must be, as I said, someone to guide you, to help you—man by himself cannot do anything. . . .

*Tarbiya* is like jumper cables, you get connected and you come to life. But *maʿrifa*, what is it? That's hard to say because you live it. It's like what the philosophers say, but they don't realize what they're saying, *maʿrifa* is realizing it, not just saying things or arguing back and forth. You live it. It's like prayer, you live prayer, it's not just the five times a day. Shaykh Ibrahim said that the *Ṣalāt al-fātiḥ* is not limited to the rosary, you eat, drink, live *Ṣalāt al-fātiḥ*. That's why we must always work hard for God, because everything we do must be for Him by Him, in Him always. . . . When you do *tarbiya* you come to know who you are, who God is, who the Prophet is, who Shaykh Aḥmad Tijānī is, who Shaykh Ibrahim is, and you see them in everything. . . .

The true knowledge is *maʿrifa*. Much has been written about *maʿrifa*, but it's something that one lives. It's like a reader; he can read a book out loud very well without understanding what it means at all. There are some things that are lived experiences. *Tarbiya* is not something you read in a book, it's something you do, you live, it's an experience of life. I don't know how I can explain it ... you can't explain it, it's something that you live. ...

In summary, [what you learn in *tarbiya*] is the Truth, the Reality, *ḥaqīqa*. You can't find that in any book. It's something that you live. It's like the philosophers say, you need to learn to read between the lines, that which is between the lines is the *ḥaqīqa*, and that you can't find in books. You can take a book and read it ten times, but if you don't read between the lines ... it's not that what is written isn't true, it's true, but appearances can be deceiving. For example, before *tarbiya*, if you speak about God, you'll think about something that is far away, on high like that—who listens to us, sees us, et cetera. But when you have done *tarbiya*, you see Him, you sense Him! You know that He is everywhere, in every place, in everything. The Infinite is the infinite—you can't measure it!

God said, "Know Me before you worship Me, if you don't know Me, then how could you worship Me?" If you don't know God, then how can you worship Him, pray to Him? If you read the Qur'an closely, you'll see that knowledge [*connaissance*] is an obligation, *I have only created jinn and men to worship me* [51:56], but that means "to know me." Knowledge is the precondition of worship or service. It [this knowledge] is certainty; you see it! There is no mistake. ...

Without *tarbiya* you can't decipher these things, it's like the Canal decoder [a French television cable/satellite decoder] that you have at your house. If you haven't "subscribed" to Shaykh Ibrahim, you can't watch. You have the decoder at your house, but if you haven't paid and you turn on the television, what do you see? The channels are encrypted, you see black and white [static]. Life is like that. Life is the white and black [static]. But when you take the *Ṣalāt al-fātiḥ*, that is the key that makes everything clear. That's subscription. Because you've subscribed to God, to Shaykh Aḥmad Tijānī, to Baye, it's a subscription. Canal Plus, that's the Tijani Fayḍa. You see? So now, you see clearly, you turn on the TV—zap! You have Canal Plus, TF1 [popular French-language channels], it's clear, you can see what it is. You see? It's easy to explain. You have the *Ẓāhir* (Outward/Apparent) and the *Bāṭin* (Inward/Hidden), but in order to peel back the husk, you have to go through Shaykh Ibrahim. They say all roads lead to Rome, we could also say that all roads lead to God, but the elevator is Shaykh Ibrahim. For a building, you have the stairs, and you have the elevator—Shaykh Ibrahim is the elevator, the fastest and most direct way to knowledge of God.

[Question: What are the conditions or qualifications for going through *tarbiya*?]

To do *tarbiya*, you have to first be Muslim, then take the Tijani *wird*, then after that you have to take the *tarbiya* in order to know God's knowledge, and when you know God, you gain *ma'rifa*. Without that you cannot gain *ma'rifa*. It's step by step. You have to go through the steps. I can't just go direct—there are steps. Be Muslim, be Tijani, take the Tijani *wird*, and take *tarbiya*. *Tarbiya* is the key that opens all doors. As I said to you, when you know God, you know everything. It's the door. Once it's open, you're there. It's like snapping your fingers, once you have that, you're finished, you have everything. But really, it's only the base, after that, there are many things, many things. . . .

[Question: So what is the point of *tarbiya*? Of knowing all of these things? Is it to go to heaven? To just know more?]

We want more than Paradise, and we know that there is more than Paradise, we know that there is more than Paradise. Because Paradise is a level, it has levels. It's like if you get eighteen out of twenty on an exam, there's still nineteen. In life, you should always try to surpass your limits, in order to discover who you really are. As soon as you stop trying to surpass your limits, as soon as you rest, you won't be able to know yourself. You should do unusual things, things that break your normal habits. When you do *tarbiya*, you cut yourself off from the world. You switch off your phone, all those good things, and sit in your corner—you are cut off. You implore God, you only seek God. Look at the Prophet Muḥammad; he did the same thing. At a certain time, he cut himself off from the world, he went up into the mountains where there was no one else. Because God, He is selfish. He is jealous. You can't associate him along with other things, no, He is too jealous, all or nothing. When you die, you leave all your things here. You go into the grave alone, you can't even go with your clothes—that is to say, God is very jealous. And so you can't do certain things. . . . You must cut off the world in order to succeed. Even the *tarbiya* can take some time if you want to keep doing this and that and other things, it takes calm and stillness, and cutting yourself off from the world.

[Question: How long does *tarbiya* take?]

It depends on the person. My own *tarbiya* took around two weeks, but I know someone who took two days, I know someone who came on Air France to Dakar for twenty hours to take the Tijani *wird* and *tarbiya*, but he believed, he believed! God will join you with what you believe in. He came, and in two hours—yes, two hours—he was done and he went back on the same plane on the same flight, the same day, because he believed in it. What you believe is what will happen. When you believe in something, do it, focus, it will happen. . . .

*Fanā'* [annihilation] and *baqā'* [subsistence] are paired like *Ẓāhir* [Outward/Apparent] and *Baṭin* [Inward/Hidden], you can't have one without the other. You can't have *fanā'* and stay out there; afterward you have to come back and put your feet on the ground. Because afterward you are a person, like others, you eat, you drink, you live like others. You are like them, but you are not like them. You live, but you don't live. You are dead, but you are not dead. You are alive—OK, because you eat, you drink, et cetera—but you are not alive because "he who does not die, does not see God." It's because you are dead that you see God. This death of which I am speaking, is not the death that puts you in the ground, but it's the death of having cut off the world, being dead to the world.³

In the above accounts, both disciples present *tarbiya* as a way of acquiring the answers to fundamental questions about life and religion. The process of *tarbiya* is also described as radically transforming basic notions of self, God, time, and space, rendering the phenomena of life recognizable or legible/intelligible as reflections or manifestations of the Real. Once one has become familiar with the Real, one can recognize it in all its manifestations.

The disciples reference, implicitly and explicitly, several texts and ideas of the Tijani and broader Sufi traditions, especially concerning the importance and significance of following the Prophet in acquiring knowledge of God. Shaykh Aḥmad al-Tijānī makes similar points in a passage of *Jawāhir al-Maʿānī*, giving a broad outline of the nature of and knowledge needed to undertake the kind of spiritual training the above accounts so colorfully describe:

> He also said: the knowledge of spiritual training [*al-ʿilm al-riyāḍī*] requires several things, the first of which is Knowledge [*maʿrifa*] of the balancing of temperament, then Knowledge of the intended goal, then Knowledge of the means of pursuing it, then Knowledge of the veils that can separate one from it, then Knowledge of the means of removing them so as to arrive at the intend goal, then Knowledge of the roots of the veils which affect him, then the effort needed to overcome these roots, then the Knowledge of that by which the veils are removed, either generally or specifically, then all that remains is for him [the servant] to unsheathe the sword of determination and mount the steed of effort, in following what is known of these matters and acting in strict compliance with them.
>
> As for Knowledge of the balancing of temperament it consists of knowing how to maintain balance in eating and drinking, equally avoiding excess and lack, being mindful of the moment and the place with respect to the heat, cold, humidity, and dryness. And likewise for age, and all that strengthens one, preventing illness.
>
> As for the intended goal, it is lifting of the veils from the Divine Spirit [*al-rūḥ al-rabbānī*], returning it to the state of purity in which it was before it was combined with the body. For it is by this that one attains all the knowledges/sciences [*ʿulūm*],

Knowledges [*ma'ārif*], and states [*aḥwāl*] and virtues, stations, openings, divine bestowals [*mawāhib*], and true nearness, and by it, one attains the happiness of this world and the next, and whosoever has lost this, has not obtained the happiness of the next world.

As for the Knowledge of the means of pursuing [this goal] it consists of following the Messenger in his speech, in his deeds, in his states, and in his character, by upholding the rights of God, Most High, secretly and openly, solely for the sake of God, not adulterating it with any worldly or after-worldly ambitions, so that it may all be for the glory and majesty of God, placing all on the cloth of contentment, submission, in delegation to and reliance upon Him, Most High, in everything, referring all to Him.

As for the Knowledge of the veils that obstruct the goals, it is [knowing how] the spirit sinks in the sea of possessions and passions and self-aggrandizement, striving for that which promotes them and repelling whatever harms them.

As for the Knowledge of the means of lifting these veils, it is striving to cut off relying on possessions and passions, giving up self-aggrandizement, and ceasing to strive for what pleases it and repelling what harms it through asceticism, but gently and with subtlety.

As for the Knowledge of the roots of these veils, they are excessive eating and drinking and attachment to things [creation], and excessive speech and sleep, and remaining neglectful of the invocation/remembrance [*dhikr*] of God.

As for the efforts needed to overcome these roots, they are hunger and thirst, in gentle moderation, in persistence in cutting off attachments to things, and remaining silent, only speaking when necessary, and keeping night vigils, in gentle moderation, and perpetual remembrance/invocation of God with the heart and tongue, and ceasing thinking about sensory things.

As for the Knowledge of that by which the veils are removed generally or specifically, it is perpetual remembrance/invocation [*dhikr*] of God with the heart and tongue, with any remembrance/invocation. Now, of the invocations that remove veils, some are general: they are those that remove any veil from the spirit, in any situation. Some are specific: they are those that only remove a veil or one type of veil. As for the general [invocations] they are "There is no god but God" [*lā ilāha illā Allāh*], prayers [*ṣalāt*] on the Prophet, "Glory be to God" [*subḥān Allāh*], "Praise be to God" [*AlḥamduliLlāh*], "God is Greater" [*Allāhu akbar*], "In the Name of God, the Merciful, the Compassionate" [*BismiLlāh al-Raḥmān al-Raḥīm*], "Allāh, Allāh, Allāh" or "God, there is no god but He, the Living, the Self-Subsistent" [*Allāhu lā ilāha illā huwa al-Ḥayyu al-Qayyūm*].

As for the specific invocations, they are all of the Beautiful Divine Names of which each one removes one type of veil without affecting the others. God is the one who grants success.

As for his statement "All that remains is to unsheathe the sword of determination...," et cetera, it is not discussed because of its obviousness. Here ends the dictation which was done by our beloved Sīdī Muḥammad ibn al-Mishrī, may God perpetuate his elevation and ascension.[4]

After quoting this passage in his *Removal of Confusion*, Shaykh Ibrahim Niasse writes, "These words of his are worthy of being inscribed in golden ink." Here, Shaykh Tijani presents the pursuit of Knowledge (*maʿrifa*) as a process of "purification," and equates the acquisition of this Knowledge with felicity. This epistemological quest is also a pursuit of ethical perfection, requiring the elimination of negative character traits and habits of thought. It is noteworthy that the "acquisition" of this Knowledge is described in negative terms, as the "removal of veils." The Knowledge is considered innate, but accessing it requires maintaining physical and psychological balance, removing negative traits and mental habits (including seeking other-worldly rewards), and the practice of certain spiritual exercises. This general outline of spiritual training involves a physical as well as psycho-spiritual regimen of discipline, which is generally defined as following the Prophet in "his speech, deeds, states, and character." This assimilation of the Prophetic example is in turn made possible through the practice of invocation/remembrance (*dhikr*) of specific formulae.

Shaykh Māḥī Niasse described the particular spiritual training program of his father, Shaykh Ibrahim, in similar terms:

> The goal of religion, all of it, is to connect man to God. From the Prophet all the way down to the great Sufi scholars, they have explained that its goal is to connect man to his Lord, so that He is with him ... so from this, scholars followed these methods to lead servants to God, from this come the Sufi orders, and the Ṭarīqa Tijāniyya is among these orders. Within the Ṭarīqa Tijāniyya, the Tijani Fayḍa appeared, to which Shaykh Ibrahim called. In short, this *tarbiya* came to emphasize the kernel of Islam, and it is the return of the servant to God, Most High, voluntarily, and not by force. "If you love God ... [then follow me and God will love you]" [3:31]—That's love. "I was a hidden treasure and loved to be known..." So since God's creation came through the door of love into existence, the return to God must also be through the way of love. And that is the basis of *tarbiya*, and that is the basis also, of all the things which the Shaykhs have taken to direct the servants to God, Most High. Shaykh Ibrahim came to purify the servants from their lusts [*shahwāt*], and from the worship of themselves (their egos), and from the worship of all that is other than God, and direct them to worship of God alone. Because, as God said in the Qurʾan, "We did not create man and jinn except to

worship" [51:56]. So this worship is the most certain of things in the world [i.e., people cannot help but worship something], but this worship is not accomplished by force, as I told you, but is only by love, voluntarily. The servant chooses, of his own volition, to turn toward God, until God is with him as it should be.

"[If you love God] Then follow me and God will love you" [3:31]. So the love of God is the foundation. So Shaykh Ibrahim came, calling people to the return of the primary foundation of the Sufi orders. Once in history, some of the Sufi scholars said, among them al-Zarrūq of Libya, who said that conventional spiritual training [*tarbiya istilāha*]—as you know—was finished, and many Sufis agreed with this opinion.[5] But Shaykh Ibrahim said, "No, this is not correct." Naturally, the scholars disagreed with one another, and he said, "*Tarbiya* will remain on earth as long God's creation does; as long as there is God's creation, there must be means of drawing them near to God, and *tarbiya* is among these means of drawing near." ...

Some said that Shaykh Ibrahim was the first to speak of *tarbiya* in the Tijāniyya, but if you go to the *Mizāb al-Raḥma al-Rabbāniyya*, you will see that the Shaykh [ibn Anbūja] said a lot about *tarbiya*—but it does not contain the full benefit—about the special Tijani methods of *tarbiya* and directing people to God. So Shaykh Ibrahim said, "This [*tarbiya*] exists, truly." Because the servant of God, in every place, is in need of God. And God is also compassionate toward His servants in every time and in every place. So at every moment, and in every time, there must be someone who can facilitate their return to God by taking them by the hand in *tarbiya*, bringing them closer to God. And this is what Shaykh Ibrahim did. ... This *tarbiya* is established on the methods, the invocations [*adhkār*] that are all known in the Ṭarīqa [Tijāniyya], and on the invocations that are known in all of the Sufi orders. It is based on the remembrance/invocation of God [*dhikruLlāh*], it is based on presence [*ḥuḍūr*], it is based on intellectual work in reflecting/meditating upon the signs/verses [*ayāt*] of God, as God has said in the Qur'an, always calling people to turn to God and to reflect on His descriptions/depictions [of Himself] in His signs/verses. And Shaykh Ibrahim also confirmed this saying that as long as people, Muslims or believers, remain on earth, God has obliged Himself to ensure that there is someone who can help them and direct them to Him.

In short, God said to his creation, in the Qur'an and in the *ḥadīth qudsī*, "Remember me, and I will remember you" [2:152]; and He also said in a *ḥadīth qudsī*, "I"—meaning God—"I am seated with he who remembers me." So God has conditioned what He gives [to his servant] by remembrance/invocation [*dhikr*] of Him. So *dhikr*, in it is a mystery [*sirr*] of God, by which he has mercy on His servant by turning him toward Him. So if you understand an invocation from among the invocations given by those who have the authorization to do so, you will find that this mystery takes you into the depths of your self, and you will find that you become freed from your carnal soul [*nafs*] [exchanging it for] God, without fabrication, and without anyone coming between you and your Lord, until you reach God and he welcomes you; as He said, "Remember me, and I will remember you," "I am seated with he who remembers me," "If you remember me in your self, I will remember you in My Self, if you remember me amongst a multitude, I will remember you amongst a multitude." So this remembrance/invocation connects the servant to God, as God has shown in the Qur'an and the ḥadīth of the Messenger of God, and that is the secret of God which is with his servants in every time.[6]

As in the accounts above, *tarbiya*, the process of acquiring *ma'rifa*, is accomplished through *dhikr* (remembrance/invocation), which frees the aspirant from the limitations that veiled him or her from the Divine Presence. But what is the actual process of *tarbiya*? Virtually all disciples request *tarbiya* only after having taken the *wird* from a shaykh or shaykha (or one of their representatives, known as *muqaddams*). If the shaykh or shaykha believes the disciple to be qualified and ready, he or she will give the disciple a certain set of invocations and prayers to recite a set number of times, at certain times of the day, alongside the standard practices of the five daily prayers, the *wird*, and the *wazīfa*. Among these prayers and invocations are the prayer known as the *Mu'awwaliyya*, the invocation of a variation of the shahāda "There is no god but God, the First, the Last, the Outward the Inward" (*lā ilāha illā Llāh, al-Awwal, al-Akhir, al-Ẓahir, al-Bāṭin*), and the celebrated prayer on the Prophet, the *Ṣalāt al-fātiḥ*, "O God blessings be upon our Lord Muḥammad, the opener of what has been closed, and the seal of what has come before, the helper of the Truth by the Truth, and the guide along Your straight path, and upon his family in accordance with the reality/right [*ḥaqq*] of his rank and his tremendous degree." These latter formulae are to be recited a specific number of times at particular times during the day and night. This particular assemblage of prayers and invocations is collectively known as the litanies of *tarbiya* (*al-awrād al-tarbiya*), and the process of transmitting them is known as *talqīn* (implantation/initiation). The precise number of times these formulae are to be recited is a closely guarded secret, and disciples are instructed to keep these details private, to avoid others attempting the process of *tarbiya* without supervision or qualification. One shaykh told me, "The best thing that can happen to someone who attempts these litanies without authorization is that he or she escapes unharmed."[7]

The shaykhs and shaykhas who dispense *tarbiya* often advise their disciples to avoid watching TV or movies, and to avoid unnecessary conversation, although they are advised to continue to go to work and school and care for their families, especially their parents and children. Due to the rigorous nature of this practice, and the unusual psychological states that often accompany it, however, disciples are often advised, and often choose, to begin this process when they are less busy. In Dakar, disciples often recite these invocations at the beach, in the mornings and evenings, due to its isolation, beauty, and the symbolism of the ocean.

The shaykhs and shaykhas monitor the disciple's state during this process, until he or she experiences a state known as rapture (*jadhb*) and eventually experiences annihilation (*fanā'*). This process can take as little as a few hours or as long as a few years, depending on the sincerity of the disciple. As Shaykh Ibrahim explains in his work *al-Sirr al-Akbar*, "The disciple can traverse these stations by the power of his sincerity [*ṣidq*], and the sincere can traverse them in the blink of an eye, or an hour, or a day or two, or a few days. And some traverse them in a month or in a year or two and some in seven years, it all depends upon sincerity."[8]

Shaykhs sometimes test disciples who seem to have experienced *fanā'* (annihilation) by asking them questions such as "Who are you? Where are you? What do you see?" or "If I offered you beer or water, which would you drink?" Disciples in a state of annihilation typically give answers such as "I am God, I am in God, there is only God" or, to the beer or water question, "It doesn't matter, both are God."[9] When the shaykh or shaykha is satisfied that the disciple has attained *fanā'*, he or she helps "bring back" the disciple, explaining and helping the disciple to interpret these unusual experiences, and attempting to help the disciple reintegrate them into a new mode of life. If the shaykh or shaykha succeeds in bringing the disciple through the state of annihilation (*fanā'*) into subsistence (*baqā'*), this stage of *tarbiya* is completed and the disciple is believed to have obtained *maʿrifa*, true knowledge of God.

While the disciples and shaykhs I interviewed made it very clear that each person's experience of *tarbiya* is unique, they all drew on a number of concepts from Sufi literature in order to describe different aspects of this process of spiritual transformation, including rapture/wayfaring (*jadhb/sulūk*), stations (*maqāmāt*), levels of the soul (*marātib al-nafs*), divine presences (*ḥaḍarāt*), and different kinds of annihilation (*fanā'*). I will include below summaries and excerpts of the most prominent and influential of these descriptions of *what* happens during *tarbiya*, before analyzing accounts of *how* these transformations occur in the next chapter.

RAPTURE (*JADHB*) AND WAYFARING (*SULŪK*)

In an interview, Imam Tijani ʿAli Cissé explained rapture and wayfaring in the following way:

As I told you, "My servant doesn't cease . . . the hand with which he grasps, the hearing with which he hears, the eye with which he sees, the foot with which he walks." How does this happen? By way of these invocations [*adhkār*], which we invoke with permission. Because there are two paths: the path of rapture [*jadhb*], and the path of wayfaring [*sulūk*]. "God draws to Himself whosoever he wills and guides to Himself those who turn [to Him]" [42:13]. The first [part of the verse] is rapture [*jadhb*], the second [part of the verse] is wayfaring [*sulūk*]. The wayfarer is the one who practices these invocations [*adhkār*] we have mentioned until he arrives at God, Most High. And the enraptured, he is the one who is attracted without *dhikr* or anything, God takes him by his attraction and he arrives at God, Most High without struggle or great effort, rather by the grace of God. That's rapture. The wayfarer is he who arrives by *adhkār* to the presence of God, Most High. When he recognizes himself, he recognizes his Lord. When he recognizes himself as nonexistent, as nothing, he recognizes his Lord as Existence, when he recognizes his meagerness, he recognizes his Lord's Majesty. And thus you find *lā ilāha illā Llāh* [there is no god but God], *lā ilāha illā anta* [there is no god but You], *lā ilāha illā Anā* [there is no god but I].[10]

In his *al-Sirr al-Akbar*, Shaykh Ibrahim Niasse explained that taking the Tijani *wird* is the beginning of *tarbiya*, the beginning of spiritual wayfaring. Thus, the disciple proceeds through this process of spiritual wayfaring—praying the prayers, reciting the general litanies or the Tijani order and the special litanies of *tarbiya*—through his or her own effort until it leads to a state of rapture (*jadhb*), in which God draws the aspirant to Himself by His own power, not the disciple's effort.

One disciple compared this transition between wayfaring and rapture to lighting something in fire or over coals: at first, the object has to be held in the fire or over the coals, which have to be fanned; but once it catches fire, the object burns on its own, without any effort. Shaykh Ibrahim was fond of quoting the following verse of the Qur'an to describe this transformation and its relation to spiritual poverty (*faqr*): "O mankind, you are the poor [*fuqarāʾ*] in relation to God, and God, He is the Rich, the Praiseworthy, If He willed, He could remove you and bring about a new creation, and that is not difficult for God" (35:16–17).[11] This "removal" and bringing about of "new creation" is understood to refer to the transformative process of *jadhb*.

In his critical edition of *al-Sirr al-Akbar*, Maigari summarizes Shaykh Ibrahim Niasse's discussion of this state of rapture:

Rapture [*jadhb*] is arrival and annihilation [*fanāʾ*] and the opening [*fatḥ*], and all of these names refer back to one named referent, and the reality of this is as he says: God does not veil anything from the seeker, because He alone exists and nothing other than He exists to veil Him.... Rather, nothing veils Him from the seeker except his imagining that there is something in existence other than Him. And so, whenever God wants to choose a servant from among his servants, to make him among those brought near to Him, He raises those imaginary veils from him, and so he doesn't see anything but God. He doesn't see himself, nor other than himself; [he sees] nothing of the created things, he doesn't see anything except for the oneness of God in everything, and this is what is referred to as the Unlimited Being of the Real [*al-wujūd al-muṭlaq al-Ḥaqq*], where there is no name, no attribute, no action, and no trace, and he becomes veiled from them [created things] by God just as before he was veiled from God by them.[12]

In the same work, Shaykh Ibrahim explains that there are three kinds of disciples who reach this state of rapture: the blind, the weak of insight, and the strong of insight. The blind, or the veiled, do not witness God as *al-Ẓāhir*, the Outward/Apparent; they are unable to recognize Him in His veils. The weak of insight remain drowned in the rapture of annihilation (*fanā'*) and are unable to go beyond it. Thus, they are unable to combine this rapture with wayfaring and are known as *majdhūb*, or enraptured. He states that this second category makes up the majority of disciples who reach this station.

Finally, the strong of insight are able to see both God and creation (*al-Ḥaqq* and *al-khalq*) at once, together. They perceive the world as having only metaphorical existence, like a shadow or a reflection, but they perceive these veils as self-manifestations of God, and so they are able to recognize God in his manifestations as well as in His Essence. He describes this as the beginning of *baqā'* (subsistence), "which is the first of the stations the wayfarer encounters in the plain of *ma'rifa*."[13]

In the same work, Shaykh Ibrahim further develops this dialectic of rapture and wayfaring by explaining that disciples can continue by practicing wayfaring in their rapture (*sulūk fī jadhb*) by "sobering up" and coming back to the world, but without losing sight of God. Then they can continue with rapture in their wayfaring (*jadhb fī sulūk*), in which the disciple continues to perform spiritual exercises, but inwardly, in a state of rapture. In this state of being "inwardly drunk, outwardly sober," the disciple perfectly combines rapture and wayfaring. Shaykh Ibrahim writes:

> Know that the people of the *ṭarīqa* are of four categories: the unenraptured wayfarer: his wayfaring dominates over his rapture, and he is apparent and outward; and the nonwayfaring enraptured: his rapture dominates over his wayfaring, and he is cut

off; and the enraptured wayfarer [sālik majdhūb], his wayfaring takes him to the station of rapture, and he has arrived at being among the Knowers if he finds one to take him by the hand; and the wayfaring enraptured [majdhūb sālik], he combines his rapture with his wayfaring, and these are the majority of the companions of the seal al-Tijānī, and they are the great ones. And there remains a fifth class—they have no place in the *ṭarīqa*—and they are those who have no wayfaring and no rapture—we seek refuge in God from this. So they, although they took the *ṭarīqa*, they took it not as Tijanis. Perhaps God will have mercy on them by giving them love for our master, the shaykh, may God be pleased with him.

As for the wayfaring in rapture it is the essence of the wayfaring previously mentioned, meaning for the Knower by God when he stops with God at the stopping places to which we have alluded, he does not perish, but he sobers up or returns to the world of metaphor and witnessing the traces and the world of exemplars and he sees two speeches: the Speech of the Divine Will and the Speech of Judgment. God's saying alludes to these two, "You don't will unless God, the Lord of the worlds, so wills" [81:29]. So he travels a path that combines establishing that which is appropriate and that which errs.[14] . . . He stands in his outward aspect, in the religious laws of Islam, and it is the appropriate speech of judgments in the physical world. But all the while, inwardly he has no movement and no stillness, and no action, and this is appropriate to the speech of the Divine Will in terms of faith, certainty, and Knowledge. So he conforms himself to the commands of God for God, from God, by God, and no movement or stillness remains for him except by the command of God, for God, and by God.[15]

Shaykh Ibrahim concludes that, "before being enraptured, wayfaring [sulūk] is a veil, and after, it is a perfection."[16] He summarizes this relationship in the following verses:

> O enraptured one! If you do not travel the difficulties of the path
> Alas for you, you are incomplete; so continue wayfaring
> O wayfarer! If you do not become enraptured
> You remain veiled, so move and bestir yourself!
> The perfected one is he who combines
> The two states of rapture and wayfaring, it is he who progresses with speed
> May God include us among such perfected ones
> Who have become truly enraptured, but continued traveling the path.[17]

## THE MAURITANIAN SERMON

In addition to these notions of rapture and wayfaring, the disciples and shaykhs I interviewed often referred to the following sermon given by Shaykh Ibrahim Niasse in Mauritania to describe this process of *tarbiya* and the relationship between spiritual practice and knowledge:

> *Taqwā* [mindfulness] is the key to all requests for the servant, the worldly of your requests and the otherworldly, outwardly and inwardly. The first thing required of the believing servant is to know knowledge, and mindfulness is the key to knowledge. God, Most High says, "Be mindful of God and God will teach you, God is of every thing knowing" [2:282]. The first thing required of man is knowledge. So whoever desires knowledge, let him be mindful of God. As Imām Shāfiʿī has said in this regard:
>
>> I complained to Wakīʿ[18] of the weakness of my memory
>> And he advised me to leave aside disobedience
>> He told me that knowledge is a light
>> And God does not give light to the disobedient
>
> Mindfulness is conforming to the commands and avoiding the prohibitions outwardly and inwardly. I say mindfulness is avoiding leaving what God has made obligatory for you and avoiding doing what God has prohibited.... Mindfulness is requesting sainthood [*wilāya*], it is the servant requesting to be among the friends [*awliyāʾ*] of God. As God said, "The friends of God neither fear nor do they grieve, [and they are] those who believe and are mindful" [10:62–63]. Abū Ḥanīfa has said about this, "If the knowers [*ʿulamāʾ*] and the doers [*ʿāmilūn*] are not the friends of God, then God has no friends." Whosoever believes in God and conforms to the commands and avoids the prohibitions, he is among the friends of God who neither fear nor do they grieve, those who neither fear in this life, nor grieve in the next.... The Messenger of God was asked, "Who are those who neither fear nor grieve?" The noble Messenger said, "They are people from among the sons of people who are gathered in the Essence of God, they sit together in God, they visit each other in God, they are those who neither fear nor do they grieve. Servants, they are neither prophets nor martyrs, yet the prophets and martyrs envy them for their closeness to the Real on the Day of Resurrection."
>
> Love in God is a mighty thing, and I swear to you that I love you for God's sake, as I swear to you that you love me for God's sake. God will shade servants on

that day when there will be no shade but His shade, He will shade seven [kinds of] servants from all the servants under the shadow of His Throne: a just leader, a young man who grows up obeying God, a person whose heart is attached to the mosque from when he leaves the mosque until when he returns, a man who refuses the call of a beautiful woman of noble birth when she offers herself to him, saying "I fear God," a man who invokes God alone and his eyes overflow with tears, a person who gives charity and hides it so that his left hand knows not what his right hand has given, and the seventh are two people who love each other in God—this [seventh kind of servant] is the easiest of the categories to achieve, and yet it the best of them. "A man is with whom he loves."[19] Whoever loves a people will be gathered with them [on the Day of Resurrection], as the Messenger of God said, "A man is with whom he loves." I testify that I love the Messenger of God, and I love Abu Bakr and 'Umar, and we, praise be to God, love them. We love these men and we are sure that they are not among the people of the fire. And this is my hope and our hope for our souls as we love one another. *Taqwā* is the key to the Garden, and the Garden is for those who are mindful, and *taqwā* is salvation from the fire. . . .

All that we seek in this world and the next, and in religion, also is *taqwā*. So I urge you and I urge myself to practice *taqwā* in secret and in public. It is conforming to the commands and avoiding the prohibitions outwardly and inwardly. God Most High says, "Be mindful of God and seek a means of access [*wasīla*] to Him" [5:35]. If you desire *taqwā*, there's no way except through a *wasīla* [means of access] that connects you to pure *taqwā*. The *wasīlas* mentioned in the Qur'an are three: following the Prophet, *dhikr* [invocation/remembrance], and keeping company with the Knowers.

[1] Following the example of prophet in all speech and action, this is a *wasīla* that connects the servant to God Most High. "Say, if you love God, then follow me, and God will love you" [3:31], and the Noble Messenger said, "If you love God, then follow me." And whoever follows the Messenger in all of His actions and words, the result is that God loves this servant. And it is said in another ḥadīth, "When I love him, I am him." If God loves a servant, then He is his hearing and seeing and tongue and hand and leg, and this is the beginning of sanctity [*wilāya*], and this is the main *wasīla* [means of access].

[2] The second Qur'anic *wasīla* is the invocation/remembrance [*dhikr*] of God, seeking only his face. God Most High said, "Restrain yourself with those who call to their Lord morning and evening seeking His face" [18:28], [that is] keep

yourself with the people who invoke God in the morning and the evening, seeking only his face. This is a *wasīla* that connects the servant to God.

[3] Keeping company with a Knower by God [*ārif biLlāh*]. The Most High says, "Follow the way of he who turns toward Me" [31:15]. And one who turns toward God in all of his states, he is a Knower by God [*ārif biLlāh*] and there is nothing for him except God. The one who keeps company with him will also find him a means of access [*wasīla*] to connect him to God.

The cosmos [*kawn*]—in reality, there is nothing in it except for God, [this is true for both] the universe and man. Man wants union with God, but between him and God there is a veil. And this veil is only the world. If he persists in *dhikr* [invocation/remembrance], with presence of his heart with God, the veils of this world are lifted from him and he arrives at God. And this world becomes "like a mirage in sandy deserts, which the thirsty man mistakes for water, until when he arrives he doesn't find anything, but he finds God with him" [24:39]. Ibn ʿArabi says: "Whoever sees creation as a mirage / has been elevated beyond the veils."

The first thing a complete shaykh does with a disciple who desires to meet God is busy him with *dhikr* [invocation/remembrance] until he arrives at the presence of God, and that is the way of *fanāʾ* [annihilation]. Because insofar as the servant has not been annihilated in the Essence of God, his faith [*īmān*] is not complete. For whatever remains is a veil, and thus there is a kind of torment attached to the servant. The Most High says, "Verily, from their Lord, that day, they will be veiled, then they will enter Hell" [83:15]. For so long as there is a veil, there is torment.[20] And if he continues in the invocation of God [*dhikruLlāh*], then he will be annihilated. There are three kinds of *fanāʾ*: annihilation in the Acts [*fanāʾ fiʾl-afʿāl*], annihilation in the Attributes [*fanāʾ fiʾl-Ṣifāt*], and annihilation in the Essence [*fanāʾ fiʾl-Dhāt*]. As for the annihilation in the acts, many believers reach this station. And whoever knows that there is no doer of actions except God, that is the completion of his annihilation in actions—he knows that there is no doer except God, and there are many believers among the common believers who have arrived at this station.

I teach students in grammar lessons; the grammarians say, "In reality the agent [*al-fāʿil*] is God,[21] and metaphorically, the one who gives existence to the action, and technically, the one on whom the action relies completely, and all of these are God." ...

Whoever knows that there is no doer but God, he is annihilated in the actions, in the presence of the actions, and has found part of faith [*īmān*]. And when he is annihilated in the Attributes, he rises from this station [*maqām*] as well. And the

Attributes of God are well-known among us. All of us have read about them in the introductory books of theology: Power, Will, Knowledge, Life, Hearing, Sight, and Speech. And when we leave these attributes to God, we arrive at annihilation in the Attributes. And we know that there is no power but God's, no will but God's, no life but God's, no knowledge but God's, no hearing but God's, no sight but God's, and no speech but God's. Whoever recognizes this also finds annihilation in the Attributes. And if he continues, he finds annihilation in the Essence; everything flees from him until nothing remains but God. The tongue of his state says:

Nothing remains but God, and nothing other than Him
To this nothing is connected, and nothing is separated.²²

Also, we have the statement of oneness [*tawḥīd*], "There is no god but God." But this statement has a shell and a kernel and a kernel of the kernel. The shell of general *tawḥīd* is found in the Qur'an, "God, there is no god but He" [2:255]. That is the truth of one who is absent from God, because God is not absent, but rather it is only you who are absent. So if the spiritual journeying continues toward God, he will arrive at the station of being present with God, and he will address Him as he does during prayer, "You alone we worship and on You we rely, guide us along the straight path" [1:5–6]—he has arrived at the station of "There is no god but You." And this is also related in the Qur'an, "There is no god but You" [21:87]. And if he continues to progress until he is annihilated in the Essence, he won't find any invocation [*dhikr*] except "There is no god but I." "There is no god but I" is also related in the Qur'an [21:27], but it is strange for a person to hear his brother say, "There is no god but I"; he may think that this person is claiming divinity for himself, but it is only the Real speaking with his tongue. So he hears the speech as if he is hearing it from him, but he is not the speaker. Similarly, God spoke to Moses through the tongue of a tree [saying] "Verily, I am God" [20:14]. If God is able to speak through the tongue of a tree saying "Verily, I am God," then He is certainly capable of saying through the tongue of an Adamite, "Verily, I am God." If he attains this annihilation, the servant Knows [*'arafa*] that there is no thing but God. And here we have the pure oneness which is the goal of the spiritual heroes [*rijāl*].

Shaykh al-Tijānī says in *Jawāhir al-Ma'ānī*, "The reality of oneness is not perceived, because as long as you continue to speak, you exist and God exists, and so there are two, and then where is the oneness? There is no oneness except when it is for God, by God, and to God. The servant has no entrance to this, and no exit from it." This is only valid for the way of annihilation. For this reason, the Knowers, their first concern for a seeker is that he finds annihilation in God, then after that he ascends until he arrives at the Shaykh, because he is an attribute of God. The goal of these two annihilations is that the servant will return to this station [annihilation in the Attributes], for if he has not met the Messenger of God and the shaykh, then he will not know what comes after. So if he continues in this way, he will return to witnessing the existents, [but] he will see the existence as nonexistent and existent at the same time. And an example of this is what we see in the cinema. Whoever among you, of the Knowers, has not seen a movie, I would love for you to see it even once, for you will witness a thing that is nonexistent [mafqūd] and yet is existent [mawjūd]. For if it were not existent, you would not see it; but it is in reality not existent. All existents are just like a movie. You witness a thing existing and not existing. And you are like this in your existence: you do good and you know that you are not doing anything, and you avoid bad things and you know that you are not doing anything. God is the one who is the agent.

After that, the heart of the seeker proceeds through the unseen, and he is neither awake nor asleep while he witnesses the unseen in which there is no thing until he is drawn [attracted] a second time, and he returns to God; he knows with certainty that there is nothing but God, not in a state of annihilation, nor drunkenness, nor rapture, but while being completely awake [aware]. He knows there is nothing but God and he perceives things as they are, and he puts every created thing in its place, in which God placed it. And he knows that he is nothing. He exalts things, while not considering them existent; and he fears things, without considering them existent; and he loves things without considering them existent. And he acquires all good actions, he prays, and he fasts, and he makes ḥajj, and he tells the truth and he spends his money. And all of that is out of good manners [adab] to God, while he knows that there is nothing there. And if the servant arrives at this, he is connected to God by a real connection—he doesn't do anything except for God.

As long as the servant doesn't find this, perhaps he does something and thinks that he is the one who has done it, and even if he does it with God in mind, if he doesn't do it for God's sake—if he moves or does some good deed, but not for the sake of God, or he avoids doing bad things out of fear of being criticized for them—this is not worship. So, therefore, the servant is one who is in need of being connected to God with a strong connection so that his actions, all of them, are acts that draw him nearer to God, in omission or in action. . . . Everything is for God, and in this regard, the Qur'an says, "They are only ordered to worship God, sincere to Him in religion" [98:5]. God commanded us to worship Him, but always with the condition of sincerity [ikhlāṣ]. And sincerity is taking everything other than the Real out of one's actions. And your self, even your self, you take your self out of this action and the action is performed by God, for God, and toward God. Thus the Qur'an says, "You alone we worship, and on You alone we rely" [1:5]. "You alone we worship," this is the station of the common; "on You alone we rely," this is the station of the elite. And the elite of the elite, they will not say anything. And the prayer [ṣalāt] is the strongest connection that connects the servant to God, and we are obliged to contemplate in prayer.

The prayer [ṣalāt], all of it is drawing near to and worship of God. The greatest recitation of the Qur'an is always praise with meditation and recitation and humble awareness of God in all the movements [of the tongue] and silences. He says, "We did not create man and jinn except to worship" [51:56]. Ibn 'Abbās said this means "except to Know." Because the actions of one who is not a Knower may not be worship of God....

I advise you—as I began—to be mindful of God in secret and in public and to be aware of Him with every breath. These are the two characteristics of everyone—those about whom you have heard and those about whom you have not heard—from among the people of goodness: they are only thus through mindfulness of God and awareness of Him. Mindfulness is conforming to commands and avoiding the prohibitions. Being aware of God is the servant being connected to God always, as if he witnesses God; as the confirmed truthful one [the Prophet] said, "That you worship God as if you see Him, for if you don't see Him, then He sees you."[23] Man worships God and calls to mind the majesty of God until he sees Him; and if he is not [i.e., if he does not exist / is annihilated], then he sees Him.[24] And if he has not arrived at this station, he calls to mind the intensity of God's awareness of the totality of the servant. Thus he knows that if he himself does not see God, then God Himself sees him always. This is the lesser awareness, and both of them are good. When he knows that God is aware of him at every moment of his life, everything that he does and does not do is within God's view. If you want to do something bad and you know that there is a great man watching you, you would consider him, and you would definitely leave aside that action. Everything bad you intended to do, you would hate him to see any of the bad things you wanted to do so you would leave that bad action; so what if you consider that God is aware each action you intend, and He is greater. God is greater [Allāhu Akbar]....

The Ṭarīqa Tijāniyya is thus [composed of] asking forgiveness [istighfār], prayers on the Prophet [Ṣalāt ʿalāʾal-nabī]—the door to God Most High—and "there is no god but God" [lā ilāha illā Allāh]. The invocation [dhikr] "There is no god but God" has three intended meanings, as I said before—the shell, kernel, and the kernel of the kernel. The shell of "There is no god but God" is "There is nothing worshipped in reality except Him"—this is the station of the generality [al-ʿāma]. Whereas in the truth of those heading toward the goal "There is no god but God" is "There is no goal in reality but God," and in the truth of those who have arrived, "There is no god but God" is "There is nothing in reality except God." The first is the possessor of "There is no god but He," the second is the possessor of "There is no god but You," the third is the possessor of "There is no god but I." And likewise for he who invokes God by saying "*Allāh, Allāh*," as I have heard you say. So the remembrance/invocation [*dhikr*] of God is the key to sanctity [*wilāya*]. Remembrance/invocation is the beginning of sanctity, the beginning and the end of sanctity; there is remembrance/invocation at the beginning and at the end always. The end is always in the beginning; where the beginning is, there, too, is the end. If the beginning is correct, the end will also be correct. Our beginning is "There is no god but He," "There is no god but You," and "There is no god but I." God, to Him you are returning, while you say, "There is no god but God, the Most High."[25]

This rich passage contains several significant epistemological principles that characterize the thought of Shaykh Ibrahim and his community. First, and perhaps foremost, is the relationship between knowledge and spiritual practice/ethics. Obeying God's commands is presented as being an important condition for the acquisition of knowledge, which is described as a "light from God." This spiritual practice involves closely following the example of the Prophet in word and deed, spending time with those who are like the Prophet, and following their example, by performing *dhikr*. This practice eventually leads to states and levels of "annihilation," in which the disciple's awareness of the Divine is radically transformed, until the disciple is aware of nothing but God, not even himself. This process culminates in the "annihilation of annihilation" wherein the disciple returns to the world but views it in a new light, as simultaneously existent and nonexistent.

Annihilation in the Prophet and Shaykh Aḥmad al-Tijānī—which disciples described as "realizing that everything is the Prophet, comes from the Prophet, even yourself" and "seeing the Prophet/the Shaykh everywhere in everything"—is described as being necessary for achieving this state of spiritual maturity, and it is only in this state of return that truly sincere worship is possible. The existential transformations of these various kinds of annihilation are identified with *maʿrifa*, real knowledge of and certainty about the way things are. It is important to note that in this process, the ethical and the epistemological converge. Knowledge is necessary to perfect the ethical, and ethical excellence is required to access the heights of knowledge. The forms of spiritual/ethical practice, which lead to annihilation and subsistence, are perfected in this ideal mode of knowing, being, and acting in the world, in God. Thus, "the end is in the beginning."

## STATIONS OF RELIGION (MAQĀMĀT)

This Mauritanian sermon substantiates its claims with several passages from the Qurʾan and ḥadīth, including one of the most quoted and foundational traditions: the ḥadīth of Gabriel. This ḥadīth is often cited to describe or define three levels of the Islamic tradition: *Islām* (Submission), *Īmān* (Faith), and *Iḥsān* (Excellence).[26] The tradition reads:

> On the authority of ʿUmar (may God be pleased with him):
> While we were one day sitting with the Messenger of God (peace be upon him), there appeared before us a man dressed in extremely white clothes and with very black hair. No traces of journeying were visible on him, and none of us knew him. He sat down close by the Prophet (peace be upon him), rested his knee against his thighs, and said, "O Muḥammad! Inform me about Submission [*Islām*]."
> The Messenger of God (peace be upon him) said, "*Islām* is that you should testify that there is no god but God, and that Muḥammad is His Messenger, that you pray the daily prayers, pay the poor tithe, fast during Ramadan, and perform ḥajj to the House, if you are able to do so."
> The man said, "You have spoken truly." We were astonished at his questioning him (the Messenger) and telling him that he was right, but he went on to say, "Inform me about Faith [*Īmān*]."
> He (the Messenger of Allah) answered, "It is that you believe in God and His Angels and His Books and His Messengers and in the Last Day, and in fate [*qadar*], both the good and the bad." He said, "You have spoken truly."
> Then he (the man) said, "Inform me about Excellence [*Iḥsān*]." He (the Messenger of God) answered, "It is that you should worship God as if you see Him, for if you do not see Him, He sees you." . . .
> Thereupon the man went off. I waited a while, and then he (the Messenger of God) said, "O ʿUmar, do you know who that questioner was?" I replied, "God and His Messenger know best." He said, "That was Gabriel. He came to teach you your religion."[27]

This tradition forms the foundation for the text most frequently cited by the disciples and shaykhs I interviewed to describe the process of the path to spiritual maturity—a treatise by Shaykh Ibrahim titled *The Three Stations of Religion* (*Maqāmāt al-dīn al-thalāth*).[28] Drawing on a long tradition of similar works, Shaykh Ibrahim describes *Islām*, *Īmān*, and *Iḥsān* as three consecutive stations (*maqāmāt*) of the spiritual path. He further divides each station (*maqām*) into three stages, yielding nine stages overall: *Islām*—repentance, integrity, mindfulness; *Īmān*—sincerity, pure devotion, serenity; *Iḥsān*—observing, direct witnessing, and Knowledge. Each of these nine stages is divided according to its meaning and nature for the masses (*al-ʿawām*), the elite (*al-khāṣa*), and the elite of the elite. The stages from serenity onward are only for the elite. However, these divisions between common and elite are not fixed; in fact, the text implies, and oral commentaries confirm, that this schema involves a kind of spiraling motion in which the disciple can go through the stages of the masses, then the stages of the elite, and then the stages of the elite of the elite. It is important to note, however, that these distinctions are largely descriptive and heuristic, and that some disciples do not experience *tarbiya* as a gradual, step-by-step process. While the initiating shaykhs will give disciples different instructions at different stages in the process, *tarbiya* appears to be more like the blooming of a flower than the construction of an IKEA chair.

*The Three Stations of Religion* was written in response to a request from a disciple to outline the stages of the spiritual path, and it reads as follows:

> In the Name of God the All-Merciful, the All-Compassionate. The blessings of God and peace upon our Lord Muḥammad and his family and companions.
>
> All praise to God, the Peace, the Believer, the Doer of Beauty [*Muḥsin*], He is the King [*al-Mālik*], the Cause and Acceptor of Repentance [*al-Tawwāb*], the Compassionate [*al-Raḥīm*], the Watcher [*al-Raqīb*], the Guardian [*al-Muhaymin*], and greetings of peace upon the straight path [*al-ṣirāṭ al-mustaqīm*], the conscientious [*al-taqī*], the pure [*al-naqī*], the truthful [*al-ṣādiq*], the purely devoted [*al-mukhliṣ*], he who is perfumed by a magnificent character, the observer [*al-murāqib*], the witness [*al-mushāhid*], the source of the most perfect divine Knowledge, the slave and the master to whom is attributed the attributes of the Supreme Master. May the complete favor [*riḍwān*] of God be on the helper of the Truth by the Truth, the guide along the straight path, and upon his family in accordance with the reality of his rank and his tremendous degree.
>
> I came upon your noble letter and sound speech, O you beloved... ʿUmar ibn Mālik..., and I came upon your question regarding the three stations of religion and their stages, and the reality of these descriptions. And you have mentioned that the Sayyid, the Knower [*ʿārif biLlāh*], ʿUbayda ibn Anbūja has discussed this in the *Mizāb*, but that after a long study of it, you didn't find anything convincing, so I will respond to you from what occurs to my mind....
>
> And he said, "There is no god but God" [*Lā ilāha illā Allāh*], makes up the three stations of religion: *Islām*, *Īmān*, and *Iḥsān*. And *Islām* [Submission] is saying "There is no god but God," *Īmān* [Faith] is knowing "There is no god but God," and *Iḥsān* [Excellence] is the flowing of "There is no god but God" through the

appropriate channels, and it is that which is said in a spiritual state, and the speech is God's. It is the noble word, the word of repentance [*tawba*], the word of mindfulness [*taqwā*], the word of excellence [*iḥsān*], the word of unity [*tawḥīd*], the word of goodness [*ṭayba*]. It has three levels, the first of which is the level of *Islām* and it is establishing the appropriate speech and wisdom in the earthly plane [*ḥaḍrat al-Nasūt*]. The second level is the knowledge of it ["There is no god but God"], and it is the station of *Īmān*. The third level is that which is the speech of God, and this is the station of *Iḥsān*. And these stations vary (from one point of view) and they don't vary insofar as they all revolve around "There is no god but God."

But as for their own distinct stages, the first stage of *Islām* is *tawba* [repentance], and it is to abandon being ungrateful [*kufr*][29] for blessings. For each blessing, the blessed should thank and acknowledge the bestower of blessing, and the opposite of thankfulness is ungratefulness. And the Sufi scholars say, it [repentance] is leaving behind every base trait for every resplendent trait. I say that in the case of the masses, the base [trait] is abandoning the obligatory and committing the forbidden [*ḥarām*] acts; and in the case of the elite, it is leaving the approved [*mustaḥabb*] [acts] and committing disliked [*makrūh*] acts; and in the case of the elite of the elite, it is turning away from the [Divine] Presence, and this is forgetfulness. And this repentance [*tawba*] [of the elite of the elite] is the reality of repentance, because its reality is slaying of the *nafs* [carnal soul/ego] as God says, "Repent unto your Creator and slay your selves" [2:54]. It is not seen, and it is not seeing your soul as really having any state or station, and that is repentance from repentance [*tawba min al-tawba*]. "Verily God loves the repenters" [2:222].

The second stage is integrity [*istiqāma*], and it is traveling along the straight path [*ṣirāṭ al-mustaqīm*] in ten qualities which God has numbered in Surat al-Anʿām: Say: "Come, I will recite that which your Lord has forbidden for you: That you ascribe no thing as partner unto Him and that you are virtuous to parents, and that you slay not your children out of fear of poverty—We provide for you and for them—and that you do not approach indecencies, whether open or concealed. And that you slay not the life which God hath made sacred, save in the course of justice. This He has commanded you, in order that you may understand. And approach not the wealth of the orphan, except in the best manner, till he reach maturity. Give full measure and full weight, in justice. We task no soul beyond its capacity. And if you give your word, do justice thereunto, even though it be [against] a kinsman; and fulfill the covenant of God. This He has commanded you that haply you may remember. And this is My straight path, so follow it" [6:151–53]. The straight path is thus described, meaning that it is the appropriate actions that characterize it. The first of these is not associating anything with God, and the lack of ingratitude [*kufr*], and not killing a soul which God has forbidden, and not killing children out of fear of poverty, and leaving lewdness, apparent and hidden, et cetera.

And integrity [*istiqāma*] is being established on the straight path, and this is the integrity of the masses. And the integrity of the elite is traveling on the straight path which is the Messenger of God, [which is] annihilation in him, loving him, and adopting his character outwardly and inwardly, and remembering and invoking blessings on and praying for him fervently and constantly—this is integrity. And the integrity of the elite of the elite is that there remains neither reticence nor grief, as God says, "those who say, 'Our Lord is God,' and afterward have integrity, the angels descend on them, saying 'Fear not, nor grieve, but hear good tidings of the paradise which ye are promised'" [41:30].

And the third stage [of *Islām*] is mindfulness [*taqwā*], and it is conforming to the commands (of God) and distancing oneself from His prohibitions outwardly and inwardly, in secret and openly. It is the greater part of integrity insofar as the commands are obligatory, recommended, prohibited, and forbidden, and the like. Conforming to the commands absolutely and avoiding the prohibitions absolutely, this is the mindfulness of the masses. And for the elite, it is that they remember Him, and do not forget Him; and thank Him and are not ungrateful to Him, and they obey Him, and do not disobey Him. God says, "O you who believe, be mindful of God as he should be minded" [3:102], and this is the level of the elite. Likewise, God says, "So be mindful of God as best you can" [64:16], and this is the level of the common. And the mindfulness of the elite of the elite is the absence of any thoughts other than God in the mind, even for a moment. As the Knower [*al-'ārif*] said:

> If a desire other than you
> Occurred to my mind inadvertently
> I would consider it
> As my apostasy.[30]

But this is the state of the Knower [*'ārif*] and the station of the unique, comprehensive pole [*quṭb*], and this is the versification of the speech of his state. However, that state is not necessary for the Knower [*'ārif*] and this mindfulness [*taqwā*] is what is alluded to in God's saying, "Verily God loves the mindful [*muttaqīn*]" [3:76].

The second station of religion is the level of Faith [*Īmān*]. Its first stage is sincerity [*ṣidq*] and it is righteous action out of obedience for God's sake; God says, "It is not righteousness that you turn your faces to the East and the West; but righteous is he who believes in God and the Last Day, the angels, the Scripture, and the prophets; and gives wealth, for His sake, to kinsfolk and to orphans and the needy and the wayfarer and to those who ask, and to set slaves free; and performs the prayer and gives alms. And those who keep their oaths when they pledge them, and those who are patient in misfortune and adversity and time of stress. Such are they who are sincere" [2:177]. This is the sincerity of the masses. The sincerity of the elite is sincerity in loving the Divine Essence, in that union with It is more beloved to him than everything in existence, Its Name is more beloved to him than any other name, and both of them are more beloved to him than all speech, and Its pleasure is more beloved to him than all pleasure, and Its beloved is more beloved to him than his beloved. This is the sincerity of the elite. God says, "Be with the sincere" [9:119]. The possessor of this station does not fix his mind on the love of anything other than God, and that is the grace of God, which he gives to whomsoever he wills, and God is the possessor of grace supreme. The sincerity of the elite of the elite is the confirmation [*taṣdīq*] of everything that the Prophetic presence received from the Divine, in terms of knowledge, spiritual states, mysteries, comportment [*adab*], rights, and functions, for whosoever's sincerity attains this level, his is the title of the truly sincere [*ṣiddīq*].[31]

The second [stage of *Īmān*] is pure devotion [*al-ikhlāṣ*], and it is performing all the commands [only] for the sake of God, the Generous, and likewise leaving the prohibitions. And wherever hypocrisy, concern for reputation, or self-satisfaction is found in a soul, that person is not truly devoted. And this is the pure devotion [*ikhlāṣ*] of the masses, and the pure devotion [*ikhlāṣ*] of the elite is not for the sake of reward nor out of fear of punishment, nor for the sake of arriving at a spiritual station; rather, it is acting out of servitude [*'ubūdiya*] and longing. Servitude is acting for no reason other than that God is deserving of worship. You are the servant, and only service is befitting for you, so do it for this reason. Don't see yourself as being deserving of anything in addition to the witnessing of blessings. It is simply witnessing actions that are from God to you. He created you and connected you to grace and blessing. The pure devotion [*ikhlāṣ*] of the elite of the elite is leaving aside all other than God in dealings with the Real, and you yourself are other than God, so therefore you see that actions are from God to God and by God, and you have no entrance to this and no exit [from it]. "God loves the purely devoted [*mukhliṣīn*]."

The third [level of *Īmān*] is serenity [*al-ṭuma'nīna*]. It is stillness of the heart by God, independence through God, and certainty by God, in that nothing remains of the heart's turning toward what benefits the soul or harms it. Rather, it casts itself, peacefully, in the hands of God. The tongue of this state says, "My God, on you I rely." This is serenity [*al-ṭuma'nīna*] and none possesses it except for the elite.

And the serenity of the elite of the elite is their certain knowledge that God alone exists, so there is no repose except in Him, and no return except to Him, and He says, "O serene soul, return to your Lord" [89:27].

The third station of the stations of religion is *Iḥsān* [excellence/perfection/beauty]. Its first stage is observing [*murāqaba*], and it is being perpetually present with God, and knowing that He is aware of the totality of the servant. This fact never leaves his mind because he sees the reality from behind a fine veil, and he understands with the understanding of taste.

The possessor of this station may speak in such a way that one who hasn't attained perfect discrimination may think that he has arrived [at the end of the spiritual path], but he has not [yet] arrived. Rather, he sees the reality from behind a fine veil, and he understands knowledge with the comprehension of tasting, not direct witnessing [*mushāhada*]. This is the observing of the elite before direct witnessing. And the observing [*murāqaba*] after direct witnessing is the observing of the elite of the elite. And the observing of the breaths[32] is a station among the stations of the spiritual heroes [*rijāl*],[33] and it is the result of Knowledge [*maʿrifa*].

The second stage [of *Iḥsān*] is direct witnessing [*mushāhada*], and it is vision of the Truth / the Real [*al-Ḥaqq*] by the Truth / the Real as it is without doubt or uncertainty or fantasy. There only remains the Truth by the Truth, in the Truth, and not one hair of the slave remains in existence. None arrives at this station except that he has been annihilated from himself and from other and otherness, and on the tongue of this state it is said:

Nothing remains except God, and nothing other than Him
To this nothing is connected, and nothing is separated.[34]

As here there is no name, no description, and no limit. This vision occurs without any "how" or "definition" or "unification" or "direction" or "comparison" or "beginning" or "union" or "separation." There is no invocation [*dhikr*] or invoker [*dhākir*] or invoked [*madhkūr*]. "The Truth has come and the false has vanished, verily the falsehood is ever vanishing" [17:81]. And this level is close to that of the opening/enlightenment [*fatḥ*], but what comes before this is not the opening—it is the door to Knowledge [*maʿrifa*], but it is not Knowledge. Every Knower [*ʿārif*] is open [has achieved *fatḥ* / spiritual enlightenment], but the opposite is not true.

The third stage [of *Iḥsān*] is Knowledge [*maʿrifa*], and it is the spirit being deeply rooted and firmly established in the presence of direct witnessing [*mushāhada*] with complete annihilation and subsistence through God. So the knower [*al-ʿārif*] among the Sufis is he who sees the other [in and by] the Essence—that is, he witnesses the Truth [*al-Ḥaqq*] in the other. For me, the Knower [*al-ʿārif*] is he who is annihilated in the Essence once, and in the Attribute twice or three times, and annihilated in the Name once. He confirms the existence of these three realities, and he confirms the Names by the Name.³⁵ And this stage is extremely difficult to reach [literally, "it tears livers to shreds, and neither wealth nor children are of any avail in obtaining this"]. The possessor of this station is perfectly awake and aware of God and His wisdom and His commandments, and satisfied with the unfolding of His decrees. For the one who is perfectly satisfied and is satisfying, it is appropriate that he address his soul with the saying "Enter among my servants, enter into My garden" [89:29–30].³⁶ And Knowledge [*maʿrifa*] is the last of the stations of religion and repentance [*tawba*] is its first. However, the reality of repentance is the absence of repentance and that is only achieved through Knowledge. In this regard, our shaykh, the seal, al-Tijānī (may God be pleased with him and us) used to say that, "by God, I have not reached the station of repentance." He, may God be pleased with him, meant that he had repented from seeing repentance. So long as the slave regards himself as repentant [in *tawba*], he has not reached the station of repentance.

This concludes the summary explanation of the stages, and if we were to continue with this, it would require a whole book. As discussed above, the reality of the stations are *Islām*, *Īmān*, and *Iḥsān*. *Islām* is saying "There is no god but God" [*La ilāha illā Llāh*], and *Īmān* is to know there is no god but God! [47:19], and *Iḥsān* is "Say: 'Allāh' [and leave them to their vain prattle]" [6:91] or "Say: He is God, the Unique, God the Eternally Independent, He neither begets nor is begotten, and there is not one like unto Him" [112] and "but none will grasp their meaning save the wise" [29:43].

These are the nine stages of religion, and if you meditate on them you will find the essence of the stations in the realities, and that they correspond to the nine Presences [*Ḥaḍarāt*], and they are the same. For if you enter the Divine pre-temporal Presence [*al-Ḥaḍrat al-Azaliyya*], you fulfill your desire for God, for the Messenger of God, and for the Shaykh [al-Tijānī]; and if you arrive at the Muḥammadan Presence [*al-Ḥaḍrat al-Muḥammadiyya*], you fulfill your desire for God, for the Messenger of God, and for the Shaykh [al-Tijānī]; and if you arrive at the Aḥmadī Presence [*al-Ḥaḍrat al-Aḥmadiyya*], you fulfill your desire for God, for the Messenger of God, and for the Shaykh [al-Tijānī], and so the Presences are nine: three within three, just as the stages [of religion] are nine: three within three. The presence of the shaykh is the station of *Islām*, the presence of the Messenger is the station of *Īmān*, and the Presence of God is the station of *Iḥsān*, "And verily unto your Lord is the final end" [53:42]. . . .

This concludes what I have received from the One who inspired it.... All praise is due to God in all cases, and the blessings and peace of God on our Lord Muḥammad and on his family and companions.[37]

As in the Mauritanian sermon, *The Three Stations of Religion* describes a process of transformation that is at once existential, ethical, and epistemological. Similarly, in both works, this process is somewhat nonlinear, with the "end being in the beginning." The different stations and stages describe various psycho-spiritual states that aspirants undergo on their way to achieving *ma'rifa*, and what they experience after having attained it. The density of Qur'anic allusions both in this treatise and the sermon also illustrate the centrality of the scripture to the thought of Shaykh Ibrahim (who was said to finish a recitation of entire Qur'an twice every week)[38] and the unique hermeneutics of the Sufi tradition to which he belonged.

## PURIFICATION OF THE SELF/SOUL (*TAZKIYAT AL-NAFS*)

The text of the Qur'an also forms the basis for a parallel descriptive schema known as the "Purification of the Soul" (*tazkiyat al-nafs*) that which appears in Shaykh Ibrahim's works, and to which his disciples frequently referred. In an interview, Shaykh Māḥī Niasse provided me with an overview of this process of purification, which I will paraphrase here.

Many people are governed by "the soul that commands evil" (*nafs al-ammāra bi'l-sū'*, mentioned in 12:53). This "inner jerk" is selfish, greedy, and wicked and pushes people toward satiating their appetites for power, wealth, position, and pleasure without any consideration of right or wrong, other people, or consequences. However, through discipline and the grace of God, one can escape from its clutches and arrive at the "blaming soul" (*nafs al-lawwāma*, mentioned in 75:2). This is the soul that reproaches itself when it does something wrong, and pushes a person toward repentance. After a person repents, and repents, and repents, he or she can reach the level of the soul known as "the inspired soul" (*nafs al-mulhama*, mentioned in 91:7–8). At this level, God inspires the soul with clear discernment between good and evil, and as a result, one's lusts and negative impulses become more manageable, and the partially purified soul begins to be characterized by praiseworthy attributes.

From this stage, one can progress to the "serene soul" (*nafs al-muṭma'inna*, mentioned in 89:27). This level of the soul is characterized by serenity and tranquility because those who have attained it see everything that happens as coming from God. For this reason, they do not get enraged or upset, or try to return evil for evil, because they perceive everything as occurring by God's will. After this comes the "satisfied soul" (*nafs al-rāḍiya*, mentioned in 89:28), the soul that is pleased with all of God's decrees. Those who have reached this stage see everything coming from God as good, and are content with whatever God does with them. This stage is followed by the "satisfying soul" (*nafs al-marḍiya*, mentioned in 89:28), which is pleasing to God just as it is pleased with God. This process of purification culminates in the "perfect soul" (*nafs al-kāmila*), which is like a perfectly polished mirror, reflecting all the qualities and attributes of God. This is the goal of the spiritual path, and of human existence; one who attains this level of purity of soul is called "The Perfect Human" (*al-insān al-kāmil*), and he or she is the goal of creation, the best of spiritual masters, and the most knowledgeable of God.[39]

According to this account, these different levels of the soul exist *in potentia* in everyone, but are only actualized through spiritual practice. As in the other descriptions, these different levels of the soul depict different modes of being through which aspirants progress on their way to achieving *maʿrifa*, the perfection of themselves and their knowledge. As above, this process of ethical perfection and spiritual purification is inseparable from the perfection of knowledge, although the latter is emphasized to a greater degree in the Mauritanian sermon and *The Three Stations of Religion*.

## PRESENCES (ḤAḌARĀT)

At the end of *The Three Stations of Religion*, Shaykh Ibrahim Niasse introduces the important Sufi concept of "presences" (*ḥaḍarāt*), which appears throughout his works and in the oral traditions of his disciples. As mentioned in the second chapter, the school of Ibn ʿArabi developed this technical vocabulary of these "presences" to describe the hierarchy of corresponding levels of consciousness or being (*wujūd*) of the human self and reality.[40] While the number and nature of these presences vary from schema to schema, in Shaykh Ibrahim's works they are typically five: *Nasūt*—the physical realm of objects and bodies; *Malakūt*—the subtle or imaginal realm, the world of exemplars (*ʿālam al-mithāl*), of dreams and visions; *Jabarūt*—the world of spirit, beyond form; *Lāhūt*—the domain of Divinity, the manifestation of the Perfect Qualities of God; and *Hāhūt*—the inscrutable Divine Essence.[41] In his *al-Sirr al-Akbar*, Shaykh Ibrahim compares each of these cosmological/existential levels to levels of the human self. *Nasūt* corresponds to the body or the soul (*nafs*), the *Malakūt* corresponds to the heart (*qalb*), the *Jabarūt* corresponds to the intellect (*ʿaql*),[42] the *Lāhūt* corresponds to the spirit (*rūḥ*), and the *Hāhūt* corresponds to the innermost secret (*sirr*).[43] However, this schema was mainly cited by shaykhs and disciples in a metaphysical or cosmological sense, in terms of explaining how they made sense of the world after *tarbiya*, and not as a description of the experience of *tarbiya* itself.

In describing the process of *tarbiya* itself, disciples made use of a different schema of presences (*ḥaḍarāt*). As quoted at the beginning of chapter 2, S. D. described the experience of four presences as follows: "*Ḥaḍrat al-Qudsi*—there is nothing, there is only one mystery here; *Ḥaḍra Aḥmadiya*, *Ḥaḍra Muḥammadiyya*, and *Ḥaḍra khutbu or Nasūt*.... After the initiation, once you know who God is, you are in what we call the *Ḥaḍrat al-Qudsi*, that *Ḥaḍra*, there is only One God, nothing except God, everything is God." He further explained that in the *ḥaḍrat al-Aḥmadiya* you "can become a Christian, a Jew, and an animist," because, in the words of another disciple, "this presence contains the essence of all religions, without any distinction."[44]

Shaykh Ibrahim alludes to this state in *al-Sirr al-Akbar*, writing that the one who has attained rapture (*jadhb*) and the opening (*al-fatḥ*) "is a disbeliever [*kāfir*] in the divine law [*sharīʿa*] because of the erasure of the Divine Names and Attributes [i.e., he is in a state where there is only God, without Name or Attribute, without any external world to which the laws can apply]. And he denies [literally, 'slays'] the prophets, while he is in reality a believer because he affirms them in reality."[45] He goes on to explain that this state is very dangerous, because the creed or belief (*ʿaqīda*) of the disciple is also effaced, and he can become a Jew or a Christian or a Magian. The disciple must be assisted by a perfected, Knowing shaykh who has already arrived, who can help bring the disciple safely back into the realms of differentiation without losing himself or his religion.[46]

This experience had such an impact on S. D. that he keeps a picture of the Virgin Mary and Christ on his phone, and in his words, "When people ask me if I am a Christian, I say, 'Yes.' But then when I go to the mosque and they ask me why, I say, 'Because I am a Muslim.'"[47]

Disciples described the *Ḥaḍrat al-Muḥammadiyya* as realizing that "everything comes from Muḥammad, from his light, and so everything is Muḥammad," and that "there's Muḥammad the son of ʿAbd Allāh and Amina, but there's also the Muḥammad who 'was a prophet while Adam was between water and clay,' so there's Muḥammad and there's Muḥammad. That's the *ḥaqīqa Muḥammadiyya* [Muḥammadan reality]."[48] Shaykh Māhī Niasse described this reality to me in the following way:

> The Muḥammadan reality—in the great Universities, you will learn that Plato was the first to speak of the First Intellect [*al-ʿaql al-awwal*], isn't that so? And this First Intellect, in his mysticism [*taṣawwufatihi*], was everything that is. And in philosophy, they call it the First Intellect. And in Christianity, they call it the Holy Spirit [*al-Rūḥ al-Quddūs*], and so on. And the Muslims, they call it the Muḥammadan

reality, because it is very close, in terms of understanding, to [what the philosophers mean by] the First Intellect, and [what the Christians mean by] Jesus the Son of God. The Muḥammadan reality is closer to the [First] Intellect and very close to what they mean by it, in any case. The Muḥammadan reality is the vault [*makman*] of the secret/mystery [*sirr*] of life, all of it. Every living thing is contained inside the Muḥammadan reality, until God wishes to manifest this reality, and so there is the first self-manifestation, the second self-manifestation, the third self-manifestation—returning to Plato, we have the First Intellect, the Second Intellect, the Third, and so on, until we reach this degree—and likewise you have the manifestation [*tajallī*] in Unicity [*al-Aḥadiyya*], the manifestation in Unity [*al-Waḥidiyya*], and so on. So the Muḥammadan reality among us, the Tijanis and the Sufis, is the vault of the divine secrets/mysteries [*asrār*]. From this reality came all that was, and from it will come all that is, to be. And thus it is the foremost of all divine matters that man seeks, because the door to [them all] is the Muḥammadan reality. The door of the Muḥammadan reality gives man access to all these detailed spiritual points.

The scholars and Sufis have said a great deal in describing this reality, and all these descriptions return to the fact that this reality is characterized by the divine secrets/mysteries [*asrār*]—it is the Divine Source/Essence of Mercy [*ʿayn al-raḥmat al-rabbānī*], the Divine Source/Essence of Mercy. And another shaykh has said that something like this in describing this Muḥammadan reality, that it is the secret in Tijānī Sufism.[49] And in the *tarbiya* of Shaykh Ibrahim also, there is annihilation [in this reality], which, if a person reaches it, perhaps he will find an opening [*fatḥ*] from God and more than that. The Muḥammadan reality is the secret/mystery [*sirr*] of the cosmos [*kawn*]. As the Christians say, "The Messiah is the son of God," as Plato has said, "The First Intellect," and so on. Each tries to explain this being in the way which suits him, some explain it with reason, others explain it with the traditions [scripture and received religious texts/sayings], some explain it with what they have taken from the prophets, and all of them are pleased with what they have.[50]

This description of the Muḥammadan reality would probably be considered as encompassing both *Aḥmadiya* and *Muḥammadiyya* in the schema S. D. presented, illustrating the many and varied ways this reality is described. In the same vein, Shaykh Ibrahim quotes the following celebrated verse to explain the various names of this "reality of realities" (*ḥaqīqat al-ḥaqāʾiq*):

> Our expressions are varied, while their meaning is one
> and all, to that perfection allude.[51]

After the Muḥammadan presence, the disciple completes this phase of the spiritual journey by returning to the *Ḥaḍrat al-Nasūt*, an "ordinary" state of consciousness, wherein he or she is aware of the sensible world around him or her, while also remaining aware of these other "presences" or levels of reality. What they see or hear on an everyday basis may be the same as before, but now they perceive it as a vast system of symbols, which are now legible, or "decoded" (to use a phrase commonly employed by the disciples themselves). This can be likened to looking at a page of a book without knowing how to read—one would only see black shapes on a white background. But after learning how to read, one could recognize letters and words, understand sentences, and even get the general meaning of the passage, all while still looking at the same black shapes on the white page. All these different levels of meaning can be perceived together or focused on separately. As M. D. put it, undergoing *tarbiya* is like "learning to read between the lines" of existence.

Having returned to "ordinary" reality, disciples are instructed to uphold the *sharī'a*, not to divulge their "extraordinary" experiences and insights to outsiders, and generally to respect the rights and nature of these different *ḥaḍarāt*, or levels of reality/consciousness (*wujūd*). For example, while it is not considered appropriate to go around saying "I am God" or "I am the Prophet" in everyday life, these statements are valid on their respective levels—those presences where there is no distinction between the self of the disciple and that of the Prophet, or the Divine Essence. The proper integration of these different levels of being/consciousness is a defining feature of *ma'rifa* and in this tradition is exemplified by the Prophet, Shaykh Aḥmad al-Tijānī, and Shaykh Ibrāhīm—all three of whom maintained the practice of the *sharī'a*, and selectively shared different aspects or levels of their inward states, thoughts, and experiences. Thus, the true Knower is one who follows this example of recognizing or "seeing" all the presences simultaneously, without confusion, in everything.[52]

As S. D. related, after *tarbiya*, "they tell you that in everything you should see the four *ḥaḍras*—in everything you should see God, the Prophet, the Shaykh [Tijānī], and Shaykh Ibrāhīm." But where do Shaykh Tijānī and Shaykh Ibrāhīm figure in all of this? The answer lies in the fact that these presences, in whatever schema they are presented, constitute a system of correspondences, such that each one is a different mode of manifestation of the Divine Essence. As such, anything that exists in one presence is both a manifestation of an aspect of the aspectless Essence, and has its own shadows or reflections in lower presences, like a light surrounded by several lampshades. Any smudge on the light bulb will appear as a dark spot on each of these shades and, ultimately, on the wall. In *al-Sirr al-Akbar*, Shaykh Ibrāhīm explains:

Firstly, the Pure Essence, which is the essence of effacement and simplicity without relation, manifests itself to itself without relation, and this is *al-Aḥadiyya* [Unicity]. In *al-Aḥadiyya*, the Divine Essence only manifests itself to itself: "Say: He is God, the Only [*Aḥad*]" [112:1]. Then it [the Essence] manifests itself in *al-Aḥmadiya* by a name of the Essence, a secret of the Essence, and an attribute of the Essence, which is *Aḥmad* [considered the esoteric or heavenly name of the Prophet]. In *al-Aḥmadiya* also, nothing is manifest in it except for *Aḥmad*. Then it [the Essence] manifests in *al-Muḥammadiyya* the forms of the Prophets and Messengers and the secret of existing things. Then it manifests in *al-Aḥmadiyya* the poles [*aqṭāb*] and Knowers, then it manifests itself in the vicegerent [*khalīfa*], the servant of the Essence for men and jinn.[53]

Shaykh Ibrahim declared himself to be this *khalīfa*, the archetypal representative and deputy of Shaykh Aḥmad al-Tijānī, who is described as the Prophet's representative. Later in the same passage, Shaykh Ibrahim compares the undifferentiated unity of *al-Aḥadiyya* to that of *al-Aḥmadiyya*, and the differentiated unity of the Divine Names and Attributes in *al-Waḥidiyya* to that of the Prophets and Messengers in *al-Muḥammadiyya*, where they are all united in the Muḥammadan reality (*al-ḥaqīqa al-Muḥammadiyya*). In the description above, there appear to be two presences named *Aḥmadiyya*, one above *Muḥammadiyya* and one below. Niasse clarifies this point a few pages later, this time describing only the "lower" presence in a slightly different schema:

When the Essence manifests Itself, It manifests Itself by Its perfection, and so the witness, through his witnessing of the manifestation in *Muḥammadiyya*, sees Muḥammad as the Essence, because there is nothing other than It, and the difference is in the thinking of the witness, in the transformation of the reality, and not in its becoming many, but rather in the characterization of the Essence and the derivation of Muḥammad from It. As God has said, "Say, if you love God, then follow me, and God will love you" [3:31]; and "Those who swear allegiance to you have sworn allegiance to God. God's hand is above their hands" [48:10]; and "Whosoever obeys the Messenger has obeyed God" [4:80]; . . . and "Verily you are of a magnificent nature" [68:4]; and "You did not throw when you threw, but God threw" [8:17]. . . .

What the one who witnesses [this] finds is that God is not other than Muḥammad, while Muḥammad is not God, but not other than Him. An example of this in the world of metaphor is what appears to someone in a mirror, except that here there is no mirror. . . .

How Is *Ma'rifa* Acquired? • 143

If Muḥammad manifests himself in *al-Aḥmadiyya*, he manifests himself with his perfection. So the witness, through his witnessing of the manifestation in *al-Aḥmadiyya*, sees Aḥmad and says that he is the same as Muḥammad, for there is nothing after God other than Muḥammad, only the thinking [*khāṭir*] of the witness is changed, the thing seen neither changes nor multiplies. So He is he, and he is He, there is no difference between the two save in its description and derivation since it [Aḥmad] is that which God brought forth as the second of two. Its [this reality's] possessor is the greatest of the sincere [*ṣiddīq*] [Qur'anic term for the highest category of believers, and also the title of the Prophet's close companion, and successor, Abū Bakr] and the "door to the city of knowledge" [a title for the Prophet's close companion, nephew, and successor, ʿAlī]. And this presence is the presence of sealhood [*al-khatmiyya*] and concealment [*al-katmiyya*],[54] and it is the presence of our lord and master Abū'l ʿAbbās Aḥmad ibn Muḥammad al-Tijānī in the realm of the senses. So he is the *barzakh* of the poles and the support of all existing things and their spirit and their secret in so far as nothing emerges from the Muḥammadan reality without him receiving it, from the pre-temporal [*al-Azal*] to the post-temporal [*al-Abad*].[55]

So the Divine Essence manifests itself as an image in a mirror, and this reflection is the Muḥammadan reality, then this Muḥammadan reality manifests itself as another image in another mirror, and this reflection is the spiritual reality of Shaykh Aḥmad al-Tijānī (as well as that of Abu Bakr al-Ṣiddīq and ʿAlī ibn Abī Ṭālib). Then this reality manifests itself in the mirror of the world producing its myriad people and things.

If we take the metaphor of the world as a dream within a dream, the Real, the Divine Essence, would be the dreamer, and the presences (*ḥaḍarāt*) would be the various levels of dreams. The Muḥammadan reality is like the dreamer in the dream; it is the self-manifestation of the Essence in this level of reality, and as the dreamer's "dream self" it both is, and is not, the dreamer. Since everything that appears in the dream is a manifestation of some aspect of the dreamer, while Muḥammadan reality is a manifestation of the dreamer itself (it is that through which the dreamer experiences the dream), this Muḥammadan reality contains within itself all the realities of the dream it occupies.

In this metaphor, the world of everyday experience would be the dream that the Muḥammadan reality dreams, and the presence of the dreamer (Muḥammadan reality) in this dream (sensory world) would be found in the Prophets and Messengers before the Prophet Muḥammad, and after him, in the supreme saints and Knowers. The idea here is that this "dreamer within the dream" was most fully actualized in the person of the Prophet Muḥammad, and after him, in the person of Shaykh Aḥmad al-Tijānī, but that the presence of the "dreamer within the dream" is always necessary for there to be a dream, a world, at all (without a dreamer in the dream, there is no dream).⁵⁶ Furthermore, the aspect of the Muḥammadan reality that appears in the dream world of senses and history as the poles (*aqṭāb*) and Knowers is most fully realized in the person of Shaykh Aḥmad al-Tijānī; and it is this aspect of the Muḥammadan reality that is described as the Aḥmadī presence, the intermediary between all of the saints, and even (in some accounts) all of existence, and the fullness of Muḥammadan reality. From this perspective, the process of *tarbiya* can be likened to successive stages of "waking up," passing from the dream within the dream, to the dream, to the dreamer; and then from the dreamer to the dreamer within the dream (in its various aspects as the Prophet, Shaykh Tijānī, and Shaykh Ibrahim), returning to the dream within the dream, but now as one who knows that he is dreaming.

It is important to remember that all of these complex schemas and metaphors have been and are employed to describe the experiences and states of consciousness that disciples undergo during and after the process of *tarbiya*. Far from being mere abstractions or flights of fancy, they draw on a long tradition of spiritual practice, associated states and modes of being/consciousness, and descriptions of these states and modes of being/consciousness.

Having covered these presences, we are now in a position to understand Shaykh Ibrahim's statement at the end of *The Three Stations of Religion*: "For if you enter the Divine pre-temporal Presence [*al-Ḥaḍrat al-Azaliyya*], you fulfill your desire for God, for the Messenger of God, and for the Shaykh [al-Tijānī]; and if you arrive at the Muḥammadan Presence [*al-Ḥaḍrat al-Muḥammadiyya*], you fulfill your desire for God, for the Messenger of God, and for the Shaykh [al-Tijānī]."⁵⁷ Because the Muḥammadan presence is a perfect reflection of the Divine Essence, and the Aḥmadī presence is a perfect reflection of the Muḥammadan presence, anything that appears in one presence is found in the others.

### ANNIHILATIONS

The process of entering these presences is often described as "annihilation" (*fanāʾ*). The French disciple Abu Ibrahim described his experience of annihilation during *tarbiya* in the following way: "You feel the unicity of everything.... To me, everything is one, even the Qurʾan says, 'Don't say three, say one.' The worshipper, the worship, the one worshipped, it's all one. *Fanāʾ* is to realize you don't exist yourself, the person, the entity you think you are, doesn't have a real existence. You realize the nonexistence of everything, yourself first and then the rest. *Baqāʾ*, to me, is to live correctly after having experienced *fanāʾ*, it's like being newborn, you live like before, but with the new knowledge." When I asked him about the different types of annihilation, he replied:

> I don't understand all that. I've probably experienced several of them, but I can't differentiate them. I mean, I can guess, but I know the most important one, I've got that: *fanāʾ* in God, in the Essence. That I'm OK with. But the others, *fanāʾ* in the Prophet, or Shaykh Tijani, or Shaykh Ibrahim, I couldn't make the difference—I might have them all or I've been through all of them or some of them, but I couldn't tell which is which. That all seems too theoretical for me.... Some people they say Shaykh Tijānī saw the Prophet with him all the time. Whether that means he saw the man, the person, or he saw himself as the Prophet—that I can understand, that we've experienced—or both, I don't know. Maybe that's *fanāʾ* in the Prophet, I don't know....
>
> To some extent, this knowledge, you have it, but to some extent, you don't have it. It's like you forget. It's not like you're in *fanāʾ* all the time. For example, sometimes if someone insults you and you're not like, "It's God who's insulting me," you get angry and you want to react. I think it's like this for most people, even *shuyūkh*, I see them get angry sometimes. Are they in *fanāʾ* or not? But also, this thing, it comes back. What I want, myself is to have it as often as possible, it's nice to have it once but the objective is to have it so that it becomes a [permanent] state that's what I'd like.... I want to have *fanāʾ* for good. I have it, but I want more of it.⁵⁸

This account highlights the individual nature of the experience of *tarbiya*, and the distinction between the "theory" and "lived experience" of the process. These distinctions should be kept in mind as we go through further schematic discussions of this process of transformation.

In his Mauritanian sermon, Shaykh Ibrahim draws on a long tradition of Sufi discourse describing three progressive kinds or stages of annihilation: annihilation in the acts (*fanāʾ fī al-afʿāl*), annihilation in the Attributes (*fanāʾ fī al-Ṣifāt*), and annihilation in the Essence (*fanāʾ fī al-Dhāt*).⁵⁹ Annihilation in the acts is to realize and experience all actions as coming from a single actor. Annihilation in the attributes is to realize and experience the seven Divine Attributes of Islamic theology (Power, Will, Knowledge, Life, Hearing, Sight, Speech) as belonging only to God. In Shaykh Ibrahim's words, it is knowing that there is "no power but God's, no will but God's, no life but God's, no knowledge but God's, no hearing but God's, no sight but God's, and no speech but God's. Whoever recognizes this also finds annihilation in the Attributes." As for annihilation in the Essence, it is the awareness of nothing but God. In describing it, Shaykh Ibrahim says, "Everything flees from him [the disciple] until nothing remains but God."⁶⁰

After describing these three levels of annihilation in the Mauritanian sermon, Shaykh Ibrahim discussed two other modes of annihilation in the Attributes: annihilation in the Prophet and annihilation in the Shaykh. Here the Prophet and Shaykh al-Tijānī are considered Divine Attributes[61] given their status as unique manifestations of the Divine Essence as discussed above. These annihilations are considered necessary for the acquisition and perfection of *ma'rifa*, as Shaykh Ibrahim said in the previously cited Mauritanian sermon:

> For this reason, the Knowers, their first concern for a seeker is that he finds annihilation in God, then after that he ascends until he arrives at the Shaykh, because he is an attribute of God. The goal of these two annihilations is that the servant will return to this station [annihilation in the Attributes], for if he has not met the Messenger of God and the shaykh, then he will not know what comes after. So if he continues in this way, he will return to witnessing the existents, [but] he will see the existence as nonexistent and existent at the same time.[62]

In fact, these annihilations define the Knower in one of Shaykh Ibrahim's most-quoted sayings from *The Three Stations of Religion*: "For me, the Knower [*al-'ārif*] is he who is annihilated in the Essence once, and in the Attribute twice or three times, and annihilated in the Name once. He confirms the existence of these three realities, and he confirms the Names by the Name."[63]

When I asked Sidi Inaya what this saying meant, he interpreted it as referring to going through the two or three circuits of the stations described in *The Three Stations of Religion*. In *The Divine Flood*, Seesemann also connects this statement to the Mauritanian sermon, interpreting the "two or three annihilations in the Attribute" as referring to annihilation in the Prophet, Shaykh Tijānī, and Shaykh Ibrahim. My own discussions with disciples seemed to confirm this interpretation. For example, S. D. explained that after *tarbiya*, "they tell you that in everything you should see the four *ḥaḍras*, in everything you should see God, the Prophet, the Shaykh [Tijani], and Shaykh Ibrahim."[64]

But why are these annihilations necessary to be a Knower? Is not annihilation in the Divine Essence enough? And what is annihilation in the Name? What does it mean to confirm the Names by the Name? Seesemann quotes a work by a Nigerian disciple of Shaykh Ibrahim Niasse that explains the relationship between name, attribute, and essence: "The name is the interior of a thing (*shay'*), and the thing is the exterior part (*ẓāhir*) of the name, in the same way as the attribute (*ṣifa*) is the interior of the name, and the name is the exterior of the attribute. The essence (*dhāt*) is the innermost core of the attribute, and the attribute is the exterior of the essence."[65]

So what is this name in which the disciple becomes annihilated? The name "Allāh" is generally considered to be the comprehensive Name of God, which includes all other Divine Names. It names the Divine Essence in its totality, which each of the other Names (with the possible exceptions of al-Raḥmān and al-Ḥaqq) designates only a particular aspect of the Divine Reality.[66] For this reason, some consider the name "Allāh" to be the Greatest Name of God, the one hundredth of the traditional ninety-nine names, which, "if God is called by it, He will answer." However, in *al-Sirr al-Akbar*, Shaykh Ibrahim connects this Greatest Name to the Muḥammadan reality:

> The expression of the People of Tastings [*ahl al-adhwāq*] differ. Some of them say that His Names, all of them are the Greatest, and the response depends on the degree of the power of sincerity [of the supplicant] ... and others among them say that the name "Allāh" is the Greatest, others say that it is "Al-Ḥayy al-Qayyūm" [the Living, the Self-Subsistent], others say that is "Hūwa," others say that it is "Dhū'l-Jalāl wa'l-Ikrām" [Possessor of Glory and Generosity], while others say that it is "Rabb Rabb" [Lord, Lord], while others say that it is "Yā Sīn" and "ḥā mīm" [Arabic letters appearing at the beginning of Qur'anic suras], while others say that it is "al-Ḥanān al-Manān" [the Kind, the Beneficent], et cetera. The expressions differ and their meaning is one:
>
>> Our expressions are varied, while your meaning is one
>> And all of them to that perfection allude.
>
> Some of them connect [the Greatest Name] to some of the separated letters [*ḥurūf al-muqaṭaʿa*] at the beginning of the suras of the Qur'an ... and the truth in that is, if God wills, that the Greatest Name is the name before every relation, and with it, and after it in terms of description. So it is established that is has that reality and meaning and form and utterance because of the perfection of its validity [*ṣidq*] in The Essence and Attributes and the Names and the Acts ... and its reality is the universal reality, in which all realties are immersed because it is the First and the Last and the Outward/Apparent [*al-Ẓāhir*] and the Inward/Hidden [*al-Bāṭin*], and *its meaning is the reality of our lord Muhammad the Opener, the Seal, that is, the Muḥammadan reality that veils the prophets and the messengers and angels from perceiving the core of the Essence*, insofar as they are not it. The ḥadīth "I have a moment with God which is shared neither by any angel brought nigh nor by any prophet sent" ... refers to this, for it [the Muḥammadan reality] is the essence of the Name, while the Names are its parts. It [the Divine Essence] manifested itself in the Muḥammadan reality and our lord Muhammad became the total meaning of the essence

of the Name, while the prophets are its parts. And It manifested Itself in perfection and the greatest of the sincere [*ṣiddiqīn*] [Shaykh Aḥmad al-Tijānī] became the form of the totality of the Essence of the Name, while the saints are its parts.[67]

In this passage, Shaykh Ibrahim draws on a long tradition within Maghrebi Sufism connecting the Greatest Name of God with the Muḥammadan reality and its various manifestations in the form of the perfected saints. Since man is made in God's image, the Muḥammadan reality / the Perfect Human (*al-insān al-kāmil*) is the greatest "name" of God in that he manifests or reflects all of the attributes, qualities, and actions of the Divine Essence in a comprehensive manner, while everything else only does so partially. In a treatise on supplications on the Prophet, the Moroccan Shādhilī-Qādirī shaykh and calligrapher al-Qandūsī (d. 1861) explains:

When we contemplated hard and long on this majestic verse ["And to God belong the Beautiful Names, so invoke Him by them" (7:180)] we found that it is not restricted to the Ninety-Nine Beautiful Names of Allah recorded [in the ḥadīth collections]. Rather the bounty is spread to the hundredth name, which is the name of His Beloved: Muḥammad! That is because the name of Allah's beloved is never separated from His Name, Exalted is He! There is no Divine Name, be it one or two or three, or ten or ninety-nine, from Allah's Names, save that the name of His Beloved is linked with It.... Consequently, a person who knows the name of Muḥammad in its essence (*dhāt*) and not just its attributes (*ṣifāt*) knows Allah's Supreme Name, for the name of the Beloved is the essence of Allah's Beautiful Names that are well-pleasing to Him; and whosoever calls upon Allah through the name of His Beloved will have his supplication answered.... Consequently, a person who knows the name of a friend (*walī*) of Allah in its essence and not just its attributes knows Allah's Supreme Name too, and knows the best supplication with which he can invoke.[68]

Similarly, the famous pole of Moroccan Sufism, ʿAbd al-Salām ibn Mashīsh (d. 1227), master of Abu'l-Ḥasan al-Shādhilī (the founder of the Shādhilī order), is supposed to have once told his illustrious disciple, "O Abu'l-Ḥasan, you want to ask about the Greatest Name of God. It is of no use to ask about the Greatest Name of God. It is important that you should *be* the Greatest Name of Allah."[69] Shaykh Ibrahim's grandson and direct disciple, Shaykh Ḥasan Cissé, commented on this saying, writing:

A man once asked Abū Yazīd al-Bisṭāmī about the greatest name. He said, "It does not have a specific definition, for it is the emptiness of your heart for the sake of

His oneness. If you were like this, then you could obtain the East and the West with any name you use." ... The affair is not to know the name, the affair is to become the essence (ʿayn) of the name. Perhaps this is the meaning of the noble narration [of God's words], "Surrender yourself to Me, O My servant, then say, Be! And it will be" ... Shaykh Abū Ḥasan (al-Shādhilī) said, "In some of God's books sent down to His prophets, God said, 'Whoever obeys Me in everything, I cause everything to obey him.'"[70]

So returning to Shaykh Ibrahim's definition of a Knower—"For me, the Knower [al-ʿārif] is he who is annihilated in the Essence once, and in the Attribute twice or three times, and annihilated in the Name once"—annihilation in the Name refers to the realization that the human state, in its perfection (the Muḥammadan reality), is the Greatest Name of God, through the annihilation in or actualization of this state. In this state, one realizes the unity of all the various Divine Names in that single reality that they all name. This is what is meant by "confirming the Names by the Name"; one becomes characterized by all of the Divine Names (confirming them), and realizes their unity in oneself, the Greatest Name. This realization is necessarily an annihilation in which one's own self-consciousness or awareness is not separate from the realization or awareness of the unity of the reality of the Greatest Name. Similarly, disciples described annihilation in the Prophet, Shaykh al-Tijānī, and Shaykh Ibrahim (the "two or three annihilations in the Attributes") as "realizing that everything—including yourself—that everything is the Prophet, Shaykh Tijani, and Shaykh Ibrahim, you see them in everything—even in yourself."[71] Annihilation in the Essence refers to a similar annihilation in which the inscrutable Divine Essence becomes the sole object and subject of consciousness.

Shaykh Ibrahim describes a visionary experience of his that further clarifies both the "three realities" mentioned in the description of *maʿrifa* in *The Three Stations of Religion*, and the relationship between annihilation in the Name and annihilation in the Prophet and Shaykh al-Tijānī as Divine Attributes:

> I witnessed the Greatest Name [al-ism al-Aʿzam] in its essence, separate from all relations, having neither end nor beginning. From this perspective, I say that the essence of the Greatest Name is the [Divine] Essence, because of the unity of the Name and the Named. I remained [in this state] for a while, and I sought out the Beautiful Names and Divine Attributes, but I saw neither Name or Attribute because of the integration of the Names and Attributes into the Greatness [of the Name].
>
> Then something from among things of the Real occurred, which cannot be described, and then with respect to the Name, the Names appeared as separate

parts—it was something like—and with God are the greatest likenesses—the appearance of the stars in the sky: the stars were the Names that appeared to me in the sky of the Essence of the Name, and each part of those parts had neither beginning nor end. So in respect to the Essence, which is the totality, I saw each Name as a part. And in respect to each Name among the Names, it meant that It [the name] was It [the Named], without any separation. So I came to know that he who says that the Name is not a name for other than the Essence has spoken truly, and he who says that [all of] the Names are great has also spoken truly. And in this place of witnessing nothing appeared to me except our lord Muḥammad.

Then another thing occurred, and I saw the pole [al-quṭb] in his multiplicity and proximity and beauty. Then something occurred, which I cannot describe, and then I found the Muḥammadan reality as I had found the Greatest Name. And I stayed [in this state] and sought out the prophets and messengers from Adam to Jesus, upon them be blessings and peace, and I saw the essence of neither prophet nor messenger because of the integration of the messengers into the Messengerhood of our lord Muḥammad. Then something occurred, and in respect to Muḥammad, the other messengers appeared as separate parts just as before [with respect to the Names]. And so, I was made to encounter the prophets, one after another, and I did not see a single one among them, except that I was told, this is our Prophet, and I only looked at our lord Muḥammad. In this place of witnessing, the Real did not manifest itself to me except as our lord Muḥammad. Then something occurred and I saw the hidden pole, and the seal of sanctity, and I found him in the place of our lord Muḥammad. So I stayed [in this state], and I sought out the saints [awliyāʾ] and I did not find a single saint apart from our lord Aḥmad [al-Tijānī], because of their integration into his [Shaykh Aḥmad al-Tijānī's] sainthood. Then something occurred and the saints and poles were seen as separate parts in him, exactly as in the first example [of the Names and the Prophets like stars in the sky]. So I came to know that our lord Muḥammad had sealed Messengerhood by his being the vicegerent [khalīfa] of the Name, while the [other] prophets were [with respect to him] like the Names [in relation to the Greatest Name]. And [I knew that] our lord Aḥmad had sealed sanctity by his being the vicegerent [khalīfa] of our lord Muḥammad, and the other saints were [with respect to him] like the prophets [in relation to Muḥammad]. This is the meaning of the seal of Muḥammadan sanctity. Some of them [the saints] existed before [Shaykh Tijānī] and some existed after [him], because this [sealhood] is not a question of temporal occurrence. For the seal of the prophets [Muḥammad] was a prophet aware of his own prophethood while Adam was still between water and clay; and likewise the seal of sanctity was a saint while Adam was between water and clay.[72]

How Is *Maʿrifa* Acquired? • 151

Disciples' accounts of the process of *tarbiya* (at least what they felt comfortable sharing with me) bore great similarities to the above description, except that many disciples also described a similar encounter with the spiritual reality of Shaykh Ibrahim Niasse as the (*khalīfa*) of Shaykh Aḥmad al-Tijānī.[73] So the Greatest Name and the spiritual realities of the Prophet Muḥammad and Shaykh Tijani all reflect or represent the Divine Essence in a particularly total or complete way in their various domains. However, it is still not yet clear why these annihilations in the Prophet, Shaykh Tijani, and the Name are necessary in order for one to qualify as a Knower (*ārif*). Why isn't annihilation in the Divine Essence sufficient?

## EPISTEMIC SIGNIFICANCE OF ANNIHILATION IN THE PROPHET

The answer can be found in a story in Ibn 'Arabi's *Futūḥāt al-Makkiya* about the early Sufi Abū Yazīd Bisṭāmī, which Shaykh Ibrahim quotes in his *Removal of Confusion*:

> Abū Yazīd was among those reported as saying things like this ["I am God" (27:9); "Verily, I am God, there is no god but Me" (20:14); and "There is no god but I, so worship Me" (27:14)] in a state of full sobriety and establishment; knowing that the Real is the One manifesting in the servant's actions within the substance of potentialities. So in some of his states, he spoke as He, and in some states, he did not mention that he was speaking as He.
>
> Some of the gnostics said in regards to the disciple (of Abū Yazīd) who considered Allah sufficient for him in his claim (to have witnessed Him), thereby disregarding seeing Abū Yazīd, that seeing Abū Yazīd one time is better than seeing Allāh a thousand times. (After the disciple was informed of this) Abū Yazīd passed in front of him, and he was told "that is Abū Yazīd." When his eyes fell on the Shaykh, the disciple died. When Abū Yazīd was informed of his death, he said, "He saw what he could not bear, for Allah manifested Himself to him in me. He could not bear it, just as Moses could not bear it (when Allah manifested Himself to him on the mountain). Allah's manifestation in me was greater than the divine manifestation the disciple used to witness in himself."[74]

Ibn 'Arabi concludes, "Since the matter is thus, we know that our vision of the Real in the Muḥammadan form by the Muḥammadan vision is the most perfect vision [of God] that there is. So we do not cease to encourage people to [seek] this."[75] It must be remembered that in Ibn 'Arabi's cosmology (and that of the vast majority of Sufis), everything that exists is a self-manifestation (*tajallī*) of God, and that the most perfect and comprehensive of these manifestations is the Prophet Muḥammad. So any vision or knowledge of God that manifested to a Sufi adept is necessarily less complete or perfect than the knowledge manifested to and through the reality of the Prophet, just as in the hours before dawn, the full moon is brighter than the faint glow of sunrise on the horizon. Elsewhere in the *Futūḥāt*, Ibn 'Arabi explains this point in greater detail, employing the metaphor of mirrors:

> You should know that God did not create the creatures with a single constitution. On the contrary, He made them disparate in constitution. This is obvious and self-evident to anyone who looks, because of the disparity among people in rational consideration and faith. God has told you that man is his brother's mirror [a reference to a ḥadīth]. Hence man sees in his brother something of himself that he would not see without him. For man is veiled by his own caprice. But when he sees that attribute in the other, while it is his own attribute, he sees his own defect in the other. Then he comes to know its ugliness if the attribute is ugly, or its beauty, if it should be beautiful.
>
> Know that mirrors are diverse in shape and that they modify the object seen by the observer according to their own shapes, whether they be tall, wide, curved, bent, round, small, large, numerous, and so on—whatever may be given by the shape of the mirror. It is known that the messengers are the most balanced of all people in their constitution, since they receive messages from their Lord. Each of them receives the message to the measure of the composition God has given him in his constitution. There is no prophet who was not sent specifically to a designated people, since he possessed a specific and curtailed constitution. But God sent Muḥammad with an all-inclusive message for all people without exception. He was able to receive such a message because he possessed an all-inclusive constitution which comprises the constitution of every prophet and messenger, since he has the most balanced and most perfect of constitutions....
>
> Once you come to know this, and once you desire to see the Real in the most perfect manner in which He can become manifest in this human plane, then you need to know that this does not belong to you. You do not have a constitution like that possessed by Muḥammad. Whenever the Real discloses Himself to you within the mirror of your heart, your mirror will make him manifest to you in the measure of its constitution and in the form of its shape. You know how far you stand below Muḥammad's degree in knowledge of his Lord through his plane. So cling to faith and follow him! Place him before you as the mirror within which you gaze upon your own form and the form of others. When you do this, you will come to know that God must disclose himself to Muḥammad within his mirror. I have already

told you that a mirror displays an effect in that which is seen from the point of view of the observer who sees. So the manifestation of the Real within the mirror of Muḥammad is the most perfect, most balanced, and most beautiful manifestation, because of the mirror's actuality. When you perceive Him in the mirror of Muḥammad, you will have perceived from Him a perfection which you could not perceive in respect of considering your own mirror.[76]

Thus, given the imperfection of our mirrors in comparison to the Prophet's, Ibn 'Arabi concludes that for us, the Real's manifestation in the Prophet will be more "perfect and balanced" than its manifestation in our own mirrors. It is as if we are in an alley whose tall buildings block the direct sight of the sun. We can perceive the sunlight in the sky, but if we were to look at a mirror that does have a direct line of sight to the sun, we would be dazzled by its brilliance. Furthermore, Ibn 'Arabi describes the "mirror of Muḥammad" as not only providing more perfect knowledge of the Real, but also of ourselves and other creatures; due to its perfect composition, it gives us a more complete picture of ourselves and other things than we could obtain without it. However, one could just as well ask if the same distorting effect our mirrors have on the image of the Real could also apply to the Prophet? Can our mirrors ever contain what is beyond their capacity to contain? If our own vision or knowledge of the Real is incomplete or weak when compared to our knowledge or vision of the Real through the mirror of the Prophet, what of our knowledge or vision of this Prophetic mirror? Is this not just shifting the goalposts?

The later Sufi tradition, including the Tijāniyya, introduces the intermediaries of the shaykhs (i.e., by one's shaykh one knows Shaykh al-Tijānī, by Shaykh Tijānī one knows the Prophet, by the Prophet, one knows God in His Essence and manifestations). But this can still be regarded as just another shifting of the goalposts, for if the mirror is still bent or imperfect, how can it not distort all that appears within?[77] As Tijani disciples often remarked, "Abu Lahab was the Prophet's uncle and saw him all the time, but did he ever really *see* him?" or in the famous story, cited by Shaykh Aḥmad al-Tijānī in the *Jawāhir al-Ma'ānī*, of the companion Uways al-Qaranī, who never physically met the Prophet but told his companions and successors, 'Umar and 'Alī, "You only saw the shadow of the Messenger of God."[78]

The answer to this question can be found in Ibn 'Arabi's previously discussed concept of "gods created in belief," to which the metaphor of imperfect mirrors alludes, and in the Shaykh al-Akbar's concept of "following Muḥammad," in which the spiritual practice of following the Prophet's example "polishes" and perfects mirrors so that they begin to approximate that of the Prophet. As discussed above, Ibn 'Arabi argues that our particular constitutions, the limitations that make us individuals, "color" and "shape" our belief and knowledge of God, just as the form of a mirror shapes the images that appear within it, or a cup colors the water poured into it. Because of this, most people simply end up worshipping a "god created in belief," a constructed idea of God, bound by one's own particular limitations.

Ibn 'Arabi bases many of his discussions of this topic on the verse of the Qur'an that states, "They did not measure God in accordance with the reality of His measure [*ḥaqqa qadrihi*] ... on the Day of Resurrection"[79] (39:67) and the related "ḥadith of transformations,"[80] in which God appears to people on the Day of Resurrection in a form in which they do not recognize Him, declaring "I am your Lord." The people reject Him in this form and say, "No! We take refuge in God from you!" Then God appears to them in a familiar form, again declaring "I am your Lord." This time, people recognize and accept Him in this familiar form, saying "You are our Lord." Ibn 'Arabi argues that these accounts do not only refer to the Day of Resurrection, but that they describe what is happening right now in regard to all of the self-manifestations (*tajālliyāt*) in which God presents Himself to us. As quoted above, Ibn 'Arabi writes:

> Generally speaking, each person necessarily sticks to a particular belief concerning his Lord. He always goes back to His Lord through his particular belief and seeks God therein. Such a man positively recognizes God only when He manifests himself to him in the form recognized by his belief. But when He manifests himself in other beliefs, he flatly refuses to accept Him and runs away from Him. In so doing, he simply behaves in an improper way towards God, while imagining that he is practicing good manners (*adab*) towards Him. Thus a person who clings to belief believes in a god according to what he has made in his own soul/mind (*nafs*). The god of beliefs comes about through the subjective act of making/positing (*ja'l*) on the part of the believers. They see naught but their own souls and what they have made therein.
>
> So contemplate the fact that the hierarchy of mankind in their knowledge of God is their very hierarchy in terms of their vision on the Day of Resurrection. So beware of being bound by a particular belief and rejecting all others as unbelief! If you do that, much good will escape you. Nay, you will fail to obtain the true knowledge of reality. Try to make yourself a (kind of) Prime Matter (*hyle*) for all forms of belief, for God is too vast and too great to be confined to one belief to the exclusion of another. For He says, *Wheresoever you turn, there is the Face of God* (2:115). God does not specify (in this verse) a particular place in which the Face of God is to be found, He only said, *there is the Face of God*. The "face" of a thing means its real essence. With this verse, God admonished the hearts of the Knowers so that they might not be distracted by nonessential matters in this lower world from

being constantly aware of this kind of thing. For no one knows at which moment he will be taken. If one is taken during a moment of forgetfulness, his position will certainly not be equal to another who dies in a state of clear awareness.[81]

Thus, for Ibn 'Arabi, the degree of one's knowledge of God is directly related to the degree to which one can recognize the Real in all of its various forms. That is, the degree to which one can transcend or go beyond one's own subjective conception of reality, one's "god created in belief." This can only be achieved through following one who has already transcended these limitations, and worshipping his absolutely unconditioned object of worship. For Ibn 'Arabi and the Tijanis, the Prophet Muḥammad is the example par excellence of one who has an infinitely receptive heart that recognizes God in all of His manifestations, and so one hoping for "knowledge of things as they are" must follow his example. Otherwise, one merely worships a creation of one's own imagination, as Ibn 'Arabi concludes: "When a person rationally considers God, he creates what he believes in himself through consideration. Hence he worships only a god which he has created through his consideration.... That is why God has commanded us to worship the God brought by the Messenger and spoken of in the Book. For, if you worship this God, you will be worshipping that which you have not created. On the contrary, you will be worshipping your Creator, and you will have fully given worship its due (ḥaqq). For knowledge of God only derives from following. It cannot possibly be derived from proofs."[82]

The real knower, the Muḥamamdan, is he who has escaped his own limitations through his heart's ability to take on any and every form. As in the example of the cup and water discussed above, the only way for the cup (the heart) to display the true color of water is for it to become transparent—that is, to transcend its coloring and become capable of taking on any color. This transformation is achieved by transcending one's own "gods created in belief" by following the Messenger of God to the point that one becomes identified with his state of perfect receptivity, achieving annihilation in him. It is only after having achieved this state of perfect receptivity to all of the divine self-disclosures that one can know and recognize God in His Essence as well as in all of His various manifestations. Thus, annihilation in the Messenger is necessary for transcending one's limits and perfecting one's Knowledge and recognition of God in this life and the next.

In the Mauritanian sermon, Shaykh Ibrahim Niasse describes these annihilations in the Prophet and the Shaykh as occurring *after* annihilation in God, as a means of establishing subsistence (*baqāʾ*) after annihilation (*fanāʾ*) in God, saying "If he [the disciple] has not met the Messenger of God and the shaykh, then he will not know what comes after."[83] It is significant that Shaykh Ibrahim's schema of annihilations follows the arc of creation of Tijani mythology: first God separates the Muḥammadan light from His Light, and the light or spiritual reality of Shaykh al-Tijānī is a hidden aspect of this Muḥammadan Light, and the spiritual reality of Shaykh Ibrahim is a hidden aspect of the spiritual reality of Shaykh al-Tijānī. From this Muḥammadan/Aḥmadī/Ibrāhīmī reality, all of the various things of the world are created. Now in this perspective, when something is created from something else, that means that the two things are identical from a certain point of view. From the perspective of eternity, this transformation appears as just the elaboration or extension of a single reality in time and space. From this atemporal perspective, the seed contains and is identical with the tree, which contains and is identical with the fruit, which contains and is identical with the seed.

Because everything is created from God, everything is God. Because everything is created from the light of the Prophet / Shaykh al-Tijānī / Shaykh Ibrahim, everything is this light. Shaykh Ibrahim and other Sufi authors have employed a number of metaphors to illustrate these relationships, such as ink and the letters formed by it, breath and spoken words, and light and images (as in Shaykh Ibrahim's metaphor of the cinema). In this perspective, the fact that the many comes from the One means that the many are still but one. In this vein, Sufi authors often cite the prophetic saying "God was and there was nothing with Him," and the commentary of ʿAlī (or Junayd), "It is now even as it was."[84] In this regard, Shaykh Ibrahim quotes the following verse of poetry:

> I was asked, "Have you ever seen anything more beautiful?"
> I said, "Is there anything else but this in existence?"[85]

The Muḥammadan reality, as the Logos, the nexus or *barzakh* between the One and the many, God and the world, the Real and its manifestations, is the key to understanding this relationship: the presence of the many in the One and the One in the many.

Thus, the annihilations in the shaykhs and the Prophet, following annihilation in the Divine Essence, permit disciples to further transcend their individual limitations and begin the stage of subsistence (*baqāʾ*), of complete *maʿrifa*, in which they can recognize God in themselves, in His Essence, and in all of His manifestations. Shaykh Ibrahim describes the one who has attained this complete degree of knowledge in the Mauritanian sermon:

> He knows there is nothing but God and he perceives things as they are, and he puts every created thing in its place, in which God placed it. And he knows that he is nothing. He exalts things, while not considering them existent; and he fears things, without considering them existent; and he loves things without considering them

existent. And he acquires all good actions, he prays, and he fasts, and he makes ḥajj, and he tells the truth and he spends his money. And all of that is out of good manners [*adab*] to God, while he knows that there is nothing there. And if the servant arrives at this, he is connected to God by a real connection—he doesn't do anything except for God.[86]

Or in the words of M. D.:

Because afterward you are a person, like others, you eat, you drink, you live like others. You are like them, but you are not like them. You live, but you don't live. You are dead, but you are not dead. You are alive—OK, because you eat, you drink, et cetera—but you are not alive because "he who does not die, does not see God." It's because you are dead that you see God. This death of which I am speaking, is not the death that puts you in the ground, but it's the death of having cut off the world, being dead to the world.[87]

Thus *tarbiya*—whether described as a journey through these different kinds of annihilations, presences (*ḥaḍarāt*), levels of the soul, or stations (*maqāmāt*)—is the process by which an aspirant's consciousness is transformed from its everyday state of perceiving self, God, and world as separate and distinct, to the state of *fanāʾ* (annihilation) in which there are no such distinctions, and finally to the station of *maʿrifa*, of *baqāʾ* (subsistence), in which the distinctions reemerge, but only virtually, as the Knower now sees all things in God and God in all things. *Tarbiya* is a process of moral, ethical, spiritual, and noetic perfection, and those who have been through it claim that it allows one to know oneself and reality with the entirety of one's being, with certainty, as it should be known.

Having covered these various descriptions of the process of *tarbiya*, we now turn to the question of how this process actually works. That is, how is it that this particular program of spiritual exercises results in the transformations described above?

CHAPTER 4

# How Does *Tarbiya* Work?

When asked how the process of *tarbiya* works, most disciples and shaykhs responded with some variation of "I know it works, but I have no idea how it works. It's like when I go to the ATM: I put in my card, I punch in my code, and the cash comes out, but how all that works, the electronics and such, I don't know. I know *tarbiya* works, I've done it myself, I've given it to others, but how it works, I don't know."[1] Sidi Inaya Niang compared the effect of reciting the litanies to a description of music he once heard from the late reggae legend Peter Tosh: "When you listen to good music it gives you a good vibration. Good vibration gives you a good feeling, a good feeling gives you a good way of thinking; good thinking makes you change your life, see the world in a new way."[2] This chapter explores several of these theories as to how *tarbiya* works, before concluding with a related discussion of how *maʿrifa* is verified and how it compares with contemporary Western epistemologies.

### FOCUS AND LOVE (*TAWAJJUH* AND *MAḤABBA*)

Disciples and shaykhs often described *tarbiya* as a process of focusing the attention and awareness of the disciple on God (and the Prophet, Shaykh Tijani, and Shaykh Ibrahim) to the exclusion of all else, and then integrating this singular awareness of unity with the awareness of multiplicity. Indeed, Shaykh Aḥmad Zarrūq begins his *Principles of Sufism* (a work popular in West Africa and frequently quoted by Shaykh Ibrahim) by defining Sufism as "sincerity in turning toward [*tawajjuh ilā*] God."[3] One contemporary disciple in her early thirties, the daughter of a prominent shaykha, described her experience in these terms:

> I was not really interested in *tarbiya* and these things, and even though I saw all the people who came to my mother for *tarbiya*, I was more interested in having fun with my friends and going to clubs. My mother never stopped me, she just said, "If you're ever interested in what I have, you can come take it." So after some of my friends took *tarbiya* from my mother, and I saw how they were different, I was curious, so I asked my mother for *tarbiya*. Then I was saying the Ṣalāt al-Fātiḥ all the time, and when I went back to the club, I could still hear the Ṣalāt al-Fātiḥ, very clearly. I just did not feel right in the club anymore, it just did not fit, so I stopped going. . . . It used to be only the greatest people who separated themselves from everything who could get a *fatḥ*, but what Shaykh Ibrahim brought, you can be a mother working in the house, a student, a worker, and say *ṣalāt al-fātiḥ* all the time and you can get the opening that people used to have to work so hard for, and only a few of them got it.[4]

For this disciple, the constant presence of the prayer in her mind and heart, and the related focus on God and the Prophet, is what led to the transformation of certain dispositions. S. D., the philosophy teacher quoted above, was even more explicit: "They have you say *lā ilāha illā Allāh* and *ṣalāt al-fātiḥ* so many times that you start saying them in your sleep. You don't watch movies or TV, you don't talk to people [any more than necessary], so you are just thinking God, God, God all the time, until eventually that is all you think or see."[5] Similarly, after explaining that the success and speed of the process of *tarbiya* depends on the sincerity (*ṣidq*) of the disciple, Shaykh Ibrahim defines the "reality of sincerity [as] the singularity of focus [*wajh*] on God."[6] Relatedly, several shaykhs described *tarbiya* as helping disciples love God and the Prophet, because "when you love someone, you think about him all the time, and would do anything for him. So love is the key to all of this. Everything Shaykh Ibrahim had, he obtained through his love of the Prophet."[7] This theme of love as the catalyst for existential transformation is a prominent one in the writings of Shaykh Ibrahim, and Sufi literature in general. As Shaykh Māḥī Niasse explained, "'I was a hidden treasure and loved to be known [therefore I created creation that I might know them].' So since God's creation came through the door of love into existence, the return to God must also be through the way of love. . . . The foundation [of *tarbiya*] is love."[8]

In many of his writings, Shaykh Ibrahim emphasized the sincerity (*ṣidq*) and zeal (*himma*) of the disciple as the main factors in determining his or her success, speed, and level of progress in *sulūk* (spiritual wayfaring). In a certain sense, the outpouring of grace (*fayḍ*) and *maʿrifa* conforms to the aspirant's degree of sincerity and zeal, on how badly he or she "wants it." If the disciple truly loves God and the Prophet above all else, then this sincerity of intention will be accompanied by zeal, the spiritual energy that gives the disciple the concentration and strength to traverse the different stages of the spiritual path.⁹

But how does the performance of certain prayers and invocations lead to this focus and love? And why these prayers and not others? Many of Shaykh Ibrahim's writings contain a kind of ritual theory that addresses such questions. For example, in his commentary on the Qurʾanic verse "Wheresoever you turn, there is the face of God" (2:155), Shaykh Ibrahim writes:

> "There is the face of God" means His direction, His Essence. The Essence of God has neither direction nor place, but it is wheresoever the servant turns in seeking the *qibla* [direction of prayer, toward the Kaʿba in Mecca]. It is this complete *maʿrifa* of the servant that dictates that he pray in any direction he wishes, but the fact that we pray in one direction is out of good manners [*adab*], conforming to the command of God, and to train the soul so that it becomes accustomed to singularity of orientation. So whenever the servant wants to worship or pray or invoke [*dhikr*], he turns toward a single direction. This is best because the servant's adopting a singular orientation outwardly affects his inner reality [*bāṭin*], until God grants him a singular orientation inwardly. The real *qibla* is the exalted Essence. What is required of the servant is that he turn his heart to this real *qibla* perpetually and eternally. Persistence in turning toward the [physical] *qibla* may discipline the inward reality of the servant until he attains the turning toward the real *qibla*. If not for this, it would be difficult for the Knower [*ārif*] to pray toward the known direction for [to him] all directions are the same."¹⁰

Thus, the outward (*ẓāhir*) discipline of facing a single direction facilitates the inward (*bāṭin*) discipline of single-pointed concentration or focus. In fact, as this passage suggests, the point of the outward discipline of turning toward the *qibla* is its effect on the inward disposition of turning toward "the real *qibla*" of the Divine Essence. This symbolic principle of correspondence underlies most of Sufi theories of ritual practice, as Shaykh Ibrahim's work and the texts from which he quotes (especially those of Ibn ʿArabi) demonstrate. For Ibn ʿArabi, this correspondence is mediated by the faculty of imagination (*khayāl*). Unlike the English meaning of "imagination," *khayāl*, for Ibn ʿArabi, denotes a kind of perception with its own corresponding ontological reality. As the *barzakh* or bridge between the formless world of spirit/meaning and the sensory world, imagination allows supra-formal realities to take on sensible forms; it is what allows us to "see" or "hear" or "taste" ideas and spiritual realities, as we do in dreams (and, strictly speaking, in everyday life). Ibn ʿArabi argues that this continuity between the spiritual and the sensible, which imagination makes possible, is why Muslims are commanded to "imagine God in the *qibla*" when they pray and to "worship God *as if* you see Him."[11] This "as if" is the key to imagination—to imagine a reality described by scripture and prophetic reports and, in doing so, to eventually realize and verify that reality.

In the case of imagining God in the *qibla*, Ibn ʿArabi and his commentators explain that those who follow reason alone reject imagination and are incapable of carrying out this particular command. Better are those "people of faith" or those who "bear witness": those who, through imagination, accept the scriptural and prophetic descriptions that seem to defy reason. They imagine God in the *qibla* and pray with the resulting humble awareness of body and soul (*khushūʿ*)—in fact, Ibn ʿArabi argues that any prayer offered without this imagined presence of the Divine and corresponding attitude of humble devotion is not valid. This is the lowest degree of "bearing witness." Better still are those who rise from this level and witness God in the *qibla* through their spiritual insight (*baṣīra*). Then comes the level in which God is witnessed in the *qibla* with both the inner eye of insight and outer eye of the senses. And in the ultimate stage, the subject and object of this witnessing become one, and God witnesses Himself in Himself.[12]

To return to Shaykh Ibrahim's commentary, paradoxically, turning in one direction leads the adept to see God in any direction, "wheresoever he turns." However, even after this realization, the adept persists in facing the physical *qibla* out of *adab* (good manners) and in conformity with God's command, maintaining the symbolic correspondence between a particular spatial orientation (toward the *qibla*) and spiritual or inner orientation (toward the Divine Essence).

### *DHIKR* (REMEMBRANCE/INVOCATION)

A similar symbolic logic is found in Shaykh Ibrahim's commentary on the verse "Those who remember God standing and sitting and lying on their sides and reflect on the creation of the heavens and the earth" (3:191):

> God described the remembers/invokers [*al-dhākirīn*] as people who pray and remember/invoke God much. In the beginning, the remembrance of God is with the tongue, and then with the heart [*qalb*], and then with the spirit [*rūḥ*]. By the remembrance/invocation [*dhikr*] of the tongue, the annihilation [*fanāʾ*] in the Acts is found. By the remembrance/invocation of the heart, annihilation

in the Attributes is found. By the remembrance/invocation of the spirit, total annihilation is found. He is annihilated, then annihilated, then annihilated, so that his annihilations are the source of subsistence [baqā']. Remembrance/invocation has a shell, and a kernel, and a kernel of the kernel. The shell is for the generality, the kernel is for the elite, and the kernel of the kernel is for the elite of the elite, and the kernel of the kernel is the oil.[13] In any case, abundance of remembrance/invocation [dhikr] is necessary.[14]

Here, Shaykh Ibrahim defines a progressive hierarchy of dhikr,[15] moving from the outward (the tongue) to the inward (the spirit). Dhikr with the tongue leads to the dhikr of the heart, which in turn leads to the dhikr of the spirit. These different modes of dhikr also lead to different kinds of realization or annihilation. The dhikr of the tongue is physical, occurring in space and time, and is limited—people have to eat, sleep, talk to one another, and so forth. The dhikr of the heart, or the internal invocation, takes place on a different, higher level of being, and is thus less limited by these constraints, although it can be limited by turning one's attention away from God. The dhikr of the spirit takes place at an even higher level of being, and as such it can be perpetual—in fact, it can barely be said to take place in time and space. One can perform the different modes of dhikr independently—that is, one can invoke with the tongue, but absent-mindedly, and thus not with the heart. Or one can invoke silently and inwardly with the heart, but not with the tongue. But the ideal dhikr is one that takes place on all levels, although from a certain perspective the higher forms of dhikr can be said to encompass the lower. Shaykh Ibrahim writes:

> The Knower by God ['ārif biLlāh] in this station is charged with filling his inner reality [bāṭin] with God perpetually though invoking/remembering with the tongue, the heart, the spirit, and the secret [sirr]. The invocation/remembrance [dhikr] of the heart is reflection [fikra], and invocation/remembrance [dhikr] of the spirit is insight ['ibra], and the invocation/remembrance [dhikr] of the secret is contemplation [naẓra].
> This is the station of "Have you seen how your Lord has extended the shadow?" [25:45][16] ... and to this station alludes the ḥadīth "The best dhikr is the hidden [al-khafī]." The best dhikr of the tongue is the Ṣalāt al-Fātiḥ—it should be practiced always with neither limitation nor [fixed] number nor limit nor set place or time.[17]

Similarly, in a passage cited frequently in Tijani sources, the Mauritanian Shādhilī Shaykh al-Yadālī writes, "It has been said that the quickest way to enter the Divine Presence is through the remembrance/invocation [dhikr] of God because the Name cannot be separated from the Named. Since the invoker [*dhākir*] ceaselessly invokes the name of God, the veils are torn to shreds bit by bit, until the heart comes to witness God directly. When this happens, the aspirant dispenses with remembrance/invocation due to his witnessing of the One remembered/invoked [*madhkūr*]."[18]

These passages presume a symbolic semiotics in which the named is present in the name and the invoked in the invocation (*dhikr*); moreover, they also presume an ontological hierarchy of the human being extending from the outward/apparent (the body) to the most inward/hidden (*al-khafī*), where the human invoker is not distinct from the divine invoked. The practice of invocation thus works by making the invoked present though its linguistic symbol (name or prayer), and by gradually leading the invoker deeper and deeper into him or herself, until he or she encounters that which is invoked directly, without any linguistic symbol.

THE SCIENCE OF LETTERS AND LANGUAGE

This ontological hierarchy—from the spiritual/supra-formal (*rūḥānī/rabbānī*) to the imaginal/formal (*khayālī/mithālī*) to the sensible (*ḥissī*)—features prominently in the "science of letters," which shaykhs and disciples frequently invoked to explain the efficacy of particular prayers and litanies. In this science, each sound/letter of the Arabic language/alphabet is associated with a number, meaning, element, aspect of life/nature, part of the body, spiritual reality or realities, and Divine Quality or qualities.[19] This science, variations of which are also found in several other religious traditions, relies on a logic of symbolism in which relationships between entities in one particular domain (such as written letters) are symbols/manifestations of relationships between entities of another domain (such as numbers or Divine Names). Connections in one domain can be mapped onto other domains.

This "science" has a certain logic to it, but its Sufi proponents claim that it can only be partially understood by reason and therefore requires spiritual unveiling and realization to master and fully understand. In a sense, one could say that this occult science appears to the uninitiated much as music theory would appear to a deaf person. He or she would have to take the hearing person's word that a minor scale sounds sad, and a major scale happy, and which intervals are harmonious and which are dissonant. On this basis, a deaf person could have some idea how a piece of music would sound on the basis of a musical score, but it is only through the power of hearing that one can truly appreciate the effects of a piece of music. Similarly, one can learn about this "science of letters," but it is only by gaining new perception through spiritual unveiling that one can truly and immediately appreciate these subtle powers of language.[20]

Ibn ʿArabi provides several different metaphors and metaphysical frameworks to explain these relationships between the world of language and various other worlds, the most prominent and influential of which is the "doctrine of the breaths" (which draws on the Qurʾanic image of God breathing His Spirit into man) and the image of the "breaths of the all-Merciful" (*nafas al-Raḥmān*) from the ḥadīth literature.

Speech is simply an articulation of breath, and according to this perspective, the divine "breath" is pure being, so everything that exists is divine speech, a cosmic array of words. Since humans are "made in God's image," we have the peculiar status of being a "talking word." To borrow an image from *The Lord of the Rings* movies, it is as if Gandalf, amid his many smoke rings, blew a smoke figure of himself blowing smoke rings. Therefore, human speech, which constitutes human language, echoes the divine speech, which constitutes the cosmos (including humanity and our language). Humanity's articulation of breath is but a reflection, in a very limited domain, of the process that brings the entire cosmos into delimited existence from undifferentiated Being.

Since God brought the world into being through His speech, people can also return to Him through His speech. Thus, the efficacy of certain prayers or invocations, like the shahāda and the *Ṣalāt al-Fātiḥ*, is attributed to or explained through these correspondences between their letters/sounds, numerical symbolism, meanings, and the spiritual realities/forces that they are believed to transmit.[21] The number of times a formula is recited also forms a part of this symbolic correspondence. One shaykh explained the symbolism of the Tijani daily office (*al-waẓīfa*) through this science of numbers and letters, pointing out that the number of recitations of this office spell out "The Prophet" (*al-nabī*), which is also (nearly) numerically equivalent to the Prophet's name, Muḥammad (M, Ḥ, M, D).[22]

In his *Removal of Confusion*, Shaykh Ibrahim quotes Shaykh Aḥmad Zarrūq's explanation of this operational symbolism:

> The special distinction of each remembrance [*dhikr*] and Divine Name derives from its meaning, and its power (*taṣrīf*) is according to what is needed. The secret of the remembrance is in the number of repetitions. Its fulfillment depends on the spiritual aspiration (*himma*) of the one practicing it (*ṣāḥibihi*). This explains why the knowledgeable person does not benefit (from a *dhikr*) unless the meaning is clear, and why the ignorant person does not benefit unless the meaning is hidden and unknown to him. In this way, their (divergent) understandings persist. As for how many times a particular formula of remembrance is repeated, this is taken from the legal sources, or derived by spiritual discovery. Success is dependent upon Allah's established custom (*sunnat Allāh*).[23]

So the efficacy of the invocations is related to the zeal (*himma*) with which it is recited, the number of times it is recited, and its meaning.

MEANING

Disciples and *shuyūkh* often referred to the inner meanings of the invocations of the Tijani litanies, especially the *Ṣalāt al-Fātiḥ* (the primary invocation of *tarbiya*), in explaining how *tarbiya* works. Several disciples told me that the inner meaning of the formula of seeking forgiveness (*istighfār*) is to seek "forgiveness" for one's own separative existence from God and asking God to "erase" this sin of the illusion of separate existence.[24] The shahāda, *Lā ilāha illā Llāh*, "There is no god but God," as discussed above, was interpreted as meaning that "there is nothing but God." Reciting it is believed to erase all illusory existence until one attains *fanāʾ* and realizes the true meaning of the shahāda.

The Tijani tradition has produced a vast body of literature on the inner meanings of the *Ṣalāt al-Fātiḥ* and the merits of its recitation, and it is widely described as "the best form of worship other than the invocation of the Greatest Name of God."[25] The late Ustadh Barham Diop told me, "The *Ṣalāt al-Fātiḥ* is such a great mystery, I am still discovering its wonders, and I can't even understand how great it is."[26] Abu Ibrahim explained his understanding of the prayer to me in the following terms:

> If you know God and the Prophet are the same thing, then you know that when Allah prays on the Prophet, it is God manifesting himself, that's it basically. That's how I understand it now. Also one of those guys who ask a lot of questions about *maʿrifa* asked, "Allah said we've got to pray on the prophet, but when we say *Ṣalāt al-Fātiḥ*, we say, 'O Allah pray on the prophet . . . ,' so how do you pray on the Prophet yourself?" . . .
>
> It's what's creating the world, it's through *Ṣalāt al-Fātiḥ* that everything exists, from the unseen, the unknown, the unrevealed. *Ṣalāt al-Fātiḥ* is what's between existence and nonexistence; when you say it, you're part of the process of expanding the universe. Did you hear this? Is this in the books? [Response: Yes, Shaykh Ibrahim wrote something like this. Shaykh Tijani and other Sufis have said things similar to this.] Because I thought it's not something to say. You see, that's something I discovered myself. I'm even surprised that it's in the books.[27]

The prayer on the Prophet (*Ṣalāt ʿalāʾl-Nabī*), of which the *Ṣalāt al-Fātiḥ* is the example par excellence for the Tijani tradition, is understood as God's outpouring (*fayḍ*) of being, consciousness, light, life, and so forth, to the Muḥammadan reality, and the subsequent outpouring from Muḥammadan reality to all existence. Thus, to recite the *Ṣalāt al-Fātiḥ* is to participate in this process, to call forth an outpouring from God, through the Prophet, to oneself, and to draw nearer to uniting with the Muḥammadan reality, which contains everything. In his article on the prayer of Ibn Mashīsh, one of the most popular prayers on the Prophet in North Africa, Titus Burckhardt explains, "According to the Sufis, the blessing or effusion of graces (*ṣalāt*) that God heaps upon the Prophet is nothing other than the irradiation (*tajallī*) of the Divine Essence, which eternally pours into the cosmos, of which Muḥammad is the synthesis. To ask for the blessing of God on the Prophet is thus to conform with the divine act and intentionally to participate in it; also, tradition provides the assurance that whoever blesses the Prophet attracts upon himself the blessing of the entire universe."[28]

Furthermore, in his *Futūḥāt al-Ilāhiya* (*Divine Openings*), from which Shaykh Ibrahim and other Tijani authors quote extensively, the Moroccan Shādhilī Shaykh Ibn ʿAjība (d. 1809) expands on this perspective:

> In the invocation of blessings [*ṣalāt*] upon the Messenger of God, people are divided into three groups:
>
> First there are those who send blessings on his human form; these are the people of rational arguments and proofs. They envisage him in their hearts as they invoke blessings on him, and as they invoke more and more (with presence of mind), the noble image becomes firmer and firmer in their hearts. Thus they see him often in their dreams; and perhaps his noble spirit might take the form of his blessed body so that they see him in a waking state.
>
> Then there are those who invoke blessings on his illuminating spirit; these are the people of witnessing who travel the spiritual path. They invoke blessings on his light, which flows down from the Realm of Domination [*al-Jabarūt*], and they witness him most of the time, as long as they have presence of mind and vision.
>
> Then there are those who invoke blessings on his primordial light, which is the light of all lights; these are the people of spiritual firmness and mastery, they of direct witnessing and vision. The Prophet never leaves them for a moment, which is why Shaykh Abū'l ʿAbbās [al-Mursī (d. 1287)], may God be pleased with him, said, "Were the Messenger of God to leave me for the blink of an eye, I would no longer consider myself a Muslim." In saying this, he was alluding to his own firmness and mastery in the Presence, and his having come back to the station of subsistence [*al-baqāʾ*] wherein one witnesses the Intermediary [the Prophet]. Such people's thoughts roam through the World of Dominion [*al-Malakūt*], and their spirits are connected to the World of Domination [*al-Jabarūt*], and in them is synthesized

all that is lacking in others, as the Prophet said: "All prey is in the belly of the wild donkey." For the wild donkey is the fattest of all hunted animals, so that whoever catches one is as fortunate as he would be to catch them all. And the poet said:

> It is not beyond God in the least
> To combine all worlds in one man.[29]

Here, and in Abu Ibrahim's account, the blessing or prayer on the prophet (*Ṣalāh*) is equated with the divine manifestation (*tajallī*) or outpouring (*fayḍ*) of the Divine Light, which is simultaneously existence and knowledge. Thus the words of the *Ṣalāt al-Fātiḥ*—"O God blessings be upon [*ṣallī 'alā*] our lord, Muḥammad, the opener of what has been closed, and the seal of what has come before, the helper of the Truth, by the Truth, and the guide along your straight path, and upon his family, in accordance with the reality/right [*ḥaqq*] of his rank and his tremendous degree"—take on a deeper significance when applied to the Muḥammadan reality, and not just the historical person of the prophet. For example, one disciple told me that in this prayer, the phrase "our Lord Muḥammad" (*sayyidinā Muḥammad*) refers to the fact (to which the verse "The Prophet is closer to the believers than their own souls" [33:6] is also believed to allude) that the Prophet is our real self, our inner reality, of which our everyday identities are but a shell or husk.[30] In the same vein, "the opener of what has been locked" can be interpreted to refer to the ḥadīth in which God says, "I was a hidden treasure . . . ," in which case the Prophet is the key that opens the hidden treasure of the Divine Reality and made it manifest. "The seal of what came before" refers not only to the Prophet Muḥammad being the "seal of prophecy," but also to the fact that since it is the reality through which all things come into existence, it is also therefore that through which all things return to God. Thus, the Muḥammadan reality both "opens" and "seals" all of existence. This arc of creation and return to God is described in the Qur'anic language of the "straight path," on which the Prophet is the guide, since he both brings forth and returns multiplicity to the Divine Unity. This Muḥammadan reality is described as the "helper of the Truth by the Truth [*al-Ḥaqq*], because through it God brings everything into existence, and through it, everything is returned to God; but this does not imply duality, since this is all accomplished in and by God, the Truth."[31] The commentaries also gloss the first "Truth" as God, the unlimited Divine Reality, and the second "Truth" as the Prophet's message, Islam, the delimited religion or way of truth, which helps bring creation back to the first Truth.[32] In the prayer, the Prophet's "family" is commonly taken to refer to his spiritual progeny or successors, the saints. "The reality/right of his rank and his tremendous degree" (*ḥaqqa qadrihi wa miqdarihi'l-'aẓīm*) echoes the previously discussed verse of the Qur'an, "They did not measure God in accordance with the reality of His measure [*ḥaqqa qadrihi*] . . .

on the Day of Resurrection" (39:67), and the associated "ḥadith of transformations," a possible allusion to the Prophet occupying "the degree beyond degrees" or the "station of no station," in which everything is synthesized.[33]

Through reciting the *Ṣalāt al-Fātiḥ*, the disciple is supposed to realize or discover its inner meanings in him- or herself, just as Abu Ibrahim claimed to have done. This is equally true of the "Pearl of Perfection" (*Jawharat al-Kamāl*), the longer prayer on the Prophet, which Shaykh Aḥmad al-Tijānī is said to have been taught directly by the Prophet Muḥammad in a waking encounter. This prayer contains an even more elaborate description of the Muḥammadan reality, and is described as being so intimately connected with this reality that reciting it seven times before sleep is believed to ensure a dream of the Prophet, and reciting it twelve times daily is believed to evoke the spiritual presence of the Prophet and lead to waking visions of him. In his *Removal of Confusion*, Shaykh Ibrahim quotes the following statement from the prominent Moroccan Tijānī scholar Shaykh Aḥmad Skīraj (d. 1944): "Know that this noble invocation [the *Jawharat al-Kamāl*] is equal in content to all the wells of gnosis and secrets."[34]

The literal text of the prayer reads:

> O God, blessings and peace be upon the source/essence [*ʿayn*] of Divine Mercy,
> The realized ruby that encompasses the center of understandings and meanings,
> The light of the existentiated existents,
> The Adamic possessor of the Divine Truth,
> The brightest flash of lightning that fills the rain clouds of blessing
> That fill all the intervening seas and receptacles,
> Your radiant light with which you have filled Your creation,
> Encompassing all possible places,
> O God, blessings and peace be upon the source/essence [*ʿayn*] of the Truth from which are manifested the thrones of realities,
> The source/essence of the most correct/precious [*al-aqwām*] Knowledges,
> Your complete and most straight path,
> O God, blessings and peace be upon the dawning of the Truth by the Truth,
> The greatest treasure, Your outpouring from Yourself to Yourself,
> The encompassing talismanic light,
> May God bless him and his family, a blessing/prayer [*ṣalāt*] through which You make him Known to us.

This highly poetic prayer primarily employs the symbolism of light and that of water, and the commentarial tradition makes much of the fact that the word *ʿayn* can at once mean "source," "essence," and "spring" to describe the Muḥammadan reality as a spring or well that waters all of creation, as the channel through which Divine Mercy and existence flow to everything that exists.

The description of this reality as a "realized ruby" alludes to the famous verse of poetry "Muḥammadan is a man, but not like mortal men / For he is a ruby, and people are like stones. This ruby is "realized" or "realizing" (*mutaḥaqqiqa*) because it is perfect in its spiritual realization and it is the means through which spiritual realization is achieved. The image of the ruby suggests facets corresponding to the Divine Qualities and Attributes, and a transparency and purity through which the otherwise invisible can be seen—just as certain lenses permit one to look directly at the sun, the "realized ruby" allows the aspirant to "see" the Divine Essence.[35]

Echoing Qur'anic language, in the Islamic intellectual tradition, knowledge (*ʿilm*) is often defined as "the encompassing of the known by the knower" (*iḥāṭa al-maʿlūm bi'l-ʿālim*), and so the commentators describe the Muḥammadan reality, the "realized ruby," as both the point in which all knowledge is synthesized, and the circle that surrounds it—its own self-awareness.

The next line of the prayer introduces the symbol of light, and the commentaries explain that the light of the Prophet was taken from the light of the Divine Essence, and the light (which is here identical to existence) of existing things is taken from the Prophet. Using Shaykh Ibrahim's cinematic analogy, the Muḥammadan reality is like the projector that contains all of the images within itself, and whose light manifests them into visibility. Light is associated with knowledge, and the analogy between visibility and intelligibility is often used in Sufism and other Islamic intellectual traditions. Light is commonly defined as that which is visible in itself—that is, self-aware—and that which makes other things apparent/intelligible. The luminous imagery of this prayer is at once cosmological and epistemological, describing the noetic and ontological dimensions of the Muḥammadan reality.

The "flashing lightning in the clouds" is a stock image of Arabic poetry and the Qur'an that evokes the contrast of light and dark and the promise of rain, which is associated with Divine Mercy. In Sufi poetry, lightning is also commonly used as a symbol of the self-disclosure (*tajallī*) of the Divine Essence (*al-dhāt*) due to its blinding brilliance, power, and instantaneity. The image of the cloud recalls the "ḥadīth of the cloud," in which the Prophet responded to the question "Where was our Lord before He created the heavens and the earth" by saying "He was in the Cloud (*al-ʿAmāʾ*) neither above nor below which was any air (*hawāʾ*)."[36] In commenting on this ḥadīth, Ibn ʿArabi explains that the cosmos in its entirety takes shape within this cloud, which he identifies with the breath of the All-Merciful (*nafas al-Raḥmān*) and calls "the supreme *barzakh*," another name of the Muḥammadan reality.[37] Thus the evocative image of the "lightning in the rain clouds" describes the Muḥammadan reality as the light of creation within the realm of the unseen, within which all of creation is waiting to be manifest through Divine Mercy, like rain in dark clouds.[38] The commentators interpret the "intervening seas and receptacles" as the hearts of the Knowers, which are filled with ma'rifa according to their different capacities or, more generally, as the immutable entities (al-'ayān al-thābita) of everything—their realities in God's Knowledge before they come into existence.

The commentators gloss the "thrones of realities" as the spiritual realities of phenomenal things. The "throne" ('arsh) is a Qur'anic term that the Sufi tradition has generally taken to refer to the reality that encompasses the entire manifest universe, connecting it to higher divine realities. In this cosmology, the visible world is something akin to a chain of islands—the landscape "above the surface" of the water is just a projection of a much larger, hidden landscape "beneath the surface." In this perspective, the "thrones of the realities" would be the "hidden" roots of the islands that connect them to the ocean floor.

The "greatest treasure" alludes to the previously discussed ḥadīth qudsī "I was a hidden treasure and loved to be known . . . ," identifying this treasure of God's unmanifest knowledge of Himself with the Muḥammadan reality; and the "outpouring from Yourself to Yourself" alludes to the description of the Muḥammadan reality as the "most holy outpouring" (fayḍ al-aqdas) and "invisible self-disclosure" (tajallī al-ghayb)—the reflection of the Real in the mirror in which It contemplates Itself in Itself. The commentators gloss "talismanic light" as "hidden light," but given that the Arabic word for talisman (ṭilism) also means "protective seal," Ibn 'Arabi's description of the Perfect Human / Muḥammadan reality is also relevant here: "He is to the world what the ringstone is to the ring, which is the place of the signet and the mark with which the king sets a seal upon his treasures. . . . For through him, the Real protects his creation, as the seal protects those treasures. No one would dare open them so long as the king's seal was still upon them, unless by his leave. It is thus that he is entrusted with protecting the world."[39]

The closing invocation of the prayer—"a blessing/prayer (ṣalāh) through which You make him Known to us"—underscores the identification of the prayer on the prophet (Ṣalāt 'alā'l-Nabī) with the outpouring of knowledge (fayḍ). Since the Ṣalāt 'alā'l-Nabī is understood to be identical to the divine outpouring of light, existence, and knowledge, the very act of reciting these prayers is regarded as receiving and participating in this outpouring of knowledge. In fact, these prayers could even be said to be or contain this Knowledge, which is, in turn, identified with the Muḥammadan reality.[40]

Another important prayer in the process of tarbiya is known by its opening phrase—Allāhumma 'alayka mu'awallī ("Oh God, on You I depend")—and is repeated by disciples after each of the five daily prayers. The text of the prayer reads as follows:

"O God, on You I depend and in You I take refuge, and with you I seek shelter, and upon You I rely and in You I place my trust. Upon Your power and might I depend, and with all the conduits of Your rulings I am satisfied, And I am confident in the ubiquity of Your eternally self-sufficient dominion [*qayyūmiyyatika*] over everything, and the impossibility of anything, small or large, escaping your knowledge and overwhelming power, until the moment of my death."[41]

This prayer underscores the fact that it is God who is behind everything that happens to the disciple, and given this knowledge, one must be pleased with all that befalls one at the hands of God's human and nonhuman agents ("the conduits of Your rulings"). In a sense, this prayer boxes in the ego (*nafs*) of the disciple, preventing it from attributing causation to itself or anything else, and forcing it to realize the reality that everything is, and must be, in the all-powerful hands of God.

Thus, the very meanings of these prayers are supposed to facilitate the realization of the realities they describe and embody in language, not only through the daily contemplation of their meanings and symbolism, but also through the mysterious power of their words. That is, the prayers are believed to be efficacious even if the reciter does not understand their meanings. When I asked shaykhs and disciples if the *Ṣalāt al-Fātiḥ* would have the same effect if recited in French or English, most of them replied, "I don't think so," or "Of course not." Some explained that this was because it was impossible to exactly translate the prayer from one language to another, and most said something like "God had put *baraka* [blessing / sacred presence] into some words, and so when you say them, they have an effect."

In response to my question "Would the *Ṣalāt al-Fātiḥ* work in French?" Shaykh Māḥī Cissé expanded on this perspective, to the different levels of *dhikr* discussed in the previous section:

> That could also work, but [saying it in Arabic] is for the *baraka* of following the Prophet Muḥammad. Because many people when they come to Islam, they say, "There is no god but Allah," because they don't know how to say *lā ilāha illā Allāh*. But to say *lā ilāha illā Allāh*, Allah put some *baraka* in some things, so that *baraka* will go with those things all the time. But even if you say *lā ilāha illā Allāh* to the point where you don't say anything, but you just have it in your heart, that will work. So what you have in your heart working, that is not French, it is not Arabic, but what they call "numerical letters," "mental letters" "imaginal letters" [*al-ḥurūf al-raqmiyya, al-fikriyya, al-khayāliyya*]—all these things are working. So you can make the *Ṣalāt al-Fātiḥ* without even mentioning anything. Because *dhikr*, as Shaykh Ibrahim mentioned in his "Conversation with His Secret,"[42] his secret asked him, "O Ibrahim, are you a friend of God [*walī Allāh*]?" He said, "Yes, and my proof for

that is that I am close to Him [wālaytuhu] through the remembrance [dhikr] in my secret, in my spirit, inwardly and outwardly [qalbān wa qāliban]." Mentioning it with your tongue [qāliban] is only the beginning, but [the goal is] to get to the *dhikr* of *qalb* [heart], to get to *rūḥ* [spirit], to get to *sirr* [secret]—even beyond the *sirr*, you can get to the *khafī* [the hidden secret].[43]

## PERMISSION AND TRANSMISSION

However, the prayers and invocations of *tarbiya* do not simply work on their own, nor are they the only way Shaykh Ibrahim led people to *maʿrifa*. Ustadh Barham Diop told me a story about a time when he and Shaykh Ibrahim traveled to Ibadan, a city in southwestern Nigeria where Shaykh Ibrahim has a large number of disciples. A certain local judge (*qāḍī*) had heard that the disciples were prone to ecstatic utterances and came to scold Shaykh Ibrahim and denounce him for promoting heresy. When the judge arrived and began arguing with him, "Shaykh Ibrahim asked him question after question, like Socrates, until that judge had a *fatḥ* and began making the same ecstatic utterances he had come to criticize Shaykh Ibrahim about!"[44]

Moreover, the *shuyūkh* I interviewed emphasized the fact that the litanies of *tarbiya* cannot be practiced without being formally transmitted from a realized shaykh, quoting the following saying of Shaykh Ibrahim: "The secret is in the permission. The best thing that can happen to someone who attempts these litanies without authorization is that he or she escapes unharmed."[45] Shaykh Ibrahim also wrote, "It is well known among the people of the spiritual path that the remembrance which benefits its practitioner is the one received from perfected shaykhs."[46] Thus, on their own, the litanies and practices of *tarbiya* do not lead to the radical transformations of consciousness described above. In fact, Shaykh Aḥmad al-Tijānī is said to have answered a disciple's question "'Is the benefit of the Tijānī litanies from the words themselves, or because of you?' He said, 'It is because of me.'"[47]

Similarly, when I asked Barham Diop how Shaykh Ibrahim devised or discovered these litanies (*awrād*) of *tarbiya*, he told me, "The litanies were known, they can be found in the books. It was because Shaykh Ibrahim was the possessor of the *fayḍa* that his *tarbiya* was so effective."[48] Thus the litanies of *tarbiya* can be understood as a means of conveying the flow of spiritual realization from master to disciple. In his *Removal of Confusion*, Shaykh Ibrahim Niasse quotes the following passage:

> Success will either come upon him suddenly, or it will take him by surprise. Allah the Exalted will favor him by removing the veil from his heart and he will become

united with the spirit of the Shaykh or that of the Prophet.... Like this, his spiritual training [*tarbiya*] comes by the outpouring (*istifāḍa*) from one of them [Shaykh Tijani or the Prophet] or both of them together. That is the grace of God, which he gives to whom He wills; and God is the owner of infinite grace (57:21). This is the meaning of what is found in the *Jawāhir al-Maʿānī* in regards to visualizing the presence of the Shaykh or the Prophet while performing the litanies.⁴⁹

The prominent shaykha Seyyida Diarra Ndiaye likened this outpouring to an electric current: "When a disciple comes to me for *tarbiya*, I feel something like electricity. With some disciples it is stronger, and other times it is less, just as the electric current can sometimes surge and sometimes be weaker, depending on the zeal [*himma*] and the capacity of the disciple."⁵⁰ This almost-sensory/physical, nondiscursive transmission of knowledge from one person to another finds its precedent in accounts of the Prophet's *miʾrāj* or heavenly ascent, where he was said to have received the totality of all possible human knowledge directly from God. Ibn ʿArabi writes, "The Prophet said, 'When God struck His palm between my shoulders, I came to know the knowledge of the ancients and the later folk' through that placing of the palm. So through that striking God gave him the knowledge he mentioned. By this knowledge he means knowledge of God. Knowledge of other than God is a waste of time (*taḍyīʿ al-waqt*), since God created the cosmos only for knowledge of Him. More specifically, this is the case with what is called 'mankind and jinn,' since He stated clearly that He created them to worship Him."⁵¹ Shaykh Babacar N'diaye commented on this account, explaining that the Prophet then transmitted some of this knowledge to all of his followers, and some of it he only transmitted to his closest companions through initiation (*talqīn*),⁵² which is the origin and source of Sufi initiations today.

In the introduction to his edition of *al-Sirr al-Akbar*, Maigari summarizes Shaykh Ibrahim's description of this process of initiation (*talqīn*) and the central role that Shaykh Aḥmad al-Tijānī plays therein:

> When the Tijani disciple reaches this, he puts himself in submission in the hands of his shaykh *murabbī* [his spiritual master] who is the representative of Shaykh al-Tijānī in the sensory world. For Shaykh al-Tijānī is his [the disciple's] spiritual trainer in reality, and he is with him always, whenever he [the disciple] remembers him [Shaykh al-Tijānī] in his heart ... So the initiator cannot initiate anyone unless he has already been effaced [*inṭimās*] in Shaykh al-Tijānī, that is, annihilated in him, from the point of view that he sees himself as being the same as Shaykh al-Tijānī. So in light of this effacement, Shaykh al-Tijānī is the one who initiates the disciple himself without an intermediary between them.... The power [of the

initiator] comes from the degree to which he is annihilated in Shaykh al-Tijānī at the moment of initiation and before it, and after it. For the goal of the disciple is none other than Shaykh al-Tijānī.[53]

Shaykh Ibrahim then goes on to explain that since Shaykh Tijānī is the real initiator, those who do the initiation are only his representatives in the sensory world, and so if these initiators leave the *ṭarīqa* or lose their state of annihilation, it doesn't affect the disciple's relationship with Shaykh Tijānī and the flow of initiatory power from him since "he is the one behind the veils of *sanad* [chains of transmission]."[54]

However, since the power of the initiation is understood to be connected to the degree of annihilation of the initiator in Shaykh Aḥmad al-Tijānī (and the Prophet and God), not all shaykhs and not all initiations are considered equal. Shaykh Māḥī Cissé likened this to studying the same subject with two different professors—those who study with the better professor will learn more:

The *wird* is the same, but the shaykhs are not the same, so the more *baraka* your shaykh has, the more *baraka* you're going to get—if you follow him! Because some people, they follow, maybe a small shaykh, and get more than the other people who follow a big shaykh, because maybe these people, they follow, while those people, they don't follow. But the *fatḥ* of a disciple depends on the *fatḥ* of his shaykh and his degree of annihilation in the presence of the Messenger and of God.[55] That is why Shaykh Ibrahim said, "Before you chose any shaykh for *tarbiya*, be sure that he is a *murabbī* [one who can dispense *tarbiya*] and that there isn't anyone better qualified to give *tarbiya* than him."[56]

This theme of annihilation features prominently in accounts of the beginning of the *fayḍa*, the special outpouring that disciples of Shaykh Ibrahim claim as the secret behind the power of his *tarbiya*. In many accounts, the *fayḍa* first became manifest in Kaolack during a *mawlid* celebration at the house of Shaykh Ibrahim's father, 'Abdallāh Niasse.[57] During the proceedings, Shaykh Ibrahim suddenly stood up and said, "Those who want anything from Shaykh al-Tijānī, know that it is me! Come to me, I am Shaykh al-Tijānī," or "This is the hand of God, this is the hand of the Prophet, this is the hand of Shaykh al-Tijānī."[58] The taking of the hand as a pact (*baʻya*) is a common form of initiation in Sufi orders, which takes its precedent from the pact of ʻAqaba, in which a delegation from Medina swore their allegiance to the Prophet by taking his hand. The Qurʼan famously refers to this event in the verse, "Those who swear allegiance to you [Muḥammad], swear allegiance to God. The hand of God is above their hands" (48:10). Commenting on this verse, Shaykh Ibrahim explains that the Prophet's hand is

God's hand because of the former's total annihilation in the latter.⁵⁹ So the outpouring of initiatory power (*walāya*) and Knowledge (*ma'rifa*), which constitutes the process of *tarbiya*, is made possible by the annihilation of the initiator in Shaykh Ibrahim, his annihilation in Shaykh Tijani, his annihilation in the Prophet, and his annihilation in God. These figures, as well as the disciple, all play an active role in the process of spiritual realization.

Thus, *tarbiya* is understood in a manner quite different from that of modern discourses about meditation or mindfulness or other "self-help" approaches to spiritual "realization." *Tarbiya* (like other processes of spiritual realization in Sufism in general) is premised on a set of social and spiritual relationships, of which, from a certain perspective, the performance of meditative practices are but a manifestation. When I asked K. S. how he joined the *ṭarīqa*, he told me his story, but then added:

> Officially you are not considered Tijani until you have taken the *wird*; it is a precondition. But a person can consider him- or herself Tijani if he or she feels deeply inside that he or she shares something with Shaykh Aḥmad Tijānī, if he or she recognizes him- or herself in the writings of Shaykh Aḥmad Tijānī, the ideas of Shaykh Aḥmad Tijānī. So, there are two ways to join the *ṭarīqa*. The official one is that you take the *wird* from a Tijani scholar who has the authorization to give you the *wird*, and the second way is more spiritual, and it is something you deeply feel inside.... The *wird* is just a concrete way to join the *ṭarīqa*, but the prerequisite is to be sincere, to feel directly connected to Shaykh Aḥmad Tijānī. The *wird* is something material; it is just a second stage. But first you have to have a strong belief in the *ṭarīqa*, in Shaykh Aḥmad Tijānī, in the ideology, in the framework in general of the Tijāniyya, and after [that], taking the *wird* is something obvious, it is just a result of this.⁶⁰

From this perspective, the performance of litanies and exercises that lead to *ma'rifa* can be understood as manifestations of these spiritual relationships or connections, and/or as a means of establishing these relationships in time and space. This may be difficult for some Western-educated readers to understand, but this may say more about the limitations of contemporary academic paradigms than it does about the coherence of these Sufi ideas. As Shahzad Bashir notes in his article on the practice of *dhikr* in fourteenth-century Central Asia:

> The ultimate purpose of following the Sufi path is to cultivate a particular form of human religious subjectivity that conjoins many different aspects of human existence.... The comparison between *dhikr* and meditation is instructive for

highlighting the fact that our commonsensical modern understanding of meditation is also premised on a particular conception of the human person that is far from a human universal valid across cultures and time periods. The idea that individual practice is localizable to a single person rests on the notion of individual sovereignty and is connected to a particular conception of rights and responsibilities that has acquired an aura of universality and inevitability only since the worldwide spread of modern, Western ideas. The modern concept of meditation is premised on this base understanding, which is why it resembles, but cannot be interchangeable with, the place of *dhikr* within a different system such as Sufi thought and practice. . . . Examining meditation in the light of presumptions coming from *dhikr* highlights meditation's connections to modern forms of human subjectivity that are ingrained in the way we think and act, but are not always easily visible.[61]

In the contemporary practice of *tarbiya*, God, the Prophet, Shaykh Tijani, Shaykh Ibrahim, and his disciples are all active participants in this process of cultivating "a particular form of subjectivity" and its associated mode of knowledge (*ma'rifa*).

## FOLLOWING THE PROPHET

This ideal "human religious subjectivity" is identified with the Prophet to such an extent that disciples and shaykhs alike usually described the process of acquiring *ma'rifa* simply as "following the Prophet." As the Prophet is reported to have said, "Were it not for the excess of your talking and the turmoil in your hearts, you would see what I see and hear what I hear."[62] The mode of being identified with the Prophet as the Perfect Human (*al-Insān al-Kāmil*) is a particular possibility among many possibilities, but for the Sufis it is like the point that contains the whole circle. It is somewhat akin to "the Aleph" from Borges's short story of the same name: the point in space that contains all other points, and from which everything in the universe can be seen from every angle, simultaneously, and without confusion or distortion.[63] Thus, following the Prophet "in words, deeds, and states" is the best way to cultivate this most comprehensive and complete mode of being/knowing.

While some Western-educated readers may find it confusing as to what fasting during a certain month, praying in a particular way, avoiding certain types of foods, or wearing certain kinds of clothes have to do with acquiring knowledge, the fact that the Prophet has done so makes it epistemically relevant. From this perspective, the many disparate things of the visible or physical world are so many phenomena or appearances of the spiritual realities, which are in turn manifestations of the Divine Essence throughout the various levels of reality. Thus actions in the physical or sensory level of reality can affect or, more precisely, are connected with[64] actions or transformations on higher levels of reality. As Shaykh Ibrahim writes, "The movement of the apparent things [*zawāhir*] is only realized by the movement of the secret things [*sarā'ir*]."[65] Thus, one's outward actions both come from, and affect, the heart, spirit, and intellect. These different levels of being each have their own characteristics and qualities, like different layers of the atmosphere. In the physical world of everyday time and space, one thing cannot be another, and things are bound in forms. This is less so in the imaginal world, where opposites can combine and forms are more fluid. The higher spiritual or intelligible worlds are those of pure meanings without forms, and about the inscrutable Divine Essence nothing can be said. Ibn 'Arabi often likens these presences or levels of reality to a horn or cone, in which the physical or sensible level is the most narrow, and the higher levels are wider and more expansive.

I mention this here because many in modern societies seem to feel a strong impulse or desire to escape the constraints of formal, outward religious practice in the name of transcending it (i.e., to be "spiritual but not religious"). This idea is completely alien to the Tijani Sufi milieu (and mainstream Sufism in general), in which the formal is transcended through formal spiritual practice. From this perspective, one can't follow more than one way of life or prescribed law (*sharī'a*), because this physical level of reality does not permit the union of opposites; however, one can transcend these apparent contradictions on the ontologically higher level of the heart, which can potentially be receptive to all forms of belief.

On the physical and mental levels, forms are inescapable. If you do one thing at a certain time that means you can't do another thing at the same time; if you think about one thing, that means that you can't think about another thing at the same time. However, the higher levels of reality, which do not partake in these limitations, can be accessed and integrated into these lower levels, through the doors of certain forms. As the Perfect Human, the model par excellence of the integration of the various levels of reality, the Prophet is considered to embody and represent the best of these forms that lead to levels of existence beyond form, and so can be said to contain all forms. If existence is envisioned as a multistory building with a rooftop terrace, then the Prophet is the staircase connecting all of its levels; if it is a mountain, then he is the stream that flows from the snowy summit to the grassy plains; if an underground cave, as in Plato's allegory, he is the tunnel that leads to the world above, and back again. This is why the practice of following the Prophet's example, often in minute detail, is given such importance, even (especially) among advanced Sufi masters. Restricting oneself to the particular form of the Prophet at one level is understood to paradoxically free one from all formal restrictions on other levels, just as the practice of turning in a single direction to pray is supposed to lead to the vision of God "wheresoever one turns." The purpose of following the *sharīʿa* of the Prophet Muḥammad outwardly is the realization of the inward states of the Muḥammadan, the Perfect Human, whose heart is receptive to all forms, and whose reality is identical with their very essence. From this perspective, the *sharīʿa* is the manifestation of this ideal mode of being in the plane of outward actions. As the Sufi saying attributed to the Prophet goes, "The *sharīʿa* is my speech, the *ṭarīqa* is my acts, and the *ḥaqīqa* is my state."[66] This is why Shaykh Ibrahim said, "The quickest way to achieve Knowledge of God is by following the Messenger of God in his statements, actions, states, and character, and in fulfilling the rights of God publicly and privately, having absolute sincerity with God without any worldly or otherworldly motives."[67]

In the *Jawāhir al-Maʿānī* the following account of "following the Prophet" is attributed to Shaykh Aḥmad al-Tijānī:

> Following the prophet is a sign of love of the servant for his Lord, and the servant's recompense for the beauty of following the Messenger is God's love for him. This love emerges from the servant's awareness of God's blessings on him, both outward and inward. The power of that love is in accordance to the degree of this awareness. Among the greatest awareness that the servant can have of the blessings of God upon him is the blessing of him being connected to Him through love and Knowledge and following His beloved. The foundation of this is a light that God casts into the heart of His servant. When that light illumines the heart, it reveals its essence to it [the heart], so he [the servant] sees in himself what corresponds to it of perfections and beauties, by which his zeal and determination are strengthened, and the darkness of his soul and nature are dissipated, for light and darkness cannot come together without one of them driving out the other. This happens to the spirit when it is between awe and intimacy with the beloved. And in accordance with this following, love and being loved are bestowed together. The affair is not complete without both of them.
>
> For what is important is not [just] for you to love God, but rather, for God to love you, and you will not be beloved unless you follow His beloved outwardly and inwardly, confirming his reports [*khabar*], obeying his commands, answering his call, preferring him, leaving aside the rulings of anyone other than him for his own rulings, leaving aside the love of and obedience to anyone else in creation in order to love and obey him alone. If you are not like this, then you do not have anything. So consider His saying, "Then follow me, God will love you" [3:31]. Following this Prophet is the nobility of the life of the hearts, and the light of the insights, and the healing of the breasts, the joy of the spirits, the intimacy of the isolated, and

the guide of the bewildered.... Among the signs of love for him [the Prophet] is love of his *sunna* and the reading of his ḥadīths. So if anyone in whose heart the sweetness of faith has entered hears a word from among the words of God or the speech of His Messenger, his spirit, soul, and heart absorb it. And when his heart and secret are illumined, waves of realization [*taḥqīq*] wash over him and proofs are manifest to him while he drinks in the affection and love he has for his beloved. Nothing could be more refreshing.[68]

Commenting on the same verse of the Qur'an (3:31), Shaykh Ibrahim similarly connects the practice of following the Prophet with love and spiritual transformation:

Say, if you love God, then follow me, and God will love you. [3:31]

This is an indication that whoever loves God will follow the Messenger of God. God has linked obeying him with obeying His messenger. "Whosoever obeys the Messenger has obeyed God." He made the sign of love of God obeying the Messenger of God. It is clear that whoever loves someone loves all of his beloveds and everything associated with him. Whoever is in love with his beloved even loves those who dress like him. When his love for Layla grew strong, Majnūn saw a dog in the desert and clothed him with a robe. When asked about it, he responded, "Truly, My eyes saw him once in Layla's neighborhood." Thus, whoever loves God, God's beloved is the Messenger of God—"If you love God, then follow me, and God will love you"—so whoever loves God, then let him follow the Messenger. The one who claims to love God and yet leaves aside the way of the Messenger, he is a false claimant.

Had your Love been sincere, you would have obeyed it
For the lover is obedient to whom he loves

The following of the Prophet through all of one's words and actions is the most elevated means [*wasīla*] that the servant can take to arrive at the presence of God. ... Whoever follows the Prophet finds the love of God, and when God loves his servant, He is him. "My servant does not cease to draw near to me through supererogatory works until I love him, and when I love him, I am him."[69]

Because the Prophet is understood as being totally annihilated in God, as having the most complete knowledge of God possible, following his example inwardly and outwardly is believed to lead to the same state. Practically, following the Prophet means following those who are annihilated in him, his representatives in one's own time and place—in this case, the shaykhs of the Tijani order. These states of annihilation, in which there is no distinction between subject and object, are only possible given the noetic/existential identity of the knower and the known, the annihilated and the "annihilated in." Thus, this perspective implies that subjectivity and consciousness are not separate, self-contained individual realities, but rather more like the tributaries of a river flowing into an ocean—distinct on one level, connected or identical on another.

Thus "following the Prophet" is a journey that is at once intellectual and existential, ethical and mystical. The fruit of this work is *ma'rifa*—certain, direct, existential knowledge of God, of self, and the intermediate realities of the Prophet and shaykhs. This process is described as a "voyage of the heart" (*sayr al-qalb*) through the world of meaning,[70] the heart being the instrument of this special and most important form of knowledge. In the same vein, Shaykh Ibrahim quotes the following verses of poetry, describing this "eye of the heart":

> My Beloved graciously manifested Himself
> What a great honor he has shown me
> Making himself known to me, until I became certain
> That I am seeing him overtly, without fantasy
> And in every state, I see Him continuously
> On the mountain of my heart, where He speaks to me
> In this embrace, there is no union
> And no separation, He is exalted above either of these
> How is it possible for the likes of me to contain the likes of Him?
> How can the tiny star be compared to the full moon?
> But I happened to see him in the purity of my secret
> There I saw Perfection, too glorious to be divided
> Just as the full moon shows its face
> In the still pond, although it shines high in the heavens.[71]

## HOW IS *MA'RIFA* VERIFIED?

Now that we have discussed *ma'rifa*, and the ways in which it is acquired, we turn to the question of verification. How do you know if someone else has *ma'rifa*? How can you tell if you yourself have acquired this knowledge? Given the close association of *ma'rifa* with certainty and the unique experiences of *fanā'* and *baqā'*, the latter question may appear trivial. However, as we will see, it is one that Shaykh Ibrahim (and the Sufi tradition in general) addresses in a nontrivial manner.

## Verification of Others' Knowledge

Given the deeply inward and personal nature of *ma'rifa* (Knowledge), it is difficult to imagine how, under "normal" circumstances, another person's Knowledge could be verified with confidence. As several disciples pointed out:

> It's difficult to say who has *ma'rifa* and who doesn't. Some people speak well, and so they seem to have *ma'rifa*, but you never know. They could just be repeating what they learned in books, what they heard from other people.... Because someone, you can hear him speak, and he speaks very well, as if he knows many things, but maybe hasn't actually experienced them.... But you go off of what you hear from him and what you see from him—does he pray, is he pious, does he have a good character—but it's difficult to judge. He can talk well and have nothing, or he can say nothing and have a great thing. You can guess, but you can't tell. As for the shaykhs, they can tell, but I don't quite know how.[72]

However, the shaykhs who administer *tarbiya* examine their disciples to determine when they have finished the process and attained *ma'rifa*, and may even give certain disciples permission to initiate others. Shaykh Māḥī Cissé compared this to taking a disciple into the ocean and teaching him how to swim. Once the shaykh is satisfied that the disciple can swim, he gives him permission to go swim in the ocean of *ma'rifa* on his own.[73]

As mentioned above, disciples told me that their shaykhs sometimes test disciples who seem to have experienced annihilation by asking them questions, such as "Who are you? Where are you? What do you see?" Disciples in a state of annihilation typically give answers such as "I am God, I am in God, there is only God." One prominent shaykha told me that when she thinks a disciple is not fully in the state of annihilation, or is faking the state, she takes a lighter or a match and holds it close to the disciple. Disciples in the state of annihilation perceive the fire, themselves, and everything as God, and so do not flinch, while those not yet in the state respond normally (i.e., flinching from the flame) and are told to continue with their *tarbiya*.[74] When I asked Shaykh Māḥī Cissé if and how he can tell if someone else has *ma'rifa*, he responded:

> If I talk with him, I know. Like the people who take *tarbiya* from me, sometimes they come, you talk to them, and they don't know. They just hear some words and want to get it [i.e., approval that they've completed *tarbiya*]. So you tell them, "Go back, go make your *dhikr* until you have *yaqīn* [certainty]." In the truth, there is

force. Words of truth have a taste, a flavor, a scent. Just as this perfume has a scent, the truth also has a scent.... If you know it, then you know it. It's like music, if you know or you've studied music, or been exposed to music, when you hear music, you'll know if that music is correct or not. Some things you know, and you can describe how you know them, and other things you know, but you cannot describe how you know them. Some things we do not have the right to describe, because they are secret, and a secret revealed is not a secret.[75]

K. S. also compared the recognition of a fellow *ʿārif* to smelling a scent or fragrance:

> It is like a fragrance—you can see if someone is very advanced in the process. If a person of that kind is about to meet another person of that kind, for example, you are in CODESRIA [an academic center in Dakar], and that person is in Tambacounda [a city in eastern Senegal] or Mermoz [a neighborhood of Dakar just north of CODESRIA], you can see his light, coming, going in this way or going in that way. And sometimes it is like a fragrance. But sometimes you can have the strong feeling that the one you are seeing is you, and you are him or her. And you were talking about *fanāʾ*, and I said that it is a process of knowing space and time; it is also a process of unification, and in *fanāʾ* there isn't any male and female, man and woman, there isn't a single thing. How do recognize someone with *maʿrifa*? If you see the person you know that he is you and you are him, you won't be able to make or to imagine two different entities—you will just see him as a part of you. Maybe he is higher or lower, so that you go to him in order to get high, or he comes to you in order to get high, and it is something complementary. But of course you will be able to know him. But it is easier for the person who is near the completion of merging—it is easier for that person to feel, to recognize someone who has just reached the ocean.[76]

Thus, it seems to take an *ʿārif* to know an *ʿārif*, and *maʿrifa* recognizes *maʿrifa*. However, as K. S. mentions, it is easier for the greater to recognize the lesser than the other way around. A large portion of Ibn ʿArabi's oeuvre is devoted to his discussion of different kinds of saints and possessors of various degrees of *maʿrifa*, and the signs by which they can be recognized. Just as one of the highest levels of *maʿrifa* is the ability to recognize the Real in all of its manifestations, the ability to recognize and correctly judge the sanctity and *maʿrifa* of others is among the characteristics of the most advanced of Sufi masters. From Ibn ʿArabi's descriptions, this appears to be due in large part to these masters' prior experience of the states and stations that they then recognize in others.[77]

### Levels of Knowledge (*Ma'rifa*)

Despite the exalted rhetoric surrounding them, completing *tarbiya* and attaining *ma'rifa* does not necessarily free one from all moral and epistemic failings. Rather, it seems to radically change one's perspective on these limitations and shortcomings by breaking one's identification with them. Moreover, as alluded to above, different people are believed to have different capacities for *ma'rifa*, and what the shaykh does through the process of *tarbiya* is help the aspirant realize his or her capacity for *ma'rifa*. *Ma'rifa* itself may be formless and unlimited, like water, but its human containers are limited—some more than others. From a temporal perspective, these limitations can be stretched through following the example of the Prophet, but from an atemporal perspective, the degree to which one can follow the Prophet (and therefore achieve annihilation in him) is the actual extent of one's limitations.

Thus, several of Shaykh Ibrahim's writings and interviews with disciples describe the experience of *fanā'* (annihilation), the completion of *tarbiya*, and the initial acquisition of *ma'rifa* as an "initiation"—a beginning, not an end. As quoted above, Shaykh Ibrahim likened it to the beginning of a perpetual "journey of the heart" (*sayr al-qalb*); Shaykh Māḥī Cissé likened it to swimming the ocean of *ma'rifa*; and others pointed out that even the Prophet, who was given the most perfect knowledge of God possible, was commanded to pray, "My Lord, increase me in knowledge!" (20:114). The journey of *ma'rifa* is thus never ending, and all the disciples I interviewed who had completed *tarbiya* expressed a desire to "know more" and "go deeper"; they admitted they had much to learn from senior or more advanced Knowers. This, in part, explains the many conflicts, disagreements, and differences of opinion among members of Shaykh Ibrahim's community who are widely regarded as Knowers (*'urafā'*): from a certain perspective, *ma'rifa* has degrees and some know more than others; and from another perspective, *ma'rifa* manifests itself differently in different contexts, and so forms that contradict each other on lower levels of Knowledge/being can be united at higher, supra-formal levels of Knowledge/being.

### Verification of One's Own Knowledge

But how do you know that you know? How do you know if you yourself have *ma'rifa*? Many disciples answered this question by insisting "If you know, then you know that you know. And if you don't, then you don't." But is it possible to have *ma'rifa* and not know it? Some disciples appealed to the atemporal perspective that *ma'rifa* opens up in order to answer this question in the affirmative. One disciple, who wished to remain anonymous, told me, "Some people have great *ma'rifa* inside of them, but they don't know it yet. They haven't realized who they are yet, but some people can see it in them now. When they realize it, then they will know who they are, what they have inside of them."[78] Abu Ibrahim held that "*maʿrifa* is always certain, but the question is whether or not what you are thinking is really *maʿrifa* or just an idea or Satan messing with you."[79]

In one of his more unique compositions, Shaykh Ibrahim discusses these issues in the form of a conversation with his secret (*sirr*) or "inner" self:

"DIALOGUE AND DISCUSSION"
WHAT OCCURRED BETWEEN ME AND MY SECRET [*sirr*] FROM MY LORD

He said, "O Ibrahim, have you arrived at God [*wāṣil ilā Allāh*]?"

I said, "Yes. My proof for that is my Knowledge by Him through the reality of certainty [*ḥaqq al-yaqīn*]. And God is too great for anything to be attached to Him or separated from Him."

Then He said, "Are you a friend of God [*walī Allāh*]?"

I said, "Yes, and my proof for that is that I am close to Him [*wālaytuhu*] through the remembrance [*dhikr*] in secret, in spirit, inwardly and outwardly [*qalbān wa qāliban*], and He is close to me [*wālānī*] through the facilitation of my affairs, being connected to me both outwardly and inwardly."

Then He said, "Are you a Knower by God [*ʿārif biLlāh*]?"

I said, "Yes, and my proof for that is my witnessing [*shuhūdī*] of the Essence [*al-ʿayn*] in otherness [*al-ghayr*] and my realization [*taḥqīqī*] by my Lord in each entification [*mutaʿayyun*] without entification [*bilā taʿayyun*] and my submission to His decree and my satisfaction with all of His judgments, and that my master and support and example who trained me in the Sufi way, al-Ḥajj ʿabd Allāh [Niasse] said to me, 'You are a Knower [*ʿārif*],' and that the master of the latter [al-Ḥajj ʿabd Allāh], Aḥmad Baddi, likewise testified to him [that he was a Knower], and likewise the notable *khalīfa*, the Ḥassān [poet] of the *ṭarīqa*, Muḥammad ibn Sayyidayn, his father, likewise testified to him [Aḥmad Baddi], and likewise Shaykh Muḥammad al-Ḥāfiẓ [al-Shinqiṭī] testified to him [ibn Sayyidayn], and likewise did the seal, al-Tijānī, bear witness to him [Muḥammad al-Ḥāfiẓ], and likewise did the master of existence [the Prophet] bear witness to him [Shaykh al-Tijānī] of that and his sealhood [*khatmiyya*] and concealment [*katmiyya*] and that is confirmed by God because he [the Prophet] did not speak out of caprice [35:3].

Then he said, "Are you among the poles [*aqṭāb*]?"

I said, "I do not know, but I heard the enraptured ones say as much to themselves. Maybe they saw in the fleeting state [*ḥāl*] of a second and witnessed what is to come."

Then he said, "Do you see the Messenger of God while awake and asleep like some of the spiritual heroes [*rijāl*]?"

I said, "I hope for that from God. But I love him and I know him with such a knowledge that were I to perceive him while alive and accompany him, it would not increase me in those two [my knowledge and love of him]. All praise be to God."

Then he said, "Do you want to meet him?"

I said, "For me, I do not want it. For if I want, I want to not want; for whatever the Willer [*al-Murīd*] wills, that is what I want."[80]

Then he said, "Do you know the Secret Greatest Name?"

I said, "The Names—all of them are great to me."

Then he said, "I testify that you are among the great men among the Knowers to whom the travelers are drawn and whom the leaders salute. So, happiness is for he who keeps your company and thinks well of you, and woe to he who opposes you because of criticism. And he departed and wished me well. Praise be to God."

I appreciated our dialogue and I set some of it down here for the beloveds.

Written by Ibrāhīm ibn al-Ḥajj ʿabd Allāh al-Tijānī [Niasse] in Kosi 1349 Hijri [1930–31 CE][81]

Among other interesting points, in this work Shaykh Ibrahim offers himself three proofs of his *maʿrifa*: his recognition of the undelimited Divine Essence, the Real, in the delimited forms of the world; his compliance with God's religious commands and his contentment with the divine rulings of fate; and finally, the testimony of the Knowers in his initiatory chain, going back to the Prophet and God. Thus the verification of one's own *maʿrifa* can have an important social or intersubjective dimension.

Disciples often mentioned the discussions they had with one another and with their shaykhs as an important means of "comparing notes" or coming to understand and find the words to describe certain experiences and intuitions. The *gammus*, other organized gatherings (such as classes with shaykhs, *dahiras*, or student group meetings), informal gatherings on Fridays after the *wazīfa*, or dinner parties with friends and family often provide the occasion for lengthy, usually nocturnal discussions about *maʿrifa*, related ideas and insights, and the different states and stages of the spiritual journey. Disciples described how satisfying it was to hear another disciple or shaykh confirm, through their own similar experiences or through quotations from the works of Shaykh Ibrahim, something they had "deeply felt" or "discovered" on their own.

Sidi Inaya Niang told me that Shaykh Ibrahim used to encourage his disciples to get together to discuss these matters as a means of perfecting their spiritual states and knowledge. For example, Sidi Inaya told me how his father had entered a station he called the *maqām al-Mahdiyya*, where he seemed to have a presentiment of everything that happened around him, and everything seemed to be obedient to his will: "Because of this, he wondered, 'Could I be the Mahdi?' He went to talk to Shaykh Ibrahim about it, who didn't answer his question directly, but instead told him to talk to three of his friends who were also disciples of Shaykh Ibrahim. When they all sat down together, they realized they were all in the same station, and they laughed about it. They were better able to understand this station and what comes after it."[82] Sidi Inaya also drew on the "scientific method" to describe the verification of *ma'rifa*, positing that the experiences of insight associated with *ma'rifa* can be confirmed by repetition under the same conditions for oneself, and by observing its reoccurrence under the same conditions in others.

Disciples with more extensive formal Islamic education often cited the Qur'an and ḥadīth as the sources to which they turned to verify their own knowledge—both in terms of the confirmation these texts provided for their experiences and ideas, and through the new levels of meaning of these texts that *ma'rifa* revealed to them. The deeper experience and understanding of the ritual prayer and Tijānī litanies, as well as the poetry and prose works of Shaykh Ibrahim, also served to confirm the attainment of *ma'rifa* for many of these Arabophone disciples (and some non-Arabophones as well).

At one point in his own Qur'anic commentary, Shaykh Ibrahim seems to take the apophatic position mentioned at the beginning of chapter 2, that "real *ma'rifa* is the inability to attain or perceive *ma'rifa*." Commenting on the verse, "We offered the trust to the heavens and the earth and the mountains, but they refused to bear it and feared it, and man bore it. Verily he is tyrannical, ignorant" (33:72), Shaykh Ibrahim interprets this "trust" to refer to man's vicegerency (*khilāfa*) of God in creation, explaining that only man could bear this burden, since only he combines the spiritual and the physical. He provides two interpretations for the second part of the verse—one obvious, negative interpretation, and one more subtle, positive interpretation:

> For were it not for his tyranny, he would not have disobeyed, and were it not for his ignorance, he would not have forgotten.[83] [He was] "tyrannical" in that he transgressed the bounds of mortal humanity [*bashariyya*] in order to be characterized by the attributes of Lordship. And [he was] "ignorant," meaning aware of God [*ārifāⁿ biLlāh*] to the point that he was ignorant of all other than He, and [this is] the ignorance of the core of the Essence. Ignorance of God, as Shaykh Aḥmad al-Tijānī says, is of two kinds: ignorance of the rank of Divinity, which makes its possessor worthy of perpetual dwelling in the Fire; and the ignorance of the core of the Essence, in terms of what It is in Itself, which necessitates the perpetual

dwelling of its possessor in the Garden. For whoever is ignorant of the rank of Divinity is an infidel, while whoever is ignorant of the core of the Essence after he has arrived there, he finds that "his inability to perceive It is his perception of it."[84] His ignorance of the reality of the core of Its Essence is his knowledge of It. And so this is the vicegerent [*khalīfa*], tyrannical and ignorant. That is, having transgressed the bounds of mortal humanity, being characterized by the attributes of Lordship, and ignorant of the core of the Essence because it has no end, and he only reaches it after having lost himself. "O Lord, how can one reach you? Leave yourself and come."[85] If you leave yourself before coming, then how can you know It? There is no one there to know it. This is the ignorance which is the utmost limit of ignorance, and it is a station of praise from this perspective.[86]

The editor notes that in this passage Shaykh Ibrahim paraphrases a statement of Shaykh Aḥmad al-Tijānī in which he described this second ignorance as "the purity of faith and the perfection of *maʿrifa*."[87] As with *tawba* in *The Three Stages of Religion*, from this perspective, the inability to verify one's own *maʿrifa* is associated with its perfection, since "none knows God but God."

Thus, for the community of Shaykh Ibrahim, *maʿrifa* is verified in and of itself, since it itself is the reality of certainty; it is verified through the confirmation of other confirmed Knowers, and the distinct intellectual content of *maʿrifa* can be confirmed through recourse to the Qurʾan, ḥadīth, and other authoritative texts of the *ṭarīqa*; personal, "empirical" testing; and consultation with other Knowers. However, from another perspective, *maʿrifa* is impossible for a person, as such, to attain, let alone verify, because it presupposes the annihilation or "leaving behind" of one's self.

CONCLUSION

In this section, we have seen how Shaykh Ibrahim Niasse and his disciples have creatively drawn on the rich epistemological tradition of Sufism to both realize and describe *maʿrifa*. In short, *maʿrifa* refers to the direct, existential knowledge of the Real / the Truth (*al-Ḥaqq*), achieved through annihilation (*fanāʾ*) and subsistence (*baqāʾ*) in Him. This knowledge can be described as self-knowledge, but the self that knows and is known is radically transformed by the process of acquisition. Or, from another perspective, the self that knows and is known is the unchanged and unchanging Divine Self.

*Tarbiya* is the primary means by which disciples of Shaykh Ibrahim Niasse acquire *maʿrifa*. During this process, the spiritual flux (*fayḍ*) from God, the Prophet, and the shaykhs; the performance of spiritual exercises; and the sincerity of the disciple (all of which are identical from a certain perspective) lead to radical transformations of consciousness. These transformations, which are described in a wide variety of schemas and metaphors, result in a unitive knowledge of God in His Essence and in His various manifestations, which constitute the phenomenal world. This unique mode of knowledge is *maʿrifa* and, in principle, is its own justification. However, practically speaking, the attainment of *maʿrifa* is verified through a number of processes, most prominently through examination by an advanced spiritual master. While *maʿrifa* stands above the level of belief or speculative thought, determining whether particular ideas or beliefs are the fruit of *maʿrifa*, ordinary human speculation, or deception/illusion is a concern of some disciples who have completed *tarbiya*. This discernment is achieved through further progress in the "journey of the heart"; consultation with other Knowers; and the examination of the Qurʾan, ḥadīth, and other authoritative texts.

As the meeting place of knower and known, subject and object, human and Divine, *maʿrifa* takes on seemingly contradictory descriptions. It is different for everyone and yet, fundamentally, the same. It is beyond all limitations, and yet limited by the knower. It is knowledge of self, of God, of the Prophet and the saints, of everything, of nothing. These various descriptions, which at times seem mutually contradictory or confusing, are not meant to be mere conceptual or poetic abstractions, but are supposed to illustrate an experiential reality.

Knowledge or knowing presupposes a properly functioning instrument of knowledge, be it heart or intellect. According to this perspective, the knower needs to be perfected in order for his knowledge to be perfect. Thus, correct knowledge coincides with, and is even identical with, a certain mode of being. This unique mode of being is identified with the Prophet. One's point of view depends on where one stands, and like the mythical "Aleph," the Prophet's point of view is understood to be that which synthesizes and comprises all possible points of view. *Tarbiya* works to cultivate this ideal mode of being in the disciple. The perfection of knowledge is knowledge of God (since there is nothing other than Him to know), and the perfection of knowledge of God is to know Him in the inscrutable Unity of His Essence and in the multiplicity of His manifestations, at once. Because these manifestations have no end, and their origin, the Divine Essence, is also boundless, *maʿrifa* (and the self of the Knower) also has no end. Thus, *maʿrifa* is dynamic, evolving as the Knower does, because it is identical with the constantly transforming being of the Knower.

The various detailed descriptions, extended metaphors, and schemas that describe the process of acquiring *maʿrifa* and the states and stations that follow its acquisition are meant as allusions (*isharāt*) to these experiential realities, with which they must be neither confused nor conflated. However, these elaborate metaphysical systems and theories emerge from "the tongue of the state" (*lisān al-ḥāl*), or the vantage point of the possessors of *ma'rifa* and their reflections on their experiences and perceptions. These theoretical expositions reveal a worldview, a metaphysics, an anthropology, an ontology, and an epistemology that differs radically from that assumed by most contemporary philosophers and scholars in the academy. In Tijani Sufism, the ratiocination and discursive speculation that is characteristic of contemporary academic philosophical thought really only begins once one's consciousness has been radically transformed through spiritual practice. Before that, such speculations can only serve as a kind of map or a postcard of the view from the summit of *ma'rifa*, calling aspirants to its heights and indicating the way.

These fundamental differences cannot be forgotten when comparing, implicitly or explicitly, Sufi epistemology with its Western, academic counterparts; moreover, these differences mean that it would be a grave mistake to try to subsume Tijani epistemology into categories that are themselves premised on and inseparable from a radically different anthropology, metaphysics, and epistemology. For example, if we tried to fit the epistemology of *ma'rifa* described in this section into the "justified true belief" paradigm of knowledge, one would have to change "true belief" to *īmān* and "justified" to *mutaḥaqqaq* (verified/realized) yielding a definition of *ma'rifa* as perfected or realized *īmān*—a description that Shaykh Ibrahim himself gives but that differs markedly from the ordinary connotation of "justified true belief." Technically, *ma'rifa* is more akin to Russell's "knowledge by acquaintance" (hence its association with *dhawq*, "tasting") than it is to propositional knowledge (which the "justified true belief" paradigm describes). However, *ma'rifa* cuts across this distinction, since it includes knowledge that would be considered propositional as well.

Tijani epistemology could be said to be foundationalist, with *ma'rifa* being the basic foundational belief on which all other beliefs rely; but strictly speaking, *ma'rifa* is not a propositional belief. It could be described as a correspondence theory of knowledge in that it implies that the reflection in the perfectly polished mirror of the heart perfectly corresponds to its object of knowledge, but in the case of God or the self (the primary "object" of *ma'rifa*) the relationship is one of identity, not correspondence.

Likewise, this Sufi epistemology could be described as being coherentist (albeit in a radical reinterpretation of this position) in that it represents a coherence with the larger context of the Real, through the knower's annihilation in the Real, and through the heart becoming "capable of accepting any form"—of the noetic "container" becoming transparent, in complete coherence with God and His Manifestations. Or more technically, *ma'rifa* could be coherentist in that it represents "a belief that receives its justification from other beliefs in its epistemic neighborhood (or their justification)," since *ma'rifa* is defined by its acceptance of all beliefs—its transcendence of belief through its immanence in all of them.

This Sufi epistemology also bears some superficial similarities with Williamson's "knowledge first" position,[88] which argues that knowledge is a fundamental psychological/epistemological state, and attempts to analyze it by breaking it down into components are mistaken. In its essence, *ma'rifa* is absolutely simple, refusing to admit any distinction of knower and known, subject and object. This is the perspective from which the perfection of *ma'rifa* is described as ignorance, or the inability to attain *ma'rifa*. However, despite these similarities, *ma'rifa* is distinct from the "factive mental state" that defines knowledge for Williamson. And furthermore, like the color of water, *ma'rifa* is paradoxically so simple that it could be said to contain its own opposite as well as everything else.

Thus, *ma'rifa* could be described as all of these theories (and many more), and none of them, because the Sufi epistemology from which it emerges is radically different from the epistemologies in which these other theories developed. Moreover, *ma'rifa* is not a theory, but designates an experiential/existential reality at the core of Sufi thought and practice.[89] Virtually all contemporary academic analyses of knowledge presuppose that it is a particular mental state among other mental states (or a relationship between a mental state and an "outside reality" or other mental states), and that the knowing subject is somehow distinct from the object of knowledge. In addition to having a different conception of what constitutes a "mental state," the epistemology described in this section posits that *ma'rifa* is quite unlike other "mental states." It is existential as well as mental, the result of the opening (*fatḥ*) of the mental plane onto higher orders of reality, which have no equivalent in contemporary academic theories of epistemology. Furthermore, the distinction between knowing subject and the known object is collapsed in *ma'rifa*. *Ma'rifa* is not a proposition among other propositions, or a kind of belief among other beliefs, but rather the transcendence of belief through realization of, and annihilation in, the Truth, and the immanence in every belief through the manifestation of the Truth in each of them. However, as this chapter demonstrates, simply because it does not fit into contemporary categories or accord with the assumptions that produce them, *ma'rifa* cannot be dismissed as mere "irrational mysticism" or "superstition."

But perhaps most important, *ma'rifa* is not merely conceptual, and so cannot merely be thought about or theorized. It must be lived and experienced, and ultimately judged only through personal "tasting"—by "being" it. As one contemporary Sufi writer aptly put it, "There is intelligence and there is intelligence; there is knowledge and there is knowledge; there is on the one hand a fallible mind that registers and elaborates, and on the other hand a heart-intellect that perceives and projects its infallible vision onto thought. Here lies the entire difference between a logical certitude that can replace another logical certitude, and a quasi-ontological certitude that nothing can replace because it is what we are, or because we are what it is."⁹⁰ Thus, discursive descriptions and debates about *ma'rifa* can only go so far—they halt on the shores where *ma'rifa* begins. As such, we will conclude this discussion of *ma'rifa* with a poem describing *ma'rifa* through the symbolism of wine, which Shaykh Ibrahim Niasse quotes in his *Removal of Confusion*:

> Say to him who condemns the people of ecstasy
> If you have not tasted the drink of passion, leave us alone
> For when we have become joyful and light-headed,
> Intoxicated by the wine of ardent yearning—you will put us to shame
> So do not blame the drunkard in his state of drunkenness
> For burdensome ceremonies are lifted from us in our intoxication
> How could we insist on patience from a woman filled with desire?
> How can one bear patience when witnessing the real meaning?
> O driver of the ardent lovers, come to the aid of the conspicuous one
> Sing for us, in the Name of the Beloved, and cheer our spirits
> Preserve our secret in our drunkenness from those who envy us
> And if you see something unworthy, forgive us
> Their stories move us, but if not for their passion
> Burning inside, such words would not affect us
> Young man, have you not seen the caged bird?
> When native lands are mentioned, it longs for its home
> So it consoles itself, giving song to the contents of its heart
> The belly shakes only with feeling and meaning
> O young man! So too the spirits of the lovers:
> They are moved by ardent yearning for the realm of radiance.⁹¹

PART 2

◇◇◇

# Ways of Knowing in Ifa

CHAPTER 5

# What Is Ifa?

> Ọsa Otura says, "What is Truth?" I say "What is Truth?"
> Ọrunmila says, "Truth is the Lord of Heaven guiding the Earth."
> Ọrunmila says, "Truth is the Unseen One guiding the
> Earth. The wisdom of Olodumare, he is using."
>
> Ọsa Otura says, "What is Truth?" I say, "What is Truth?"
> Ọrunmila says, "Truth is the character [iwa] of Olodumare.
> Truth is the word that cannot fall. Ifa is Truth. Truth is the word
> that cannot spoil. Might surpassing all. Blessing everlasting"
> was the one who cast Ifa for Earth.
> They said they should come and speak the truth.
>
> "Speak the truth, tell the facts;
> Speak the truth, tell the facts;
> Those who speak the truth are those whom the gods will help."
> —ODU ỌSA-OTURA

> Yoruba ethics means: to become through ritual,
> a being who knows more and understands more,
> a person who lives more and is more.
> —ULLI BEIER

Of the thousands of different religious traditions of African origin, those of the Yoruba-speaking peoples of southwestern Nigeria, Benin, Togo, and the Atlantic diaspora have emerged as the most influential, and the most studied. The sophistication, beauty, and power of these traditions have impressed colonial explorers, missionaries, scholars, and generations of adherents and admirers on both sides of the Atlantic, ensuring their survival and growth in the face of wars, enslavement, and the increasingly competing claims of other religious traditions and ways of life. Of all the various sacred traditions of the Yoruba, Ifa has come to be regarded as the most important and authoritative. So what is Ifa?

Like many terms in Yoruba religious discourse (indeed in the Yoruba language itself), the term "Ifa" has many meanings, and this polyvalence is of deep metaphysical significance. First and foremost, the word "Ifa" refers to the divinatory wisdom tradition associated with Ọrunmila, the orisa (or deity/prophet) believed to have founded it. Second, "Ifa" refers to this deity, who is revered by his followers as Ibikeji Olodumare, "second only to Olodumare," the transcendent, Supreme Divinity who is also known as Ẹlẹda, the Creator, and Ọlọrun, the Lord of Heaven.

Third, and perhaps most formally, "Ifa" is used to refer to the religious tradition established by Ọrunmila. The priests and leaders of the tradition of Ifa are known as babalawo (literally, "father of secrets" or "master of mysteries")[1] and must train for years to master this multifaceted tradition. One of these facets, also known as Ifa, is the vast oral corpus that babalawo (the term is both plural and singular) spend their lives memorizing, reciting, and contemplating.[2] This living oral tradition is organized into 256 Odu, or sections, each of which is associated with a particular divinatory sign, and is said to have at least 256 ẹsẹ or verses,[3] which can themselves be quite long. This vast body of orature is regarded as the most authoritative source of traditional Yoruba mythistory, ritual, and moral prescriptions, and serves as a treasury of proverbs, songs, stories, wisdom, and philosophical meditations. Much of Yoruba popular oral art and literature comes from the orature of the Odu, and there is scarcely a deity, cultural practice, town, or even plant or animal found in Yorubaland whose myth of origin is not found in the ẹsẹ of Ifa.

But this vast orature is not the only facet of the Ifa tradition, which also involves the knowledge and performance of various rites, rituals, and sacrifices, and a veritable pharmacopoeia of herbal medicine. These other elements are often described, mentioned in, or closely associated with particular ẹsẹ and are sometimes also referred by the term "Ifa." In the most popular usage, however, "Ifa" refers to the system of divination associated with this religious tradition and its vast orature and bodies of knowledge. However, before turning to Ifa divination, we must first discuss the traditional Yoruba cosmology in which this tradition functions.

## YORUBA RELIGION(S) AND COSMOLOGY

Although particularly important, Ifa is but one tradition of Yoruba spirituality.[4] The traditions of sacred kingship; the traditions of the orişa such as Ọbatala, Ogun, Ọşun, Şango, and Eşu; the numerous secret societies such as the Ogboni fraternity; as well as ancestral masquerade societies (Egungun) and the numerous traditions of local deities, all provide unique perspectives on this world. Each tradition is like a planet in the religious solar system of the Yoruba (and neighboring ethnolinguistic groups and traditions). The view from each of these traditions is different, but deeply interconnected. What is central for one is peripheral for another; what is terra firma for a priest of Ọbatala is but a star in the firmament for a priest of Ọşun or a babalawo.

At the center of this spiritual universe is Olodumare, the ineffable, transcendent deity, who is also mysteriously immanent in *aşẹ*, the divine force that animates the cosmos.[5] Olodumare is described as the Ultimate Source (Orise), the Owner of Life/Spirit (Ẹlẹmi), the Creator (Ẹlẹda) of everything in heaven and earth. Seminal scholar of Yoruba religious traditions, Bolaji Idowu, writes, "Yoruba theology emphasises the unique status of Olodumare. He is supreme over all on earth and in heaven, acknowledged by all the divinities as the Head to whom all authority belongs and all allegiance is due.... His status of supremacy is absolute. Things happen when He approves, things do not come to pass if He disapproves. In worship, the Yoruba holds Him ultimately First and Last."[6] However, unlike the Supreme Deity in Abrahamic religions,[7] Olodumare is not the main focus of ritual worship or sacrifice. This role is played by the orişa, who are described as creations of Olodumare and have distinct personalities, histories, functions, rituals, natural phenomena, and even days of the week associated with their worship. For example, the orişa Ọşun has been described as the goddess of sweet waters, love, fertility, beauty and the arts, brass, and honey (the latter two are frequently used in her worship). Her tradition is closely connected with the river identified with her[8] and is centered in the towns of Oşogbo, home to many of her sacred groves through which the river flows, and Ado-Ekiti, where the source of the river is found. One myth tells us how, when offended by the other deities, Ọşun withdrew from the earth, causing the rains to cease and leaving pregnant women unable to deliver their children,[9] thereby demonstrating two of her many functions.

It is significant that the Yoruba apply the verb *sin*, meaning to serve or worship,[10] to Olodumare, but not the verb *bọ*, meaning to offer sacrifice or venerate through ritual offering. Both verbs are applied to the orişa. The orişa have specialized priesthoods and traditions of worshippers/followers, whereas Olodumare has no specialized priesthood and his cult is either universal or nonexistent.

The major orisa, or those whose worship has become widespread throughout various Yoruba cities and the diaspora, include Ọbatala, the old, wise, gentle archdeity of white cloth who fashions the bodies of people; Ẹṣu, the mischievous and powerful trickster deity of the crossroads who delivers sacrifices to their divine recipients and serves as a divine policeman and messenger; Ogun, the powerful, hot-tempered, solitary deity of iron, war, and justice; Ọṣun, the charming and strong-willed goddess of wealth, beauty, magic, and the river that bears her name; Ọrunmila, the wise and patient god of Ifa divination and messenger of Olodumare; Ọsanyin, the mysterious god of plants, medicine, and magic; Olokun, the deity of riches, the lagoon, and/or the deep sea; Ṣango, the fiery, proud god of thunder, lightning, and retributive justice; and Yemọja, the gentle, maternal goddess of the Ogun River in Nigeria, the ocean, and its fish in the Americas.[11]

Ulli Beier summarizes the perspective of Susanne Wenger—the late, renowned Austrian-born artist, longtime priestess of Ọbatala, and architect of the sacred grove of Ọṣun in Oṣogbo—on the relationship between Olodumare and the orisa:

> Olodumare contains all the complexities of the world within him. He is the egg from which the world breaks out. As a creator, Olodumare is called Ẹlẹda (ẹda = creature). With a gesture of creation Olodumare splits himself up and becomes multiple beings through his innumerable creatures. Olodumare in his pure form cannot be perceived by the senses or understood by intelligence—that is why he receives almost no direct worship and no sacrifice. But as Ẹlẹda we can begin to understand him....
>
> In Susanne Wenger's vision, the *orisha* are part representations of Olodumare. Each *orisha* is the universe looked at from another angle. Olodumare is the sum total of all the complexities, he is the universe concentrated into one intelligence. Susanne Wenger says that one could conceive God as the force from which everything emerges—or else one could see him as the coexistence of all the complexities.[12]

Wenger herself writes, "Ọṣun can be described as the goddess of the waters of life. As she is an Oriṣa she is supernaturally intense, a metaphysical concentration of a distinct force which also is contained not only in man and in all that lives, in all that exists physically, but also in Olodumare, God himself."[13] Thus Ọbatala can be understood as the god of creativity and as the creativity of Olodumare; Ọṣun as the goddess of bewitching beauty and as Olodumare's bewitching beauty; Ọrunmila as the god of wisdom and as the embodiment of the wisdom of God; Ẹṣu as the god of transformation and communication as well as the embodiment of the unpredictable transformative and communicative power (aṣẹ) of the divine.

The orisa, however, are not just understood as rarified divine powers, but are also believed to have come down to the world and lived as human beings. Moreover, the ranks of orisa are not closed, but can be joined by exceptional human beings. In his seminal essay on Ifa, Fela Sowande writes:

> For the definition of Orisa we turn once more to . . . Chief Ajanaku, Araba Eko, who defined Orisa as "*Awọn ẹniti Ori ṣa da yatọ si awọn ẹlẹgbẹ rẹ iyoku*," namely, "he whom Ori has created in a manner different to that in which his contemporaries have been created." Such a person has an added something which makes him stand out among his fellows. . . . We have the following Eji-Ogbe [the first Odu of the Ifa corpus] stanza: "Ọrunmila said: Human beings become Orisas! I responded: human beings become Orisas. He said, Oduduwa, that you hear so much of, he was a human being; because he did good while on earth as a man, he was remembered after his death and worshipped. Ọrunmila said: Human beings become Orisas! I responded: human beings become Orisas. He said, Orisanla, for example, was a human being; but he was wiser than his fellows, and did good while on earth; therefore he was remembered and worshipped after his death. Therefore human beings become Orisas; only the wise ones are worshipped. Human beings become Orisas."[14]

**The Orisa in Comparative Perspective**

The characters of these orisa and their relationship to one another, and to people on earth, is chronicled in the many myths, songs, dances, and rituals of their traditions. The orisa, indeed Yoruba religion and civilization as a whole, have been productively compared to that of the ancient Greeks, and with good reason. Both have diverse mythological and ritual traditions, which vary significantly from one region to the next, reflecting the diversity of the many culturally distinct city-states that made up each civilization. Both traditions are home to initiatic mystery cults, priesthoods, and shrines/temples associated with different gods, and in both traditions people commonly worship multiple deities while usually having a particularly strong affiliation with a particular god or goddess. Both pantheons place some deities in heaven (ọrun/Olympus) and others under the earth (ilẹ or ọrun odo / chthon). Both sets of mythology are replete with tales of the gods misbehaving and interacting with mortals, as well as mortal and semi-divine heroes becoming deified after death. Both pantheons have inspired remarkable works of theater, sculpture, music, dance, poetry, song, festivals, food, and crafts.

Despite these many and profound similarities, Greek and Yoruba mythology have three fundamental differences that are worth discussing. The Greek pantheon contains no Supreme Deity like Olodumare; the deeds of the Yoruba pantheon have only recently begun to be set down in written form, whereas the Greek gods have been bound to paper for millennia; and, finally, the orisa are still actively worshipped and sacrificed to by millions of people around the world, while the Olympians, although revered in modern literature, probably haven't smelled a burnt offering in over a thousand years (excluding certain recent neo-pagan groups).

The significance of the first difference is seen in the various quarrels between the divinities, as well as their seeming flaws and faults. Although Zeus is the arch-divinity of Mount Olympus, he, too, makes mistakes and can be outwitted, overcome, or defied by other deities. The Zeus of Homer or Hesiod is a far cry from Olodumare; instead, he is more like a Ṣango with the authority of Ọbatala, in that he can settle disputes between other deities by virtue of his strength or seniority, but he is decidedly one of them. As such, Olympian feuds are settled, and mistakes are punished, based on personal strength and cunning. The orisa, on the other hand, are firmly under the dominion of Olodumare, whose moral reign is as certain and natural as physical law. The justice of Olodumare is impersonal, and the punishment/redemptive penance a natural result of the offense, whereas that of the Olympians tends to be described in more personal terms of offense.

Wọle Ṣoyinka notes, "Like the Yoruba deities, but to a thousandfold degree, the Greek gods also commit serious infractions against mortal well-being.... Punishments, when they occur among the Olympians, take place only when the offence happens to encroach on the mortal preserves of another deity."[15] The Yoruba gods, however, are generally held to the same natural laws of justice that they enforce.[16] In the Yoruba universe, Olodumare's moral dominion would have cut Socrates's dialogue with Euthyphro rather short: the gods love the good because it is good, because it is in accordance with the nature of Olodumare, the supreme arbiter of right and wrong.

The process of writing facilitated a standardization and canonization of the Greek mythology. Dynamic, different, and seemingly contradictory mythologies can easily exist and are readily found in oral traditions, which are often discretely conveyed via particular speech events in particular contexts. Whereas in writing, mythology becomes more fixed and less dependent on context, making seeming contradictions more apparent, and the need for their "resolution" more pressing. The remarkable variation in the mythology found in the works of Homer, Hesiod, Aeschylus, and Plato is but a small snapshot of what must have been an even more diverse and dynamic body of oral Greek mythology. The diversity of Yoruba mythology, as a tradition that is still evolving and remains primarily oral, is much greater than can ever possibly be represented in our scholarly writings. The canonization of mythical narratives in the strictly memorized verses of Ifa is as close as the tradition comes to an authoritative collection of myths, but even the Ifa corpus is still a living and intentionally dynamic body of orature. Moreover, most babalawo memorize, recite, and transmit mythological narratives of Ifa that seem contradictory or variants of the same story without much cognitive dissonance, in part due to the oral and "performative" nature of the tradition.[17]

The living nature of the Yoruba mythological tradition also makes it much more dynamic and diverse than the remnants of the Greek mythological tradition that have been preserved in writing. The myths about the orişa are being told and retold, revised and reinvented every day in Yoruba, Spanish, Portuguese, English, and other languages. The mythology, conceptualization, and worship of Yemọja in Brazil differs significantly from that in Nigeria, and can even differ greatly from town to town, or temple to temple, within one country. This diversity is actually proof of the tradition's vitality; only dead trees produce no new branches. Moreover, for practitioners, the orişa are still very much alive, acting in the world and interacting with their devotees. When we discuss orişa, it is important to remember that we are describing living realities, not ancient, aestheticized abstractions. These differences between Greek and Yoruba mythology are important to keep in mind when trying to understand the role that the orişa play in traditional Yoruba religions.

The diasporic traditions, such as Santería (Cuba) and Candomblé (Brazil), have often identified the orişa with Catholic saints, and there are in fact many ritual similarities.[18] Catholic saints have an essentially intercessory function, which is often eclipsed in their veneration, just as happens with the orişa. Many devotees have a particularly close relationship with one saint while simultaneously venerating several others, mirroring patterns of worship among the abọrişa (those who worship the orişa). The highly practical nature of the veneration of Catholic saints also shares much with that of the orişa. Miracles, which are required for canonization, sustain the popularity of the cult of a particular saint, which finds its parallel in the Yoruba saying *Orişa ta kẹ kẹ kẹ, ti o gbọ, ta gẹ gẹ gẹ, ti o gba, oju popo ni ngbe*, which roughly translates to "The orişa that doesn't hear you when you cry, or doesn't help you when you worship it, get rid of it!"[19] The calendar of Catholic saints include angels (Saint Michael, Saint Gabriel), mythological heroes (Saint George the Dragon Slayer), and exceptional spiritual men and women, just like the pantheon of orişa. Those saints who walked the earth become apotheosized into a spiritual principle and function, guarding particular regions and sectors of humanity, while maintaining a distinct personality and human history, much like the orişa.

Although the cults of Catholic saints bears a number of ritual similarities to those of the oriṣa, they are doctrinally quite distinct. The oriṣa occupy a central role in worship, veneration, and salvation, more comparable to that of Christ and the Virgin in the Catholic Church. Moreover, the language used to describe the oriṣa tends to be more mythological and less historical, more symbolic and less factual, than the hagiographies of the saints. Although both genres are more concerned with describing spiritual archetypes and moral exemplars than with prosaic facts, this feature is even more greatly accentuated among the myths of oriṣa than with the sanitized tales of the saints. The oriṣa lie, cheat, get drunk, steal wives, beat people up, get jealous, and kill. The saints never seem to behave like this, at least not after their conversion, and so the myths of the oriṣa require a different kind of hermeneutic to understand how such a seemingly rough-and-tumble crowd can uphold and impose strict moral injunctions on their followers.

The oriṣa can also be compared with the prophets of the Abrahamic world, particularly the esoteric Islamic understanding of them as created spiritual realities having a pretemporal existence.[20] In many schools of Sufism, the lives of the prophets are not confined to their time on earth, as they occupy the heavenly spheres above time and exert spiritual influence in the world both before after their deaths. Similarly, the oriṣa are simultaneously described as spiritual realities dwelling in heaven or under the earth, and also as earthbound people who experienced the vicissitudes of human existence and traveled through familiar landscapes, especially Ile-Ifẹ. The places associated with the prophets and oriṣa are made special due to their association and are frequently the sites of shrines and pilgrimage (e.g., Jerusalem, Mount Sinai, Medina, Mecca; Oṣogbo, Oke-Igẹti, Ile-Ifẹ). Like the oriṣa, the prophets have distinct histories and personalities, and they are associated with certain natural phenomena (e.g., Moses with water, Abraham with fire, Solomon with wind, David with iron).

But perhaps most significant, the prophets, like the oriṣa, establish a particular way of life and mode of sanctity that is closely imitated by their devotees, often in minute detail. The devotees of oriṣa ritually reenact their particular deity's rites of passage, and take them as moral and aesthetic exemplars in ordinary life, much as pious Muslims do vis-à-vis the Prophet of Islam. Very pious *abọriṣa* seldom make any major decision—or a minor one for that matter—without consulting their oriṣa through divination or by recalling a mythological precedent for the action. In fact, in both traditions, piety and sanctity are each measured by the degree to which one assimilates into the archetype of the prophet or the oriṣa. More than one babalawo explained that "Ọrunmila is for us what Muḥammad is for Muslims, what Jesus is for Christians—he is the messenger of Olodumare," and that "we are all just striving to be like Ọrunmila—no one can ever be like him, but we are all trying."[21]

Furthermore, in certain schools of Sufism, each saint is said to be "on the foot" of a particular prophet, meaning that he manifests the same kind of sanctity and wisdom as that particular prophet. For example, some saints, like al-Ḥallāj, are said to be ʿĪsawī or Christ-like, tend to be inward-focused and ascetic, and are often persecuted or martyred. Likewise, among the Yoruba, every person is said to have an orisa who "owns his or her head," meaning that the he or she manifests the characteristics of that particular divinity, who governs his or her destiny. Unlike the orisa, however, the prophets are not worshipped directly or sacrificed to; however, the veneration of Christ in Christianity and the invocation of blessings and praises on the Prophet of Islam in prayers and poems bear close resemblance to similar practices among the devotes of the orisa.

Esoteric Islamic traditions, particularly the school associated with Ibn ʿArabi, share another particularly fascinating feature with Yoruba religion, one that has caused a great deal of confusion for scholars of both traditions. The Yoruba proverb *Bi o s'eniyan, imale o si*, or "If not for people, the gods would not be," reflects an important aspect of the Yoruba worshipper's relationship with the orisa. It is widely assumed, and often explicitly stated, that the orisa depend on humanity for their existence. In some rituals, worshippers even threaten the orisa that if they do not answer their prayers, they will go worship another deity and the orisa will be left without devotees.[22] However, Yoruba mythology, particularly that of Ifa, describes the deities as being temporally and ontologically prior (in myth, it amounts to the same thing) to human beings, and much more powerful than them. Given this fact, how are the orisa dependent on people?

Wọle Ṣoyinka sees this as a kind of humanist strain within traditional Yoruba thought,[23] but this seems a bit of a stretch in the ritual, mythical, and even historical context. I believe Karin Barber comes closer to the mark in her explanation of this as a West African version of Hegel's master-slave dialectic (the clients or followers of a "Big Man" or patron derive their status from him, but he, in turn derives his status from them, because without followers he would not be a "Big Man") applied to relationships with the orisa.[24] However, Barber is careful to explain that this attitude is not one of skepticism, and that to the Yoruba, the orisa really are existing, powerful deities, just as the popular, human "Big Men" and their power are real. She also points out that this relationship of mutual dependence, or the not-so-secret "secret" that man makes the gods, does not apply to Olodumare. Citing examples from neighboring ethnic groups whose social structures mirror the structure of their worship, she argues that these social relationships serve as the model for relationships with the deities.[25] She concludes, "The Yoruba conviction that the òrìṣà need human attention in no way questions the existence of spiritual beings as a category.... It is rather because of the element of choice in the system, the survival in the human community of any òrìṣà depends on human collaboration."[26] The orisa and humanity exist in a relationship of mutual dependence, and although Olodumare remains independent, the forms in which people chose to worship and relate to the Supreme Deity are many and "made by human hands."

Similarly, in the Islamic context, Ibn 'Arabi explains that there can be no lord (*rabb*) without a vassal, or one who is lorded over (*marbūb*), and that there can be no divinity (*ilāh*) without something for whom it is a divinity (*ma'lūh*), so that without the creation over which he is lord, God could not be God. However, mirroring the Yoruba exception of Olodumare to this rule of reciprocity, Ibn 'Arabi insists that God's unknowable Essence remains independent of all relationships. The Andalusian mystic further explains that all objects of worship are actually "gods created in belief," writing, "No individual can escape having a belief concerning his Lord. Through it he resorts to Him and seeks Him. . . . No believer believes in any God other than what he has made in himself, for the God of beliefs is made. The believers see nothing but themselves and what they have made within themselves."[27] In a poem whose sentiments and metaphors would not seem too out of place in a Yoruba context, Ibn 'Arabi summarizes this perspective:

> We are His food
> since He feeds upon our existence,
> just as He is the food of created things, without doubt.
> He preserves us in creation
> and we preserve the fact that He is a god.[28]

This concept of the mutual interdependence of man and gods also find a home in the vast universe of Hinduism, whose pantheon bears some resemblance to that of the Yoruba, not least of all in its dizzying diversity and regional variance. The intense personal devotion that Hindu deities receive at shrines in households, workplaces, and markets, as well as the elaborate rituals of sacrifice and festivals conducted in their honor, bear a strong resemblance to practices among the Yoruba. The phenomenon of possession by deities, which forms an important part of the worship and spiritual practice of many of the oriṣa (but not that of Ọrunmila) also finds parallels in the vast world of Hindu practice, unlike in most Abrahamic traditions. The notion of the "avatar"—a particular divine descent or incarnation—is also a familiar one to the world of oriṣa, each of whom has multiple stories of birth and ascent into heaven or disappearance into the earth. This, or a similar notion, seems to be implicit in the many variations in name, myth, and ritual practice for what is considered to be a single deity. For example, Oriṣa Funfun, Oriṣanla, and Ọbatala all have distinct but similar myths and rites associated with them, but are often understood to be the same deity. Barber recounts several examples of this phenomenon, including a myth in which Ogun and his wife

Ọya (a powerful female orișa) fought, breaking each other into pieces (seven and nine, respectively), each of which inspired a distinct cult of the god or goddess.[29] The diasporic concept of different "roads"(*caminos* in Spanish) or "aspects" (*qualidades* in Portuguese) or incarnations of a given orișa is even closer to the notion of an avatar.

The close connection and even identification of Hindu deities with natural phenomena and features—such as the Himalayas, the Ganges River, and natural rock formations—finds close parallels in the Yoruba world. The natural or "discovered" shrines of Hinduism both look and are used in a manner very similar to the shrines of the orișa. While it is difficult to make generalizations about either tradition, both seem to emphasize the worship of one particular deity,[30] which becomes a window onto Absolute Divinity, and consequently shares many appellations with the Supreme Divinity. For example, the babalawo refer to Ọrunmila by many praise names shared with Olodumare, such as Ọbarisa, "The King of the Orișa"; Ọlọjọ-oni, "The Owner of Today"; and Ar'inu r'ode, Olumọ ọkan, "He who sees inside and outside, the Knower of hearts."

However, the Yoruba tradition differs from the Hindu in that the orișa, by and large, remain distinct from and subordinate to Olodumare, whereas for their devotees, Shiva and Vishnu tend to be none other than the Absolute itself. In the Yoruba setting, the relationship between the devotee, the orișa, and Olodumare is summarized in the following saying: "People praise the babalawo, the babalawo praises Ifa [the orișa Ọrunmila], Ifa praises Olodumare."[31] Thus Beier concludes:

> The relationship between the Yoruba and his *orisha* is essentially different from the relationship of a Christian worshipper to his God. The Christian demand for "faith" in God has no meaning in terms of Yoruba religion. A Yoruba never says "I believe" [*mo gbagbọ*] in *orisha*. One can believe or disbelieve another man's story or excuse. But in a religious context, the word cannot be used....
>
> The relationship between a Yoruba and his *orisha* is expressed in the complex, multivalent verb *li* or *ni* that is contained in the word *olorisha*. *Olorisha* is usually translated into English with the approximation "*orisha* worshipper," but strictly speaking it could mean "One who *has orisha*," "One who *is* orisha," or "One who *makes orisha*."
>
> To *have orisha* expresses the simplest and most obvious relationship. Most people have simply inherited their *orisha*, and a failure to serve him would result in dangerous *disorder*, the symptoms of which could be disease or death in the family, failure in business and so on. These misfortunes are not punishments because the *orisha* is angry. But the neglect of the *orisha* has put things out of joint, and life cannot function again properly unless the right relationship is reestablished.

To *be orisha* is an equally correct translation of the word *olorisha*. The worshipper offers his body as a vehicle to *orisha*, he allows the *orisha* "to mount his head," to ride him, and he strives to become, for brief moments, the personification of the *orisha*. Only few and very powerful priests could really represent the *orisha* all the time. But every *olorisha* must become the *orisha* some time.

To *make orisha* is an expression that signifies the interdependency between *orisha* and worshipper. The *orisha* cannot exist for man without the *olorisha* through whom he can manifest himself. He must be strengthened through the ritual activities of the *olorishas*. In the praise names of Ogun this is very poetically expressed:

> Does the woman who spins ever reject a spindle?
> Does the woman who dyes ever reject a cloth?
> Does the eye that sees ever reject a sight?

> The function of ritual is partly to increase the *orisha*, to make him more *orisha*. The more his force is built up, the more strength he can return to the community of worshippers. The simplest and most common way of strengthening the orisha is to pronounce [*ki*] him. The verb *ki* means to greet, to call, perhaps to evoke [or invoke]. *Oriki* are the poetic formulae with which the *orisha* is being addressed, greeted, identified, strengthened.... A dialogue must take place every day through the medium of divination.[32]

As the oriṣa and owner of the most elaborate and trusted system of divination (Ifa) that contains *oriki* for nearly every member of the vast Yoruba cosmos, Ọrunmila and his followers (the babalawo) are the models par excellence of this intimate, dynamic relationship between devotee, oriṣa, and the transcendent divinity of Olodumare.

**"Theology" and Symbolism in Yoruba Religion**

Further evidence of this telescoping model of divinity is found in the etymology of the term "oriṣa" favored by Idowu in his seminal work, *Olodumare, The Concept of God in Yoruba Belief*. He writes:

> I am very inclined to the view that the name *Oriṣa* is a corruption of an original name *Oriṣẹ* (*Ori-ṣẹ*)—"Head-Source"... an ellipsis of *Ibiti-ori-ti-ṣẹ*—"The Origin or Source of Ori [head/essence]." Now what is this Origin, or "Head-Source"? It is the Deity Himself, the Great *Ori* from whom all *ori* derive, inasmuch as he is the Source and Giver of each of them. In Yoruba, the name *Oriṣẹ* (the original form), then

refers to Olodumare. This is borne out by the fact that the name *Orisa* is applied to Him in some parts of Yorubaland.... The original *Orise* is His common name in Owo and among the Itsekiri and the Western Ijaw.... Thus the divinities would be small *orise*, taking their name as their origin from *Orise*, Olodumare Himself.[33]

In this view, the orisa derive their name, as well as their divinity, from Olodumare.

Another mythical etymology of the name "orisa" reveals one more aspect of their divinity and relationship to one another and Olodumare. According to the myth,[34] Olodumare sent Orunmila and Orisa, the original arch-deity, into the world to keep it running smoothly. One day, Orisa bought a slave at the market named Atowoda (or Atunda, in some other versions), who served him well. Atowoda asked his master for a piece of land to farm on his own, and Orisa agreed, giving him some land on a hill. Atowoda began to till his land, digging up the large rocks that were buried there. However, Atowoda harbored the desire to murder his master, and one day, while Orisa was walking by the bottom of the hill, he seized his chance. He rolled a huge boulder down the hill at his master, who was subsequently smashed to bits and scattered to the four winds. Orunmila came along looking for his friend, surveyed the scene of the disaster, and began traveling all around, collecting the pieces of Orisa, which he gathered in a calabash. He deposited some of these at the spot of the accident, and distributed the rest throughout the world, each piece becoming a different orisa, and each place where it fell, a center of worship for that divinity. The name "Orisa" is then derived from the phrase *Ohun-ti-a-ri-sa*, "the thing that was found and scattered." The deity formed at the spot of the accident was called Orisanla, "the great or arch-deity." The other scattered pieces of him, the other orisa, are considered his "children."

Another version of the myth begins with a universe peopled only by the single divinity, Orisa, and his slave, Atunda. Again, Atunda rolls a boulder on top of his master, smashing him into 401, or 601, or 1,001 pieces that became the pantheon of the Orisa and all the other living things on earth. Idowu interprets these myths as symbolizing the necessary fragmentation that occurs when the human mind (symbolized by Atunda) tries to conceptualize, understand, or mentally encompass or master the awesome unity of the Divine. Ever the ritual dramatist, Soyinka interprets the myth as the origin of the gods' unrest and incompleteness, which fuels their epic and tragic labors. In both interpretations, divinity is derived from a single, unified source, and this fundamental unity of all divinity, and all life, is emphasized.

Traditional sources vary in their enumeration of the orisa:[35] some count 1,700; the numbers 400 and 200 (and their sum, 600) are also common; as are 401 and 201. All of these are symbolic numbers indicating the indefinite and unlimited number of divinities. In fact, anything can become an orisa.[36] In the traditional Yoruba cosmos, the supernatural is not separate from the natural (this distinction does not really exist in Yoruba), and the physical world is inextricably linked and identified with the metaphysical, which is nearly always symbolized by elements of common experience. Wọle Ṣoyinka points out that the language of Yoruba symbolism is not one of ethereal stars and planets, but rather "the imagery of peat, chalk, oil, kernels, blood, heartwood and tuber, and active metaphors of human social preoccupations."[37]

The traditional Yoruba worldview is centered around human experience and is markedly intuitive. The experience of sky's all-encompassing transcendence is a natural symbol for Ọlọrun ("the owner of heaven," another name for Olodumare), who is described as "He Whose Being spreads out over the whole world, the Owner of the mat that is never rolled up." In fact, the sky is called Oju Ọlọrun, "the face/eyes of Ọlọrun," and when it brightens, people say Ọlọrun nṣeju, "Ọlọrun is winking."[38] Feelings, emotions, and the unseen aspects of human experience are described as being "inside" (inu) where they are felt. After people die, they are buried in the earth, and thus the depths of the earth are also a natural symbol for the unseen realm of the dead and other invisible beings. The vault of the sky, the "inside" of the body/self, and the earth's recesses are three convergent symbols of the unseen in the Yoruba cosmos.

Thus the traditional Yoruba worldview is highly symbolic, in the sense that nearly everything is, or can become, a symbol for (or identified with) a metaphysical or spiritual reality. As one babalawo explained to me, "Everything has an *inu* [an inner, hidden dimension], and the *inu* of a thing is its heavenly or spiritual self."[39] According to this worldview, a tree is not just a physical tree, but is also a spirit or an abode of spirits, symbolizing or embodying certain spiritual realities. Or rather, the tree is the spirit, and the spirit, the tree. These symbolic relationships are enshrined and expressed in religious orature such as myths, the verses of Ifa, or the hunter's chants known as *Ijala*; and in rituals, which are often connected to these myths and verses. As Ṣoyinka writes, "Ijala celebrates not only the deity but animal and plant life, seeks to capture the essence and relationships of growing things and the insights of man into the secrets of the universe."[40]

This rich symbolic web interweaves the physical and the spiritual, and connects its various elements in a particular but dynamic pattern. This pattern is the source of the logic of ritual. For example, each orisa has his or her favorite "foods" or sacrifices that are symbolically and mythologically connected to the character of that particular orisa. Anyone with a passing familiarity with the music and mythology of Ọṣun, the lovely orisa of sweet waters and fertility, can immediately see why honey is used to worship her. Ọṣun is like honey: sweet, golden, and strong. Or rather, honey simply *is* Ọṣun. Likewise, iron isn't just a symbol or manifestation of Ogun—it *is* Ogun. Numerous rituals, myths, and songs connect and identify Ogun and iron and Ọṣun and honey, making these intuitive connections official and explicit.

It is not unlike the connections we intuitively draw between moods, colors, friends, characters in movies, and so forth. The oriṣa represent a particularly fundamental set of these archetypes, and the more one becomes familiar with their embodiments in myth, music, dance, sculpture, sacrifices, and devotees, the easier it becomes to recognize their manifestations in the natural world, other people, and oneself.

The Ifa corpus describes these connections with and between the oriṣa (and the other inhabitants of the Yoruba cosmos) as interpersonal relationships, and thus babalawo and devotees of other oriṣa inhabit a complex web of relationships within which they constantly interact with the oriṣa in their various forms of manifestation. This web of relationships is remarkably dynamic and adaptable. For example, Ogun, the strong, trailblazing deity of iron and war is experienced in and identified with cars, trucks, and trains; while Ṣango, who was traditionally associated with lightning, became the demiurge of the new phenomenon of electricity.

However, it is important to note that although new myths and rituals emerge all the time, and old ones are constantly being reformulated, these symbols, myths, and rituals are not considered mere creative inventions of a literary or performative imagination. Rather, their significance lies in the fact that they reveal, rather than invent, the "deep" or hidden connections between the inhabitants of the densely populated Yoruba cosmos.[41]

Ultimately, everything in the world is a creation of Olodumare and reveals or manifests something of the deity; in Yoruba terms, everything has its aṣẹ.[42] Moreover, nearly everything one would encounter in Yorubaland (and by extension, many things that one would not) has a symbolic, and therefore mythical, and therefore ritual connection with various Oriṣa and other spiritual beings and forces. Although everything has the potential to be worshipped, to become an oriṣa, not everything is actually worshipped at once, in the same way, otherwise there would be no pattern or structure. As a verse of Ifa from Odu Ogbe Okanran says, "Not every palm nut drinks blood like *ikin* [the palm nuts used in Ifa divination that symbolize Ọrunmila and are therefore worshipped with sacrifices]."

All of this is strikingly similar to historian of religion Mircea Eliade's description of *hierophanies*—that is, places, people, objects, performances, or things that manifest the "Sacred" in the "profane," or ordinary, world. He writes, "The dialectic of hierophany implies a more or less clear choice, a singling-out. A thing becomes sacred in so far as it embodies (that is, reveals) something other than [merely] itself."[43] Thus, each hierophany is described as a "paradoxical coming-together of being and non-being, absolute and relative, the eternal and the becoming."[44] This seems an apt characterization of the Yoruba religious world in which anything can become an oriṣa at any time, but not everything all at once, in the same way. Unlike Eliade's account however, the

Yoruba cosmos is not divided into domains of "sacred" and "profane"; everything is sacred, everything has its aṣẹ, but some things have a more intense aṣẹ. Typically these alaṣẹ (possessors of aṣẹ and authority) are associated with an oriṣa, verse of Ifa, or myth because to become part of a myth or an oriṣa is to participate in eternal mythical time, in the sacred, and it is these myths and associated rituals that give everyday objects—like palm nuts, termite dust, honey, and chalk—their profound meanings. From one perspective, it is what these "everyday objects" really are. Eliade explains that hierophanies such as these "acquire their reality, their identity, only to the extent of their participation in a transcendent reality."[45] In the Yoruba cosmos, this participation is mediated by ritual and myth.

Because ritual myth is what gives things their meaning, it is important to separate the latter word from the connotation of falsehood that it has accrued over the years in English (as in "that's just a myth"). In traditional Yoruba worldviews, and for Eliade, myth has the exact opposite connotation. From these perspectives, the mythical (or ritual) truth is the only one that matters, that gives things meaning. Comparing an actual historical event (the tragic death of a young Romanian man on the eve of his wedding) with the myth that quickly grew up around it, Eliade writes, "It was the myth that told the truth: the real story was already only a falsification. Besides, was not the myth truer by the fact that it made the real story yield a deeper and richer meaning, revealing a tragic destiny?"[46] "The myth" is more true and of greater consequence than "the fact" because it deals with truths of a loftier nature, those truths that give meaning and structure to the world. Without these mythical truths, facts would be completely meaningless.[47] The myths and their associated rituals of the Yoruba world bind its various elements together, giving them order, meaning, and significance.

This is why Ifa—the tradition that, more than any other, gives discursive structure to these structuring myths—is so important in the Yoruba universe.[48] Eliade writes, "In such a perspective this is not a closed Universe, no object exists for itself in isolation; everything is held together by a compact system of correspondences and likenesses."[49] Ifa might very well be described as this "compact system of correspondences and likeness" that holds everything together. Since Ifa is regarded as the wisdom and expressed will of Olodumare, devotees of other oriṣa (and many Christians and Muslims as well) come to consult babalawo. Ifa is understood to speak for all oriṣa, and its indefinite number of verses, to contain the myths of origin and relationships between the indefinite number of oriṣa.

The organization of the vast pantheon described in Ifa is often depicted in the orientation shown in figure 3.

In figure 3, Olodumare stands above and beyond good (represented by the right side) and evil (represented by the left side), encompassing everything. The structure

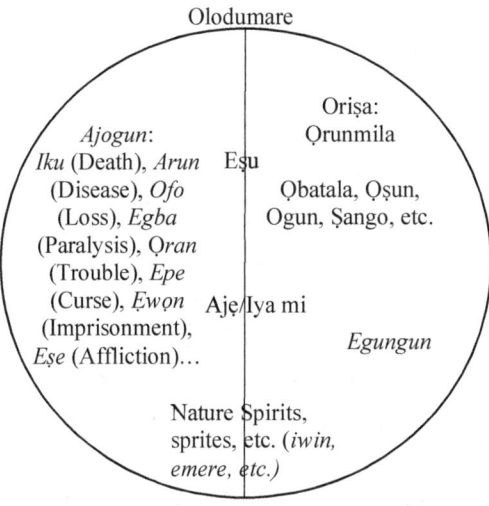

FIGURE 3 Diagram of the Yoruba cosmos.

of this schema comes (among other sources) from the following popular invocation, variants of which are often heard at the start of rituals such as sacrifice or divination:

> Iba irunmalẹ ojukọtun
> Iba igbamalẹ ojukosi
> Iba ọta-le-n-irun Irunmalẹ
> Ti o ja atari ọna ọrun gbangba[50]

> Praise to the 400 divinities of the right hand (the "benevolent")
> Praise to the 200 divinities of the left hand (the "malevolent")
> Praise to the 460 divinities
> Who line the very road of heaven

The major orisa are usually considered benevolent forces[51] and ministers of Olodumare who, however, can punish and harm those guilty of ritual and moral transgressions. Gentle, patient Ọbatala will punish his devotees for drinking alcohol; Ọrunmila, although patient and understanding, can punish his devotees who disregard his taboos by lying or committing adultery; Ogun is swift to punish liars and oath-breakers, as is Ṣango, but of no orisa is this more true than Eṣu. Eṣu is simultaneously a mischievous trickster and a strict enforcer of the will of Olodumare and the law of sacrifice. Whenever a sacrifice is offered, it is Eṣu who takes the sacrifice to the intended recipient—thus the saying *Ẹni o rubo l'Eṣu gbe*, "Eṣu supports the one who sacrifices."[52] However, if a sacrifice is not made, or is not done correctly, Eṣu will side with the ajogun

What Is Ifa? • 211

(the malevolent powers on the left side of the diagram) and wreak all kinds of havoc on the offending party. Eṣu also punishes the other oriṣa for their refusal to sacrifice, for their hubris, and sometimes just for fun.

"No respecter of persons," Eṣu is a notoriously ambivalent figure and is only consistently allied with Ọrunmila, the god who prescribes sacrifices (and even this god of wisdom suffers Eṣu's wrath on occasion), and of course Olodumare. For this reason, he is placed neither on the left nor on the right, but in the middle.[53] Eṣu is both good and evil, a reflection, on a lower plane, of Olodumare's transcendence of both good and evil. The chaos that Eṣu is so fond of creating is a shadow of the undifferentiated "chaos" of Olodumare's transcendence of all categories and divisions.

Turning to the left side of the diagram, we find the ajogun, who are the calamitous spirits and enemies of humankind. They are legion, and led by eight warlords:[54] Iku (Death), Arun (Disease), Ofo (Loss), Ẹgba (Paralysis), Ọran (Trouble), Epe (Curse), Ẹwọn (Imprisonment), Eṣe (Affliction). The ajogun are opposed and held at bay by the oriṣa and other benevolent spiritual forces with whom man can ally himself through sacrifice and good conduct/character. The *ajẹ*, often euphemistically called *ara aye* or *iya mi* (literally, "the people of the world" or "my mothers"), are sometimes added to the list of ajogun, but I believe this is not correct. *Ajẹ* is often translated as "witch," but as numerous studies[55] and my own conversations with babalawo have demonstrated, the English word "witch" does not map well onto the Yoruba concept of *ajẹ*, unless the original Old Germanic meaning[56] of "one possessing special knowledge or uncommon skill" is intended. Despite their name and this unfortunate translation, the *iya mi* or *ajẹ* are not exclusively female, and one babalawo I interviewed even told me that they are mostly male.[57] In short, the *ajẹ* are people of exceptional spiritual power who have the ability to curse or bless those around them, and they can be propitiated by certain sacrificial rituals.

The Yoruba cosmos is also home to various tree, river, rock, and nature spirits, as well as a host of other sprites, spirits, and ghosts who range from the helpful to the mischievous to the downright wicked. Although seldom the object of worship or veneration (with certain important exceptions), certain sacrificial rites are used to elicit their support, bind or block them, or avoid them altogether.

The ancestral collective known as Egungun receive sacrifice and are venerated, and are sometimes included in the pantheon of oriṣa. The cult of Egungun is virtually all male,[58] as is the related cult of Oro, but both men and women can, and are expected to, make offerings to this ancestral collective. Usually one's deceased parents and/or grandparents are worshipped individually, with more distant ancestors being absorbed into the collective Egungun. However, not every dead person becomes an ancestor. Only those who reach adulthood, die a "good" death, receive a proper burial, and are known for good character qualify for this veneration. As one babalawo explained to me, "Only people who have completed the task for which Olodumare sent them into the world are worshipped after death. We don't sacrifice to [or] worship those who die in childhood or wicked people."[59] The Egungun occupy their own realm, which is sometimes described as the "heaven below" (ọrun-odo)[60] and other times as the world of the unborn and the "heaven above" (ọrun) of the orișa and Olodumare. In the time of myth, these domains and the "land of the living" were traversed by all with relative ease, and something of this porous nature remains today.[61]

The transition from the realm of the unborn, or heaven (ọrun), into the world (aye), is one of the main themes of Yoruba mythology. The things people and the orișa do in heaven and on their way down to the world are of the utmost consequence. It was on his way down to earth that Ọbatala got drunk and fell asleep, denying him the honor of being the first king on earth, and causing his lifelong abstinence from alcohol. It was on the way down from heaven that Ọrunmila acquired the "calabash of wisdom," and his important position in the pantheon.[62] But perhaps no myths illustrate the importance of heaven more than those surrounding *ori*, the head.

The term *ori* is used to refer both to a person's physical or "outer" head (*ori ode*) and his "inner head" (*ori inu*). The latter is one of the most important elements of the Yoruba cosmos and of the traditional Yoruba conception of personhood. The *ori inu* is at once one's destiny, fate, guardian angel, personal divinity, and source. It is one's *ori*, more than anything else, that determines one's outcome in life. As the myths of the Ifa corpus tell us, each person chooses an *ori* in heaven. Some are good and lead to long life and prosperity, while others end in ruin. In one variant of the myth, on the way out of heaven, each person stands at the "Tree of Forgetfulness," *Igi Igbagbe*,[63] and declares the fate he has chosen for himself. But after passing under its branches, and descending into the world, all recollection of one's fate is lost. In all versions of the myth, Ọrunmila alone witnesses the choice of *ori* and is thus called *ẹlẹri ipin*, "witness of the choice [of destiny]." For this reason, Ọrunmila can be consulted through divination to determine the content or wishes of one's *ori*. In fact, Abimbola writes, "It is important for every individual to consult Ifa from time to time to find out the true path of one's destiny. By consulting Ifa, one is merely trying to find out what has been kept in store by one's *ori*. Divination is therefore regarded as the communication of the wishes of one's *ori* to Ifa, who will then reveal this to the client through the appropriate chapter and verse of the Odu system."[64]

As another babalawo explained, "Everyone, even the orișa, have an *ori*; it is only Olodumare who does not, because He is the original source of all *ori*."[65] As witness of the choice of *ori*, Ọrunmila stands in a unique position to advise all of the other deities, as well as human beings. The myths of Ifa recount that he was the first creation of Olodumare, and as such, has eternal knowledge of all that was and is and is to come. He declares the will of Olodumare to man and god alike, and serves as the mouthpiece of the other oriṣa. Since leaving the world, Ọrunmila speaks through Ifa divination, one of—if not the—main mode of communication between humankind, the oriṣa, and Olodumare, and between heaven and earth.

Babalawo often cite the proverb *Aye l'ọja, ọrun n'ile*, or "The world is a market, heaven is home,"[66] to explain the relationship between life in the world and that in heaven. The world, or *aye*, has a somewhat ambivalent nature: it is the stage of action, of life, of enjoyment, but it is also a place of death, decay, trouble, and torment. However, as bad as life in this world may get, it is better than life in *ọrun apadi*, "the heaven of broken pot shards," where the wicked go after death.[67] However, ọrun, or the realm of the ancestors, seems to be a pleasant place, although many verses of Ifa, as well as rituals and popular belief, point to the desirable possibility of return to the world from this realm, through reincarnation as a child of one's descendants.[68]

Heaven (ọrun) and earth (ilẹ) are frequently depicted as two half-sphere calabashes, with that of heaven lying on top of that of the earth, with the world (*aye*)[69] serving as the plane where the two halves meet. As Margaret Thompson Drewal explains, "The Yoruba conceive of the cosmos as consisting of two distinct yet inseparable realms—*aye* (the visible, tangible world of the living) and ọrun (the invisible, spiritual realms of the ancestors, gods, and spirits). Such a cosmic conception is visualized either as a spherical gourd [calabash], whose upper and lower hemispheres fit tightly together, or as a divination tray with a raised figurated border enclosing a flat central surface."[70]

Like the cosmos, human beings are similarly symbolized by calabashes, which are also used to house or "enthrone" the physical presences of oriṣa (such as the sacred palm nuts of Ọrunmila) in homes and temples. As one babalawo explained, "Man is a small world, everything in the world, all the powers of the world exist inside him"[71]—so people are understood to contain or carry the presence of the oriṣa and the inner realities of the myriad things of the world within themselves, just as calabashes contain the physical presence of the oriṣa. This explains the symbolic imagery of the posthumous abode of the wicked, ọrun apadi, "the heaven of broken pot shards"—the place of those fragmented and fractured souls who have fallen beneath the human state. In several verses of Odu Ofun-Ọsa, the broken or cracked calabash also serves as a symbol of the world or life gone awry, which only Ifa can repair, restoring the cosmos, and the individual human, to order and wholeness.[72] Between the two halves of the cosmic calabash, the drama and mystery of life and death, both human and divine, unfolds according to the will of Olodumare, under the knowing gaze of Ọrunmila. The totality of this cosmic drama is summarized and encoded in the 256 Odu of Ifa divination.

## IFA DIVINATION

The historian of religion Joachim Wach described divination as the "exploration and interpretation of the will of the Godhead ... done in the spirit of devotion and submission rather than coercion and manipulation."[73] This definition certainly applies to Ifa divination, with the qualification that the submission is not a passive process, but is nearly always active, requiring deep contemplation and interpretation, the performance of specified rituals, and/or changes in behavior.

Ifa divination is based on the production of 256 divinatory signatures (one for each of the 256 Odu) through a few ritual processes. The basic structure of Ifa divination is relatively simple, and it is shared by a number of divinatory systems in West Africa and around the world.[74] The client or seeker presents his or her question or problem in a ritualized manner to the instruments of divination, not the diviner.[75] After performing an invocation, the diviner manipulates the instruments of divination in a semi-random manner to produce a divinatory signature or sign that corresponds to a specific body of orature. Then further divination is done to determine a particular verse or narrative among those associated with this signature. These verses are then recited and interpreted for the seeker, often diagnosing the seeker's issue and advising a specific course of action (most commonly a sacrifice). Then the seeker confirms or rejects the diagnosis of the divination (which can be further clarified through additional divination) and either performs the prescribed ritual actions or does not.

Ifa divination is usually performed either with sixteen palm nuts, known as *ikin*, or with a chain called an *ọpẹlẹ*, which is made of a metal or cotton chain or thread linking eight shells of the fruit of the *ọpẹlẹ* tree. Each shell is curved, creating a convex and concave side. To perform divination with the *ikin*, the babalawo takes all sixteen nuts in one hand and then tries to snatch all of them with the other hand. If two nuts remain in his hand, he makes one mark in the sawdust-like camwood powder (*iyẹ-irosun*) on his divination tray (*ọpọn Ifa*). He then repeats this process, and if only one nut remains in his hand this time, then he makes two marks in the *iyẹ-irosun* directly to the left of the first mark. If, however, no nuts or more than two remain in his hand, no mark is made. The babalawo repeats this process as many times as is necessary to make two columns of four sets of marks (or four rows of two sets of marks). First, he marks the top row, starting with the right, and then he continues on down, marking each row, starting from the right, making a total of eight sets of marks. These eight sets of marks constitute the sign of the Odu. For example, figure 4 shows the sign of the Odu Otura Meji.

These eight sets of marks, each with two possibilities (one or two marks), yields $2^8$ or 256 possible signs. Taken separately, each row has $2^4$ or 16 possible signs, each of which has a name. For example, the name of each of the rows below is Otura. Since

|   |   |   |   |   |   |
|---|---|---|---|---|---|
| I | I | 2nd | 1st | FIGURE 4 | Order of markings. |
| II | II | 4th | 3rd | | |
| I | I | 6th | 5th | | |
| I | I | 8th | 7th | | |

|   |   |   |   |   |   |
|---|---|---|---|---|---|
| I | II | I | I | FIGURE 5 | Ranking of Odus. |
| II | I | I | I | | |
| I | II | I | I | | |
| II | I | I | I | | |
| Odu Ofun Ọsẹ, the 256th Odu | | Odu Eji Ogbe, the 1st Odu | | | |

this row appears twice in the Odu above, the Odu is known as Otura Meji, or "Two Oturas." The sixteen "twinned" Odus, like *Otura Meji*, are considered the principal or primary Odus, from which the other 240 Odus, called *amulu*, are derived. The Odus are all ranked in terms of seniority from Eji Ogbe (two Ogbes), the most senior, occupying the first place, to Ofunsẹ, the 256th Odu. Ofunsẹ comprises Ofun on the right and Ọsẹ on the left (see fig. 5). This ranking of the Odu plays an important role in the divination process, as we will discuss shortly.

Although the *ikin* are used in the manner above for public and special ritual occasions because it is believed to be the most effective and reliable—if time-intensive—method, babalawo usually use the *ọpẹlẹ* to divine. Grasping the chain or thread of the *ọpẹlẹ* in the middle, so that four shells hang down on either side, the babalawo will toss it forward onto his *apo Ifa* (the bag in which he normally keeps his Ifa paraphernalia) so that the two ends of the chain point toward him, and the middle of the chain is pointing away from him.[76] The two sides of the chain make up the two columns of the sign of the Odu (see fig. 6).

The concave or smooth side of the *ọpẹlẹ* shell is equivalent to a single mark, and the convex or rough side of the *ọpẹlẹ* shell is equivalent to two marks. Therefore, if the *ọpẹlẹ* is tossed and all the shells land with their concave sides up, the sign produced is that of *Eji Ogbe* (see above). The *ọpẹlẹ* is quicker, easier to use, and more portable than the *ikin*, which are usually reserved for special occasions.[77]

Once the figure of the Odu is produced, either by the *ọpẹlẹ* or *ikin*, the babalawo can recite one or more of the verses (*ẹsẹ*) of that particular Odu.[78] Most senior babalawo have at least eight verses of each Odu memorized, and many have significantly more in their repertoire. The diviner will typically then recite the beginning, invocatory part of the chosen ẹsẹ verbatim, and then recite the mythical narrative (*itan*) of the ẹsẹ in his own words. This narrative usually takes the form of a mythological figure (a god, animal, person, inanimate object, etc.) seeking out a particular mythical babalawo (often with a highly evocative name given in *oriki* form) to perform Ifa divination because of a particular need or problem (going on a journey, sickness, barrenness, etc.). The Odu to which the narrative belongs is the one that emerges, and the mythological babalawo tells the seeker to make a certain sacrifice. The figure either performs or does not perform the sacrifice, resulting in his or her success or failure, respectively. The consequence of the performance or neglect of the sacrifice is often connected to the way things are in the present.[79] After the story is complete, the babalawo will recite the closing verses of the ẹsẹ, which also seldom vary.[80]

After this recitation, the babalawo will summarize the story and the main message of

FIGURE 6 *Ọpẹlẹ* in the position of Odu Ika-Iwori.

the ẹsẹ for the client or seeker, giving advice in the following form: "Ifa says such-and-such is happening, you must not do such-and-such, and make a sacrifice of such-and-such for so-and-so." Then, and only then, will the seeker/client explain his problem to the babalawo, who will then help the seeker interpret the ẹsẹ of Ifa in light of his particular situation.[81] Then, if the seeker has further questions, or if the sacrifice is not specified by the ẹsẹ, they can ask Ifa further "yes" or "no" questions through the use of *ibo*. The *ibo* usually consist of a piece of bone, which stands for "no," and two cowries tied together, which represent "yes." The babalawo will ask Ọrunmila the question and then touch the *ibo* to each of the shells of the ọpẹlẹ before handing them to the seeker. The seeker cups the bone and the cowries between his palms, shakes them, and then separates them, taking one in each fist. Then the babalawo casts the ọpẹlẹ twice. If the Odu that appears first is senior to that which appears second, the seeker opens his left hand to reveal the answer. If the junior Odu appears first, the right hand is opened.[82] In this way, the seeker can ask Ọrunmila

What Is Ifa? • 217

a number of direct, "yes-or-no" questions and make the answer quite specific. The babalawo can also use the *ibo* after the very first cast of the ọpẹlẹ, before the babalawo recites verses from that Odu, in order to select the verses from that Odu to recite by asking Ifa if the situation is "good" or "bad" or by asking if the situation concerns "enemies," "children," "money," and so forth. In this way, the message of Ifa becomes ever more specific, from Odu to ẹsẹ to the particular situation of the seeker, which could itself become an ẹsẹ one day.

This process provides insight into the metaphysics and cosmology assumed by Ifa divination. The Odu themselves are considered to be deities,[83] spiritual principles, and archetypes from which the world and all of its inhabitants are created. For example, babalawo often refer to the orişa Eşu as Ọsẹtura, the Odu that contains the story of his creation. During a babalawo's initiation, divination is performed to determine which Odu the initiate is "a child of." In fact, the babalawo call their personal Odu *Odu to bi mi*, "the Odu that gave birth to me." The babalawo in question is understood to be a particular manifestation of that particular Odu, and must endeavor to learn and follow all the principles, taboos, and lessons of the many verses of that Odu, because in learning about that Odu he is learning about himself.[84] But this dynamic is not limited to babalawo—everything in the world is created through the Odu; the fundamental, organizing principles of the universe; and Ifa. One babalawo explained, "Ifa is the word from the mouth of Olodumare which he used to create the world, which he uses to mend the world."[85] The Odu are the metaphysical archetypes or principles that form the basis of the world. They are like the fundamental forces of physics or the Platonic archetypes—once you understand them, everything else in the universe comes down to the details of their application. Every babalawo I interviewed said the following in one way or another: "The whole world is in Ifa—everything that will ever happen and everything that has ever happened." The Odu of Ifa are the alphabet of existence.[86]

The process of divination mirrors the cosmic process of creation: things go from a heavenly unity of universals to an earthly multiplicity of particulars. In Ifa divination, first the Odu governing the seeker's situation is determined through divination, taking his or her particular circumstance and connecting it to its original archetype. Then, through divination, this heavenly archetype is brought down into the realm of the particular and the practical. Since these particulars were created through the Odu in the first place, it is through the Odu that they can be "mended"—that is, reconnected with their origin, with their true selves. It is because Olodumare created the world through his word of Ifa that the world can be mended by Ifa.

## HISTORIES OF IFA

> *Ifa l'o ni Oni*
> *Ifa l'o ni Ọla*
> *Ifa l'o ni Ọtunla*
> *Ifa l'o ni Ireni*
> *Ọrunmila l'o ní ọjọ mẹrin*
> *Orișa da si aye*
>
> Ifa is the owner of today
> Ifa is the owner of tomorrow
> Ifa is the owner of the day after tomorrow
> Ifa is the owner of the day after that
> Ọrunmila is he who owns the four days
> The Orișa created on earth
> —ODU OGUNDA MEJI

### Time and Eternity in Yoruba Cosmology

A history implies a metaphysics of time and place, a cosmology.[87] Different cosmologies will necessarily entail different conceptions of time and space, and the events that occur therein, and therefore produce different histories. A child of the related scientific and industrial revolutions, the modern concept of history has become increasingly abstract, linear, homogenous, and quantitative, a line of identical quantized seconds running from the big bang off into the oblivion of the future.[88] The traditional Yoruba concept of history, *itan*, however, is inseparable from myth, and the cosmology described therein. Time in Yoruba cosmology has often been described as cyclical or spiral. In one of his most metaphysically insightful passages, Ṣoyinka writes:

> This seeming cosmic anachronism is in fact a very handy clue to temporal concepts in the Yoruba world-view. Traditional thought operates, not a linear conception of time, but a cyclic reality.... But the degree of integrated acceptance of this temporal sense in the life-rhythm, mores and social organization of Yoruba society is certainly worth emphasizing, being a reflection of that same reality which denies periodicity to the existences of the dead, the living, and the unborn.... The world of the unborn, in the Yoruba world-view, is as evidently older than the world of the living as the world of the living is older than the ancestor-world. And, of course,

What Is Ifa? • 219

the other way around: we can insist that the world of the ancestor is older than the world of the unborn in the same breath as we declare that the deities preceded humanity into the universe.[89]

Yoruba cosmology assumes multiple realms of existence that often overlap and are simultaneous—that is, they exist "on top" of one another, rather than one after the other. Those yet to be born are above us right now, and those who have already lived are below us in the earth or above us in heaven (depending on the particular mythological perspective adopted). In Yoruba thought, the afterlife is not so much "after" life as it is above or below it; likewise, our preexistence is not just "before" life, but also above it. Myths of reincarnation[90] equate the realm of the ancestors with that of the unborn, so the ordinary temporal succession we experience in everyday life is like an island surrounded by the timeless ocean of pre- and post-existence. Ritual brings us to the shores of this sea of eternity. Taking another perspective, Drewal writes:

> If in Yoruba thought life on earth is merely a temporary segment in a human spirit's journey, then all time would have to be classified as cyclical, not just ritual time. What Benjamin Ray terms "ordinary linear time" would not exist in Yoruba consciousness, since, conceptually, the human spirit is always coming into the world and returning in one unending cycle. On the other hand, since nothing ever repeats itself, and since from this ontological perspective there is always change and transformation ... then existence in time would be more appropriately conceived in spatial terms as a spiral—neither cyclical, nor linear. There is no time-out-of-time, properly speaking that is, if I have understood the concept.[91]

While I agree with Drewal that in Yoruba thought no particular thing repeats itself, and that change and transformation are a perpetual part of the world (*aye*), I would refine her description slightly. This is a delicate metaphysical point, but one that is essential to a complete understanding of traditional Yoruba conceptions of time. The transition from *aye* (the world) to *ọrun* is not just an ordinary transition in time, but rather the transition from time to "outside of time."[92] In Yoruba, *aye* means at once world, space, and time. Closely examining Drewal's statement provides another way of approaching this point. She writes, "The human spirit is *always* coming into the world ... there is *always* change and transformation." This "always" (*lailai* in Yoruba) is the boundary between the timeless and time. If something "happens" in eternity (outside of time), then it *always* happens in time. In Yoruba myth, the human being comes into time as she comes into the world (*aye* designates both), and so she is *always* coming into the world/time.[93] This is why people know everything that they will do in the world when they choose their *ori* in heaven; they are above or outside of ordinary time and can choose and perceive their lives "all at once."[94] If we picture time or the world as a river, then heaven could be a cloud that extends over the entire length of the river, sending down rain and receiving evaporating water. Because the motion of rain is vertical, it doesn't participate in the horizontal motion of time until it enters the river of the world, and can fall or evaporate up at any point along the river—just as in the Yoruba worldview, people enter and leave the world at every point in time.

But this is not the whole story; there remains what Ṣoyinka calls the "fourth stage,"[95] the liminal realm of myth and ritual. If time is a river, and heaven is a cloud, then myth takes place at the source of the river, in the heights of the hills, where the river meets the cloud. What looks like a succession of reincarnations from the perspective of *aye* (the world) is simultaneous and parallel from the perspective of *itan* (myth), and utterly undifferentiated from the heavenly vantage point of Olodumare. When combined, these three perspectives—the temporal, the mythical, and the eternal—produce something like Drewal's "spiral" time.[96] What is a point in eternity is spun to make a circle in the mythical time of heaven, which the linear time of the world stretches out into a spiral. However, it is important to remember that this spiral is only how things appear from the perspective of the world of living human experience. The point is still a point; it merely appears to be a circle or a spiral, like the patterns produced when you wave a stick pulled from the fire.

The meaning and the etymology of the Yoruba word for history, *itan*, can help shed some light on this concept. *Itan* is the verbal noun of *tan*, a verb that means "to light" or "to spread"—the metaphorical implication of which is that myths and historical narratives are like lights that shine forth to illuminate the present, or that they are like a fire that can be brought from one "place" (or time) to another to give light and warmth.[97] The fire is the same even if the fuel is different.

These images and metaphors are meant to convey the epiphanic nature of *itan*, myth/history. In Ifa, and in Yoruba culture in general, moments or historical events appear as different manifestations of eternal realities or archetypes. Myths, rituals, proverbs, and divination connect these different manifestations and make them intelligible. As the Yoruba proverb says, *Ẹni ti ko mọ itan, yoo mọ itan*, "The one who doesn't know myth/history, won't know his relations[hips]."[98]

Eliade's characterization of the relationship between "myth" and "history" has strong resonances with this perspective. He writes, "though it may seem paradoxical, what we may call the 'history' of primitive societies consists solely of the mythical events which took place in *illo tempore* and have been unceasingly repeated from that day to this."[99] In *Cosmos and History*, he elaborates: "An object or an act becomes real only insofar as it imitates or repeats an archetype. Thus, reality is acquired solely through repetition or participation."¹⁰⁰ Furthermore, "to know the myths is to learn the origin of a thing. . . . For knowing the origin of an object, an animal, a plant, and so on is equivalent to acquiring a magical power over them by which they can be controlled, multiplied, or reproduced at will."¹⁰¹ Yoruba *itan*, like Eliade's myth, connects a given object or act with its origin, and with its related iterations throughout history, imbuing it with meaning, reality, and power.

Given this fact, let us consider what Ifa says about the creation of history and the ritual calendar, in order to get a better understanding of these abstractions. Odu Oturupọn-Otura describes the creation of the four days of the Yoruba ritual calendar. According to this myth, originally there was only one day, which repeated over and over. Ọrunmila asked Olodumare to make different days, and Olodumare agreed and dedicated the four new days to four different orisa. As the most senior, Orisanla received the first day; Ọrunmila took the second; Ogun had the third; and Jakuta (eventually Ṣango)¹⁰² took the fourth. Each deity held a big celebration on his day with his followers.

Odu Ika-Ogbe, however, tells another story. In this myth, Ọrunmila used to hold meetings with the other Orisa every seventeen days (sixteen days in English reckoning, as the Yoruba include the present day when counting time). Since only he could reckon time, Ọrunmila would call all the other deities to meet him on the appropriate day with a special charm (like a mythological cell phone). However, at that time, the days were very short, and the gods didn't have enough time to get anything done, so Ọrunmila decided to go to heaven to ask Olodumare for more time. He asked Orisanla, Ogun, and Ṣango to accompany him, and each rudely rebuffed him. So Ọrunmila set off to meet Olodumare alone. Olodumare responded to his request by giving him four days to take back to earth. When he returned to earth, Ọrunmila gave three of the days to the three deities who had refused him, keeping one for himself. When Eṣu, Ori, Egungun, Ọṣun, and Olokun (Ọrunmila's close friends and wives) found out that he had given away the days of the week to other orisa, they were upset. But Ọrunmila calmed them down by explaining that he wanted them all to share the same day so they could celebrate together. That is why these deities are worshipped on Ọrunmila's day.¹⁰³

In these myths, we again find the transition from the undifferentiated synthesis of a universal to a set of particulars, and the myth connecting these particulars back to their primordial origin establishes the mythological precedent for ritual action. In particular, these myths establish the Yoruba four-day ritual calendar as well as the congregation of Ifa priests that takes place every four (four-day) weeks. The myths also emphasize the role of Ọrunmila as the mediator between Olodumare and the other deities, and the origin of the ritual calendar, underlining Ifa's role as the source of cosmic and ritual structure for the Yoruba cosmos.

The action described in these narratives of the differentiation of time and the creation of a ritual calendar is like that of a prism that separates white light out into different colors. The days of the week are not identical; rather, they are qualitatively different, and these differences have ritual consequences. This "prismatic" structure is very common in Yoruba myth (such as in the story of Atunda and Orisa above), as it substantiates or organizes ritual actions in time and space, as well as connecting them with a universal origin, and therefore with one another.

As illustrated above, Eliade's description of myth as the irruption of the eternal into the temporal is particularly apt in the case of *itan*. *Itan* always contains a sense of the timeless in its description of events in mythical place and time. Within Ifa, as with many other mythological traditions, the history of a thing is not just a factual chronicle of events, but rather the story of its coming into being—often with the accent placed on its coming into time rather than its becoming within time. So when babalawo describe the myths, stories, and narratives as being literally true, they mean something slightly different from what a modern European or American presumably would.

For example, when asked about the different and seemingly inconsistent myths about the creation of the world or the apotheosis of Orunmila, many of the babalawo I interviewed had no problem explaining that all the accounts were both different and true. The babalawo who had little to no formal Western education refused to make any distinction between "literal" and mythological truth, while those who had attended university seemed relatively uninterested in the historicity of the myths of Ifa compared to their moral and metaphysical content.[104]

**History of Ifa**

Given these facts, we must discuss two distinct histories of Ifa: first, the mythological history that Ifa ascribes to itself; and second, the nonmythological, external history of Ifa. While several verses of Ifa refer to the heavenly origins of the tradition, I will only discuss two here—one that describes Orunmila's descent into the world (Oturupon Meji), and another that describes his departure (Iwori Meji):

Not long after the orisa came down to earth in Ile-Ife, things started going wrong. People fell ill and couldn't bear children, and no one knew what to do. Olodumare told the orisa to come back to heaven so he could give them something that would help them solve their problems. All the orisa rejoiced and got ready to travel back to heaven, except for Orunmila, who wanted to do divination before they set off on the journey. The other deities mocked and abused him, saying that it was Olodumare himself who had called them, so there was no need to perform divination.

So while Ọrunmila went to see a diviner, they left without him. The diviner gave Ọrunmila the mysterious advice that "when you lose something from your hand, don't use your hand to find it, use your feet," and told him to leave a meal of goat meat at the crossroads for Eṣu as a sacrifice. Ọrunmila did as he was told and left the sacrifice at the crossroads.

On the way to heaven, Eṣu saw the sacrifice Ọrunmila had left at the crossroads, and realizing what had happened, he quickly went down and ate it, and rejoined the other oriṣa on their way to heaven without anyone noticing. When they reached heaven, Olodumare asked the oriṣa where Ọrunmila was. They replied, "He was taking too long, so we left him behind." Olodumare looked at them knowingly for a while, and then handed them the "calabash of wisdom" [*Igba iwa*]. The oriṣa were so happy to finally have the solution to their problems that they started going back to earth without asking Olodumare how to use the calabash.

On their way down, they met Ọrunmila at *bode*, the river separating heaven from earth. They began to mock him again for wasting his time doing divination on earth while they got the calabash from Olodumare. One of them even taunted Ọrunmila by waving the calabash in his face. Just then, Eṣu knocked the calabash out of the oriṣa's hands into the river. The other oriṣa all started frantically groping in the river with their hands, trying to recover the calabash. Suddenly, Ọrunmila remembered the advice of the diviner, and started feeling around with his feet under water. Sure enough, he found the calabash and pulled it up out of the river. The other oriṣa demanded that he give it back, but instead Ọrunmila swallowed the calabash whole.

The oriṣa were furious and wanted to rip him open to get the calabash back. However, Eṣu would not let anyone touch Ọrunmila because of the sacrifice he had made for him, and so they all went back to ask Olodumare to settle the matter. When Olodumare heard their case, he declared that the oriṣa would have to treat Ọrunmila better from now on since he possessed all the wisdom Olodumare had sent down into the world, and that whenever they needed anything, they would have to go to Ọrunmila to find the answer to their problems. That is why everyone today goes to see babalawo, the children/disciples of Ọrunmila, to solve their problems.[105]

This myth is significant for several reasons. First, the journey of the oriṣa (and possibly people) to and from heaven to see Olodumare illustrates the "bringing together" of heaven and earth, of the eternal and the temporal in myth and ritual, which reenacts the myth. The ritual reenactment of this myth would be the performance of Ifa divination that produces this Odu, and the performance of the same sacrifice that Ọrunmila made for Eṣu. The seeker would be advised that although people look down on him now, he is about to attain a very high position—but he must make sacrifice, and continue doing things in his own unique way, and not follow those around him. If he does this, then he will be greatly blessed by Olodumare, and the mockery of those around him will turn to respect.

This myth also illustrates one of the more peculiar features of Ifa divination: the fact that Ọrunmila goes to see babalawo to perform divination for him. Since Ọrunmila is supposed to be the one who speaks through Ifa divination, this seems like something of a paradox. Why would he ask himself something through divination? This paradoxical reflexivity is actually a feature of many mythologies,[106] and in the case of Ifa, it serves to establish the ritual precedent of consulting Ifa. All of the babalawo I interviewed also told me that for important matters, one should not just divine for oneself, but also consult other senior babalawo for additional divination and insight into the result of one's own divination. The precedent for such a practice is established in this and other myths where Ọrunmila seeks out babalawo for divination. Several babalawo also explained that when we go to have divination done, it is Ọrunmila who answers; but when Ọrunmila goes to have divination done, it is his heavenly double (one babalawo identified him with Ọrunmila's *ori*), known as Ajagunmale, who responds through the divination.

This myth also emphasizes the "physical" integration of Ọrunmila with the wisdom of Olodumare and their inseparability. Ọrunmila eats the calabash of wisdom, integrating it into his very being. This also serves as the mythical precedent for a practice in the early training of a babalawo, called "eating the Odu" or "eating Ifa," in which the *ọpẹlẹ* is put in the position of Eji-Ogbe, the first Odu, and a ritual preparation of alcohol and pepper is placed on each of the shells. The babalawo-in-training must eat this preparation off the *ọpẹlẹ*. This is repeated for each of the sixteen major Odu, so the apprentice actually "eats" all sixteen principal Odu. This physical, ritual internalization of the Odu is believed to assist and complement the internalization of the Odu through memorization. Most significantly, however, this myth establishes the origin of Ọrunmila's possession of the transcendent knowledge of Olodumare, the access that Ifa divination grants to this knowledge, and the power of this knowledge to resolve problems through counsel and sacrifice.

Odu Iwori Meji gives a complementary account of the origin of Ifa divination and describes how Ọrunmila returned to heaven:

> It is the *apa* tree that grows in the forest, lighting the wizards' fire
> It is the *oruru* tree that is clothed in blood from top to bottom
> It was on the earth that I pressed the marks of Ifa

> Before I used the divining tray
> The slender palm tree atop the hill
> Which branches this way and that in sixteen heads
> Performed divination for Ọrunmila
> When they said that Baba would never have children in the city of Ifẹ

When Ọrunmila was living in Ile-Ifẹ, people mocked him because he had no children. But Ọrunmila simply laughed and performed divination. He soon gave birth to eight children, each of whom became important kings of Yoruba city-states [most of which still exist today; the myth explains how the titles of the kings of these cities are contractions of the original names of Ọrunmila's children]. One day, Ọrunmila called all his children to join him for a festival. They all came to join him and paid their respects, but the youngest child challenged Ọrunmila's authority by coming to the festival with the same symbols of authority that his father wore and refused to bow to him. Ọrunmila was incensed by this rejection of his authority, so he withdrew to the foot of a particular kind of palm tree and climbed up into heaven. As a result, the earth fell into chaos, women couldn't get pregnant, those who were pregnant couldn't deliver, the sick didn't recover, the rain stopped falling, the rivers dried up, the crops failed, the animals started behaving strangely. Everything was falling apart. The people begged Ọrunmila's children to convince him to come back, and they went to perform divination. Ọrunmila's children made the prescribed sacrifice and went to the foot of the palm tree their father had climbed and began to implore him to return to earth, reciting a litany of his praise names. However, Ọrunmila had made up his mind not to return to earth. But pitying his children, he told them to stretch out their hands so he could give them something to ease their distress. He gave them the sixteen *ikin*, the palm nuts used in Ifa divination, telling them, "All the good that you want in this world, this is the one you must consult." When they returned to Ile-Ifẹ, things started to go well again and they attained all the good things they were seeking.

> Ọrunmila, fluent-in-every-language,
> Ẹla of Isode [praise name of Ọrunmila]
> Ifa went to the home of Olokun and never returned
> He said, "The one that you see, call him Baba."[107]

This myth is remarkable for several reasons. Most obviously, it explains the origin of the divination with *ikin*, and identifies the particular kind of palm tree from which they must be sourced. This establishes the "Ifa palm" as an axis mundi, because

Ọrunmila climbed it to return to heaven, and because its palm nuts connect the people of earth with Ọrunmila in heaven.[108] Furthermore, the myth establishes and explains the meaning and origin of several important titles of rulers in Yorubaland. In addition to describing the ritual paraphernalia of Ifa, the myth serves as a warning of the consequences of hubris against Ifa (and one's elders in general). But most strikingly, this particular narrative's graphic description of a world without Ifa underscores the fundamental Yoruba belief that the order and proper functioning of the world is dependent on a continual close relationship with heaven.[109] The consequences of Ọrunmila's departure recalls what Eliade calls the "terror of history," the descent of humanity into a desacralized, chaotic world of meaningless, endless, linear time.[110]

The myth also establishes a number of profound praise names of Ọrunmila, one of the most famous of which is Afedefẹyọ, which translates to "Fluent in every language," referring to the universality of Ifa. This myth is also connected to a few other narratives in which Ọrunmila, instead of going to heaven by climbing a palm tree, enters the lagoon, the domain of his wife, Olokun, to remain there forever. Like the underground, the underwater is a symbol of occultation in an unseen realm, and babalawo do not see a contradiction in saying that Ọrunmila is in heaven and that he is underwater with Olokun.[111] Most importantly, however, the myth establishes the "vertical" history of Ifa divination, the authority of his priests ("the one you see, call him Baba"), and its power to mend the world.

The "horizontal," or external, history of Ifa is much more difficult to reconstruct. It seems possible that the tradition of Ifa was a later addition to the Yoruba religious universe, as Ọrunmila rarely appears in the myths associated with the cults of the other orisa, while they all appear in the myths of Ifa. But this evidence is circumstantial at best. The most promising method of dating Ifa would probably be some kind of glottochronological study of the variants of particular verses from particular Odu; however, given the special linguistic status of verses of Ifa, such an effort would require a great deal of work. Ifa, like Yoruba religion and culture in general, is remarkably dynamic and easily integrates and domesticates new and foreign elements, customs, and ideas. Some verses of Ifa from the Odu Otura Meji mention Islam explicitly and display a great deal of familiarity with Muslim ritual practice and doctrines. Therefore, we can conclude that these verses emerged no earlier than the seventeenth century, when Islam began to take root in Yorubaland. Ifa is also mentioned in some of the earliest colonial and missionary accounts of the mid-nineteenth century that deal with traditional Yoruba religions.[112] Archaeological evidence may also shed some light on the history of Ifa. For example, Suzanne Blier's *Art and Risk in Ancient Yoruba* hypothesizes that some artifacts from ancient Ifẹ (ca. thirteenth–fifteenth centuries CE) contain symbols of the Odu and other signs of Ifa divination. If this is correct, it could undercut Louis

Brenner's hypothesis that the tradition of Ifa is derived from Islamic geomancy, since the earliest known Islamic presence in the region occurs in the seventeenth century CE.[113] Nevertheless, all we know for certain is that the origins of Ifa as we know it today[114] are situated somewhere between the emergence of Yoruba civilization and the mid-nineteenth century.

Babalawo often recount an interesting myth, illustrating Yoruba mythology's remarkably integrative nature, which identifies the origins of Ifa divination with the mysterious figure of Setiu,[115] the first diviner. In some versions of the myth, Setiu was a Tapa (i.e., Nupe, a ethno-linguistic group bordering the Yoruba to the north) man who was very unusual due to the fact that he had no bones in his body. According to the myth, it was this extraordinary figure who introduced Ifa divination among the Yoruba.

Another version of the myth puts the boneless Setiu in Mecca during the time of the Prophet of Islam. When the Prophet was fleeing Mecca for Medina he hid in a cave with his close companion, Abu Bakr, because the people of Mecca, the Quraysh, were trying to assassinate him. The myth tells us that the Quraysh came to Setiu and had him perform divination to determine Muḥammad's whereabouts. Setiu told them that the Prophet was hiding in a particular cave, so the Quraysh went to check the cave, carrying Setiu with them. When they arrived, they found that a spider had woven a web over the entrance of the cave, so they berated Setiu, telling him that he had obviously gotten it wrong. Setiu insisted that the Prophet was actually inside the cave, but the Quraysh refused to listen and left. In fact, the Prophet and Abu Bakr were in the cave, and because the Quraysh ignored Setiu, the Prophet and his companion were able to make it to Medina, where they gathered an army and converted or expelled all the idol-worshippers in Mecca. Setiu was taken with those who fled to Africa and taught Ifa divination there. One babalawo explained to me that the Prophet Muḥammad and Ọrunmila are friends and brothers, and that the only reason there are problems between Muslims and babalawo today is because of what happened between Setiu and Muḥammad back in Mecca.[116]

Some scholars have speculated that Ifa emerged as an indigenous Yoruba response to the presence of Islam (like Islam, it has a "scripture" of sorts that is memorized and recited); while others have explored Ifa's relationship to and possible origins among other forms of divination, such as the Islamic tradition of geomancy known as *khaṭṭ al-raml*, which is widespread in the Muslim world, and other distant but similar forms of divination, including the *I Ching* and a Melanesian form of divination also based on sixteen figures.[117] William Bascom also compares Ifa with several other divinatory systems employed in and around Yorubaland among the Yoruba and neighboring Fon, Ewe, Yagba, Nupe, Igbo, Itsekeri, Ijaw, Tiv, Jukun, and Hausa peoples.[118] It is likely that many of these systems of divination have a common historical ancestor, while some, like the *khaṭṭ al-raml* employed by the Hausa and Muslim diviners among the Yoruba, may have a different, or more distant, common origin,[119] although it may have influenced the way in which the Odu of Ifa are marked. Some of these other divinatory traditions are acknowledged by Ifa and often mythically connected to Ọrunmila himself, and the practitioners of these presumably Ifa-derived divination systems often accept these mythical accounts of the origin of their art.[120] The Fa tradition of the Fon-speaking people is an adaptation of the Ifa tradition to the context of Dahomey, beginning when the king brought several Yoruba-speaking babalawo to his court. Despite its differences, as Maupoil, Bascom, and others have noted, the predominantly Fon-language Fa tradition still remains closely linked to the tradition of Ifa, with priests exchanging knowledge and even initiations.[121]

## CONCLUSION: IFA TODAY AND PRESENT FOCUS

While the history of Ifa divination remains shrouded in mystery, further studies and new methods of analyzing oral history may lead to some progress in this arena. However, I believe the most fascinating aspect of Ifa is not its history, but its continued resilience in a world that is increasingly modern, Christian, and Muslim (on the continent) and increasingly secular and Pentecostal (in the Americas and Europe). In Nigeria, Ifa is often reviled as "devil worship" or "pagan idolatry," or regarded as an archaic holdover from a pre-"civilized" past—a cultural curiosity, like the ruins of an old palace. Yet despite such opposition and indifference, Ifa continues to be practiced across southwestern Nigeria and, in some ways, to even thrive. Every single Yoruba town still has its council of babalawo who advise the traditional king and their communities. Moreover, the babalawo are not going out of business anytime soon. At some point in nearly every single interview I conducted, I was interrupted by a seeker who had come to see the babalawo with whom I was speaking, or called him on the phone to ask him to perform divination for a particular issue. Many of these seekers were affluent, respected members of their towns, many were highly educated, many were Muslim or Christian, and virtually all of them seemed confident in the power of Ifa to resolve their problems.

While this, in and of itself, was fascinating (e.g., how does an engineer with a PhD, trained in a science based on Cartesian dualism, reconcile his scientific training and worldview with that of Ifa?), I was more fascinated by the babalawo themselves. I was impressed by their rigorous honesty, compassion, and work ethic, and their incredible breadth and depth of knowledge. I wanted to understand, philosophically, how these babalawo came to be who they are, how they know what they know, and how these ways of knowing, so radically different from anything I had encountered in my academic training, "work." In answering these questions, I hope to provide a compelling account of the epistemology of the tradition of Ifa, and to make its worldview (and the intellectual reasons for its continued resilience) more understandable and accessible to a general audience.

It is important to recognize that Ifa is an extremely heterogeneous, diverse, and dynamic tradition. Traditions, myths, and rituals can vary widely over a small area and within a generation or two. However, the babalawo and other practitioners of Yoruba traditions recognize a continuity between these varying manifestations, and I believe anyone who spends enough time in communities of practitioners will notice it as well. The cosmology and mythology outlined above is largely schematic and based on the principles extracted from my own various experiences, impressions, research, and study.[122] Other scholars and practitioners will necessarily have different perspectives, having been exposed to other aspects of these traditions. My goal in this chapter was not to write *the* exposition of the doctrines of Ifa (a task as impossible as writing an exposition of *the* doctrines of the contemporary academy), but rather to present an accessible introduction to Ifa that would be acceptable and illuminating to both scholars and babalawo.

CHAPTER 6

# Knowledge in Ifa

Truth is a sacred water from Ile-Ifẹ; there
are not many who drink from it.
—ODU ỌWỌNRIN DAGBON

Deep knowledge [imọ ijinlẹ] is the word [ọrọ] from the mouth
of Olodumare that He gave to Ọrunmila to mend the world
—AWO FANIYI

If we knew the reality of things, we would
be the masters of our own lives.
—GEDEGBE, *Awo* OF THE ROYAL COURT OF ABOMEY

"A small child works his way off the edge of the sleeping mat
A bird soars above it all"
Divined for the elders
When they were preparing to leave heaven to come to the world
They said, "What are we going to do?"
They asked themselves, "Where are we going?"
We are going in search of knowledge [imọ],
truth [otitọ], and righteousness [ododo]
In accordance with our destined lot [kadara ayanmọ]
over the top [ori] of the hill
and the plateau
We are going to the palace of the king of goodness
We will reach a holy land
We will reach a land that is beautiful
We are seeking knowledge everyday
Knowledge has no end
—AWO ỌṢITỌLA, CITING UNNAMED ODU

## KNOWLEDGE IN IFA

The priests of Ifa, known as babalawo, are widely regarded as being among the foremost traditional intellectuals of Yoruba society. People seek their counsel and insight on practical and personal matters, affairs of state, and all manner of ritual, mythological, theological, and philosophical questions. Babalawo undergo a rigorous training, which can last as long as thirty years, and spend most of their life researching, studying, performing, and contemplating the oral corpus of Ifa and its associated sacrifices and rites. In fact, these similarities between babalawo and contemporary academics account in no small part for the fact that Ifa is perhaps the most studied religious tradition of the Yoruba.

Knowledge is of paramount importance to the babalawo, and knowledge of the mysteries of Ifa is what makes one a babalawo, a "father of secrets/mysteries." The knowledge that is central to this tradition is multidimensional, involving the procedural, creative knowledge of divination and ritual; the medical knowledge of pharmacology (*ewe Ifa*); the memorization and interpretation of a vast body of orature; as well as self-knowledge (*imọri*), all of which is intimately connected to the cultivation of good or gentle character (*iwa pẹlẹ*). In this chapter, I will discuss the distinctions the babalawo I interviewed made between various types of knowledge, before moving on, in the following chapter, to describe the process through which these forms of knowledge are acquired, then concluding with a discussion of how this knowledge is verified.

**Forms of Knowledge**

In their landmark study, Barry Hallen and J. Olubi Ṣopido demonstrated the critical nature of the discourse about knowledge among traditional *oniṣẹgun* ("medicine men").[1] Among other things, this study underscored the distinction between *igbagbọ* (secondhand or received knowledge) and *imọ* (firsthand or empirically verified knowledge). The babalawo I interviewed drew nearly identical distinctions, explaining that *igbagbọ* is "something that you hear [*gbọ*] and accept [*gba*]. But it is not knowledge [*imọ*]. When you yourself see something, then you know it, that is knowledge [*imọ*]."[2] As Hallen and Ṣodipo demonstrate, this distinction between *igbagbọ* and *imọ* does not map neatly onto the English terms "belief" and "knowledge," as many things that we would ordinarily consider knowledge (e.g., the structure of atoms or the existence of giant squid) would be classified as *igbagbọ* unless we have seen and evaluated the evidence ourselves, without relying on the reports of others. As members of a predominantly oral society, traditional Yoruba intellectuals were and are more attuned to the secondhand nature of most of the information we receive. The babalawo I met were highly critical and careful about their claims to knowledge, and this does not seem to be a function of the influence of Western education or culture—by far the most critical and epistemologically cautious babalawo I interviewed, the Araba of Modakẹkẹ, was the one with the least exposure to formal Western education, having only attended primary school for three years in his youth.

The babalawo also differentiated *imọ* and *igbagbọ* through the related concept of *otitọ* (truth): "If you accept something that you hear [*gbagbọ*], perhaps it is true, perhaps it is not; however, if you know [*mọ*] something, then it must be true."[3] Similarly, *imọ* was described as being certain (*daju*), whereas *igbagbọ* was described as being somewhat uncertain (*aidaniloju*).

Speaking the truth or being truthful is a sine qua non of being a babalawo. Strict honesty is a condition of being one who relates the words of Ifa, and babalawo often told me that lying is much more "dangerous" for a babalawo than for other people. Since they carry the burden of accurately communicating the speech of Ọrunmila, and therefore Olodumare, lack of respect for or distortion of speech (*ọrọ*) and truth (*otitọ*) fundamentally compromises this function. The babalawo I interviewed frequently cited this verse of Odu Ọsa-Otura—*S'otitọ s'ododo, s'otitiọ o si tun s'ododo, ẹni s'otitọ ni Imale yoo gbe o*, "Speak the truth, speak justly, speak the truth, and also speak justly; those who speak the truth will be helped by the gods"—and this praise name of Ọrunmila from Odu Ọkanran-Wọnrin—*Otitọ inu o ja ju oogun lọ*, "The truth inside is more efficacious than medicine"—to underscore the essential importance of honesty in the tradition. One babalawo even defined being a babalawo as "speaking the truth and having a good/gentle character [*iwa pẹlẹ*]."[4] The existential danger of distorting speech is related to the ontological dimension of speech and truth, to which we will turn shortly.

### *Imọ* and *Imọ Ijinlẹ*

Babalawo also described a special type of *imọ* called "deep knowledge," or *imọ ijinlẹ*. The Araba of Modakẹkẹ compared it to "ordinary knowledge," explaining that *"imọ ijinlẹ* is knowing the origin of something, to go deep. The mechanic has *imọ*, but the engineer has *imọ ijinlẹ*. The doctor has *imọ*, but the professor [of biology or medicine] has *imọ ijinlẹ*."[5] Thus, in this account, *imọ ijinlẹ* is described as principial or foundational knowledge. Similarly, Professor Agboola, a babalawo from Ọyọ and instructor of agriculture at Ọbafẹmi Awolọwọ University in Ile-Ife, described *imọ ijinlẹ* as "fundamental knowledge, knowledge of your self / destiny (*ori*), of the world (*aye*), of the gods (*irunmọle*), the knowledge of Ifa, which is the wisdom of Olodumare." Professor Agboola also described *imọ ijinlẹ* as a combination of *imọ* (knowledge), *oye* (experience), and *ọgbọn* (wisdom), and as going deep into the Odu Ifa, interpreting them deeply, and applying these deep interpretations to one's own life.⁶ Awo Faniyi, a young babalawo from the town of Iseyin and recent graduate of Ọbafẹmi Awolọwọ University, equated *imọ ijinlẹ* with Ifa itself:

> Deep knowledge [*imọ ijinlẹ*] is the speech [*ọrọ*] from the mouth of Olodumare that He gave to Ọrunmila, when he was coming from heaven to earth, to use to mend the world. This is the basis of the knowledge for which the babalawo who can recite all 256 Odu of Ifa are called deep knowers [*onimọ ijinlẹ*] among the priests of Ifa. For example, Odu Ofun Meji says:
>
>> "Speech is the one responsible for things
>> Even if you see that it is him
>> Even if we see that he has not left it"
>> Performed Ifa divination for Olodumare
>> Who will bring speech so that you can have an orientation/explanation.
>
> This verse of Ifa can help us understand that since speech [*ọrọ*] is what Olodumare used to create the world, speech is also what He gave to Ọrunmila to mend the world. This speech is the totality of the verses [*ẹsẹ*] of Ifa, which we can never finish knowing, whose depths we can never plumb; this speech from the mouth of Olodumare, which is Ifa, is *imọ ijinlẹ*.⁷

*Ọrọ*, which I have rendered here as "speech," has a much wider and more profound significance than the English term suggests. In everyday Yoruba, *ọrọ* refers to "speech" or "the topic of discussion or thought"; however, in the mythology of Ifa, *ọrọ* refers to the fundamental, supra-formal, Logos-like⁸ reality of the spoken word through which God creates the cosmos and all of its inhabitants. Rowland Abiọdun relates the following narrative from Odu Osa Ogunda, which explains the genesis of *ọrọ* and its relationship to wisdom (*ọgbọn*) knowledge (*imọ*), and understanding (*oye*):

> There-were-no-living-things
> Was the priest on earth
> That-which-was-suspended-but-did-not-descend,
> Was the priest in heaven
> All-was-just-empty-space-with-no-substance,
> Was the priest of Midair
> It was divined for Earth and Heaven
> When they both existed,

With no inhabitants
In the two empty shells
There were neither birds nor spirits
Living in them
Odumare[9] then created himself,
Being the Primal cause,
Which is the reason we call Odumare
The only wise one on earth
He is the only cause in creation
The only wise one in heaven,
Who created humans.
When He had no companions
He applied wisdom to the situation
To avert any disaster
You, alone,
The only one in Heaven
Is the name of Odumare
The only wise one,
We give you thanks,
The only wise one
Without listening to anyone else
You judge, and are pleased

Odumare sat back and thought about how to create more things in his universe. For this purpose, he realized he needed an intermediary force, since he was too charged with energy to come into contact with any living thing and have it survive. Therefore he created *Ogbon* (Wisdom), held it in his palm and thought where it could live. After a while, Odumare released *Ogbon* to fly away and look for a suitable place to lodge. When *Ogbon* could not find a suitable abode, it flew back, humming like a bee, to Odumare who took *Ogbon* and swallowed it. Similarly *Imo* (knowledge) and *Oye* (understanding), which were also created, returned for lack of suitable abodes, and were swallowed for the same reason.

Odumare then slept, but not in the human sense of the word. . . .

After several thousand years during which Odumare was disturbed by the incessant humming of *Ogbon*, *Imo*, and *Oye*, he decided to get rid of them in order to have some peace.

So he ordered *Ogbon*, *Imo*, and *Oye* to descend (*ro*) making the sound "*hoo*." Thus the three heavenly bodies, now known as *Hoo-ro* or *Oro*, were evacuated and set for their descent for earth. Since they were heavily charged lifeforces from heaven, their descent was accompanied by lightning and thunder. All solid matter melted and became jelly-like. For a while, Ọrọ was suspended in midair like an egg and did not melt, but then it dropped to the earth and split (*la*).

In Ọrọ's new state it is identified with Ẹla [of whom Ọrunmila is regarded as an aspect], the deity that functions in the Ifa divination complex and is regarded by the Yoruba as the embodiment of wisdom, knowledge, and understanding.... Hence Ifa confirms,

> Who was the first to speak?
> Ẹla was the first to speak
> Who was the first to communicate?
> Ẹla was the first to communicate
> Who is this Ẹla?
> It was the Họọ which descended
> That we call Ẹla[10]

In this verse of Ifa, wisdom, knowledge, and understanding are described as inherent qualities of Olodumare in and of himself, which he then created as intermediaries to serve as a buffer between him and creation, to allow creation to have its own existence. Olodumare combined these three entities into a single complex known as *ọrọ* and commanded them to descend to earth (the name of this complex is characteristically derived from the sound, *họọ*, it made as it descended [*rọ*]). Upon its descent, Ọrọ split open (*la*) and acquired the name Ẹla, the origin of meaning, speech, and communication. The Logos-like entity of Ọrọ/Ẹla is identified with Ọrunmila and Ifa, and is often described as a kind of pure meaning beyond formal expression. Nevertheless, it is that which is expressed through the various modalities of the spoken, musical, plastic, and other art forms. Abiọdun explains:

> Ẹla utters through *Owe*, literally "proverbs," but which in broad usage can metaphorically apply to the communicative properties of sculpture, *aroko*, dance, drama, song, chant, poetry, incantations like *ọfọ, ogede, ayajọ epe, odu, ẹsa* and many others which make heavy and esoteric use of metaphors in ritual contexts. ... *Owe* operates between *ọrọ* on the spiritual plane and the earth-level where Ọrọ can be understood, assimilated, and used by humans. Similarly, communication with the *Orisạ*, ancestors, and invisible bodies in heaven is made possible through the channel of *owe*.... With the aid of Ẹla, Ọrọ is made manifest, and it is beautifully "clothed" in poetry, maxims, and wise sayings, all of which are *owe*.

For as the saying goes, *kolombo ni Ọrọ n rin*, "*Ọrọ* moves around naked," and it is forbidden to see it in that state.[11]

In the same vein, Abiọdun quotes the following adage:

> Proverbs (metaphorical/poetic speech) is the steed of *ọrọ*
> If *ọrọ* is lost
> Proverbs are what we will use to find it[12]

So in summary, *owe*—the poetic, metaphorical, proverbial, symbolic mode of speech (and other forms of expression) of the orişa (particularly Ẹla/Ọrunmila)—is what manifests and gives us access to the enigmatic *ọrọ*—the composite of wisdom (*ọgbọn*), knowledge (*imọ*), and understanding (*oye*), which in turn manifest and give us access to Olodumare. The ineffable reality of Olodumare is rendered intelligible through the creation and descent of wisdom (*ọgbọn*), knowledge (*imọ*), and understanding (*oye*) as *ọrọ*, which is in turn made tangible and sensible through the symbolic arts of *owe*. These parallel processes of "ascent" and "descent" form the animating logic of ritual practice. As Abiọdun writes, "This, in fact, is what happens in the worship of *Orişa* where sculpture, mime, dance, drama, and poetry of an appropriate character combine to raise consciousness above and beyond the physical into the spiritual realm for the vivid realization of an abstract idea."[13]

Wisdom (*ọgbọn*) and understanding (*oye*) also have more prosaic meanings, which the babalawo I interviewed described for me in strikingly congruent fashion. *Oye* was characterized as a form of understanding that is the result of wide experience and exposure: in the words of the Araba of Modakẹkẹ, "We cannot say that a child has *oye*."[14] *Ọgbọn* was often glossed as "wisdom," or as the Araba succinctly put it, "*Ọgbọn* is *imọ* plus *oye*." This description of wisdom (*ọgbọn*) as knowledge (*imọ*) plus understanding (*oye*) met with strong approval among the other babalawo I interviewed, all of whom stressed the supremacy of Ọrunmila's wisdom (*ọgbọn*), which they related to the fact that he was the first creation of Olodumare. Since Ọrunmila has directly witnessed everything and has more experience than any other creation, his wisdom is supreme.

The mythological narrative about the "calabash of wisdom" (*igba iwa*) from Odu Oturupọn Meji (cited in the previous chapter) was also invoked to explain the supremacy of Ọrunmila's wisdom and its relationship to character (*iwa*). When I asked the Araba of Modakẹkẹ about the relationship between character and wisdom, he recited part of this narrative, and explained that "Ọrunmila could handle the calabash of wisdom [*igba iwa*] because of his good character [*iwa*]." Discerning readers may notice that the word for "character," *iwa*, and the word glossed as "wisdom" (*iwa*) in the "calabash of wisdom" (*igba iwa*), are identical. Thus, wisdom could be said to be the content that the "calabash of character" (*igba iwa*) contains; that is, good character is a necessary condition, and the fruit, of wisdom.[15]

Furthermore, the etymology of the word *iwa* (character) is particularly revealing. This word *iwa* (character), is undoubtedly related to the verb *huwa*, which roughly means "to behave." But, more interestingly, it is also a homophone of the verbal noun of the verb *wa*, which means "to be" or "to exist." Thus *iwa* could be understood to mean "being" or "existence," revealing the close relationship between morality/ethics and ontology in traditional Yoruba thought.[16] The better one's character (*iwa*), the "more" one is—or conversely, to lack character, to have a bad character (*iwa buruku*), is to be "less," to have a lesser existence.

As the source or origin of all existence, Olodumare is the foundation of the moral/existential order. Professor Agboola explained that "*Otitọ* [truth/reality] is the *iwa* [character/being] of Olodumare,"[17] and so speaking the truth and behaving truthfully is to align one's own character, or mode of being, with that of Olodumare, the Absolute Being or Lord of Existence (*Olu-Iwa*). To have good character (*iwa*) is to be like Olodumare, and to be like Olodumare is to be more real, to have a greater share of existence (*iwa*). Citing a verse from Odu Eji Ogbe, the Araba of Modakẹkẹ similarly commented:

> Good/gentle character [*iwa pẹlẹ*] is what Olodumare likes when Olodumare comes to take *ẹmi* ["the breath of life" or spirit] at the time of death.
>
> > Coming into the world is easy
> > Later, when returning, the last gasps are difficult
> > There is no comforter
> > No one to whom we can complain, what remains is the work of one's hands
> > Gentle character is what Eledumare likes.
>
> When Olodumare comes to take *ẹmi*, if the person's character is not good, the *ẹmi* will get stuck in the throat, he will gasp and choke, and death will be difficult.[18]

If one's character or mode of being is not in conformity with that of Olodumare (Absolute Being itself), then the reintegration of the individual self (*ẹmi*) with its origin will be difficult.

### Yoruba/Ifa Anthropology and Psychology
#### Ẹmi

The *ẹmi* is a central element of the traditional Yoruba conception of personhood as articulated in the oral corpus and rituals of Ifa. *Ẹmi* is often rendered into English as "self";[19] however, in the context of Ifa, and traditional Yoruba thought in general, ẹmi has a significant mythological, metaphysical dimensions that the English term "self" seldom carries. The Araba of Modakẹkẹ explained that ẹmi is the child of Olodumare (ọmọ Olodumare), a bit of himself that he "blows" (fẹ) into the bodies of people in heaven, bringing them to life. The orișa Ogun is credited with forming the bones of people; the orișa Ọbatala, with forming their bodies;[20] and Olodumare provides ẹmi, the animating "breath of life," which is also the defining element of consciousness, subjectivity, and selfhood. A myth from Odu Obara-Ọturupọn tells how Eṣu, Ogun, and Orișanla conspire and create a fake bride to scam Ọrunmila into giving them money as a brideprice; Ogun provided the structure of the body and gave it motion, Orișanla gave her speech, and Eṣu used his wiles to make her charming and attractive—but without Olodumare's ẹmi, the fake bride started to fall apart after two days, though that was long enough to scam Ọrunmila into paying her dowry.[21] Upon death, the ẹmi is said to leave the body and return to Olodumare. However, the Araba explained that this only takes place for those who have lived long, full, good lives. The ẹmi of those who died untimely deaths, or who died before developing good character, is believed to linger on earth before eventually leaving to take on a new body and return to the world.

Ori

According to Ifa, before coming into the world, the newly animated person chooses an ori, a "head" or "destiny." As one of Hallen's collaborators explained, "It (ẹmi) chooses what it will come to do.... So also it is the act of the self (ẹmi) when it is with the supreme deity (Ọlọrun)."[22] This ori inu or "inner head" is differentiated from the physical or "outer head," ori ode, which serves as a symbol and vessel for the former. The inner head is regarded as the essence of one's individual personality and destiny. This ori is at once a personal divinity or guardian angel, the divine aspect of a person, one's fate or destiny, and one's own personal archetype of a felicitous and successful life. This is illustrated in the following myth (in summary form) from Odu Ogbe-Ogunda (Ogbe-Yọnu):

> It is a snare which strikes suddenly
> Ifa divination was performed for Orisẹẹku, the son of Ogun
> Ifa divination was also performed for Orileemere, the son of Ija
> Ifa divination was performed for Afuwapẹ, who was the son of Ọrunmila
> On the day they were going to the house of Olodumare to choose their heads

> The three of them were good friends and decided to go down to earth to settle, because perhaps it would be a better place for them than heaven. They sought

the advice of elders who told them to go directly to the house of Ajala, the potter who mould heads to choose their heads and then go down to the world. Afuwapẹ ignored the advice and went to see his father Ọrunmila who performed divination for him. Ogbe-Yọnu came out and the Ifa priests in Ọrunmila's household interpreted the Odu for him, saying that his son was going on a journey and that he should perform a sacrifice so that he would choose a good head. The sacrifice was three bags of salt, and three bags of twelve thousand cowries. When he came out of his father's house, Afuwapẹ could not find his friends, Orisẹẹku, the son of Ogun and Orileemere, the son of Ija. They had gone on ahead to find Ajala's house. On the way they met a gatekeeper and asked him to show them the way, but he said that it was too far, so they went alone and eventually found Ajala's house. However, they could not find the potter there, so Orileemere choose a brand-new head, not knowing that it had not been baked yet. Orisẹẹku chose a big head, not knowing that it was broken. They both put on their heads and hurried on down to the world. On their way down into the world they were beaten by rain, which saturated their heads, causing them to break apart. They entered the world with these small heads. In the world, they worked hard, but did not get anywhere. They consulted babalawo, who told them that the fault was in the bad heads they had chosen. The babalawo told them that they had chosen bad heads, and that all the work they had been doing was just to mend the worn off parts of their bad heads. Only after this had been accomplished, would their works begin to prosper.

On the way to Ajala's house, Afuwapẹ met the gatekeeper cooking soup. He saw the man putting ashes into his soup, and he offered him the salt to use instead. The man thanked him and told him that he would walk him to Ajala's house. When they arrived, they heard someone shouting. The gatekeeper explained that Ajala's creditor was the one shouting, because he was looking for Ajala. Afuwapẹ went to the creditor and paid off Ajala's debt with one of the bags of twelve thousand cowries. The creditor left and Ajala hopped down from the ceiling where he had been hiding and thanked Afuwapẹ. Ajala took him to his storehouse of heads and began to hit various heads with his iron rod, until he found a good, strong one, which he gave to Afuwapẹ. Afuwapẹ fixed it on his head and went down to the world. He also passed through heavy rains, but they did not damage his head. When Afuwapẹ arrived on earth, he worked hard and his works bore fruit. He became wealthy, had many wives and children, and was honoured with a title. When Orisẹẹku, the son of Ogun, and Orileemere, the son of Ija, saw him they started to weep.

Each said, "I don't know where the lucky ones chose their heads,
I would have gone there to choose mine

I don't know where Afuwapẹ chose his head"
Afuwapẹ answered them saying
"You don't know where the lucky ones chose their heads,
You would have gone there to choose your own
You don't know where Afuwapẹ chose his head
You would have gone there to choose your own
We chose our heads from the same place
But our destinies (*kadara*) are different"[23]

Within the Ifa corpus, misfortune in life is often attributed to having chosen a bad *ori* in heaven or to having "missed the road" (i.e., not followed the path of one's destiny), and both descriptions are really just two different ways of saying the same thing. From the human side, looking "up," we have forgotten the nature of our *ori*, and so it would seem that either one's bad actions spoiled one's good destiny, or that one's bad destiny thwarted one's good efforts (hence the saying *ẹni l'ori rere ti ko ni iwa, iwa l'o ma b'ori reje*, "For the person with good destiny but no character, it is character that will ruin his good destiny"). But from the divine side, looking "down," all of a person's decisions are really just repetitions of his primordial choice of *ori*—in fact, the person is just a manifestation of his *ori*, an unfolding in time of all of its potentialities, hence the verse of Ifa that says *ori ẹni l'Ẹlẹda ẹni*, "One's *ori* is one's Creator." So from the heavenly side, destiny is character (destiny manifests itself as character), but from the human side, character is destiny (character seems to determine one's destiny).[24] Hence a song derived from Odu Ogbe-Yọnu says:

If Ori marries Iwa [character]
And Iwa marries Ori
The world will be well

And the following verse from the same Odu makes a similar point:

"Nothing comes from getting angry
Patience is the father of character
An elder who has patience
Has everything"
Performed Ifa divination for *ori*, and likewise for character [*iwa*]
It is only cultivating character that is difficult
There is not one bad *ori* in Ile-Ifẹ [the primordial city, symbolizing heaven]
It is only cultivating character that is difficult[25]

Knowledge in Ifa • 241

*Ori* is also worshipped as a divinity in its own right, and the Ifa corpus is replete with myths emphasizing its superiority to other divinities and its close connection to Olodumare. For example, Abimbola cites the following verses of Ifa from Odu Oyẹku Meji and Odu Ogunda Meji (respectively):

[Odu Oyẹku Meji]
A child is not tall enough to stretch his hand to reach the high shelf
An adult's hand cannot enter the mouth of a gourd
The work an adult begs a child to do
Let him not refuse to do.
We all have work to do for each other's good
Ifa divination was performed for Ọrunmila
About whom his devotee
Would make a complaint to Olodumare
Olodumare then sent for Ọrunmila
To explain the reason why
He did not support his devotee
When Ọrunmila got to the presence of Olodumare
He explained that he had done all in his power for his devotee
But that the destiny chosen by the devotee made his efforts fruitless
It was then that the matter
Became quite clear to Olodumare
And he was happy
That he did not pronounce his judgment on the evidence of only one of the
    two parties.[26]

[Ogunda Meji]
Ori I hail you
You who do not forget your devotees
Who blesses a devotee more quickly than other gods
No god blesses a man
Without the consent of his Ori
Ori, I hail you
You who allow children to be born alive
One whose sacrifice is accepted by Ori
Should rejoice abundantly[27]

Likewise, the Araba recited the following verse of Ogunda Meji:

Ori is the only one. Ọrunmila says you cover a dirty person with dyed cloth, the one who makes the elephant blow its horn [praise names for ori], Ori is the only one who can complete the journey. If you have money, it is the work of Ori. If you want a wife, it is Ori. If you want children, it is Ori. If you are searching for any blessing, it is to Ori that you must bring your supplications! O my Ori! Ori is always the first to remember me, who will quickly carry me to the orișa, my helper. There is no orișa who supports us like Ori. My Ori, I salute you!

They say when a babalawo dies, we must bury him with his Ifa. When a devotee of Șango dies, we throw away his effects. When a devotee of Ogun dies, hunters take his effects and perform the *ipa* rituals with them. When a devotee of Orișanla dies, we throw his effects into the bush. However, when a person dies, nobody will take away his head. A person is buried with his/her head. Ori is the only one who can make the journey like Alasan. I greet you Ori, who is always the first to remember me, who will quickly carry me to the orișa, my helper. There is no orișa who supports us like ori. Ori, I salute you![28]

In fact, *ori* is often described as our "heavenly self" or "double" (*ẹnikeji t'o wa l'ọrun*) that exists with Olodumare and in the depths of our being (*inu*).[29] The worship of *ori* is central to the practice of Ifa, as Abimbola explains: "It is important for every individual to consult Ifa from time to time to find out the true path of one's destiny. By consulting Ifa, one is merely trying to find out what has been kept in store by one's *ori*. Divination is therefore regarded as the communication of the wishes of one's *ori* to Ifa who will then reveal this to the client through the appropriate chapter and verse of the Odu system."[30]

Thus, even Ifa serves as an intermediary between oneself and one's own *ori*, the connection or nexus between one's individual self and Olodumare. Ifa makes much of the natural symbolism of the physical head to illustrate the nature of the "inner head," pointing out that most children come into the world headfirst; while alive, our heads are usually the closest part of our bodies to heaven; even in death, our heads go with us into the grave, unlike other objects of worship; furthermore the body cannot function without the head, which is also traditionally used to carry heavy loads.[31] The following verse of Ifa, which also functions as a praise-poem, illustrates this point:

> All the good things that will bless me
> I will seek from my *Ori*
> He who cuts a narrow path to the world
> He who cuts a narrow path to heaven.
> *Ori* cause and creator

> *Ori* the one and only, who makes bean cakes but never sells them at Ejigbomẹkun market[32]
> The great companion who never deserts one
> *Ori* the master of all
> It is the *Ori* we should praise
> The rest of the body comes to naught
> When *Ori* is missing from the body
> What remains is useless
> What remains is incapable of carrying any load.
> It is the *Ori* which bears the load
> *Ori*, I plead with you
> Do not desert me
> You, the lord of all things[33]

Susanne Wenger summarized these various aspects of *ori* as follows: "Ori is that part of one's complex identity which is an imperishable part of God. . . . Ori is a part of God, Olodumare, in His quality as the Creator, in which capacity he is called Ẹlẹda; but he is also our very own self. From this, our self, depends not only our fate, but our active participation in our fate. Ceremonially we address Ori as '*Ori mi Ẹlẹda mi*,' 'My Ori, my creator!'"[34]

However, the babalawo I interviewed emphasized the fact that no discussion of *ori* can be complete without a discussion of *ẹsẹ*, a word that at once means "leg," "struggle," or "effort." As the Araba of Modakẹkẹ put it, "Have you ever seen a head [*ori*] rolling around by itself without any legs [*ẹsẹ*]? It takes legs/effort [*ẹsẹ*] to walk the path of your destiny." Abimbola cites a verse from Odu Oturupọn Meji that illustrates the inseparability and complementarity of *ori* and *ẹsẹ*, destiny and effort:

> Ọpẹbẹ, the Ifa priest of legs [*ẹsẹ*],
> Performed Ifa divination for legs
> On the day he was coming from heaven to earth
> All heads [*ori*] called themselves together
> But they did not invite legs
> Ẹsu said, "Since you did not invite legs,
> We will see how you will bring your deliberations to success."
> Their meeting ended in a quarrel
> They then sent for legs
> It was then that their deliberations became successful.
> They said that was exactly what their Ifa priests had predicted

> Ọpẹbẹ, the Ifa priest of legs [ẹsẹ],
> Performed Ifa divination for legs
> On the day was coming from heaven to earth
> Ọpẹbẹ has surely come,
> Ifa priest of legs
> No one deliberates
> Without the reckoning with legs
> Ọpẹbẹ has surely come,
> Ifa priest of legs[35]

Professor Agboola cited the following verses of Odu Irẹtẹ Meji describing the necessity of struggle, even for those blessed with good destinies:

> "You imprint one leg [ẹsẹ] of Irẹtẹ
> I, too, imprint one leg of Irẹtẹ
> When the imprint becomes two, then the true Irẹtẹ-Meji is formed."
> Performed Ifa divination for "One with a good *ori* but lacking good legs"
> He was told to offer sacrifice
> He heard, he made the sacrifice
> My sacred palm nuts [*ikin*], the protruding tooth,
> Ifa, please let me have a good *ori*
> Together with good legs.[36]

Like *ori*, *ẹsẹ* illustrates an important aspect of the worldview articulated by Ifa: the symbolic relationship that connects everything in the outer/physical (*ode*) world (*aye*) to a corresponding inner or heavenly (*inu/ọrun*) reality that shares the same name. While conceptually distinct, the outer reality has an ontological continuity with its inner aspect, for which it serves as a manifestation or appearance. More strictly speaking, the things in heaven (*ọrun*) all have their mirror images or manifestations in the world (*aye*), just as the inner aspects or realities of a person (*inu*) have their counterparts or manifestations in the person's outer appearance (*ode*).

*Inu*

This inner dimension is another important constituent element of the Yoruba conception of personhood. *Inu*, which can literally refer to the stomach or intestines,[37] is more generally used to refer to one's "insides," the inner dimensions that might be called "psychological" or "spiritual" in English. *Inu* is the stage of one's inner life: feelings, thoughts, as well as the promptings or impulses that manifest as conscious behavior are all described as taking place or inhering in *inu*. For example, the most common way of expressing happiness in Yoruba is *inu mi dun*, which literally means, "my insides are sweet." *Inu* designates the subjective, interior dimension of human existence.

### Ọkan

One of the most important inhabitants of the *inu*, the *ọkan* (heart) is the seat of cognition, whereas feelings are usually described as occurring in *inu*. *Ọkan* literally means "heart,"[38] and as in other languages (e.g., classical Arabic, Chinese, and Hebrew) it also denotes "the mind." In addition to pumping blood throughout the body, the heart is also the instrument and location of thoughts (*ẹro*), intention, and attention. Closely related to this "heart/mind" is *ẹri ọkan*, which is often glossed as "conscience," but which literally means "witness of the heart." This faculty is the instrument of introspective moral self-evaluation. In the words of one babalawo, "When you are doing something, maybe after you have done it, it is the *ẹri ọkan* that tells you if what you have done is good or not good. It can even tell you if what you are going to do is good or not."[39] A related but distinct faculty is the *oju inu*, the "inner eye" or "insight," by which one infers, interprets, understands, or perceives the nonapparent aspect of phenomena from their appearances. The *oju inu* is used to do things as commonplace as intuiting a child's character on the basis of a few interactions to recognizing the working of the orișa or other invisible powers in one's own life and others.

### Ero/Ironu

"Thought" and "thinking" are used to translate *ero* and *ironu*, which are usually described as taking place in the *ọkan* (heart/mind) and/or *inu*. Segun Gbadegesin speculates that *ero* is derived from the verb *ro*, meaning "to stir," and therefore *ironu* (*ro+inu*) would literally mean "to stir up one's insides"[40]—the implication being that thinking or cogitation stirs up one's insides, bringing thoughts and ideas to the surface like pieces of meat in a stew. Relatedly, *ronupiwada*, which is commonly translated as "repentance," refers to the process of introspection or self-reflection that leads to a change in behavior and character (*iwa*).

### Ọpọlọ

*Ọpọlọ*, which refers to the physical organ of the brain, is also commonly used to refer to intelligence, especially as regards creativity and production. For example, when I explained the mnemonic strategies I used to memorize the order of the Odu of Ifa, my babalawo interlocutors complimented me by saying "Your brain is complete/correct!" (*Ọpọlọ rẹ ti pe*). Awo Faniyi cited the following verse from Odu Eji Ogbe recounting the process of the self's coming into being in the womb/heaven to explain the relationship between these different aspects of the self:

> "The day that the body was created from water
> The day that water was created, so was blood
> The day that blood was created, so was the whole body"
> Performed Ifa divination for the heart [*ọkan*]
> And likewise for the self [*ẹmi*]
> [He] performed Ifa divination for the inner head [*ori inu*]
> And likewise for the brain [*ọpọlọ*]
> When the four of them were coming from heaven to the world

The verse goes on to describe the different functions of these four elements, which Awo Faniyi summarized as follows: "*Ẹmi* is the king of the whole body/person [*ara*]. *Ori inu* says everything that the person will do in life. *Ọkan* circulates the blood and thoughts [*ero*] throughout the body/person [*ara*]. *Ọpọlọ* applies wisdom/intelligence [*ọgbọn*] to situations in order to accomplish things."[41] Similarly, the Araba explained, "*Ẹmi* is the king, it is like the king of the whole body. *Ẹmi* comes from Olodumare and returns to Him when the person dies. . . . *Ori inu* is very important; it is the fate or destiny [*kadara, ayanmọ*] of a person, which he or she chose in heaven before coming into the world. Everything good in life comes from one's *ori*, so it must be worshipped. We do divination and Ifa tells us what we should do, what Olodumare wants us to do, what our destiny [*ori inu*] is so that we can find the blessings of life [*ire aye*]."[42]

*Ara/Eniyan*

*Ara* is used to designate a person's physical body as well as his or her totality as a person. As mentioned above, the physical body is understood not only as the vessel of the inner self (*inu* or *ẹmi*), but also as a symbolic representation, reflection, or manifestation of this inner reality. This symbolic relationship is not merely mental, but also ontological: the physical or outer head (*ori ode*) has an existential connection to the inner head (*ori inu*), and the various rituals and rites of Ifa make use of these connections, which are also encoded in the language of the Odu Ifa. The babalawo I interviewed emphasized the fact that "everything has its counterpart [*ẹnikeji*] in heaven, inside a person [*inu eniyan*]. Head [*ori*], legs [*ẹsẹ*], hands [*ọwọ*], eyes [*oju*]—all the parts of the body."[43] *Eniyan* is usually translated as "person," but in Yoruba it has a distinctive, normative moral and ethical connotation, like the term "human" or "humanity" in English. Someone who exhibits bad character is said to "not be a person" (*Kii ṣe eniyan*). Illustrating this normative dimension of the concept of personhood, B. A. Ademuleya quotes the following verse of Odu Irosun Iwori, which provides a mythical derivation of the word *eniyan*, from the phrase *ẹni a yan*, "one who is chosen":

> ... a wa gegebi eniyan,
> a wa ni Olodumare yan
> lati lo tun ile aye se,
> Eni-a-yan ni wa ...
>
> We as human beings,
> We the ones God has chosen,
> To renew the world,
> We are the chosen ones.[44]

Thus, to be truly human is to fulfill the task for which we were chosen, thereby renewing/repairing the world. For the babalawo, this is accomplished through their deep knowledge (*imọ ijinlẹ*) of Ifa, the source of wisdom (*ọgbọn*) and the fundamental principles through which the inner self (*inu*), the world (*aye*), and heaven (*ọrun*) were created. As Awo Faniyi explained, "Deep knowledge [*imọ ijinlẹ*] is the word [*ọrọ*] from the mouth of Olodumare that He gave to Ọrunmila to mend the world [*tun aye ṣe*]."[45] This knowledge is acquired by studying and being initiated into the priesthood of Ifa, which involves the cultivation of a good character characterized by honesty, gentleness (*pẹlẹ*), diligence, and patience (*suuru*). The acquisition of this wisdom (*ọgbọn*) is presented as being inseparable from the cultivation of this character or mode of being (*iwa*), since both this wisdom and character are said to belong to Ọrunmila (and ultimately to Olodumare), and, in the words of one babalawo, one must "become like Ọrunmila in order to know what he knows."[46]

**Knowledge of God / Knowledge of Self**

Knowing one's *ori* (*imọri*) is one of the stated goals of Ifa divination and practice. Deepening one's knowledge (*imọ*) of Olodumare and the orisa is also a part of the process of becoming a mature babalawo; however, this is not so much a matter of knowing whether Olodumare and the orisa exist—to a babalawo such a question is as nonsensical as asking whether or not reality, love, wind, gravity, or consciousness exist. It is a question of acquiring deep firsthand knowledge (*imọ ijinlẹ*) of what these fundamental aspects of human experience are like. Wọle Ṣoyinka and Ulli Beier once commented on this distinctive feature of traditional Yoruba worldviews:

> Ṣoyinka: I believe that the truly liberated mind is never aggressive about his or her system of beliefs. Because it is founded on such total self-confidence, such acceptance of others, that there is no need to march out and propagate one's

cause. That is why Yoruba religion has never waged a religious war, like the Jihad or the Crusades.[47]

Beier: In fact they never make converts! It is the orisha himself who chooses his devotees....

Ṣoyinka The person who needs to convert others is a creature of total insecurity.

Beier: There is this beautiful Yoruba proverb: "The effort one makes of forcing another to be like oneself, makes one an unpleasant person!" ...

Beier: It is significant that when a Yoruba says "Igbagbo" (a believer) it means "Christian," because it is nonsensical to say "I believe in Shango" or "I believe in Ogun." One is too secure in one's worldview. I think I have mentioned to you once that remarkable reply of an old olorisha, to whom his grandchild said: "The teacher said, your Ọbatala doesn't exist!" He simply answered. "Only that for which we have no name does not exist." He could not be shaken.

Ṣoyinka That is a brilliant way of putting it. And you have been to Brazil and Cuba. In that part of the world you find Europeans ... who accept the humanism of this religion and who recognize it as their own way of truth. And they cannot conceive of any other way of looking at the world. This proven ability of this religion is well documented.[48]

Relatedly, Susanne Wenger writes, "But the term 'to believe' which automatically implies the opposite, namely to not believe, does not exist for the Yoruba, to whom the idea that one may deny God's existence is too absurd for words and the epitome of madness."[49] Similarly, when I asked babalawo if and how they knew that Olodumare or Ọrunmila existed or were real, the responses tended to consist of a scoff followed by some variation "Of course!" and a counterquestion invoking close personal relationships such as "How do you know I exist?" "How do you know you exist?" or "How do you know your father or brother exists?" The Araba of Modakẹkẹ explained, "No one can say he has seen Olodumare or Ọrunmila, but we see the work of their hands and we speak with them every day in prayer [adura]. Olodumare speaks to us through Ọrunmila, and Ọrunmila speaks through his palm nuts [ikin] and divination chain [opẹlẹ]."[50]

So asking a babalawo whether he believes in Olodumare or Ọrunmila is as nonsensical as asking someone if he believes in existence or the color red. The question, rather, is "What does one know of or about these realities?" and, most importantly, "What is the nature of one's relationship with them?" The specific ways in which this knowledge is acquired and these relationships are established will be the subject of the next chapter.

CONCLUSION

Knowledge (*imọ*) in Ifa is multifaceted, and situated within the unique Yoruba cosmology, anthropology, and psychology that has been outlined in this chapter. *Imọ* is differentiated from *igbagbọ* (belief), in that the former must be the result of direct perception or verification, and thus many things that would ordinarily count as "knowledge" in English (such as the number of Jupiter's moons) would be regarded as *igbagbọ* for all but the specialists who directly verify these facts. Moreover, *imọ ijinlẹ* (deep knowledge) is described as a knowledge of foundational principles, and is identified with Ọrọ, the Logos-like word through which Olodumare created the world, and with Ọrunmila and the Odu of Ifa itself. Through acquiring and applying this deep knowledge, babalawo are said to "mend the world," returning it to its sacred origin. Closely related to *imọ ijinlẹ* is *imọri*, the knowledge of one's *ori*, which is also described as one of the most important goals of the tradition of Ifa. The following two chapters will examine the ways in which babalawo cultivate and verify these forms of knowledge, which they identify as the goal of their tradition.

CHAPTER 7

# How Is Knowledge Acquired in Ifa?

*A kọfa mọfa*
*Babalawo t'o ba kọfa mọfa*
*A maa di Babalawo*
*Onişegun t'o ba kọogun-mọogun*
*A maa di agbalagba işegun*

One who studies Ifa, knows Ifa
A babalawo who studies Ifa and knows it
Will become a [senior] babalawo
A traditional doctor, if he studies medicine and knows it
He will become a revered elder in medicine
—ODU OTURA-OGBE

Truth is the character [*iwa*] of Olodumare
Otitọ [*truth*] is more than saying the truth, it is being true
—AWO AGBOOLA

*Ifa ki ko nii mu ni mọ Ifa*
*Ọna sisi nii mu ni mọ ona*
*Ọna ti a ko rin ri*
*Nii se ni sibasibo*

It is through learning Ifa that one understands Ifa
It is by missing one's way that one becomes
acquainted with the way
It is the road that one has not walked before
That makes one wander here and there
—ODU OKANRAN-TURUPON

When I first began my program of research in Ifẹ and the neighboring town of Modakẹkẹ, I conducted daily interviews with the Araba of Modakẹkẹ, who very patiently endured my seemingly endless barrage of questions about knowledge and learning in Ifa. On our third day of interviews, however, he interrupted my latest line of inquiry with a suggestion: "These things that you want to know, you can see them all for yourself if you take initiation and go to the sacred grove [*igbodu*]. But since I know you do not want to do that, I think you should learn the first sixteen Odu of Ifa. This is how we begin to teach children. Once you know these, you have the foundation; everything else is derived from these sixteen Odu."[1]

So for the next few months, in addition to the interviews I conducted with other babalawo in the area, I spent a few hours a day, five or six days a week, memorizing the sixteen main divinatory signs of the Odu, their order, and learning two or three verses for each of these sixteen main Odu. This process introduced me to some dimensions of the process of studying Ifa that would be difficult to access through questions alone. Studying the Odu of Ifa began to change the way I perceived my surroundings; given that virtually all the flora and fauna, all the cultural, economic, artistic, and social practices of Yorubaland, are described in the Odu of Ifa, I daily came across things that brought the verses I had just learned to mind. After a few weeks, I began to recognize the Odu Ifa in the phenomena and situations around me, and my perception of them became intertwined with the verses of the Odu that described them.

For example, while walking home one day, wondering whether an acquaintance of mine had overcharged me for some cloth, I saw a butterfly flapping in front of me and immediately remembered the following verse of Odu Irẹtẹ Meji:

> "Big hill at the end of the straight way"
> Performed Ifa divination for the Moth
> And also for Locust
> But only Butterfly sacrificed
> After he made the sacrifice, he said:
> "Look at my belly, look at my back." [because I am concealing nothing]
> The butterfly has no scheme in mind
> "Look at my belly, look at my back."

Ifa says that the mind (*inu*) of this person should be open, that he should not have two minds (*inu meji*) [i.e., have second thoughts] about someone. Ifa says that life should be easy for this person.[2]

The sight of the floating butterfly; the onomatopoeic sound of the Yoruba word for butterfly, *labalaba*, which resembles its playful flapping; and the descriptive verse of Ifa that portrays the butterfly as innocent and carefree, all combined into a single perceptual event that allayed my suspicions and set my mind at ease. I didn't think anything of it at the time, and it was only later that I realized that I was subtly beginning to perceive the world in a new way—even only after a few weeks—and without the benefit of initiation.

### EARLY TRAINING OF A BABALAWO

The babalawo I interviewed all explained that their relationship with Ifa began before birth and extended beyond death. As mentioned above, before descending to the world from heaven, each new person is said to choose his or her own unique destiny/head (*ori*), and each *ori* has a particular set of relationships with the various Odu of Ifa and with the orişa. A particular orişa is said to "own" the head of a devotee, who is also said to have an Odu that gives birth to him or her. On the way to the world down from heaven, the person is said to pass underneath the "tree of forgetfulness" (*igi igbagbe*) or cross the river at the boundary of heaven and forget his choice of *ori*. The physical process of birth is paralleled by and identified with the process of passing from heaven to the world (*aye*). The *ori* of those destined to become babalawo are said to be "owned" by Qrunmila.

According to Professor Agboola, after birth, the infant's feet are kept off the ground until the third day (or fifth day in some places, and these days it is often combined with the naming ceremony on the seventh or eighth day of the child's life),[3] when a ceremony called *ęsę n taye* ("feet touching the world") or *ikọsę waye* ("stepping into the world") is held, which he described as "a spiritual look into the life of a newborn."[4] Part of this ceremony is known as *imọri*, or knowing the *ori* of the child.[5] During this ceremony, a babalawo will perform Ifa divination for the child to determine the Odu that will guide the child's early life. The verses of this Odu will prescribe the sacrifices that the child's parents will perform for him, as well as the taboos (*eewọ*) they will observe for the child (such as not wearing red, not eating certain foods, etc.). For example, if Irętę Meji comes up when divination is performed and the following verse is recited—

> "The dry season comes and the river quickly leaves"
> Performed Ifa divination for *Atọka* [a large bird of prey]
> The one who is the messenger of Ęlędumare
> The king's messenger does not go to the farm

> The king's messenger does not go to the river
> If I am the messenger of Ifa
> I will be happy
> The king's messenger does not go to the farm
> The king's messenger does not go to the river
> Travelers to Ipo, travelers to Ọffa[6]
> Who doesn't know that I am the messenger of Ifa?[7]

—the babalawo will instruct the parents that the child should become a babalawo, meaning that instead of doing customary chores and work, he or she should be sent to study Ifa.[8]

During this ceremony, which takes place near sunrise, the presiding babalawo will also perform divination to determine which orisa the child should worship to assist him or her in fulfilling his or her destiny. These orisa will then be "made" for the child, formally establishing their relationship by embodying their presence within the child. The family of the child will also then observe the taboos associated with the worship of this orisa (e.g., alcohol is forbidden to children of Ọbatala, while sorghum or guinea corn is forbidden to children of Ọsun).

During this ritual, divination will also be performed to determine which, if any, of the ancestors of the mother or father have returned in this new child. If the child is destined to become a babalawo, the child's *oluwo* ("master of secrets")—or godfather, the one who will train and initiate him into Ifa—will also be determined through divination. Professor Agboola recounted his own experience, explaining that since he was born into a family of babalawo, he was expected to become a babalawo as well: "For example, when they did my *ikọse-aye*, Ifa said I should be given Ọsun, so to this day I am close to Ọsun, and I have a brass *ọpẹlẹ* [brass is sacred to Ọsun]. Ifa also said who my *Oluwo* should be—it is usually not your father, although it can be. I used to watch my father and assist him, and at four years old I began memorizing verses of Ifa with my *oluwo*, who lived around the corner from my father's house in Ọyọ."[9]

Professor Agboola went on to explain that the family and surrounding society influence the child based on the results of this divinatory ritual determining the Odu and orisa that are said to govern the child's life. For example, children of Odu Otura Meji, known as the "Muslim Odu," were sometimes dressed in white on Fridays and given an Islamic education, even if their parents were practitioners of an orisa tradition.[10] Children of Ṣango are thought to be headstrong, fiery, and virtuosic, like Ṣango himself, and are treated as such. This socialization, or "passive training," as Professor Agboola called it, is, in the case of children destined to become babalawo, complemented by the "active training" they receive at the hands of their *oluwo*. While most children born to worshippers of orisa undergo the ritual of *ẹsẹ n taye / ikọse aye*, only those born to babalawo families and those destined to become babalawo undergo training with an *oluwo*. Even among those destined to become babalawo, the divinatory orature of this early ritual creates a highly specialized socialization for each child.

People also frequently become initiated when they receive the "call" of an orisa, which often takes the form of a personal crisis such as an illness. Through divination they discover that they are meant to be initiated. This is increasingly common in contemporary times as hereditary orisa worship appears to be dwindling in Nigeria.

### EARLY TRAINING WITH *OLUWO*

Even before they begin their apprenticeship, all the children of a babalawo family, both male and female, begin their training by assisting their father and mother with chores relating to the practice of Ifa: fetching the instruments of divination and running errands, especially to collect or assist in preparing the ingredients of sacrifices (*ẹbọ*) and herbal medicines (*ewe*). During this time, children also observe and imitate the bodily postures, intonation, greetings, and general comportment of their parents and/or *oluwo*. Babalawo-in-training usually begin their apprenticeship with their *oluwo* between the ages of four and ten, often spending all day at their *oluwo*'s house and returning to their parents' home in the evenings. The children and apprentices of babalawo are also disciplined to adopt certain behaviors as a result of their father's profession.

For example, one afternoon I gave some money to the Araba's young children to buy ice cream; however, when the children came back and were playing with the remaining money, the Araba scolded them severely for having bought the ice cream themselves and for playing with the money out in public. He then turned to me and explained, "Children of babalawo shouldn't be seen outside playing with money or buying frivolous things. People will think that their father is just taking money from people and using it anyhow."[11]

### CULTIVATION OF CHARACTER

Furthermore, apprentices and children of babalawo are held to a higher standard than their peers. The virtues of obedience (*igbọran*), respect and deference toward elders (*itẹriba/ibọwọ*), humility (*irẹlẹ*), patience (*suuru*), honesty (*otitọ*), discretion (*lakaye/ isọra*), thinking well of others (*inu rere*), bravery (*igboju*), diligence, eloquence, and intelligence that characterize the Yoruba aesthetic/ethical ideals of *ọmọluwabi* (often glossed as ọmọ ti Olu iwa bi, "a child of God," meaning a well-raised, cultured person) and iwa pẹlẹ (good/gentle character) are especially expected and cultivated in the children and apprentices of babalawo. Given that they may be privy to the secrets of many members of their community who come to their parent or oluwo for divination, as well as some of the "secrets" of practicing Ifa, the stakes of good character are particularly high for these children. As a verse of Odu Iwori-Ọkanran says, "Careless talk usually kills an ignorant person. There is nothing the eyes of a babalawo cannot see. There is nothing a babalawo cannot know. A babalawo cannot be garrulous."[12] Furthermore, as representatives and potential successors of their priestly fathers and mothers, the children and apprentices of babalawo are expected to embody these ethical ideals that are regarded as a necessary precondition and complement to receiving the knowledge of Ifa.

Abimbola cites a story from Odu Ogbe-Alara (Otura) to underscore the importance of the cultivation of iwa pẹlẹ for babalawo:

> "If we take a wooden object to bash the calabash
> Let us hail Iwa [character]
> If we take up a wooden object to bash the calabash
> Let us hail Iwa
> If we take a wooden object to strike a stone
> Let us hail Iwa"
> Performed Ifa divination for Ọrunmila
> When Baba [Ọrunmila] was going to marry Iwa
> The first time that Ọrunmila married a wife
> Iwa was the one he married
> And Iwa herself
> Was the daughter of Suuru (patience)
> When Ọrunmila proposed to marry Iwa
> She said it was alright
> She said that she would marry him.
> But there was one thing to observe:
> No one should send her away from her matrimonial home.
> No one should use her carelessly as one uses rainwater
> No one should punish her unnecessarily
> Ọrunmila exclaimed, "God will not let me do such a thing."
> He said that he would take care of her
> He said that he would treat her with love
> And he would treat her with kindness
> He then married Iwa

After a very long time,
He became unhappy with her...
He therefore started to worry Iwa
If she did one thing
He would complain that she did it wrongly
If she did another thing,
He would also complain
When Iwa saw that the trouble was too much for her,
Iwa said alright,
She would go to her father's house
And her father was the first-born son of Olodumare
His name was Suuru (patience), the father of Iwa
She then gathered her calabash utensils
And left her home
She went to heaven (ọrun)
When Ọrunmila returned, he said,
"Greeting to the people inside the house!
Greeting to the people inside the house!
Greeting to the people inside the house!"
But Iwa did not show up
Baba [Ọrunmila] then asked around for Iwa
The other neighbors said that they had not seen her
"Where has she gone?
Did she go to the market?
Did she go somewhere?"
He asked these questions for a long time until he added two cowries to three[13]
And went to the house of an Ifa priest
They told him that Iwa had run away
He was advised to go and find her in Alara's household
When he got to the house of Alara he said,
"If we take up a wooden object
To bash it against the calabash
Iwa is the one we are seeking.
Let us hail Iwa.
If we take up a wooden object
To bash it against the calabash
Iwa is the one we are seeking
Let us hail Iwa

If we take up a wooden object
To strike a stone
Iwa is the one we are seeking
Let us hail Iwa
Alara if you see Iwa, let me know
Iwa is the one we are seeking
Iwa"
Alara said that he did not see Iwa
The father then went to the house of Orangun, king of the city of Ila
Offspring of the bird with plenty of feathers
He asked whether Orangun saw Iwa
But Orangun said that he did not see her.
There was hardly any place he did not go
After a long time
He turned back
And inquired from his divination instruments
He said that he looked for Iwa in the house of Alara
He looked for her in the house of Ajero . . .
. . . But they told him that Iwa had gone to heaven [ọrun]
He said that he would like to go and take her from there
They said that was alright
Provided he was prepared to perform sacrifice
They asked him to offer a net,
And give honey to Eṣu
He offered honey as a sacrifice to Eṣu
When Eṣu tasted the honey
He said, "What is this which is so sweet?"
Ọrunmila then put on an Egungun costume
And went to heaven
He started to sing again
Eṣu then played the game of deceit
And went to the place where Iwa was
He said, "A certain man has arrived in heaven,
If you listen to his song,
He is saying such and such a thing . . .
You are the one he is looking for . . ."
Iwa then left (her hiding place)
And went to meet them where they were singing

Ọrunmila was inside the Egungun costume
He saw Iwa through the net of the costume
And he embraced her . . .
Those who change bad luck into good [a praise name for Ọrunmila] then
　　opened up the costume
"Iwa why did you behave like that?
You left me on earth and went away."
Iwa said that was true
She said that was because of how he mistreated her
That she ran away
So that she might have peace of mind
Ọrunmila then implored her to please
Have patience with him,
And follow him [back home]
But Iwa refused
But she said that was alright
She still could do something else
She said, "You Ọrunmila,
Go back to the earth
When you get there
All the things which I have told you not to do,
Don't try to do them
Behave very well
Behave with good character
Take care of your wife,
And take care of your children.
From today on, you will not set your eyes on Iwa anymore.
But I will abide with you
But whatever you do to me
Will determine how orderly your life will be."[14]

Among the many profound points in this verse, two stand out: the genealogy of character—that is, its intimate relationship with patience (*suuru*) and Olodumare—and the utmost importance attributed to the difficult task of cultivating and maintaining the intangible quality of good character. Abimbola concludes, "The man who has *iwa pẹlẹ* will not collide with any of the powers both human and supernatural and will therefore live in complete harmony with the forces that govern the universe. This is why the Yoruba regard *iwa pẹlẹ* as the most important of all moral values, and the greatest attribute of man. The essence of religious worship for the Yoruba consists therefore in striving to cultivate *iwa pẹlẹ* [good/gentle character]. This is the meaning of the saying, *Iwa l'ẹsin* [Worship/religion is character]."[15]

## LEARNING THE ODU

Like the cultivation of character, the process of memorizing the Odu of Ifa is a lifelong process that begins in childhood. Although some babalawo begin this process in adulthood, most start before that. Initially, the apprentices (*ọmọ awo*, "child of secrets") are taught how to properly use the divining chain (*ọpẹlẹ*) and the sacred palm nuts (*ikin*).[16] Then they are taught the sixteen names of the principal Odu (see fig. 7), from which the other 240 Odu are derived, and how to make the signs for these Odu with the divining chain and in the camwood powder (*iyẹ irosun*) on the divining tray (*ọpọn Ifa*). This process of learning to make the marks of the Odu in the powder is known as *ẹtitẹ alẹ*.[17]

Mastering the names, signs, and order of all 256 Odu can take as little as a few days or as long as a year,[18] depending on the intelligence, dedication, and time the apprentice has to devote to this task. The Araba told me that the availability of pen and paper has made this task easier for his apprentices, and he actively encouraged me to write down the names and signs of the Odu in my notebook to accelerate the learning process, which took a couple of days. After mastering and memorizing the names, signs, and order of all 256 Odu, the apprentice performs a ritual known as *ṣiṣi-ọpẹlẹ-ja* (opening and grabbing the divining chain), which involves a sacrifice and, among some babalawo, the ritual known as *jijẹun Ifa* or *jijẹun Odu* (eating Ifa or eating Odu).

In this ritual, the wife of the *oluwo*—who, like all wives of babalawo, is known as an *apẹtẹbi* (a title in its own right with its own responsibilities and rituals)—prepares a "hot" solution of alcohol, pepper, and herbs, which she places on the *ọpẹlẹ* in the position of Eji Ogbe, the most senior Odu. The apprentice must then lick the solution off the eight shells of the *ọpẹlẹ*, and do so for each of the sixteen principal Odu. Professor Agboola recalled doing this around the age of ten and barely being able to finish: "I think I had to do it over the course of two or three days, it tasted so bad, and made me sick. But they say it gives you the power of the spoken word [*ọrọ sisọ*] and puts the Odu inside of you."[19] This kind of physical embodiment and literal internalization of the Odu plays a prominent role in many of the rituals in Ifa, with the camwood powder (*iyẹ irosun*) in which the Odu is marked serving as the most common vehicle of this process of literal incorporation.

Next (although these stages of learning may co-occur), the apprentice memorizes the verses of the Odu. Professor Agboola explained that the standard practice is to start

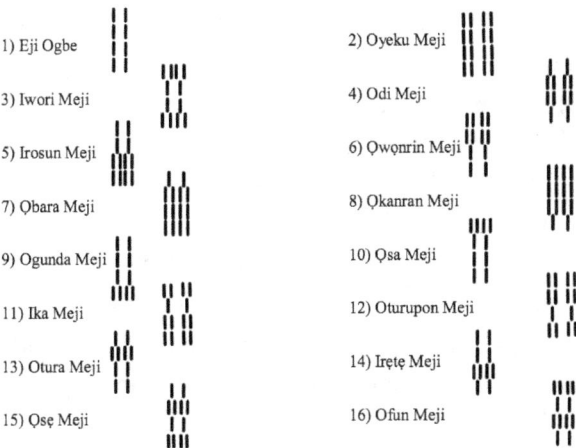

FIGURE 7 The sixteen primary Odu (in order of seniority).

from Eji Ogbe and learn one or two verses (usually one positive verse and one negative) for each Odu, in order of seniority, until the apprentice has "gone all the way around" and memorized a verse or two for each of the 256 Odu. Each verse (*ęsę*) comprises a complete narrative, and ranges in length from a few sentences to epic narratives of hundreds of lines that may take over a half hour to recite. This process of memorizing and mastering the oral corpus is known as *Ifa riran* (seeing Ifa) and primarily done through in-person oral repetition: the *oluwo* corrects mistakes in pronunciation and then tells the apprentice to keep reciting the verse to himself until he memorizes it. While the meanings of a verse may sometimes be discussed, at this stage of training the focus is on memorization and correct recitation.

After the apprentice has memorized and can competently recite a verse from each of the 256 Odu, a special ceremony is held for the *oluwo*, and the apprentice begins his next round, learning another set of verses for each of the Odu. During this process, apprentices often move in with their *oluwo* to devote themselves to the study of Ifa "full-time." The *oluwo* often assist their apprentices in this process through a special herbal/incantatory preparation believed to enhance memory known as *isǫye* (*isǫ+oye* = speaking+understanding). There are various types of *isǫye*, each associated with a particular Odu, such as Eji Ogbe or Ǫbara Iwori, whose verses encode the incantation and ingredients of the formula, which is usually ingested.[20] Similarly, the practice of memorizing the Odu is also thought to improve one's memory. The prominent babalawo Yęmi Ęlębuibǫn writes, "It is a belief that as the acolyte or priest memorizes these verses, his capacity to memorize is increased every day. Ajagunmǫle (he-who-teaches-the-priest-through-dreams) is the great Ifa priest in heaven. He holds the responsibility for guiding the righteous and the upright by giving them retentive memory. It is believed that those who lose their memory or are unable to recite the Odu very well might have offended Ajagunmọle."[21]

Professor Agboola recalled that he began memorizing the verses of Ifa around the age of four and finished his "first round" around the age of ten, taking him six years to memorize one verse for each of the 256 Odu. He explained that he would have been able to do it faster, but that his father enrolled him in Western school at the age of six, so he had less time to devote to his study of Ifa. The "second round" of learning a verse for each of the 256 Odu took him another two or three years, after which, as he recalled, "My father [himself a babalawo] called me inside and told me, 'Now you can call yourself a babalawo, but only inside our house. Don't say you are a babalawo to anyone outside.'"[22]

Relatedly, the Araba of Modakẹkẹ told me, "If you know the sixteen [principal] Odu, you will be a babalawo; the others [i.e., the other Odu] will come out of you. When you see the ọpẹlẹ, Ọrunmila will come out of your mouth and speak, and what you say will be true."[23] However, on another occasion, the Araba explained that to be a practicing babalawo, one must know at least eight verses for each of the Odu, and that knowing sixteen was more complete. Abimbola also gives sixteen as the number of verses of each Odu that must be memorized before the babalawo can move on to the next step of his or her training.[24] Awo Faniyi opined that in order to really be a babalawo, one must know at least four verses for each Odu, but that the process of learning new verses is a lifelong pursuit. Prof. Agboola and the Araba concurred, explaining that studying and learning verses of Ifa extends from "cradle to grave."

Concurrent with this process of memorization, the apprentice also learns the basic interpretation of each verse, and how to perform the various sacrifices associated with each (ẹbọ riru). This process is known as ọkanran ẹbọ and involves mastering the sacred taxonomy of Ifa, which includes a vast array of the flora and fauna native to Yorubaland (and many species that are not) as well as a vast array of artifacts (farming, domestic, and ritual implements), and the incantations (ọfọ) that accompany each item, which may differ depending on the sacrifice or preparation. This vast body of practical knowledge is learned through observation, imitation, and then performance under observation.

The Odu themselves are not regarded as mere chapters of text or collections of words, but are understood as spiritual entities with distinct "personalities" and characteristics in their own right. For example, before the Araba taught me verses from the sixteenth Odu, Ofun Meji (also known as Ọrangun Meji), he explained to me that he had to ask Ofun Meji if it would be alright to teach me its verses, explaining that it was a very powerful and "hot-tempered" Odu given the fact that it was once the most senior of all Odu but is now the sixteenth. The Araba explained that in heaven, Orangun Meji was the most senior of the Odu, but in a case of the "last becoming first," the youngest Odu, Eji Ogbe, was the first to arrive on earth, followed by Oyęku Meji and the other Odu.[25]

When Eji Ogbe arrived at Ile-Ifę, its people made him the paramount chief. Each of the other sixteen primary Odu came down, with Orangun Meji arriving last. When he arrived, he was incensed to learn that his junior sibling had been made king in his stead, and began to fight and then defeat the other Odu. Eventually a truce was reached, and since they could not dethrone Eji Ogbe it was agreed that Ofun Meji's seniority would be recognized in other ways (e.g., after saying his name, he is always hailed with the honorific "Eepa," and Ofun Meji is always considered the senior Odu when casting the opęlę to determine specific alternatives (ibo). Ofun Meji is always propitiated before his verses are recited as a result of this primordial slight and in recognition of his seniority.

After relating this myth, the Araba then went into his backroom, to where his *ikin* (which are used for divination and represent the deity Ifa) are kept in a porcelain pot, and offered a propitiatory sacrifice (*etutu*) of alcohol, palm oil, and a rooster to Ofun Meji. He then asked Ofun Meji for permission to recite its verses to me, performing kola nut divination to ascertain Ofun Meji's response. The response was positive, and so "everything was open" for us to proceed with studying Ofun Meji.

Similarly, Ofun-Ogunda is regarded as a "dangerous" Odu, to which propitiatory sacrifice (*etutu*) must be made before its verses are recited.[26] Another Odu is considered too dangerous for its name to be said aloud and is euphemistically referred to as Odu *Iru-ękun*, or "leopard's tail."[27] Odu Osę-Otura is considered to be the Odu that gave birth to Ęsu and, as the incantatory embodiment of this divine messenger, is invoked when sacrifices are performed, even if the sacrifice is associated with another Odu. The Odu are regarded both as children of Orunmila and as divinities in their own right. They feature as characters in many of the myths of Ifa, and their distinct power (*ase*) and personalities are manifest in their verses, signatures, and associated sacrifices/preparations (*ęb* and *akoşe*). Thus, learning the Odu is more like getting to know a family of people or a set of characters in a novel than it is like learning the periodic table of the elements (although some chemists and small children may relate to the elements in a somewhat similar interpersonal manner).

While memorizing the Odu and assisting their *Oluwo*, apprentices also join their *Oluwo* or their families in worshipping Ifa every fourth day (Ifa's day in the traditional four-day week) through sacrifice, reciting verses of Ifa, and singing *orin Ifa* (songs of Ifa) from the Odu of Ifa. Every sixteenth day, the babalawo of a town or local area gather together to worship Ifa communally in a meeting known as *itadoogun* (meaning the seventeenth—the Yoruba method of counting days counts both the first and last day). Iyanifa (women initiated into Ifa), ọmọ awo (apprentices), babalawo, their wives (apẹtẹbi), and even their children all participate in these gatherings during which they exchange news, stories, and ẹsẹ Ifa (verses of Ifa); seek one another's advice; and address issues affecting their communities. On the rare occasion when I had a question that the Araba could not answer, or about which he was not sure, he would consult with other babalawo at this gathering to see what they had to say.

INITIATION: *ITẸFA* AND *IGBODU*

But perhaps the most important ritual in the training of a babalawo is the *itẹfa*, or initiation into Ifa, which takes place in a temporary space constructed for that purpose, known as the *igbodu*, the grove of mysteries, or *igbo aiku*, the immortal grove. The highest level of this initiation involves witnessing the unutterable secret of Odu (which is distinct from the 256 Odu of Ifa), sometimes described as the mythical wife of Ọrunmila, who gave birth to the 256 Odu, who bear her name.[28] In many places in contemporary Nigeria, women can be initiated into Ifa and become *elegan Ifa* (the most basic degree of initiation), but they are typically forbidden from witnessing Odu and joining the highest ranks of initiates, who are called *olodu* (possessors of Odu). We will return to this point later, but here we should mention that the initiation of women into Ifa is still relatively rare in Nigeria (there appear to be far more babalawo than iyanifa) and is somewhat controversial in the diaspora.[29] There are however, many women in Nigeria who are very knowledgeable about Ifa and are called on to recite and interpret its verses, having studied the Odu and their rituals with their fathers, husbands, or brothers.

In any event, women play an integral role in the *itẹfa* ceremony,[30] which is traditionally a fourteen-day affair involving many elaborate rituals, the details of many of which are closely guarded secrets.[31] While it appears that, traditionally, the *itẹfa* ceremony would take place after the apprentice had memorized one or two verses of each of the 256 Odu, many children of babalawo families in Ijẹbu are initiated during childhood before completing this first round of memorization.[32] In other areas, children go through initiation at a young age if a verse of Ifa calling for it emerges during divination for the child, such as this verse of Odu Irẹtẹ Meji:

"The row [in planting] goes like this
The boundary line goes like this."
Performed Ifa divination for cricket, who pressed two tracks

> That would open wide [the way]
> They said he should perform a sacrifice
> He understood and offered the sacrifice there
> And not long after
> Cricket-presses-two [Irẹ-tẹ-meji] opened wide [the way]
> Ifa says that this person should be initiated [tẹ], that the babalawo should take him to Igbodu, so that his life will go smoothly.[33]

Even if this occurs, the expense of the ceremony (which can run over $1,000) may delay the child's initiation, and even those of adults. This was the case for one of the Araba's younger sons, whom divination revealed should enter the Igbodu as soon as possible, but whose initiation was delayed for several years due to its expense and inconvenience. Sometimes, when adults come for divination about a typical problem (usually lack of money or children, or problems at work or in the family) and a verse recommending initiation into Ifa emerges, the adult may be taken for initiation before studying the Odu. This was the case for a Christian Nigerian friend of mine (who is not from a babalawo family) who came to consult the Araba of Modakẹkẹ about his plans to try to move to the United States after a series of career disappointments and frustrations.

Bascom records a similar story about the Agbọnbọn of Ifẹ, the second highest ranking of the king's diviners (Awọni), whom Bascom described as "the most respected diviner in Ifẹ until his death in 1947." As a child, the future Agbọnbọn was told by his father, described as one "who had been to heaven and returned" (ayọrunbọ), to study Ifa, but he refused. Before the father died, he gave his son a divining chain, again reiterating that although the young man was a Christian, he was meant to be a babalawo (as his father had been). Again, the young man ignored his father's advice and prospered as a farmer outside of Ifẹ, marrying seven wives and fathering many children. However, when he returned to Ifẹ in 1894, all of his wives and children died. Distraught, he walked out of town into the bush to die. On the way, he met a chief who discovered his intentions and proclaimed, "You are a coward and a lazy man, do you know what you were made for?" advising him to visit a diviner. The diviner told him that unless he became a babalawo, he would continue to lose everything. So the distraught young man was initiated into Ifa and became wealthy and highly respected, and by 1937 he had so many wives that he said he had lost count of them.[34]

This Job-like story is of interest here not only for its unique historical details, but because it illustrates a common motif among the stories of many babalawo and ọmọ awo (apprentices) I encountered: even a century ago, the long and intensive training and expensive initiation rituals deter many children of babalawo families from becoming babalawo themselves, and it is often only later in life, when "Ifa fights with them," that they eventually decide to undertake the discipline and study of Ifa.

In the case of both adult and child apprentices, the babalawo I interviewed all seemed to agree that the normal course of action would be to memorize the Odu before initiation. Professor Agboola remarked:

> The knowledge should come first before initiation. You should go around once [i.e., memorize at least one verse for each of the 256 Odu] . . . because if you do not have the knowledge, how can you call yourself [a] babalawo? Because coming out of Ifa grove does not empower you—it empowers you spiritually in another way—but that does not empower you to acquire Eji Ogbe, to know how to say yes or no. Even if I come out of Ifa grove and I throw Irẹtẹ Otura, what will I say? I can't say anything. . . .
>
> And the person [receiving initiation] is already old, unlike the one who was asked to do it at a young age—that is what will make you a complete babalawo. Even if you have gone around ten times [i.e., memorized ten verses for each Odu] and you don't do Ifa initiation, you are not a babalawo, you are just calling yourself babalawo, but you don't actually have it. You need to have knowledge and then you go for Ifa initiation. But some people, a lot of cruel people in Nigeria they go to the United States and they harvest people, whether they have knowledge or not, they initiate them, and what is that? There are some of them that cannot even recite one verse of their Odu. Not to speak of the other 255, so how can they be called a babalawo?[35]

While the ritual details and even the length of the initiation ceremonies vary greatly, the babalawo I interviewed concurred that the ritual ideally takes fourteen days, although in recent times it is often abbreviated to three or even two days.[36] Essentially, the initiation serves to establish the relationship (and even identity) between the initiate's *ikin*, his *ori*, and his Odu, and to empower him with the force (*aṣẹ*) of *Odu*, the mythical wife of Ọrunmila and mother of babalawo.[37] In describing the initial rituals of *itẹfa*, Drewal writes, "The inner head [*ori inu*] of the individual was elevated to the status of a personal deity; the palm nuts [*ikin*] are its shrine."[38]

The rituals that accomplish this vary significantly from initiation to initiation, due to the fact that many of these rituals are determined by divinations performed during the ceremony itself. Thus, no two initiations are ever entirely alike. Nevertheless, the babalawo I interviewed sketched similar broad outlines of the initiation: an initial stage of preparation that takes place publicly or semi-privately in which the initiating babalawo, their wives and *ọmọ awo* (apprentices), as well as the initiate and his mother or wife participate, involving sacrificial rituals, purification by jumping over fire, and sung and chanted invocations of Ifa (*iyẹrẹ Ifa*) both preparing the initiate and his *ikin*, and seeking permission to enter the sacred grove of *igbodu*.[39] Only initiated babalawo are allowed to enter the *igbodu*, and this initial stage of preparation culminates in the entrance of the blindfolded initiates into the sacred space.

In the *igbodu*, the initiates are said to witness secret wonders, culminating in the opening of the container holding Odu and, after having washed one's face and eyes (*oju*) with a special herbal infusion, witnessing Odu.[40] The calabash or pot containing Odu is known as *Igba Odu*, and is identified with the "calabash of wisdom/existence/character" (*Igba Iwa*) that was the source of Ọrunmila's wisdom in the previously mentioned myth from Odu Oturupọn Meji.[41] While the Araba of Modakẹkẹ was reluctant to discuss the details of the ceremonies inside the *igbodu*, especially those relating to Odu herself, he explained that

> *igbodu* is the greatest title and initiation. There is nothing after that. It is greater than the highest initiation of *Ogboni* [a secret religiopolitical society related to the worship of the Earth to which the Araba previously belonged]. It is greater than anything else. Anything you are seeking in life, you will find it in *igbodu*. There is nothing after that. If you go to *igbodu*, everything will open for you in life, good things will come to you.... One of my friends who was *Alhaji* [had performed the ḥajj to Mecca], he told me that what they have in Mecca, in the Ka'bah, is the same as what is in *igbodu*.[42]

Professor Agboola described his own experience of Odu in the following way: "When you go in, you will feel the energy; in that part of the *igbodu*, it is already charged with Odu. They take you in blindfolded, then they remove the blindfold and you see something. It enters you. You will see something shaking your body. Science will probably say it is your feelings or something, but I felt it. And not only that time, when you are feeding Odu, after, after you have done that you can feed Odu, you can join other babalawo to feed Odu, during that time you will feel that energy."[43]

Awo Faniyi likened the ceremonies inside the *igbodu* to being reborn, and equated Odu with the "sacred power of one's heavenly choice of destiny" (*aṣẹ ipin ọrun*) and one's own "spiritual" or "inner head" (*ori inu*):

> Odu is the *igba iwa* [calabash of wisdom/existence/character] that Olodumare gave to Ọrunmila to mend the world. Ọrunmila is the witness of the choice of destiny [*ẹlẹri-ipin*] while Odu is the sacred power [*aṣẹ*] of that choice of destiny [*ipin*]. This choice of destiny is the thing that Olodumare has chosen for each and

every creature [ẹda] coming into the world; this destiny is one's inner head [ori inu]. The sacred power of the choice of destiny [aṣẹ ipin], Odu, is the choice that one made while coming into the world; it is everything that one will or should do, and everything that one will not or should not do.[44]

Again invoking the myth of the choice of destiny (ori/ipin), which one forgets on the way into the world, Awo Faniyi elaborated: "When you see Odu, you meet everything that you left behind on the way down to earth at the tree of forgetfulness [igi igbagbe]."[45] Thus in witnessing Odu, the initiate comes face to face with his own destiny, his innermost or divine self (ori inu), and the power it contains to fulfill this destiny. The initiatory process can be likened to the construction of a metaphysical mirror in which the initiate glimpses and recognizes his inner self (ori inu) and becomes empowered to fulfill this destiny.

The particularities of this destiny or inner self (ori inu) are revealed through the verses of the Odu of Ifa that emerges when divination is performed for the new initiate in the igbodu. Drewal writes, "The belief is that once the divination palm nuts [ikin] have been ritually associated with the individual, then when cast they will reveal what his inner head prefers."[46] This Odu of Ifa is said to be the "Odu which gave birth" to the babalawo, and the verses that are recited from it are a kind of personal revelation meant to guide the initiate throughout the rest of his life: establishing his taboos (eewọ), describing the initiate and his life trajectory, giving advice and counsel on how to fulfill this destiny. Initiates will spend the rest of their lives contemplating these verses, and collecting more verses from this particular Odu to better understand themselves.[47] As Drewal writes, "Indeed, the more meaning a person reads into his personal texts, the better he knows himself."[48]

Professor Agboola explained this process through the metaphor of medical surgery:

> It's like you take a patient to the operating theatre, and you open the patient. When you open the patient, then the medical doctors who are around are able to see the arrangements of organs and everything, then they put you back and then you come out.... When we are in the grove, we open you up and say that "oh, OK, this is this; this is this..." And then this thing will come up with an Odu, and when we know the Odu we can say, "OK, OK." [*nodding head*] We are now able to precisely monitor your full step. The first one, ikọse aye, is just to guide the child, but this one, this is for life. And with that one, I can tell you everything about you. Someone will say, "Ah, ah! How do you know that [about me]?" I can say, "Well, you said your Odu was this..." *Ti Ifa ko ba joni ko nibi yii*—if Ifa did not resemble you, then it would not have come out in the initiation day. Ifa that comes out on the initiation day is the one that looks like you, it came out because it resembles

you. So, for example, if someone says, "I am a child of [Odu] Ogbe-Atẹ," oh OK, don't eat cock [rooster], don't eat amaranthus vegetables, you meet your prosperity on the road, you are not the kind of person that sits down, you must always be on the move, always check your friends, not everyone who calls himself your friend is your friend. . . .

They [i.e., the verses of the Odu] tell you everything. And the wife, for the children of Ogbe-Atẹ, they tell you have just one of two options, at extreme ends. If you are lucky you will marry the one who is submissive; if not, you will have one who is arrogant. No in-between. Either the wife of Ogbe-Atẹ is respectful or [*shakes head*] they say, if the wife is like this [respectful], build a palace, you have to build a palace for her. If the other one . . . [*throws hands up in the air*] So everything is now exposed.[49]

Another babalawo told me that his Odu was Ogbe-Yọnu (Ogbe-Ogunda), which is also known as Ogbe-Suuru, "Ogbe-Patience," because many of its verses prescribe the patient endurance of suffering. As I was soon to be married, he recited the following verse for me from his Odu, explaining the origins of the Yoruba word for wife, *iyawo*:

> "Nothing comes from getting angry
> Patience is the father of character
> An elder who has patience
> Has everything"
> Performed Ifa divination for Ọrunmila
> When he was going to seek the hand of Iya [suffering]
> The daughter of the king of Iwo [a Yoruba town]
> He was told to offer sacrifice
> He accepted and offered the sacrifice
> Not long after, not far
> Meet us in the midst of all good
> The suffering [Iya] which Ọrunmila faced at Iwo
> Is not worth mentioning at home
> Ọrunmila began to dance and rejoice
> That Suffering, the suffering [Iya]
> That Ifa faced in Iwo became his wife [*iyawo*]
> That Suffering, that suffering [Iya] became his wife

Ọrunmila was traveling to the kingdom of Iwo, and he went to see a babalawo. They told him he should perform a sacrifice and that he should marry Iya, the firstborn child of the king of Iwo. Iya was a child with very bad character. No one could stand her, and even though she was a princess all of her suitors, including Orisa like Sango and Ogun, ran away from her rough treatment. The babalawo told him that he should not get angry, that he should not complain. That trouble would befall him, but if he was patient and calm, then the bad things would become good.

When Orunmila reached Iwo, and met with Iya, she did not greet him properly; instead she abused him and did not give him any food or water, and showed him no hospitality. Orunmila remained calm and said nothing. Then when he went out to find food for himself, Iya insisted that she come along and that Orunmila carry her on his back. Orunmila agreed and carried her. While he was carrying her, she peed on him. Orunmila remained calm and said nothing. On the way back, he carried her again; this time, she shat on him. Orunmila remained calm and said nothing. When they reached her house, Orunmila went to sleep. When he woke up the next day, he found that she had broken his wooden divining tray [opon Ifa] and tapper [iroke] and used them as firewood to cook her breakfast. Orunmila was angry, but he remained calm and said nothing. Then she took his Ifa pouch [apo] and used it as a rag. Orunmila was upset but he remained calm and said nothing.

Then Iya and Orunmila went back to see her father, the king of Iwo. The King thought that Orunmila had come to return Iya because of her bad character. Everyone was amazed to see that Orunmila had tolerated Iya, who had now become calm. Everyone was amazed to see Iya behaving gently. The king of Iwo gave Orunmila another wife and divided his kingdom into two and gave Orunmila half. Orunmila began to dance and rejoice; the Iya of Iwo [the Suffering of Iwo] became his wife.

This is the meaning of the word "wife" [iyawo]. Ifa says that you must be patient, that you should not get angry, that you should endure suffering, and if you are patient, you will find all kinds of good things. Did you understand everything Orunmila went through? No one could endure that and be patient. His wife did this and that, and he did not get angry, he did not complain, not even once. None of us could do that, but we have to try. A child of Ogbe-Yonu will have to face a lot of suffering, people will always be disappointing him, but he must be patient and endure, and then he will find all good things.[50]

True to his Odu, this babalawo has endured a great deal, especially during a local conflict in the late 1990s, during which he lost one of his wives, his house, and much of his wealth. And yet, despite these and many other disappointments, he is one of the most patient, gentle, and jovial teachers I have ever encountered.

Drewal recounts how Oyẹku Meji was the Odu divined for Awo Ọṣitọla's eldest son in the *igbodu* during the *itefa* ceremony she witnessed in Imodi, Ijẹbu, in 1986. Ọṣitọla narrated an *ẹsẹ* about the coming of Sunrise into the world whose symbolism is simply too lovely and illustrative to omit here:

> He lives a full, complete life, and he was bright and prosperous and loved. He had everything in life.
>
> Words of wisdom were spoken to Sunrise early in his life [i.e., when he was rising]. They said that he would complete his journey, that his journey would be bright; everybody would like his brightness. And he would also be powerful. But if he wanted to ensure this success, his parents must make a sacrifice on his behalf. They should sacrifice a bunch of brooms, a bundle of white cloth, and a sheep.
>
> Sunrise gathered the items and was told, as you are rising, as your life becomes bright, there will be some enemies who will be jealous, who will try to dim your brightness. They will use the power of dangerous inner eyes (*oju buruku inu*) to stare at you. But if you can satisfy the divine mediator, Eṣu, then he will assist you to prevent those dangerous eyes from dimming your brightness.
>
> Sunrise's parents, named Eṣuwata [devotees of Eṣu], made the sacrifice on his behalf. They prepared Sunrise for his journey right from his rise. When he arrived at his destination, everything went well. People understood his light. Everybody admired him, for they did better as a result.
>
> But, as he moved higher in the sky, as Ifa predicted, some people attempted to dim his light by staring at him with their dangerous eyes. Immediately, Eṣu, the divine mediator who was by Sunrise's side, inquired from wise men, "Things are now topsy-turvy, what happened? What is the matter with these troublesome people?" The wise elders responded, "it is Sunrise they want to trouble." But Sunrise had been well-prepared, he had been well-established, he had performed the necessary sacrifices. Eṣu asked, "where is the evidence of the sacrifices?" The wise men showed him the bunch of brooms prepared with medicines, instructing him to put the brooms on Sunrise's forehead so that no one can see his inner head well.
>
> Because Eṣu blessed the brooms, when anyone stared at Sunrise they saw only the brooms, which scratched and hurt their eyes [i.e., the bright beams of sunlight, the "eyelashes" of Sunrise]. It is the broom straws scattered in the Sunrise that injure people's eyes and prevent them from looking into it; it is the broom straws that prevent people from dimming sun's brightness. The broom blinds the evil inner eyes of onlookers. Extraordinary eyes cannot penetrate a prepared person. If they dare disturb the child, they will be blinded.[51]

This beautiful verse establishes the mythological precedent for the life of the initiate, and would seem to indicate that the initiate's parents should perform a sacrifice to Eṣu and/or prepare some sort of medicine or charm, presumably involving a broom or the eyelashes of the initiate to protect him against the "evil eye." However, Drewal also recorded Awo Oṣitọla's interpretation of this verse, which was somewhat different:

> You see the interpretation of Ifa just provides us a model to follow, not just exactly what should be done. You can perform in the "changing world manner." You don't have to do exactly what Ifa did historically. Our own knowledge, our own power, our own *aṣẹ* may not be as powerful as the one they used for the broom in the past. And again, it may be more powerful than that. And it may not be [in the manner of] that broomish preparation. We have to look at what to do. How can we do it? For instance, we are not in a world where we can give a child a broom to be carrying all the time. Then we have to do it in the changing world fashion.[52]

This creativity in interpretation, doing things in "the changing world fashion," is one of the characteristic features of the hermeneutics babalawo employ in interpreting their own verses, those of their initiates, and those of the clients who come to them for divination and counsel. Divination can also be employed to ask Ifa to clarify or amplify the taboos to be observed or sacrifices to be performed, as is done in the *igbodu* during initiation.

The initiating babalawo perform the sacrifices specified by the verse of Ifa divined for the initiate, and they provide the initiate with an interpretation of these verses and an explanation of the taboos these verses indicate he or she should observe. After the initiation rituals are complete, the new initiates emerge from the sacred grove with shaven heads, in white cloth, symbolizing their rebirth as initiated babalawo. They can now return to the grove of Odu to participate in the initiation of other babalawo, further reflecting on the rites and rituals of the *igbodu*.

### GENDER AND INITIATION

> *O ni gbogbo ohun ti eniyan ba nṣe*
> *Ti ko ba fi ti obinrin kun un*
> *O ni ko le ṣeeṣe*
> He said, "In every thing that we do.
> If we do not include women in it
> It cannot succeed."
> —ODU OṢẸ-OTURA

As Drewal points out, the structural motif of female container, male contained is common across a wide range of art forms and rituals of Yoruba-speaking peoples.[53] The *igbodu* represents a womb from which the (usually male) initiates emerge. The *ikin* are kept in an *agẹrẹ* (carved container) that usually incorporates a female form, just as women carry and dance with the *ikin* during the preliminary stages of the initiation. Many other oriṣa initiations (such as the initiations of Ṣango and Yemọja) involve the symbolic wedding of the initiate (whether male or female) as a "bride" (*iyawo*) to the oriṣa. In these initiations, however, not only is the oriṣa "made" and kept in a calabash or container to serve as the shrine of the initiate, but the initiate him- or herself also serves as such a shrine (and is often decorated in a similar fashion to a shrine), as the presence of the oriṣa is physically built up in him or her through medicines that are placed in incisions in the scalp; thus the initiate serves as a "container" for the oriṣa. However, in the *igbodu* of Ifa, this mystical marriage or encounter of male and female principles takes place not only between the initiate and Ọrunmila, but also between the male initiates, and Odu, the mythical wife of Ọrunmila and "mother" of babalawo.

The role of women in Ifa has become a somewhat contentious issue among Ifa practitioners around the world,[54] with some scholars reading the gendered distinctions and prescriptions of the tradition as an example of patriarchy, and some Western practitioners of Ifa regarding gendered norms as patriarchal importations from Islam and Christianity.[55] However, it is important to understand the Ifa tradition's conception of "gender," which is markedly different from modern and postmodern approaches. In the traditional Yoruba context, gender is regarded as something like a complementary, metaphysical bipolarity (there can be no male without female, just as there can be no left without a right) that is manifest through symbol and metaphor in the interconnected spiritual, political, social, and physical domains of life and the cosmos.[56] As Oyeronke Olajubu writes in the introduction to her excellent *Women in the Yoruba Religious Sphere*:

> Gender as construed by the Yoruba is essentially culture-bound and should be differentiated from notions of gender in some other cultures. It is a gender classification that is not equivalent to or a consequence of anatomy at all times. Yoruba gender construction is fluid and is modulated by other factors such as seniority (age) and personal achievements (wealth and knowledge acquisition).... For instance, just as the Yoruba construct gender, they also deconstruct it through ritual. Moreover, the flexibility of Yoruba gender constructs is vividly displayed in the assumption that the occupant of any gender role need not absorb the prevalent attitude of the sex for whom such gender roles was delineated. For example,

female "husbands" in Yorubaland do not have to display aggressiveness and strong physical features to fulfill their roles as husbands to wives in the lineage....

The existence of gender constructs among the Yoruba does not translate to notions of oppression and the domination of women by men, because it is mediated by the philosophy of complementary gender relations, which is rooted in the people's cosmic experience. A complementary gender relation is entrenched at every level of the Yoruba socio-religious consciousness, as both male and female principles are crucial to a smooth living experience. Social, political, and religious structures reflect this perception in both their membership and their modes of operation.... This neutral complementarity is here taken to refer not to equality or parity but to cooperation and specified areas of control for the female as well as the male. Therefore, among the Yoruba, the question to ask about the state of sexes is not which sex is dominant, but rather, over which areas do the sexes enjoy prominence. Further, it should be noted that the prominence that one sex enjoys in a particular area of human activity does not make the people of that sexual category independent of those of the other.[57]

The tradition of Ifa is no exception, with masculinity and femininity characterizing the various Odu, and structuring the logic and symbolism of many of the rituals of the tradition. However, there are far more male priests of Ifa (babalawo) than female priests (iyanifa), and far more male priests who perform divination than female priests. In fact, a few babalawo told me that some babalawo have accused others of inventing the idea of a female Ifa diviner as a means of getting money from foreign women who wish to be become diviners. Other babalawo defended this as an uncommon but traditional practice, supported by the verses of the Ifa corpus and Ifa divination itself, as Ifa is consulted through divination during the initiations of these women. Oyeronke Olajubu records a verse of the Odu Eji-Ogbe that explicitly states that there is no taboo against women performing Ifa divination, citing the precedent of Ọrunmila's firstborn daughter, who was a diviner along with her twin brother.[58] Olajubu attributes the overwhelming preponderance of male priests to the time-consuming rigors of becoming an Ifa priest, which few women could afford to combine with their domestic duties.[59] She also notes that those women who become iyanifa typically only marry babalawo, the explanation being that "only someone with an equal knowledge and the power that such knowledge bestows could marry them."[60] However, there does seem to be a consensus that women must not witness Odu, or at the very least that they cannot witness it without losing the ability to bear children.

The Araba of Modakẹkẹ told me that his own daughter has studied Ifa and practices it, but that he did not know of any other female diviners. He also remarked that he knew several women (from babalawo families) who could recite (*ki*) the verses of Ifa very well, and knew the Odu so well that they could interpret them for clients when divination was performed by a babalawo. He also confirmed the taboo on women seeing Odu, explaining that if a woman looked at Odu, she would lose the ability to bear children; and that if a male noninitiate were to look at Odu, he would go blind. However, he said that he would not forbid a qualified woman from entering *igbodu* if she wanted to, as long as she was aware of the consequences.

The secondary literature also contains several references to the historical presence of women who performed Ifa divination. Bernard Maupoil's work on the Fa tradition in 1930s Benin records several female diviners who traveled widely in their training,[61] and Karin Barber's landmark study *I Could Speak until Tomorrow* describes the career of Fakẹmide of Okuku, a celebrated female babalawo[62] who traveled widely, regularly performed divination for the king, and trained students (both male and female) of her own. Moreover, Barber notes that "no one ever suggested that there was anything odd about [her practice of Ifa]. Men and women alike asserted that no code was transgressed by her actions and that no disapproval was directed at her."[63] Barber also contextualizes this fact within the broader practice of Yoruba gender norms (supporting Olajubu's above characterization): "There are few situations in which women are told they *cannot* pursue a certain course because they are women.... Despite the disadvantages that weigh down an ambitious woman, if she decides to do something, it is accepted that she can do so."[64]

However, women typically participate in the tradition of Ifa in two main ways: as an *apẹtẹbi*, or wife of a babalawo; or as an iyanifa (which literally means "wife of Ifa"), a female initiate and practitioner of Ifa. A woman can become an *apẹtẹbi* if the divination performed shortly after birth indicates that she should be married to a babalawo. If this is the case, then a ritual called *isodẹ*, "tying the bracelet,"[65] is performed, in which the young woman is "married" to the *ikin* of a babalawo. The young woman is then under the protection of this babalawo until she marries her husband (who must also be a babalawo), and then a ritual known as *itudẹ*, "cutting the bracelet," is performed. The *apẹtẹbi* is then "wedded" to her new husband's *ikin*. *Apẹtẹbi* have several official functions, including cleaning the area where the family worships Ifa (the "house of Ifa," or Ifa shrine, *ile Ifa*) every five days (four days in English reckoning); worshipping Ifa herself (there are particular *ọrin Ifa*, "songs of Ifa," which are only for *apẹtẹbi*); and standing in for her husband in his absence and even divining for clients (using sixteen cowrie shells) if she is able. Typically, when a married man undergoes initiation into Ifa, his wife undergoes the rituals to become an *apẹtẹbi*, and when a woman marries a babalawo, she is also expected to become an *apẹtẹbi* by performing the *isodẹ* ritual. However, many of the babalawo I interviewed remarked that these rituals are not as common as they once were.

In contrast to an *apẹtẹbi*, an iyanifa is a woman who has studied, and been trained and initiated into Ifa, regardless of who her husband may be. The only difference between an iyanifa and a babalawo is that the former is typically forbidden from entering the grove of Odu and witnessing Odu, whereas this is the essential component of the highest degree of initiation for the latter. Since this level of initiation is barred to women, some have interpreted this as meaning that the greatest iyanifa are still inferior to the greatest babalawo;[66] other babalawo argue that as a "feminine energy," Odu complements or completes the male's initiation, whereas it is unnecessary for the female initiate, since she already possesses "feminine energy." For example, Professor Agboola explained:

> The Ifa initiation, what makes the difference between *elegan* and *olodu*—for the women, they must be *elegan*, not because of this story, but because of the story of Odu, mystical wife of Ọrunmila. I hope you have read this. One day a woman, who was ugly, came to Ọrunmila's house and asked for water. Then later she said, "I would like food." Ọrunmila gave her the food. Then she said, "You know I am traveling, and I can't continue, I need a place to sleep." Ọrunmila gave her a place to sleep. She said, "Where I come from, I don't sleep alone. Come and sleep with me." That was when Ọrunmila's wife said, "Ah! Look at this ugly woman, she asked for water, we gave her, she asked for food, we gave her, she asked for room, we gave her, but now, she's now asking for our husband!" Ọrunmila said, "Well, that is what she wants. I have to." Because Ọrunmila has done Ifa divination that has guided him. So she [Odu] said, "Yes, I'm coming here to marry you, but not a regular marriage, no sexual intercourse." That's Ofun Meji. "But I know that you need additional power, that's why Olodumare sent me. So I will be your wife, but no sexual intercourse. When you want to see me, none of your wives must see me. If you want to see me, you must do this, this, this, and wash your eyes before you come in. But whatever you ask, I can do it for you." But Ọrunmila's other wives they started getting jealous, saying, "Who is this woman that is inside the room?" One day, when Ọrunmila was not around, they went in and that is when they were destabilized. The interpretation is that their energy was already there; when they opened the door, the additional female energy that was there just . . . [*claps hands together*] The energy that is balanced, which is what we are, we have both male and female, it's already balanced, so if you now bring additional female energy, it will throw it out of balance. So they couldn't have children again. So that is the story that prevented women from looking into Odu. If the boys, the men, are not up to your level, let us give them additional power so that they are equal to you. So, for example, if I take you and

Funmilayo [a common girl's name] to the grove, I have to give you additional energy so that you will be equal to her.[67]

Thus, according to Professor Agboola, entering the *igbodu* makes babalawo equal and not superior to iyanifa. Aside from Awo Faniyi, all of the babalawo emphasized the feminine nature of Odu,[68] and the son of a prominent babalawo from the Oṣogbo even told me that Odu was the first *Iya mi* (name for the members of the female secret society of Ajẹ), which literally means "My Mothers." Odu is associated with the power of giving birth, as it is only *olodu* (babalawo who have seen Odu) who can initiate or "give birth" to new babalawo. Some babalawo, such as Professor Agboola above, seem to argue that receiving Odu is necessary for babalawo to equal their female counterparts, iyanifa. Others see the acquisition of Odu as giving babalawo a degree of superiority since they now have both male and female power, pointing out that because they are not *olodu*, iyanifa are unable to perform several rituals, such as initiating new babalawo (*itẹfa*) and the *imọri / ikọse aye* ritual.[69] However, the contemporary iyanifa Ifaboyede M. Ajisebo McElwaine Abimbola writes in her essay on the subject, "The case of Odù is not a justification to disallow women from the priesthood of Ifá. Women are always *Babalawo Elegan*, as are the men who do not have Odù. Only babalawo who have Odù are known as *Babalawo Olodu*. So, although women as well as uninitiated men are excluded from seeing Odù, no male or female Ifá priest is excluded from the responsibility of learning *odù Ifá*, the literature."[70]

All of the babalawo interviewed emphasized that menstrual blood was so powerful that it could "spoil" many sacrifices, rituals, and shrines, and by virtue of this, premenopausal iyanifa would be excluded from performing certain rituals, although menstruation (and femininity in general) was understood as being its own extremely potent spiritual force. However, it should be mentioned that Ifa is but one tradition among the many spiritual traditions of Yoruba-speaking peoples, and in several other prominent and widespread spiritual/political traditions—like those of the Oriṣa such as Yemọja, Ọṣun, the *Iya mi*, the *Iyalọde* (chief of the market), and certain chieftaincies—women typically occupy the highest ranks, and can perform rituals that men cannot.

In any event, the taboo against women seeing Odu seems to be widely recognized and agreed on, although I did encounter some stories about women who had breached this taboo and "looked Odu in the face." These stories typically involve a foreign woman who either pays a babalawo an exorbitant sum of money to see Odu; or ignores the advice of the babalawo, looks at Odu, and ends up becoming barren, facing problems in Nigeria, and then leaving. I cite these stories here not to claim them as historical fact, but because they function as a kind of commentary on the verses of Ifa prohibiting women viewing Odu, a contemporary echo or manifestation of the myths that established this taboo. For example, one verse, from Odu Irẹtẹ Ogbe, says:

> When the time had come, Odu said, "You, Ọrunmila"
> She said, "Quickly, come know my taboos"
> She said that she wanted to teach him her taboos
> She said that she didn't want his other wives
> To look her in the face
> She said that he should tell all his other wives
> That they should not look her in the face
> She said that if one of them looks her in the face, she will find a fight
> She said that she does not want anyone to look her in the face
> Ọrunmila said, "Not bad"
> He also called all of his wives
> He warned them
> Ọrunmila's wives, they will not look her in the face
> Odu told Ọrunmila that
> She had come to make his burden easier[71]

In conclusion, while women play an important role in the tradition of Ifa, and while some babalawo regard iyanifa as their equals, the highest stage of initiation, the encounter with Odu, is typically forbidden for women, and so the highest ranks of the tradition are virtually all male. However, some babalawo reported their willingness to perform this initiation ceremony for women, as long as they understood its consequences, and were willing to forego having any more children. Finally, it should be noted that while Ifa is, de facto, a predominantly male tradition, it is not an *exclusively* male tradition, and that several other Yoruba traditions are predominantly or even exclusively female.

### AFTER INITIATION

Whether male or female, leaving the sacred grove of Ifa (*igbo Ifa*) marks the beginning of the initiate's life as a babalawo or iyanifa, and his or her lifelong journey in search of the "deep knowledge" of Ifa. As Awo Ọsitọla told Drewal, "The sacrifice we make at the sacred bush is the beginning of one's life. The journey does not finish there. That is not the end of everything for that man. . . . Ifa says do such-and-such this time, just for a moment, for the time being, in order to start life properly. The first sacrifice that we can do at the sacred bush is [in order] to start life properly."[72]

Furthermore, the knowledge acquired through the experiences of the *igbodu* (for babalawo) and during the initiation rituals is not final and comprehensive, but is rather described more like a seed of knowledge whose branches and leaves of meaning and understanding grow and blossom through lifelong contemplation, reflection, and practice. As Awo Ọsitọla remarked, "even if you were allowed to see inside of the *igbodu*, you would see only the impotent part of it. The knowledge is the potentiality, the knowledge you must sustain, the knowledge you must learn—not just the materials."[73] Several verses of various Odu of Ifa emphasize this aspect of continuous reflection and contemplation after initiation, even comparing the continuous practice of Ifa to reinitiation. For example, an *ẹsẹ* (verse) from Odu Eji Ogbe says:

> It is we who have initiated you into Ifa
> [Now] you must renew your initiation
> This was the initiation that was performed for Eji Ogbe
> Who used his head [*ori*] to enter the grove [*igbo*]
> It is we who have initiated you
> [Now] you must renew your initiation
> If you haven't reached the top of the palm tree
> Don't open your hands [i.e., let go][74]

In this *ẹsẹ*, the mention of the palm tree recalls the various myths in which Ọrunmila left the world by climbing a palm tree into heaven (see chapter 5). Thus "climbing the palm tree" here refers to following in the footsteps of Ọrunmila. Just as one cannot loosen one's grip before one reaches the top of a palm tree, a babalawo or iyanifa cannot stop practicing Ifa until he or she reaches *ọrun* (the heavenly ancestral abode) at the top of Ifa's palm tree. Moreover, Ifa is identified with this palm tree, so clinging to the palm tree symbolizes clinging to Ifa until one "reaches the top" and has all of Ọrunmila's knowledge. Eji Ogbe's "delving into the bush" is a reference to initiation, as well as the fact that Eji Ogbe was the first Odu to descend into the world. As for the "renewal of initiation," the following *ẹsẹ* from Odu Ogbe-Atẹ seems to equate it with observing one's taboos:

> "Ogbe come and be initiated so that you will be at ease
> 'I accepted, I was initiated,' is the blessing of Ifa"
> Performed Ifa divination for Ọrunmila
> Baba, when he was going to initiate his child into Ifa

They said that he should perform a sacrifice
He understood, He sacrificed
When I accept
[That is when] Baba will initiate me
Lack of wisdom inside
Lack of deep thought inside
This is what makes people enter the *igbodu* three times
If we have completed initiation into Ifa
What issue of Eṣu Odara remains?
If we have completed initiation into Ifa
We must not use a worn rope to climb the palm tree
We must not jump into the river without knowing how to swim
We must not risk death needlessly
We must not marry the wife of [another] babalawo
We must not take the wife of a medicine man [oniṣegun]
We must not lie with the wife of [another] babalawo
We must not plot against a friend with his wife
We must not lie to our Oluwo
Or second-guess him
Ọrunmila initiated Akọda
He initiated Aṣẹda[75]
He initiated Araba [mahogany tree, the title of the chief babalawo of a town]
Ọrunmila, Agbonniregun [another name for Ọrunmila], the owner of the day
He alone we do not know who initiated [him]
Now, if I have completed my initiation,
I will renew my initiation
The taboos that have been given to me
I will accept
I have been initiated
I will renew my initiation[76]

Echoing the symbolism of climbing the palm tree in the previous verse, in this ẹsẹ, not observing one's taboos is likened to trying to climb a palm tree with a worn rope, to jumping into a river without knowing how to swim, and to risking death. One renews one's initiation through observing the taboos decreed for one during initiation, and any subsequent taboos that may emerge from learning more about one's Odu.

Similarly, an ẹsẹ from Odu Otura-Irẹtẹ associates this reinitiation with the virtue of moderation (iwọn), which it describes in detail:

> Renew yourself and your initiation
> If we have been born, we must also try to be reborn
> The moderate one, the moderate one
> One who knows moderation will not be disgraced
> I said, "Who knows moderation?"
> Ọrunmila said, "One who works hard"
> I said, "Who knows moderation?"
> Ọrunmila said, "One who does not waste all of his money"
> I said, "Who knows moderation?"
> Ọrunmila said, "One who does not steal"
> I said, "Who knows moderation?"
> Ọrunmila said, "One who does not owe excessive debts"
> I said, "Who knows moderation?"
> Ọrunmila said, "One who does not drink alcohol,
> One who does not break his word to his friend
> One who rises early, reflects upon himself [banu ara rẹ] and contemplates his
>     actions [ṣiro niroti iṣẹ rẹ]
> Amongst the thorns and brambles, the palm frond will be seen rising above
> The cautious one [amẹsọ] is the moderate one [amuwọn]⁷⁷

Echoing a common image in the verses of Ifa, the palm frond (moriwo ọpẹ) rising above the other flora (in this case thorns) represents the babalawo rising above the troubles of life and/or his peers who do not adhere to the ethical standards of Ifa. Perpetual reflection on the verses of Ifa and one's actions so as to develop understanding and good character is part and parcel of the daily life of a babalawo.

Through the rituals of igbodu, the initiate comes face to face with his own inner reality (ori inu). The nature and wishes of this self are then elaborated in the poetic and symbolic language of the verses of the Odu divined for the initiate in the grove. By learning more about this Odu, contemplating its verses, as well as performing the sacrifices and avoiding the taboos prescribed therein, the new babalawo or iyanifa both becomes "more" him- or herself and knows him or herself better. This process of self-cultivation and discovery through the practice of good character, divination, as well as contemplation on and performance of rituals and ritual orature is thus likened to reinitiation or "re-creation," as the following verse of Odu Ogbe–Atẹ indicates:

> If I am created,
> I will re-create myself
> I will observe all the taboos
> Having been created,
> I shall now re-create myself.[78]

The study and practice of Ifa are understood to be inseparable lifelong processes, from which one can never take a break. As a verse in Odu Odi-Iwori says:

> If we have wisdom and fail to apply it
> We become ignorant
> If we have power and fail to exercise it
> We become indolent[79]

### TRAVELING AND BOTANICAL MEDICINE (EWE ỌSANYIN)

After the period of apprenticeship with the *oluwo*, which often takes around ten years to complete, the young babalawo or iyanifa travels widely, seeking specific knowledge from well-known babalawo through further apprenticeships. Professor Agboola likened this stage of a babalawo's training to a "postdoctoral fellowship" or "residency for doctors," explaining that babalawo seek knowledge to complement their training with their *oluwo*, and often start to specialize in one of Ifa's many branches of practical/medicinal knowledge.[80] For example, the Araba of Modakẹkẹ told me how he spent a few years traveling in Ilọrin and the north of Yorubaland, learning about the treatment of the mentally ill (*were*). Other babalawo may specialize in the treatment of infertility, various other maladies, or forms of malevolent "magic." The study of the pharmacology of Ifa, *ewe Ọsanyin* ("leaves of Ọsanyin, the orișa of plants and herbal medicine") is often an integral part of these "advanced studies." Babalawo keep a shrine of Ọsanyin in the corner of their rooms, and a few of the verses of Odu Ọbara Meji explain how and why Ọsanyin became the servant of Ọrunmila, and thus why babalawo possess his knowledge of plants and herbal medicine.[81] One of these narratives describes how plants used to speak to people and share their names, natures, and various uses. However, over time, people began to abuse plants to poison one another and make bad charms (*oogun*) to harm and kill one another. Then Olodumare intervened and ordered plants to stop speaking to people. Only Ọsanyin, the orișa of plants and herbal medicine, and his children (initiates) were allowed to continue to communicate with plants. As a result of the special relationship between Ọrunmila and Ọsanyin, babalawo share in this deep knowledge of plants.

Perhaps more than any other branch of knowledge in Ifa, *ewe Ifa* (the herbal/incantatory medicine of Ifa) clearly illustrates the unique theories of language and ritual that animate the tradition's practice. As Verger's masterful study demonstrates, the plants and other natural ingredients, their names, the name and figure of the Odu with which they are associated, and the "activating" incantation (*ọfọ*) are usually inseparably linked in the preparation and administration of *ewe Ifa*. These incantations, which often involve puns and other wordplay, symbolically and poetically describe features of the plant and link these features to the desired result of the medicinal preparation. For example, Verger records the following formula:

> The Odu Ọsẹ-Otura requires one to bring together *ewe anamu ọga*, stretch-to-take-chameleon (*Ipomoea sp. Convolvulaceae*), *ewe aṣẹ*, "power" (*Iodes Africana, Iacacinaceae*), and *ile kokoro* (worm). Pound them and mix with *ọṣẹ dudu*, black soap that must be put in a horn. Lick the soap when expressing a wish. Its incantation is:
>
> *Anamu ṣẹ ni ti ọga*
> *Aṣẹ jẹ ki ọrọ temi o ṣẹ*
> *Nijọ ti kokoro ba lu ilẹ ni i ja ọrun*
> Stretch-to-take is like a chameleon
> Power, allow my words to be fulfilled (*o ṣẹ*)
> When the worm falls to the ground it travels beyond [literally, "snatches heaven"][82]

Note the assonance between *o ṣẹ* (to be fulfilled), *ọṣẹ* (soap), and the name of the Odu, Ọsẹ-Otura. Furthermore, the buds of *ewe anamu ọga* (commonly known as morning glory)[83] resemble a chameleon's head, and the reddish-pink flowers that emerge therefrom recall the chameleon's tongue, which stretches out quickly and takes its prey. The worm symbolizes the incantatory words that move invisibly, like a worm through soil, and reach their destination. Bascom describes a similar feature of the verses of Ifa:

> A special type of pun which similarly contributes to internal consistency is that designated here as word magic, in which the name of an object sacrificed resembles the words expressing the result desired by the client. Thus the figure Iwori Meji, who has sacrificed a mortar and tẹtẹ and gbegbe leaves in order to find a place to live, recites the formula: "The mortar (*odo*) will testify that I see room in which to settle (*do*), the tẹtẹ leaf will testify that I see room in which to stretch out (*tẹ*),

the gbegbe leaf will testify that I see room in which to dwell (*gbe*)." Water (*omi*) is sacrificed so that the client can breathe (*imi*), ochra (*ila*) so that he will gain honor (*ọla*), and salt, used to make food tasty or "sweet" (*dun*), so that his affairs will be sweet (*dun*)."[84]

Thus, within Ifa, the relationship between signifier and signified is not arbitrary, but rather symbolic.[85] The name of a given plant within the pharmacopeia of Ifa, its active properties, and the incantation used to actualize these properties are all connected through relations of similarity, not a network of difference, as in Saussurean semiotics. The invocatory words of the verses of Ifa, the name and figure of the Odu that contains them, as well as the plants and other objects that they name are all related or even identified with one another symbolically. That is, the same principle that takes the form of a particular plant or herbal concoction in the material domain, takes the form of an activating incantation in the domain of language, and another form in the visual domain of the signs of the Odu. The same symbolic logic animates the rituals of Ifa, and the dynamism and improvisation that highly skilled babalawo display in performing these rituals[86] is a result of the recognition of and deep familiarity with these "principles" across various domains (plant, animal, mineral, material, verbal, visual, etc.).

For example, Verger highlights several of these incantatory formulae that involve foreign plants and names such as "*Ilémú* [which] is derived from 'lime' in English or from 'lima' in Portuguese. It is used in formulae to obtain money, *awure owo*, with the incantation: *lemu mu owo wa*. 'Lime bring (*mu*) money.'"[87] While I assisted the Araba of Modakẹkẹ in preparing a medicine to combat fever (*iba*) for a young neighbor, he explained, "We don't just use the plant itself, we use the coolness in it, and the incantation provides the power [*aṣẹ*] for the medicine. It is prayer [*adura*]. It is not just with words that you can pray. The words give the materials power and the materials give the words power so that they can be effective. All these sacrifices [*ẹbọ*] that Ifa tells you to do, even these medicines [*oogun*], they are prayer [*adura*]."[88] Similarly, Professor Agboola explained, "It's not the plant, it's the power in the plant that is used. *Ododo* [a kind of flower] is cool and calm, and that [coolness] is what you extract. It is the same thing in *ẹsẹ Ifa* [verses of Ifa], you extract the meaning and use that."[89] As Verger concludes, "The objects symbolically represent the incantation, but the spoken word realizes the action of the ingredients. A magical composition seems to be thought of as a collection of material things, articulated by language. The spoken incantation provides the description as well as the explanation for their meaning."[90] Thus, the semiotics of Ifa (like that of the early Western "doctrine of signatures") is based on a symbolic logic of resemblance or similarity. This same symbolic logic also structures the verses and rituals of Ifa, including divination and sacrifice (*ẹbọ*).

The babalawo I interviewed were all eager to distinguish between the sacrifices prescribed by Ifa (ẹbọ Ifa), the medicinal preparations associated with Ifa (oogun Ifa/ewe Ifa), and the commonplace charms and magical preparations prepared by non-babalawo specialists (onis̩egun and others). Professor Agboola explained that "in the old days, babalawo only did Ifa. Ifa is just sacrifices and leaves (ewe), not charms (oogun); but nowadays, people are more interested in charms and flashy things, so many babalawo learn these other charms. But these things are not from Ifa, they are outside of it."[91]

Similarly, Bascom records the following verse of Odu Ofun-Ọkanran—"Open for all to see, open for all to see; Ifa is the one who does things we can hear about; only curses we should not know about; curses are the voice of Ife"—for which he provides the following interpretation: "This means that the Ifa diviners do not work with bad medicine or do other evil things which have to be concealed, while those who use curses keep their work a secret. Ifẹ is reputed as a place where curses are strong and commonly used, as the Ijẹbu people are known for using bad medicine (oogun). Spells or incantations (ọfọ) whose purpose is to kill someone are known as igede, ogede, or egẹde."[92]

Professor Agboola also explained that the efficacy of Ifa sacrifices (ẹbọ Ifa), unlike charms (oogun), depends more on the person who performs it and less on the actual materials: "It is the nonmaterial aspect of the sacrifice that is the one that is most important. . . . If there is no alignment between ori inu and ori ode, then the sacrifice cannot be accepted."[93] He also explained that the intention of the person performing the sacrifice was the most important element of the ritual, and that even if you fail to gather all the necessary materials, if you have a sincere intention your sacrifice will be accepted. He also opined:

> Knowledge can substitute for sacrifice. The first and greatest sacrifice is honesty/righteousness [tootoo fun un]. . . . My students don't have to go through what I went through to get knowledge, but it requires more seriousness, spiritual focus, and concentration. For example, there is a complicated ritual that I learned how to perform, but I learned that you can just invoke those who performed that ritual and it will have the same effect; you can still tune into that energy, that power. So instead of teaching my students that complicated ritual, I teach them to invoke my oluwo, my father, the ancient babalawo and the Odu from which it comes.[94]

Bascom also recorded accounts of similar ritual simplification or innovation on the part of babalawo in the early twentieth century: "The clients say that Ifa teaches the diviners to be kind and that if they know a client is poor, they may suggest a hair in place of a horse, some wool in place of a ram, or a feather in place of a chicken; or they may suggest a calabash of water, or sixteen pebbles, or something else of no value.

As noted earlier, one informant said that sacrifices are generally more expensive when they are not modified, suggesting that the diviners usually propose reductions."[95]

While the ẹbọ (sacrifices) and ewe (botanical preparations) of Ifa operate within a similar system of symbolic logic as the ọfọ (incantations) and oogun (charms) of other Yoruba-language occult traditions, intention seems to play a larger role in the former, which are regarded as the "proper" work of babalawo who are qualified to ritually modify or reinterpret these sacrifices in accordance with their own insight or inspiration.

## INDEPENDENT CAREER

After traveling the countryside to learn *ewe Ifa* and further hone their knowledge and skills, babalawo settle down to establish their own independent practice and take on their own apprentices (*ọmọ awo*). Babalawo may spend fifteen to thirty years studying and practicing Ifa under the tutelage of more senior babalawo before they begin to practice on their own and take on their own apprentices. These priests of Ifa usually make their livings through divination and as medical and ritual specialists, performing ceremonies for infants and consulting for other *olorisa* and the general public. The most senior and respected babalawo may become part of the official hierarchy of babalawo of the town in which they settle, the highest position of which is the Araba. These official positions carry a small government stipend and require the titleholders to perform rituals on behalf of the king and the entire town. Being a babalawo is often a full-time occupation. As Susanne Wenger explains, "The *olorisha* must *intensify* his life through constant preoccupation with the deity. The concentration that is needed for the dialogue with the deity can only be built up through perpetual training. That is why a real *olorisha* cannot have many occupations besides serving his god. All these activities of *olorishas*: ritual, divination, sacrifice, and magic are entirely a means. The final purpose of *orisha* worship is to extend the natural limits of human experience into the sphere of the metaphysical. Man becomes more than man."[96]

In the same vein, she is also quoted as explaining the primacy of one's relationship with the orisa: "My late friend, the priestess of Oganla, was right when she said to me: your strength comes from your love of human beings. But you must know that you love people because they are part of *orisha*. Do not do anything because of human beings as such. Do everything because of *orisha*."[97] The Araba of Modakẹkẹ expressed similar sentiments, explaining that to be a good babalawo, one must "do everything because of Ifa, do it for Ifa, because everything is in Ifa; if you have Ifa, then you have everything."[98]

Professor Agboola, a babalawo who also has a separate full-time job as a university professor of agriculture, similarly described a continuum running from "spiritual" to "secular" babalawo:

> The babalawo nearer the spiritual pole, they are trying hard to be like Ọrunmila, he is the most spiritual. For these kinds of people, life is very hard. They usually don't have many material possessions or modern conveniences. They consult Ifa about everything. For example, "Should I go to an event?" They ask Ifa. "Should I travel to this town?" They ask Ifa. They are very conservative and strictly adhere to the moral code of Ifa and follow the example of Ọrunmila. For example, if they had a conference in Ghana and Ifa said they couldn't go, they wouldn't even ask Ifa for a sacrifice to allow them to go. . . . Babalawo nearer to the secular pole are more liberal, not rigid. They are more lax. You can see them enjoying life with nice cars and things. You wouldn't know that they are babalawo from their picture, from just seeing them. They modify Ifa to fit the situation, they modify what Ifa says to fit their needs.[99]

The Araba of Modakẹkẹ similarly opined, "We are all trying to be like Ọrunmila, but it is very hard. People today are not strong enough to do it. If someone were to be like Ọrunmila today, he would suffer greatly, he would barely have clothes to cover his body. No one today is strong enough to endure that. So we are all just trying."[100] The tension between the often extreme financial pressures of life in contemporary Nigeria and the demanding and time-intensive practice of Ifa was felt acutely by the babalawo with whom I interacted, and is addressed directly by a verse from Odu Ọbara-Iwori:

> Ọrọbanta-awuwobi-owu divined Ifa for the world on the day all the world's people declared that money is the most important thing in the world. They would give up everything and continue to run after money. Ọrunmila said: Your thoughts about money are right, and your thoughts about money are wrong. Ifa is what we should honor. We should continue to adore both of them. Money exalts a person; money can spoil a person's character. If anyone has too much love for money, his character will be spoiled. Good character is the essential adornment of a human being [iwarere li ọṣọ eniyan]. If you have money, it does not prevent you from becoming blind, mad, lame, and sick. You can be infected by diseases. You should go and increase your wisdom, readjust your thinking. Cultivate good character, acquire wisdom, go and perform sacrifice in order that you may be at ease.[101]

Similarly, the Araba told me that doing what Ifa says and following Ọrunmila's example was the surest way for babalawo to be successful in life.[102] The babalawo whom

How Is Knowledge Acquired in Ifa? • 287

I interviewed resolved this tension between the "good life" promised by Ifa and the difficulties and hardships that attempting to live up to this standard entail, in four ways: (1) The intense difficulty of practicing Ifa sincerely may last a long time, but it is eventually rewarded with the blessings of long life, children, health/peace, and wealth (irẹ aiku, irẹ ọmọ, irẹ alaafia, irẹ ọla); (2) The contemporary time is one of turmoil and confusion where everything is upside down, and the life of a righteous babalawo is harder than that of careless and corrupt babalawo, but still character is what matters most in the end; (3) Those who seem to be enjoying life (the corrupt) may actually be suffering, and those who seem to be suffering (those with good character) may be enjoying life, we cannot know; and (4) The good character and knowledge achieved through personal sacrifice is its own reward. As one verse of Odu Ofun Meji says, "The babalawo have never been rich in money, although they are rich in wisdom";[103] and another verse of Odu Iwori-Atẹ says, "Anyone who does good, does it for himself; anyone who does evil, does it for himself."[104]

The Araba explained that Ọrunmila is patient, but that he eventually punishes those babalawo who ignore his taboos and misuse or make light of Ifa (or that acting in such a way brings down disaster on one's own head). He recounted the story of his own predecessor, the former Araba of Modakẹkẹ. This former Araba had a young Christian wife who convinced him to become more involved in the church and neglect his worship of Ifa. Other babalawo consulted Ifa for him about this change, and Ifa issued a strong warning that he had gone too far and needed to return to the practice of Ifa and fulfill his duties as Araba. However, he ignored these warnings and sadly died in a car accident shortly thereafter. His death was widely interpreted as resulting from his ignoring Ifa's warnings—not necessarily that Ifa had punished him, but rather that Ifa had warned him that disaster waited for him if he continued along his present course. In the same vein, Afolabi Epega cites the following verse of Odu Ọkanran Ọwọnrin:

> Jẹkoṣeka ("let him do evil") favors Oṣika ("the evildoer"); Jẹkoṣebi ("let him practice cruelty") favors Aṣẹbi ("the cruel").
>
> Performed Ifa divination for those who would not listen, who say that Ọrunmila is full of warnings, but that they will do as they please. They are doing evil, they are doing wickedness; the things of the world are good for them. This was reported to Ọrunmila. He said, "However long it takes, the master of vengeance (ẹlẹsan) is coming, rolling in like the waves of the ocean, he relieves people of their burdens and deals gently as he works. When he comes, they will run away."
>
> They said that a sacrifice should be made to prevent Jẹkoṣeka ["let him do evil"] and Jẹkoṣebi ["let him practice cruelty"] from entering into us, so that our

companions and peers will not mock us in the end. The sacrifice: sixteen snails, palm oil, and eighteen thousand cowries. They heard and they sacrificed.[105]

When asked if a babalawo with bad character could know everything that a babalawo with good character could, Professor Agboola explained, "If you become a babalawo, any kind of priest really, your character has to change. You can't curse people, you can't fight. You can't curse people because your words have *aṣẹ*. It is also not befitting your status and role in society to curse and fight. People expect better of you. You must model *iwa pẹlẹ*. A babalawo with bad character is not a babalawo."[106]

When pressed, however, he clarified further: "A babalawo who lies or has bad character, we say 'his clothes will be stained' [*aṣọ rẹ maa pọn ni wọn*]. Ọrunmila used to punish people immediately, but now it can be as long as sixteen years [a symbolic designation for a long time], but Ọrunmila will punish those who break his taboos."[107] Similarly, Ulli Beier wrote:

> Being a priest also involves the merging of one's personality into a much bigger whole. Humility, subjugation to *orisha* and to *the discipline of ritual* are the essential qualities a priest has to achieve. For he knows that where a man is himself, he is foolish and where he is a part of the whole, he is wise. So for the *orisha* priest, modesty and a complete lack of selfishness are the prerequisites of wisdom.
>
> A prime function of the priest is to restore harmony, and it is a very difficult and responsible one. More so than any other person, the priest must watch his every step and action, even his thoughts—so that he can remain close to the *orisha* himself. A senior priest once told Susanne Wenger: "You are now an *olorisha*. Therefore you have to be very careful what you are thinking because thought is creation."[108]

The Araba of Modakẹkẹ opined that a babalawo with bad character could theoretically learn (*kọ*) anything (verses of Ifa and ritual procedures) that a babalawo with good character could, but that practically speaking, his bad character would make it unlikely that other babalawo would want to share their knowledge with him. However, he emphasized that because his bad character put him out of alignment with his *ori* and with Ifa, he would not be as effective and his knowledge would not be as deep as a babalawo with good character. Awo Faniyi concurred, explaining that a babalawo who knows a little but has good character can be stronger (i.e., have more powerful *aṣẹ*) than a babalawo who knows a great deal but lacks good character. However, all agreed that there were many fraudulent or "wicked" babalawo operating around the world, some of whom were quite wealthy, and some of whom had a great deal of power (*agbara* or *aṣẹ*) and knowledge (at least of a superficial kind). But as a verse in Odu Ofun Otura says:

> The liar casts the kola, and it is blocked/opaque
> The oath-breaker casts the kola, and does not yield a clear choice
> *Oninure* ["One who is good inside"] casts the kola
> And it is clearly befitting.[109]

Awo Faniyi cited this verse to underscore the relationship between the character of a babalawo and the quality of the divination and interpretation he performs. The greater the harmony between the babalawo's *ori inu* (inner head / destiny) and *ori ode* (outer head/actual life), the stronger the relationship between the babalawo and Ọrunmila, the better his divination and other ritual performances will be.

### REPETITION, CONTEMPLATION, AND INTERPRETATION

Having memorized these vast bodies of knowledge associated with the practice of Ifa (the orature of the Odu; the procedures of divination and sacrifice; the rituals for festivals, newborns, and new initiates; the pharmacopeia of Ifa) and cultivated *iwa pẹlẹ* (gentle character) through these ritual practices, the mature babalawo or iyanifa is now in a position to contemplate the symbolism and "deep meanings" of these words and practices. Professor Agboola explained:

> When you are young, you just memorize it and repeat it back. Then you know if this verse comes out, this is the situation and you must do this and that. Then as you get older and you go over it again and again, you start thinking about the meanings, and you go deeper and deeper.... It's like when you memorize Ifa, you go around once, then you go around again [learning one verse for each Odu, from the first to the 256th]. The same thing with the meanings [*itumọ*], you go around once and get one kind of meaning, then you go around again and get a deeper meaning.[110]

Each divination for a client, each day of worship for Ifa, each sacrifice, each preparation of medicine, each ceremony of a newborn, each new initiation provides the senior babalawo an opportunity to reflect on and contemplate these rituals and the music and verses of Ifa that form an integral part of these ceremonies. The point is to develop a unique mode of being, a particular character (*iwa pẹlẹ*) characterized by patience, gentleness, and honesty. This mode of being is identified with wisdom (*ọgbọn*), with deep knowledge (*imọ ijinlẹ*), and with Ọrunmila. From this vantage point, the senior babalawo contemplate the tradition of Ifa, and life in general, and delve into the deep meanings of both. As the proverb says, "Like proverbs, like proverbs is how Ifa speaks" (*Bi owe, bi owe n'Ifa sọrọ*). As Abiọdun points out in the quotes cited above, "proverb" (*owe*) has a wide semantic field, covering all forms of sacred art that "clothe" the numinous *ọrọ* (meaning), itself a manifestation of the even more inscrutable Olodumare. Thus the hermeneutic process is understood as a movement of return, of reintegration, from the manifest *owe* to the hidden *ọrọ* through its constituent knowledge (*imọ*), wisdom (*ọgbọn*), and understanding (*oye*), back to Olodumare.

For example, I had the great pleasure of discussing with Awo Faniyi and Professor Agboola the following verse of Odu Otura Meji: "When God does good we call it bad; when God does bad we call it good." It was a fascinating discussion between a senior and junior babalawo, both of whom had attained the highest degree of initiation (*olodu*), and both of whom have university degrees. Although the battery on my recorder died early in our discussion, I will try to recall the main points of our discourse as best I can here:

Awo Faniyi: But how can Olodumare do bad?
Awo Agboola: Bad and good are just what we call bad and good, everything Olodumare does is good.
Me: Even in the verse itself, when it says "When God does good," "When God does bad," we are already calling what He is doing "good" or "bad."
Awo Agboola: Ha! That is interesting.
Awo Faniyi: But, excuse me sir, I think the verse means that people often don't like what happens to them, even if it is for their good, and sometimes enjoy things that happen to them, even if they are bad for them.
Awo Agboola: Yes, but it is also saying that Olodumare is beyond good and evil. The "good" and "evil" of his actions are just what we call them, from our perspective, our point of view.
Awo Faniyi: But, sir, you can't just call anything "good" and call whatever you want "evil," can you?
Me: Yeah, it's not completely relative is it? You can't kill someone and say that it is good. Although I guess people do that. So is the verse saying that there are two kinds of good and bad: that which people think is good and bad, and that which actually is good and bad? Or is it that Olodumare is beyond good and evil?
Awo Agboola: Yes, I understand it like that. Everything comes from Him, what we call good and what we call bad.[111]

Similarly, the signatures of the Odu Ifa and the divining tray (*ọpọn Ifa*) on which they are marked are often the subject of "deep" interpretation and speculation. The principle of male-female (*takọ-tabọ*) and senior-junior (*ẹgbọn-aburo*) complementarity, which structures many of the rituals of Ifa, is also central in these interpretations. For example, when preforming divination with the sixteen *ikin*, if one palm nut remains in the diviner's hand, two marks are made on the divining tray; and if two palm nuts remain, the babalawo will make one mark on the tray. The single mark is interpreted as "male" and "senior" to the double mark, which is "female" and "junior." Hence, Odu Eji Ogbe, which consists entirely of single marks, is considered as "male" and senior to Odu Oyẹku Meji, which is considered "female." However, these are relationships of complementarity, so no babalawo would claim that Eji-Ogbe is "better" than Oyẹku Meji, but rather that they are part of an intricate network of complementary relationships: the signature of Ogbe (four marks of one) is associated with beginnings, birth, light, clarity, masculinity, the right, and seniority; that of Oyẹku (four marks of two) is associated with death, darkness, obscurity, femininity, the left, and being junior. In the pairings of these signatures that make up each Odu, the right position is considered senior (being marked first), and that on the left, as junior (being marked second).

The divining tray is often interpreted as a symbol of the entire cosmos, and babalawo touch different parts of the tray (the top, bottom, right, left, and center) before divination when invoking the different powers of the cosmos. For example, the following invocation is typical:

> The front of the diving tray, hear [us]
> The back of the divining tray, hear [us]
> The ones on the right
> The knowing ones on the left
> The center of the divining tray is the center courtyard of heaven[112]
> The dawning of the day
> The setting of the sun
> Let it be good, let it be good, o![113]

Similarly, babalawo often press a line into the camwood powder on the tray, dividing it into halves, and then another line, dividing into quarters, before many rituals. Each of these places on the divination tray (top, bottom, right, left, center) is associated with various signatures of the Odu, cardinal directions, fundamental attributes, and types of *aṣẹ* (dynamic force). For example, Epega and Neimark include the diagram presented in figure 8 at the beginning of their book *The Sacred Ifa Oracle*.[114]

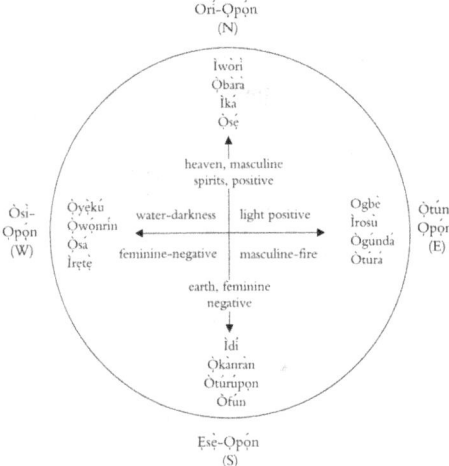

FIGURE 8 Ọpọn cosmogram. Reprinted from Afolabi Epega and Philip John Neimark, *The Sacred Ifa Oracle* (San Francisco: Harper, 1995), xvi.

THE SIXTEEN BASIC FIGURES OF IFA

A. Using Sixteen Palm Nuts

| 1 | 2 | 3 | 4 | 5 | 6 | 7 | 8 |
|---|---|---|---|---|---|---|---|
| Ogbe | Oyẹku | Iwori | Edi | Ọbara | Ọkanran | Irosun | Ọwọnrin |
| 1 | 1 1 | 1 1 | 1 | 1 | 1 1 | 1 | 1 1 |
| 1 | 1 1 | 1 | 1 1 | 1 1 | 1 1 | 1 | 1 1 |
| 1 | 1 1 | 1 | 1 1 | 1 1 | 1 1 | 1 1 | 1 |
| 1 | 1 1 | 1 1 | 1 | 1 1 | 1 | 1 1 | 1 |

| 9 | 10 | 11 | 12 | 13 | 14 | 15 | 16 |
|---|---|---|---|---|---|---|---|
| Ogunda | Ọsa | Irẹtẹ | Otura | Oturupọn | Ika | Ọsẹ | Ofun |
| 1 | 1 1 | 1 | 1 | 1 1 | 1 1 | 1 | 1 1 |
| 1 | 1 | 1 | 1 1 | 1 1 | 1 | 1 1 | 1 |
| 1 | 1 | 1 1 | 1 | 1 | 1 1 | 1 | 1 1 |
| 1 1 | 1 | 1 | 1 | 1 1 | 1 1 | 1 1 | 1 |

FIGURE 9 The Ifẹ numbering of the sixteen basic figures. Based on a chart from William Bascom, *Ifa Divination: Communication Between Gods and Men in West Africa* (Bloomington: Indiana University Press, 1969), 4.

However, such schematics can be highly idiosyncratic and differ from babalawo to babalawo. When I showed and explained figure 8 to the Araba of Modakẹkẹ, he strongly objected to it; whereas Professor Agboola explained that while he agreed with the grouping of the Odu, he would put Ogbe at the top, Iwori on the right, Oyẹku on the bottom, and Idi/Odi on the left, or potentially have Ogbe at the top, Iwori on the right, Idi/Odi on the bottom, and Oyẹku on the left. Each signature or Odu represents a particular archetype exemplified in the verses and narratives of that Odu. Even the forms and the order of the signatures of the Odu are objects of interpretation and speculation. As figure 9, reproducing a chart from Bascom, shows, each Odu signature (Ogbe, Oyẹku, Iwori, etc.) is paired with another signature that is either its inverse, swapping single marks for double (Ogbe-Oyẹku, Iwori-Odi/Edi, Irosun-Ọwọnrin) and/or 180° rotation (Irosun-Ọwọnrin, Ọbara-Ọkanran, Ogunda-Ọsa, Ika-Oturupọn, Otura-Irẹtẹ, Ọsẹ-Ofun).[115]

Thus, the progression through the signatures Odu of Ifa is marked by the same logic of complementary pairing: opposites beget or follow each other. Furthermore, each Odu has a special relationship with its complementary Odu, which is recited when performing a sacrifice (from the original Odu), according to Professor Agboola. For example, many verses from the Odu Ogbe-Irẹtẹ discuss initiation into Ifa (*itẹfa*); while several verses of its complementary Odu, Irẹtẹ-Ogbe, discuss Ọrunmila's wife, Odu, and how they came to be married.

How Is Knowledge Acquired in Ifa? • 293

Like the figures of the *I Ching*, the progression through the different signatures of the Odu is understood to represent the different stages of change, cycles of life, death, and rebirth in which opposites inevitably follow each other: what goes up comes down, what goes down comes up; joy is followed by sorrow, which precedes joy; weakness precedes strength, which is followed by weakness; light comes before darkness, which is followed again by light. This symbolism is also found in the process of Ifa initiation, which involves a kind of union or "marriage" with Odu. The following verses of Ifa allude to this dynamic of complementarity:

[Odu Iwori-Ọsẹ]
"Tribulation does not come without its good aspects
The good and bad are always together . . .
sweetness usually ends the taste of a bitter leaf"[116]

[Odu Irosun-Iwori]
"Fire likes inside
Darkness likes outside
The roof or the back [of the house] only"
Performed Ifa divination for Fire
When he was going to take darkness as a wife
Fire entered, and darkness disappeared[117]

The Araba explained that fire loves darkness and seeks it out, only to banish that which it seeks, but eventually fire always dies down and darkness returns, just as night always follows day.

These associations and diagrams are the result of years of experience reciting, contemplating, and performing the Odu and their associated rituals. Similarly, in addition to the meanings and signatures of the verses of Ifa, the sacrifices prescribed therein are also the subject of interpretive speculation. For example, some babalawo classify the elements of prescribed sacrifices according to the three main colors of the Yoruba language: white (*funfun*: chalk, snails, shea butter, etc.), black (*dudu*: indigo cloth, black animals, ashes, dark leaves, etc.), and red (*pupa*: blood, palm oil, camwood powder, etc.). Each category has its own associations and effects. Similarly, the elements sacrificed are also classified in accordance to whether they belonged to the animal (*ẹran*), plant (*ewe*), or mineral (*okuta/ilẹ*) kingdoms. These elements were also classified as "hot" (*gbọna*)—such as alcohol or pepper—or "cool" (*tutu*)—such as snails, water, and certain leaves. The dynamics of these categories of sacrifice and the relationship to the verses that contain them are illustrated by the following related pair of verses from Odu Iwori-Ọsa and Odu Oturupọn-Odi, respectively.

> [Odu Iwori-Ọsa]
> Akitaraṣẹtẹ, the diviner of heaven
> Performed Ifa divination for Olodumare and the world
> When people were running to Olodumare to seek his advice on various problems
> Crying, "Father, Father, I have come. Save me, please save me."
> He said, "What is the problem?"
> Those to whom I gave power [agbara] did not use the power. Those to whom I gave wisdom, did not use the inner wisdom (ọgbọn inu) I gave them."
> He was asked to offer sacrifice in order to place a veil of darkness over the earth.
> The sacrifice: a black cloth, a black sheep, twenty thousand cowries, and Ifa leaves.
> He heard and performed the sacrifice.
> It was assumed that if a child did not see his father, he would defend himself.[118]

> [Odu Oturupọn-Odi]

> The world is good (dara). Heaven is magnificent. Odudua [i.e., Olodumare] advised the people of the word to come back to him for reincarnation. The children refused to go. The elderly people also refused to go. We asked why. They said, "It is not easy to go to heaven and come back." Ọrunmila said, "Heaven is good and it is the home of beauty." Odudua would never live in a despicable place. Oriṣa is always found in decent places. Anyone who is called should answer his call. No mother would call her child to suffer. The people of the world were still hesitating. They were advised to sacrifice so that the veil of darkness might be removed from their eyes. If they are working, they should always look up to heaven. The sacrifice: sixteen limestones, a piece of white cloth, twenty thousand cowries, and Ifa leaves. If the prescribed sacrifice is performed, they should abstain from blood. They refused to sacrifice.[119]

In the first verse, Olodumare places a veil between himself and the world because His children were not using the "inner wisdom" (ọgbọn inu) and "power" (agbara) He had given them. By separating Himself from His children, He forces them to rely on their own inner resources that He has bestowed on them. He achieves this veil of separation through a sacrifice of a black cloth, a black sheep, twenty thousand cowries, and

Ifa leaves. In the next verse, the "veil of darkness" (*okunkun*) is removed through a sacrifice of sixteen limestones, white cloth, twenty thousand cowries, and Ifa leaves. These "white" (*funfun*) elements have the opposite effect of their "black" (*dudu*) counterparts, lifting the veil of obscurity from heaven. The "black sheep" (an unusual animal, as sheep are normally white) is here counterbalanced by "sixteen limestones" (an unusual mineral, as stones are usually black).

These verses are also fascinating in that the second explains the common fear of death and the return to heaven as being a result of ignorance. Heaven is described as the "home of beauty," suggesting that the beauties of the world have their home, their source and origin, in heaven, the home of Olodumare and the oriṣa. Nevertheless, because people did not perform the sacrifice, they remained veiled, and thus fear Olodumare's call to return home.

The first verse explains the origins of this "veil of darkness" that hides Olodumare and heaven from people dwelling in the world. Instead of relying on the power and wisdom that Olodumare had given them, people returned to heaven to ask Olodumare about every little thing. Both the Araba of Modakẹkẹ and Professor Agboola emphasized that Ifa divination is no substitute for one's own discernment, wisdom (*ọgbọn*), and hard work. The practice of Ifa should develop these qualities in a babalawo, not make them completely reliant on divination to make every decision. This may seem to be somewhat in tension with the extreme devotion that respected babalawo and other *oloriṣa* display, often consulting their deities about decisions as small as whether to travel or even what to have for dinner. This tension can be somewhat resolved through the metaphor of intimate interpersonal relationships, which characterizes much of Yoruba religious discourse. Consulting one's wife or husband regarding dinner or travel is not a sign of a lack of independence, but rather of intimate concern, consideration, and respect. So it is with devoted babalawo and other *oloriṣa*. Moreover, this verse suggests that because God and heaven are obscured, we must apply our own "inner wisdom" and strength in order to know them; this was, in fact the reason for the imposition of the "veil of darkness." The verse also implies that knowledge of God and heaven is the normal state of affairs, and that something (in this case a "veil of darkness") has to intervene to keep us from having direct access to Olodumare and heaven.

DEATH, BURIAL, AND REBIRTH

For babalawo, like elders of other spiritual traditions among Yoruba-speaking peoples, old age is typically understood as the zenith of one's spiritual prowess, even as it marks the nadir of one's physical strength. As Ulli Beier remarks:

In traditional Yoruba life, a man did not lose his strength as he grew older. His strength was transposed: as his physical strength weakened, his psychic power increased. The really old men became centres of power. They might sit at home on the same spot, without taking physical part even in the ceremonies. But they become the embodiment of wisdom and knowledge. It was from them that the younger more active people had to receive advice and strength. It was important for the community to be exposed to their radiation, because these people were really close to the *orisha*, they achieved the semi-divine state of "dynamic relaxation": a perfected state of mind where intense concentration results in a state of complete repose. Yoruba sacred images are always represented in this state. When such a man dies it is a cause for great rejoicing, because he is becoming divine and is on his way to being ultimately reborn again.[120]

The most senior babalawo are regarded as having achieved a kind of union with Ọrunmila. As the living representatives of Ifa, they exemplify his character, behavior, and wisdom, and they carry out his functions. Their words can even be regarded as the words of Ifa and can become new *ẹsẹ Ifa*. This merging of babalawo and Ifa/Ọrunmila in a state of "dynamic repose" is especially evident during festivals and when these senior babalawo perform divination and recite verses of Ifa. While I would not call these states of trance or possession (possession is a major taboo for babalawo, unlike some other *olorișa*), I noticed marked changes in posture, facial expressions, and overall disposition (that seemed consistent with Wenger's and Beier's description of "dynamic relaxation") when babalawo recited verses of Ifa. Perhaps one could say that the most advanced babalawo achieve this perpetual state of intense concentration/repose, which is like that of Ọrunmila. In the words of Susanne Wenger, who had a great deal of personal experience with orișa possession/trance:

> The limits of human existence have been extended and man has become divine for a brief moment. Man has been reassured of his participation in creation, man has reassured himself that he is a part of god. And this is what gives man his pride: that he is able to be more than man. This is his greatness: that he has the courage to transcend the natural limits of his existence....
>
> Only the really great priests, when they become old, achieve a permanent state of union with the god. They become like shrines, and even when their bodies have become so weak that they spend years lying on the mat of a dark room, they may still radiate power. Death does not "happen" to such people. They finally pass into the other sphere when they have decided to let go of their magical hold on this world. The Yoruba ritual that leads the worshipper towards taking part in the

god's identity explains why an *olorisha*'s physiognomical features are gradually being moulded by some kind of archetypal image of the *orisha*. Anybody who has lived close to Yorubas would be able to identify worshippers of Ọbatala, Shango, or Ogun simply by looking at their eyes. The spiritual identity finally finds visible expression in a person's physiognomy.[121]

Thus, a lifetime of imitation of and devotion to an orişa shapes not only the inner (*inu*) but also the outer (*ode*) aspects of a person. The Araba confirmed this observation, noting that serious babalawo "resemble Ọrunmila more and more as they get older, just like Şango priests resemble Şango, Ogun priests resemble Ogun, and Ọşun priests resemble her."[122] Likewise, as Babatunde Lawal writes, quoting Frank Willett, "It is indeed one of the surprises of living in Yorubaland that one does frequently see people whose features remind one very forcibly of a particular sculptural style, yet the sculptures are not portraits of individuals, but they are supposed to look as if they might be."[123] Taking these two perspectives together, ritual sculpts the inner and outer dimensions of babalawo and other orişa devotees in the image of orişa, just as sculptors carve wood in the images of the orişa. The sculptures resemble the orişa because they also resemble their devotees, and the sculptures resemble the devotees because they resemble their orişa.

Death merely returns or transposes such people to the realm of the orişa, at which point, their identification with the orişa may become ritually complete: such people can be remembered and worshipped as "parts" or manifestations of particular orişa, and such babalawo may become enshrined in the mysterious names of the diviners that begin most verses of Ifa, often in the Odu with which they are associated. Many of these proverbial names appear in many different verses of the same Odu. For example, the proverb/name (*oriki*) "Nothing comes from getting angry. Patience is the father of character. An elder who has patience has everything," appears as the diviner in many of the verses of Odu Ogbe-Yọnu cited in this chapter, and many others that are not. As the proverb says, "It is death that turns an individual into a beautiful sculpture; a living person has blemishes" (*Oju a ku la a d'ere, eniyan ko sunwon laaye*).[124]

The verses of Ifa repeatedly describe death as an inevitable return home, and for mature babalawo, an anticipated transition (whereas premature death is feared and avoided). In this vein, Professor Agboola quoted the following proverbs, commonly cited when hearing news of the death of an elder: "The child sent on an errand has come back," "The world is a market, heaven is home," and "When someone dies, the people of heaven don't cry, [just as] we rejoice when a new child is born."[125] Likewise, a verse from Odu Irosun-Ofun says:

Ofun is giving out goodness

Ofun does not make any noise about it

People like Ofun are hard to find on earth

Anyone who wants to perform wonders should look up to heaven. Heaven is the home of honor.

Ifa divination was performed for human beings who were told that death would always bring them to see the wonders in heaven

They were asked to sacrifice so that darkness and sorrow might be banished from their paths

The sacrifice: four hens, four tortoises, four pieces of white cloth, and four bundles of kola nuts

They heard, but did not sacrifice[126]

## Burial (*Isinku*)

The funerary rites of babalawo are all centered on facilitating this transition from the world (*aye*) to heaven (*ọrun*), anticipating the eventual return to the world. Not every babalawo is given a funeral. Only those who are understood to have reached maturity and achieved exemplary character and wisdom qualify for the elaborate funerary rituals,[127] which last seven days, often at great cost to the deceased's family. While some of the rituals are secret, and specific to Ifa, many of the funerary rites of babalawo are shared by members of other Yoruba traditions such as washing the corpse with a special solution of water, herbs, and blood (of a rooster for men, a hen for women); rubbing chalk on the palms of the corpse; wrapping the body in a special cloth; washing the coffin; feasting; and playing music. These rituals are typically conducted by the eldest members of the deceased's family and ritual group (Ifa, Ogboni, Ogun, Egungun, etc.). As Drewal explains, "This ritual is the deceased's initiation by the society of elders into the group of the ancestors."[128] Awo Agboola described the funerary process for babalawo as facilitating the deceased's "transition to the level of orisa":

> Anyone we feed with sacrifice to is an orisa. . . . In the ancestral realm, in heaven [*ọrun*] we appear in a new body. But we have to do some things to help the soul, the spirit of the person to get there. . . . After the third day, we perform a ceremony called *itufa* [burying Ifa]. At midnight we go and ask the deceased what we should do with his Ifa [his instruments of divination]. The only language that a babalawo will understand after death is Ifa, the Odu of Ifa. So we chant seven Odu: Odu

Ofun-Ọbara, Odu Oyẹku-Ofun, et cetera, to guide the person to a certain point, after which he can guide himself.[129]

**Reincarnation**

The newly deceased person who has joined the ranks of the ancestors and orișa is expected to choose a new *ori* in heaven and return to the world, being reincarnated among their descendants. As a verse from Odu Iwori-Odi says, "Our father, if he gives birth to us in full, inevitably we shall, in time, give birth to him in turn. Our mother, if she gives birth to us in full, inevitably we shall, in time, give birth to her in turn."[130] This new incarnation is understood to choose a new *ori* and to receive a new body from Ọbatala and a new *ẹmi* from Olodumare, so in one sense it is a bit like the mythical ship of Theseus, which retains a certain continuity of identity, even as all of its constituent parts are replaced.

Some verses of Ifa suggest a kind of teleology to this cycle of reincarnation: that the purpose of all of this coming and going between heaven and the world is to perfect one's character and wisdom. Once this "good position has been achieved," one has found his or her raison d'être, putting an end to the now unnecessary reincarnation. For example, a verse from Odu Irosun-Iwori says:

> Let's do things with joy. Those who wish to go may go. Those who wish to return may return. Definitely, human beings have been chosen to bring good fortune to the world. "Omniscience," the diviner of Ọrunmila, performed Ifa divination for Ọrunmila, who was told that human beings would come and ask him a particular question. He was advised to offer a sacrifice of fish and two hundred grains of cornmeal. Ọrunmila heeded the advice and performed the sacrifice.
>
> One day all kinds of people, including robbers and other evildoers gathered themselves together and went to Ọrunmila to complain, they said that they were "tired of going back and forth to earth. Ọrunmila! Please allow us to take refuge in heaven."
>
> Ọrunmila said that they could not avoid going to and coming back from the earth until they had attained the good position (*ipo rere*) that Odudua [in this case, another name for Olodumare] had ordained for every individual; only then could they reside in heaven. They asked, "What is the good position?" Ọrunmila asked them to admit their ignorance. They said, "We admit our ignorance and would like to be given knowledge by God (*Oluwa*)."
>
> Ọrunmila said, "The good position is a life/world (*aye*) with full knowledge of everything, joy everywhere, without anxiety or fear of enemies, attack from

snakes or other dangerous animals, without fear of death, disease, accusations, losses, wizards, witches, Eṣu, accidents from water and fire, without the fear of misery or poverty, because of your inner power, good character, and wisdom....

All evil acts have their repercussions. Individually, what is needed to attain the good position is: wisdom that can adequately govern the world as a whole; sacrifice or cultivating the habit of doing good to the poor or those who need your help; desire to increase the world's prosperity rather than destroy it.

People will continue to go to heaven and return to the world after death until everyone attains the good position. There are a lot of good things in heaven that are still not available in the world, and will be obtained in due course. When all the children of Odudua are gathered together, those chosen (*yan*) to transfer the good things to the world are called *eniyan*, human beings.[131]

Thus, this verse defines the telos of humanity, or the purpose of life, to be the attainment of this "good position," which is at once individual and communal. This "good position" is characterized by "full knowledge" (*amọtan*), "joy" (*ayọ*), "wisdom" (*ogbọn*), "inner power" (*agbara inu*), and "good character" (*iwa rere*). Human beings in general, and babalawo in particular, have been chosen to develop these qualities and use them to "bring the good things from heaven to the world." The Araba of Modakẹkẹ and Awo Faniyi identified this "good position," the perfection of the human condition, with Ọrunmila, separately commenting that "Babalawo are all praying to be with Ọrunmila after death" and "the goal of a babalawo to do the work of Ọrunmila, to mend the world with the word of Olodumare, which is Ifa."[132] This, in short, is the ultimate goal of a babalawo: to reach the "good position" of full knowledge and joy through the cultivation of wisdom, inner power, and good character, and to help others to do the same.

CONCLUSION

Thus, the process of acquiring knowledge in Ifa begins before birth with the choice of *ori* and can continue after death with the return to the world. This knowledge is acquired through memorization, study, ritual practice (prayer, recitation, divination, sacrifices, etc.), cultivation of good character, initiation, as well as contemplation and interpretation of the rituals and orature of Ifa. This process is inherently social, involving interaction with and the participation of other babalawo, family and community members, and the orisa and other spiritual entities. Nevertheless, self-knowledge, or knowledge of one's *ori*, is essential and even foundational to this process, the purpose of which is to become like Ọrunmila, to perfect oneself and serve as a bridge between heaven and the world, bringing them together and repairing the world. As a verse from Odu Iwori Odi says:

> "There is no childbearing woman who cannot give birth to an Ifa priest. There is no childbearing woman who cannot give birth to Orunmila. Our father, if he gives birth to us in full, inevitably we shall, in time, give birth to him in turn. Our mother, if she gives birth to us in full, inevitably we shall, in time, give birth to her in turn." Performed Ifa divination for Orunmila who said he would bring heaven down to the world, he would take the world back to heaven.
>
> In order for him to accomplish his mission, he was asked to offer everything in twos, one male and one female—one ram and one ewe, one he-goat and one she-goat, one cock and one hen, and so on. Orunmila heeded the advice and performed the sacrifice. Thus the earth became fruitful and multiplied greatly.[133]

The following *oriki* (praise-prayer)[134] of Orunmila (from Odu Oyeku Meji), one of the many that babalawo recite daily upon waking in the morning, summarizes the role and importance of Orunmila in this enterprise:

> Orunmila! Eleri Ipin
> Ibikeji Olodumare;
> A-je-ju-Oogun,
> Obiriti, A-p'ijo- iku-da
> Oluwa mi, A-to-i-ba-j'aye
> Oro a-bi-ku-j'igbo
> Oluwa mi, Ajiki,
> Ogege a-gb'aye-gun;
> Odudu ti ndu ori emere
> A-tun-ori-ti-ko sunwon se,
> A-mo-i-ku
> Olowa Aiyere
> Agiri ile-Ilogbon
> Oluwa mi: amoimotan
> A ko mo o tan kose
> A ba mo tan iba se ke[135]
>
> Orunmila, Witness of the choice of destiny
> Second to Olodumare
> More potent than medicine [charms]

The vast sphere, who averts the day of death
My Lord! Who can prevent the world's ruin
The mystery who fought death in the bush
My Lord, whom I greet upon awakening
The balance that set the whole world aright
The one who strives to repair the heads of spirit children
Who repairs ill-made heads/destinies
He who knows you never dies
Lord, the unopposable king
Perfect in the house of wisdom
My Lord, whose knowledge is without end
Not knowing you fully, we [our lives] are in vain
If we could but know you in full, all would be well[136]

As the "witness of the choice of destiny" Ọrunmila can help "repair" ill-made heads (*ori*), and help one come to know oneself, one's *ori inu*. Thus, he who knows Ọrunmila knows his or her own heavenly or eternal self, and "never dies."[137] One comes to know Ọrunmila by following his example as set forth in the orature and rituals of Ifa, by cultivating a character like his, through intense devotion to him, and deep contemplation of his embodiment in the Odu of Ifa. Ọrunmila's wisdom is "perfect" and his knowledge is "without end," and to know him is to participate in this perfect knowledge, which is the purpose of life and "makes all things well."

The following verse from Odu Ọwọnrin Ọbara emphasizes the close relationship between this most important form of knowledge and self-knowledge, and Ọrunmila's role as the facilitator of the latter:

"He sees me, I don't see him
Ọwọnrin'Bara"
Performed Ifa divination for Ọwa
They said that what we are seeking is near us, but our lack of knowledge
    prevents us from recognizing it
They said that we should make a sacrifice so that Baba Agbọnniregun
    [Ọrunmila] can show it to us
Ọrunmila, Witness of the choice of destiny, Second to Olodumare, said:
What we are seeking is near us, but our lack of knowledge prevents us from
    recognizing it.
They said that he should sacrifice a hen, twenty thousand cowries, and Ifa
    leaves [*ori awọnriwọn meji*—two guana heads]

He heard and sacrificed
They said: Enough! From now on, Ọwa will find what he is seeking[138]

The opening epithet—"He sees me, I don't see him"—suggests that this verse can be interpreted as describing self-knowledge, knowledge of one's *ori/ipin*. As Ẹlẹri ipin (the witness of the choice of destiny), Ọrunmila (who sees us and our destinies, to which we are blind) alone can help us recognize that which is closest to us. The *ewe Ifa* (Ifa leaves) specified for this sacrifice further reinforce this symbolism, for it takes a head to see another head, and the name of the plant (*ori awọnriwọn*) can be glossed as "heads, they see each other." Through the practice and study of Ifa, Ọrunmila shows babalawo that "what they are seeking is near." Like a mirror, unseen himself, Ifa witnesses the heads (*ori*) of his devotees, facilitating self-knowledge, by making them seen and known. Thus, the oracle of Ifa, like its counterpart at Delphi, directs its supplicants to "know themselves."

CHAPTER 8

# How Is Knowledge Verified in Ifa?

*Ọbẹ t'o mu ki gbẹ kuku ara rẹ.*
However sharp the knife, it cannot carve its own handle.
—YORUBA PROVERB

Contrary to common assumptions, knowledge in Ifa (and other indigenous intellectual traditions) is not merely memorized, but is also verified, often empirically. For something to even be considered *imọ* (knowledge) instead of *igbagbọ* (accepted hearsay), it must be experienced and verified firsthand. So how is this knowledge, some of which may seem quite unusual and far-fetched to Western-educated readers, verified in Ifa?

## HOW DOES DIVINATION WORK?

Going back as far as Plato, scholars have divided divination into two different categories: those characterized by technique or mechanical manipulation (casting lots, augury, etc.) and those characterized by inspiration or possession (e.g., the Oracle at Delphi).[1] Babalawo's own explanations of Ifa blur this dichotomy, describing the process of divination as Ifa or Ọrunmila speaking directly through them or through the instruments of divination and, quite obviously, as the mechanical or technical use of these instruments to produce a figure that is then interpreted. It must be remembered that in the process of divination, the client or seeker does not reveal the reason for his or her consultation to the diviner until the end of the consultation, when the client and diviner work together to interpret the oracular pronouncements of Ifa.

Babalawo draw on the verses and rituals of Ifa itself to provide several different, complementary accounts of how Ifa divination works. As Eze writes, "Odu, however, is not a dead document merely repeated from one generation to the next. It contains elaborate exegesis on the text, but more importantly, it contains... theories about how to do the work of interpretation."[2] These different accounts of interpretation seem to be regarded as different perspectives, not mutually contradictory or competing theories. In one account, as mentioned above, Ifa divination reveals the wishes or direction of the seeker's *ori*, as symbolized by the seeker touching money or the instruments of divination to his or her head before handing them over to the babalawo for divination.

In another closely related account, Orunmila, as the witness of the choice of destiny (*eleri-ipin*), communicates and guides the seeker in accordance with his or her own destiny, by speaking through the instruments of divination and the babalawo. In another account, it is Orunmila himself who hears and answers the question of the seeker, while yet another account portrays Ifa divination as a means, introduced or founded by Orunmila, of gaining insight into the situation at hand.

In all of these accounts, however, the process of divination is the same, and is highly symbolic. Mirroring the accounts of creation in the Odu Ifa (one of which is cited above), the divination process begins by a division of undifferentiated unity into a binary opposition of possibilities. With each cast of the *ikin*, the figure of the Odu becomes more and more specific, until one of the 256 possibilities is marked on the divination tray. This figural representation of the archetypal Odu can then be further elaborated through the use of *ibo*, in which the babalawo will perform additional divination to determine if the pronouncement is good (*ire*) or bad (*ibi*), and then what type of good or bad is specified. However, it is common for the babalawo, as in the examples in the previous chapter, to interpret the Odu, recite the narrative, and interpret it for the client before resorting to the lots (*ibo*) for further clarification. Finally, the client explains his or her situation in light of the recited narrative, and in consultation with the babalawo (and Ifa, if subsequent divination is performed) determines the appropriate course of action.

Thus, the divination procedure re-presents the coming into being of the client's situation. The unseen and unknown intention existing in the client's *ori inu* is first manifested in a whispered word to the instruments of divination, which then manifest in a particular figure of an Odu, then in a particular verse and narrative, through which the client's situation is interpreted and into which it is integrated through consultation and the performance of ritual (usually a sacrifice) of mythological precedent. Ifa divination reveals the unspoken archetype from which the client's situation has emerged, and with each step becomes more specific and particular until there is a meeting and merging of the "descent" of the meaning/matter at hand (*oro*) and the "ascent" of interpretive understanding (*oye*).

Since the whole world is understood to be contained in Ifa, and everything is said to be created through a combination of the Odu (which are themselves created through a combination of the binary pair: I II), any given situation, just like any person, plant, animal, or town, is understood to have an Odu that gave birth to it. Ifa divination identifies this Odu, or archetypal principle, which is then elaborated through the proverbial speech (*owe*) of the *ẹsẹ* of that particular Odu. Then this narrative is applied to the client's particular situation, as both client and diviner interpret the situation through the lens of this mythological/proverbial narrative, reintegrating the particular situation with its mythological/archetypal precedent and completing the cycle of creation and interpretation. This hermeneutic reverses the process described in Odu Ọsa Ogunda above, in which knowledge (*imọ*), wisdom (*ọgbọn*), and understanding (*oye*) combine to form *ọrọ*, which descends and is clothed in *owe*, the proverbial, metaphoric, symbolic register of speech and art. To quote Rowland Abiọdun again, "With the aid of *Ẹla* [Ọrunmila], *Ọrọ* is made manifest, and it is beautifully 'clothed' in poetry, maxims, and wise sayings, all of which are *owe*. For as the saying goes, *kolombo ni Ọrọ n rin*, 'Ọrọ moves around naked,' and it is forbidden to see it in that state."[3] Ifa clothes *ọrọ* in the Odu and their verses (*ẹsẹ*) giving the client and the diviner access to the metaphysical root of the situation. As the previously cited verse from Odu Iwori-Odi explains, Ọrunmila said he would "bring heaven down to the world, he would take the world back to heaven."[4]

In this way, Ifa divination serves as a kind of metaphysical mirror reflecting the archetypal origins of the client's situation in the Odu, then specifying the particular mythological narrative and ritual course of action to achieve the desired result. And yet, one may still ask how this process is accomplished. How is it that seemingly random throws of a divining chain or palm nuts can yield profound insight into any given situation? And how can the interpretive claims of babalawo be verified, if at all?

As alluded to above, these claims are only incredible or fantastical given certain metaphysical assumptions about causality, symbolic correspondences, and so forth; given other assumptions (those outlined above, which undergird Ifa) these claims are more commonsensical. Nevertheless, one can still ask how babalawo account for and verify the efficacy of this particular system of divination. The babalawo I interviewed discussed several different ways in which the accuracy of the system of divination is verified and even tested; however, first we will discuss the two complementary forms of explanation they offered on how Ifa divination "works," before covering these different methods of verification. In the first, or "incantatory," explanation, the act of divination and recitation of certain verses of Ifa affects the client and puts him or her into the situation described in the verse. Professor Agboola explained: "*Ẹsẹ Ifa* are coded stories from the time of Ọrunmila. The spiritual power [when they are divined and recited] will transfer what happened in that time to the current situation. It's like [the Qur'anic account] of Yunus [Jonah] and the whale.[5] The prayer is, what happened then, let it be the same here and now.... Babalawo have power of the spoken word (aṣẹ ọfọ), what they say comes to pass. The words of Ifa are powerful."[6]

In the second, or "mirroring," explanation, through the system of symbolic correspondences between the seeker's ori, Ọrunmila, the instruments of divination, and the babalawo described above, Ifa divination reveals the nature of the client's situation. Both the Araba and Professor Agboola frequently cited the maxim "If Ifa did not resemble you, it would not have come out" to summarize this perspective.

But Ifa divination is not only descriptive, it is also prescriptive. In fact, the vast majority of people who come to consult Ifa with a babalawo are just as, if not more concerned with how to resolve their problems, than they are with their root causes. The interpretive process of Ifa is then applied to prescribe the appropriate ritual intervention and/or change in behavior. Professor Agboola explained, "It's not the plant, it's the power of the plant that is used.... It's the same thing with ẹsẹ Ifa, you extract the meaning and use that.... With sacrifice you change the environment by inviting some forces and clearing out others."[7] In another interview, he similarly commented, contrasting charms (oogun) with Ifa: "Ifa goes to the root of the problem, which we may not be seeing. Charms only deal with the surface, with the symptoms, but Ifa goes to the root, that is why some people do not have the patience for Ifa today. Maybe it will tell them to change their behavior or character, or other things they don't want to hear or understand. So they just go for charms to do what they want."[8]

**Verification of Divination**

In the same interview, Professor Agboola responded to my question "What if Ifa makes a prediction that doesn't make any sense or that is wrong?" by telling me about a man for whom he performed divination in the United States. According to Professor Agboola, the man came to see him about a new job he was hoping to get, but the verse of Ifa that came out was about a troublesome child. The man was confused and skeptical, but performed the sacrifice anyway. Sure enough, the man got the job, but a few months later, his son did some foolish things and was arrested. The extra money the man had from his new salary was just enough to cover the bail and lawyer's fees to get his son out of trouble. Professor Agboola concluded his story:

> So you see Ifa dealt with the root of the problem. The man came to ask about a job, but Ifa saw that there was no issue with the job, the problem was with the child. Sometimes a woman may come seeking children, but Ifa will talk about a job or

*ori* or money, and eventually you will see. So sometimes when you are thinking that Ifa has given a wrong answer or when it doesn't make sense, maybe in a few weeks or months or years, something will happen, and you will say, "Ah! That is what Ifa was saying." This happens often.⁹

So the predictions of Ifa are expected to be verified over time; however, as its predictions are not always obvious, neither is this process of verification.

Sometimes, however, the process of verification is much clearer. The Araba told me how a man once came to him for divination, and the verse of Ifa that emerged indicated that he was a thief seeking help with his next robbery. So the Araba said, "You are a thief, and I don't help thieves. Come back when you want to do something good with your life." The man admitted that this was true and left. Sometimes the predictions of Ifa are even more specific. The Araba told me that he once interpreted a verse of Ifa for a man explaining that "he wanted to marry a light-skinned woman with a birthmark on her left thigh," which the man excitedly confirmed.¹⁰ During most of the divinations I observed during my time with the Araba, the clients immediately identified the interpretation the Araba gave as clearly and directly applying to their situation.

For example, several students from the nearby Ọbafẹmi Awolọwọ University interrupted one of our sessions asking the Araba to divine for them. The university was on strike and so they had little to do. The Araba explained to them how the divination process would work and the first one came forward and whispered his problem to a twenty-naira note, which he then placed on his head and handed to the Araba. The Araba then touched this note to each of the shells on his *ọpẹlẹ* (divining chain), invoked Ọrunmila, and then cast the chain. He announced the name of the Odu, then cast lots to specify if the pronouncement was one of good or bad. The Araba then gave a summary of the pronouncement, explaining that "Ifa says you want to fight two people, but you must not do this: one of them is very powerful, and the other is very good. Whatever you are trying to do to them will come back on your head. However, if you make a sacrifice, and don't fight with them anymore, you can avoid this." The students were noticeably surprised and a few of them gasped. The Araba then began reciting the verse of Ifa that he had just summarized, and then interpreted it again for the student, remarking that "Ifa says you want to fight a person, a girl"—at this point one of the student's friends hit him and said, "Rebecca!"¹¹ The Araba continued, "But you must not fight her, she is a very powerful person. Ifa says you are also trying to fight another woman, a girl, but this person is very good, she has not done anything wrong to anyone, so you must not fight her." At this point the student looked back at his friends and said, "Korede!" The Araba then explained the sacrifice that they must make in order to prevent bad things from happening to them in this quarrel. The students then explained that they were having some sort of quarrel with other students and that they were planning to fight them later that week. The Araba advised them not to fight, especially not to fight the two women mentioned in the verse he had recited.

In the few cases where the pronouncements of Ifa did not seem to match the problem that had led the clients to the Araba, neither he nor they seemed particularly bothered. While such predictions that seem to "miss the mark" may lead some clients to seek the help of other specialists, many others simply trusted that Ifa's pronouncements would make sense in the end, often citing their previous positive experiences with the Araba or other babalawo as justification for this confidence. The Araba admitted to sometimes being puzzled by the pronouncements of Ifa, but also cited his innumerable experiences of divining accurately (especially those instances when an unclear pronouncement became clear a few months or years later) as justification for his confidence in the system of divination.[12] Moreover, as previously mentioned, if the diviner has a bad head (*ori*), or is considered unskilled, he may also be blamed for a bad interpretation that seems to "miss the mark."

**Direct Testing of Instruments of Divination**

Babalawo sometimes "test" the instruments of divination, especially the *ọpẹlẹ* (divining chain), which is regarded as less reliable than the *ikin* (divination palm nuts). They typically do this by asking questions to which they already know the answer and casting *ibo* (alternatives). As Bascom records:

> The reason for maintaining that the divining chain is an inferior and less reliable instrument may derive from the fact that it is more often used for the technique of specific alternatives. If many questions are asked, conflicting answers may be given, and occasionally the answers may contradict what is said in the verse. In the instance cited earlier, where the figure Otura Irosun was cast for a client who wished to learn about taking a trip, the verse selected (183–84) warned that he would lose his way if he did not sacrifice. However, in the inquiries through specific alternatives, good rather than evil was indicated, and the kind of good specified was children. In discussing this with the diviner, he indicated that such contradictions were not infrequent, but when either good or evil is confirmed, the prediction is more certain. Nevertheless, a sacrifice would still be required.
>
> He was more puzzled by the reference to children in this context, though he showed little concern, pointing out that the correct answer had come out eventually through the verse, and citing the proverb "Like proverbs, like proverbs, is how Ifa speaks." [*Bi owe, bi owe n(i)-Ifa sọrọ.*][13]

## Human Error and Fraud

However, when the results of Ifa divination appear to lack coherence or applicability, human error or dishonesty is usually the first suspected culprit. In his essay on Ifa divination, Bade Ajayi cites the following verse of Ifa (without giving the Odu to which it belongs) and comments:

> Ọpẹ [the palm tree] (Ọrunmila) is not dishonest,
> It is the chanter who is not versed in Ifa,
> Whatever we ask Ifa
> Is what Ifa reveals

If this happens, it is the babalawo who has "misrepresented the divinity." Anyone who has successfully passed through the rigours of Ifa training would be able to identify the problem of his clients. The babalawo should base his expertise on the training he has acquired. Those who use charms to find out the hidden problems of their clients are not true babalawo and in fact, they are not fit to be one. This class of babalawo (if any), are being dishonest, and they pay dearly for it. In the later part of their life, emphasised our informants, such babalawo lose their sight permanently.[14]

Nevertheless, the babalawo whom I interviewed complained of many fraudulent babalawo operating in Nigeria today, explaining that because contemporary people have less knowledge of Ifa and the orisa than their ancestors, they are easily exploited. However, even Bascom's work, conducted in the mid-twentieth century, records the presence of false or fraudulent diviners from contemporary testimony and the verses of Ifa itself:

> However, that there are dishonest diviners who falsify their predictions is believed by both clients and diviners, and this belief is confirmed by the precautions that the clients take to conceal their problems. A case in point is cited in one of the Ifa verses in which a king's diviner, who was having an affair with the king's wife, heard that another diviner was coming; he instructed that the new diviner was to be killed as a human sacrifice because he feared that his guilt would be revealed, as indeed it was. In another verse, a false diviner pleased his clients by promising them blessings, whereas a truthful diviner correctly warned them against evil spirits. Wishing to believe the first prophecy, they bound the truthful diviner and left him in the forest until the evil spirits arrived and they saw that he had been telling the truth. Eshu intervened to save the truthful diviner, who, in turn, saved the clients. . . .

It appears easiest for a diviner to falsify the results in the recitation of the verses. Here he might select from all the verses he has learned, regardless of the figures with which they are associated, in order to find one that fits the problem with which he believed the client to be concerned, or he might improvise one to fit it. It would be even easier for him simply to keep on reciting verses memorized for other figures until he came to one that touches on the client's problem; but any of these subterfuges might be detected if his apprentices or another diviner were present. The diviner is expected to recite the verses for the figure as he learned them, without knowing which applies to the client's problem. He may alter their order if he wishes; but if he is honest, he must recite only the verses belonging to the figure that is cast....

There is no question in my own mind, on the basis of my experience, that most of the babalawo are honest, as both diviners and clients assert. They operate in perfectly good faith, employing a system in which they believe implicitly and in terms of which they themselves offer sacrifices, make decisions, and in fact order their own lives. They believe that they can best serve both their clients' and their own interests by transmitting the message of their deity, Ifa, as accurately as possible....

It is possible for clients to test a diviner's accuracy through specific alternatives, and in two of the verses this is done by the mythological character. In the latter, when the cow of the Sea Goddess died she had it covered with cloths like a human corpse, and told her followers to announce her own death. When they called the diviners to learn if any sacrifice was required, they all announced, because they were not skillful in the use of specific alternatives, that the kind of evil with which they were confronted was death. The followers of the Sea Goddess asked if there were not another diviner; and when he came, he announced that the evil involved a loss. The Sea Goddess then revealed herself, rewarded him, and chose him as her diviner.[15]

The pragmatic and even empirical attitude demonstrated by the Sea Goddess in the above narrative is a distinct characteristic of Yoruba spirituality that has caught the attention of many scholars of religion and Yoruba culture. For example, Karin Barber recorded the following song, sung by Ṣango worshippers: "Ṣango, if you don't bless me, I will make an Oṣun image. Ṣango, if you don't bless me, I'll go and turn Christian."[16]

In fact, in the historical accounts cited in J. D. Y. Peel's *Religious Encounter and the Making of the Yoruba*, the reason most commonly cited for converting to Christianity from the worship of the oriṣa, and sometimes back again, is the inability of a particular mode of worship to provide the worshipper with what he or she is seeking, be it children, wealth, or peace of mind and understanding.[17] This attitude is succinctly captured in the popular Yoruba saying *Orișa ta kẹ kẹ kẹ, ti o gbọ, ta gẹ, gẹ, gẹ, ti o gba, oju popo ni ngbe*, which, roughly translated, means, "If your god doesn't listen when you praise it, or doesn't help you when you worship it, get rid of it!"[18] This "empirical" and "skeptical" attitude is a significant cause of the dynamism of Yoruba spiritual, intellectual, and artistic traditions, and underlies the "verification" of the efficacy of these traditions in the everyday lives of their adherents.[19]

## VERIFICATION OF SACRIFICES AND MEDICINES

While the efficacy of the sacrifices (*ẹbọ*) and pharmacopoeia (*ewe*) of Ifa is implicitly trusted (when received from authoritative sources), and is assumed to usually be more efficacious than other forms of medicine/charms (*oogun*)—hence the expression *ẹbọ s'agba oogun*, sacrifice is senior to medicine/charms[20]—the babalawo I interviewed would generally not say that they know (*mọ*) a sacrifice or herbal preparation unless they had tried it out for themselves and verified its efficacy. Leaving aside the case of "false positives" where the cure or resolution of the problem had some other cause (or no cause at all in the case or preventative sacrifices and herbal medicines), I asked the Araba what happens when the *ẹbọ* or *ewe* appear to not have worked. He explained that he would first check to see if the people involved had correctly followed their instructions and done the sacrifice appropriately and/or that the *ewe* had been prepared and administered correctly. Some of the *ẹbọ* and *ewe* have specific taboos associated with them, such as not eating certain kinds of food or refraining from sexual activity or entering certain places for a period of time. The violation of these taboos is often suspected as the reason some *ẹbọ* and *ewe* do not seem to work. Professor Agboola quoted the following saying to explain this point: "One who offers sacrifice but does not observe the taboo is no better off than if he had thrown away the money he spent on the sacrifice."[21]

If everything appears to have been performed correctly, the Araba explained that the next step would be to try to discover, by consulting Ifa and perhaps by visiting the home of the affected person, if there are other factors or agents at play. Are there enemies (*ọta*) using bad medicine (*oogun*), curses, and the like to spoil the person's health or efforts? Are there things in the home and family environment that are obstructing the work of the *ẹbọ* or *ewe Ifa*? Finally, the Araba explained that in some particularly difficult cases, consultation with other specialists is necessary. Babalawo are particularly ecumenical, and frequently consult with other ritual specialists such as other babalawo and *olorișa, ajẹ, onișẹgun* (experts in traditional medicine), *alfa* (Muslim scholars versed in esoteric sciences), pastors, and even practitioners of modern, "Western" medicine. The Araba only singled out evangelical Christian pastors and modern Salafi imams as those with whom he would not like to work, explaining that he did not think they had any useful "deep knowledge" (imọ ijinlẹ).[22] The Araba is sometimes hired by local government officials in Ọṣun state to work in consultation with other ritual specialists to "disinfect" their offices when they suspect someone (usually the previous occupant of their position) of having left negative charms there.

In any event, the Araba clearly distinguished between those medicines and incantations he had tried himself and seen work (those that he said he "knew," mọ), and those few he had only received from others and had yet to verify (those he said he "accepted," gbagbọ).[23] But what if after all of this, a sacrifice or herbal preparation still did not work, would that be cause to doubt the legitimacy of the verse of Ifa that prescribed it? Of Ifa itself? Isn't it possible that false, ineffective, or distorted verses could work their way into the oral corpus? How could you tell a "true" verse from a false one?

Since more than one verse from the Odu that emerges in divination can be employed in prescribing sacrifice and herbal preparations, and since the babalawo often determine themselves what the sacrifice or herbal preparation should be, the Araba explained that even if something didn't seem to work, that would not lead him to doubt the efficacy of Ifa divination, since another verse or sacrifice from the same Odu should be able to succeed if the other one seemed to have failed. The Araba explained that this seeming failure would then be chalked up to the error of the babalawo in determining the appropriate sacrifice—perhaps he should have asked Ifa to specify things more clearly, or perhaps he made a mistake or misremembered something. As for the issue of "false" verses, the Araba rejected this possibility, explaining that a real babalawo (babalawo gidi) would be able to tell a real verse from a false one just by hearing it, and that in any event, verses could be "cross-checked" with other babalawo. However, one's success is ultimately due to one's ori inu (as the previously cited verse of Odu Ogunda Meji says, "No god blesses a man without the consent of his ori") and the will of Olodumare.

### CONSULTATION WITH OTHER BABALAWO AND AUTHORITY OF ẸSẸ IFA

When they get together for ritual festivals or worship, babalawo frequently engage in competitions of reciting Ifa, in which each babalawo will recite a verse from a particular Odu, one after the other, until they have exhausted all of the verses in their memory. One cannot recite a verse that has already been recited, and so the junior apprentices (ọmọ awo) and babalawo usually begin such competitions, since they will typically only have a few verses of any given Odu memorized, which are often commonly known, whereas more senior babalawo will know more, and more rare verses of Ifa. Participants drop out when all the verses they know have been recited, and the "last man standing" wins. While regional and other variants of similar verses are admitted without any problem, senior babalawo will often correct their juniors where they think they have made a mistake by incorrectly attributing a verse to a particular Odu, by misremembering the details of a verse, or by conflating/combining one narrative with another. Younger babalawo whose learning is widely respected may also correct older babalawo for similar lapses. Such competitions and sessions of reciting and chanting verses of Ifa and singing Ifa songs are important for maintaining the integrity of the oral corpus, and actively establish and authenticate this dynamic body of orature. As Noel Amherd explains, "The apprenticeship of babaláwo requires the utmost conformity to the conservative practices of the profession where recitations should conform to the master's teaching. Nearly every researcher who has dealt with babaláwo has commented on their high ethical behavior, reinforced by the fact of a babaláwo's being immersed in a community, locally and extensively, which provides a checks-and-balance conservatism that inhibits the gratuitous invention of texts by those who are unable to live up to the intellectual and ethical rigor that Ifá requires."[24]

This process of "authentication" is of great importance, given that the ẹsẹ Ifa constitute perhaps the most authoritative body of oral tradition among not only babalawo, but also other oloriṣa and Yoruba-speakers worldwide. Babalawo most commonly justify their claims about mythistory, metaphysics, epistemology, theology, and correct ritual practice by referring to and interpreting ẹsẹ Ifa,[25] not unlike the way they conduct divinatory consultations, except in this case they select the relevant Odus to recite. These interpretations of and insights drawn from the verses of Ifa can be remarkably unique and even idiosyncratic, but are often cause for lively discussion and debate, as the discussion between Awo Faniyi and Professor Agboola cited in the previous chapter demonstrates. In such discussions, personal experience and other ẹsẹ Ifa are used to support interpretations, and such consultations and discussions with other babalawo, especially respected and senior babalawo, are an important means of verifying these interpretations and insights.

Consulting with other babalawo is an important part of every stage of a babalawo's career. The babalawo I interviewed emphasized that for important matters, one should not just divine for oneself, but also seek out other senior babalawo for additional divination and insight into the result of one's own divination. The precedent for this practice is established in the many mythological narratives of Ifa wherein Ọrunmila consults babalawo for divination. Just as our interactions with other people teach us things about ourselves we could never learn otherwise, and just as we need a mirror in order to see our face, for babalawo, divination with other babalawo can reveal things that divination for oneself cannot. As the proverb at the beginning of this section says, "However sharp the knife, it cannot carve its own handle."

Thus we can see that the tradition of Ifa is critical and dynamic, and one in which verification plays an important role. While these modes of verification differ significantly from the "null-hypothesis-rejecting" paradigm that supposedly governs contemporary scientific research, those of Ifa have their own internal consistency and logic, as the sections above demonstrate.

### VERIFICATION THROUGH DIRECT/LIVED EXPERIENCE

However, by far the most commonly cited, and important, form of verification was the actual experience of the practice of Ifa. Babalawo cited the things they had felt and seen during the practice of Ifa, and the profound insight that Ifa gave them into their lives and themselves as the primary basis of their confidence in their own knowledge. The experience of initiation in the *igbodu*—wherein one is confronted with Odu, one's own *ori*, and the Odu "which gave birth to one"—was often cited as being at once the source and verification of the knowledge that babalawo had previously learned and would later acquire. As the encounter with one's own *ori inu*, one's inner/heavenly self, everything that follows is understood as a kind of exposition of that single moment or reality, just as it is a confirmation of everything that has come before. The verses of the Odu that are determined to have "given birth to one" further clarify and construct this "destiny" and conception of the self through their words, advice, and behavioral prescriptions. Reflecting on one's own self, character, and life through the lens of these *ẹsẹ*, living out these prescriptions and taboos (*eewọ*), and observing what happens when one fails to perform these actions, were all cited as important ways that one "verified" this self-knowledge, and by extension, the "deep knowledge" (*imọ ijinlẹ*) of Ifa, of the Odu, which govern the other inhabitants of the cosmos. One's knowledge of Ifa, of one's destiny, is verified the only way it can be—by living it.

The following narrative, from Ogbe-Atẹ, is instructive in this regard. In this *ẹsẹ*, a man became initiated into Ifa and performed all the sacrifices, but his life did not really seem to change or get noticeably better. Frustrated by the apparent fruitlessness of all his efforts in Ifa, he decided to give up on it and go back to his old way of life. So he went to the river and threw away his *ikin*. But soon things got even worse for him, and he thought that maybe he had made a mistake in abandoning Ifa. He went to see a babalawo to ask for help. The babalawo performed divination for him and told him that he should sacrifice to his *ikin*, but the poor man told the babalawo that he had thrown away his *ikin*, so he was told to make the sacrifice with the *ikin* of the babalawo who performed divination for him. The sacrifice required a large fish, so he went to the river, caught a fish, and brought it back to the babalawo to prepare the sacrifice for him to make things easier. When the babalawo opened up the fish, he found a complete set of *ikin* inside. The man recognized his own *ikin*, and concluded that Ifa was telling him something. The babalawo agreed. They washed the *ikin* and the babalawo told him that he should be reinitiated. He was indeed reinitiated and given a new Odu.[26]

In this narrative, a babalawo doubted Ifa to the point of giving it up because it did not seem to change his life in any noticeable way, but then decided to return to seek Ifa's counsel because of the changes in his life after he threw away his *ikin*. The prescribed sacrifice led the man back to his own *ikin*, and to Ifa. On a more symbolic level, the things that seemed to lead him away from Ifa or take his Ifa away from him (changes in life or lack thereof, the river, the fish) actually led him back to Ifa. In any event, his knowledge of Ifa was inseparable from his practice of it, and the verification of this knowledge (once negatively, once positively) lay in his life experiences and his interpretation thereof.

Thus, to verify the knowledge of Ifa, especially its deep knowledge (*imọ ijinlẹ*), one must practice Ifa. As the *ẹsẹ* says, *a kọfa mọfa*, "to study/practice Ifa is to know Ifa." To practice Ifa is to participate in a process of self-transformation and self-knowledge (*imọri*), which is necessarily unique. To study Ifa is to cultivate a particular mode of being and a distinct form of self-knowledge through the mediation of the Odu. Thus, there is a point at which any academic or "objective" study of Ifa and its knowledge must halt, and it is at this point that the real study and knowledge of Ifa—the study of and engagement with one's inner self and destiny (*ori inu*) through the mediation of Ifa—begins.

CONCLUSION

Stories are powerful things. Stories can inspire us, awaken latent possibilities within us, expand our horizons, and make us reevaluate our priorities, our outlook on life, and our very selves. Stories keep us going, give us new ways to understand ourselves and our lives, and shape our imagination. Stories can give us the strength and guidance we need to live out and make sense of our own. When we recognize ourselves or one of the situations that make up our lives in the mirror of a story, a poem, a song, or a movie, it is a unique moment of self-discovery wherein a new aspect, a new facet of our reality is revealed to us. Stories make and shape who we are, and this is perhaps more true of the initiates of Ifa than anyone else. For babalawo and iyanifa, the indefinitely numerous and dynamic narratives of the Odu not only hold a mirror up to the whole cosmos, they also reveal and structure their individual lives and destinies.

Through a lengthy and rigorous training, babalawo memorize, learn, and become acquainted with the Odu and their associated ritual practices, and cultivate a particular mode of being (*iwa*) specified by and congruent with the Odu of Ifa "that gave birth" to them. This received body of knowledge (*igbagbọ*) is transformed, along with the apprentice (*ọmọ awo*), into realized or verified knowledge (*imọ*) by putting it into practice in ritual, and by living it through cultivating good character (*iwa pẹlẹ*). The cultivation of character is essential to this process of acquiring knowledge not only because babalawo do not like to share their knowledge with ill-mannered apprentices, but because good character (*iwa pẹlẹ*) is the existential or ontological concomitant of knowing the truth. To have good character (*iwa*) is not just to be "better" than one who lacks character, it is to be "more," to have a greater share of "existence" or "being" (*iwa*). This greater capacity of being is both a condition and a result of the process of acquiring knowledge. As Beier writes, "Yoruba ethics means: to become through ritual, a being who knows more and understands more, a person who lives more and is more."[27] Character is so central to the epistemology of Ifa that Professor Agboola defined truth (*otitọ*) as "the character [*iwa*] of Olodumare. Truth is more than saying the truth, it is being true."[28]

This cultivation of character is not identical for everyone, since each of us has a unique destiny or inner head (*ori inu*). The rituals of initiation are meant to establish the relationship between the initiate's *ikin*, *ori*, and Ọrunmila, and to give the initiate (and the other initiating babalawo) a glimpse into himself, into his destiny, his chosen purpose in life (*ipin*), to remember "everything he left behind at the tree of forgetfulness (*igi igbagbe*)" when coming into the world from heaven. By encountering his *ori inu* in the grove of Odu, and by the elaboration of this choice of destiny (*ipin*) through the revelation of the Odu that "gave birth" to him and will structure the rest of his life, the initiate acquires knowledge of himself (*imọri*), his destiny, and purpose in life. Babalawo come to embody this Odu through memorizing and contemplating its verses, observing the taboos associated with these verses, and becoming defined by the character traits exemplified in the Odu. By embodying their Odu, they come to know it (and thus Ọrunmila and Olodumare) and themselves more fully.

This is *imọ ijinlẹ*—the deep knowledge that mends the self, connecting the outer or everyday self (*ori ode*) with its inner or heavenly counterpart (*ori inu*), and that ultimately mends the world, bringing the things in the world back together with their heavenly principles (Odu and orișa), and through them, back to Olodumare. As Awo Faniyi explained, "Deep knowledge [*imọ ijinlẹ*] is the Word [*ọrọ*] from the mouth of

Olodumare that He gave to Ọrunmila, when he was coming from heaven to earth, to use to mend the world. This is the basis of the knowledge for which the babalawo who can recite all 256 Odu of Ifa are called deep knowers [onimọ ijinlẹ] among the priests of Ifa."²⁹

As the verse from Odu Ọsa Ogunda quoted in the previous chapter illustrates, this ọrọ is composed of the wisdom (ọgbọn), knowledge (imọ), and understanding (oye) of Olodumare through which he created the world. To acquire deep knowledge is to reverse the cosmogonic process and return to Olodumare through the intermediary of Ẹla/Ọrunmila, the owner of this deep knowledge, this Divine Word. Through imitation of and devotion to Ọrunmila, through contemplating the Odu and rituals of Ifa, babalawo come to resemble, to know, and to participate in the endless knowledge of Ọrunmila, who is hailed in his *oriki* from Odu Oyẹku Meji:

> Perfect in the house of wisdom
> My Lord, whose knowledge is without end
> Not knowing you fully, we [our lives] are in vain
> If we could but know you in full, all would be well.³⁰

But this deep knowledge of Ọrunmila is not other than self-knowledge, because as the Araba of Modakẹkẹ explained, "Ọrunmila is inside of everyone." Mythologically, Ọrunmila is the father of the 256 Odu, and each babalawo is a child of a particular Odu. Thus, Ọrunmila is the principle or origin of all babalawo. For a babalawo or iyanifa, to become more like Ọrunmila in knowledge, character, and actions is to become more oneself.

This close relationship and even identification with Ọrunmila is the result of a lifetime of learning and devotion, as Susanne Wenger explains: "The *olorisha* must *intensify* his life through constant preoccupation with the deity. The concentration that is needed for the dialogue with the deity can only be built up through perpetual training.... All these activities of *olorishas*: ritual, divination, sacrifice, and magic are entirely a means. The final purpose of *orisha* worship is to extend the natural limits of human experience into the sphere of the metaphysical. Man becomes more than man."³¹ This state, which Beier describes as "the semi-divine state of 'dynamic relaxation': a perfected state of mind where intense concentration results in a state of complete repose,"³² is identified in Odu Irosun Iwori as the "good position" (*ipo rere*), the goal of human existence.³³

The tradition of Ifa is critical and dynamic in part because of this emphasis on existential and even empirical verification of the deep knowledge (*imọ ijinlẹ*) that is its foundation and goal. While this knowledge cannot be contained in books or tested in a laboratory, it is tested, verified, and sometimes rejected—in the lives of the millions of people who seek out Ifa's counsel, and in the lives of those who dedicate themselves to pursuing, cultivating, and disseminating the wisdom of Ọrunmila, the ọrọ of Olodumare. As the proverb says, *Ẹni t'o ba f'eyin t'ọpẹ ni gbọ ohun Olodumare*—"Those who rest their backs against the palm tree (Ifa) will hear the voice of Olodumare."

Through the study and practice of Ifa, babalawo cultivate a very particular mode of being (*iwa*) defined by their Odu, the mythological precedent of Ọrunmila. This self-transformation leads to a deep knowledge of self, of the world, and of Ọrunmila and Olodumare. In so doing, babalawo accomplish the mission of Ọrunmila as described in the Odu Iwori Odi, to "bring heaven down to the world" and "take the world back to heaven," to make existence whole again by bringing together the two halves of the cosmic calabash.

PART 3

❖❖❖

# Comparing Ifa and Tijani Sufism

CHAPTER 9

# Comparing Ifa and Tijani Sufism

> Surely there is a window from heart to heart:
> they are not separate and far from each other.
> Two earthenware lamps are not joined,
> but their light is mingled as it moves.
> —RUMI, *Mathnawī*

> If a Muslim were to know what an idol is
> He would know that religion is idol-worship
> And if the associator [*mushrik*] were to know what an idol is
> Where would he have gone wrong in his religion?
> —MAḤMŪD SHABISTARĪ

> *Dagadamba n fura, oseye oko ogbo male. Awo Rokonjobi*
> *A difa fun Ọrunmila nijọti ti o lọ re gba gambi*
> *A gba gambi o, a gba wa*
> *A le we lawani,*
> *a gbede bọrun*
> *Ifa wa di male*
> *Dagadamba n fura* makes a bird in the bush understand Islam
> The babalawo Rokonjobi performed Ifa divination for Ọrunmila
> When he went to collect Gambi
> We received Gambi, we brought it back
> We can don the turban
> We can speak their language
> Our Ifa became Muslim
> —ODU OTURA MEJI

## WHY COMPARE SUFISM AND IFA?

The project of the comparative study of religion has rightly been criticized for its checkered past, in which many, if not most, of its studies failed to balance the pole of similarity and universality with that of difference and particularity. More recently, comparative studies have also come under (justified) attack for their colonial and Christian triumphalist heritage of categorization, control, domination, and defeat (in which religions were classified, ranked, seen through the lens of, and unfavorably compared to Protestant Christianity or secular rationalism), and for their tendency to overgeneralize and fit data into its preconceived categories. In the introduction to their anthology of essays on contemporary comparative religion, *A Magic Still Dwells*, Kimberley Patton and Benjamin Ray summarize this postmodern critique:

> The standpoint of the comparativist was once privileged as a vantage-point of objective description, classification, and comparison of "other peoples" and their beliefs. The focus of deconstructive scrutiny "reveals" it instead, at worst, as a subjective mélange of culturally biased perception that cannot but distort or, at best, as an act of imaginative, associative "play." . . . To compare is to abstract, and abstraction is construed as a political act aimed at domination and annihilation, obliterating the cultural matrix from which it "lifts" the compared object. Thus to compare religious traditions, particularly unhistorically related ones . . . is to attempt to control and ultimately destroy them.[1]

Most characteristically, however, the comparative project has been criticized for its "unscientific" methodology that emphasizes similarity over difference. As J. Z. Smith wrote in his 1982 essay "In Comparison a Magic Dwells," "For as practiced by scholarship, *comparison has been chiefly an affair of similarity*. . . . The issue of difference has been all but forgotten."[2] There are, however, two sides to this coin.

The postmodern perspective is characterized by its own totalizing dogmas of difference and particular theories of semiotics (free-floating signifiers) and metaphysics (there is nothing beyond the text / discourse / power relations), which are not shared by many traditions, including Sufism and Ifa. Thus, as mentioned in the first chapter, subjecting these traditions to the "gaze" of postmodern theory recapitulates the same colonial logic of domestication and destruction. How many undergraduate or graduate students have stopped practicing or even abandoned the worldviews of their traditions, regarding them as "naïve" or "backward," in the wake of courses on the postmodern study of religion? How many more students and professors hide their religious affiliations and convictions in academic settings for fear of being judged and dismissed by their colleagues? Shaykh Ibrahim Niasse and the Araba of Modakẹkẹ would strongly disagree with Derrida and Foucault on their characterizations of language, power, ethics, aesthetics, truth, and so forth. So why must the former pair be subjected to the theories of the latter and not the other way around? Ironically, the postmodern theorization of religious traditions, especially those of the African continent and diaspora (in many ways, the ultimate "other" of this Western tradition), can be yet another, but less self-aware and honest, attempt to control and destroy them. In the name of "giving them a voice" it silences them, in the name of freeing them from colonial hegemony, it subjects them to the hegemony of (post)colonial, (post)modern theory.[3]

So what does all of this have to do with comparison? As Foucault and others have demonstrated, postmedieval Western thought has been governed increasingly by the logic of difference, discursivity, and analysis. As the previous chapters demonstrate, both Ifa and Sufism are largely characterized by symbolic logics of resemblance, which have a much greater affinity with the western classical and medieval epistemes than those of the modern and postmodern West. Describing the transition from the classical/medieval approach based on resemblance to the modern taxonomy based on difference, Foucault writes:

> All this was of the greatest consequence to Western thought. Resemblance, which had for long been the fundamental category of knowledge—both the form and the content of what we know—became dissociated in an analysis based on terms of identity and difference; moreover, whether indirectly by the intermediary of measurement, or directly and, as it were, on the same footing, comparison became a function of order; and, lastly, comparison ceased to fulfill the function of revealing how the world is ordered.... The activity of the mind... will no longer consist *in drawing things together*, in setting out on a quest for everything that might reveal some sort of kinship, attraction, or secretly shared nature within them [*resemblance*], but, on the contrary, in *discriminating*.[4]

Thus, the contemporary aversion to comparative studies (which are typically governed by resemblance) must be understood in the broader context of the rise of analysis and difference as the governing principles of modern/structuralist and postmodern/poststructuralist thought. Most contemporary arguments against comparison are based on a privileging of difference, a position that is not shared by the traditions of Sufism and Ifa.[5]

From the perspective of Sufism, especially that of Ibn 'Arabi, analysis and discrimination is the domain of the rational faculty (*'aql*), whereas synthesis and perceiving similarity is the domain of the imaginal faculty (*khayāl*) and the heart (*qalb*); thus the current academic climate could be characterized by a hypertrophy of *'aql* (reason) and an atrophy of *khayāl* (imagination) and *qalb* (heart/intellect). The ideal, according to Ibn ʿArabi, is to "see with two eyes," to combine the synthetic perception of similarity of the imaginal faculty (*khayāl*) with the discriminative and analytic power of reason (*ʿaql*). Thus, any exercise in comparative religion must involve both comparison and contrast, and resist the tendency to reduce all to incomparable difference or sheer identity.

So now we return to the titular question of this section: why compare Ifa and Sufism? First of all, not only do these traditions compare themselves to each other, but their interpretive frameworks provide means of interpreting and comparing these and other traditions. Comparison is an inescapable aspect of human cognition, and when learning about traditions such as Sufism and Ifa, we unconsciously and automatically compare and contrast them with and to each other, and with the other intellectual and religious traditions with which we are familiar. Since this is happening anyway, we might as well attempt to do it consciously and carefully. Furthermore, in Nigeria and the African diaspora, these two traditions exist side by side and are sometimes even found within the same family. For many of us who encounter both traditions in our daily lives, their relationship to each other (and to ourselves) can be a matter of personal and existential concern.

Moreover, Tijani Sufism and Ifa represent two important kinds of non-Europhone African intellectual traditions: on the one hand, the written/oral Arabophone and indigenous-language (and now somewhat Europhone) traditions of Sufism and Islamic learning, and on the other, the oral (and now somewhat written) indigenous language (and somewhat Europhone) indigenous religious traditions. Careful comparison can help dispel the lingering colonial myth of a syncretic *islam noir*, and help us better understand the similarities and differences between these two kinds of traditions—a prerequisite to undertaking any study of their mutual influence.[6] Likewise, comparing Tijani Sufism and Ifa brings into sharper focus their similarities and differences, and the ways in which contemporary academic practice, discourse, and theory differ significantly from thoseof these two traditions.

But perhaps most important, the way the comparison is conducted in this chapter—reporting what each tradition has to say about the other, and then writing from the perspective of each tradition—provides a concrete example of how both Sufism and Ifa can and do interpret themselves as well as other traditions—how both traditions serve as theoretical perspectives that can interrogate other traditions. Moreover, these examples make more salient the particularities and limitations of the categories and perspectives of contemporary academic theories often naïvely assumed to be universal. This mode of comparison makes it easier to see that the contemporary academy is just one intellectual tradition among many others, such as Ifa and Sufism.

Finally, from the lens of Ibn 'Arabi's "theory," studying reality's self-portraits side by side, comparing and contrasting them, is an important means of recognizing and transcending our own limited conceptions of reality. To quote him again:

> So beware of being bound by a particular belief and rejecting all others as unbelief! If you do that, much good will escape you. Nay, you will fail to obtain the knowledge of reality *as it is*. Try to make yourself a (kind of) Prime Matter (*hyle*) for all forms of belief, for God is too vast and too great to be confined to one belief to the exclusion of another. For He says, *wheresoever you turn, there is the Face of God* (2:115).[7]

And also:

> It is incumbent upon the Folk of Allah to know the doctrine of every sect and creed concerning God, in order to witness Him in every form and in order not to stand in the place of denial. For He permeates existence, so no one denies Him except those who are limited. But the Folk of Allah follow Him whose folk they are, so His property flows over them. And His property is the lack of delimitation. Hence He possesses all-pervading Being (*wujūd*), while they possess all-pervading witnessing (*shuhūd*). That person who delimits His Being delimits the witnessing of Him; he is not one of the Folk of Allah.[8]

And elsewhere:

> He who counsels his own soul should investigate, during his life in this world, all doctrines concerning God. He should learn from whence each possessor of a doctrine affirms the validity of his doctrine. Once its validity has been affirmed for him in the specific mode in which it is correct for him who holds it, then he should support it in the case of him who believes in it.[9]

From this perspective, the study and comparison of different religious traditions and doctrines (all considered as "self-portraits" of reality) is essential to the proper understanding of the reality they intend to describe.

However, there are several difficulties involved in this kind of comparison, which I believe the method described above and below helps to address. One of the most important is that of determining the corresponding category of comparison for Ifa: is it Islam, Sufism, Tijani Sufism, or Shaykh Ibrahim's branch of the Tijāniyya? Conversely, given that Ifa does not (so far as I am aware) have "schools," in the same way that Sufism and other traditions do,[10] what is the category that corresponds to Shaykh Ibrahim's branch of the Tijāniyya? The strategy of shifting between the perspectives of these traditions allows one to make comparisons across multiple categories, and to deal with other significant differences, such as the role of orality and literacy in these two traditions.

With this in mind, we will begin our comparison with a brief summary of how Ifa and babalawo have described Islam, before turning to a creative interpretation of Tijani Sufism from the perspective of Ifa. Then we will summarize the ways in which Muslims have described Ifa, before turning to a creative interpretation of Ifa from the perspective of Tijani Sufism. Next, we will turn to a discussion of seemingly similar elements in both traditions, again alternating between the perspectives of Ifa and Tijani Sufism. Finally, we will conclude with a comparison of these two traditions with contemporary academic epistemologies and theories, keeping in mind that when writing in English, western Christianity, along with its Greco-Roman and Germanic heritages and secular philosophical descendants, are always "silent interlocutors." This concluding discussion will focus on contrasting features common to Ifa and Tijani Sufism with those of contemporary academic theories in order to prevent the reduction of the former to the latter, and to highlight the ways these traditions reveal limitations of contemporary academic discourse about knowledge, ritual practice, and philosophy, and even potentially point the way out of some of these particular limitations.

TIJANI SUFISM AS SEEN BY IFA

**What Does Ifa Say About Sufism/Islam?**

Islam plays a fairly prominent role in the oral corpus of Ifa, a testimony to the centuries of interaction between the two traditions, especially in the northern areas of Yorubaland such as Ilọrin and Ọyọ, which are now predominantly Muslim. The general impression one gets upon surveying the references to Islam in the verses of Ifa is that Islam is regarded as another orișa tradition, like that of Ọșun, Șango (who, in some narratives, is said to have been Muslim himself), or Ogun. Some verses appear to be critical of Islam and mock its rituals;[11] while others, such as the one cited at the beginning of this chapter, appear to praise it and its Prophet. This is characteristic of other orișa traditions whose adherents and orișa are almost equally humiliated and lauded in the verses of Ifa.[12]

Moreover, in a manner similar to other verses that explain the origins of various rituals of *olorișa*, a verse from Odu Okanran-Oturupọn provides a mythological description of the origin of the sacrificial ritual of the Muslim festival of Ileya ('Eīd al-Kabīr).

In this narrative, Muslims used to make the long journey to heaven annually to sacrifice a ram to Olodumare. Over time, the trip became more and more difficult, and many of them would die along the way. A babalawo performed divination for them and told them the good news that Olodumare would accept a sacrifice made on earth, thus establishing the festival of Ileya.[13]

But perhaps the clearest evidence of Islam being considered as an orisa tradition is the case of so-called predestined Muslims. During the ritual of *ęsę n taye/ikǫse aye* ("stepping into the world"), some babalawo interpret the Odu Otura Meji as indicating that the child should be dressed in white on Fridays and given an Islamic education, regardless of the traditions to which his or her parents belonged.[14]

Even more explicitly, a verse from Odu Otura-Yapin (Otura-Oyęku) describes how Islam came into the world (an abridged version of this long verse follows):

"Bit by bit we hoe the farm, bit by bit, we clear the path, it was in private that Otura met Oyęku on the ǫpǫn." Performed Ifa divination for Ǫrunmila when he went to work as a diviner in heaven and took an entire person as a sacrifice.

Eledumare [Olodumare] sent for Ǫrunmila to come up to heaven to conduct an examination. This is because Eledumare created Ǫrunmila as the first prophet [*wǫli*][15] to come down to earth in primordial time [*igba iwasę*]. He also entrusted Ǫrunmila with dominion over the whole world. As a result, Eledumare gave Ǫrunmila everything in the way of knowledge, foresight, wisdom, good character, and so on. When Eledumare made humans, we multiplied, and after we became numerous, our behavior was not pleasing to Eledumare anymore. . . .

Eledumare is Kabiyęsi, that is "the one who is not questioned," the person who takes action that we cannot question. That is Eledumare. Ǫrunmila said, "Kabiyęsi o!" He said he had come because he heard Eledumare's message. Eledumare said he should bring out his divining instruments because He [Eledumare] wanted to investigate a problem. Ah! Ǫrunmila laughed, and said, "Baba, but this is You . . ." Eledumare cut him off and said, "This is not a joking matter. This is quite serious." Ǫrunmila understood and began to look into the matter. He said to Eledumare, "Baba, Kabiyęsi, there is something you created with your own hands that is causing you sadness. Ifa says that the sacrifice You are to make now is a slave from Your own house. That is what is required for the sacrifice. Then Your power will control all that your hand has created and is saddening you." Eledumare said, "Very well." Ǫrunmila said, "When you bring out your servant for the sacrifice, that is when Your power will control all that your hand has created and is saddening you." Eledumare said, "A slave in my house?" Ǫrunmila said, "Yes, he has a long beard. He has a long beard like this. This baba with the long beard is a slave [*ęru*] in your house."

Eledumare said, "Yes, it's true. He brought Aafa[16] out. He was the man with the long beard. This man with the long beard, he was Eledumare's slave. He was Eledumare's messenger [iranṣe].

When they reached earth, Aafa watched closely when Ọrunmila practiced Ifa. When Aafa was coming from heaven, he tucked the Qur'an underneath his arm and brought it to earth. Ọrunmila said, let us do on earth as we did in heaven. When Ọrunmila was worshipping Ifa, the man with the long beard would also come into the Ifa shrine. He would watch how Ọrunmila would wash himself, and he, too, would wash himself before entering the Ifa shrine. He would also copy Ọrunmila when he would touch his head to the ground in prayer. One day Ọrunmila called God's slave, that is the man with the long beard or Aafa [the Prophet Muḥammad], and told him that he gave him permission to practice his religion just as he had been doing in heaven. That is how Ọrunmila ordered Aafa. The way Aafa was worshipping, the language he spoke when he was worshipping in heaven, that is how he then began to separate the two religions.

Ọrunmila instructed God's slave [the Prophet Muḥammad] that he should pray just as he had been doing previously in heaven, but Aafa very much liked to imitate what Ọrunmila did when he practiced Ifa. All of the prostrations [rakʿat] that Muslims do in the mosque, Aafa learned from Ọrunmila. Before anyone can enter the house of Ifa, he [or she] must wash. When Aafa goes to pray in the morning, he must wash himself. Before entering Ifa's house, one must wash his [or her] backside thoroughly, and everything that the babalawo did appealed to Aafa, and he has continued to do so until today.

Aafa and Ọrunmila did everything together. Aafa learned his practice of praying in the mosque from Ifa. The two loved each other very much, and they intermarried. Aafa married Ọrunmila's children, and Islam began to expand. When it came time for the annual Ifa festival, Aafa and his wives and children would come and join the celebration. When the Ileya festival [ʿĪd al-Kabīr] arrived, Ọrunmila, his wives, and his children would join Aafa in the celebration. When the Muslims would finish their fast [ʿĪd al-Fiṭr] they would all again take part in the festivities. That is how they came to live so closely to one another. They were so close to the extent that when the Ifa festival arrived and the babalawo began reciting Ifa verses, Ọrunmila praised the babalawo, and the babalawo in turn praised Ifa, all because of the babalawo who cast Ifa for Ọrunmila on the original day.

That is how Ifa brought the man with the long beard, whom we call Aafa, down to earth. This Aafa is the messenger of God in heaven. They say that they are slaves of God. There are no children of God, but rather Aafa's followers are slaves of God. They were slaves in heaven before Ọrunmila brought them down to earth. That is how Ọrunmila brought Aafa down to earth in Odu Otura Yapin. That is also the time when the religion/worship [ẹsin] was split [pin] into two. Islam and Ifa, traditional worship [ẹsin ibilẹ, ẹsin abalaye]. That is how it came to be. They did everything together, but the religion/worship was split into two.¹⁷

While this verse is fascinating for many reasons, here we are most interested in the way it describes the Prophet (Aafa) and Islam. This verse describes and defines the mythological origins of a fairly amicable and close relationship between Muslims and babalawo, as well as highlighting several similarities in ritual practice (ablutions, prostrations, and recitations in prayer) and the fact that they participate in one another's festivals. It is also fascinating that the Prophet is described as Aafa or Alfa, the Yoruba word designating a Muslim scholar, shaykh, or religious specialist. Just as Ọrunmila is regarded as the archetypal babalawo, the Prophet Muḥammad is regarded as the archetypal alfa. Moreover, he is described as having a "long beard" and a "book" (identified as the Qur'an), and as being a "slave" (ẹru) and messenger (iranṣẹ) of Olodumare. This description closely matches Islamic accounts of the Prophet as the slave (ʿabd) and Messenger (rasūl) of God. Furthermore, Ọrunmila's close relationship with Aafa (the Prophet) is described as beginning in heaven, and their earthly friendship and that of their followers is understood as a reflection of this heavenly relationship and even unity, since it is only in coming into the world that the worship/religion (ẹsin) of Ọrunmila and the Prophet Muḥammad split into two separate traditions. Thus, in this account, Ifa presents Islam as a form of worship brought into the world by and derivative of Ọrunmila/Ifa, the original prophet/messenger of Olodumare, for the purpose of mending a world full of wicked people.¹⁸ Ifa describes Islam as united with it in principle, and separate, but similar, in manifestation in the world—this similarity being a reflection of the original, heavenly unity of the two traditions.¹⁹

**What Babalawo Say About Islam / Tijani Sufism**

A few contemporary babalawo describe themselves as Muslim and observe the Islamic rites of prayer and fasting to varying degrees. Ayọdeji Ogunnaike's unpublished undergraduate thesis explores this phenomenon of "Muslim babalawo," explaining that some babalawo accept the practice of Islam together with the practice of Ifa, just as they may combine the worship of Ọṣun, Ogun, Ṣango, or other oriṣa with that of Ifa. However, this work also records a kind of consensus that one cannot "go deep" into both traditions simultaneously—that is, most babalawo seemed to agree that if one is to become an imam, alfa, or join a Sufi order (such as the Tijāniyya), then one must leave aside serious practice of Ifa; and conversely, if one is to become a serious babalawo, then one must focus on Ifa alone.[20] Nevertheless, opinions on this matter vary greatly.

The Araba of Modakẹkẹ generally had high praise for Islam and Muslims: he is close friends with several local imams and many, if not most, of his clients were Muslim. He also said that Muslims were generally more respectful of Ifa and of him than were Christians. In fact, he told me that he became a babalawo on the advice of a Muslim diviner who practiced the geomantic tradition of *yanrin* (*khaṭṭ al-raml*). According to the Araba, a babalawo performed divination shortly after he was born that indicated he should study Ifa and become a babalawo, but his parents forgot about this advice, so as he grew up he studied herbal medicine (*oogun ewe*) instead. However, he was frequently plagued by illnesses and headaches, so his father took him to a Muslim diviner, who told him that the reason he was getting sick was that he was supposed to be studying Ifa, and if he seriously studied Ifa his health problems would go away and things would go well for him. His father then remembered the babalawo's earlier prediction and having it confirmed in this way by a Muslim diviner sent the Araba to study with a babalawo. So it was actually a Muslim diviner practicing an Islamic form of divination that led the Araba to his current practice of Ifa.[21]

The Araba's wife told me how she pulled one of her children out of a Christian school because of the negative things the teachers and other students said about Ifa, and enrolled the child instead in a local Islamic primary school where she felt he would not be discriminated against as the child of a babalawo. As in the verse of Odu Otura-Yapin cited above, the Araba explained that he and other babalawo celebrate the ʿEīds with Muslims, and that many Muslims join the babalawo and other *oloriṣa* in celebrating the annual Ifa festival. When I asked him about initiation in the *igbodu*, he explained that his friend, who had performed hajj and then later been initiated in the *igbodu*, had said that the Kaʿba and the *igbodu* were "the same."[22] Generally, his opinions seemed to be very much in line with those expressed in the above narrative in which Islam is regarded as a derivative tradition of Ifa, and one that remains very close to it.[23] In fact, many, if not most, babalawo regard Islam as a derivative offshoot of Ifa.

The Araba's main criticism of Muslims was their refusal to acknowledge or accept Ifa's validity; he particularly criticized those who "came to see him by night, and denounced Ifa by day." He also criticized Muslims for not taking their tradition as seriously as babalawo take Ifa, but then added, "Today there are also many babalawo who are not serious."[24] This attitude is characteristic of senior priests of oriṣa traditions, many of whom accept the validity of traditions that reject the validity of their own. Susanne Wenger recalls the reaction of the Ajagẹmọ, the chief priest of Ọbatala in Ẹdẹ, who initiated her into oriṣa worship, to one such unpleasant encounter with Muslims: "Rebuked for not retaliating for abusive and aggressive comments on Oriṣa in the mosque in Ilobu, the very wise and senior priest of Ọbatala said 'you will not succeed in teasing a true ọlọrisa into retaliation, since this cannot take place in Orisa-life. If we do as they do now, we are what they are, that is enemies of the spirit and of wisdom (imọ). We would join them in the destruction of Ọrisa and be, as traitors, more guilty than the ignorant.'"[25]

The Araba was not very familiar with Tijani Sufism as such, but had seen Shaykh Ibrahim Niasse's picture (which is ubiquitous in Muslim shops and on minibuses in northern and southwestern Nigeria), and had a good opinion of him as a "great imam" and "a true aafa" (*aafa gidi*). However, the Araba was critical of some elements of the Tijani tradition. When I asked him if babalawo ever saw or spoke to Ọrunmila in dreams, adding that Tijanis claim that reciting certain prayers regularly can lead to an encounter with the Prophet in a dream, the Araba responded:

> Araba: No one can see Ọrunmila in a dream. There is *agbalamọ*, a medicine you can make to learn things in dreams, but no one has seen Ọrunmila in a dream, no one knows what he looks like. We know [from descriptions of him in the verses of Ifa] that he was short and dark, but you cannot see him in a dream. Some people receive messages from him in dreams, but they do not see him. These prayers you mentioned, have you tried them for yourself? Did they work?
> Me: No, I have not tried them.
> Araba: Eh-hen, so you see?[26]

In addition to demonstrating the critical spirit and high standard for *imọ* (knowledge based on direct experience) that characterized the Araba's discourse in general, this exchange illustrates the implicit similarity the Araba assumed to exist between Ifa and Tijani Sufism / Islam. Since babalawo do not see Ọrunmila in dreams, he was skeptical of the claims of Tijani Sufis to be able to see the Prophet in dreams. However, had I "verified" these prayers for myself and informed the Araba of this fact, he would probably accept (*gba*) what he heard (*gbọ*) from me—but he certainly would not consider it *imọ*, and I imagine he would remain somewhat skeptical. Having summarized these perspectives of Ifa and babalawo on Islam and Tijani Sufism, we will now turn to the creative exercise of interpreting Tijani Sufism from the perspective of Ifa.

**Tijani Sufism from the Perspective of Ifa**

From the perspective of Ifa, Shaykh Aḥmad al-Tijānī and Shaykh Ibrahim Niasse could easily appear as rebirths or reincarnations of the orisa Aafa, or as particularly powerful devotees of Aafa who became orisa in their own right and were somewhat amalgamated with Aafa. The precedent for this amalgamation can be seen in the case of the orisa Ṣango, the mythical fourth king of Ọyọ,[27] who after death became amalgamated with the older orisa Jakuta, sharing many of his attributes and of whom Ṣango was possibly a devotee. From the perspective of Ifa, Ṣango can appear as a reincarnation of Jakuta.

Within the Ifa corpus, it seems likely that many of the myths and stories about Ọrunmila are actually about very powerful babalawo, who embodied or represented Ọrunmila to such an extent that they were similarly amalgamated with him after death, or seen as a manifestation or "child" of his during life. The ritual veneration Shaykh Aḥmad al-Tijānī and Shaykh Ibrahim Niasse receive in the form of pilgrimage, celebration of their birth- and death-days (among other important days in their lives), and their continued spiritual interactions with their followers would easily qualify them as orisa from the perspective of Ifa.

Babalawo also frequently likened the oral corpus of Ifa to the Qur'an, and in both Sufism and Ifa the Qur'an and the oral corpus of Ifa are understood, respectively, to contain all knowledge and the principles of everything that exists. Within Sufism, the different surahs of the Qur'an are commonly described as having their own attributes and "personalities"—Ibn ʿArabi describes visionary encounters with different surahs in a mythical language not unlike that which Ifa uses to describe the Odu. Ritually, the verses (*ayāt*) of the Qur'an and those (*ẹsẹ*) of Ifa are used in similar fashion: they are recited as worship, as protection, and as incantations for various effects for everything from easing childbirth to escaping enemies and witchcraft. Like the oral corpus of Ifa, the Qur'an is typically (in a traditional Tijani Sufi context) memorized in childhood and contemplated throughout the rest of one's life. The process of memorization of the Qur'an, which often involves drinking or licking the ink of its verses off of a wooden tablet (*lawḥ*) and other special prayers to aid in memorization, could be likened to the rituals of "eating" the Odu off of the ọpẹlẹ (divining chain) and the memory-enhancing medicines (*isọye*) given to apprentices. The strong emphasis Shaykh Ibrahim placed on the Qur'an in his personal life and teachings—he is said to have prayed for "the miracle of his community to be knowledge of the Qur'an, since the Qur'an was the miracle of the Prophet";[28] he is also said to have recited the entire Qur'an twice a week, and also emphasized memorization of the Qur'an among his own children and early disciples—is certainly similar to the centrality of the oral corpus of Ifa for babalawo. From the perspective of Ifa, both the Qur'an and the Odu Ifa are primarily oratures, which happen to have symbolic, written representations that are ritually potent. The Qur'an's physical pages or wooden board and text could thus be likened to the divining tray (*ọpọn Ifa*) and camwood powder (*iyẹ irosun*) into which the signatures of the Odu are pressed. Thus, from the perspective of Ifa, the Qur'an, Islam in general, and Tijani Sufism in particular, would appear to be a repetition of the oral corpus of Ifa, albeit in a different language and in a different form.

The different Sufi orders of Islam, with their different practices, emphases, and taboos, could appear to play the same role as the Odu "that give birth to" babalawo do in Ifa, structuring their moral and ritual formation in different but converging ways.[29] Perhaps the central practice of the Tijāniyya—that of invoking prayers on the Prophet, especially the Ṣalāt al-Fātiḥ—could be seen from the perspective of Ifa as reciting *oriki Aafa*. Karin Barber describes *oriki* as "collections or strings of name-like attributive epithets, 'praises' which are neither narrative nor descriptive, but vocative. They are addressed to their subject or 'owner,' and are felt to encapsulate, and evoke in some way that subject's essential powers and qualities."[30] Thus the Ṣalāt al-Fātiḥ and the *Jawharat al-Kamāl*, as well as other symbolic invocations of the Prophet's qualities and attributes that are believed to evoke the presence and reality of the Prophet, would naturally be understood as (or at the very least likened to) *oriki*.

From the perspective of Ifa, the accounts of *fanā'* in Tijani Sufism could appear as descriptions of forms of possession (*igun*), made possible by the initiatory rites that "make" or "put" the oriṣa Aafa into the initiate, allowing this potential identification to become actualized in possession/annihilation. However, the idea of being directly "possessed" by God (i.e., annihilated in God) would strike babalawo as bizarre, especially since possession is taboo for and strongly looked down on by babalawo. The goal of a sober *baqā'* would be much more appealing to babalawo and more in line with the way babalawo understand and articulate their practice.

The Islamic notion of *baraka* (blessing, spiritual presence) would most likely be translated as *aṣẹ*, since both flow from Allah or Olodumare through the channels of sacred places, people, and rituals. From the perspective of Ifa, the *asrar* of Tijani Sufism would be seen as various types of *oogun* (medicine), *akoṣe* (a "prayer" of a combination of specific items), *ọfọ* (incantation), *ewe* (herbal/ incantatory medicine), or even *ẹbọ* (sacrifices) depending on the ingredients used and intention involved.

From the perspective of Ifa, the central doctrine of the *ḥaqīqa al-Muḥammadiyya* (Muḥammadan reality) would appear as another description of Ọrunmila and his heavenly counterpart, Ajagunmọle, the diviner of heaven; or Ẹla, the Logos-like Word (*ọrọ*) of Olodumare, "the first to speak," from which everything is created. In many myths of Ifa, it is for and through Ọrunmila/Ẹla that the cosmos is created (just as is the case of the Muḥammadan reality), and the descriptions of the Muḥammadan reality as the possessor of knowledge of God / all existence closely mirror those of Ọrunmila. Moreover, just as the Prophet Muḥammad (and the other prophets) are regarded as manifestations of the Muḥammadan reality, so, too, is Ọrunmila (and the other oriṣa) sometimes regarded as an aspect of Ẹla.

The close relationship between ethics, epistemology, and memory in Tijani Sufism as articulated by Shaykh Ibrahim's quotation of the poem of Imām Shāfiʿī in his Mauritanian sermon—"I complained to Wakīʿ of the weakness of my memory / And he advised me to leave aside disobedience / He told me that knowledge is a light / And God does not give light to the disobedient"—could easily be identified with Yemi Elebuibon's assertion that "those who lose their memory or are unable to recite the Odu very well might have offended Ajagunmọle [the diviner of heaven]."[31] In both cases, knowledge and the ability to retain and incorporate it are granted by a divine figure, who can withdraw it when one's ethical comportment does not conform to the model of this figure.

Despite these similarities, many aspects of Tijani Sufism would appear odd from the perspective of Ifa. Perhaps most obviously, as discussed above, the prohibition on participating in other religious traditions (or Sufi orders) would seem strange to babalawo, who are often themselves initiates of other orisa and help initiate devotees into the traditions of other orisa. Relatedly, the relative uniformity of the *sharīʿa* and rites of the Tijānī *ṭarīqa* differs markedly from the highly individual nature of the ritual program of taboos (*eewọ*) as well as the sacrifices prescribed by Ifa, and such a "one-size-fits-all" approach would seem peculiar from the perspective of Ifa. The comparative lack of sacrifices in Tijani Sufism would also strike babalawo as odd,[32] as would the fact that the Qurʾan is seldom used for divination or conversation with the Prophet/Deity (although the practice known as *istikhāra* and the contemplative recitation of the Qurʾan approach something like this). While the "deep" or "esoteric" (*bāṭin*) hermeneutics of the Qurʾan would be familiar and welcome to babalawo, the fixed nature of the Qurʾan (no new verses are added to surahs) would be seen as different and even strange. However, the continuing presence of the Prophet in dreams and waking visions of Tijanis, in a certain sense, extends the canon of ḥadīth (although these encounters are never included in canonical ḥadīth collections, and are not regarded as authoritative in the same fashion) such that babalawo could find it reminiscent of the emergence of new verses of Ifa. Nevertheless, as mentioned above, at least some babalawo are skeptical of these kinds of visionary encounters.

In summary, from the perspective of Ifa, Islam in general, and Tijani Sufism in particular, appear as a tradition of the orisa Aafa (or even as a peculiar form of Ifa deriving from Odu Otura Meji), characterized by the recitation/invocation of *oriki*, leading to a kind of possession by Aafa and even Olodumare. As the Araba remarked, "There is only one God, and that God is the same God that sent Ọrunmila and sent *Musulumi* [the Prophet Muḥammad] into the world."[33]

While we will compare and contrast various other features of Ifa and Tijani Sufism later in this chapter, the above exercise of interpreting Tijani Sufism from the perspective of Ifa provides a new way of looking at Sufism, illustrates the interpretive strategies of Ifa, and demonstrates the tremendous influence a particular choice of interpretive tradition can have on the portrayal and understanding of another tradition.

## IFA AS SEEN BY TIJANI SUFISM

### What Do Yoruba Muslims / Tijani Sufis Say About Ifa?

Turning now to the Islamic tradition, the Qur'an does not mention Ọrunmila or Ifa explicitly, although some Yoruba Muslims identify him with the prophet Idrīs or the figure of Luqmān, whom the Qur'an describes as a righteous man and possibly a prophet to whom God gave wisdom (*al-ḥikma*) (31:12). Most of the Tijani *shuyūkh* and disciples I interviewed were not familiar with Ifa, however, and tended to take one of three positions when it came to non-Abrahamic, African religious traditions: (a) these traditions were once valid religions, but had since fallen into decay and/or been abrogated (i.e., rendered spiritually ineffective and/or not accepted by God) by the coming of Islam; (b) these traditions were not really religious, but rather a kind of "animism," intuitions about the unseen, magic (*siḥr*), and interactions with *jinn*; or (c) these traditions were sheer superstition with no reality whatsoever. Proponents of positions (b) and (c) sometimes compared these non-Abrahamic African traditions to the idol-worship of the pre-Islamic Arabs in the "Age of Ignorance" (*al-jāhiliyya*). The opinions of the Yoruba Muslims with whom I spoke included these three broad perspectives, but they also spanned a wider spectrum. Their opinions tended to cluster around the following six positions:

1. Ifa is mere superstition with nothing behind it at all. It is a clever collection of Yoruba orature with no real spiritual power.
2. Ifa is evil and dangerous magic and medicine (*oogun*) from which good Muslims must keep their distance, and/or Ifa is a form of *kufr* (disbelief) and *shirk* (polytheism), a "false religion."
3. Ifa is the corrupted remnant of a now-abrogated tradition that was brought by a Prophet (either Luqman or one of those prophets who is not explicitly mentioned in the Qur'an).
4. Ifa is a valid, accepted spiritual tradition brought by a prophet sent to the Yoruba people, either Idrīs or Luqman or one who is not mentioned in the Qur'an, but which cannot be practiced together with Islam.
5. Ifa is *ḥikma*, or an occult science, which one may or may not be able to practice alongside Islam.
6. Ifa is an integral part of Yoruba culture and something in which one should participate, to some level, as a Yoruba person. Ifa is a way of achieving inner peace, success, prosperity, and children, and avoiding disasters and the machinations of one's enemies. According to this view, any Yoruba person, irrespective

of religious affiliation, and many non-Yoruba people, can and should consult with Ifa in order to have a better life.

This last position was the one most commonly expressed by the Yoruba Muslims I encountered in the Araba's neighborhood in Modakẹkẹ. They would often cite some variant of the proverb "I will practice the custom of my house [ọrọ ile mi]. Christianity will not stop me, Islam will not stop me, from practicing my traditional rites," or they would emphasize that they were "born Yoruba, but chose to practice Islam" implying a certain priority to their Yoruba identity and traditions, which encompass those of Islam and Christianity. A few local alfas expressed opinions that could be categorized as position 5, whereas most other alfas and Muslims with whom I spoke held positions ranging between 1 and 4, often in combination, and sometimes with a great deal of uncertainty.

Many Muslim university students with whom I spoke explained that they did not know what the "official" opinion on Ifa was from an Islamic perspective, but that even though Ifa and traditional religion had a bad reputation, they knew of many pastors and imams who were "crooks" and "wicked people," and that they also had elder family members who still practiced Ifa and other oriṣa traditions who were very pious and had "good character." One student even mentioned a ḥadīth—that "the weightiest thing on the scales on the Day of Judgment is good character [Arabic akhlāq; Yoruba iwa]"—concluding that it didn't matter what one believed or practiced, as long as one had good character, God would be pleased.[34] However, the more Salafi / "Ahl us-Sunna" (reformist) Muslim students I encountered invariably advocated positions 1 or 2.

The perspective of Alfa Akurede of Ogbagba was typical of many alfas:

> Lā ilāha illā Llāh that we say is the language, everybody knows it [means that] "the somebody that created you is God. We don't know any other person to be divine like God, more than God." That is the meaning of Lā ilāha illā Llāh. When we call Lā ilāha illā Llāh, we say Muḥammadun Rasūlu Allāh. This Muḥammad, it is [an] intermediary between us and God, just as Ọrunmila is the intermediary between the babalawo and God. . . . If you take a sentence that is true and translate it into many languages, the sound has changed, but the meaning is the same, and it is true![35]

As in the accounts of Ifa, Alfa Akurede also described Islam and Islamic knowledge as being derivative of Ifa and traditional Yoruba religion: "Maybe I cannot use Ifa, but the people who have the most knowledge, all the Islamic spiritual peoples, they come from Ifa, because when the Prophet Muḥammad, our forefather in Islamic knowledge, comes from traditional religion, then all of us, too, come from traditional religion."[36]

However, it is in the person of Shaykh Abdul-Hameed Akorede, the late leader of the Qadiri Sufi order in Modakẹkẹ, that we see the most intimate nexus of the two traditions. Baba Akorede, as he was known, was raised in a family of orisa worshippers, learning Ifa divination as a child, and it was through Ifa that he became a Muslim. In the words of one of his former disciples, Ismaheel Bakare:

> The man [Shaykh Akorede] told me that his father was an *elebo* [person who worships orisa], an idolater or traditional religionist. He said that they all knew Ifa very well. So he (the shaykh), while a little boy, was on the *ọpẹlẹ* checking [doing divination]. Then he got to a point and said, "*Baba mi, aṣe afaa ni mi!*" (My father, I am to be an Alfa) [most likely Otura Meji had emerged and he asked Ifa for clarification of his intuition that he should become an alfa and Ifa confirmed it]. So the father brought out a charm and hit the boy with it, and ever since he was paralysed and he couldn't walk again. So he told me that "*Mo wo lọ ilekewu ni*" (I crawled to the Arabic school). And later he became the grand shaykh of the town. . . . He was a *murid* [disciple] of Alfa Nda Salaty and died some years ago around 2011 or so.[37]

In this account, it was Ifa that led Baba Akorede to embrace Islam and eventually to become one of the most respected spiritual leaders in the local Muslim community. This account also illustrates the hostility that some practitioners of Yoruba religious traditions felt—and feel—toward Islam. Nevertheless, Baba Akorede separated his treatment at the hands of his father from the tradition of Ifa itself, and is reported to have said that "Ifa is an ancient knowledge, and it has nothing to do with idolatry."[38]

Across the Atlantic, the story of an African American man named Yusuf Jones parallels that of Baba Akorede. In his own words:

> For a time, I was strongly drawn back to the African traditions, specifically the Yoruba. . . . I made the decision to pursue initiation into the Yoruba spiritual tradition through a priest in Houston, Texas. After determining his authenticity and sincerity, I made a trip with my (then) wife and son to Houston. When I arrived at the home, my wife decided to wait in the car while I knocked on the door with my $300 offering. A young woman in white answered the door and welcomed me into the home. Statues surrounded me; images and implements of the Yoruba tradition. Not long after the Babalawo emerged from the back room. He was friendly and after a brief discussion with the young woman, who presented him with the money, he sat down opposite a large roundtable. We had corresponded by email several times and he was eager to help me find my way.

After a few preliminary ceremonial observances, he placed a bag on the round table and emptied the contents. He asked me some questions about my life and journey and after lighting some candles, he told me that he was going to use divination to find out which Orisha ruled my head. He closed his eyes and took the divination bones [perhaps an ọpẹlẹ] into his hands, chanting in Yoruba for a few minutes, he cast the bones across the table. He studied them carefully, wrote down a few notes, looked at me and smiled. He picked them up a second time and threw them down again. He did this three times and then called for the young woman to come to the side of the table. To my surprise, they seemed to argue for a minute because the man had asked her to do something she obviously didn't want to do. She left and came back.

Then he took my hands firmly and looked into my eyes silently for about five minutes. Then he said the words that have shaken me to tears whenever I have recalled them since. Here it is as best I can remember from what I wrote down at the time: "Your path to knowledge you have been seeking and the power that will heal you, guide you, comfort you and strengthen you, protect you and where you will find your spiritual family and home is not with the Orisha. When I was casting divination for you I had to do so three times because I did not understand what I was seeing. Time and time again a vision appeared in my mind of you wearing all white and following those who wear all white. You and your companions were traveling East to the house of the One. I also had a vision that my family and I would experience dire consequences if I tried to tell you otherwise. This is why I am giving you back your money. My daughter doesn't understand but I have to do what I was told to do. I was told to give it back. The Orisha did not reject you but Affa, the man from the East, claimed you. You are a child of Africa but also a son of the East. You must find He who has claimed you until you become one of those in white."[39]

This pronouncement would eventually lead Mr. Jones to convert to Islam and join Ibrahim Niasse's branch of the Tijāniyya. It is interesting to note that these accounts are almost the exact mirror image of the Araba's story—whereas Ifa led Baba Akorede and Yusuf Jones to Islam and Sufism, an Islamic form of divination led the Araba to Ifa.

Like the Qadiris, the Tijanis of West Africa have lived in relatively close quarters with practitioners of various indigenous traditions, and have been responsible for the conversion of many of these people to Islam. al-Ḥājj ʿUmar Tall's correspondence during his conquests of the non-Muslim polities of Tamba, Kaarta, and Segou and his accusations against the Muslim polity of Ḥamdullāhi describe the practitioners of Bamana religious traditions as "unbelievers" (kuffār) and "polytheists/idolaters" (mushrikūn). After conquering the kingdom of Segou, he ordered a public burning of the "fetishes" of the chief priest and king, and held a public display of the "fetishes" of ruling families to prove they were not true Muslims by virtue of their continued adherence to traditional Bamana customs.[40] Thus, one would be safe in assuming that al-Ḥajj ʿUmar Tall and his followers would reject positions 4–6 (and probably also position 3).

However, al-Ḥājj ʿUmar's grand-nephew, the Tijani shaykh Tierno Bokar (d. 1939), seems to have advocated a more universal perspective. His biographer and disciple, Amadou Hampâté Bâ, records him as having made statements such as:

> The rainbow owes its beauty to the variety of its shades and colors. In the same way, we consider the voices of various believers that rise up from all parts of the earth as a symphony of praises addressing God, Who alone can be Unique. We bitterly deplore the scorn that certain religious people heap on the form of divine things, a scorn that often leads them to reject their neighbor's hymn because it contrasts with theirs. To fight against this tendency, brother in God, whatever be the religion or the congregation to which you are affiliated, meditate at length on this verse: *"The creation of the heavens and the earth, and the diversity of your languages and of your colors are many wonders for those who reflect"* (30:22). There is something here for everyone to meditate upon....
>
> Are children of the same father, although physically different from one another, any less brothers and legitimate sons of he who fathered them? In accordance with this law-truth, we pity those who deny believers from different confessions a spiritual identity and brotherhood under one single God, the unique and immutable Creator. Although it may not please those attached to the letter, for us one thing alone counts above all others: to profess the existence of God and His unity.[41]

As well as:

> You will gain enormously by knowing about the various forms of religion. Believe me, each one of these forms, however strange it may seem to you, contains that which can strengthen your own faith. Certainly, faith, like fire, must be maintained by means of an appropriate fuel in order for it to blaze up. Otherwise, it will dim and decrease in intensity and volume and turn into embers and then from embers to coals and from coals to ashes. To believe that one's race or one's religion is the only possessor of the truth is an error. This could not be. Indeed, in its nature, faith is like air. Like air, it is indispensable for human life and one could not find one man who does not believe truly and sincerely in something. Human nature is such that it is incapable of not believing in something, whether that is God or Satan, power or wealth, or good or bad luck. So, when a man believes in God, he is our

brother. Treat him as such and do not be like those who have gone astray. Unless one has the certitude of possessing all knowledge in its entirety, it is necessary to guard oneself against opposing the truth. Certain truths only seem to be beyond our acceptance because, quite simply, our knowledge has not had access to them....

Avoid confrontations. When something in some religion or belief shocks you, instead seek to understand it. Perhaps God will come to your aid and will enlighten you about what seems strange to you.[42]

However, Tierno Bokar was known to actively proselytize among the non-Muslim Dogon people of his hometown of Bandiagara.[43] This does not necessarily mean that he did not regard them as being "believers in God," but it does indicate that he thought they had something to gain by converting to Islam. Bâ deeply studied the traditions of Bamana and Peul (Fulani) religious traditions in Mali and Upper Volta (Burkina Faso), and in the conclusion of his seminal *Aspects de la Civilisation Africaine* he gives his own account of the relationship between African traditional religions and Islam:

The animist religions prepared Mali, like the other African countries south of the Sahara, for the idea of the Sacred and of a mysterious creative force of the universe. The revealed religions, notably Christianity and Islam, found there a fertile ground for their propagation.... The empire of Islam in Africa was established, I will not say on the ruins of animism—for it still survives despite the blows it has suffered at the hands of the [revealed] religions and by the technical and philosophical civilization brought to it by Western colonization—but on its foundations. The main principles of animism (the sacred and non-profane character of everyday life, a sense of being a part of a whole of which one is an integral part—the human community or the universe—the existence of a Supreme Being, transcendent and yet immanent in His Force in all things and all places ... ) found their continuation in Islam, although in a simplified and purified form....

Prepared by his ancestral tradition to detect all around him a living presence hidden behind the appearance of things, perhaps the black African Muslim, while directing his body ritually to the image of the Center which is the Ka'ba, is particularly capable of realizing the mystery contained in this Qur'anic verse:

To Him (God) belong the East and the West
And wherever you turn, there is the Face of God.[44]

According to Bâ, African Islam was established on the "foundations" of these preexisting traditions, which were "simplified" and "purified" by the coming of Islam, which unified and organized the diverse forces of the cosmos, replacing the fear of "mysterious forces" with the "reverential awe" and "love" of the transcendent and yet omnipresent "One God." Nevertheless, these "animist" traditions are described as playing a role in predisposing African Muslims toward spiritual realization. These accounts probably represent the most positive written appraisals of indigenous African religious traditions from the perspective of a Tijani Sufi.

Turning now to Shaykh Ibrahim Niasse's branch of the Tijāniyya, which has a large following among the Yoruba-speaking peoples of Nigeria, while I was unable to find anything in the literature of Shaykh Ibrahim and his disciples directly dealing with Ifa during the course of my research, I did find a few brief references to traditional religions in Nigeria and West Africa. In a speech, Shaykh Ibrahim Niasse explains the relationship of "Islam" to other religions:

> Islam is the belief in One God. The resignation to the will of Allah is the realization of justice among the people. The Qur'an reveals that all of the Prophets of Allah have used the same word to describe their religion: *al-Islām* or "submission." Islam is surely the universal religion, encompassing all the other religions. The stains of man cannot obscure or modify its essential beauty. Islam was the belief and method of worship prescribed for Abraham, Moses, and Jesus Christ. Its meaning has not changed: release yourself into the worship of Allah, and do not divide yourselves to its purpose. As for those religions the Qur'an mentions as having been altered by later followers, these religions had already become irreparably distant from the essential truth of Islam before becoming nullified by successive revelations. The last revelation, which abrogates the previous revelations, is the religion of Muḥammad.[45]

In this perspective, the religion brought by the Prophet Muḥammad is but the latest iteration of the "one, true religion" of "Islam." New prophets with successive revelations are sent when the practice of people has become "irreparably distant" from the "one true religion." These new revelations and dispensations abrogate their forerunners whose "essential truth" has become obscured. Thus, from this perspective, Ifa and other indigenous African religions could be seen as "altered" forms of "abrogated" revelations. Elsewhere, Shaykh Ibrahim Niasse describes those practitioners of indigenous African traditions as "unbelievers and idol-worshippers": "And I—and all praise is for Allah—know of tens of millions of Muslims who took this Ṭarīqa through me; and even more who were unbelievers, idol-worshippers and Christians before coming in contact with us; and even more who attained the Opening (of the Knowledge of Allah) through witnessing and beholding (the Presence of Allah) without any proof or reasoning."[46] This account implicitly likens the practitioners of indigenous African religious traditions to the idol-worship of the pre-Islamic Arabs.

But it is in a semi-hagiographical account of the Yoruba shaykh Muḥammad Jami'u Bulala of Shaykh Ibrahim Niasse's branch of the Tijāniyya that we see an explicit reference to Ifa:

> Both parents were pagans. His mother especially was an Osun worshipper. This could be the reason for naming their son Osundare. Before and after the birth of a child in Yorubaland in those days, it was the practice then to consult the Oracle to know what the future held for the child. It was predicted to Shaykh's parents that the pregnancy carried by the mother would be a male child who would acquire knowledge of the new religion (as Islam was being called then). Also that the child in question will have the ability to know what he was not even taught and many people would be blessed through him. [The] Shaykh didn't tread the path of his parents. . . . [The] Shaykh in his own case was a Muslim who lived according to the dictates of the Qur'an. He believed in the oneness of Allah. One shouldn't be surprise[d] that a pagan might give birth to a saint. We have seen such example in the personality of prophet Ibrahim.[47]

Interestingly, the pronouncements of the "Oracle" (most probably Ifa) are used here to bolster the supernatural credentials of the shaykh, while his "pagan" parentage is excused or explained by reference to the Qur'anic account of Ibrahim, whose father is also described as "taking idols for gods" (6:74). This account is particularly fascinating because while it seems to denigrate the "pagan" worship of Oṣun, it relies on and assumes the authority of the Ifa oracle in order to make the point that, from birth, Bulala was destined for greatness in Islamic scholarship and sanctity.

The above passages demonstrate the diversity of perspectives on Ifa and indigenous African religious traditions in general among Yoruba Muslims and West African Tijanis. While this is a rich topic that deserves further inquiry, for the purposes of the present study we can conclude that West African Tijanis would tend to regard Ifa as "unbelief" (*kufr*), "idol-worship," "paganism," or as an abrogated or former revelation. Some Tijanis (such as Tierno Bokar and Amadou Hampâté Bâ) would perhaps regard Ifa as being among "the diverse forms of religion" and babalawo as being among the "brotherhood of believers in God."[48] Having summarized these perspectives, we now turn to the task of creatively interpreting Ifa from the perspective of the Tijani tradition.

## Ifa from the Perspective of Tijani Sufism

As the accounts above demonstrate, the Qur'an is central to the Tijani tradition's interpretation not only of itself, but also of other traditions.[49] A superficial or outward (*zāhir*) acquaintance with Ifa (and the orisa traditions in general) would lend itself to interpreting the practices of the babalawo through the lens of verses describing the "intermediary deities" of the pre-Islamic Arabs, such as "Surely pure religion is for God only. And those who choose protecting friends beside Him [say]: 'We worship them only that they may bring us near unto God.' Lo! God will judge between them concerning that wherein they differ" (39:3).[50] Or even if Orunmila and other orisa were to be interpreted as "angels" or "prophets," the fact that they are worshipped and sacrificed to would suggest the condemnation of the following verse: "And he commanded you not that you should take the angels and the prophets for lords. Would he command you to disbelieve after you had surrendered [to God]?" (3:80).

Similarly, the divinatory aspects of the Ifa tradition would call to mind the following verses forbidding the pre-Islamic Arab practice of "arrow divination":[51] "Forbidden to you are carrion, blood, the flesh of swine ... as also things sacrificed to idols, and divination by the divining arrows [*al-azlām*]: that is ungodliness" (5:3); and "O you who believe! Strong drink and games of chance and idols and divining arrows [*al-azlām*] are only an infamy of Satan's handiwork. Leave it aside in order that you may succeed" (5:90). The divinatory aspect of Ifa would also recall the strong Islamic prohibition against jinn-inspired fortune-telling or soothsaying (*al-kihāna*). Seen through the lens of these traditions, Ifa would appear to be a reiteration of pre-Islamic idolatry and its related practices of soothsaying by means of communication with jinn.

On the other hand, as mentioned above, Ifa bears a striking resemblance to the Islamic occult sciences of geomancy (*khaṭṭ al-raml*) and divinatory tables (*ziyārij*), and its sacrifices and incantations bear a kind of family resemblance to the talismanic tradition of secrets (*asrār*), popular among Tijani Sufis and other West African Muslims. Many of these occult sciences draw on pre-Islamic Greek, Persian, Indian, Babylonian, and indigenous African sources (just as the Islamic sciences of astronomy, astrology, and mathematics do); therefore, from this perspective, Ifa could be seen as a pre-Islamic tradition of *asrār*, as an occult science. Alternatively, Ifa could also be seen as a creative Yoruba adaptation of these Islamic divinatory sciences.

From another perspective, given the fact that Ifa describes a unique, Supreme, Transcendent Deity who is all-knowing, a "reckoning" of sorts after death, and prescribes "right actions" through the imitation of the figure of Orunmila, a more charitable reading of Ifa could consider babalawo and iyanifa as "believers" (*mu'minūn*), Orunmila as a prophet or sage whose "book" or message of Divine Unity (*tawḥīd*) is the Odu of Ifa.

Thus, when interpreted through the lens of verses such as "Verily We sent messengers before thee, among them those of whom We have told thee, and some of whom We have not told thee" (40:78); "For We assuredly sent amongst every People a messenger, [with the command], 'Serve God, and eschew evil'" (16:36); "There is not a nation but a warner hath passed among them" (35:24); as well as "And for every nation there is a messenger. And when their messenger comes (on the Day of Judgment) it will be judged between them fairly, and they will not be wronged" (10:47),[52] Ọrunmila could appear as a prophet/messenger/warner sent to Yoruba-speaking people.

Moreover, the famous "ḥadīth of the slave-woman" (ḥadīth jāriya) provides a Prophetic example for considering babalawo as "believers." In this tradition, a companion of the Prophet asks him to examine a captured enslaved woman to see if she is a believer (if she is, then she is to be freed); the Prophet asks the woman (who in some narrations is described as a "black woman"), "Where is God?" To which she replies, "In the sky." Then the Prophet asks, "And who am I?" To which she responds, "You are the Messenger of God." The Prophet then says, "Free her, for she is a believer."[53] Babalawo, who by and large consider the Prophet to be a "divine messenger" of sorts, who also hold that God symbolically exists "in" or "above" the sky would easily pass this test.

Furthermore, taking Ọrunmila to be a prophet, Ifa's recognition of the Prophet Muḥammad and its encouragement of children of Odu Otura Meji to follow his religion could even be read as a fulfillment of the "covenant" described in the following Qur'anic verse: "When God made [His] covenant with the prophets, [He said]: 'By that which I have given you of a Book and Wisdom, should a messenger then come to you, confirming that which is with you, you shall believe in him and you shall help him.' He said: 'Do you agree, and take on My burden on these conditions?' They said: 'We agree'" (3:81).

Thus, Ifa could even be interpreted in light of the following verses of the Qur'an, considering its devotees as believers who need not fear the punishment of the afterlife:[54] "Those who believe, and those who are Jews, and Christians, and Sabaeans—whoever believes in God and the Last Day and does right—surely their reward is with their Lord, and there no fear will come upon them neither will they grieve" (2:62; 5:69); and "For every one of you We have appointed a revealed law and a right way" (5:48).

By this line of reasoning, the devotees of Ifa could be considered among those who "believe in God and the Last Day and do right." From this perspective, Ọrunmila would be a prophet, not a deity or partner set up alongside God; the taboos and prescriptions of Ifa would constitute a "revealed law and right way"; and the posthumous fate of babalawo, like all other believers, would be in the hands of God: "Unto God [belongs] whatsoever is in the heavens and whatsoever is in the earth; and whether ye make known what is in your minds or hide it, God will bring you to account for it.

He will forgive whom He will and He will punish whom He will. God is able to do all things" (2:284); "He will not be questioned as to that which He does, but they will be questioned" (21:23).

Leaving aside these soteriological considerations, from another perspective, the orişa could be seen as personified Divine Names or Attributes (*ṣifāt*), each representing a different divine facet or activity. The interaction between Divine Names is sometimes described in Sufi literature in mythological language similar to that of the myths of Ifa.[55] Furthermore, just as Sufi doctrine describes how different people are governed by different Divine Names at different times, Ifa describes how different people and situations are governed by different orişa at different times.

On an even deeper/inner (*bāṭin*) level, Ọrunmila could be seen as yet another manifestation of the Muḥammadan reality (*al-ḥaqīqa al-Muḥammadiyya*) or Muḥammadan light (*nūr Muḥammadī*) that encompasses all the prophets (including the Prophet of Islam) without distinction. As the Qur'an says, "We believe in God and that which is revealed unto us and that which was revealed unto Abraham, and Ishmael, and Isaac, and Jacob, and the tribes, and that which Moses and Jesus received, and that which the prophets received from their Lord. We make no distinction between any of them, and unto Him we have surrendered" (2:136; 3:84); "The messenger believes in that which hath been revealed unto him from his Lord and [so do] believers. Each one believes in God and His angels and His books and His messengers—We make no distinction between any of His messengers" (2:285); and "But those who believe in God and His messengers and make no distinction between any of them, unto them God will give their wages; and God is ever Forgiving, Merciful" (4:152). To use Tierno Bokar's analogy of the rainbow, from this perspective, all the prophets (and by extension all the prophetic messages and religious traditions) are the same in that they are all light, but each is unique and distinct in that it has a unique color and, in the case of the rainbow, its own place of shining or manifestation (*maẓhar*). Thus this seemingly contradictory verse of the Qur'an—"Of those messengers, some of whom We have caused to excel others, and of whom there are some unto whom God spake, while some of them He exalted in degree" (2:253)—can be understood as referring to the distinct degree of superiority that each "messenger" or "message" has over the other by virtue of representing a certain possibility that is not found in the others (i.e., red "has a degree" above blue because it has something that blue does not, and likewise blue "excels" red in that it represents something not found in red). Here we come to a very delicate point: most Tijani (and Sufi) writings identify the historical Prophet Muḥammad with the Muḥammadan reality to such a degree that the historical person is seen as the "fullest" embodiment or manifestation of the Muḥammadan reality, containing the perfections of all others like the "white light" of a prism contains all colors. From the perspective of Sufism this is certainly true, but only relatively so.

The levels or *ḥaḍarāt* at which the Prophet Muḥammad is distinct and different from the other prophets are "lower" or "less real" than the levels or *ḥaḍarāt* in which they are all united in the same reality (the *ḥaḍrat al-Aḥmadiyya*). Insofar as degrees of superiority or inferiority have to do with the historical person of a prophet, they are limited to those things having to do with that visible, outward level of reality, bound by time and space—such as number of followers, years of life, statements made, books written/recited, and so forth. Insofar as degrees of superiority or inferiority have to do with the inner or spiritual reality of a particular prophet, they remain distinct but begin to converge; and insofar as statements about degrees of superiority concern the innermost reality of a particular prophet, they all merge into one another, so on this level the praises of one apply to all. As Rumi writes, "The name of Aḥmad is the name of all the prophets, when the hundred come, ninety is with us as well."[56] When you follow the rays of different colors back into the prism, they eventually converge into a single white light. This helps explain the apparent contradiction in the following two statements of the Prophet: "I am the best of the children of Adam, without boast, Adam and those who come after him will be under my flag on the Day of Resurrection";[57] and "Do not say that I am better than Yunūs ibn Matta [Jonah]."[58] In the *ḥaḍrat al-Aḥmadiyya*, in the *ḥaqīqa al-Muḥammadiyya*, there is no distinction between prophetic lights, there is only the all-comprehensive "white light" of the *nūr Muḥammadī*. That is why Shaykh Ibrahim Niasse and his disciples say that "during *tarbiya*, a disciple becomes a Christian, a Jew, a Magus, an animist." At this level, one simultaneously transcends and realizes the "transcendent unity" of all forms of prophetic guidance.

From another perspective, which appears to be shared by the likes of Tierno Bokar, Ibn ʿArabi addresses the issue of abrogation, comparing other religions to the stars and the "all-inclusive" religion of Muḥammad to the sun:

> All the revealed religions [*sharāʾiʿ*] are lights. Among these religions, the revealed religion of Muḥammad is like the light of the sun among the lights of the stars. When the sun appears, the lights of the stars are hidden, and their lights are included in the light of the sun. Their being hidden is like the abrogation of the other revealed religions that takes place through Muḥammad's revealed religion. Nevertheless, they do in fact exist, just as the existence of the light of the stars is actualized. This explains why we have been required in our all-inclusive religion to have faith in the truth of all the messengers and all the revealed religions. They are not rendered null [*bāṭil*] by abrogation—that is the opinion of the ignorant. (3.153.12)[59]

On an even deeper level, in the "black light" of the Divine Essence (*al-dhāt*), the *ḥaḍrat al-Quds*, all such distinctions are obliterated. All forms of belief are transcended, and even this transcendence is transcended, so that one sees nothing but God. More precisely, God sees nothing but Himself in Himself by Himself.

For Tijani Sufis, however, the truest perspective comes from "coming back down" and journeying "with God in creation" (*maʿ al-Ḥaqq fiʾl-khalq*) through *baqāʾ*. This necessitates combining the undifferentiated perspective of *fanāʾ* or the *ḥaḍrat al-Quds* with the more differentiated perspectives of the other *ḥaḍarāt*, including the "everyday" reality of the *ḥaḍrat al-Nasūt*, where each thing, including each revealed law, is irreducibly different, distinct, and even opposing. Thus, Tijanis, like other Sufis, may acknowledge and recognize the validity and identity of other traditions with their own at one level, while denying this validity and identity on another. It is a question of levels of reality, of *ḥaḍarāt*. Ibn ʿArabi gives one explanation for inwardly recognizing a tradition while outwardly denying it:

> As for those who know the affair *as it is*, they are manifest in a form that rejects the [other] forms that are worshipped [i.e., idols and other traditions of worship]. Their station in knowledge grants them that they be determined by the moment, owing to the determination over them of the Messenger in whom they believe. It is by virtue of this that they are called believers. They are worshippers of the moment, though they know that they [the idol-worshippers] did not worship those forms [idols] themselves, but only worshipped God in them by virtue of the influence of the self-disclosure which they knew to be found in them. The denier, who has no knowledge of what self-discloses, is ignorant of it, while the perfected knower—prophet, messenger, or heir—veils it.[60]

Likewise, the Knower (*ʿārif*) inwardly recognizes that everything is God or the Prophet, but veils this knowledge outwardly, giving each thing its due on its own level by following the Prophet in outward actions and speech as well as in inward states and knowledge. So in this respect, Tijani Sufis could potentially inwardly recognize the validity or even identity of Ifa with their own tradition, while outwardly denying or veiling this fact. This should not be understood as some kind of a Straussian concealment of esoteric truths for fear of political oppression, nor can it even be reduced to Aristotelian concern for exposing the hoi polloi (*al-ʿāma*) to that which they cannot understand (i.e., "casting pearls before swine," although this is certainly an important consideration), but should rather be understood as the epistemological imperative of following the example of the Messenger, which leads to the most perfect possible realization and recognition of the Real in all its forms.

Thus, from the perspective of Tijani Sufism, Ifa appears outwardly (*zāhiran*) as pagan idol-worship / unbelief (*shirk* or *kufr*), or sorcery (*siḥr*), or a non-Islamic occult science, or as an abrogated/altered tradition brought by a prophet sent to the Yoruba people or their ancestors. However, inwardly (*bāṭinan*), Ifa could appear as a star in the sky of prophetic lights, a distinct band of color in the rainbow of prophetic guidance—Ọrunmila could be seen as a particular manifestation of the Muḥammadan reality—and Ifa, as one of the many forms of belief through which God knows Himself.

Through the above examples, we can see how both Ifa and Tijani Sufism can be used to interpret each other, demonstrating their own "comparative theories of religion." Interestingly, both traditions contain perspectives that can be used to interpret the other as being united or identical with it "in heaven" (*ọrun*—Ifa) or "in the Aḥmadi presence" (*ḥadrat al-Aḥmadiyya*) or "in the Divine Presence" (*ḥadrat al-Quds*—Tijani Sufism), while being distinct, different, and even opposing "in the world" (*aye*—Ifa) or in the outward presence of apparent reality (*ḥadrat al-Nasūt*—Tijani Sufism). Now we will turn to the comparison of certain dimensions of Ifa and Tijani Sufism. These "dimensions of comparison" are constructed by exploring the relationship between seemingly similar or related concepts from the two traditions.

CHAPTER 10

# Comparative Conclusions

> To study the Way is to study the self. To study the self is to forget
> the self. To forget the self is to be enlightened by all things of
> the universe. To be enlightened by all things of the universe
> is to cast off the body and mind of the self as well as those of
> others. Even the traces of enlightenment are wiped out, and
> life with traceless enlightenment goes on forever and ever.
> —DOGEN

DIMENSIONS OF COMPARISON BETWEEN IFA AND TIJANI SUFISM

### Knowledge (*'Ilm-ma'rifa / Igbagbọ-imọ*)

The distinctions between *'ilm* and *ma'rifa*, rational speculation (*fikr/naẓar*) and unveiling (*kashf*), book knowledge (*'ilm al-awrāq*) and knowledge by taste (*'ilm al-adhwāq*) that characterize Tijani epistemology do not exactly map onto the *imọ* (direct knowledge) versus *igbagbọ* (secondhand knowledge) distinction that characterizes the epistemology of Ifa (and traditional Yoruba thought and language in general). Within Sufism, the epistemological contrast is between a merely mental or sensory form of knowledge achieved through the senses or rational speculation, on the one hand, and an existential/metaphysical form of knowledge or self-knowledge achieved through the heart (*qalb*), spirit (*rūḥ*), or Divine Intellect (*al-'aql al-rabbānī*), on the other. In

Ifa, the distinction is rather between direct/firsthand knowledge (sensory or otherwise) (*imọ*) and secondhand knowledge of a primarily propositional nature (*igbagbọ*).

These distinctions are similar in that they both privilege direct, intimate, and nondiscursive knowledge (*maʿrifa* and *imọ*) over knowledge that tends to be indirect, secondhand, and discursive (*ʿilm* and *igbagbọ*).[1] It is notable that while in everyday language, both *maʿrifa* and *imọ* are used to refer to the knowledge that one has of another person, it would be a bit odd to use *ʿilm* and absurd to use *igbagbọ* to refer to this kind of interpersonal knowledge. This is significant as it indicates that the object of both *maʿrifa* and the deepest mode of knowledge (*imọ ijinlẹ*)—which is at once the Divine (Allāh/Olodumare) and the self (*ʿayn*/*ori*)—is understood to be an active knowing subject and not a passive object of knowledge.

Characteristically, the language of Ifa is more polysemic and synthetic (e.g., *imọ ijinlẹ* can be used to refer to the principial knowledge of medicine or geometry as well as the sacred "word that Olodumare gave to Ọrunmila to mend the world"), while that of Tijani Sufism is more analytic and technical, in part due to the Sufi tradition's long engagement with the even more analytic and discursively technical disciplines of *falsafa* (Islamic philosophy) and *kalām* (Islamic theology). Within Ifa, there is less of a distinction between esoteric and exoteric knowledge than there is in Sufism. For example, a babalawo who has not memorized several verses of each of the 256 Odu and their rituals, would rarely, if ever, be called a "deep knower" (*onimọ ijinlẹ*), whereas I met many a Tijani disciple described as being a "Knower by God" (*ʿārif biLlāh*), who had not memorized the Qurʾan and had little more than a basic knowledge of Islamic rituals and jurisprudence (*fiqh*), not to mention the other Islamic sciences.

Thus, being a "Knower by God" in Tijani Sufism does not seem to require a mastery of other, more "exoteric" sciences, whereas being a "deep knower" (*onimọ ijinlẹ*) in Ifa is not similarly separated from the memorization of the Odu and the extensive procedural knowledge of their associated rituals. However, as mentioned above, some initiates of Ifa enter the *igbodu* before having mastered or even memorized the Odu of Ifa, acquiring direct and deep knowledge of their *ori*. Moreover, one of the distinguishing characteristics of Shaykh Ibrahim and his close disciples (including many contemporary *shuyūkh* as well as Shaykh Aḥmad al-Tijānī, Ibn ʿArabi, and Sufi masters in general) was/is their unification or combination of *dhawq* ("tasting" or experiential knowledge) and *dirāya* (discursive knowledge). The vast majority of *shuyūkh* I interviewed had memorized the Qurʾan and were masters of many other Islamic sciences.

In any case, the epistemologies of both traditions privilege and are founded on these direct modes of (self-)knowing, which both aim to cultivate through a highly structured program of ritual practice, a way of life and being. In fact, these forms of knowledge (*ma'rifa* and *imọ ijinlẹ*) can also be described as distinct modes of being whose perfections are identified with the Prophet Muḥammad and Ọrunmila, respectively.

**Acquisition of Knowledge and Ritual Practice**

Thus in both traditions, the process of acquiring or cultivating these ideal modes of knowing/being involves the transformation of the self through ritual practice. Since these modes of knowing are at once self-knowledge and modes of being, the self's mode of being must be changed or actualized through transformative ritual practices. These practices are invariably linked to or done in imitation of the founder of the tradition, who is identified with this most perfect mode of being/knowing. In self-knowledge, the knowing subject is the same as the object known; therefore, to change or increase what you know, you must change or increase your self. In Tijani Sufism, the most intense and deepest levels or aspects of the self are identified with God, the Prophet, and Shaykh Aḥmad al-Tijānī / Shaykh Ibrahim; while in Ifa, the most intense and deepest levels of the self are identified with Olodumare ("the *ori* of all *ori*"), one's *ori*, Ọrunmila, and one's Odu. If you want to know me, walk a mile in my shoes; if you want to know the Ọrunmila or the Prophet Muḥammad, walk a life in their footprints—and in doing so, you become who *you truly are* and thus know yourself *as you truly are* and know things *as they truly are*.

**Initiation (*Tarbiya/Igbodu*)**

Initiation (*tarbiya* in Tijani Sufism and *itẹfa/igbodu* in Ifa) is of central importance to this process of transformation or realization in both traditions. However, just because both terms are translated as "initiation" does not mean that they should be assumed to be identical. As the descriptions in chapters 3 and 7 demonstrate, the rituals of *tarbiya* and those of *itẹfa* and *igbodu* are clearly very different. Nevertheless, they share certain similarities despite their obvious differences. The exact rites and realizations of both are closely guarded secrets, with strict taboos governing what initiates can and cannot disclose about their experiences to noninitiates. As mentioned above, this is closely related to the inner/invisible–outer/visible distinction and complementarity that is important to both Ifa (*inu-ode*) and Sufism (*bāṭin-ẓāhir*). Within both traditions, the knowledge of the inner is ineffable to a certain degree, and thus can only be expressed outwardly through symbol and allusion, which is liable to be misunderstood by those who have not had the same experiences. This implies a special symbolic theory of language and communication that will be taken up in the next section of this chapter. Furthermore, the rites of initiation are also kept secret to prevent the uninitiated from trying to initiate themselves, an impossible and dangerous proposition in both traditions.

Interestingly, babalawo liken going to the *igbodu* to performing the ḥajj, a comparison that is suggested not only by the similarity of the clothes of the Ifa initiates to those of the Meccan pilgrims (white cloth tied over one shoulder), but also by the symbolism of the Kaʿba as the heart within Sufism. According to Shaykh Ibrahim Niasse, the real ḥajj is the journey to the heart, to the dwelling place of God in the innermost depths of one's being; while for babalawo, the *igbodu* is the place where one encounters one's true self (*ori inu*) and the Odu that gave birth to one. Likewise, in *tarbiya*, the initiate comes to know his or her inner reality and identity with God, the realities of Prophet, Shaykh Aḥmad al-Tijānī (and Shaykh Ibrahim). Thus, both initiatory rites are likened to a "rebirth" and radically alter the way initiates perceive and interact with themselves and the world around them. In both Tijani Sufism and Ifa, initiation is described as opening the soul, the self, up to the higher levels of its being.[2] If a noninitiate can be likened to a person locked in a room with a few small windows, initiation unlocks the door and allows the person to go outside and look around. It gives the initiate the spiritual power (*aṣẹ* in Ifa, *fayḍ* or *walāya* in Tijani Sufism) to open the door and transcend the limits of his or her "everyday" self.

Thus, in both traditions, initiation is described not as an end, but rather as a beginning (as even the English word "initiation" suggests). Interestingly, both traditions contain sayings that describe initiation as a never-ending process. The journey of knowledge in both traditions is endless, "from the cradle to the grave" and beyond. Since the object of knowledge (the Real [*al-Ḥaqq*] / the Muḥammadan reality [*al-ḥaqīqa al-Muḥammadiyya*] in Tijani Sufism and Olodumare/Ọrunmila in Ifa) is both infinite and identified with the knowing subject, the journey of knowledge is boundless "on both sides," in both traditions.

Initiation and the daily, weekly, and annual rites of both traditions are both described as establishing an intimate relationship and communication/communion with these divine realities. As a result, both traditions are extremely dynamic because of the continued "vertical" connection with these sources of orthodoxy and orthopraxy. Tijani *shuyūkh* and disciples report regularly seeing the Prophet, Shaykh Aḥmad al-Tijānī, and Shaykh Ibrahim in dreams and visions, and babalawo consult with Ifa multiple times a day. As mentioned above, these intimate interactions are made possible by the "putting," "making," or "actualizing" of these realities within the initiate. In both of these traditions, you cannot really or directly know something or someone that is not inside of you, so in Ifa (and oriṣa traditions in general) the oriṣa are "made" and "put" inside the initiate, enabling him or her to interact with their physical shrines and metaphysical presences. In the Tijani Sufism of Shaykh Ibrahim, the *talqīn* or "implantation" of the general *wird* and the special *awrād* (litanies) of *tarbiya* transmit the flux of light and knowledge (*fayḍ*) from shaykh to disciple, actualizing the initiate's inner connection (*rābiṭa*) to, and ultimately identity with, Shaykh Ibrahim, Shaykh al-Tijānī, the Prophet, and God.

Without this connection or transmission, one is not authorized to perform the rites of the Tijāniyya; similarly, without this "implantation" of Ifa (or other oriṣa), one is not authorized to perform the rites of Ifa (or other oriṣa). This provides another perspective from which we can understand that the modes of knowing cultivated in both traditions are akin to the intimate way in which one knows another person—as a part of oneself—not as an object, but rather intersubjectively, or ultimately, as a part of one's own knowing subject.

While the symbolic logics that structure and animate the discursive and nondiscursive rituals of these traditions will be discussed in the next section, a note is in order here about the role that discursive, conceptual thought plays in the ritual processes of realization in Ifa and Tijani Sufism.

### The Role of Conceptual/Discursive Thought in Realization

> *Fikr* (thought) leads to *dhikr* (remembrance/invocation)
> from *dhikr* combined with *fikr*
> a hundred good thoughts (*afkār*) arise
> —JĀMĪ

> You are now an olorisha. Therefore you have to be very careful what you are thinking because thought is creation.
> —SUSANNE WENGER

The rituals of Ifa and Tijani Sufism are not only spiritual and physical exercises, they also shape the inner realities (*inu/ọkan* and *nafs/qalb/'aql*) from which thought (*ero* and *fikr*) emerge. But what role do concepts and speculative thought play in these ritual processes of realization? Both traditions set forward not only a program of ritual exercises to be performed, but also elaborate doctrines, sets of concepts to be learned, as well as hermeneutics, means of interpreting and making sense of oneself and the surrounding world. While these doctrines (which are described in detail in the previous chapters) are not usually taught to noninitiates, they can be learned and understood, to a certain extent, without participating in the traditions themselves. However, in both traditions, these doctrines are verified and transcended through the direct realizations experienced during initiation (*igbodu* and *tarbiya*) and afterward.

The doctrines of Ifa and Tijani Sufism thus serve as a kind of "map" of the cosmos and self, of reality as such, pointing out the best means of navigating through the different levels and aspects of existence and beyond. The narratives and rituals of the Odu and festivals of Ifa; the discourse of the babalawo; and the Qurʾan, ḥadīth, writings, poetry, and oral instruction of Sufi masters, profoundly shape the imaginations and minds of devotees, providing them with a wealth of concepts, images, and symbols to both contemplate and think with throughout their lives.

These concepts and ideas serve as motivation and reminders, provide a basic sense of "what's going on," orient practitioners' intentions (a key component of ritual practice in both traditions), answer questions, remove doubts and false certainties, and eliminate errors and habits of thinking that inhibit realization, replacing them with those that anticipate and facilitate realization and spiritual maturity. These concepts and ideas are not considered to be speculative, but are rather understood to be "inspired": coming directly from God, the founder of the tradition, or the realized masters of the traditions. These concepts, insights, and means of interpretation are thus understood to both come from and lead back to a Divine Truth that is considered as both origin and goal in both traditions. Thus, when examining either tradition, it is important to distinguish between these "inspired" concepts, on the one hand, and the everyday speculative concepts that have a merely mental or more commonplace origin, on the other. The former come from and lead beyond concepts, while the latter lead only to more concepts.

The supra-formal Truth (*al-Ḥaqq*) of Sufism or the Divine Word (*ọrọ*) of Ifa take on a wide variety of forms in the minds of babalawo and Sufis, and because thought or the inner life (*inu*) is regarded as the origin or father of one's outward behaviors in both traditions, eliminating false patterns of thought, false stories we tell ourselves about ourselves and others, is considered just as, if not more, important than eliminating or curbing wrong or false behaviors. In both traditions, adepts are first introduced to these "inspired" concepts, which gradually come to replace other concepts and patterns of thought, and through the combination of study and practice, these "inspired" concepts transform the very being of the initiate, further illuminating other concepts and practices.[3] For both traditions, "real" thinking seems to begin after initiation.

Drawing an analogy from the world of orisa spirituality, this mental transformation can be likened to the dances practiced by some *olorisa* seeking to become possessed by their orisa. As the dancer's steps become more and more like that of the orisa, the orisa eventually possesses the dancer, whose steps are now perfected under the divine control of the orisa. Within the tradition of Ifa, thinking (*ironu*) seems to function in a similar way: proper thinking leads to understanding, which leads to proper action, which leads back to proper thinking.

Within the Tijani tradition, Shaykh Ibrahim's commentary on the verse "If you love God, then follow me, and God will love you" (3:31) illustrates this point in similar fashion: "The following of the Prophet through all of one's words and actions is the most elevated means [*wasīla*] that the servant can take to arrive at the presence of God.... Whoever follows the Prophet finds the love of God, and when God loves his servant, He is him. 'My servant does not cease to draw near to me through supererogatory works until I love him, and when I love him, I am him.'"[4] In his *Removal of Confusion*, Shaykh Ibrahim comments on the same ḥadīth:

> The heart has become the abode of the Manifest Truth, and God is his tongue with which he speaks. If such a person remembering [God in this way] were to strike a blow, God becomes his hand with which he strikes, and if he hears, God is his ear with which he hears. The Most High who is remembered has taken possession of the heart, so He controls it. He has taken possession of the limbs of the body, so He uses them for what is pleasing to Him. He has taken possession of the servant's character traits, so He operates them however He wills for the sake of His pleasure.[5]

The ḥadīth cited in these passages reads, "My servant does not cease drawing near to me through supererogatory acts of worship until I love him. Then when I love him, I become his hearing with which he hears, his seeing with which he sees, his hand with which he grasps, and his foot with which he walks," to which one could easily add "the thinking with which he thinks."[6] Shaykh Ibrahim appears to make this precise connection in the previously quoted passage in which he defines different kinds of "thought" or mental activity: "Thought [*khāṭir*] is what descends on the heart either with the acts of meditation [*fikr*] or not. The real thought [*al-khāṭir al-ḥaqīqī*] is the thought united with God when the slave ceases to exist and his being is annihilated so that nothing remains except the thought which roams, freed from its restrictions, wherever it wants."[7]

For Shaykh Ibrahim, "real thought" only takes place after annihilation; and in this regard, it is interesting to note that he used to comment on and teach some of the intellectual classics of Sufi literature, such as Ibn 'Aṭā Allāh's *Ḥikam*, to his disciples *after* they had completed their *tarbiya*. This emphasizes the continued role and importance of discursive thought even after *tarbiya*, when joined with spiritual realization. For the disciples of Shaykh Ibrahim, *tarbiya* marks the beginning, not the end, of "real thought."

Thus, in both Tijani Sufism and Ifa, conceptual or discursive thought plays an essential role as the activity of a person's inner reality (*inu/ọkan* in Ifa and *nafs/qalb/'aql* in Sufism). Given that the goal of both traditions is to establish a total and radical transformation of one's being, all aspects of one's being, including the "mind," must be engaged and involved. This engagement takes the form of the "inspired" concepts of the doctrines embedded in the orature and literature of the traditions, whose theoretical understanding and contemplation, when combined with other forms of ritual practice (this contemplation is itself a form of ritual practice) facilitates the deeper, existential realization and verification of these doctrines. In his *Ringstones of Wisdom*, Ibn 'Arabi explains the function and transformation of these beliefs or "concepts": "Regarding the Selfhood, some slaves judge, in their belief, that God is such and such, and when the covering is removed, they see the form of what they believe which is true, and they believe in it. Then the knot is undone and the belief disappears, and becomes a knowledge through witnessing. After this sharpening of sight, dull vision shall not return."[8]

In both traditions, the ideas we have about ourselves, who we are and what we can become, strongly determine our development during life and after death. This is particularly true of the "revealed" or "inspired" concept of self (*ori*) in Ifa, which bears some similarity to the concept of *'ayn thābit* (immutable entity, identity or essence) in Sufism.

### The Eternal Self (*Ori/'Ayn*)

> Any life, however long and complicated it may be, actually consists of a single moment—the moment when a man knows forever more who he is.
> —JORGE LUIS BORGES

> The essence of all sciences is only this: that you know who you are on the Day of Resurrection.
> —RUMI

> The end of knowledge is that man comes to the point where he was at the origin.
> —DHŪ'L-NŪN AL-MIṢRĪ

> There is no head that is without a Divine Secret
> —HĀFIẒ

To briefly summarize the reality of *ori* described in the previous chapters, the *ori inu* (inner head) is chosen by each person in heaven before coming to the world. This choice (*ipin*) comprises everything that the person will ever do, experience, and become, and is often glossed as "destiny" or "fate." On the way down to the world, people pass beneath the tree of forgetfulness and forget their destinies, but they can still commune and communicate with them through Ifa divination and by worshipping and "feeding" their *ori inu* (inner heads, destinies), which also serve as a kind of guardian angel, muse, and spiritual double. At the apex of their initiation ceremony, babalawo encounter their own *ori inu* and the *aṣẹ* of this choice of destiny (*ipin*) in the *igbodu*.

In Ibn ʿArabi's work, and Sufi traditions (such as the Tijani) influenced by it, the *ʿayān al-thābita*, or immutable entities/identities of people or things, play a remarkably similar role. Drawing inspiration from Qurʾanic verses such as "And Our word unto a thing, when We intend it, is only that We say unto it: Be! And it is [*Kun fayakūn*]" (16:40) and "But His command, when He intendeth a thing, is only that He says unto it: Be! and it is [*Kun fayakūn*]" (36:82). Ibn ʿArabi explains that these "things" or "entities" (*ʿayān*) are in God's Knowledge before He creates them or the world, and that He only gives them existence in the forms they have chosen or determined for themselves. In the *Ringstones of Wisdom*, he writes:

> He does not determine our properties except through us. Or rather, we determine our own properties. Or rather, we determine our own properties through ourselves, though within Him. . . . The Divine Will becomes connected only to a single thing. Will is a relationship which follows knowledge, while knowledge is a relationship that follows the object of knowledge. The object of knowledge is you and your states (*aḥwāl*). Knowledge displays no effect within the object of knowledge. On the contrary, the object of knowledge displays its effects in knowledge. The object gives to knowledge what it actually is in itself. . . . *None of us there is but has a known station* (37:164). This "*known station*" is what you are in your immutability. . . . Even though the Real determines the property, He only effuses [*fāḍa*] existence upon you, and you determine your own property. Hence you should praise none but yourself and blame none but yourself. For the Real, only praise remains for effusing existence, since that belongs to Him, not to you.⁹

That is, our immutable identities—what we are in God's eternal knowledge of us and all of our states (*aḥwāl*), everything that we are, will be, and will happen to us—determine God's Knowledge of us. All God does is bring us into existence. So, in a sense, we "choose" to be what we are, and then God gives us existence in the form we have chosen or determined. However, it is important to remember that all of this takes place *in Divinis*, in God (*ʿinda Allāh*), so the "we" that chooses or determines our immutable identities is none other than the Divine "We."

In fact, this act of determination is elsewhere described as the first "entification" or "determination" (*al-taʿayyun al-awwal*) of Divine Essence (*al-Dhāt*).¹⁰ In the same work, Ibn ʿArabi explains, "All He does is emanate existence upon you, and the determination is yours and is over you."¹¹ That is, you determine what God existentiates through what you are in your immutable entity, and the Divine Essence determines this immutable entity through its own determination in Itself or self-disclosure to Itself. Then, through a second determination or self-disclosure called the "Breath of the All-Merciful" (*nafas al-Raḥmān*) or the "Holy Effusion" (*al-fayḍ al-muqaddas*), God brings the hidden realities of the immutable entities, and thus all of creation, into existence. This whole process is often likened to a person speaking: first you form the words you want to say in your mind, where they are inaudible; then you externalize and enunciate these words on your breath through your vocal chords and mouth, and they become audible.

All of this is strikingly similar to the way *ori* is described in the Yoruba context. Wenger's definition of *ori*—"that part of one's complex identity which is an imperishable part of God"—could just as well apply to the immutable entity (*'ayn thābit*) of Sufism. Moreover, as one of Barry Hallen's collaborators explained, "It (*ẹmi*) chooses what it will come to do.... So also it [*ori*] is the act of the self [*ẹmi*] when it is with the supreme deity (*Ọlọrun*)."[12] Furthermore, the *oniṣegun* interviewed by Hallen also described *ori* in the following ways: "It is the person who has chosen for himself or herself what he or she has come to do on earth.... The Supreme Deity (*Ọlọrun*) merely says that it should be so [the *aṣẹ*]"; "Destiny is everything that the person will do on earth. The self (*ẹmi*) chooses all the things that the person will do, without leaving anything aside."[13]

Thus the choice (*ipin*) of *ori* can be likened to the determination of the immutable entities (*al-'ayān al-thābita*), and the creative power of Olodumare (*aṣẹ*) that "says that it should be so" is like the creative or existentiating command of "Be!" (*Kun!*), the effusion of existence through the "Breath of the All-Merciful" (*nafas al-Raḥmān*) or the "Holy Effusion" (*al-fayḍ al-muqaddas*). But the similarities do not end here.

Much as the *ori* is worshipped as a "personal god" or "personal aspect of divinity," the immutable entity (also called "preparedness" [*isti'dād*]), although not consciously worshipped as such, determines each person's object of worship. Ibn 'Arabi explains:

> The Real becomes manifest in the measure of the preparedness of the slave... for the slave becomes manifest to the Real in the measure of the form within which the Real self-discloses to him.... God has two self-disclosures: an invisible self-disclosure and a visible self-disclosure. From the disclosure of the invisible He grants the preparedness of the heart. This is the self-disclosure of the Essence, whose reality is the invisible, and is the Selfhood.... When this preparedness is actualized in it—that is, in the heart—He discloses Himself to it through a self-disclosure of the visible in the realm of the visible, and it sees Him. It is manifest in the form of what was disclosed to it, as we have already said....
>
> He then lifts the veil from between Himself and His servant, who then sees Him in the form of what He believes. It is identical with what he believes. Neither the heart nor the eye ever witness anything but the form of what one believes

concerning the Real. The Real of what is believed is that whose form is encompassed by the heart. The eye only sees the Real of belief.... The identity of the form that discloses itself is the identity of the form that receives that self-disclosure.[14]

The "god of belief," the god that is worshipped, is defined by and identical to the form of the "preparedness of the heart," which is identical to the form of the immutable entity in which the servant presents him- or herself to the Real. In simpler, more poetic language, "Every creature has a face turned to God, which is also the Face of God turned to that creature, bestowing being upon that creature."[15] Thus what one is *in God*, one's immutable entity or the preparedness of one's heart, determines how God appears *in* and *to* one—the form in which one conceives and worships God. This individual aspect of divinity is often referred to as one's *rabb* or Lord.

This bears strong similarities to Susanne Wenger's description: "Ori is He [Ẹlẹda] in us, through Ori everything is imperishably part of His sanctity and thus divine. ... God's own archetypal self is imperceptible, remote to mortal mind, but is utterly intimate—the very nucleus of all and everything, of all that is created individually."[16] Moreover, the encounter with the realities of *ori* and one's immutable entity during initiation in Ifa and Tijani Sufism also contain some fascinating similarities. One disciple described the *fatḥ* or opening experienced during *tarbiya* as "when you discover who you really are, everything about you, what you have come into the world to do, what will happen to you, how you will live and die, everything that Allah will do with you, and so after that, you will not be afraid or worry."[17]

Ibn 'Arabi similarly describes this realization, relating it to the Knower's immutable entity (*'ayn*):

> Among them is one who knows that God's knowledge of him, in all of his states, is what he is in his identity's state of immutability prior to its existence, and he knows that the Real grants him nothing but what the knowledge of his identity grants Him, which is what he is in his state of immutability. He knows from whence God's knowledge of Him is realized. There is no category of the Folk of God more exalted or more unveiled than this category.... For he knows what is contained in God's knowledge of him ... through the unveiling to him of his immutable identity and the infinite transitions of the states it encounters.... As concerns his knowledge of himself, he is at the degree of God's knowledge of him, because what is received comes from a single source [his immutable identity (*'aynihi al-thābit*)].[18]

This is remarkably similar to Awo Faniyi's description of the encounter with Odu in the *igbodu*: "The sacred power of the choice of destiny [*aṣẹ ipin*], Odu, is the choice that one made while coming into the world, it is everything that one will or should do, and everything that one will not or should not do. . . . When you see Odu, you meet everything that you left behind on the way down to the world at the tree of forgetfulness [*igi igbagbe*]."[19] Thus, encountering and knowing one's *ori* (*imọri*) in Ifa seems strikingly similar to the description of knowing one's immutable entity ('*ayn thābit*) in Ibn 'Arabi's thought and to the description of *fatḥ* (enlightenment) in the Tijani tradition. In a sense, in Ifa, all knowledge (both *igbagbọ* and *imọ*) is not only founded on, but is also contained in *imọri* (direct knowledge of one's *ori*), since all of these forms of knowledge and related experiences are contained in one's *ori*. Similarly, Ibn 'Arabi explains that everything one experiences or comes to know is nothing other than one's identity ('*ayn*).

Even if this knowledge appears to be different or distinct from oneself, it is only in the same way an image one sees in a polished surface is different from oneself: the image may appear different in different places because of the different nature of the surfaces, but it is still identical with the figure who casts the reflection. Ibn 'Arabi poetically describes this point when he writes, "From the tree of his self, he harvests the fruit of his knowledge."[20]

Knowing one's *ori* and knowing one's '*ayn* are both described as the deepest form of self-knowing possible, as both are defined as knowing one's "eternal self," or knowing oneself as God knows one, which is ultimately identical or related to how one knows God. Moreover, this mode of self-knowing is defined as the epistemological foundation of all other modes of knowing, which, from a certain perspective, are nothing other than it. In both traditions it seems that "he who knows himself, knows his Lord" and that the fruit of this (and all) knowledge is harvested from the tree of this self.[21] Or in the famous words of T. S. Eliot, "And the end of all our exploring / Will be to arrive where we first started / And know the place for the first time."[22]

**The Goal (of No Goal)**

However, this "goal" of self-knowledge is not a fixed target—it is not a static object or station that is attained once and for all, but is rather a dynamic mode of being. In the eternity of heaven (*ọrun*) or the Divine Essence (*al-Dhāt* or *al-Aḥadiya*), the *ori* and the '*ayān* are "fixed" or "static" (*thābita*); but in the world of time and becoming, they manifest as the fluid, perpetually changing states and conditions of the heart (*qalb*) or inner reality (*inu*) of the Sufi Knower ('*ārif*) or babalawo. Both Ifa and Tijani Sufism present a variety of "goals" as the raison d'être of their respective traditions—moral, epistemological, and soteriological ends to which their adherents aspire: "mending the world," "knowing the Truth," "knowing oneself," "knowing

God," "cultivating good character," "having a good life and afterlife," and so forth. However, in both traditions, all of these diverse goals are united in the goal of following the example of (or becoming like) the founder of the tradition: Ọrunmila through one's Odu for babalawo, the Prophet Muḥammad through Shaykh Aḥmad al-Tijānī through Shaykh Ibrahim for Tijanis. This goal is simultaneously described as unattainable (no babalawo can attain the rank of Ọrunmila, no Tijani can surpass Shaykh Ibrahim or Shaykh Aḥmad al-Tijānī or the Prophet) and ever present, since these founding figures are understood to be identical to the innermost realities of their followers in a certain respect. Thus, becoming a sage, becoming like the all-knowing founder of the tradition, is no ordinary goal. Perhaps these contradictions can be better understood by examining the ways in which these traditions describe these perfected modes of being and knowing.

In a speech, Shaykh Tijani 'Ali Cissé described the perfect Knowers (*ārifūn*) by referring to the classical Sufi tradition: "Junayd was asked about the saying of Dhū'l Nūn al-Miṣrī describing the gnostic [*Ārif biLlāh*], 'he was here but now he has gone.' Junayd replied, 'One spiritual state does not hold the gnostic back from another spiritual state, and one spiritual station does not veil him from changing stations. Thus, he is with the people of every place just as they are, he experiences whatever they experience, and he speaks their language so that they might benefit by his speech.'"[23]

And later he explains that this dynamic mode of knowing is only possible through entirely disinterested, "goalless" love: "Love is the attachment of the heart to the exalted Divine Essence, enamored with Him for His sake, not for any other purpose. This is not the case except for the perfected gnostics. May Allah make us among them by his blessing."[24] Similarly, as quoted above, when asked what he wanted, Shaykh Ibrahim said (echoing Abu Yazīd), "I want to not want." Ibn 'Arabi similarly describes this state of human perfection as the "station of no station" (*maqām lā maqām*) and identifies it with the Prophet Muḥammad, calling those who have attained it "Muḥammadans."

This highest class of Knowers are those who have undone all of the "knots of belief," who have transcended the "gods created in belief," and through the infinite flexibility of their hearts, come to recognize God in His Essence and in every single one of His self-disclosures. They are those who know Reality in Its inscrutable Essence and in Its infinite self-portraits in the beliefs of others. These Muḥammadans do not hold a particular kind of belief about God or Reality, but rather have transcended the limitations of all beliefs by becoming infinitely receptive to all of them. Taking the image contained in the aphorism "the water takes on the color of its vessel," the vessels of these Muḥammadans have transcended all limited colors by becoming transparent like water, capable of taking on any color. Ibn 'Arabi explains this "goalless" and dynamic "station of no station":

Comparative Conclusions • 363

The highest of all human beings are those who have no station. The reason for this is that the stations determine the properties of those who stand within them, but without doubt, the highest of all groups themselves determine the properties. They are not determined by properties....

This belongs to no human being except the Muḥammadans.... Hence the possessors of stations are those whose aspirations have become limited to certain goals and ends. When they reach those goals, they find in their hearts other, new goals, and these goals which they have reached become the beginning stages for other goals. Hence the goals determine their properties, since they seek them, and such is their situation forever.

But the Muḥammadan has no such property and witnesses no goal. His vastness is the vastness of the Real, and the Real has no goal in Himself which His Being [or Consciousness] might ultimately reach. The Real is witnessed by the Muḥammadan, so he has no ultimate goal in his witnessing. But other than the Muḥammadan witnesses his own possibility. Hence he stands in a state or station which, in his eyes, may come to an end, or change, or cease to exist. He sees this as the ultimate goal of knowledge of God.... [But] the Muḥammadan has no ultimate goal in mind which he might reach.[25]

And in another section, he concludes:

The most all-inclusive specification is that a person not be delimited by a station whereby he is distinguished. So the Muḥammadan is only distinguished by the fact that he has no station specifically. His station is the station of no station. The meaning of this is as follows: A man may be dominated by his state so that he knows only by means of it, is attributed to it, and is designated by it. But the relationship of the stations to the Muḥammadan is like the relationship of the names to God. He does not become designated by a station which is attributed to him. On the contrary, in every breath, at every moment, and in every state, he takes the form which is required by that breath, moment, and state. Hence his delimitation does not last. For the divine properties are diverse at every moment, and he is diverse in accordance with their diversity.[26]

Thus, the Muḥammadan does not hold a static belief or concept of reality, nor does he or she reside in a particular station of enlightenment or attainment; but rather these most perfect of Knowers perpetually transform with and perfectly respond to "every breath, moment, and state." As Shaykh Ibrahim writes, "Allah may manifest in a tree, but the next moment, this manifestation may move to another tree, or something else.

The manifestations of Allah are constantly evolving and never at a standstill.... Allah says in the Qur'an, *You see the mountains you deem to be solid, but they are moving like clouds* (27:88)."²⁷

A similar notion can be seen within the descriptions Ifa gives of Ọrunmila, one of whose praise names is Afedefẹyọ, or "fluent in every language." Through divination and the symbolic language of the Odu, Ọrunmila speaks the language of everyone who comes to him, according to the conditions of the moment or state—this is the function and goal of the best of babalawo. Moreover, in one Odu, Ọrunmila is described as "having no bones," and another Odu describes the mythical figure of Setiu, who introduced Ifa divination to the Yoruba as "a Nupe man without bones in his body," while some babalawo gloss another one of Ọrunmila's titles, Agbọnniregun, as "the wise man with no bones."²⁸ This description of Ọrunmila as "boneless," can be interpreted as referring to the fluid, dynamic, and supra-formal nature of his knowledge, and Ọrunmila himself. One can also say that his speaking every language is a function of his embodiment of perfect knowledge, which implies possessing exactly what every situation requires and allows him to perform the sacred function of the perfect oracle.

Similarly, some babalawo gloss the name Olodumare as a contraction of *Olo odu ọṣumare*, "the owner of the pot of the rainbow serpent,"²⁹ and in some Odu, Ọrunmila is closely associated with Ọṣumare, the oriṣa of the rainbow, who is sometimes represented as a serpent eating its own tail (like the Greek *ouroboros*). One verse of Odu Ọsẹ-Ogbe describes Ọrunmila as the child of Ọṣumare, the rainbow, while other verses describe Ẹla (understood as the heavenly aspect of Ọrunmila) as a pure, unseen light, from which the differentiated lights of the rainbow, Ọṣumare, emerges. The union of all colors in the rainbow and the "numinous light" of Ẹla/Ọrunmila, as well as the circularity of the rainbow serpent, Ọṣumare, recall this transcendent form of knowledge.

The same symbolism is suggested by one of the most common symbols on the divining tray, the chameleon (*agẹmọ*). His ability to take on the color of his surroundings and see in all directions at once, as well as his infinitely spiraling tail, all recall this infinite, dynamic receptivity. Moreover, the chameleon frequently appears in the Odu Ifa as a messenger or servant of Olodumare, Ọrunmila, or Oriṣanla, the god of white cloth. In a verse from Odu Ogbe-Yẹku, Oriṣanla gets into a dispute with Olokun, the goddess of the seas, over who should rule the land. They decide to settle their dispute by seeing who has more cloth. Ọrunmila performs divination for Oriṣanla and tells him to treat his servant, the chameleon, well, since he will be the key to his victory. At the appointed time, instead of going out to meet Olokun himself, Oriṣanla sends the chameleon to lay in wait for her in the bushes. Every time Olokun comes out with a new bundle of colorful cloth, the chameleon would snatch it away with his quick tongue. After this happened several times, Olokun realized what was happening, but by this point, the chameleon had more clothes than she did, so she gave up, declaring, "Orișanla, you must surely be the ruler of the land! If I cannot defeat the apprentice, how could I ever defeat the master?"[30]

In this myth, the supra-formal wisdom that transcends color, represented by Orișanla, the god of white cloth, is able to take on and demonstrate its superiority to the multiple forms of manifest knowledge, perspectives, or beliefs, represented by Olokun, the goddess of the boundless seas and her vast collection of colorful cloth. This is achieved through the mediation of Agẹmọ who, like Ọrunmila, like the Muḥammadan, is capable of taking on any cloth, any color, any form.[31] As the "witness of creation" and "second to Olodumare" Ọrunmila is understood to comprehend all of the orișa, indeed everything in creation. Hence, he is praised as:

> He who knows you never dies
> Lord, the unopposable king
> Perfect in the house of wisdom
> My Lord, whose knowledge is without end
> Not knowing you fully, we [our lives] are in vain
> If we could but know you in full, all would be well[32]

Thus the position of Ọrunmila and the babalawo compared to the other orișa (from the perspective of Ifa) is like that of the Prophet Muḥammad and the Muḥammadans compared to the other prophets and messengers (from the perspective of Sufism). Ibn 'Arabi writes:

> The perfect friend calls upon God in every station and tongue, but the messengers—who are many—stop with that which was revealed to them. What has been revealed to one of them may not have been revealed to another. But the Muḥammadan gathers together through his level every call that has been dispersed among the messengers. Hence he is non-delimited because he calls with every tongue. For he is commanded to have faith in the messengers and that which was sent down to them [Qur'an 2:136]. So the Muḥammadan friend does not stop with a specific revelation.[33]

Likewise, the babalawo know and can communicate with—and on behalf of—all the orișa; they can "call with every tongue" (*Afedefẹyọ*) and understand from every perspective.

In general, Ifa has less of a soteriological or even explicitly goal-based orientation than Tijani Sufism. Outwardly, babalawo study and practice Ifa in order for their lives (and the world) to go well, so they do not run afoul of their destinies (*ori*). Inwardly, they do so because the study and practice of Ifa is simply the performance of their destinies (*ori*). However, as seen above, in some of its deepest formulations, Tijani Sufism similarly advocates a "goal of no goal": there is nowhere to arrive since we are all already there, or the goal is to give up all of one's goals.³⁴ As Shaykh Ibrahim writes, "Whoever wants nothing except what God wants, he is a true servant of God. The Knower [*'ārif*] is he who has left his own desires for the desire of the Real."³⁵

**Why Practice?**

Here we come to a variation of the question famously asked by the founder of one of the major schools of Japanese Zen Buddhism, Dogen (d. 1253): "If all beings are inherently enlightened, then why do the enlightened beings work so hard to attain enlightenment and keep practicing after they have attained it?" In other words, "If there is no goal, or we are already identical with the goal, then why do all of these practices?" The Tijani tradition offers a number of answers to this question. First, according to Shaykh al-Tijānī and Shaykh Ibrahim, the intention or foundation of the acts of worship should be one of disinterested *shukr* or gratitude, not out of any desire to attain anything, even spiritual enlightenment (*fath*). Shaykh Ibrahim derides this functional approach to spiritual practice as "a depravity of the depravities of the *nafs* [ego] that one should worship and invoke God with the expectation of obtaining by that, the opening/enlightenment [*fath*]."³⁶ Instead he advocates that God be worshipped simply "for His own sake"— that is, one should simply worship God because He is who He is, and we are who we are, and by virtue of this, one accepts and is pleased with whatever God grants one. Elsewhere, Shaykh Ibrahim says that one should ask "Allah for Allah":

> The only thing that can truly satisfy the servant of Allah is the possession of Allah Himself. May Allah grant us His Person. May Allah give us Himself. Indeed Allah has promised this to those of us who request it. As humans, our needs are certainly exceptional. We need nothing less than Allah Himself. Other living things are not even aware of the existence of such a need or desire, so their hearts are at rest. The one who is awake—whose heart's eye is open—becomes enraptured by the beauty of Allah's Countenance and longs for nothing else. Allah said, "I created man and made him weak." This weakness is the individual's admiration, his love, and longing for Allah, which creates in him an infinite need for Him. What is left for the people of knowledge? We want only Allah.³⁷

However, even this desire is to be abandoned or is subsumed in desiring only what God desires. If God desires the feeling of distance or the apparent absence of *ma'rifa* and realization, then, paradoxically, this is what the true Knower desires.[38] In the broader tradition of Sufi poetry this is often compared to a devoted lover who prefers separation to union, if that is what his beloved desires, since a true lover follows the desires of his beloved instead of his own.[39]

This point—that the apparent distance from God is actually a form of nearness to Him, since God is both the Outward (*al-Ẓāhir*) and the Inward (*al-Bāṭin*), and that even the seeming veils of ignorance are nothing other than His self-disclosures of Himself to Himself[40]—points to another response of the Tijani tradition to Dogen's question: namely, the union of practice (*sulūk*) and realization (*taḥqīq/wuṣūl*). Ultimately, the attainment of *ma'rifa* is really just God revealing Himself to Himself through Himself, and so, ultimately, there is no separation between the process of acquiring *ma'rifa* and the *ma'rifa* itself. Furthermore, from this perspective, there is no distinction between the process of coming to Know, the Knower, the Knowledge, and the Known. All are God. Shaykh Ibrahim alludes to this "union of practice and realization" in the following passages: "Remembrance/invocation [*dhikr*] is the beginning of sanctity, the beginning and the end of sanctity, there is remembrance/invocation at the beginning and at the end always. The end is always in the beginning, where the beginning is, there, too, is the end. If the beginning is correct, the end will also be correct. Our beginning is 'there is no god but He,' 'there is no god but You,' and 'there is no god but I.' God, to Him you are returning, while you say, 'there is no god but God'";[41] and "'You don't will unless God, the Lord of the worlds, so wills' [81:29]. . . . So he conforms himself to the commands of God for God, from God, by God, and no movement or stillness remains for him except by the command of God, for God, and by God. . . . Before being enraptured, wayfaring [*sulūk*] is a veil, and after, it is a perfection."[42]

Once the veil of individual existence and effort has been lifted and the disciple realizes that all his efforts are from God and toward God, his practice or wayfaring ceases to be a veil and becomes a perfection. This suggests a third response to Dogen's question: that practice is simply the outward expression of inward realization. If one has inwardly realized the "station of no station" of the Muḥammadan, then one's outward actions will simply be those of the *sunna* (example) and *sharī'a* (law and way) of the Prophet. From this perspective, the practices of Islam and Sufism are just the manifestation of this ideal mode of being in the plane of outward actions. As the previously quoted Sufi saying attributed to the Prophet asserts, "The *Sharī'a* is my speech, the *Ṭarīqa* is my acts and the *Ḥaqīqa* is my state."[43] Thus one could say that before realization, one prays on the way to achieving annihilation (*fanā'*) in God and the Prophet; and afterward, in *baqā'*, God and the Prophet pray through one, and one realizes that this was the case all along. As the famous adage attributed to Rumi goes, "For years I knocked at the door, but when it finally opened, I found I had been knocking from the inside!"[44]

While questions such as these are more foreign to the climate of Ifa, certain verses of the Odu Ifa can be read as alluding to similar points, such as this one from Odu Ọkanran-Oturupọn: "It is through learning Ifa that one understands Ifa. It is by missing one's way that one becomes acquainted with the way. It is the road that one has not walked before that makes one wander here and there."[45] The previously cited verses from Odu Ogbe-Atẹ (and others) on the perpetuity or renewal of initiation through practice also can be interpreted in this light:

> Now, if I have completed my initiation
> I will renew my initiation
> The taboos that have been given to me
> I will accept
> I have been initiated
> I will renew my initiation[46]

Remembering that Ifa initiation involves a profound moment of "realization" in the initiates' encounter with his own *ori*, this initiatory realization is then prolonged through practice, by living out one's *ori* or destiny.

Thus, both traditions appear to claim that if you follow in the footsteps of the founders of the tradition (Ọrunmila for Ifa; the Prophet Muḥammad, Shaykh Aḥmad al-Tijānī, and Shaykh Ibrahim for Tijani Sufism), you will attain an ideal mode of being that grants you true knowledge of yourself, your origin and destiny, and the Divine Reality of Olodumare or *al-Ḥaqq*. Ibn ʿArabi writes:

> Here a certain question arises: how does the person who has the aptitude for the state of gnosis understand his own reality? It is answerable in this way: It is necessary that he finds a gnostic who knows his own self and after he has found him, from the bottom of his heart, and with all his soul, make his character to be his character. The person of gnosis, to find his own origin, should hold on to this way and the following Qurʾanic verse points to this meaning: "Search for the means that will take you to Him" [5:35]. The explanation of this may be as follows: There are of My servants those who have found Me. If you want to find Me follow in their footsteps. They become a means for you and they finally lead to Me. If this is so, then by serving those people, a person comes to know himself. He will understand whence he came and where he is going, and he will have an inkling of the station of the present state.[47]

It is from the "perspective of no perspective" of this ideal mode of being that the founders and realized masters of Sufism and Ifa elaborate theories of metaphysics, cosmology, and anthropology: descriptions of the metacosm (Divine Reality), macrocosm (the world[s]), and microcosm (the self) that are intimately related to the "Book" (the Qur'an in Tijani Sufism) or "Word" (ọrọ and/or the Odu of Ifa) that contain and describe all three.

**Metaphysics/Cosmology/Anthropology**

In this "theoanthropocosmic" perspective that characterizes both Ifa and Tijani Sufism, there is a close symbolic relationship between God, humanity, the cosmos, and the Divine "Word" or "Book" that describes and provides the key to understanding these realities and the relationships among them. As Awo Faniyi explained, "Man is a small world, everything in the world, all the powers of the world exist inside him,"[48] and similarly, Shaykh Ibrahim explained, "There are some who say man is a small world (microcosm), but in reality, he is the large world (macrocosm) since all the worlds are contained in him."[49] In the same vein, all the babalawo I interviewed affirmed that all knowledge and every thing is in, and was created through, the Odu of Ifa, while Shaykh Ibrahim quotes the verse "We have left nothing out in the Book" (6:38) to demonstrate that the Qur'an similarly contains all knowledge of every thing.[50]

From the "perspective of no perspective" described above, God, the Self, the world, and the Divine Word/Book appear as so many reflections of the same ineffable reality, as different perspectives or windows onto that which is both Being and Consciousness, that which is at once knowledge, knower, and known. Thus the different levels or aspects of the self/consciousness described in both traditions (*inu-ode* in Ifa and *bāṭin-ẓāhir* [among others] in Tijani Sufism) correspond to levels of reality, and to levels of meaning, interpretation, and understanding of the Odu Ifa and the Qur'an. In this way, learning the Odu Ifa or the Qur'an grants one a better understanding of God, oneself, and the world; knowing God grants one an understanding of oneself, the world, and Odu Ifa / the Qur'an; and so on, through all the other possible permutations. As Andrew Apter notes, "The 'levels' of knowledge in Yoruba ritual are in fact infinitely deep and polyvocal, grounded in the hermeneutical axiom: 'Secret surpasses secret, secret can swallow secret completely.'"[51]

In both traditions, this multidimensional reality is synthesized into something akin to what Ibn 'Arabi calls "The Perfect Human" (*al-Insān al-Kāmil*), the fullness of the realization of the unity of God, Self, cosmos, and Divine Word/Book. In Ifa this "Perfect Human" is Ọrunmila/Ẹla, who is identified with the Odu of Ifa, with the entire world, with the *ori* or innermost self of babalawo, and—from a certain perspective—with Olodumare (given that he possesses all of the knowledge of Olodumare). In Tijani Sufism, this "Perfect Human" is the Muḥammadan reality (*al-ḥaqīqa al-Muḥammadiyya*) and its manifestations in the persons of the Prophet, Shaykh Aḥmad al-Tijānī, and Shaykh Ibrahim.

Shaykh Ibrahim describes this reality as follows: "In a *Ḥadīth Qudsī*, Allah says, 'If not for you, O Muḥammad, I would not have brought forth the creation. I created you for Myself and I created the rest of creation for you.... All of creation—believers and nonbelievers, the heavens and the earth—came from his light and his light came from Allah."[52] Similarly, in a narrative of Eji Ogbe, Olodumare creates the world for, at the request of, and through the Odu of, Orunmila.[53] When the babalawo memorize and internalize the Odu, which are like the "alphabet" of existence, they acquire *imo ijinlẹ* ("deep knowledge"); like Orunmila, they acquire principial knowledge of God, the world, and the self, and can "read" them at will. Orunmila became Orunmila by eating *Igba Iwa* (calabash of wisdom/existence/character) and acquiring all of Olodumare's knowledge. He found this calabash by using his feet to search for it in the waters of the river separating heaven and earth, which, remembering the symbolic meaning of feet/legs (*ẹsẹ*) in Ifa as struggle or effort, can be understood as the internal, hidden struggle through ritual practice and contemplation to achieve wisdom. This struggle takes place beneath the surface of the ever-changing river of the inner self (*inu*), which is the boundary between the world (*aye*) and heaven (*ọrun*).

When babalawo similarly acquire the Igba Iwa through internalization of the Odu, through initiation in the *igbodu*, they become like Orunmila and can see and know like him. Similarly, when Tijanis acquire *ma'rifa* through internalizing the Qur'an / the Prophet through *tarbiya*, they become annihilated in the Prophet and both know and know like him. Then from this perspective, the sages of Ifa and Tijani Sufism describe these realities through the elaborate and intricately connected descriptions and accounts of metaphysics/theology (What is real? / Who is God?), cosmology (What is the world?), and psychology/anthropology (Who am I? / What is human?), usually through interpretation of the descriptions already contained in the Odu or the Qur'an and ḥadīth (which are themselves understood to be accounts emanating from this central reality of Orunmila for Ifa and the Muḥammadan reality for Tijani Sufism).

The ritual nature and function of these inspired descriptions and revealed accounts (which can involve all kinds of forms: poems, songs, prayers, bodily positions and dispositions, as well as written and oral texts in Tijani Sufism and dances, music, sculpture, and complicated ritual procedures in Ifa) is of the utmost importance. They are not merely meant to describe or represent reality, but are meant to symbolize and be used ritually to lead initiates back to the profound reality from which they come. The Odu of Ifa, their signs, verses, rituals, implements and *oriki* of Orunmila—are all identified with Ifa/Orunmila (that is why they are all called Ifa), and are understood to come from and lead back to him. Similarly, the *Ṣalāt al-Fātiḥ*, the Qur'an, and the various rites and rituals of Islam are identified with, and understood as coming from and leading back to, the Muḥammadan reality, and this identity is "proved" through various numerical and other symbolisms and correspondences.[54] In the words of Ifa, these "inspired descriptions" are meant to "bring heaven down to the world" and "take the world back to heaven."

### Aṣẹ/Baraka

As a result, these descriptions are understood to transmit the presence and power of the Divine. Telling certain Ifa narratives, even in English, is believed to have ritual consequences, which can range from angering the oriṣa to spoiling shrines, to driving away or attracting certain influences. Reciting verses of Ifa in Yoruba is believed to be even more potent, and certain verses can put people into a trance, others are used to sacrifice animals without touching them, while other verses are used to assist in childbirth (and babalawo are careful not to recite them around pregnant women for fear of inducing labor). Interestingly, within various traditions of Sufism (including those found in West Africa), these same functions are also shared by certain verses of the Qur'an and other Islamic talismanic preparations.[55] Many Tijanis carry copies of Shaykh Ibrahim's book *The Removal of Confusion* with them as protection when traveling, as many Muslims do with the Qur'an. In Ifa, the markings of the Odu and the camwood powder in which Odu are pressed are used for a variety of purposes including protection, blessing, healing, destroying enemies, etc. and are an essential part of many of the sacrifices prescribed by Ifa divination.

This presence and power that animates this kind of ritual is known as *aṣẹ* in Ifa (and in Yoruba more generally). *Aṣẹ* is understood as the power of the presence of Olodumare (*agbara ọdọ Olodumare*), the divine sanction or creative power that brings things to pass. "*Aṣẹ*" is the refrain repeated during prayers, and is used to translate the Christian "amen" and the Islamic "*amīn*." This is very similar to the concept of *baraka* in Sufism, and Islam in general, which is generally understood as an aspect or manifestation of sacred presence associated with a person, place, or tangible thing. Different people and places have different degrees and kinds of *baraka*, as Shaykh Ibrahim explains, "in reality Allah is everywhere, but His manifestations vary in degrees from one place to another."[56] Olodumare flows through everything in the cosmos via *aṣẹ*, and God's manifestation of Himself in every place and thing grants them their *baraka*. It is this *aṣẹ* or *baraka* that is the domain or subject of the various esoteric or occult sciences of Ifa and Tijani Sufism that manipulate combinations of actions, words, objects, flora, and fauna in order to achieve a particular effect in the soul or in the world. The flows of *aṣẹ* and *baraka* are both governed by the intricate symbolic relationships between

Divine Reality, the world, the self, and the Divine Word/Book, often in the form of letters, words, numbers, shapes, and elements of the natural world.

However, the sciences of symbolic correspondence associated with both traditions can and are used for baser purposes, such as acquiring power, or even hurting, seducing, and killing people. However, in recent years, this "dark side" of both traditions appears to be most commonly used to amass wealth. In Nigeria, politicians are particularly known to patronize these "dark arts," known as *oogun ika* ("wicked medicine") in Yoruba. However, both Tijani *shuyūkh* and babalawo view such disciplines as being "outside" their traditions and strongly condemn their use in no uncertain terms. For example, in an interview with the Nigerian newspaper *Punch*, the popular Araba of Oṣogbo, Yẹmi Ẹlẹbuibọn, answers the following blunt question:

Reporter: Have you killed anybody with your charms before?
Ẹlẹbuibọn: Why will I kill anybody? I don't do that, I have never killed anybody and I will never kill. You see, Babalawo don't kill. Although Babalawo have an immense power, they are capable of doing so many things, but killing is against the rules in this religion. There are things that are forbidden here. It is wrong to blame killings on the doorstep of Babalawo. Those involved in killing may be *oloogun-ika* [those who use "wicked medicine"]. Babalawo are priests, just like you have Catholic priests, Imams. We don't use Ifa divination and sacrifice to kill. Sacrifices are offered for atonement, for healing of diverse diseases and ailments. But all the religions have some parts they can use to do evil things. There are portions like that used by some wicked Muslims and also the Seven Books of Moses are used by some Christians to do evil. All the religions have positive and their negatives uses.[57]

Shaykh Aḥmad al-Tijānī and Shaykh Ibrahim were even more strict when it came to the use of these *asrār* (secrets), even for seemingly "laudable" ends, forbidding their use in virtually all cases, save for those complete Knowers whose individual wills have been completely surrendered to the Divine. In a letter to a disciple who had figured out an elaborate "secret"—a complicated talismanic diagram believed to have great power—and sent it to him, Shaykh Ibrahim wrote, "As for those who occupy themselves with the esoteric sciences ['ulūm al-sirr], which Shaykh al-Tijānī described as sciences of evil ['ulūm al-sharr], they would arrogate this diagram to themselves, drawing it for people seeking the ephemeral things of this world. This is like selling the religion for the world. I forbid myself and I forbid you to draw this for anybody. I do not give permission for this, and I do not give permission, verily I do not give permission!"[58]

## Modernity and the Nature of the Contemporary Time

Both Tijani Sufism and Ifa seem to have a "tale of two cities" evaluation of the contemporary situation: "It is the best times, it is the worst of times." Both traditions have a generally conservative view of history and time: the world (and the people in it) were at its best when it was closest to God/heaven, and this closeness was at its greatest in the mythical time after creation, of the earliest ancestors, and during the time of the founders of the tradition (the Prophet/Qrunmila and the orisa). Thus, each generation is generally thought to be superior to the one that follows it, being closer to the source or origin. However, within Ifa, the more cyclical, mythical understanding of time implies that, from a certain perspective, one never leaves this mythical time. However, the Yoruba saying "We met Ifa when we came to the world. We met Islam when we came to the world. It was at noon that Christianity arrived on the scene" alludes to the fact that many babalawo regard the colonial encounter as a kind of unprecedented qualitative change in (and descent into) time. In the Islamic tradition, this general decline is interrupted by periods of renewal (*tajdīd*).[59] Similarly, Shaykh Aḥmad al-Tijānī and Shaykh Ibrahim presented themselves and their spiritual traditions as "renewers," reversing the general decline of history.[60]

The followers of Shaykh Ibrahim commonly described the present time as one of "corruption" and "the greatest spiritual difficulty," conditions that are compensated for by the *fayḍa* of Shaykh Ibrahim.[61] Because of this "flood of *maʿrifa*," however, the present time was also often described as one of renewal, as "the best time in the history of humankind after the Prophet's time." Disciples cited the dearth of spiritual guidance, the difficulties of practicing Islam in a world that is no longer of its making, as well as the religious and political oppression of the colonial and postcolonial states around the world as the difficult conditions for which the *fayḍa* is a compensation.

The twentieth- and twenty-first-century explosion of technology and technical knowledge was often described as the complement or sign (*ayah*) or even result of the *fayḍa*'s explosion of mystical knowledge. Many of these explanations took the following form: "Before, it took you years of hard traveling to make ḥajj, to go to Mecca and come back; now, you can fly there in a plane in a few hours. That is a sign [*ayah*] for what Shaykh Ibrahim brought. Before, it would take you years of hard work and discipline to attain *maʿrifa*, now with the *tarbiya* of Shaykh Ibrahim people arrive in a few weeks, days, or even hours."[62] Nevertheless, the ambivalence of this "acceleration of time" was also recognized, with several disciples commenting that "in this time, there is no time." Shaykh Ibrahim is even reported as saying that "these technologies will one day bring about the End of Time."[63]

Nevertheless, many Tijani disciples in Dakar pointed out to another condition of postcolonial Senegal that gave many young disciples ample time for spiritual practice: unemployment. One disciple half-jokingly told me, "There are no jobs, no good work for people with degrees, so you have nothing better to do, why not try *tarbiya* and spend all your time with your *kurus* [prayer beads], going to *gammus*, et cetera. It doesn't cost much and it's not like you have anything better to do, you can only drink so much tea and play so much football and watch so many movies."[64] Shaykh Ibrahim's branch of the Tijāniyya is also especially popular among urban youth in Senegal in large part due to the rapid and direct access to *maʿrifa* that *tarbiya* promises and the resulting "democratization" of mystical knowledge: a young disciple with no formal training in Arabic or the Islamic sciences can be considered "senior" to, or a "more advanced" Knower (*ʿārif*) than, an elder who has studied and practiced for years, but has not gone through *tarbiya*. In certain ways, the tradition's emphasis on rapid, individual, and "empirical" verification (*taḥqīq*) of the meanings of the Qurʾan, ḥadīth, and the Tijani tradition itself, bear some resonances with certain elements of post-Enlightenment, Western scientific and intellectual traditions—and, thus, exposure to these originally Western modes of thought and life may account for some of the remarkable appeal of this tradition in contemporary West Africa and the diaspora.

Similarly, as J. D. Y. Peel and J. Lorand Matory have noted, due to its relative similarity to modern Christian traditions (as compared with other oriṣa traditions, Ifa has a "scripture" of sorts, and a mostly male, professional "priesthood" that spends much of its time memorizing and interpreting said "scripture"), Ifa was more easily legible to and more easily fit into the modern category of "religion" by missionaries, colonial administrators, and Western-educated Yorubas, many of whom emphasized these similarities in order to secure recognition and prestige for Ifa and "Yoruba civilization." These dynamics contributed in no small part to Ifa's current prominence in both practice in and academic literature about Nigeria and much (though not all) of the diaspora.[65]

However, several Tijani *shuyūkh* also described the difficulties presented by the encounter with Western education and ideologies. One Mauritanian shaykh told me how he had stopped praying and was a committed secular, Marxist revolutionary until he read Shaykh Ibrahim's *Removal of Confusion*;[66] while others described their interest in modern French philosophy, especially existentialism, Marxism, and *négritude*. All of these *shuyūkh* described their coming to Shaykh Ibrahim's tradition as a "return." Ustadh Barham Diop described these people as "the generation of people who went abroad to France to be educated, but came back to their tradition,"[67] and this encounter is perhaps most fully described in Cheikh Hamidou Kane's *Ambiguous Adventure*.[68]

Shaykhs and disciples more commonly complained of the difficulties caused by modern Salafi and Salafi-inspired movements and propaganda, which they claimed led to misunderstandings of Sufism, the Tijāniyya, Shaykh Ibrahim, and even Islam in general. These misunderstandings were characterized as being "modern," and as coming from those who have little contact with or grounding in "tradition," and who were thus stuck on the outward surface of things (*al-ẓāhir*). However, shaykhs do not seem to advise disciples to avoid Western education or technology but rather encourage engagement with it. According to his son, Muḥammad al-Makkī (who studied in Egypt), Shaykh Ibrahim was initially reluctant to send his children to study abroad in the Middle East, because he feared they would be negatively influenced by the growing Salafi presence there, but eventually decided they would be fine and sent many of his children, disciples, and grandchildren to study the Islamic sciences, Arabic literature, and modern disciplines abroad in Egypt, Morocco, France, the United Kingdom, and the United States. Shaykh Muḥammad al-Makkī also explained to me that Shaykh Ibrahim was always keen to learn about and use the latest technologies, such as radio and cassette recorders, in order to spread his message and to help his disciples—and the tradition—adapt to the changing times.[69]

For the Tijani disciples I interviewed, modernity was characterized by a dominance of the outward (*al-ẓāhir*), the acceleration of time, changes in lifestyle and labor, and encounters with Western and Western-influenced ideas and ideologies. These extraordinary challenges were met with the extraordinary occurrence of the *fayḍa* and the adaptations to spiritual training and religious education brought by and through Shaykh Ibrahim and his community.[70]

Babalawo also seemed to bemoan the current state of affairs, using the English word "modernism" or the Yoruba word *ọlaju* ("civilization") to describe a Western-influenced mode of life, education, religious practice, and outlook that, in the words of the Araba of Modakẹkẹ, "makes people greedy and stupid" and "not serious."[71] Virtually all of the babalawo complained that there are no babalawo living today who could compare with those of the past few generations, and in the Araba's words, "the real babalawo are getting old and dying, and the young ones, very few of them are serious."[72] Western education and the new modes of life and thought it facilitates, coupled with the demonization of Ifa by evangelical Christians and some Muslims, have made times more difficult for babalawo, and have made the already arduous process of becoming a babalawo even less appealing to potential apprentices. As the Araba explained, "There is only one God, and that God is the same God that sent Ọrunmila and sent Musulumi [the Prophet of Islam] into the world. But many Muslims [and Christians], they do not have that understanding, and because of this modernism, people just believe that, 'no, what I'm doing should be the best.' This is a big problem for many people today."[73]

Moreover, babalawo complained that this "greed and stupidity" typical of "modernism" had corrupted many of their own ranks, producing a bumper crop of charlatans who deceive and fleece people. The babalawo I interviewed characterized the contemporary time as one of extreme confusion and disarray, a breakdown of the normal order, in which the life of a righteous babalawo is much more difficult than that of a careless and corrupt one. Moreover, the proliferation, prominence, and notoriety of these impostors and corrupt babalawo, combined with the denunciation of Ifa by Christians and Muslims, has seriously eroded the support for and respect of babalawo among the general populace, especially in urban areas.

The dwindling community support for babalawo and other *oloriṣa* is a substantial threat to their traditions, as many of their important rituals require substantial communal investment and support. However, the growing influx of foreigners coming to Nigeria to learn about and be initiated into Ifa has brought significant support, money, and prestige to the babalawo. This has led some Nigerians to reevaluate their opinion of Ifa. Independently, however, many younger Nigerians—feeling dissatisfied with (post)colonial modernity and what they perceive as the inherent racism and "foreignness" of secular, Christian, and Muslim traditions—have turned to Ifa and other orisa traditions as a "return" to an "authentic, African" spiritual way of life. The Araba even told me about reports across Yorubaland from babalawo and Muslim non-babalawo that "Orunmila has been telling people that he is coming back. In dreams he is telling them this. He is coming back among his followers, not physically, but spiritually. That is why so many people are coming from all over the world to learn Ifa—it is Orunmila inside of them that is making them want to study Ifa. Orunmila is coming back and they are coming back to Ifa."[74]

Although outside the scope of the current project, Ifa also contains several fascinating critiques of colonial modernity, usually in the form of describing Europeans and their "belief," Christianity (*igbagbọ*). In one such narrative from Odu Eji Ogbe, white people (*oyinbo*) are described as *ọmọ aṣogun dere* or "the children of those who made Ogun into an idol."[75] In the Yoruba pantheon, Ogun is the voracious god of war, iron, technology, and progress. He is often described as clearing the brush with his iron cutlass, and he is so violently ravenous that he can consume anything placed before him, even his friends and family. While this highly evocative description is deserving of further attention, it seems that in their early experience with Europeans the sages of Ifa recognized the violent, technologically fueled worship of progress and described it in the language of "making Ogun become an idol."[76]

Being a babalawo was, and is, a full-time profession for most practitioners, but the exigencies of contemporary Nigerian life (and/or their own proclivities and destinies) have led some babalawo to take "day jobs" as professors, bank clerks, artists, and businessmen. This is, however, considered neither normative nor ideal.[77] While being a Sufi shaykh was seldom considered a profession in and of itself, many *shuyūkh* in western Africa traditionally earned their living through serving as the imam of a mosque, as *qāḍīs* or *fuqahā'* (judges or jurists), scholars and teachers of the Qur'an, Arabic, or other Islamic sciences; doctors and "occult specialists"; or as traders and farmers. Many *shuyūkh* in the precolonial and colonial periods performed all of these professions at once. However, the spiritual leadership of some Sufi *shuyūkh* was combined with political and economic leadership so that, by virtue of their status as a shaykh, many Sufi masters were also the founders and heads of sizeable polities and networks of people. The demands of these functions often precluded them from having a separate career, and the contributions of their followers provided for their expenses.

In contemporary times, shaykhs of the *fayḍa* seem to roughly fall into one of three categories with regard to their professional lives. The first group makes their living as government officials, professors, businessmen, administrators, and shopkeepers, and their status as a shaykh may not be immediately apparent. The second group makes their living teaching the Qur'an or other Islamic sciences, or as occult specialists, and while their professional work may overlap with their role as spiritual master (they may have students who are also disciples), these roles are largely distinct and their identity as a shaykh may or may not be public. The third group makes their living as Sufi *shuyūkh*, they devote themselves full-time to the spiritual training of disciples, spreading the *ṭarīqa*, giving public lectures at *gammus*, appearing on television and radio, and writing, editing, and publishing works on the doctrines and history of Tijāniyya and Shaykh Ibrahim. The work of this third group is supported by their disciples, followers and devotees, and sometimes grants from governments and international organizations.

Thus, both traditions explicitly recognize a similar set of challenges of colonial and (post)colonial modernity, but both traditions—especially the Tijanis of the *fayḍa*—also emphasize the unique advantages of this latest dispensation. It is the "worst of times" in terms of the material, cultural, intellectual, and spiritual assault of modernity and its associated ideologies, but it is also the "best of times"—due to the increased connectivity and ease (in certain domains) that characterize modernity, and the special conditions of the *fayḍa* in Tijani Sufism. I doubt many babalawo would refer to the current situation as "the best of times," but the rumored "spiritual return of Ọrunmila" in Ifa and the increased numbers of people from around the world coming to Nigeria for initiation are regarded by some as something of a compensation. Both traditions have creatively adapted to the rapidly changing conditions of contemporary times in order to provide their initiates access to the "timeless truths" that are their foundation and raison d'être.[78] As such, I believe these traditions have much to offer contemporary academic institutions as they move into a new period of closer contact and connection with non-Western intellectual traditions. It is important to remember that neither Ifa nor Tijani Sufism are small, local sects, but rather global traditions with tens of millions of adherents scattered across every inhabited continent. In fact, one estimate puts the number of people in Shaykh Ibrahim's branch of the Tijāniyya alone at over one hundred million.[79]

## COMPARISON WITH CONTEMPORARY ACADEMIC PERSPECTIVES

> The encounter between African and European had been abrupt,
> not so much in historical terms as in philosophical ones.
> —Cedric Robinson

> To know is to possess and any fact is
> possessed by everyone who knows it,
> whereas those who feel the truth are possessed, not possessors.
> —E. E. CUMMINGS

> *Aye l'a ba 'Fa*
> *Aye l'a ba 'mọle*
> *ọsan gangan ni 'gbagbọ wọle de*
>
> We met Ifa when we came to the world
> We met Islam when we came to the world
> It was at noon that Christianity arrived on the scene
> —YORUBA PROVERB

> There are two kinds of intelligence.
> One is like that acquired by a child at school,
> from books and teachers, new ideas and memorization.
> Your intelligence may become superior to others,
> but retaining all that knowledge is a heavy load....
> For the other kind of intelligence is the gift of God:
> its fountain is in the midst of the soul.
> —RUMI

As discussed in the first chapter of this book, the theories and worldviews that form a kind of "unarticulated consensus" of most contemporary academic discussions differ significantly from those of Ifa and Tijani Sufism. Moreover, these differences cannot merely be reduced to these traditions having different histories in different places—such a reduction would ignore and subsume the self-proclaimed transhistorical dimensions of Ifa and Sufism into the post-Christian secular historicism that characterizes so much of modern academic thought. Moreover, many of the points on which Ifa and Tijani Sufism (not to mention other oriṣa traditions, or other Sufi orders, or other premodern or non-Western spiritual/intellectual traditions) appear to agree are precisely those points wherein they diverge from or disagree with the various traditions dominant in the Western academy. Many studies that have sought to compare traditional Islamic or indigenous African thought with contemporary Western thought have emphasized the similarities between Western and non-Western traditions, usually in the hopes of winning recognition and validation of these traditions as rising to the level of "rational thought" or "philosophy"—or, more modestly, to demonstrate their "rationality."[80] The more avant-garde works of anthropology have often compared and domesticated the "exotic conceptions" of African thought with the latest trends in postmodern theory—again, often in an attempt to achieve recognition for these African or Islamic traditions.[81] However, in this section, I will take a different approach. I intend to focus on those points where Ifa and Tijani Sufism appear to agree with each other, and disagree with prevailing trends in contemporary academic theory and practice, in order to highlight the limitations of contemporary academic approaches and the ways in which I think the traditions of Ifa and Tijani Sufism can be useful not only in critiquing these limitations, but also in moving beyond them.

### *Theoria* Versus Theory

First and foremost, contemporary academic discussions and works are based on the application and development of "theories," whereas Ifa and Sufism are concerned with the cultivation of what could be (and in the West once was) called *theoria*—a "vision of the truth," a blissful mode of being, knowing, and contemplating reality in its fullness. The former goal is mental and theoretical (and political), whereas the latter, while including the mental, is more encompassing and existential. Hadot differentiates *theoria* from theory using the example of Porphyry: "In the same context, Porphyry insists strongly on the importance of spiritual exercises. The contemplation (*theoria*) which brings happiness, he tells us, does not consist in the accumulation of discourse and abstract teachings [theory], even if their subject is true Being. Rather, we must make sure our studies are accompanied by an effort to make these teachings become 'nature and life' within us."[82]

These fundamentally distinct goals can and have been described in different ways—in St. Augustine's distinction of *scienta* (rational knowledge) and *sapientia* (experiential wisdom); in later Islamic philosophy as "knowledge by representation" (*'ilm al-ḥuṣūlī*) versus "knowledge by presence" (*ʿilm al-ḥuḍūrī*); in Sufism as *ʿilm* or *dirāya* (theoretical knowledge) versus *maʿrifa* or *dhawq* (taste)—and although distinct, this even bears some relationship to the distinctions between *igbagbọ*, *imọ*, and *imọ ijinlẹ* (deep knowledge) in the context of Ifa.[83] All of these traditions privilege the latter over the former. In the Buddhist tradition, this distinction is made through the poetic image of "the finger pointing at the moon." The following verse of Oturupọn Meji can also be interpreted as alluding to this distinction between the limits and futility of merely theoretical knowledge and essential nature of existential self-knowledge (*imọri*):

"No wise man can tie water into a knot at the edges of his garment
No sage knows the number of grains of sand on the earth"
Ifa divination was performed for Ori
And also for Character
Ori we hail you
You who allow children to be born alive
A person whose sacrifice is accepted by Ori
Should rejoice exceedingly[84]

The Sufi tradition also provides us with several rich illustrations of the distinction between the merely theoretical and the existential approaches to knowledge and reality, and the inescapable primacy of the latter. Shabistarī compares those who seek to understand reality through discursive reasoning alone to one who "seeks the blazing sun by the dim light of a torch in the desert"; the early Sufi Abu Bakr al-Wasiṭī said, "If someone says, 'I recognized God through the evidence,' ask him how he recognized the evidence";[85] and Shaykh Tijānī and al-Ghazālī compare *maʿrifa* to health and theory to knowledge of medicine. The same distinction is found in the previously cited discussion of knowing versus being the Greatest Name of God. Theory is like a map of a mountain, while *theoria* is the vision from its summit. The theoretical approach that characterizes contemporary academic work is very useful in its place, but it also has its limits, and implicitly relies on (both historically and epistemologically) a very different approach to knowledge, which has different goals.[86] It is important to remember this distinction when studying traditions such as Ifa and Sufism, so as to not reduce them to mere sets of doctrines, theories, and ideas, interpreting them as some kind of "indigenous" attempt to theorize like modern academics.

Moreover, even when recognizing this distinction, and the fact that these traditions constitute a "way of life," it is important not to subject this *theoria*, the mode of knowing and being of these traditions, to a theory that denies anything beyond its own scope. That is, when presented with a "finger pointing at the moon," scholars should not, on the basis of theories that reject the existence of anything above the trees, reduce the tradition in question to "the finger," and go about their business constructing an elaborate anatomical representation. To paraphrase a poem quoted by Shaykh Ibrahim, "If you have not seen the newborn crescent moon, at least *listen* to those who claim to have seen it."[87] For example, one cannot reduce the tradition of Ifa to its observable practices and doctrines, but must also find a way to take seriously its metaphysical or inner (*inu*) dimensions that lie outside the scope of most modern theories of physics, history, language, and so forth.

Furthermore, this distinction between the *theoria* of traditions such as Ifa and Sufism and the theory of contemporary Western philosophy and academia presents a potentially constructive challenge to the way in which we do academic work. In his *Empty Words*, philosopher Jay Garfield begins one of the chapters with insightful quotes from his Tibetan colleagues and students he encountered during his work in cross-cultural philosophy:

> If Western philosophers don't think that philosophy can lead to liberation from cyclic existence, why do they do it?
> *A question asked by dozens of Tibetan students and colleagues and students*

> I am worried that these students are just getting religious indoctrination. I mean, they are learning Buddhism, right. And aren't most of the teachers monks?
> *A dean of a small Western secular college at which the works of Aquinas, Augustine, Farabi, and Maimonides are taught in philosophy classes, in response to a proposal that students have an opportunity to study Buddhist philosophy at a Tibetan university*

> I can understand why you have come to India to study Buddhist philosophy. For our tradition is indeed deep and vast. But I frankly don't see what we have to learn from you. For Western philosophy is very superficial and addresses no important questions.
> *The Ven. Gen Lobzang Gyatso, director of the Institute of Buddhist Dialectics, in response to an offer of lectures on Western philosophy at his college*[88]

From the standpoint of *theoria*-based traditions such as Sufism and Ifa, modern and postmodern theories of knowledge can never achieve certain or "deep" knowledge of reality as it is. Modern theories of knowledge celebrate the power of a particular mode of reasoning, while postmodern theories celebrate the inescapable contradictions and relativity of this mode of reasoning, but both are limited by the limited scope of their epistemological methods. Ibn ʿArabi and the Tijani and Ifa traditions suggest that it is only through ritual exercises that these epistemic limitations can be overcome. As Peter Coates concludes his study of Ibn ʿArabi's thought in relationship to Western philosophy:

> When Giddens asserts that "modernity is enigmatic at its core, and there seems to be no way the enigma can be 'overcome,'" he is perhaps not only attesting to the inability of the "circularity of reason" to overcome this enigma but implicitly recognizing also the boundaries of reason's "own proper playing field." According to Ibn ʿArabī, it is a kind of progress for reason to recognize its own epistemological boundaries, for it attests to the incapacity of human beings to reach knowledge of the Real via unaided reason. The enigma of modernity can therefore be seen as indicating that we take seriously the possibility of alternative epistemic means.[89]

While I am not suggesting that Western philosophy has "nothing to offer," I am arguing that Western academics should recognize and respect these traditions, and that Western universities should create a space for these traditions to be taught on their own terms,[90] especially given the role that the Western academy has played in destroying and marginalizing many of these traditions, even in their lands of origin. More immediately, the work of our colleagues in more *theoria*-oriented traditions should inspire us to use nondiscursive as well as discursive means in our search for truth, as well as give us pause in the midst of the hustle and bustle of the "grant-and-paper mill" to reflect on why we are doing what we are doing, and what kind of effect we hope our work has on our readers, students, colleagues, families, and, perhaps most importantly, ourselves.

I believe academic work—especially philosophy, the study of religion, and the humanities—can and should combine *dhawq* (taste) and *dirāya* (theoretical knowledge). While I personally know many practicing Sufis and *olorişa* in academia, the vast majority of them feel constrained to write and deliver lectures like white, secular, post-Protestants, even though this does not appear to be the way they think and speak outside these academic performances.[91] Our works can and should be more than maps or representations; they should also be invitations to different ways of seeing and being in the world. This does not mean lapsing into a kind of apologist or dogmatic confessionalism or abandoning the enterprise of critical inquiry. On the contrary, as I hope the previous chapters have demonstrated, the "radical openness" and the "two-eyed" approach of combining reason and imagination advocated and demonstrated by Ibn ʿArabi's ideas is in no way incompatible with critical acumen and can even sharpen it.

In short, I argue that traditions such as Ifa and Tijani Sufism invite us to make our scholarly work about more than bringing new facts and data to light, but also about helping our readers and students reappraise, rediscover, and love "old truths" (perhaps even the "truths" of their "selves"). As Hadot wrote, "Vauvenargues said, 'A truly new and truly original book would be one which made people love old truths.' . . . There are some truths whose meaning will never be exhausted by the generations of man. It is not that they are difficult; on the contrary, they are often extremely simple. Often, they even appear to be banal. Yet for their meaning to be understood, these truths must be *lived*, and constantly re-experienced. Each generation must take up . . . the task of learning to read and to re-read these 'old truths.'"[92] Some of these "old truths" which I believe Ifa and Tijani Sufism can help us love and live again include the identity between knowledge and being and the concomitant "wisdom of the body"; the importance of ritual and community in intellectual work; and finally, the understanding that reality (like nature or the self) is not a passive object of inquiry, but rather an active subject that reveals and conceals itself through its own will.

As the previous chapters demonstrate, both Ifa and Sufism posit an identity, on the highest or most profound level, between knowledge and being. The most direct and trustworthy form of knowledge is self-knowledge, and in this self-knowledge there is no separation between knower, known, and knowledge, thus the knowledge must be identical with the being of the knower and the known. Both traditions posit a kind of loss of this primordial knowledge through the descent into the world of bodies and time. Within Ifa this is symbolized by passing under the "tree of forgetfulness" (*igi igbagbe*), and Shaykh Aḥmad al-Tijānī similarly writes, "The spirit [*rūḥ*] of every human being has been created initially endowed with a conscience and a perfect knowledge of God. An intense degradation then follows, by biological contact with the corporeal substance; and this soul becomes ignorant, losing its original memory."[93] Thus, the process of recovering this knowledge is akin to remembering, to Plato's *anamnesis*,[94] and the masters of these traditions serve as "philosophical midwives," to borrow another metaphor from Plato, to bring out, rear, and cultivate this knowledge within their charges. Certain modes of thought and behavior are more conducive to (or stem from) forgetfulness than the remembrance and self-knowledge that is the goal of these traditions, and so the practice of virtue is inseparable from the acquisition of this knowledge. In fact, one could even say that this knowledge is both the foundation and fruit of lived virtue. Since knowledge and being are ultimately one in these perspectives, true modes of knowledge imply and are identical with true modes of being (virtue), uniting epistemology, ontology, and ethics.[95]

## The Wisdom of the Body

> Secrets [*asrār*] are in the chests [*ṣudūr*] of spiritual heroes [*rijāl*], not in the bellies of books.
> —SHAYKH IBRAHIM NIASSE

> Body is not veiled from soul, nor soul from body
> —RUMI, *Mathnawī*, 1.8

One important corollary of this unity of knowledge and being is the epistemological role of the body, a role that has been relatively neglected and misunderstood in mainstream contemporary academic practices.[96] Although Shaykh Aḥmad al-Tijānī's quote above seems to imply that the body is a cause of the soul's ignorance, and a great deal of Sufi literature describes the body as a kind of "prison" of the soul or spirit, this is only part of the story. One of the characteristics of West African Sufism (and West African traditional religions, and one could even hypothesize African spiritualities in general) is its strongly "embodied" character: its emphasis on the integration of the body into spiritual life and practice, and the immanence of the spirit (*rūḥ*) in, or rather as, the human body both during and after life.[97] Rudolph Ware's *The Walking Qur'an* has demonstrated the centrality and importance of this "embodied epistemology" in West African Qur'anic education in particular and Islamic pedagogy in general.[98]

Much as certain physical postures both express and facilitate certain emotional states (e.g., making yourself smile makes you happier, stretching your arms above your head makes you feel more confident), in both Ifa and Tijani Sufism, certain bodily positions, movements, and embodied ritual actions are understood to both express and facilitate certain inner, spiritual states and knowledge. Thus, the body plays an important role as a support for and ultimately as both a self-disclosure (*tajallī*) and place of manifestation (*maẓhar*) of spiritual/intellectual realization.

Tijani disciples frequently described a physical feeling of being "filled to bursting" or a kind of "heat" during the process of *tarbiya* and afterward. At dinner, one group of disciples in Medina Baye even teased one of their friends who had just completed *tarbiya* by touching him as if he were a hot stove, making hissing noises and waving their fingers in the air as if they had just been burned. Shaykh Ibrahim describes similar bodily sensations accompanying realization in the following poem:

> There I called upon Him with The Greatest Name
> Approaching [Him], seeking guidance, until heat
> Spread out in the center of my breast from my invocations

> And how could it not, as it was filled with lights,
> And with realities and gnoses (*ma'ārif*),
> And the secret of the secret of the secret and Knowledge (*ma'rifa*)
> I carried the secret of the Seal of Sainthood,
> I have united tasting (*dhawq*—experiential, esoteric knowledge)
> And comprehension (*dirāya*—formal, exoteric knowledge)
> The tongue of my state sang hymns to me,
> Telling of the gifts of the Creator.
> The basin filled up and my abdomen said:
> "Go easy, go slowly, you have already filled my belly!"
> He gave me distinction through knowledge and the power of disposition (*taṣrīf*)
> If I say, "Be!" it comes about without delay!⁹⁹

We must not forget that the practice of *tarbiya* itself is physical as well as spiritual (and leads to the disappearance of distinction between the two): the disciple recites prayers with his or her mouth, performs the canonical prayers with his or her body, until God "becomes" his or her body ("I become . . . the hand by which he grasps, the foot by which he walks, the tongue with which he speaks"). This integral role of the body in Sufi spiritual practice and intellectual realization finds its precedence in the nocturnal ascent (*mi'rāj*) of the Prophet through the heavens to the Divine Presence, which many Muslims believe to have taken place bodily. That is, it is understood as a physical and metaphysical ascent and return in which the entirety of the Prophet's being participated, including his physical body.[100] In his *Removal of Confusion*, Shaykh Ibrahim quotes the following account of the *mi'rāj*, emphasizing the embodied nature of the Prophet's acquisition of knowledge: "I approached my Lord until I was as He said, *two bow-lengths or nearer* (53:9), and my Lord asked me, but I was unable to respond. So He put his hand between my shoulder blades, without qualification (*takyīf*) or delimitation (*taḥdīd*), until I discovered the coolness (*bard*) of the Divine Presence upon my heart. Then I inherited the knowledge of everything that came before and everything that was to follow. He taught me all the sciences, which had been scattered and dispersed."[101]

The integration of all knowledge that characterizes the Prophet was accomplished through the integration of all levels of the being of the person of the Prophet, from his body to the Divine Presence. In this perspective, the body finds its perfection along with the entirety of the human being in spiritual/intellectual realization, which is identified with the being of the Prophet. Elsewhere Shaykh Ibrahim writes:

> The body [*jasad*] without the spirit [*rūḥ*] is a corpse. The body with the spirit, but without intellect [*'aql*], is insane. If there is intellect but no *ma'rifa*, that

intellect is completely lost, and it is useless. If there is *maʿrifa*, the goal is obtained. *Maʿrifa* is the spirit of the intellect, and the intellect is the spirit of the spirit, and the spirit is the spirit of the body. So in this way, man has an animal spirit [*rūḥ ḥayawānī*] and a human spirit [*rūḥ insānī*]; if you like you can say soul [*nafs*] and spirit [*rūḥ*].[102]

Thus, the body finds its fulfillment and perfection in *maʿrifa*. In the same work, Shaykh Ibrahim gives a detailed exposition of the correspondences between various parts of the body, aspects of the cosmos, and divine attributes.[103] In fact, in the Sufi tradition, human beings are described as having different bodies corresponding to the different levels of reality or *ḥaḍarāt*. Just as the body one has in a dream is connected and even continuous with the body lying in bed dreaming, one's physical body and imaginal/spiritual "subtle bodies" or "bodies of light," as they are often called, are symbolically and ontologically related, especially in the cases of Knowers and the Prophet who have integrated them.[104] Thus, the physical body is seen as just "the tip of the iceberg" of the human being, the aspect of its being that emerges into space and time.

But the body is not just a symbol or privation of the soul and spirit in space and time. It also has its own special qualities and attributes that, from a certain point of view, perfect and complete the spirit and soul. Shaykh Ibrahim quotes a tradition in his *Removal of Confusion* describing the height of the Prophet's ascension into heaven: "It is related that when the Prophet reached the highest levels and distinguished stations, God revealed to him, 'with what shall I honour you?' The Prophet said, 'by relating me to You through servanthood (*ʿubūdiyya*).'"[105] Ibn ʿArabi connects this servanthood to the body in particular and physical matter in general, explaining that the body exhibits perfect servanthood, perfect receptivity to the Divine, since it only moves and acts as it is commanded, and itself issues no commands. Thus, the body is more noble and exalted than any of the other elements or levels of being that attempt to arrogate aspects of lordship (*rubūbiyya*) for themselves, when in reality it only belongs to God. The appropriate attitude before the absolute lordship of God is that of the body, of matter, of the Prophet—the attitude of perfect servanthood.

Because of this attitude, and the perfect integration of all the levels of his being, the Prophet's body is the perfect body, and his perfect body perfects Being itself. As the author of the *Ibrīz*, an oft-quoted source of Tijani doctrine, writes, "In his pure body (*dhāt*)—God's blessings and peace be upon him—the spirit has settled down in contentment, love and acceptance, and the veil between the spirit and the body has been removed. Thus, the state of the Prophet's noble spirit, in its perfection and penetration of the worlds, is firmly rooted in his pure, earthen body (*dhāt al-tūrabbiyya*). This is perfection beyond which no perfection exists."[106]

Like the black surface at the back of a mirror, matter is the completion of the human being that makes possible his or her task of reflecting the Divine Image, of bringing together heaven and earth. From this perspective, the body is the completion and perfection of the human being, the human being is the completion and perfection of creation, and creation is the perfection of the Divine Nature as the Infinite and Manifest (al-Ẓāhir).[107] But the body itself is also perfected through the acquisition of *ma'rifa*, through which it is reunited with the spirit, transcending these divisions in the unity of the Real, which becomes the "hand by which it grasps, the foot by which it walks, and the tongue by which it speaks."[108] This is one of the reasons why the bodies and tombs of Sufi saints and Knowers are believed to be such powerful sites of *baraka* and grace.[109] Al-Ghazālī writes, "The heart of the believer does not die, and his knowledge is not obliterated when he dies, nor is the heart's clarity blurred. Hasan (al-Basri) alluded to this when he said, 'Earth does not swallow up the dwelling place of faith; rather, it becomes a means and a source of nearness to God.'"[110] Thus, within the Sufi tradition, the body is integral to the acquisition of knowledge and, as a mode of being, identical with the knowledge it achieves.[111] As a result, *ma'rifa* and the related, embodied *adab* (comportment) are typically achieved through extended time in the physical presence of a master or masters.

Within Ifa, the epistemological significance of the body is even more apparent. Ọrunmila acquired the wisdom of Olodumare by eating the *igba iwa* (calabash of wisdom/existence/character), physically incorporating it into his body, and *ọmọ awo* (apprentices) follow suit by "eating the Odu." During initiation and other rituals, the orisa and other forces are physically put into the bodies of babalawo and others through incisions and ingestion. Through the elaborate taboos (*eewọ*) and rituals associated with each Odu, the bodies of babalawo become transformed through the things they do and do not eat, the places they do and do not go, the kind of clothes they can wear, the dances they perform, et cetera. Like the rituals that "build up" or "fix" the presence and power (*aṣẹ*) of an orisa in a shrine, the rituals performed by and on babalawo "build up" and "fix" the presence of Ifa within their bodies, which then transmit the words (*ọrọ*) and character (*iwa*) that Olodumare gave to Ọrunmila to "mend the world." This is why the funerary rites of babalawo (and their Ifa instruments) are so intricate, involved, and important; their bodies are much more than biological material. From this perspective, a babalawo's body, like his *ikin* (sacred palm nuts) and other instruments, is Ifa itself.

Moreover, in Ifa, virtually every part of the body, like the head (*ori*) and mouth (*ẹnu*), is worshiped as orisa in its own right. Different Odu are associated with different parts of the body (e.g., Eji Ogbe with the head), and different parts of the body are said to belong to and thus contain the presence of different orisa—Ogun makes the bones, Ọbatala the flesh, and so forth—and these different body parts are seen and understood as outer forms of inner realities, which is why they often feature as separate characters in the myths of Ifa.

In both Ifa and Tijani Sufism, the physical presence of the master or teacher is considered extremely important, and is often indispensable in acquiring knowledge. The body helps to realize, and through its solidity, "to fix" and to convey or express the deepest forms of knowledge of these two traditions. From a certain perspective, the bodies of the masters of Ifa and Sufism are identical with the knowledge of these traditions.

While these radically different conceptions of body, being, and knowledge may not find wide reception in contemporary academia, they can invite us to reconsider the importance of physical presence and activities in the age of massive open online courses and Zoom. Moreover, the very different physical postures, gestures, rituals, and general physical habitus cultivated by these two traditions should make us aware of just how particular, modern, and profoundly European our contemporary academic embodied practices (e.g., sitting in chairs in a classroom, standing at a podium) and "professional demeanor" truly are, and how profoundly significant this fact is. Both Ifa and Tijani Sufism have radically different "languages" of embodied practice and gesture (prayers, offerings, greetings, dances, postures during study[112] and recitation, etc.) that both express, facilitate, and constitute the realization of the state and knowledge of the founder of each tradition (the Sunna of the Prophet for Sufism, the *iwa pẹlẹ* of Ọrunmila). As Yolanda Covington-Ward writes in her study of embodied performances in Congo, they "are not about just *meaning-making*, but also *meaning-doing*."[113]

These different perspectives can also draw our attention to the way in which the increasingly virtual rituals of modern scholarship—hours and hours of researching and writing on a computer, reading and sending e-mails, sitting at tables during meetings and conferences, reading the occasional physical book and journal, and lecturing to students—affects our bodies, and how our bodies and bodily practices affect and even define our intellectual life. Personally, I know that after too much time at my computer writing or reading, I start to feel like a disembodied Cartesian rational faculty, and I have to do something else to come back to myself to think and "be" more clearly.

**Importance of Ritual**

This points to another concomitant of the identity of knowing and being in these traditions: the importance of ritual practice in acquiring or cultivating knowledge. As the previous chapters demonstrate, ritual practice is an essential component of the acquisition and expression of knowledge in both Tijani Sufism and Ifa; since both are founded on a kind of self-knowledge that is identical with a mode of being, ritual exercises that transform the mode of being of the knowing subject are central to these traditions. As Ulli Beier wrote, "Yoruba ethics means: to become through ritual, a being who knows more and understands more, a person who lives more and is more."[114]

But one does not have to be a babalawo or Sufi to appreciate the epistemological power and importance of ritual. The way in which we live, the rituals we perform (consciously or not), profoundly influence the way we experience and understand ourselves and the world. Rare indeed are the articles, books, or classes that change the way we see the world as profoundly as falling in love, having a child, witnessing tragedy, or even traveling and living in a different society. I cannot help but wonder how different Kant's thought would have been had he gotten out of Prussia and worked as a sailor for a few years, seeing the world and living with different kinds of people.

Reflecting on Ifa and Tijani Sufism, we as academics should take stock of the way the rituals and experiences of our lives affect our own and our students' work and intentionally try to use this immense epistemological power in order to make our work better. What rituals can we perform, what experiences can we seek out, for ourselves or for our students, to give us a better understanding of our subject matter and maybe even ourselves? As one would expect, the anthropological literature is very rich in this regard. For example, the work of Paul Stoller on magic and healing among the Songhay in Niger and Robert Rozehnal's work on contemporary Chishti Sufis in the Indian subcontinent clearly illustrates how transformative ritual experiences encountered during research can lead scholars to rethink their own personal theoretical and metaphysical assumptions, as well as those of their professional practice.[115]

These examples also illustrate the inherently social nature of the process of acquiring and producing knowledge. Our socialization can and does profoundly influence what and how we know. Even with the legacy of the hermetically sealed Cartesian/Kantian subject, and the often isolated and isolating nature of academic work (especially in the humanities), socialization and discussion remain an important cornerstone of academic training. However, this is even more true of Ifa and Sufism, where communal practice and interpersonal relationships (some of which are metaphysical) are an integral part of the acquisition and cultivation of knowledge.

Given the epistemic power of social interaction, the academy could greatly benefit from conferences, courses, symposia, and even casual conversations with representatives of these and other traditions. I believe that contemporary philosophers and scholars of religion should spend some time in the context of another intellectual tradition, even if only for a little while. A couple of weeks living and interacting with one's counterparts in a Tibetan monastery, Sufi zawiya, or meetings of babalawo is bound to make one see the world differently, or at least make one less smug. Such interactions and encounters can and have been crucial in revealing and subjecting to inquiry many of the academy's most hidden assumptions and biases. As Goethe pointed out, "Anyone who doesn't know foreign languages knows nothing of his own."[116]

**The Real as an Active Teacher**

One of the most pervasive of these assumptions, which goes all the way back to Kant (or even Descartes), is that the object of knowledge, qua external object, is a passive object of inquiry. While scientists may poetically speak about patterns or data "revealing themselves," in reality, the way scientists treat the *res existans* of nature (whether particles, protozoa, plants, pigs, or human bodies) is as a passive, inert object that can and should be manipulated at will until we can "dig up" or "get out" the data we are looking for. Across the campus lawn, in the humanities, with the "death of the author" and the rise of the "hermeneutics of suspicion," texts, especially those from non-Western traditions, are typically deconstructed, historicized, pulled apart, read into and from every perspective—except that of the tradition to which they belong (with certain glowing exceptions). In between, the social sciences have the unique burden of directly dealing with fellow human subjects as objects of knowledge. But while the colonial and racist horrors of previous generations of social science research have made some researchers more aware and conscious of the dangers of dehumanizing and objectifying the people and societies they study, the increasingly quantitative nature of the field (under the influence of the models from the "harder" sciences) is moving some of its disciplines away from intersubjective encounter to a more "scientific" relationship of researcher and data.

These dynamics aside, the philosophical assumptions that serve as the foundations of the theories of these fields generally posit a kind of naïve realism in which the objects of knowledge are inert and passive vis-à-vis the researcher/theorist, or a Kantian position wherein the object of inquiry must conform to the knowing subject and not the other way around. According to these perspectives, the objects of knowledge are mere things, concepts, or representations, and seldom, if ever, knowing, active subjects in their own right. Even where such agency is acknowledged and theorized (as in ethnography), relations of dominance, conquest, and extraction predominate.[117] For example, in his seminal *Witchcraft, Oracles, and Magic Among the Azande*, E. E. Evans-Pritchard writes, "In the long run, however, an ethnographer is bound to triumph. Armed with preliminary knowledge nothing can prevent him from driving deeper and deeper the wedge if he is interested and persistent."[118]

However, Ifa and Tijani Sufism present us with radically different perspectives in which the Real (*al-Ḥaqq*) and the Prophet or Olodumare and Orunmila are actively involved in the human quest to achieve knowledge of them. As conscious, knowing subjects themselves, God / the Real, the Prophet, the Qur'an, and Olodumare,

Ọrunmila, and the Odu of Ifa conceal and reveal themselves to, and shape, their would-be knowers. As Michel Foucault succinctly notes, "If we define spirituality as being the form of practices which postulate that, such as he is, the subject is not capable of the truth, but that, such as it is, the truth can transfigure and save the subject, then we can say that the modern age of the relations between the subject and truth begins when it is postulated that, such as he is, the subject is capable of truth, but that, such as it is, the truth cannot save the subject."[119] Or as Rumi more poetically explains:

> The Qur'an is like a bride. Although you pull the veil away from her face, she does not show herself to you. When you investigate the Qur'an, but receive no joy or mystical unveiling, it is because your pulling at the veil has caused you to be rejected. The Qur'an has deceived you and shown itself as ugly. It says, "I am not that beautiful bride." It is able to show itself in any form it desires. But if you stop pulling at its veil and seek its good pleasure; if you water its field, serve it from afar and strive in that which pleases it, then it will show you its face without any need for you to draw aside its veil.[120]

Similarly, the Araba had to ask the Odu Ofun Meji's permission and propitiate it with sacrifices before he could teach me its verses. Moreover, in both of these traditions, through serving the desired object of knowledge, by becoming like it and drawing near to it, one eventually comes to recognize that it is not other than oneself, and that this "object" is actually a subject knowing itself through one's very self. This knowledge is not conceptual, and so one never arrives at a perfect "theory of everything" or comes to possess ultimate knowledge, but rather, ultimate knowledge (or the ultimate Knower) comes to possess one. In the words of the ḥadīth, "The Real becomes one's hearing, sight, hand foot, and tongue." Or as the Araba said, "Ọrunmila will come out of your mouth and speak, and what you say will be true."[121]

Such perspectives are worthy of consideration, especially by scholars of religion, art, and culture. The way a tradition, a people, or a culture present themselves to us often says a great deal about us and our relationship with the object of our study, but this relationship has two sides—that is, it is not entirely up to us. Thus, the "responsive reverence" and service that Rumi recommends for would-be readers of the Qur'an seems as good a description of responsible/responsive scholarship and issues of agency as any I have come across in the anthropological literature.

### (Post)Colonial (Post)Modernity

Despite contemporary academics' deep ambivalence toward the related Enlightenment and imperialist projects, especially those in the fields of anthropology and area studies, the dogma of progress still runs deep in academia, and apologists for Western modernity—whether subtle (such as Charles Taylor)[122] or less so (such as Steven Pinker and Jared Diamond)[123]—are largely well received and even lauded. Moreover, one can almost excuse Francis Fukuyama for his triumphalist "end of history" hypothesis: virtually every human being in the world now lives under the rule of a modern nation-state, participates in a capitalist economy, and has received or been exposed to some form of Western-style education; and the crusaders of "development" have devoted their significant resources to ensuring that everyone can become assimilated into these new (post)colonial modes of life, leisure, labor, and learning. The remarkable economic, political, and military dominance of this (post)colonial (post)modernity is only matched by its seeming intellectual dominance. Thanks to international schools, brain drain, the prestige of European and American institutions of higher learning, and the somewhat successful colonial enterprise to destroy the authority of non-Western intellectual traditions, many of the best and the brightest (and wealthiest) young students from around the world now receive shockingly similar intellectual formations, regardless of their backgrounds. Moreover, this intellectual formation of the elites often has a trickle-down influence on their societies. And so Margaret Thatcher's Borg-like ultimatum that "there is no alternative" seems inescapable. It looks as if the different "languages of thought" represented by the world's different intellectual traditions, like the diverse sociopolitical and economic structures that supported them, will become mere "accents" of the universal language of Western postindustrial (post)modernism.

However, studying Ifa and Tijani Sufism reveals that far from going the way of the dinosaur, these traditions, like West African clothing, have adapted and in some cases even thrived in this new environment, spreading across the continent and even the world. Moreover, much of the interest in these two traditions is driven by those one would assume least likely to embrace such traditions (at least according to the perspective outlined above): members of the African diaspora in the Caribbean, North and South America, as well as many Europeans and Euro-Americans in the case of Ifa, and educated, urban youth in Senegal, Nigeria, South Africa, Egypt, Indonesia, and the African diaspora in Europe and North America in the case of Tijani Sufism. These traditions are not going anywhere, and their continued resilience poses a unique intellectual challenge to the totalizing narrative outlined above, not only because they continue to exist, but because these traditions actively articulate their own theories of history, progress, and knowledge in which they are not relics of a bygone age clinging to the periphery of modernity, nor reactionary appropriations of modernity, but are rather in the center of the spiritual and intellectual movements that are subtly but powerfully shaping the world.

These different approaches to knowledge also direct us to reconsider those perspectives that were repressed and occluded in the West's own intellectual history, such as the neo-Platonic and Pythagorean, medieval Scholastic, Christian and Jewish mystical and kabbalistic traditions, and so forth. These perspectives give us a very different view on the "inevitable march of progress and knowledge," and they, along with traditions of Islamic, Native American, Chinese, and Indian and Buddhist philosophy, as well as traditions such as Ifa, will undoubtedly become more important as the enthusiasm for and confidence in the (post)colonial, (post)modern, neoliberal project fades. Just because the military and economic machinery that supports and defends modern academic institutions is more powerful than those of other intellectual traditions does not mean that our ideas are better, more profound, or more true, and it is becoming increasingly difficult to ignore this fact.

Finally, in reflecting on the ways in which Ifa and Sufism differ so markedly from the intellectual traditions of the academy—all the metaphysics, the rituals, the spirits, the poetry, the seemingly impossibly lofty claims of knowledge and certainty—one is reminded of Aesop's cautionary tale of the fox who could not reach the grapes and so declared them sour. We must be careful not to fall into the trap of, "in the name of wisdom, vilifying one's neighbour's wisdom to console oneself—or to take one's revenge—for not having found it oneself."[124]

## CONCLUSION

Ifa and Tijani Sufism represent different and distinct approaches to knowledge and knowing that are compelling, sophisticated, and dynamic in their own right. In Tijani Sufism, disciples acquire Knowledge (*ma'rifa*) by undergoing an initiatory process called *tarbiya*, which leads to a profound shift in their perception and understanding of the self, the world, and God. They experience the radical unity (*tawḥīd*) of the Divine Reality, and then "come back" to themselves and the world of multiplicity, which they now see with new eyes, as manifestations or reflections of this single Divine Reality. Thus, they are known as Knowers by God (*'ārifūn biLlāh*), for it is ultimately God who does the knowing through them. This marks but the beginning of an endless spiritual/intellectual journey whose goal is the infinitely receptive mode of being and knowing exemplified by the Prophet, Shaykh Aḥmad al-Tijānī, and Shaykh Ibrahim Niasse.

In Ifa, babalawo acquire "deep knowledge" (*imọ ijinlẹ*) by memorizing verses from all of the sacred 256 Odu. During their initiation in the "grove of mystery" (*igbodu*), they encounter their innermost self and destiny (*ori*) and are given the power (*aṣẹ*) to fulfill it. This initiation is but the beginning of a lifelong journey of knowledge through the cultivation of character, practice of divination, and contemplation of the Odu. The goal of this practice is the being/character (*iwa*) and knowledge of Ọrunmila, hailed as "My Lord, whose knowledge is without end. Not knowing you fully, we [i.e., our lives] are in vain. If we could but know you in full, all would be well."

Like the philosophy of Western antiquity, Ifa and Sufism are at once ways of knowing and transformative ways of life. Hadot's description of ancient philosophy is remarkably applicable to both traditions: "Philosophy was a method of spiritual progress which demanded a radical conversion and transformation of the individual's way of being. Thus, philosophy was a way of life, both in its exercise and effort to achieve wisdom, and in its goal, wisdom itself. For real wisdom does not merely cause us to know: it makes us 'be' in a different way."[125] But beyond these similarities, what is perhaps of greatest interest to Western-educated readers is the fact that Ifa and Tijani Sufism represent markedly different perspectives on knowledge and knowing than those in which we have been trained. For example, most modern, Western theories of knowledge assume that reality is like (or simply is) the way it reveals itself to our rational faculties and our senses (aided by our scientific instruments). That is, human beings, more or less as they are, are capable of discovering or constructing truth (or what approximates it), whereas in Ifa and Tijani Sufism human beings must conform themselves to and be transformed by the Truth through ritual means in order to see things "as they truly are" instead of how they ordinarily appear. While similar perspectives can also be found within the so-called Western tradition (in ancient Greek, Roman, and medieval Christian philosophy), as Hadot points out, we have to move beyond the Enlightenment caricatures of these traditions in order to better understand them, the intellectual heritage of the West, and similar traditions from other civilizations. The racist and triumphalist ideologies of the Enlightenment rendered opaque and unintelligible not only ancient and classical philosophy, but also the philosophical and intellectual traditions of other civilizations. Difference from the newly defined "rational" and "enlightened" modes of thinking and being was interpreted as lack and imperfection, and the specter of this unfortunate legacy still haunts us today.

However, in the contemporary academy, we can also approach and understand difference not as a defect or lack in the other, but as an abundance, a plenitude that can not only reveal our own limitations, but help to transcend them as well. However, the traditions of Tijani Sufism and Ifa do not exist solely as a resource for Western scholars; rather their goal is to cultivate ideal modes of knowing and being in their initiates, and to "mend the world." Approaching these traditions and their representatives as teachers and colleagues is much more productive than approaching them as intellectually passive informants or sources of ethnographic or historical "data," as I hope the current work demonstrates.

Nevertheless, the careful study of Ifa and Tijani Sufism can serve as powerful correctives to the "colonial hangover" that continues to cloud much of our thinking by revealing our assumptions and illustrating alternative approaches to knowledge. Much of the troublesome heritage of the Enlightenment came from the elevation of an immanent, particular mode of knowing and being (that of rational, white, post-Christian, rich, eighteenth-century [or future] men from northern Europe) to a transcendent, universal standard of knowledge. From the perspective of Ifa, Enlightenment thinkers have tried to put themselves in the place of Ọrunmila. And from the perspective of Sufism, they put themselves in the place of the Perfect Human / Muḥammadan reality—or more specifically, they confused their particular, limited "station" with the transcendent "station of no station" (*maqām lā-maqām*). However, both Ifa and Tijani Sufism outline specific programs of practice and thought that claim to be able to lead initiates to the realization of this "station of no station," which is not a particular perspective or theory, but rather a mode of being characterized by the ability to take on, accept, and recognize the validity and limitations of every partial perspective. Within both Ifa and Sufism, you never fully come to know God and the Prophet or Olodumare and Ọrunmila, but rather these transcendent figures come to know themselves through and in you.

Thus, Ifa and Tijani Sufism present us with a wisdom that is both timeless and timely in a world where knowledge is increasingly externalized and shallow and many battles are fought and lives are ruined due to the resulting inability to recognize the limitations of one's own perspective and the possibility and validity of other ways of knowing and life. So, in conclusion, we can only add our voice to the prayers of the masters of these traditions:

> "What we beg for from God is this: that He preserve all His servants from a belief which goes no further than imitation and pretence..."[126]

*ḥaqqa qadrihi wa'l-miqdarihi'l-aẓīm*

In accordance with the reality of His rank and his tremendous degree
*Abọru, Abọye*
May our sacrifice reach heaven, May our sacrifice be accepted,
*Abọye, Abọṣiṣẹ*
May our sacrifice be accepted and allow our intentions to come to pass.

# Notes

INTRODUCTION

Unless they are part of a quotation from another work, all translations of the Qur'an in this volume are taken from Marmaduke Pickthall's 1922 translation, *The Meaning of the Glorious Qur'an*, and in some cases from the 2015 HarperCollins *Study Qur'an*, often modified to fit the context in which they are cited. Unless otherwise stated, all English translations of interviews and works in Arabic, French, and Yoruba are the author's.

1. The only articles in *African Philosophy: An Anthology*, ed. Emmanuel Chukwudi Eze (Hoboken, N.J.: Wiley-Blackwell, 1998) that piqued my interest and sincere appreciation at the time were Chinua Achebe's articles on Igbo cosmology and art, Wọle Ṣoyinka's piece "The Fourth Stage," Kwame Gyeyke's article on the Akan conception of the "self," and my favorite reading of the book, the seventeenth-century Ethiopian philosopher Zera Yacob's reflections on "God, Faith, and the Nature of Knowledge."

2. Amadou Hampâté Bâ, *Amkoullel, l'enfant Peul: Memoires* (Arles: Actes Sud, 1991), 197.

3. Shaykh Tijānī 'Alī Cissé, interview with the author, conducted in Arabic, January 14, 2012, Medina Baye, Senegal. This quote appears to be derived from the thirteenth-century Andalusian scholar al-Shāṭibī's (d. 1388) saying, al-'ilm yu'khidhu min ṣudūr al-rijāl lā min suṭūr al-kutub, "knowledge is taken from the chests of men, not the strokes of the pen"; or al-'ilm kāna fī ṣudūr al-rijāl thumma intaqala ilā al-kutub wa ṣārat mafātiḥahu bi aydayy al-rijāl, "knowledge was in the chests of men, then it was transferred to books, with its keys in the hands of men."

4. However, some scholars, drawing on evidence from the Greek tradition itself, locate the origins of the Greek traditions of philosophy, and even the origin of the term *philosophia* itself, in ancient Egypt. For example, see Théophile Obenga *Ancient Egypt and Black Africa* (Chicago: Karnak House, 1992), 49–53.

5. Pierre Hadot, *Philosophy as a Way of Life: Spiritual Exercises from Socrates to Foucault* (Oxford, UK: Blackwell, 1995), 266.

6. Ibid., 128–29:

In order to understand the phenomenon under consideration, it is essential to recall that there was a widespread Christian tradition which portrayed Christianity as a *philosophy*.... The Apologists considered Christianity a philosophy, and to mark its opposition to Greek philosophy, they spoke of Christianity as "our philosophy" or as "Barbarian philosophy." They did not, however, consider Christianity to be just one philosophy among others; they thought of it as *the* philosophy. They believed that that which had been scattered and dispersed throughout Greek philosophy had been synthesized and systematized in Christian philosophy. Each Greek philosopher, they wrote, had possessed only a portion of the *Logos* whereas the Christians were in possession of the *Logos* itself, incarnated in Jesus Christ.... The identification of Christianity with true philosophy inspired many aspects of the teaching of Origen, and it remained influential, throughout the Origenist tradition.... Under the influence of Greek tradition, the monastic life continued to be designated by the term *philosophia* throughout the Middle Ages. Thus, a Cistercian monastic text tells us that Bernard of Clairvaux used to initiate his disciples "into the disciplines of celestial philosophy." Finally, John of Salisbury maintained that it was the monks who "philosophized" in the most correct and authentic way.

7. For example, Ash'arī theologians arguments for occasionalism preceded Hume's similar arguments, which were probably indirectly influenced by theirs.

8. The Islamic philosophers saw themselves and their discipline as being directly descended from figures such as Plato, known in the tradition as "The Divine Plato" (*Aflāṭun al-Ilāhī*).

9. As Seyyed Hossein Nasr notes in *Islamic Philosophy from Its Origin to the Present: Philosophy in the Land of Prophecy* (Albany: SUNY Press, 2006), 95:

The Islamic intellectual tradition has usually not seen a dichotomy between intellect and intuition but has created a hierarchy of knowledge and methods of attaining knowledge according to which degrees of both intellection and intuition become harmonized in an order encompassing all the means available to man to know, from sensual knowledge and reason to intellection and inner vision or the "knowledge of the heart." If there have appeared from time to time thinkers who confined knowledge to what can be attained by reason (*istidlāl*) alone and who have denied both revelation and intuition as sources of knowledge, they have for that very reason remained peripheral within the integral Islamic intellectual tradition.

10. One could draw a comparison with the contemporary situation in which the incredible wealth of translated texts and practicing communities from the different philosophical traditions around the world is now leading to new understandings of philosophy. Moreover, the efforts to create space to think and work outside the dominion of modern and postmodern Western thought are somewhat reminiscent of those employed by the early humanists to create a space to think outside the dominion of the Church.

11. Hadot, *Philosophy as a Way of Life*, 28–29.

12. Ibid., 26–30.

13. See, e.g., Feuerbach's *The Essence of Christianity*.

14. Including a fatigue with destructive internecine wars and certain trends in late Scholasticism; see Gilbert Durand, *On the Disfiguration of the Image of Man in the West* (Ipswich, UK: Golgonooza Press, 1977).

15. Richard King, *Orientalism and Religion: Postcolonial Theory, India, and the Mystic East* (London: Routledge, 1999), 15.

16. Relatedly the modern categories of "secular" and "religious" were also formed during this period through a similar process. See Talal Asad, *Formations of the Secular: Christianity, Islam, Modernity* (Stanford: Stanford University Press, 2003).

17. Emmanuel Chukwudi Eze, ed., *Race and the Enlightenment: A Reader* (Oxford, UK: Wiley-Blackwell, 1997); Peter K. J. Park, *Africa, Asia, and the History of Philosophy: Racism in the Formation of the Philosophical Canon* (Albany: SUNY Press, 2014).

18. See H. Lovejoy, *The Great Chain of Being: A Study of the History of an Idea* (Cambridge: Harvard University Press, 1950).

19. The elaborate angelologies of medieval Europe were thus replaced by the elaborate racial hierarchies of the eighteenth and nineteenth centuries. This also had profound implications for the understanding of gender, since not man as human, but man as male was put atop the Great Chain of Being. See Thomas Laqueur's *Making Sex: Body and Gender from the Greeks to Freud* (Cambridge: Harvard University Press, 1990).

20. G. W. F. Hegel, "Lectures on the Philosophy of World History," in *Race and the Enlightenment*, ed. Eze, 122.

21. James Beattie, "An Essay on the Nature an Immutability of Truth, in Opposition to Sophistry and Skepticism," in *Race and the Enlightenment*, ed. Eze, 36.

22. "One can take the classification of organic and living beings further. Not only does the vegetable kingdom exist for the sake of the animal kingdom (and its increase and diversification) but humans, as rational beings, exist for the sake of others of a different species (race). The latter stand at a higher level of humanity, either simultaneously (as, for instance, the Americans and Europeans) or sequentially." Quoted in Stuart Elden and Eduardo Mendieta, eds., *Reading Kant's Geography* (Albany: SUNY Press, 2011), 1.

23. Hegel, "Lectures on the Philosophy of World History," 112–53.

24. Similarly, Uday Mehta has compellingly argued and demonstrated the imperialistic urge inherent in the modern liberal project and ideology. See Uday Mehta, *Liberalism and Empire: A Study in Nineteenth-Century British Liberal Thought* (Chicago: University of Chicago Press, 1999).

25. Nor could they, since European rationality and philosophy were so narrowly and self-referentially defined, and yet paradoxically proclaimed as universal. The only way to qualify as a philosopher would be to already be a European philosopher.

26. Jay Garfield, *Empty Words: Buddhist Philosophy and Cross-Cultural Interpretation* (Oxford: Oxford University Press, 2001), 260.

27. For example, see Henry Odera Oruka "The Fundamental Principles in the Question of 'African Philosophy,'" *Second Order* 4, no. 1 (1975): 44–55; Barry Hallen, *A Short History of African Philosophy* (Bloomington: Indiana University Press, 2009); Kwasi Wiredu, ed., *A Companion to African Philosophy* (Oxford, UK: Blackwell, 2006); Souleymane Bachir Diagne, *L'encre des savants: Réflexions sur la philosophie en Afrique* (Dakar: CODESRIA; Paris: Présence Africaine Éditions, 2013). For a more detailed analysis of the history of the field African philosophy in relation to this project, see Oludamini Ogunnaike, "African Philosophy Reconsidered: Africa, Religion, Race, and Rationality," *Journal of Africana Religions* 5, no. 2 (2017): 181–216.

28. For example, my great-great-grandfather never thought of himself as an "African."

29. But perhaps after many generations, if a distinct "school" of Lagos Buddhism developed, one could consider such a tradition as an example of "African philosophy."

30. William E. Abraham, "Amo," in *A Companion to the Philosophers*, ed. Robert Arrington (Oxford, UK: Blackwell, 2001).

31. Gbemisola Olujobi, "Austrian Artist Becomes Nigerian Ancestor" *Truthdig*, May 21, 2009, http://

www.truthdig.com/report/item/20090522_austrian_artist_becomes_nigerian_ancestor.

32. Like traditional African philosophies, many traditional African musical traditions have ritual functions and psycho-spiritual dimensions beyond those commonly theorized for their modern counterparts in the West. Neither Copeland nor Chopin's music is understood to speak to spirits or bring rain.

33. I employ this term—a translation of the honorific Arabic term (*ummī*), used to describe the Prophet of Islam, who neither read nor wrote—instead of the terms "illiterate," or "nonliterate," which imply a privation or lack, or "oral," which implies that the spoken word is the tradition's only means of representation. For all of the benefits of writing, the distinction between a "literate" and an "unlettered" society or tradition is not simply the subtraction of writing, as "unlettered" societies and traditions have many features and qualities seldom found in their literate counterparts. See Ananda Coomaraswamy's excellent article "The Bugbear of Literacy" in *The Bugbear of Literacy* (London: Dennis Dobson, 1949), 23–41. Moreover, many "unlettered" African traditions employ forms of symbolic representation other than writing (such as adinkra symbols, dance, music, and sculpture) to encode ideas and principles.

34. V. Y. Mudimbe, *The Invention of Africa: Gnosis, Philosophy, and the Order of Knowledge* (Bloomington: Indiana University Press, 1988).

35. For those having difficulty in imagining this, or any other, alternative to the Kantian divide between noumena and phenomena, I offer the following story of Zhuangzi as a key:

> Zhuangzi and Huizi were strolling along the bridge over the Hao River. Zhuangzi said, "The minnows swim about so freely, following the openings wherever they take them. Such is the happiness of fish."
> Huizi said, "You are not a fish, so whence do you know the happiness of fish?"
> Zhuangzi said, "You are not I, so whence do you know I don't know the happiness of fish?"
> Huizi said, "I am not you, to be sure, so I don't know what it is to be you. But by the same token, since you are certainly not a fish, my point about your inability to know the happiness of fish stands intact."
> Zhuangzi said, "Let's go back to the starting point. You said, 'Whence do you know the happiness of fish?' Since your question was premised on your knowing that I know it, I must have known it from here, up above the Hao River."

Brook Ziporyn, *Zhuangzi: The Essential Writings with Selections from Traditional Commentaries* (Indianapolis: Hackett, 2009), 76.

36. Walter Benjamin, "The Task of the Translator," in *Walter Benjamin: Selected Writings*, vol. 1, *1913–1926*, ed. and trans. Edmund Jephcott (Cambridge: Belknap Press of Harvard University Press, 2002), 261–62.

37. See the works of Algis Uždavinys and Pierre Hadot for a fuller account of the spiritual and religious dimensions of these Greco-Roman philosophical traditions. Nigerian scholars Sophie Oluwole and Omotade Adegbindin have already begun work on such comparisons in *Socrates and Ọrúnmìlà: Two Patron Saint of Classical Philosophy* (Lagos: Ark, 2015) and *Ifa in Yoruba Thought System* (Durham, N.C.: Carolina Academic Press, 2014), respectively. While these books have many issues, they also contain many important insights and I hope that more scholars will take up this line of inquiry.

38. Biọdun Jeyifo, "Oguntoyinbo: Wole Soyinka and Igilango Geesi." *Philosophia Africana* 11, no. 1 (2008): 29.

39. Or to give another analogy, if we compare Western academic traditions of philosophy and theory to Euclidean geometry, I am arguing that we should consider these African intellectual traditions as being analogous to modes of non-Euclidean geometry, based on different axioms and/or means of demonstration, but nonetheless consistent and compelling.

40. Babatunde Lawal, *The Gèlèdé Spectacle: Art, Gender, and Social Harmony in an African Culture* (Seattle: University of Washington Press, 1996), xvi. Similarly, another scholar (I cannot remember who) said, "Far too often, theory becomes a celebration of ourselves, a tool of subjugation and domestication."

41. Toshihiko Izutsu, *Sufism and Taoism: A Comparative Study of Key Philosophical Concepts* (Berkeley: University of California Press, 1984).

42. See William Chittick, *The Sufi Path of Knowledge: Ibn Al-'Arabi's Metaphysics of Imagination* (Albany: SUNY Press, 1989); and William Chittick, *The Sufi Path of Love: The Spiritual Teachings of Rumi* (Albany: SUNY Press, 1983).

43. Moreover, this style is also in keeping with the way these traditions discursively express themselves. The vast majority of Tijani texts and oral discourses consist mostly of quotations from earlier Sufi works and masters, as well as Prophetic sayings and passages of the Qur'an, creatively arranged with authorial commentary. The oral discourses of babalawo are similarly composed of verses and narratives of Ifa, stories of other babalawo, and relatively light individual commentary. This point is significant and alludes to the fact that in both traditions, truth is not constructed or individually authored; rather, one conforms to and becomes identified with the truth embodied in these sacred texts.

44. Valerie Hoffman, *Sufism, Mystics, and Saints in Modern Egypt* (Columbia: University of South Carolina Press, 1995).

45. William Chittick, *Imaginal Worlds: Ibn Al-ʿArabī and the Problem of Religious Diversity* (Albany: SUNY Press, 1994), 6. On the same page he adds:
> Even scholars who speak as Christian theologians tend to bow to the assumptions of modern thought. If they refuse to do so, they often assume the superiority or ultimacy of the Christian religion and devalue other religions appropriately, and of course they are likely to be ignored by the academy. . . . [In relation to what modern scholarship does not assume] one might reply that Christian fundamentalists, for example, do presuppose some or most of these things, and that they do not play an honored role in academic circles. I would add that they are also not known for the subtlety of their interpretative techniques or their positive evaluation of religious plurality.

46. Ibid., 174.

47. Ibid., 174–75.

48. Quoted in ibid., 176.

49. Quoted in ibid.

50. See Eduardo Batalha Viveiros De Castro, *Cannibal Metaphysics: For a Post-Structural Anthropology*, trans. Peter Skafish (Minneapolis: Univocal, 2014) for a related effort based on the "perspectivism" of indigenous Amazonian peoples. This approach also bears some resemblance to the Jain principle of *Anekāntavāda*, or the "many-sidedness" of reality.

51. Sīdī ʿAlī Harāzim al-Barrāda, *Jawāhir al-Maʿānī wa Bulūgh al-Amānī fī Fayḍ Sidi Abī ʿAbbās al-Tijanī*, trans. Ravane Mbaye (Dakar: Dar Albouraq, 2011).

52. Shaykh Aḥmad al-Tijānī, *Aḥzāb wa Awrād*, ed. Muḥammad al-Ḥāfiẓ al-Miṣrī (Cairo: n.p., 1983).

53. Shaykh Ibrāhīm Inyās, *Jawāhir al-rasāʾil wa-yaliyya ziyādat al-jawāhir al-ḥāwī baʿḍ ʿulūm wasīlat al-wasāʾil*, ed. Aḥmad Abū'l-Fatḥ, 3 vols. (Borno: Aḥmad Abī'l-Fatḥ, n.d.).

54. Shaykh Ibrāhīm Inyās, *Fī Riyāḍ al-Tafsīr li'l-Qurʾān al-Karīm*, 6 vols. (Tunis: al-Yamāma, 2010).

55. Shaykh Ibrahim Niasse, *Kāshif al-ilbās ʿan fayḍat al-khatm Abī l-ʿAbbās*, ed. Tijānī Cissé (Cairo: al-Sharika al-Dawliyya, 2001). Translated as *The Removal of Confusion Concerning the Flood of the Saintly Seal Aḥmad al-Tijānī* by Zachary Wright, Muhtar Holland, and Abdullahi Okene (Louisville, Ky.: Fons Vitae, 2010).

56. Shaykh Ibrāhīm Inyās, *al-Sirr al-Akbar wa'l Kibrīt al-Aḥmar*, ed. Maigari, in Muḥammad al-Ṭāhir Maigari, *Shaykh Ibrāhīm Aniyās [sic] al-Sinighālī ḥayatuhu wa arāʾuhu wa taʿlīmuhu* (Beirut: Dar al-ʿArabiyya, 1981), 410–98.

57. Oludamini Ogunnaike, *Poetry in Praise of Prophetic Perfection: A Study of West African Madīḥ Poetry and Its Precedents* (Cambridge, UK: Islamic Texts Society, 2020).

58. African Sources of Knowledge—Digital Library, Odu Ifa Collection, Harvard University, http://ask-dl.fas.harvard.edu/odu-ifa.

59. While many of the doctrines or aspects of the worldviews of Ifa and Tijani Sufism presented here have been discussed in the secondary literature, they have usually been covered with an emphasis on their historical, sociopolitical, or anthropological significance, and not their intellectual or philosophical relevance. That is, from the secondary literature, one can get a general sense of what Tijani Sufis and babalawo claim to know and do, but it is difficult to get a sense of the intellectual rigor, rhetorical force, and internal logic and coherence of the traditions from these accounts because they seldom focus on these philosophical dimensions. For example, many works on Tijani Sufism describe the concept of the *Quṭb*, an axial saint or friend of God, but I am not aware of any that demonstrate (or seek to) the logical necessity of a *Quṭb* given certain fundamental premises of the tradition. While Ifa and Tijani Sufism have been admirably represented in the secondary literature, what I am attempting to do in this work is to "think through" and "think with" these traditions the way Izutsu has done with Ibn ʿArabi and Chuang Tzu, Bernard Faure has done with Chan/Zen traditions, or the way a book presenting the thought of Plotinus, Spinoza, or Wittgenstein would.

60. See Bernard Faure and Janet Lloyd, *Double Exposure: Cutting Across Buddhist and Western Discourses* (Stanford: Stanford University Press, 2004) for an exposition and examples of "thinking with" Buddhist traditions.

61. Quoted in Chittick, *Imaginal Worlds*, 176.

62. It is possible that Ifa developed from, or was substantially influenced by, Islamic forms of geomancy (*khaṭṭ al-raml*) or that Islamic geomancy and Ifa are derived from a common ancestor, or that Ifa influenced *khaṭṭ al-raml*, in which case Sufism and Ifa would have a closer shared history.

63. Amadou Hapâté Bâ, "The Living Tradition," in *General History of Africa*, vol. 1, *Methodology and African Prehistory*, ed. J. Ki-Zerbo (Berkeley: University of California Press, 1981), 202–3. What I am suggesting here is not a kind of phenomenological bracketing or "suspension of disbelief," but rather a potential "forgetting" of theories and methods such as phenomenology itself.

CHAPTER 1

1. Some have hypothesized that it is derived from *Ṣuf*, meaning wool, referring to the woolen garments that early ascetics often wore. Others connect it to the word *Ṣafā'*, which means purity. Still others think it refers to *Ṣuffah* (bench) and the *Ahl al- Ṣuffa*, the famous members of the early Islamic community who lived on this bench outside the Prophet's mosque in Medina. Still others think the name comes from *Ṣaff*, meaning line or rank, the implication being that Sufis are the foremost in religion, like the first few rows in a mosque. The polymath al-Birūnī famously suggested that the term was derived from the Greek *Sophia*.

2. Aḥmad Zarrūq (d. 1493) writes, "Sufism has two thousand definitions." Quoted in Ibrahim Niasse, *Pearls from the Divine Flood: Selected Discourses from Shaykh Al-Islam Ibrahim Niasse*, trans. Zachary Wright (Atlanta: African American Islamic Institute, 2006), 41.

3. Ibn al-Jalā', quoted in Eric Geoffroy, *Introduction to Sufism: The Inner Path of Islam* (Bloomington, Ind.: World Wisdom, 2010), 1.

4. Ismā'īlism and Twelve Imām Shi'ism also contain important esoteric Islamic traditions that are distinct from Sufism, not to mention earlier traditions of Islamic piety and esoteric thought that were not called *taṣawwuf*, but whose adherents and authors later came to be categorized as Sufis, as well as the traditions of Islamic philosophy and occultism whose connection to Sufism is not necessarily explicit or clear (e.g., the Brethren of Purity and the Illuminationists).

5. Most Sufis would say that it is the essence of Islam, such as in the saying of Aḥmad Zarrūq, "Sufism is to religion what the spirit is to the body." Quoted in Niasse, *Pearls from the Divine Flood*, 47.

6. The term "mysticism" is derived from the Greek *mysterion*, meaning "a secret rite or doctrine," which is in turn derived from *mystes*, meaning "an initiate," which itself is derived from *muen*, meaning "to close or shut (the mouth or eyes)." Unfortunately, this term has been clouded by connotations of subjective, emotive irrationality since the standard-bearers of the Enlightenment defined their "rationality" against "mysticism." Furthermore, William James's influential *Varieties of Religious Experience* largely served to reduce mysticism to a particular category of personal, psychological experience, and Bertrand Russell's *Logic and Mysticism* categorized it as a special kind of irrationality. These particular prejudices notwithstanding, if figures in the so-called Western tradition such as Plotinus, St. Theresa of Avila, St. John of the Cross, and Meister Eckhart are "mystics" then Sufis are also mystics. Here I take the term "mystical" to denote a spiritual/intellectual tradition that emphasizes union or direct connection with the Divine or the Transcendent, and to connote the importance of initiation and secrecy—either of things not to be said or things that cannot be said—in these traditions.

7. 'Alī Hujwīrī, *Kashf al-mahjúb: The Oldest Persian Treatise on Sufism*, trans. R. A. Nicholson (London: Luzac and Co, 1911), 44.

8. Namely the second century Hijri, circa eighth and ninth century CE.

9. Traditionally each Islamic science was classified according to its definition (*ḥadd*), subject matter (*mawḍū'*), founder (*wāḍi'*), name (*ism*), derivation (*istimdād*), legal status (*ḥukm*), topics (*masā'il*), relationship to other sciences (*nisba*), distinguishing trait/virtue (*faḍīla*), and fruit/benefit (*thamara*).

10. Niasse, *Pearls from the Divine Flood*, 43. Similarly, Sufism has also been described as the "science of intention (*niyya*)," since, according to a ḥadīth, "actions are [judged] by their intentions." Thus even performing all the actions required by Islamic law could be judged as sinful, if one's intention is not correct. The famous Sufi Shaykh al-Shādhilī (d. 1253) is said to have remarked, "If someone does not become immersed in this science of ours, he will die as one who persists in the major sins, without being aware of his condition." Quoted in Niasse, *Removal of Confusion*, 21.

11. From the oft-quoted verse of the Qur'an (33:21), "Verily, you have in God's Messenger a beautiful model for whosoever hopes for God and the Last Day and remembers God much."

12. *Ṣaḥīḥ Muslim*, 6.168.

13. In Arabic, *Kāna al-Qur'ān yamshī 'alā'l-ard*.

14. W. Montgomery Watt, *Imam Al-Ghazali's Deliverance from Error and the Beginning of Guidance* (Kuala Lumpur, Malaysia: Islamic Book Trust, 2005), 52.

15. See William Chittick, *The Self-Disclosure of God: Principles of Ibn Al-'Arabī's Cosmology* (Albany: SUNY Press, 1998), 57–90.

16. Aḥmad ibn 'Ajība, *Tafsīr Fātiḥa al-Kabīr* (Beirut: Dar al-Kutub al-'Ilmiyya, 2004), 244.

17. This is why descriptions of Sufi doctrine tend toward the allusive and mythopoeic; allusion and symbol are necessary when experience is not shared.

18. Chittick, *Sufi Path of Knowledge*, 169.

19. Jalāl al-dīn Muḥammad Rūmī, *Mathnawi of Jalaluddin Rumi*, trans. R. A. Nicholson (London: Luzac, 1972), 3.3637–39.

20. In imitation of the Prophetic supplication *Allāhuma aranā al-ashyā' kamā hiya*, "O God, show us things as they really are."

21. See Watt, *Al-Ghazali's Deliverance from Error*, 73–78; as well as the introduction of al-Suhrawardī's *Ḥikmat al-Ishrāq* in John Walbridge and Hossein Ziai, *The Philosophy of Illumination: A New Critical Edition of*

*the Text of Hikmat al-Ishrāq* (Provo: Bringham Young University Press, 2007), xxxviii–5; and the introduction to Mulla Sadra's *Hikmat al-ʿArshiyya*, in James Winston Morris, *The Wisdom of the Throne: An Introduction to the Philosophy of Mulla Sadra* (Princeton: Princeton University Press, 1981).

22. Titus Burckhardt, *Universal Man: Extracts* (Roxburgh, Scotland: Beshara, 1995), 42. Jīlī was one of the most prominent authors of Ibn ʿArabi's school.

23. These three terms are taken from Qurʾanic passages (the first two from sura 102 and the last from 69:51). See Martin Lings, *The Book of Certainty: The Sufi Doctrine of Faith, Vision, and Gnosis* (Cambridge, UK: Islamic Texts Society, 1992).

24. Lings, *Book of Certainty*.

25. Martin Lings, *Sufi Poems: A Mediaeval Anthology* (Cambridge, UK: Islamic Texts Society, 2004), 29.

26. Schimmel, *Mystical Dimensions of Islam*, 266.

27. Sufis often quote the verse of the Qurʾan "Wheresoever you turn, there is the Face of God" (2:115) to justify the orthodoxy of this state.

28. Burckhardt, *Universal Man*, xii.

29. Inyās, *Jawāhir al-rasāʾil*, 1:60.

30. Maḥmūd Shabistarī, *Gulshan-I Rāz: The Mystic Rose Garden*, trans. E. H. Whinfield (London: Trübner, 1880), 46.

31. Inyās, *Jawāhir al-rasāʾil*, 1:60.

32. See Chittick, *Sufi Path of Knowledge*, 13–30, 213–17.

33. Lings, *Sufi Poems*, 88.

34. Awhad al-din Balyani, *Know Yourself: An Explanation of the Oneness of Being*, trans. Cecilia Twinch (Oxford, UK: Windrush, 2011), 17–18, 26–27.

35. While Arabic word *insān* refers to humankind, both male and female, the word is grammatically male, and is thus often translated as "man" in English. In the quotes and text below, I generally render *insān* as "human" and sometimes "man" depending on the context. In any event, it should be remembered that *insān* refers to the human being, both male and female.

36. William C. Chittick, "The Five Divine Presences: From Qunawi to Qaysari," *Muslim World* 72, no. 2 (April 1982): 110.

37. Izutsu, *Sufism and Taoism*, 220–21; al-Barrāda, *Jawāhir al-Maʿānī*, 395–401.

38. Cheikh Tijani Chiekh Elhadi, interview with the author, conducted in Arabic, January 2008, Rabat, Morocco. See also Niasse, *Removal of Confusion*, 237.

39. Chittick, *Sufi Path of Knowledge*, 16–18.

40. See Niasse, *Removal of Confusion*, 155: "The Prophet said, 'the Final Hour will not arrive as long as there is a perfect human (*insān kāmil*) upon the earth.' He is the delegated spiritual pillar. If you want, you could call him the one for whose sake the universe is kept intact. If (this position) were taken away, the sky would be shattered, the sun would be divested of life, the stars would fall, the pages (*ṣuḥuf*) would be scattered, the earth would split asunder, and the Resurrection would be at hand."

41. Ibn al-ʿArabi, *The Ringstones of Wisdom (Fuṣūṣ al-ḥikam)*, trans. Caner Dagli (Chicago: Kazi, 2004), 6.

42. For a list of ḥadīth and other early sources dealing with this concept, see al-Barrāda, *Jawāhir al-Maʿānī*, 395–401; and Michel Chodkiewicz, *Seal of the Saints: Prophethood and Sainthood in the Doctrine of Ibn ʿArabī* (Cambridge, UK: Islamic Texts Society, 1993), 60–73.

43. Chodkiewicz, *Seal of the Saints*, 60–73.

44. Chittick, *Sufi Path of Knowledge*, 169, 85.

45. Burckhardt, *Universal Man*, x.

46. Chodkiewicz, *Seal of the Saints*, 50.

47. Although these of course are regarded as important, given that they serve as the "door" to and outward expression of the inner sainthood of the prophet.

48. See the introduction of Vincent Cornell's *Realm of the Saint: Power and Authority in Moroccan Sufism* (Austin: University of Texas Press, 1998); and Chodkiewicz's *Seal of the Saints* for a detailed discussion of the two terms.

49. See Chodkiewicz, *Seal of the Saints*, 89–115.

50. Inyās, *Jawāhir al-rasāʾil*, 1:132.

51. There is a subtle difference here between Ibn ʿArabi's conception of the seal of the saints and that of the Tijanis. For Ibn ʿArabi, the seal of the saints appears to be the source of sainthood even for the prophets (although not superior to them, standing in relationship to them as the "keeper of the treasury in relationship to the King and Nobles," according to al-Kāshānī, a prominent commentator within the Akbarī school), whereas in the Tijani schema the Prophet Muḥammad receives his sanctity directly from God, while the other prophets receive from him and serve as a secondary source for the seal of sainthood. See figure 1.

52. See Chodkiewicz, *Seal of the Saints*, 136.

53. In this respect, *walāyah* is closely connected to the concept of *fayḍ*, the divine outpouring or effulgence.

54. Quoted in Niasse, *Pearls from the Divine Flood*, 105.xxx.

55. *Ṣaḥīḥ Bukhārī*, 81.91, https://sunnah.com/bukhari/81/91.

56. This is but one heuristic division among many other schemas describing the wide diversity of Sufi practice.

57. Martin Lings, *What Is Sufism?* (London: George Allen & Unwin, 1975), 59.

58. Shaykh Ibrahim Niasse wrote, "We have been commanded to pray because it constitutes the remembrance of Allah (20:14).... The remembrance of Allah

constitutes the highest stage in religion" (Niasse, *Pearls from the Divine Flood*, 118).

59. This distinction between *dhikr* and *fikr* is more analytic and heuristic than substantive—they are combined in practice and seldom discussed separately, and *dhikr* is used to name dances, songs, visualizations, and other "meditative" practices.

60. See Inyās, *Jawāhir al-rasā'il*, 1:10.

61. However, in many regions, such as West Africa, the older, more informal networks and family lineages continued to be the main vectors of Sufism and other traditions of Islamic spirituality up through the nineteenth century.

62. It is also interesting to note that Sufi doctrine also became more formalized and fully elaborated in writing shortly after this period, and undoubtedly, the two trends are connected. However, this was not seen as a form of "progress" or development by those who participated in it. Just before this period, 'Alī Hujwīrī, the author of the early Sufi treatise, *Kashf al-Maḥjūb*, lamented that Sufism went from being "a name without a reality to being a reality without a name." Seyyed Hossein Nasr resolves these seemingly opposite trends by asserting that the need for exposition of the truth increases with our ignorance, not our knowledge. See Seyyed Hossein Nasr, *Three Muslim Sages: Avicenna, Suhrawardī, Ibn 'Arabī* (Cambridge: Harvard University Press, 1964), 91.

63. The precedent for this being the pact of 'Aqabah in which a delegation of people from Medina pledged their allegiance to the Prophet and about which the Qur'an says, "God's hand was over their hands" (48:10).

64. If music is involved, it is often called a *samā'*.

65. See Zachary Wright, *On the Path of the Prophet: Shaykh Ahmad Tijani and the Tariqa Muḥammadiyya* (Atlanta: African American Islamic Institute, 2005).

66. The complete name of which is the Ṭarīqa Aḥmadiyya Muḥammadiya Ibrāhīmiyya Ḥanifiyya Tijāniyya.

67. Sīdī 'Alī Harāzim, *Kitāb Jawāhir al-Ma'ānī wa-bulūgh al-amānī fī fayḍ Sīdī Abī'l al-'Abbās al-Tijānī*, trans. Ravane Mbaye (Dakar: Dar al-Bouraq, 2011).

68. John O'Fahey and Berndt Radtke, "Neo-Sufism Reconsidered," *Der Islam* 70, no. 1 (1993): 52–87; and Nehemia Levtzion, *Eighteenth-Century Renewal and Reform in Islam* (Syracuse: Syracuse University Press, 1987), 117–32.

69. Which became widespread in the central Sahara, namely in Libya, Chad, and Niger.

70. Also known as the Mirghaniyya, this order spread and is still active in Sudan, Ethiopia, and Eritrea.

71. Founder of the Sammāniyya order, which is popular in Sudan.

72. Or even earlier, as Fritz Meier identifies their origins in the eleventh century; see B. Radtke, "Fritz Meier's Unpublished Papers and the Tijāniyya," *Sudanic Africa* 11 (2000): 125–30.

73. For example, Shādhilīs claim that all *aqṭāb* (poles or axial saints) are Shādhilī; the Naqshbandīs claim that their *silsila*, which goes through Abu Bakr, grants them easier and superior spiritual realization; and Qādirīs claim that the founder of their order, Shaykh 'abd al-Qādir Jilānī, is superior to all other saints.

74. Amadou Hampâté Bâ, *Vie et enseignement de Tierno Bokar: Le sage de Bandiagara* (Paris: Presence Africaine, 1980), 230.

75. See Roman Loimeier, *Islamic Reform and Political Change in Northern Nigeria* (Evanston: Northwestern University Press, 1997); and Jean Triaud and David Robinson, eds., *La Tijânîyya: Une confrérie musulmane à la conquête de l'Afrique* (Paris: Karthala, 2000).

76. Niasse, *Pearls from the Divine Flood*, 82.

77. For an excellent discussion of the term *fayḍ* and its use in Tijānī contexts, see Rüdiger Seesemann, *The Divine Flood: Ibrahim Niasse and the Roots of a Twentieth-Century Sufi Revival* (New York: Oxford University Press, 2011), 41–66.

78. The central prayer of the Tijānī tradition, the *Ṣalāt al-Fātiḥ* is actually believed to have been revealed to the Egyptian Sufi Muḥammad al-Bakrī (d. 1585) when he took a retreat seeking the best way to invoke blessings on the Prophet. Shaykh Aḥmad al-Tijānī is said to have been instructed in the merits of this prayer by the Prophet Muḥammad in a vision. The Tijānī order popularized the *Ṣalāt al-Fātiḥ*, which they hold to be the best prayer on the Prophet, and the best form of invocation (*dhikr*) aside from the Supreme Name of God (*al-ism al-A'ẓam*).

79. For example, see Titus Burckhardt, "The Prayer of Ibn Mashish," *Studies in Comparative Religion* 12, nos. 1–2 (Winter–Spring 1978), http://www.studiesincomparativereligion.com/public/articles/The_Prayer_of_Ibn_Mashish-translation_and_commentary_by_Titus_Burckhardt.aspx.

80. Recall that *ma'rifa* is literally existential knowledge. In the *Jawāhir al-Ma'ānī*, Shaykh Aḥmad al-Tijānī is recorded as saying that "*fayḍ* embraces all forms of knowledge ['ulūm], all mysteries [asrār], all realities [haqā'iq], all realizations [ma'ārif], and all lights [anwār]" (1047).

81. Inyās, *Jawāhir al-rasā'il*, 1:113.

82. Niasse, *Pearls from the Divine Flood*, 17. *Fayḍa* is the *ism marra* of the term *fayḍ*, and refers to a particular instance of this outpouring, which according to a Tijani prophecy would come at a time when humanity was in great distress, and bring a great multitude of people into the *ṭarīqa* and to knowledge of God.

83. This diagram is modified from that found in Seesemann, *Divine Flood*, 56, and from those found in the *Rimāḥ* (from which Seesemann's diagram is also derived). Many Tijani disciples interviewed during the course of my research would modify this diagram to make Shaykh Ibrahim the intermediary between Shaykh Aḥmad al-Tijānī and everyone/everything else.

84. Consisting of the standard one hundred *AstaghfiruLlāh*, one hundred *Ṣalāt ʿalā'l-nabī*, and one hundred *Lā ilāha illā Llāh*, separated by and concluded with standard Qur'anic passages.

85. Consisting of one recitation of the *Fātiḥa*, thirty recitations of *Istighfār*—*AstaghfiruLlah al-ʿAẓīm aladhī lā ilāha illā Huwa al-Ḥayyu al-Qayyūm* ("I ask forgiveness from God, the Supreme, whom no God exists but He, the Living, the Self-Subsistent")—fifty recitations of the *Ṣalāt al-Fātiḥ*, one hundred recitations of the shahāda *Lā ilāha illā Allāh*, followed by one recitation of *Muḥammadun RasūluLlāh ʿalayhi SalāmuLlāh*, then twelve (or eleven) recitations of the *Jawharat al-Kamāl*—all separated by and concluded with standard Qur'anic passages.

86. Held between the afternoon and sunset prayers, in which the shahāda is recited at least one thousand times, begun and concluded with standard Qur'anic passages.

87. *Tarbiya* is a word that means spiritual training or rearing and is the process by which the shaykh brings the initiate to spiritual realization and maturity. This term took on special significance in Shaykh Ibrahim Niasse's branch of the Tijāniyya, as will be discussed in the next chapter. For an overview of the history and debates surrounding this term in Tijani sources, see Seesemann, *Divine Flood*, 67–100.

88. Although the way *tarbiya* is practiced in some places might be described as a kind of *khalwa*.

89. When reciting this prayer, said to have been revealed to Shaykh Aḥmad al-Tijānī by the Prophet, Tijanis must be in a state of ritual ablution, sit in a clean place, and observe certain other conditions because after seven recitations the Prophet, the first four caliphs, and Shaykh Aḥmad al-Tijānī are believed to become present with the reciter.

90. This distinction between the "way of gratitude" and the "way of asceticism" was characterized in the influential work *al-Ibrīz* by the eighteenth-century Shādhilī scholar of Fes, Aḥmad al-Lamaṭī, about his shaykh, ʿabd al-ʿAzīz al-Dabbāgh. The way of gratitude (*shukr*) was described as being the way of Shaykh al-Shādhilī, and the way of asceticism (*zuhd*) was described as being the way of al-Ghazālī. The *Ibrīz* says:

> And from the start, emigration (*hijra*) on the path of thankfulness was to God and to His Apostle, not to illumination and the acquisition of unveilings. Emigration on the path of self-mortification, however, was aimed at illumination and the acquisition of spiritual ranks. Journeying on the first path is a journey of hearts, while on the second path is a journey of bodies. And illumination on the first path is a sudden onslaught that the bondsman hadn't been desiring. While the bondsman was in the station of seeking repentance and forgiveness of sins, behold, clear illumination came over him! Both paths are correct but the path of thankfulness is more correct and more sincere.

John O'Kane and Bernd Radtke, *Pure Gold from the Words of Sayyidi ʿAbd al-ʿAzīz al-Dabbagh* (Boston: Brill, 2007), 623.

91. See Niasse, *Removal of Confusion*, 154.

92. *Ṣaḥīḥ Muslim*, 52.78, https://sunnah.com/muslim/52/78. In the same vein, the famous early female Sufi saint Rābiʿa al ʿAdawiyya is said to have walked around with a bucket of water and a torch in order to "set fire to heaven and put out those of hell, so people worship God for His own sake alone."

93. Niasse, *Pearls from the Divine Flood*, 91–98, 125–26.

94. See Seesemann, *Divine Flood*, 106–8.

95. See Annemarie Schimmel, *Mystical Dimensions of Islam* (Chapel Hill: University of North Carolina Press, 1975), 86–87.

96. See Chittick, *Sufi Path of Knowledge*, 372–75. In a passage reminiscent of Taoist descriptions of a sage, Chittick writes of the *malāmī*, "In him, nothing stands out, since he flows with all created things in perfect harmony and equilibrium. . . . He is like a tree or a bird in his ordinariness, following the divine will wherever it takes him, with no friction, no protest, complete serenity, no waves" (372).

97. See Ghislaine Lydon, *On Trans-Saharan Trails: Islamic Law, Trade Networks, and Cross-Cultural Exchange in Nineteenth-Century Western Africa* (Cambridge: Cambridge University Press, 2012).

98. Ibn Anbūja, *Mizāb al-Raḥma al-Rabbaniyya fī al-Tarbiya bi'l-Ṭarīqa al-Tijāniyya* (Casablanca: Dar al-Rashad, 2009).

99. Amir Syed, "Al-Ḥājj ʿUmar Tāl and the Realm of the Written: Mastery, Mobility and Islamic Authority in 19th Century West Africa" (PhD diss., University of Michigan, 2017).

100. For more on the *Rimāḥ*, see B. Radtke, "Studies on the Sources of the *Kitab Rimah hizb ar-rahim* of al-Ḥajj ʿUmar," *Sudanic Afrika* 6 (1995): 73–113.

101. The Ḥamawwiya also had its fair share of scholarly adherents, but they did not constitute the majority of the order. See Sean Hanretta, *Gender and Agency in the History of a West African Sufi Community: The Followers of Yacouba Sylla* (Cambridge: Cambridge University Press, 2009).

102. See Amadou Hampâté Bâ, *A Spirit of Tolerance: The Inspiring Life of Tierno Bokar*, trans. Gaetani, Roger (Bloomington, Ind.: World Wisdom, 2008); and Louis Brenner's more scholarly *West African Sufi: The Religious Heritage and Spiritual Search of Cerno Bokar Saalif Taal* (Berkeley: University of California Press, 1984).

103. David Robinson, *Paths of Accommodation: Muslim Societies and French Colonial Authorities in Senegal and Mauritania, 1880–1920* (Athens: Ohio State University Press, 2000); Ravane Mbaye, *Pensée et action: Le grand savant El Hadji Malick Sy* (Ozoir-la-Férrière, France: Albouraq, 2003).

104. See Seesemann's *Divine Flood* for an in-depth scholarly description of the early history of this phenomenon.

105. Abdallah Schleifer, ed., *The Muslim 500: The 500 Most Influential Muslims* (Amman, Jordan: Royal Islamic Strategic Studies Center, 2013), 70–71. While the figure given for the number of disciples is very much a matter of debate, the influence that the various successors of Shaykh Ibrahim Niasse wield in West Africa and the diaspora is indeed immense.

106. In the *Theaetetus* Socrates says, "Take a look round, then, and see that none of the uninitiated are listening. Now by the uninitiated I mean: the people who believe in nothing but what they can grasp in their hands, and who will not allow that action or generation or anything invisible can have real existence."

CHAPTER 2

1. Actually a *ḥadīth qudsī*, frequently cited by disciples of the Fayḍa: "Seek to know me before you worship me, for without knowing Me, how can you worship Me?"

2. S. D., interview with the author, conducted in French and English, February 16, 2014, Dakar, Senegal.

3. "the greatest opening/enlightenment," a term designating supreme realization.

4. Abu Ibrahim, interview with the author, conducted in English, February 24, 2014, Dakar, Senegal.

5. For example, see Qur'an 2:186, 12:58, and 5:83, which reads, "You will see their eyes overflow with tears as they listen to what is revealed to the Messenger, for they recognize [*'arifū*] the Truth."

6. Quoted in Reza Shah-Kazemi, "The Notion and Significance of *ma'rifa* in Sufism," *Journal of Islamic Studies* 13, no. 2 (2002): 161.

7. Ibid.

8. Hujwīrī, *Kashf al-mahjūb*, 267–68.

9. That is, the cosmological proofs of God's existence of peripatetic philosophy and theology. In the words of the early Baghdadi Sufi Abū Bakr al-Wāsiṭī (d. 932), "If someone says, 'I recognized God through the evidence,' ask him how he recognized the evidence." Quoted in William Chittick, trans., *Kashf Al-asrār: The Unveiling of the Mysteries* (Louisville, Ky.: Fons Vitae, 2015), 295.

10. A reference to the state of annihilation, *fanā'*, discussed above.

11. Hujwīrī, *Kashf al-mahjub*, 269–71.

12. An early Persian Sufi of Nishapur, Abū Ḥafṣ 'amr ibn Salmā Ḥaddād (d. ca. 879) was described by other early Sufi writes (e.g., Sulamī and Qushayrī) as an ascetic and a *malāmī* (see previous chapter) of the first order.

13. Hujwīrī, *Kashf al-mahjub*, 266–67.

14. The Qur'an refers to God as al-*'Alīm*, "The Knowing," deriving from the same root as *'ilm*. Moreover, in a famous ḥadīth the Prophet says *al-'ilmu nurun*, "Knowledge is Light," which was taken by Sufi authors to imply a scope for *'ilm* beyond mere conceptual knowledge.

15. And in other specialized contexts, *'ilm* is considered to be superior to *ma'rifa*—the former referring to God's perfect knowledge, the latter referring to man's "recognition" of the Divine, which is regarded inferior because it implies a coming to know after ignorance. Ibn 'Arabi characteristically took the position that these distinctions were merely verbal and that whether a Sufi author referred to *'ilm* as being superior to *ma'rifa* or *ma'rifa* as being superior to *'ilm*, he referred to the same distinction between divine and merely human knowledge. See Chittick, *Sufi Path of Knowledge*, 148–49.

16. See Hujwīrī, *Kashf al-Maḥjūb*, 267; and Abū Naṣr al-Sarrāj, *Kitāb al-Luma' Fi'l-Ṭasawwuf of Abū Naṣr 'Abdallah B. 'Alī Al-Sarrāj Al-Ṭúsī*, trans. R. A. Nicholson (London: E. J. Gibb Memorial Series, 1963), 40.

17. Inyās, *Jawāhir al-rasā'il*, 2:62.

18. The two ḥadīth, while not found in the canonical collections, have been cited so often by Sufis that they have become part of the popular canon of narrations attributed to the Prophet. Ibn 'Arabi claimed to have asked the Prophet about this narration in a dream, and that the Prophet told him that its meaning is sound even though he never said it. Thus Ibn 'Arabi considered it a saying whose authenticity is proven by unveiling (*kashf*) but not by historical transmission (*naql*). See Chittick, *Sufi Path of Knowledge*, 391n14 and 250–51.

19. The first chapter of Ibn 'Arabi's influential *Ringstones of Wisdom* is essentially a commentary on this tradition.

20. Shaykha Maryam Niasse, daughter of Shaykh Ibrahim Niasse, told me that "love is a station that precedes *ma'rifa* and is also the fruit of the union of *ma'rifa* to which it leads." Interview with the author, conducted in Arabic, March 7, 2014, Dakar, Senegal.

21. Chittick, *Sufi Path of Knowledge*, 345.

22. Ibn al-ʿArabi, *Ringstones of Wisdom*, 134–35.

23. Ibn al-ʿArabī, *Futūḥāt al-Makkiyya* (Cairo: Bulaq, 1911), 2:297.

24. Ibid., 2:297–98.

25. Ibid., 2:298–99; cf. Chittick, *Sufi Path of Knowledge*, 167–78.

26. Ibn al-ʿArabī, *Futūḥāt al-Makkiyya*, 2:299.

27. Chittick, *Sufi Path of Knowledge*, 149.

28. Inyās, *Jawāhir al-rasāʾil*, 1:47.

29. Inyās, *Fī Riyāḍ al-Tafsīr li'l-Qurʾān al-Karīm*, 5:250–51. Similarly, Ibn ʿAṭā Allāh's *Ḥikam* no. 246 reads, "The cosmos is large in respect to your body, but it is not large in respect to your soul." See Ibn ʿAṭā Allāh al-Iskandarī, *Kitāb al-ḥikam* (Cairo: Maktaba Madbūlī, n.d.), 41.

30. Sidi Mohamed Kane, interview with the author, conducted in French, April 26, 2014, Dakar, Senegal.

31. Chittick, *Sufi Path of Knowledge*, 341.

32. Ibid.

33. *Ṣaḥīḥ Bukhari*, 97.35, https://sunnah.com/bukhari/97/35.

34. A reference to the ḥadīth "My Heavens and My Earth do not contain me, but the heart of My believing servant contains Me" and "The heart of the believer is the throne of the All-Merciful." See Chittick, *Sufi Path of Knowledge*, 339–40.

35. Ibn al-ʿArabi, *Ringstones of Wisdom*, 226.

36. Ibid., 115–16.

37. Rumi similarly writes, "Know that the outward form passes away, (but) the world of reality remains forever. / How long will you play at loving the shape of the jug? Leave the shape of the jug: go, seek water" and "When the many-coloured glasses are no more, then the colourless Light makes thee amazed. / Make it thy habit to behold the Light without the glass, in order that when the glass is shattered there may not be, blindness (in thee)." *Mathnawi*, 2.1020–21 and 2.990–91.

38. Ibn ʿArabi here plays with the meaning of the root of the word "heart" (*qalb*), q-l-b, which means to change, transform, or turn over. William Chittick, "Ibn ʿArabī's Own Summary of the Fuṣūṣ: 'The Imprint of the Bezels of Wisom,'" *Journal of the Muhyiddin Ibn ʿArabī Society* 1 (1982): 26.

39. One is reminded of the short stories by Jorge Luis Borges and Lewis Carroll that explore the futility of creating a map that is the same size as the country or the world it is meant to represent. One of Carroll's characters notes, "We now use the country itself, as its own map, and I assure you it does nearly as well." Lewis Carroll, *The Complete Illustrated Works* (New York: Gramercy Books, 1982), 727.

40. Rumi makes a similar distinction in his Mathanwi in the story about the Greek and Chinese painters. In summary, a king once held a contest between Greek and Chinese artisans to see who could create the most beautiful room. The Chinese artists asked the king for hundreds of shades of paint and supplies, but the Greeks only asked for polish. When the Chinese artists were finished, the king inspected the room and was astounded by its beauty, but when the screen separating it from the Greeks' room was removed, he was even more amazed. The reflection of the Chinese works of art on the polished Greek walls was even more beautiful than the Chinese room itself. Rumi concludes this story with the following verses:

> The Greeks, O father, are the Sufis: without study and books and erudition / But they have burnished their breasts pure from greed and cupidity and avarice and hatreds. / That purity of the mirror is, beyond doubt, the heart which receives images innumerable. / That Moses (the perfect saint) holds in his bosom the formless infinite form of the Unseen (reflected) from the mirror of his heart . . . / know that the mirror of the heart hath no bound. / Here the understanding becomes silent or (else) it leads into error, because the heart is with Him (God), or indeed the heart is He." (1:3484–89)

41. Ibn al-ʿArabi, *Ringstones of Wisdom*, 115.

42. Seesemann, *The Divine Flood*.

43. Zachary Wright, *Living Knowledge in West African Islam: The Sufi Community of Ibrahim Niasse* (Leiden: Brill, 2015), 132.

44. Joseph Hill, "Divine Knowledge and Islamic Authority: Religious Specialization among Disciples of Baay Ñas" (PhD diss., Yale University, 2007).

45. I am grateful to William Chittick and James Morris for suggesting this translation and its advantages.

46. al-Barrāda, *Jawāhir al-Maʿānī*, 979–80.

47. Ibid., 1045–49.

48. K. S., interview with the author, conducted in English, March 26, 2014, Skype.

49. Shaykh Tijānī ʿAlī Cissé, interview with the author, conducted in Arabic, January 14, 2013, Medina Baye, Senegal. The "lamp" is a reference to the celebrated "verse of light" (24:35) which reads, "God is the Light of the heavens and the earth, the likeness of His Light is like a niche wherein is a lamp—the lamp is in a glass, the glass is as it were a shining planet—kindled from a blessed tree, an olive neither of the East nor West, whose oil would almost shine forth, though no fire touched it. Light upon light. God guides unto His light whom He will. And God strikes likenesses for mankind and God is of all things, Knowing."

50. Inyās, *Jawāhir al-rasāʾil*, 2:58.

51. Ibrahim Niasse, *Maqāmāt al-Dīn al-Thalāth* in *Sa'ādat al-Anām* (Cairo: al-Sharikat al-Dawliyya, 2006), 129.
52. Ibid.
53. Shaykh Tijānī 'Alī Cissé, interview with the author, conducted in Arabic, January 14, 2013, Medina Baye, Senegal.
54. Sidi Inaya Niang, interview with the author, conducted in English and French, March 13, 2014, Dakar, Senegal.
55. Sidi Mohamed Kane, interview with the author, conducted in French, April 26, 2014, Dakar, Senegal.
56. Sidi Inaya Niang, interview with the author, conducted in English and French, March 13, 2014, Dakar, Senegal.
57. K. S., interview with the author, conducted in English, April 6, 2014, Skype.
58. "La conscience de toutes les sciences: science sans conscience n'est que ruine de l'âme."
59. Sidi Inaya Niang, interview with the author, conducted in English and French, March 13, 2014, Dakar, Senegal.
60. Cissé, *What the Knowers of Allah Have Said*, 20.
61. Ibid., 61.
62. Shaykh Barham Diop, interview with the author, conducted in Arabic, April 4, 2014, Dakar, Senegal.
63. Chittick, *Sufi Path of Knowledge*, 249.
64. Sidi Mohamed Kane, interview with the author, conducted in French, April 24, 2014, Dakar, Senegal.
65. For a detailed discussion of this work, its reception, and context, see Wright, *Living Knowledge in West African Islam*, 223–31.
66. Similarly, Sidi Inaya Niang told me that Shaykh Ibrahim often quoted an adage attributed to Imām Mālik, founder of the Mālikī school of jurisprudence (*fiqh*): "Whoever engages in Sufism [*taṣawwuf*] and does not learn *fiqh* is a heretic; whoever learns *fiqh* but does not engage in Sufism is depraved; and whosoever joins the two of them is correct."
67. Sidi Inaya Niang, interview with the author, conducted in English, March 4, 2014, Dakar, Senegal.
68. Inyās, *Jawāhir al-rasā'il*, 2:61.
69. This idea is also mentioned in Ibn 'Arabi's letter to Fakhr ad-Dīn al-Rāzī and Ibn 'Ajība's commentary on the widely used grammar text *al-Ajrūmiyya*.
70. Inyās, *Jawāhir al-rasā'il*, 2:59.
71. Ibrahim Niasse, *Rūḥ al-Adab* (Kano, n.d.), vv. 46–48.
72. M. D., interview with author, conducted in French, March 19, 2014, Dakar, Senegal.
73. Cissé, *What the Knowers of Allah Have Said*, 30–31.
74. Chittick, *Sufi Path of Knowledge*, 169–70.
75. Ibid., 169.
76. K. S., interview with the author, conducted in English, April 6, 2014, Skype.
77. The passage in question is a part of a commentary on a famous poem attributed to Junayd.
78. al-Barrāda, *Jawāhir al-Ma'ānī*, 893–97.
79. This point of view was prominent in Sufi discourse as early as al-Ghazālī (d. 1111), and increased in prominence as the tradition deepened its engagement with, and incorporation of, Islamic philosophical discourse.
80. Shaykh Aḥmad al-Tijānī, *Aḥzāb wa Awrād*, ed. Muḥammad al-Ḥāfiẓ al-Miṣrī (Cairo: n.p., 1983), 15.
81. Shaykh Māḥī Niasse, interview with author, conducted in Arabic, January 14, 2012, Medina Baye, Senegal. In this interview, Shaykh Māḥī also contrasted philosophy (*falsafa*) with Sufism, describing the former as being concerned with doubt and the latter with certainty: "The philosophers seek doubt in everything even to the extent of asking 'Is white black?' The Sufis seek certainty, they seek the Truth / the Real, as it is, they don't try to go into doubt. But as for philosophy, you always think in your mind trying to create these doubts."
82. Abu Ibrahim, interview with the author, conducted in English, February 24, 2014, Dakar, Senegal.
83. K. S., interview with the author, conducted in English, April 6, 2014, Skype.
84. *Sidi Ahmad Zarruq's Commentary on Shaykh al-Shadhili's Ḥizb al-Baḥr*, trans. Khalid Williams (London: Visions of Reality, 2013), 106–7. Shaykh Ibrahim quotes a similar passage in *The Removal of Confusion*, 30–31. For a more thorough discussion of these esoteric sciences and their status amongst the Tijāniyya, see also Wright, *Living Knowledge in West African Islam*, 233–36.
85. Inyās, *Jawāhir al-rasā'il*, 1:19.
86. Nevertheless, these talismanic traditions are widely practiced among the community of Shaykh Ibrahim and in the wider context of West African Sufism, in which many shaykhs have quite lucrative careers utilizing these secrets for wealthy clients, whether local or from the Middle East (especially the Gulf).
87. Niasse, *Removal of Confusion*, 88.
88. Shaykh Tijani 'Ali Cissé, interview with the author, conducted in Arabic, January 14, 2014, Medina Baye, Senegal.
89. Chittick, *Sufi Path of Knowledge*, 353.
90. Inyās, *Fī Riyāḍ al-Tafsīr*, 3:345.
91. Ibid., 1:350–51.
92. Inyās, *al-Sirr al-Akbar*, 447–48.
93. Niasse, *Removal of Confusion*, 21.

94. Mohammed Rustom, "Ibn ʿArabi's Letter to Fakhr al-Din al-Razi: A Study and Translation," *Oxford Journal of Islamic Studies* 25, no. 2 (2014): 113–37.

95. It is worth noting that the manuscript copies of this letter differ somewhat from what is found in this quotation from the *Jawāhir al-Maʿānī*, highlighting the fact that these classical Sufi texts and ideas are mediated by their transmission from master to disciple and by their quotations in other works. Thus the Tijani reception of Ibn ʿArabi's legacy differs from that of other Sufi orders or philosophical schools.

96. This refers to one of Ibn ʿArabi's favorite ḥadīths in which God presents himself to people on the Day of Judgment in a form in which they do not recognize Him, and they deny Him and seek refuge. Then God transforms Himself and appears to them in a form in which they do recognize Him, and so they acknowledge Him after having denied Him. See Chittick, *Self-Disclosure of God*, 440.

97. Niasse, *Removal of Confusion*, 167–68. See Rustom, "Ibn ʿArabi's Letter to Fakhr al-Din al-Razi" for a translation of a different version of this letter.

98. Hill, "Divine Knowledge and Islamic Authority," 249–50.

99. Shaykh Ibrāhīm Inyās, *Dawāwīn al-Sitt* (Beirut: Dār al-Fikr, 2009), 61.

CHAPTER 3

Portions of this chapter have been previously published in Oludamini Ogunnaike, "Annihilation in the Messenger Revisited: Clarifications on a Contemporary Sufi Practice and Its Precedents," *Journal of Islamic and Muslim Studies* 1, no. 2 (2016): 13–34, reproduced here with permission.

1. K. S., interview with the author, conducted in English, March 26, 2014, Skype.

2. Shaykh Ibrahim Niasse's first work, a short didactic poem advising Tijani disciples on how to achieve success in their spiritual lives.

3. M. D., interview with the author, conducted in French, March 19, 2014, Dakar, Senegal.

4. Harāzim, *Kitāb Jawāhir al-Maʿānī*, 1412. Also quoted in Niasse, *Removal of Confusion*, 37–38.

5. For an overview of this controversy and the different ways in which *tarbiya* was understood, see Niasse, *Removal of Confusion*, 89–95 and 151–68, and Rüdiger Seesemann, *The Divine Flood: Ibrahim Niasse and the Roots of a Twentieth-Century Sufi Revival* (New York: Oxford University Press, 2011), 75–87.

6. Shaykh Māḥī Niasse, interview with the author, conducted in Arabic, January 14, 2012, Medina Baye, Senegal.

7. Shaykh Babacar N'Diaye, interview with the author, conducted in Arabic, February 16, 2014, Arabic. This exact quote is also attributed to Ibrahim Niasse in Wright, *Living Knowledge in West African Islam*, 232.

8. Inyās, *al-Sirr al-Akbar*, 418.

9. Such ecstatic utterances are known as *shaṭaḥāt* and are a well-documented feature of Sufism throughout the ages. See Carl Ernst, *Words of Ecstasy in Sufism* (Albany: SUNY Press), 1985.

10. Shaykh Tijānī ʿAlī Cissé, interview with the author, conducted in Arabic, January 14, 2013, Medina Baye, Senegal.

11. Niasse, *Removal of Confusion*, 31, 35.

12. Inyās, *al-Sirr al-Akbar*, 392. Although Maigari wrote this work as a refutation of Shaykh Ibrahim's views, some of his summaries of the chapters of Niasse's work are quite accurate and concise syntheses of Niasse's more extended discussions.

13. Ibid., 427.

14. See Ibn al-ʿArabi, *Ringstones of Wisdom*, 87–95, for a more detailed discussion of this distinction and relationship between the Divine Creative Command (*al-ʿamr al-takwīnī*, here called the Divine Will), which makes things as they are, and the Divine Prescriptive Command (*al-ʿamr al-tadwīnī*, here called the Divine Judgment), which divides deeds into good and bad, and their consequences into felicitous and infelicitous. In this passage, Shaykh Ibrahim describes how the Knower is inwardly aware that everything happens according to the Divine Will, even those actions that go against the Divine Judgment; and yet he upholds and closely conforms to this Divine Judgment, even though he knows it is "out of his control" from a certain point of view.

15. Inyās, *Jawāhir al-rasāʾil*, 1:81.

16. Ibid.

17. Niasse, *Removal of Confusion*, 95.

18. The ḥadīth scholar and jurist Wakīʿ ibn al-Jarrāh (d. 812) was the teacher of Imām Shāfiʿī (d. 820), the eminent scholar, poet, and founder of the Shāfiʿī *madhhab*, one of the four main schools of Sunni jurisprudence.

19. A ḥadīth of the Prophet related in both *Ṣaḥīḥ Bukhārī*, 78.94, https://sunnah.com/bukhari/78/94; and *Ṣaḥīḥ Muslim*, 45.213, https://sunnah.com/muslim/45/213.

20. This references the common Sufi idea, expressed by many disciples, that people who are veiled in this life are in hell, and do not realize it until after they die.

21. This same idea is found in the previously cited letter from Ibn ʿArabi to Fakhr ad-Din al-Razi as well as Ibn ʿAjība's commentary on the famous grammar text, *al-Ajrūmiyya*.

22. This is probably another verse of Ibn ʿArabi's, as he quotes it in his *Ringstones of Wisdom*, 83.

23. This is a quotation from the famous ḥadīth of Gabriel, which will be discussed in further detail below.

24. The last phrase of this ḥadīth can be parsed in two ways: "if you do not see Him" or "if you are not, [then] you see Him." This latter interpretation has been interpreted by Sufis throughout the centuries as referring to the noetic aspect of *fanāʾ*, annihilation in God. The only way to see God is to be annihilated in God, since only God sees God.

25. Inyās, *Jawāhir al-rasāʾil*, 2:56–69. A recording of this sermon can be accessed at https://www.youtube.com/watch?v=zsOWmEOk7fI.

26. This tradition is the source of the "five pillars of Islam," and Sufis usually identify *iḥsān*—which literally means "doing the good/beautiful"—with Sufism.

27. *Ṣaḥīḥ Muslim* (*Kitāb al-Īmān*), 1:1, http://sunnah.com/muslim/1/1.

28. As Seesemann points out in *The Divine Flood*, Niasse's treatise is a synthesis of an earlier Tijānī work, ibn Anbūja's *Mīzāb al-Raḥma*, which is in turn largely based on a fourteenth-century work by the Andalusian scholar Muḥammad al-Anṣārī al-Sāḥilī (d. 1353). A similar schema can be found in Ibn ʿAjība's *Book of Ascension to the Essential Truths of Sufism* (and in his commentary [*Iqāẓ al-himam*] on the *Wisdoms* of ibn ʿAṭāʾ Allāh). This genre of Sufi literature, describing the different stages or stations of the spiritual path, is found in some of the earliest of Sufi works, most notably Khwājah ʿAbd Allāh Anṣārī's (d. 1088) Persian treatise *The Hundred Plains* (*Ṣad Maydan*) and his Arabic *Waystations of the Travelers* (*Manāzil al-Sāʾirīn*), which also divides each station into three degrees or levels (the generality, the elite, and the elite of the elite). Seesemann takes this work of Niasse's as being constitutive of the method or process of *tarbiya*: "Drawing on earlier models within and outside the Tijani tradition (most notably the Andalusian fourteenth-century mystic Abu ʿAbdallāh Muḥammad al-Sāḥilī), Niasse devised a method of spiritual training (*tarbiya*)." Rüdiger Seesemann, "Sufism in West Africa," *Religion Compass* 4, no. 10 (2010): 611. However, I believe that this work represents, not so much a program or method of spiritual training, but rather one description amongst many of the process of this transformation. While Niasse's description in *The Three Stations of Religion* is indirectly derived from the description given Sāḥilī's work, these descriptions should not be confused for the process itself, which can, and is, divided up into several different conceptual schemas, as this chapter demonstrates.

29. The root *k-f-r* literally means to cover over, and *kufr*, translated as disbelief in other contexts, is contrasted to *īmān*, faith or belief.

30. A verse of the Egyptian Sufi poet Ibn al-Fāriḍ (d. 1235).

31. This was the title of the first caliph and close friend of the Prophet, Abu Bakr, as well as a Qurʾanic category of the best of the saints, second only to the Prophets and Messengers as described in 4:69: "And he who obeys God and the Messenger, they are with those whom God has favored: the prophets, the sincere [*ṣiddīqīn*], the martyrs, and the righteous. What lovely company."

32. The breaths (*anfās*) is a technical term in Sufism that simultaneously alludes to the verbal creative act through which God perpetually re-creates the cosmos (the breath of the merciful, or *nafas al-Raḥmān*) and the subtle states of the most accomplished Sufis who are perpetually aware of their (and the entire cosmos') re-absorption and re-creation through these breaths. In his Sufi lexicon, Ibn ʿAjība writes:

> Al-Qushayri says, by breath (*nafas*) the Sufis mean the repose which hearts find in the subtle emanations of the unseen. Someone who is granted breaths is at a higher level than someone granted a state (*ḥāl*) or a moment (*waqt*). We could say that the one granted moments is at the beginning [of the way], the one granted breaths is at its end, and the one granted states is intermediary, [or that] "moments" are for people of the heart, "states" are for people of the spirit, and "breaths" for people of the innermost being (*sirr*). A breath, then, is more delicate than a moment. Keeping moments from being wasted is for devotees and ascetics, keeping breaths from being wasted is for gnostics who have reached the goal, and making use of states is for aspirants.

Ibn ʿAjība, *The Book of Ascension to the Essential Truths of Sufism: A Lexicon of Sufic Terminology*, trans. Mohamed Fouad Aresmouk and Michael Fitzgerald (Louisville, Ky.: Fons Vitae, 2012), 64–65.

33. While this term literally means "men," it does not refer to gender, but rather significant spiritual achievement. ʿAttar famously wrote that on the Day of Judgment, God will call for the men (*al-rijāl*) to stand forth, and the first to step forward will be Mary, the mother of Jesus. For more on this notion see Joseph Hill, "All Women Are Guides: Sufi Leadership and Womanhood among Taalibe Baay in Senegal," *Journal of Religion in Africa* 40, no. 4 (2010): 375–412.

34. A variant of a verse found in Ibn ʿArabi's *Fuṣūṣ al-ḥikam*, likely composed by Ibn ʿArabi himself: *fa lam yabqa ilā al-ḥaqq lam yabqa kāʾin / fa mā thumma mawṣūl fa mā thumma bāʾin*.

35. See Ibn ʿAṭāʾ Allāh's *Ḥikam*, no. 250:

> The existence/finding [*wujūd*] of His traces points to that of His names. The existence/finding of His

names point to the establishment [*thubūt*] of His attributes. The establishment of His attributes point to His Essence since it is impossible for an attribute to subsist by itself. For the enraptured [*arbāb al-jadhb*], the perfection of His Essence is unveiled to them; then, He makes them witness His attributes. Then, He returns them to attachment to His names. Then, He makes them witness His traces. And it is the reverse for the wayfarers [*al-sālikūn*]. So the end of the wayfarers is the beginning of the enraptured. And the beginning of the wayfarers is the end of the enraptured, but not in the same sense. So, perhaps the two groups may meet on the path, these going up and those going down. (al-Iskandarī, *Kitāb al-ḥikam*, 41)

36. The full context is this verse is as follows: "O you serene soul, return to your Lord, well-pleased and pleasing, enter thou amongst my servants, enter into My garden" (89:27–30).

37. Shaykh Ibrāhīm Inyās, *Maqāmāt al-Dīn al-Thalāth*, in *Saʿādat al-Anām* (Cairo: al-Sharikat al-Dawliyyah, 2006), 123–30.

38. Zeynabou Kane, personal communication on behalf of Shaykha Mariama Niasse, September 23, 2014.

39. Shaykh Maḥī Niasse, interview with the author, conducted in Arabic, January 14, 2013, Medina Baye, Senegal. A similar account can be found in Inyās, *al-Sirr al-Akbar*, 419.

40. See Chittick, "Five Divine Presences"; and Izutsu, *Sufism and Taoism*, 11–20.

41. Inyās, *al-Sirr al-Akbar*, 429. This same passage also describes a parallel schema of seven levels of "divine descents" (*tanazzulāt*):
 1. Absolute Simplicity (*al-sādhij*)
 2. Divine Unicity (*al-Aḥadiyya*)
 3. Divine Oneness (*al-Waḥda*)
 4. Divine Unity (*al-Waḥidiyya*)
 5. The level of the spirits (*al-Arwāḥ*)
 6. The imaginal realm (*al-ʿĀlam al-Mithāl*)
 7. The level of the sensory (*al-Ḥiss*).

42. Shaykh Ibrahim makes it clear that this is the Divine Intellect (*al-ʿaql al-rabbānī*) described in the previous chapter.

43. Inyās, *al-Sirr al-Akbar*, 434.

44. S. D., interview with the author, conducted in French and English, February 16, 2014, Dakar, Senegal.

45. Inyās, *al-Sirr al-Akbar*, 426.

46. Ibid.

47. S. D., interview with the author, conducted in French and English, February 16, 2014, Dakar, Senegal. I should emphasize here that S. D. does not attend masses or church services, and by all appearances he behaves like any other pious, urban Muslim man in Dakar—he prays five times a day, fasts during Ramadan, neither drinks nor smokes, et cetera.

48. M. D., interview with the author, conducted in French, March 12, 2014, Dakar, Senegal.

49. Probably a reference to the following passage from a letter of Shaykh Ibrahim Niasse's: "Know that the purpose of the shaykhs of *tarbiya* is to connect to the Prophet, who is the greatest means of access to God. Sidi Abdullah wuld al-Ḥajj al-ʿAlawī once said to me, 'The purpose of the Tijani litanies is to get a whiff of the Muḥammadan reality [*al-ḥaqīqa al-Muḥammadiyya*]'" (Inyās, *Jawāhir al-rasāʾil*, 1:113).

50. Shaykh Māḥī Niasse, interview with the author, conducted in Arabic, January 14, 2012, Medina Baye, Senegal.

51. Inyās, *al-Sirr al-Akbar*, 439.

52. This mode of "seeing" can have practical consequences, as Sidi Ben Omar Kane, Shaykh Ibrahim's grandson and director of a prominent Franco-Arab school founded by his mother, Shaykha Maryam Niasse, explained: "Shaykh Ibrahim once told me the story of ʿAisha, may God be pleased with her, who when she gave a gift to a beggar, perfumed it, and wrapped it up nicely. When the Prophet asked her why she had done this, she said, 'Because I knew that it is the hand of God that will receive it.' The Prophet smiled when she said this and told her that she had understood things well." Sidi Ben Omar then went on to link this story to the rise of Islamic sectarian groups, explaining that outwardly, physically, we are all separate and different, and unity is only conceptual or imagined. However, inwardly our hearts and spirits mingle together and are actually united in the Prophetic reality, and in God. The reason there is so much divisiveness and sectarianism today, he argued, is that people are less aware of this inward dimension in which there is real unity, and are only aware of the outward dimension in which unity is less apparent. The ways in which we are different, he explained, are less real than the ways in which we are the same, and this synthetic way of seeing, of understanding the world, is what Shaykh Ibrahim taught, because it is also the message of the Qurʾan, of the Prophet. Sidi Ben Omar Kane, interview with the author, conducted in French and Arabic, February 16, 2014, Dakar, Senegal.

53. Inyās, *al-Sirr al-Akbar*, 427. On the relationship between Aḥad and Aḥmad, Shabistari writes, "And of them [the prophets] our lord Muḥammad is the chief, / At once the first and the last in this matter. / The One (*Aḥad*) was made manifest in the [letter] *mīm* of *Aḥmad*. / In this circuit the first emanation became the last. / A single *mīm* divides *Aḥad* from *Aḥmad*. / The world is immersed in that one *mīm*." Shabistarī, *Gulshan-i Rāz*, 3.

54. Two titles of Shaykh Aḥmad al-Tijānī, who among Tijanis is known as the "concealed seal of Muḥammadan sanctity" (khatm al-walāyah al-Muḥammadiyah al-maktūm); see chapter 1.

55. Inyās, al-Sirr al-Akbar, 432.

56. Shaykh Ibrahim Niasse explains that the relationship between saintly pole (quṭb) and the rest of existence is like that of the spirit to the body: "He is for them like the spirit for the physical body. If his spiritual reality (rūḥāniyya) departed from them, the whole of existence would pass into extinction. He is the spirit of existence and the entirety of its properties.... None of the elements of existence can exist unless the spiritual reality of the saintly pole exists within them. If the saintly pole's spiritual reality was removed from them, the whole of existence would cease, becoming a featureless corpse" (Niasse, Removal of Confusion, 263).

57. Inyās, Maqāmāt al-Dīn al-Thalāth, 130.

58. Abu Ibrahim. interview with the author, conducted in English, February 24, 2014, Dakar, Senegal.

59. Ibn ʿAjība gives a similar account of levels of annihilation in his commentary on Ibn ʿAṭāʾ Llāh's Ḥikam. See chapter 3 of Īqāẓ al-Himam fī Sharḥ al-Ḥikam (Rabat: Dār al-Fikr, n.d.).

60. Inyās, Jawāhir al-rasāʾil, 2:58–59.

61. Disciples and shaykhs often cited the Qurʾanic verse, "We only sent you as a mercy to the worlds" (21:107)—"mercy" being one of God's primary attributes in the Qurʾan—to substantiate this claim.

62. Inyās, Jawāhir al-rasāʾil, 2:60.

63. Inyās, Maqāmāt al-Dīn al-Thalāth, 129.

64. S. D., interview with the author, conducted in French and English, February 16, 2014, Dakar, Senegal.

65. Seesemann, Divine Flood, 296n89, from Ilyās al-Wālī's Afḍal al-wasāʾil fī al tawassul bi sayyid al-awākhir wa al-awāʾil. See also Ibn ʿAṭāʾ Allāh's Ḥikam, no. 250:
> The existence/finding [wujūd] of His traces points to that of His names. The existence/finding of His names point to the establishment [thubūt] of His attributes. The establishment of His attributes point to His Essence since it is impossible for an attribute to subsist by itself. For the enraptured [arbāb al-jadhb], the perfection of His Essence is unveiled to them; then, He makes them witness His attributes. Then, He returns them to attachment to His names. Then, He makes them witness His traces. And it is the reverse for the wayfarers [al-sālikūn]. So the end of the wayfarers is the beginning of the enraptured. And the beginning of the wayfarers is the end of the enraptured, but not in the same sense. So, perhaps the two groups may meet on the path, these going up and those going down." (al-Iskandarī, Kitāb al-ḥikam, 41)

66. Ibn ʿArabi writes:
> Abū'l-Qāsim al-Qaṣī alluded to this in his Removal of the Sandals, saying, "Every Divine Name can be named by all of the Divine Names, and can be described by them." This is so because every Name indicates the Essence as well as a meaning that is proper to it and requires it. By virtue of its indicating the Essence it possesses all the Names, and by virtue of it indicating a meaning by which it is unique it is to be distinguished from what is not itself, such as Lord, Creator, Giver of Forms, and so forth. The Name is the Named by virtue of the Essence, and the Name is not the Named in virtue of the meaning specific to it, by which it is set apart. (Ringstones of Wisdom, 57–58)

67. Inyās, al-Sirr al-Akbar, 439–40.

68. Shaykh Muḥammad B. Al-Qasim Al-Qandusi, The Drink of the People of Purity (Singapore: Muḥammadan Press, 2014), 21–23.

69. See Hoffman, Sufism, Mystics, and Saints in Modern Egypt, 23. In some variants of this tradition, it is ibn Mashīsh's son who tells Shaykh al-Shādhilī this.

70. Ḥasan Cissé, "Kanz al-awliyāʾ wa aḥādīth al-ism al-aʿẓam," in Ibrāhīm Niasse, Kanz al-maṣūn, 173–74. Quoted in Wright, Living Knowledge in West African Islam, 151.

71. M. D. interview with the author, conducted in French, March 12, 2014. Dakar, Senegal.

72. Inyās, Jawāhir al-rasāʾil, 2:126–27.

73. Shaykh Ibrahim gives a similar account in which he explicitly describes himself taking on the role of khalīfa through his annihilation in the Prophet and Shaykh Aḥmad al-Tijānī. See Cissé, What the Knowers of Allah Have Said, 94–95.

74. Niasse, Removal of Confusion, 233.

75. Valerie Hoffman, "Annihilation in the Messenger of God: The Development of a Sufi Practice." International Journal of Middle East Studies 31, no. 3 (1999): 354.

76. Chittick, Sufi Path, of Knowledge, 351–52.

77. This ultimately goes back to the question raised in the discussion of Ibn ʿArabi's definition of maʿrifa at the beginning of this section: before you know, how can you know the way that will lead you to know? Practically, the answer usually comes in the form of some kind of deep intuition or recognition of the truth or liberating potential of a practice, doctrine, text, or person, living or dead. Within Shaykh Ibrahim's branch of Tijani Sufism, this most commonly takes the form of Shaykh Aḥmad al-Tijānī, Shaykh Ibrahim Niasse, or one of their living representatives who will serve as the foundation and touchstone of the disciple's confidence in the ṭarīqa and its methods, until he or she comes to verify them for him- or herself (or does not). Ultimately, however, even this initial intuition, and every

other stage in the process, is dependent on God, who is understood to be an active participant in this process, seeking the seeker even more than the seeker seeks Him, as the following ḥadīth qudsī illustrate: "I desire them more than they desire Me"; and "I am as my servant thinks of me and I am with him as he remembers me. If he remembers Me in himself, then I remember him in Myself. . . . If he draws near to me by the span of his hand, I draw near him by the length of an arm. If he draws near me by the length of an arm, I draw near him by the length of a fathom. If he comes to me walking, I come to him running." Quoted in William A. Graham, *Divine Word and Prophetic Word in Early Islam: A Reconsideration of the Sources, with Special Reference to the Divine Saying or ḥadîth Qudsî* (The Hague: Mouton, 1977), 129, 175–76.

78. al-Barrāda, *Jawāhir al-Maʿānī*, 227, 397.

79. This phrase (*ḥaqqa qadrihi*) appears at the end of the Ṣalāt al-Fātiḥ, the primary prayer of Tijani *tarbiya*, where it is probably an allusion to this verse, and possibly an allusion to this notion of a rank (*qadr*) beyond all limitations. Similarly, Shaykh Tijani ʿAli Cissé writes, "Concerning the words of the Most High, 'They did not measure God with the reality of His measure' [39:67, 6:91], al-Akhfash said, 'It means they have not Known him with the reality of His Knowledge [*maʿrifa*]'" (*What the Knowers of Allah Have Said*, 21).

80. See Ibn al-ʿArabī, *Divine Sayings: 101 Ḥadīth Qudsī, The Mishkāt al-Anwār of Ibn ʿArabī*, trans. Stephen Hirtenstein and Martin Notcutt (Oxford, UK: Anqa, 2008), 27; and Chittick, *Sufi Path of Knowledge*, 100; Chittick, *Self-Disclosure of God*, 440. For additional references, see Graham, *Divine Word and Prophetic Word in Early Islam*, 134–35; and Ṣaḥīḥ Muslim, 1.361, https://sunnah.com/muslim/1/361.

81. Quoted in Izutsu, *Sufism and Taoism*, 254; for an alternate translation, see Ibn al-ʿArabi, *Ringstones of Wisdom*, 115–16. In his *Futūḥāt*, Ibn ʿArabi also writes:

> But it is incumbent upon the Folk of Allah to know the doctrine of every sect and creed concerning God, in order to witness Him in every form and in order not to stand in the place of denial. For He permeates existence, so no one denies Him except those who are limited. But the Folk of Allah follow Him whose folk they are, so His property flows over them. And His property is the lack of delimitation. Hence He possesses all-pervading Being (*wujūd*), while they possess all-pervading witnessing (*shuhūd*). That person who delimits His Being delimits the witnessing of Him; he is not one of the Folk of Allah. (Chittick, *Sufi Path of Knowledge*, 110–11)

82. Chittick, *Sufi Path of Knowledge*, 350.

83. Inyās, *Jawāhir al-rasā'il*, 2:60.

84. Niasse, *Removal of Confusion*, 87–88.

85. Ibid., 65.

86. Inyās, *Jawāhir al-rasā'il*, 2:61.

87. M. D., interview with the author, conducted in French, March 19, 2014, Dakar, Senegal.

CHAPTER 4

1. Sidi Mohamed Kane, interview with the author, conducted in French, April 24, 2014, Dakar, Senegal.

2. Sidi Inaya Niang, interview with the author, conducted in English, April 26, 2014, Dakar, Senegal.

3. Aḥmad Zarrūq, *Qawāʾid al-Taṣawwuf* (Beirut: Dār al-Kutub al-ʿIlmiyya, 2005), 21.

4. Anonymous disciple, interview with the author, conducted in French, April 20, 2014, Dakar, Senegal.

5. S. D., interview with the author, February 16, 2014, conducted in English and French, Dakar, Senegal.

6. Inyās, *al-Sirr al-Akbar*, 418.

7. Ustadh Barham Diop, interview with the author, conducted in Arabic, April 4, 2014, Dakar, Senegal.

8. Shaykh Māḥī Niasse, interview with the author, conducted in Arabic, January 14, 2012, Medina Baye, Senegal.

9. Inyās, *al-Sirr al-Akbar*, 418.

10. Inyās, *Fī Riyāḍ al-Tafsīr*, 1:134–35. This commentary is remarkably similar to Ibn ʿArabi's commentary on this verse in *The Ringstones of Wisdom*, 115–16.

11. Ibn al-ʿArabī, *Ringstones of Wisdom*, 289–91.

12. Izutsu, *Sufism and Taoism*, 260.

13. An allusion to the "verse of light" (24:35).

14. Inyās, *Fī Riyāḍ al-Tafsīr*, 1:352.

15. A similar hierarchy is also found in the works of Ibn ʿAṭāʾ Allāh. See *The Key to Salvation and the Lamp of Souls: Miftāḥ al-Falāḥ wa Miṣbāḥ al-Arwāḥ*, trans. Mary Ann Koury Danner (Cambridge, UK: Islamic Texts Society, 1996), 53–55.

16. The next verse reads, "Then we withdraw it unto ourselves with a gentle withdrawal." Ibn ʿArabi's discussion of this verse compares the world and the human being to a shadow, and the Real to the object that casts the shadow (*Ringstones of Wisdom*, 99–101). The allusion here seems to be comparing the "lengthening shadow" to *dhikr* extending through the various levels of the human being, and gradually withdrawing from the outward to the inward. The best invocation being the "most inward/hidden," the place where the shadow (*dhikr*/invocation) and the object (God/the one invoked) meet.

17. Inyās, *al-Sirr al-Akbar*, 446–47.

18. Cissé, *What the Knowers of Allah Have Said*, 18.

19. See Chittick, *Self-Disclosure of God*, xviii–xxx.

20. "For Ibn ʿArabi as well as a number of other Sufis, the science of letters is properly speaking the science of the [saints] *âwliyâʾ*, and it is one of the surest signs of the authenticity of their spiritual realization." Clause Addas, "Ship of Stone," *Journal of the Muhyiddin Ibn ʿArabi Society* 19 (1996), http://www.ibnarabisociety.org/articles/shipofstone.html.

21. For an exposition of the numerological symbolism of the *Ṣalāt al-Fātiḥ*, see "Décryptage de Salatoul Faith" (presentation), January 14, 2015, https://www.youtube.com/watch?v=3yYNioSTdKM.

22. The *waẓīfa* consists of one recitation of the *Fātiḥa*, thirty recitations of *AstaghfiruLlāh*, fifty recitations of the *Ṣalāt al-Fātiḥ*, one hundred recitations of the *Shahāda*, and twelve recitations of *Jawharāt al-Kamāl*. In Arabic numerology, 1=*Alif*, 30=*Lām*, 50=*Nūn*, 2=*Bāʾ*, and 10=*Yāʾ*. So 1+30+50+12=*al-nabī*=93; removing the one recitation of the *Fātiḥa* gives 92. The four letters of the Prophet's name, "Muḥammad," have the following numerical values: *Mīm*=40, *Ḥāʾ*=8, *Mīm*=40, *Dal*=4. Hence, 40+8+40+4=92. The one hundred recitations of the *Shahāda* are excluded/numerically incorporated for esoteric reasons. Similarly, many disciples and shaykhs were fond of pointing out the numerical equivalence of the Prophet's name with a phrase from a variant of the *ḥadīth qudsī* "I was a hidden treasure and I loved to be known, so I created the creatures, and by Me [*fa bī*] they know Me." In Arabic numerology, the three letters that make up the phrase "by Me" (*fa bī*) have the following numerical values: *Fāʾ*=80, *Bāʾ*=2, and *Yāʾ*=10. Hence, 80+2+10=92, which is the numerical equivalent of the name "Muḥammad." The implication here is that the Prophet is the means through which God is known, and through which He knows himself. This numerical symbolism underscores the close identity between God and the Prophet, and the latter's central role in epistemology. Shaykh Babacar N'Diaye, interview with the author, conducted in Arabic, February 16, 2014, Dakar, Senegal.

23. Niasse, *Removal of Confusion*, 29.

24. This is a common theme that appears in early Sufi literature, perhaps beginning with the aphorism attributed to Rābiʿa al-ʿAdawiyya, who told a self-righteous would-be disciple, "Your very existence is a sin with which no other sin can be compared." See also Niasse, *Removal of Confusion*, 185.

25. Niasse, *Removal of Confusion*, 193.

26. Ustadh Barham Diop, interview with the author, conducted in Arabic, January 10, 2012, Medina Baye, Senegal.

27. Abu Ibrahim, interview with the author, conducted in English, February 24, 2014, Dakar, Senegal. See also al-Barrāda, *Jawāhir al-Maʿānī*, 1408–31.

28. Titus Burckhardt, *Mirror of the Intellect: Essays on Traditional Science and Sacred Art*, trans. William Stoddart (Albany: SUNY Press, 1987), 188.

29. Ibn ʿAjība, *Al-Futūḥāt al-Ilāhiyyah fī Mabāḥith al-Aṣliyya* (Cairo: ʿĀlam al-Fikr, n.d.), 6.

30. M. D. interview with the author, March 26, 2014, conducted in French, Dakar, Senegal. See also Niasse, *Removal of Confusion*, 212.

31. In his commentary on Qurʾan 8:17, "You [the Prophet] did not throw when you threw, but God threw," Shaykh Ibrahim explains that due to the perfection of his annihilation in God, the Prophet did absolutely everything by God, so even his "help" of God in the prayer is only achieved through and by God. Inyās, *Fī Riyāḍ al-Tafsīr*, 2:367.

32. Other oral commentaries gloss the first "Truth" as God, and the second as the Muḥammadan reality.

33. This phrase also appears in 6:91, "And they measure not God in accordance with the reality of His measure when they say, 'God has not sent down anything to a human being' [in terms of revelation]." Thus, in the prayer, the reality of his/His measure possibly alludes to this "measure," including both God's transcendence and immanence, especially His immanent manifestation in the form of the "Perfect Human."

34. Niasse, *Removal of Confusion*, 215. The *Jawharat al-Kamāl* belongs to a genre of prayers (*ṣalawāt*) on the spiritual reality of the Prophet popular in North African Sufism. The aforementioned prayer of Ibn Mashish is perhaps the oldest and best known of this type of prayer containing an elaborate and poetic description of the Prophet's metaphysical and cosmological dimensions. The celebrated *Dalāʾil al-Khayrāt* of the Shādhilī Shaykh al-Jazūlī also contains several such prayers. These prayers were often said to be received from the Prophet in some form of visionary experience, as was the *Jawharat al-Kamāl*.

35. Shaykh Ibrahim comments on this part of the prayer in another prayer of his: "Allow this scintillating ruby to take possession of my heart, so that by it I come to realize (*ataḥaqqaqu*) the Greatest Name and Its secret. Illuminate my heart until it emits light, so that by this ruby I see the unseen worlds of the universe, until neither the unseen external worlds nor the subtleties of the hidden worlds are hidden from me. By this ruby let me see the perfection of Your essence (*dhāt*)." Quoted in Wright, *Living Knowledge in West African Islam*, 157.

36. Related in Ḥanbal and Tirmidhī; see Chittick, *Sufi Path of Knowledge*, 125.

37. Chittick, *Self-Disclosure of God*, 70; Chittick, *Sufi Path of Knowledge*, 125. The allusion here is to the two outpourings (*fayḍān*) through which the world is existentiated. In the first, "the most holy outpouring"

(*al-fayḍ al-aqdas*), the absolutely undifferentiated Divine Essence differentiates itself into the immutable entities (*al-ʿayān al-thābita*) without existentiation; and in the second, "the holy outpouring" (*al-fayḍ al-muqaddas*), the breath of the All-Merciful grants these immutable entities their existence. The "lightning" can refer to the first effusion, and the "rain" to the second.

38. This image could also possibly allude to the verse "And you see the mountains, which you deem to be solid, passing away as the passing away of the clouds" (22:78), which Shaykh Ibrahim frequently quotes as an allusion to another aspect of the doctrine of the breaths of the All-Merciful (*nafas al-Raḥmān*), through which everything is created and returned to God at each instant, like a kind of instantaneous divine inhalation and exhalation (Niasse, *Jawāhir al-Rasāʾil*, 2:126).

39. Ibn al-ʿArabi, *Ringstones of Wisdom*, 6; Chittick, *Sufi Path of Knowledge*, 184–86.

40. For commentaries on these and other Tijānī prayers, see Niasse, *Removal of Confusion*, 177–222; al-Barrāda, *Jawāhir al-Maʿānī*, 1408–31; and al-Tijānī, *Aḥzāb wa al-Awrād*, 1–21.

41. Ibn Anbūja, *Mīzāb al-Raḥma al-Rabbaniya fiʾl-tarbiya biʾl-Ṭarīqa al-Tījāniyya* (Beirut: Dar al-Kutub al-ʿilmiyya, 2014), 42.

42. This short treatise is translated in full in the following section.

43. Shaykh Māḥī Cissé Medina Baye, interview with author, conducted in Arabic, April 21, 2014. Medina Baye, Senegal.

44. Ustadh Barham Diop, interview with the author, conducted in Arabic, April 4, 2014, Dakar, Senegal.

45. Quoted in Wright, *Living Knowledge in West African Islam*, 232.

46. Niasse, *Removal of Confusion*, 23.

47. ʿUmar al-Fūtī, *Rimāḥ*, 419. Quoted in Wright, *Living Knowledge in West African Islam*, 245.

48. Ustadh Barham Diop, interview with the author, conducted in Arabic, April 4, 2014, Dakar, Senegal.

49. Niasse, *Removal of Confusion*, 91, quoting Sidi al-ʿArabī al-Sāʾiḥ's *Jawāb al-Shāfiʿ*.

50. Seyyidah Diarra Ndiaye, interview with the author, conducted in Wolof and French, April 20, 2014, Dakar, Senegal.

51. Chittick, *Sufi Path of Knowledge*, 150. Also Shaykh Babacar N'Diaye, interview with the author, conducted in Arabic, February 16, 2014, Dakar, Senegal. Also quoted in Niasse, *Removal of Confusion*, 85–86.

52. A term that literally means "implantation."

53. Inyās, *al-Sirr al-Akbar*, 389. Niasse's more extended discussion can be found on pp. 416–20.

54. Ibid., 390. He also explains that the disciple must show reverence and respect to one's shaykh because it is the same as showing reverence to Shaykh Tijānī and to the Prophet.

55. However, some disciples told me that they saw other disciples following shaykhs whose degree of realization was less than theirs, "like the moon following a star" or "an ocean following a river."

56. Shaykh Māḥī Cissé Medina Baye, interview with the author, conducted in Arabic, April 21, 2014, Medina Baye, Senegal.

57. Other accounts locate the beginning of the *fayḍa* at the nearby village of Kossi.

58. Shaykh Babacar N'Diaye, interview with the author, conducted in Arabic, February 16, 2014, Dakar, Senegal. See also a similar account in Seesemann, *Divine Flood*, 60.

59. Inyās, *Fī Riyāḍ al-Tafsīr*, 5:346–47. He also describes this annihilation as being the secret of the *Ṣalāt ʿalāʾal-nabī* (the prayer on the Prophet), explaining that it is not permitted to perform the ritual prayer toward or upon someone, with the exception of the funeral prayer, because in that case, the person is not there. Because of the totality of the Prophet's annihilation in God, it is permissible to pray toward or upon him, just as it is permissible to perform the prayer toward or upon a dead person in the funeral prayer.

60. K. S., interview with the author, conducted in English, March 26, 2014, Skype.

61. Shahzad Bashir, "Movement and Stillness," in *Meditation in Judaism, Christianity, and Islam: Cultural Histories*, ed. Halvor Eifring (New York: Bloomsbury, 2013), 210–11.

62. Quoted in James Morris, *The Reflective Heart: Discovering Spiritual Intelligence in Ibn ʿArabi's Meccan Illuminations* (Louisville, Ky.: Fons Vitae, 2005), 42. For a similar statement, see Niasse, *Removal of Confusion*, 238.

63. Borges has the characters in the story describe the Aleph and the experience of seeing it as follows:

> The only place on earth where all places are—seen from every angle, each standing clear, without any confusion or blending.... I saw the circulation of my own dark blood; I saw the coupling of love and the modification of death; I saw the Aleph from every point and angle, and in the Aleph I saw the earth and in the earth the Aleph and in the Aleph the earth; I saw my own face and my own bowels; I saw your face; and I felt dizzy and wept, for my eyes had seen that secret and conjectured object whose name is common to all men but which no man has looked upon—the unimaginable universe. (Jorge Luis Borges, "The Aleph," in *Collected Fictions*, trans. Andrew Hurley [New York: Penguin Books, 1999], 283–84)

64. For Ibn ʿArabi's influential and fascinating theory of causality across different levels of reality, see Izutstu, *Sufism and Taoism*, 256–59.

65. Inyās, *al-Sirr al-Akbar*, 390.

66. See Schimmel, *Mystical Dimensions of Islam*, 99.

67. Quoted in Cissé, *What the Knowers of Allah Have Said*, 21; cf. pp. 25–26 (for an alternate English translation).

68. al-Barrāda, *Jawāhir al-Maʿānī*, 1309–11.

69. Inyās, *Fī Riyāḍ al-Tafsīr*, 1:272–74.

70. Inyās, *al-Sirr al-Akbar*, 447.

71. Niasse, *Removal of Confusion*, 237. The poem appears to be by Abū l-ʿAbbās ibn al-Bannā al-Marrākushī, and it is cited by ibn ʿAjība in his *al-Futūḥāt al-Ilāhiyya*, which is itself a commentary on another one of Ibn al-Bannā's poems. See ibn ʿAjība, *al-Futūḥāt al-Ilāhiyya*, 32.

72. Abu Ibrahim, interview with the author, conducted in English, February 24, 2014, Dakar, Senegal.

73. Shaykh Māḥī Cissé, interview with the author, conducted in Arabic, April 21, 2014, Medina Baye, Senegal.

74. Seyyida Diarra Ndiaye, interview with the author, conducted in Wolof and French, April 20, 2914, Dakar, Senegal.

75. Shaykh Māḥī Cissé, interview with the author, conducted in Arabic, April 21, 2014, Medina Baye, Senegal.

76. K. S., interview with the author, conducted in English, March 26, 2014, Skype.

77. For example, see Claude Addas, *Quest for the Red Sulphur: The Life of Ibn ʿArabī* (Cambridge, UK: Islamic Texts Society, 1993).

78. Anonymous disciple, interview with the author, conducted in English and French, March 24, 2014, Dakar, Senegal.

79. Abu Ibrahim, interview with the author, conducted in English, February 24, 2014, Dakar, Senegal.

80. This is a paraphrase of a famous saying attribute to Abū Yazīd: "I want to not want except what He wants."

81. Niasse, *Jawāhir al-Rasāʾil*, 124–25.

82. Sidi Inaya Niang, interview with the author, conducted in English, March 4, 2014, Dakar, Senegal.

83. In the Qurʾanic account of the Garden of Eden, Adam's sin is sometimes described as forgetfulness (20:115).

84. A famous Sufi aphorism, often attributed to Abu Bakr. See Cissé, *What the Knowers of Allah Have Said*, 49.

85. Another famous saying of Abū Yazīd al-Bisṭāmī, also attributed to the Prophet David in the Sufi tradition. See Cissé, *What the Knowers of Allah Have Said*, 16.

86. Inyās, *Fī Riyāḍ al-Tafsīr*, 5:87.

87. Ibid.

88. Timothy Williamson, *Knowledge and Its Limits* (Oxford: Oxford University Press, 2000).

89. *Maʿrifa* could even be described as the pure experience of pure existence.

90. Frithjof Schuon, *To Have a Center* (Bloomington, Ind.: World Wisdom, 1990), 67.

91. Niasse, *Removal of Confusion*, 64–65.

CHAPTER 5

The epigraph from Awo Epega is quoted in William Bascom, *Ifa Divination Communication Between Gods and Men in West Africa* (Bloomington: Indiana University Press, 1969), xii. The epigraph from Ulli Beier comes from *The Return of the Gods: The Sacred Art of Susanne Wenger* (Cambridge: Cambridge University Press, 1975), 49.

1. Both men and women worship and practice Ifa and have done so traditionally. Female priests of Ifa are called iyanifa (wife/mother of Ifa). The children and spouses of babalawo and iyanifa often have extensive knowledge of the oral corpus and rituals of Ifa, even if they have not been initiated as priests and do not perform divination. Today, there are some (but not many) iyanifa who practice divination, but they typically do not perform all the initiatory rituals that men do.

2. Some babalawo, however, consider this to be the principal and original meaning of Ifa. I frequently heard variations of the phrase *Ifa ọrọ ẹnu Olodumare, ti a fi da aye*, or "Ifa is the word of the mouth of Olodumare, by which he created the world," and a narrative from the Odu Eji-Ogbe in which Ọrunmila makes a distinction between himself and Ifa, cited as proof of the fact that Ifa is first and foremost the divine message and Ọrunmila is the bearer of this message.

3. This number, however, is largely symbolic and refers to the potentially infinite number of verses in each Odu. Many of the babalawo I interviewed compared Ifa to an ocean, saying that no one can know the beginning or end of its verses or wisdom. In his *Sixteen Great Poems of Ifa*, Abimbola estimates that each Odu contains six hundred *ẹsẹ*.

4. Some accounts attribute the introduction of Ifa to the Yoruba-speaking people to a Nupe (or Arab, in some versions) man named Ṣetilu. Ifa was introduced to the Kingdom of Dahomey during the reign of Agaja (1718–40), where its practice (known as Fa) persists among the Fon-speaking people of Benin to this day (see Edna Bay, *Wives of the Leopard: Gender, Politics, and Culture in the Kingdom of Dahomey* [Charlottesville: University of Virginia Press, 2012], 94). It is presently practiced by hundreds of thousands of people around

the world from nearly every imaginable ethnolinguistic background. What makes Ifa "Yoruba" (itself a complicated, exogenous category) is that Yoruba is the ritual language of the particular tradition in question.

5. See Rowland Abiodun, "Understanding Yoruba Art and Aesthetics: The Concept of Ase," *African Arts* 27, no. 3 (1994): 68–103. Some scholars, such as J. D. Y. Peel and Kola Abimbola (in his book *Yoruba Culture: A Philosophical Account* [Birmingham, UK: Iroko Academic, 2005]) argue that Olodumare's role in Yoruba mythology and religion is the result of Islamic and Christian influence; while this is possible, it is of little concern to the present study, which seeks to describe the contemporary tradition, not those of the past.

6. Bolaji Idowu, *Olodumare: God in Yoruba Belief* (London: Longmans, 1962), 56.

7. With the possible exception of Christianity, depending on the particular formulation of Christology.

8. The river is actually an embodiment of Ọṣun; several myths describe how she transformed herself into this particular body of water. Thus, for practitioners, Ọṣun *is* the river and the river *is* Ọṣun.

9. This myth is found in Odu Ọṣẹ-tura of the Ifa corpus.

10. This verb is very similar in connotation to the Arabic verb *'abada*.

11. The traditions of these later two orisa, although still prominent in Nigeria, seem to be even more central in diaspora, especially in Cuba and Brazil.

12. Beier, *Return of the Gods*, 33.

13. Susanne Wenger, *The Timeless Mind of the Sacred: Its New Manifestation in the Ọṣun Groves* (Ibadan, Nigeria: Institute of African Studies, University of Ibadan, 1977), 7.

14. Fela Sowande, *Ifa Guide, Counsellor, and Friend of Our Forefathers* (Oja, Yaba East: Forward Press, 1964), 43–44.

15. Wọle Ṣoyinka, *Myth, Literature and the African World* (Cambridge: Cambridge University Press), 14.

16. This does not mean, however, that the orisa never get away with acts of seeming wickedness. Many myths involving Eṣu describe how he causes unprovoked mayhem with impunity, and in more than one myth Ọrunmila scams people without punishment, but these actions are often only peripheral to the main thrust of the myth. In fact, the orisa are usually able to avoid punishment only by performing some sort of sacrifice, and so must follow the same moral law as the mortals for whom they are exemplars. As far as I know, there are no sympathetic Promethean figures in Yoruba mythology.

17. This, however, does not imply that the babalawo are uncritical vis-à-vis the myths of Ifa. Some of the liveliest discussions I had during my research revolved around these apparently contradictory myths. Sometimes, contradictory variants of a myth were rejected as false, but more often, the apparent contradictions were resolved by synthesizing the seemingly opposing perspectives.

18. For more on a traditional Yoruba perspective on "syncretism," see Ayodeji Ogunnaike, "What's Really Behind the Mask: A Re-examination of Syncretism in Brazilian Candomblé," *Journal of Africana Religions* 8, no. 1 (2020): 146–71.

19. Ayodeji Ogunnaike, "The Myth of Purity," *Harvard Divinity Bulletin*, Summer–Autumn 2013, https://bulletin.hds.harvard.edu/articles/summerautumn2013/myth-purity.

20. For example, consider the famous saying of the Prophet of Islam, "I was a Prophet while Adam was betwixt water and clay."

21. Professor Agboola, interview with the author, conducted in English and Yoruba, November 24, 2013, Ile-Ifẹ, Nigeria.

22. See Karin Barber's "How Man Makes God in West Africa," *Africa* 54, no. 3 (1981): 724–44.

23. Ṣoyinka, *Myth, Literature and the African World*, 10.

24. Barber, "How Man Makes God."

25. I suspect, however, that traditional Yoruba perspectives would turn it around so that the relationships with the deities serve as the model for human relationships, or that the two are mutually dependent and reinforcing.

26. Barber, "How Man Makes God," 744.

27. William Chittick, *The Sufi Path of Knowledge: Ibn al-'Arabi's Metaphysics of Imagination* (Albany: SUNY Press, 2010), 355.

28. Ibid., 30. However, this concept is not limited to Islamic mysticism and Traditional West African religions, it also appears in Christian mysticism. The seventeenth-century German Catholic poet Angelus Silesius writes, "I know God couldn't live a moment without me; if I should disappear, He would die, destitute." The daring words of his predecessor and countryman, Meister Eckhart, closely parallel the Yoruba proverb cited above, "If I were not, God would not be either. I am the cause of God's being God: if I were not, then God would not be God." Meister Eckhardt, *The Complete Mystical Works of Meister Eckhart*, ed. and trans. M. Walshe (New York: Crossroad, 2009), 424.

29. Barber in "How Man Makes God" (732–34) gives a detailed description of this phenomenon.

30. While by and large respecting other divinities, although they may be denigrated in the myths of the cult to show the superiority of its particular divinity

(e.g., the famous myth of Shiva's endless phallus [*lingam*] bewildering Vishnu and Brahma, or myths about Şango taking the orişa Ọya away from Ogun to be his wife).

31. Idowu, *Olodumare*, 52.

32. Beier, *Return of the Gods*, 44–45.

33. Idowu, *Olodumare*, 60.

34. See ibid., 58–60; and Şoyinka, *Myth, Literature and the African World*, 27.

35. See Idowu, *Olodumare*, 67. The number 200, in Yoruba, *Igba*, and 400, *Irinwo*, both symbolize totality, while the numbers 200+1 and 400+1 symbolize the transcendence of this totality.

36. Professor Agboola, interview with the author, conducted in English and English and Yoruba, November 27, 2013, Ile-Ifẹ, Nigeria. Olumọ rock outside Abẹokuta is worshipped as an orişa, as is Agẹmọ, the chameleon, and most rivers in Yorubaland are worshipped as goddesses. It is important to remember however, that the orişa are not limited to these physical objects, nor are these objects of worship mere "physical" objects.

37. Şoyinka, *Myth, Literature and the African World*, 25.

38. See Idowu, *Olodumare*, 40–41.

39. Araba of Modakẹkẹ interview with the author, conducted in Yoruba, November 2, 2013.

40. Şoyinka, *Myth, Literature and the African World*, 28.

41. Or more precisely, the act of discovery is a creative act that can establish a new ritual or mythological form if it has enough *aşẹ*. Ultimately, there is no distinction between inventing a connection and revealing a connection; it is simply a matter of perspective. In any event, what establishes the connection and makes it efficacious is the *aşẹ* of the people and elements involved.

42. This notion of *aşẹ* is closely related to power and beauty as insightfully described in the following passage:

> Susanne Wenger believes the aesthetic concepts of the West are "merely a substitute for these other things about which we no longer permit ourselves to talk. Why is a tree beautiful? One tree is beautiful because it is regular. Another is beautiful because it is irregular. When we say beautiful we simply describe our reaction to the tree that has a strong *identity* [or character]. The Yoruba 'worships' this identity, if you want to use a Christian term here. Where we respond with superficial aesthetic remarks, the Yoruba feels a profound fusion of human intelligence with tree intelligence." It is no accident, perhaps, that the most sacred spots on the Oshun river, the *ibu*, are also the ones which the European observer regards as the most "beautiful" sites. (Beier, *Return of the Gods*, 89)

43. Mircea Eliade, *Patterns in Comparative Religion*, trans. Rosemary Sheed (Lincoln: University of Nebraska Press, 1996), 12–13.

44. Ibid., 29.

45. Mircea Eliade, *Cosmos and History: The Myth of the Eternal Return*, trans. Willard Trask (New York: Harper Torchbooks, 1959), 5.

46. Ibid., 46.

47. This is not just true of mythical worldviews like that of the Yoruba; so-called scientific facts only have worth and meaning because of myths such as "the worth of human life," "the quest to understand the universe," and "development."

48. In practice, rituals seem to play an even more important role than myths, many of which seem to exist as a commentary on or explanation for these rituals. Many *abọrişa* are relatively unconcerned with their tradition's mythology, but I have yet to meet one unconcerned with ritual performance, which is a primary constituent of their relationship with their orişa and their world. In fact, the pride of place that Ifa enjoys in contemporary scholarship on African religions is likely due, in part, to the fact that its more discursive and "scriptural" dimensions are easier for Western-trained scholars to get a handle on than those traditions that are more ritually and less discursively orientated. In any event, the distinction between myth and ritual is a tenuous one in the Yoruba case, as myths are embodied and creatively reworked in ritual practices, and the act of learning and reciting mythological narratives is itself a ritual performance.

49. Mircea Eliade, *Images and Symbols: Studies in Religious Symbolism*, trans. Philip Mairet (Princeton: Princeton University Press, 1961), 178.

50. Idowu, *Olodumare*, 67.

51. However, this distinction between "benevolence" and "malevolence" is relative and heuristic and therefore must be taken with a grain of salt, for as Barnes notes, "In West Africa, positive and negative power is not separate. Power is singular, and therefore what we in the West see as dual and capable of being divided into two mystical notions cannot be divided in African thought. For the latter, power exists in a single supernatural representation." Sandra Barnes, "The Many Faces of Ogun," in *Africa's Ogun: Old World and New*, ed. Barnes (Bloomington: Indiana University Press, 1997), 19.

52. Araba of Modakẹkẹ, interview with the author, conducted in Yoruba, November 11, 2013, Modakẹkẹ, Nigeria; Professor Agboola, interview with the author, conducted in Yoruba and English, November 26, 2013, Ile-Ifẹ, Nigeria.

53. Hence his appellation "Eṣu, the one who belongs to the right and left sides of a matter without any shame." Abiodun, "Understanding Yoruba Art and Aesthetics," 68–78, 45.

54. This number, and the nature of the ajogun, also varies widely.

55. For example, see Barry Hallen and J. Olubi Ṣopido, *Knowledge, Belief, and Witchcraft: Analytic Experiments in African Philosophy* (London: Ethnographica, 1986); Barry Hallen *The Good, the Bad, and the Beautiful: Discourse About Values in Yoruba Culture* (Bloomington: Indiana University Press, 2000); Teresa Washington, *Our Mothers, Our Powers, Our Texts: Manifestations of Aje in Africana Literature* (Bloomington, Indiana University Press, 2005).

56. The word "witch" may come from the Old German *witjan* or *wizzen* (meaning "knowledge," "intelligence," or "skill"—from which the word "wit" is also derived), which has its origins in the Proto-Indo-European *wid-* or *vid-* meaning "to see" and, metaphorically, "to know."

57. Araba of Modakẹkẹ, interview with the author, conducted in Yoruba, November 11, 2013, Modakẹkẹ, Nigeria.

58. Female participation is not unheard of, but it is the exception rather than the rule.

59. Professor Agboola, interview with the author, conducted in Yoruba and English, November 24, 2013, Ile-Ifẹ, Nigeria.

60. This lower heaven is also identified with the earth, *Ilẹ*, in Yoruba cosmology.

61. To these three domains of human experience (the world of the unborn, the world of the dead, and that of the living) Ṣoyinka adds what he calls the "fourth stage"—the liminal realm between these three more stable abodes. The fourth stage is the place of ritual, of intercourse between the different realms and the forces that inhabit them. See Ṣoyinka, *Myth, Literature and the African World*, 140–60.

62. It should be noted that it is but one of many myths explaining the source of Ọrunmila's wisdom and supremacy amongst the oriṣa.

63. In other versions of this myth, this declaration takes place at *bode*, the boundary or gate of heaven.

64. Wande Abimbola, *Sixteen Great Poems of Ifa* (New York: UNESCO, 1975), 33–34.

65. Awo Faniyi, interview with the author, conducted in Yoruba, November 27, 2013, Ile-Ifẹ, Nigeria.

66. Professor Agboola, interview with the author, conducted in Yoruba and English, November 24, 2013, Ile-Ifẹ, Nigeria.

67. Peel and others conclude that this conception of the afterlife is the result of Islamic influence. See J. D. Y. Peel, *Religious Encounter and the Making of the Yoruba* (Bloomington: Indiana University Press, 2003), 187.

68. Upon the birth of a new child, Ifa divination is performed to determine which of the child's ancestors has returned to the world "through" the child. Even amongst Christians and Muslims, the names *Babatunde*, "The Father has come again," and *Yẹtunde*, "The mother has come again," are common for children born shortly after the death of a relative.

69. Yoruba mythology generally differentiates between the world (*aye*) and the earth (*ilẹ*), which is a divinity in her own right, as well as acting as a symbol for unseen realms of being.

70. Margaret Thompson Drewal, *Yoruba Ritual: Performers, Play, Agency* (Bloomington: Indiana University Press, 1992), 14.

71. Awo Faniyi, interview with the author, conducted in Yoruba, November 27, 2013, Ile-Ifẹ, Nigeria.

72. See Afolabi Epega and Philip John Neimark, *The Sacred Ifa Oracle* (San Francisco: Harper, 1995), 479–83.

73. Joachim Wach, *The Comparative Study of Religions* (New York: Columbia University Press, 1958), 111.

74. See William Bascom, *Ifa Divination: Communication Between Gods and Men in West Africa* (Bloomington: Indiana University Press, 1969), 3–13; and Wande Abimbola, *Ifá Divination Poetry* (New York: Nok, 1977), 37–39.

75. This is usually accomplished by whispering the request to a small amount of currency, which is then placed on the divining instruments. Money is a common (and effective) concrete symbol of will or desire.

76. There is also regional variation here, as many Ifẹ diviners cast the ọpẹlẹ the opposite way.

77. All the elements used in this process of divination are also known as Ifa, and are regarded as embodiments of the deity Ọrunmila. This is the aforementioned metaphysical significance of the polyvalence of the term "Ifa": Ọrunmila contains the entire tradition, with all of its facets and historical unfoldings, within himself, and conversely, is present in every aspect and every person of the tradition.

78. When I asked the babalawo how they selected the ẹsẹ they recite out of the hundreds or thousands in each Odu, the answers ranged from *imisi*, "Inspiration," to "You recite whatever comes into your head," to "You can recite as many as you remember, all of them apply." Not one of them ever mentioned examining the client for clues or, as far as I could tell, ever tried to "cold read" anyone who came seeking divination. Such practices were seen to be interfering with Ifa and therefore were practiced only by false babalawo.

79. For example, one myth of Odu Odi-Ọkanran explains how the lizard went to a babalawo because he

wanted to marry a certain beautiful woman. He partially completed the sacrifice, and so the woman agreed to marry him. However, since he didn't complete the sacrifice, the people of the town told the woman not to marry him because his home was a crack in the wall. She asked him if this was true, and when he admitted it, she left. Now the lizard runs all around, bobbing his head up and down (a characteristic behavior of this particular species) looking for his lost wife. See Bascom, *Ifa Divination*, 330–31.

80. See chapter 3 of Noel Amherd, *Reciting Ifá: Difference, Heteregeneity, and Identity* (Trenton, N.J.: Africa World Press, 2010) for a detailed account of the fixed and variable aspects of recitation of *ęsę Ifá* during divination.

81. If the babalawo "misses the mark" and the recites a verse that seems to have nothing to do with the seeker's secret request, the babalawo may be blamed for not knowing enough verses of the Odu. However, usually this seemingly unrelated narrative is understood to be the answer that "the seeker needs to hear" even if it is not what he originally came to ask Ifa about. I heard several stories from babalawo and seekers about seemingly strange predictions of Ifa that actually proved to be connected to the seeker's situation, such as a man who came to ask about his job, but Ifa responded with a story about children. The man later found out that his girlfriend was pregnant but had not yet told him. More skeptical or casual visitors of babalawo will simply ignore predictions that do not make sense and go seek another solution to their problem, often from another babalawo or spiritual specialist such as a Muslim *alfa* or a Christian prophet or pastor.

82. There are several further intricacies to this process that are outside the scope of this chapter, however; for a more detailed explanation of the procedure, see Bascom, *Ifa Divination*, chapters 4, 5, and 6.

83. The Odu appear in many verses of Ifa as mythological characters. They are often interpreted as disciples or children of Ǫrunmila.

84. Awo Faniyi even equated a babalawo's Odu with his *ori*.

85. Awo Faniyi, interview with the author, conducted in Yoruba, November 27, 2013, Ile-Ifę, Nigeria.

86. The babalawo often identified certain events in their life with particular Odus, and explained or justified their behavior by citing a myth from the Odu. Once they recognized the pattern of the Odu or one of its myths in their present situation, the babalawo would use it to analyze the situation and make moral judgments about the best course of action even without performing divination. It was as if a kind of internal Ifa divination was occurring.

87. The epigraph for this section is drawn from Abimbola, *Ifá Divination Poetry*, 170.

88. The history of the concept of time in Western thought is a fascinating and multifaceted one, as the originally mythical or cyclical time of the Greeks and other peoples of antiquity was transformed by the introduction of writing; the spread and dominance of Christianity, in which a particular historical event (the crucifixion and resurrection) redefined the nature of time; and finally the Enlightenment and the scientific revolution, which largely stripped time of its qualitative and sacred aspects, reducing it to an independent measure of change. These trends ultimately led to the industrial revolution and digital age, whose modes of labor and leisure radically altered the way most people experience time. Nevertheless, even this understanding of time is not entirely without its cyclical and mythological nature: the years are all still counted from the mythological year of Christ's birth, the twelve months have loose astrological correlations and repeat each year, and the seven days of the week cycle through the names of Norse and Roman deities. The units of measurement of time are still based on the earth's rotation and revolution, and have not yet become a completely abstract set of numbers ticking off into infinity. For an excellent overview of these trends and the emergence of modern, secular conceptions of time, see Richard Amesbury, "Secularity, Religion, and the Spatialization of Time," *Journal of the American Academy of Religion* 86, no. 3 (2018): 591–615.

89. Şoyinka, *Myth, Literature and the African World*, 10.

90. Odu Irosun Iwori says, "People will keep going to heaven and returning to earth after death until everyone arrives at that good position." Similarly, when someone dies, the people of heaven are supposed to say, "The child sent on an errand has come back." Professor Agboola, interview with the author, conducted in Yoruba and English, November 27, 2013, Ile-Ifę, Nigeria.

91. Drewal, *Yoruba Ritual*, 47.

92. Or perhaps more accurately, a qualitatively different sort of time—the *nigba lailai* or *nigba naa*, the "mythical time" of Ifa and *itan*. See the discussion of Şango and Jakuta below for an illustrative example.

93. J. D. Y. Peel makes the same point in his "Making History: The Past in the Ijesho Present," *Man* 19, no. 1 (1984): 118. Likewise, Odu Eji Ogbe describes how the eternal Olodumare created time (*igba*) when he created the primordial day (*Ǫjǫ*).

94. Odu Eji Ogbe also explains that Ǫrunmila's presence at the creation of everything else is the reason for his knowledge of everything that has happened or will happen in the world.

95. Ṣoyinka separates the worlds of the unborn and the ancestors, creating four realms: the land of the living, the unborn, the ancestors, and the fourth stage. Although the ancestors and the unborn are treated separately in ritual, for the reasons cited above, I believe Ifa combines the realm of the unborn and that of the ancestors into one realm (ọrun), so I describe three realms of human experience: heaven (ọrun), the world (aye), and the transitional mythical/ritual (igba naa).

96. See also Peel's excellent article "Making History," whose findings closely parallel the above discussion.

97. I am indebted to Jacob Olupọna for this insight. Amherd makes a similar point by arguing that the "past" tense of Yoruba most commonly used in myths can refer both to "present" and "past" action. The elision/fusion of the present and the mythical past, or their collapse into each other, is one of the main functions of Yoruba myth and ritual. See Amherd, *Reciting Ifa*.

98. Ṣola Ajibade, interview with the author, conducted in Yoruba and English, November 19, 2013, Ile-Ifẹ, Nigeria.

99. Eliade, *Patterns in Comparative Religion*, 397.

100. Eliade, *Cosmos and History*, 34.

101. Mircea Eliade, *Myth and Reality* (New York: Harper & Row, 1963), 13–15.

102. Ṣango's apotheosis and amalgamation with Jakuta also proves the timelessness of Ọrun. Ṣango, a historical figure (the fourth king of Ọyọ), became deified upon his death and identified with the older thunder god Jakuta, to such an extent that his name has almost completely replaced that of Jakuta in their shared mythology. Jakuta's name is essentially only preserved in the name of his day of the week. According to his devotees, Ṣango, the king, did not die—in ascending to heaven, he became timeless.

103. Araba of Modakẹkẹ, interview with the author, conducted in Yoruba, November 20, 2013, Modakẹkẹ, Nigeria.

104. Similarly, after recalling the myth of the Buffalo Woman and the coming of the sacred pipe, Black Elk succinctly notes, "This they tell, and whether it happened so or not I do not know; but if you think about it, you can see that it is true." John Neihardt, *Black Elk Speaks* (Albany: SUNY Press, 2008), 4.

105. Araba of Modakẹkẹ, interview with the author, conducted in Yoruba, November 20, 2013, Modakẹkẹ, Nigeria.

106. See Kimberly Patton's *Religion of the Gods: Ritual Paradox, and Reflexivity* (Oxford: Oxford University Press, 2009), which, among many other rituals, describes and explains similar accounts of this kind of reflexivity in ancient Greek religions, such as deities making sacrifices to themselves.

107. Professor Agboola, interview with the author, conducted in English and Yoruba, November 24, 2013, Ile-Ifẹ, Nigeria. See also Wande Abimbola, *Sixteen Great Poems of Ifa* (London: UNESCO, 1975), 50–72.

108. Abimbola notes that these particular palm trees are not harvested by cultivators of palm oil, even to this day (*Sixteen Great Poems of Ifa*, 12–13).

109. In fact, this could be regarded as a mythological equivalent of the argument first put forward by Seyyed Hossein Nasr in *The Encounter of Man and Nature: The Spiritual Crisis of Modern Man* (London: George Allen and Unwin, 1968); and in Lynn White's famous essay "The Historical Roots of Our Ecologic Crisis" (*Science* 155, no. 3767 [1967]: 1203–7), identifying the ecological crisis with the desacralization of the scientific view of nature.

110. See chapter 4 of Eliade's *Cosmos and History*. The Araba of Modakẹkẹ described the present day in similar terms, describing the chaos and injustice of postcolonial Yorubaland as the result of the general abandonment of the traditions of Ifa and the orisa.

111. Araba of Modakẹkẹ, interview with the author, conducted in Yoruba, November 10, 2013, Modakẹkẹ, Nigeria and Professor Agboola, interview with the author, conducted in English and Yoruba, November 24, 2013, Ile-Ifẹ, Nigeria. Babalawo often say that "Christians and Muslims pray to go to heaven with Jesus and Muḥammad when they die; babalawo pray to go to Olokun to be with Ọrunmila."

112. P. R. McKenzie's *Hail Orisha! A Phenomenology of a West African Religion in the Mid-Nineteenth Century* (Leiden: Brill, 1997), 302, provides the earliest detailed written account of Ifa practice I have been able to find, dating from 1846. Bascom cites the descriptions of Ifa appearing in Sarah Tucker's 1853 work *Abeokuta or Sunrise Within the Tropics: An Outline of the Origin and Progress of the Yoruba Mission* and the surprisingly accurate account found within E. G. Irving's 1853 "The Yoruba Mission" from the *Church Missionary Intelligencer* as the earliest recorded accounts of Ifa (Bascom, *Ifa Divination*, 13).

113. However, it is entirely possible that Islamic geomantic traditions could have spread from neighboring Muslim areas before Islam was established in Yorubaland.

114. It is possible that Ifa could have been introduced to the Yoruba-speaking people from the outside (as several myths suggest); however, its current form of practice is inseparable from the Yoruba language, and it is this form with which the present study is concerned.

115. This figure is probably derived from the legendary Arab diviner Satih, whom Ibn Khaldun mentions in his *Muqaddimah*: "The Arabs used to repair to soothsayers in order to learn about forthcoming events. They

consulted them in their quarrels, to learn the truth by means of supernatural perception.... In pre-Islamic times,... Satih, of the tribe of Mazin b. Ghassan, were famous (soothsayers) (the latter) used to fold up like a garment, as he had no bones save for his skull." Ibn Khaldun, *Muqaddimah: An Introduction to History*, 3 vols., trans. F. Rozenthal (Princeton: Princeton University Press, 1980), vol. 1, chap. 1, disc. 6, http://www.muslimphilosophy.com/ik/Muqaddimah/Chapter1/Ch_1_06.htm. The inclusion of this arcane figure in the mythology of Ifa may indicate a deep knowledge of Islamic lore among babalawo; the influence or even origin of Ifa in the tradition of Muslim geomancy known as *khaṭṭ al-raml*; or merely babalawo's recognition of the similarity of their tradition with that of Islamic geomancy.

116. Araba of Modakẹkẹ, interview with the author, conducted in Yoruba, November 12, 2013, Modakẹkẹ, Nigeria. See Martin Lings, *Muḥammad: His Life Based on the Earliest Sources* (Rochester, Vt.: Inner Traditions, 1983), for the Islamic version of the story from which the myth is derived.

117. See Louis Brenner, "Histories of Religion in Africa," *Journal of Religion in Africa* 30, no. 2 (2000): 143–67; and Bascom, *Ifa Divination*, 3–12.

118. Bascom, *Ifa Divination*.

119. As evidenced by its radically different process and logic of divination, although the geomantic figures produced by both Ifa and *khaṭṭ al-raml* are nearly identical. Given the common Yoruba myths of origin that describe the ancestors of the Yoruba as originally coming from Egypt or the Middle East, it is also possible that *khaṭṭ al-raml* and Ifa may share a more ancient, Egyptian or Middle Eastern common ancestor.

120. For example, Odu Ogbe-Sa describes how Ọrunmila taught his wife, Ọṣun, the art of sixteen-cowrie divination, which is commonly practiced by priests of nearly all oriṣa. Agbigba, a form of divination common among the Yagba and northeastern Yoruba, was said to be a slave of Ọrunmila, who taught him the simplified form of divination that now bears his name.

121. Bernard Maupoil, *La Geomancie à l'Ancienne Côte des Esclaves* (Paris: Institut d'ethnologie, 1943).

122. Largely conducted with babalawo from Modakẹkẹ, Ile-Ifẹ, Oṣogbo, and Iseyin, and drawn from scholarly works in English, Yoruba, and French.

CHAPTER 6

The verse of Ifa presented in the epigraph comes from Drewal, *Yoruba Ritual*, 33–34. Translation modified by the author.

1. Hallen and Ṣopido, *Knowledge, Belief, and Witchcraft*.

2. Araba of Modakẹkẹ, interview with the author, conducted in Yoruba, November 11, 2013, Modakẹkẹ, Nigeria.

3. Ibid.

4. Professor Agboola, interview with the author, conducted in English and Yoruba, November 26, 2013, Ile-Ifẹ, Nigeria.

5. Araba of Modakẹkẹ, interview with the author, conducted in Yoruba, November 11, 2013, Modakẹkẹ, Nigeria.

6. Professor Agboola, interview with the author, conducted in English and Yoruba, November 24, 2013, Ile-Ifẹ, Nigeria.

7. Awo Faniyi, interview with the author, conducted in Yoruba, November 27, 2013, Ile-Ifẹ, Nigeria.

8. In fact, Logos could be a good translation of *ọrọ*, in that they are both used to refer to both "primary cosmic principle" and "speech, word."

9. A contraction of "Olodumare."

10. Rowland Abiodun, "Verbal and Visual Metaphors: Mythical Allusions in Yoruba Ritualistic Art of Ori," *Word and Image* 3, no. 3 (1987): 254–55.

11. Ibid., 256. There is also the proverb *Bi owe, bi owe n Ifa sọrọ*, "Like proverbs, like proverbs is how Ifa speaks."

12. Ibid. Translated by the author.

13. Ibid., 257.

14. Araba of Modakẹkẹ, interview with the author, conducted in Yoruba, November 11, 2013, Modakẹkẹ, Nigeria.

15. Araba of Modakẹkẹ, interview with the author, conducted in Yoruba, November 20, 2013, Modakẹkẹ, Nigeria.

16. For example, Ṣoyinka describes the nature of the "moral order" in Yoruba (and African) thought and society as follows: "It must not be understood in any narrow sense of the ethical code which society develops to regulate the conduct of its members. A breakdown in the moral order implies, in the African worldview, a rupture in the body of Nature just like the physical malfunctioning of one man" (*Myth, Literature and the African World*, 52).

17. Professor Agboola, interview with the author, conducted in English and Yoruba, November 26, 2013, Ile-Ifẹ, Nigeria.

18. Araba of Modakẹkẹ, interview with the author, conducted in Yoruba, November 11, 2013, Modakẹkẹ, Nigeria. The Araba also connected this central ideal of *iwa pẹlẹ*, or gentle/good character, with the popular Yoruba ideal of *ọmọluwabi*, "a well-mannered or cultured child." The Araba glossed *ọmọluwabi* as "child of God" in English, highlighting a possible etymology of

the word ọmọ ti Olu Iwa bi—the child born to the Lord of existence/character; that is, the child who resembles his progenitor, God, in character.

19. See Hallen, *The Good, the Bad, and the Beautiful*, 87–90.

20. This takes place in heaven, before birth. Ogun, as the principle of firmness, hardness, and strength, is naturally manifest in the bones, while Ọbatala, the gentler orișa of creation and creative expression, is manifest in the fleshy and expressive body.

21. Araba of Modakẹkẹ, interview with Ayọdeji Ogunnaike, conducted in Yoruba, 2011.

22. Hallen, *The Good, the Bad, and the Beautiful*, 52.

23. Wande Abimbola, *Ifa: An Exposition of a Literary Corpus* (London: Oxford University Press, 1977), 125–32. The Yoruba word *kadara* is derived from the Arabic verb *qadara*, which literally means to measure out or apportion, and theologically refers to destiny, lot, fortune, or fate.

24. See Adegboyega Orangun, *Destiny: The Unmanifested Being* (Ibadan, Nigeria: African Odyssey, 1998), for more on this aspect of *ori*.

25. Awo Faniyi, interview with the author, conducted in Yoruba, November 27, 2013, Ile-Ifẹ, Nigeria.

26. Abimbola, *Ifa*, 145–46.

27. Ibid., 142.

28. African Sources of Knowledge—Digital Library, Odu Ifa Collection, Harvard University, http://ask-dl.fas.harvard.edu/content/90-ogunda-meji.

29. Araba of Modakẹkẹ, interview with the author, conducted in Yoruba, November 11, 2013, Modakẹkẹ, Nigeria.

30. Abimbola, *Sixteen Great Poems of Ifa*, 33–34.

31. Ibid., 158–77.

32. A mythical market that features in several narratives of Ifa.

33. Abiodun, "Verbal and Visual Metaphors," 264.

34. Wenger, *Timeless Mind of the Sacred*, 53.

35. Wande Abimbola, *Ijinle Ohun Enu Ifa, Apa Keji* (Ibadan, Nigeria: University Press Limited, 1976), 149. In addition to illustrating the relationship between destiny and effort, this verse of Ifa contains several other characteristic features: the "coming into being," which is the setting of many verses of Ifa; the frustrating but ultimately instructive role of Eṣu in preventing or facilitating communication; and the final moral, explanatory conclusion, "No one deliberates without reckoning with legs."

36. Professor Agboola, interview with the author, conducted in English and Yoruba, November 24, 2013, Ile-Ifẹ, Nigeria.

37. *Inu* is also used to designate "inside," as in *inu ile*, "the inside of the house."

38. Suggestively, this word also means "one."

39. Awo Faniyi, interview with the author, conducted in Yoruba, November 27, 2013, Ile-Ifẹ, Nigeria. The heart is also associated with bravery and perseverance, so that in ordinary Yoruba speech, to say that someone "has a heart" is not unlike the English expressions, common in sporting contexts, "he showed a lot of heart" or "she has a lot of heart."

40. Segun Gbadegesin, *African Philosophy: Traditional Yoruba Philosophy and Contemporary African Realities* (New York: Peter Lang, 1996), 32.

41. Awo Faniyi, interview with the author, conducted in Yoruba, November 27, 2013, Ile-Ifẹ, Nigeria.

42. Araba of Modakẹkẹ, interview with the author, conducted in Yoruba, November 11, 2013, Modakẹkẹ, Nigeria.

43. Ibid.

44. B. A. Ademuleya, "The Concept of Ori in the Traditional Yorùbá Visual Representation of Human Figures," *Nordic Journal of African Studies* 16, no. 2 (2007): 214.

45. Awo Faniyi, interview with the author, conducted in Yoruba, November 27, 2013, Ile-Ifẹ, Nigeria.

46. Professor Agboola, interview with the author, conducted in English and Yoruba, November 24, 2013, Ile-Ifẹ, Nigeria.

47. However, the written record of the encounters between Yoruba-speaking Olorișa, Muslims, and Christians in the nineteenth and early twentieth centuries is replete with examples of religiously motivated persecution and violence on all sides. See Peel, *Religious Encounter and the Making of the Yoruba*.

48. "Wole Soyinka on Yoruba Religion A Conversation with Ulli Beier," *Isokan Yoruba Magazine* 3, no. 3 (1997): 5.

49. Wenger, *Timeless Mind of the Sacred*, 29.

50. Araba of Modakẹkẹ, interview with the author, conducted in Yoruba, November 12, 2013, Modakẹkẹ, Nigeria.

CHAPTER 7

The third epigraph is drawn from Epega and Neimark, *Sacred Ifa Oracle*, 412.

1. Araba of Modakẹkẹ, interview with the author, conducted in Yoruba, November 11, 2013, Modakẹkẹ, Nigeria.

2. Araba of Modakẹkẹ, interview with the author, conducted in Yoruba, November 21, 2013, Modakẹkẹ, Nigeria.

3. The Araba of Modakẹkẹ insisted that the traditional way to do it was on the fifth day, but that people today do not have the time, money, or diligence to do all the proper ceremonies, so it is typically combined

with the naming ceremony and circumcision on the eighth day.

4. Professor Agboola, interview with the author, conducted in English and Yoruba, November 24, 2013, Ile-Ifẹ, Nigeria.

5. Based on her fieldwork with a babalawo in Ijẹbu, Drewal's *Yoruba Ritual* records that this first ceremony was called as *ikọsẹ waye*, "stepping into the world," and was performed between the third and seventh days after birth; while the *imọri* was a separate ritual performed during the baby's third month (52–56). Such ritual variants are common from region to region, and between babalawo in the same region; in fact, many babalawo even perform these ceremonies and rituals in different ways depending on the context, time, and financial constraints of the families and individuals.

6. These are Yoruba towns, and this phrase is an Ifa idiom that roughly translates as "people far and wide."

7. Araba of Modakẹkẹ, interview with the author, conducted in Yoruba, November 18, 2013, Modakẹkẹ, Nigeria.

8. Ibid.

9. Professor Agboola, interview with the author, conducted in English and Yoruba, November 24, 2013, Ile-Ifẹ, Nigeria.

10. See T. G. O. Gbadamosi, "Odu Imale: Islam in Ifa Divination and the Case of Predestined Muslims," *Journal of the Historical Society of Nigeria* 8, no. 4 (1977): 91–92; and Gbadamosi, *The Growth of Islam among the Yoruba, 1841–1908* (Ibadan, Nigeria: University of Ibadan, 1978), 68–69.

11. Araba of Modakẹkẹ, interview with the author, conducted in Yoruba, November 21, 2013, Modakẹkẹ, Nigeria.

12. Epega and Neimark, *Sacred Ifa Oracle*, 204.

13. An Ifa idiom that means something like "he put two and two together."

14. Wande Abimbola, "Iwapele: The Concept of Good Character in Ifa Literary Corpus," in *Yoruba Oral Tradition: Poetry in Music Dance and Drama*, ed. Abimbola (Ile-Ifẹ, Nigeria: Department of Languages and Literatures, 1975), 395–414.

15. Ibid., 395. Similarly, both Awo Faniyi and Professor Agboola in interviews with the author said that "a babalawo without good character is not a babalawo"; and the Araba also cited the proverbs *iwa l'ẹwa*, "character is beauty," and *iwa l'ọba awure*, "character is the king of all [good luck] charms," to make a similar point.

16. Although some babalawo wait to teach their apprentices how to handle the *ikin* during the initiation ceremony (*itẹfa*), since the *ikin* are regarded as a more direct embodiment of Ifa and therefore must be handled with even greater care than the *ọpẹlẹ*.

17. This order has some regional variance: in Ifẹ, Ekiti, and Ijẹsa, Ọbara Meji is fifth, Ọkanran Meji is sixth, Irosun Meji is seventh, and Ọwọnrin is eighth (see fig. 9); whereas babalawo in Ọyọ, Egba, and Ijẹbu areas use the order presented above.

18. There are some subtleties pertaining to the order of the 240 *Odu amulu* (compound Odu) that are a bit more complicated and therefore take some more time to memorize.

19. Professor Agboola, interview with the author, conducted in Yoruba and English, November 26, 2013, Ile-Ifẹ, Nigeria.

20. Pierre Verger and Anthony Ming, "Isọye: Medications de la mémoire chez les Yoruba en Afrique et au Brésil," in *Médicaments et aliments: Approche ethnopharmacologique*, ed. E. Schröder et al. (Paris: Orstrom, 1966), 174–177.

21. Ifayemi Elebuibon, *Ìyẹ̀rẹ̀ Ifá: Tonal Poetry, the Voice of Ifá: An Exposition of Yorùbá Divinational Chants* (San Bernardino, Calif.: Ilé Ọrúnmìlà Communications, 1999), 101.

22. Professor Agboola, interview with the author, conducted in English and Yoruba, November 24, 2013, Ile-Ifẹ, Nigeria.

23. Araba of Modakẹkẹ, interview with the author, conducted in Yoruba, November 21, 2013, Modakẹkẹ, Nigeria.

24. Abimbola, *Sixteen Great Poems of Ifa*, 10.

25. This is a common trope in Yoruba mythology and culture. When twins are born, the one who emerges from the womb last is considered the eldest.

26. Bascom, *Ifa Divination*, 85.

27. Fatumbi Pierre Verger, *Ewé: The Use of Plants in Yoruba Society* (Rio de Janeiro: Odebrech, 1995), 46. This is also the name of a large forest tree whose leaves and sap are used in herbal/incantatory preparations associated with this Odu.

28. See Drewal, *Yoruba Ritual*, 73.

29. Many orișa traditions are dominated by one gender or another. For example, J. L. Matory noted that the priesthood of Yemọja in Old Ọyọ is almost exclusively female, while the priests of the Ogun and Ifa traditions are overwhelmingly male. He also notes that women tend to be central in those traditions in which possession is important (e.g., those of Șango, Yemọja, Ọsun, Ọya, and arguably Aladura Christianity), while they are more marginal in those traditions in which possession is taboo or does not play a central role (e.g., those of Ifa, Ogun [in Ọyọ], Islam, and mission Christianity). See Matory, *Sex and the Empire That Is No More: Gender and the Politics of Metaphor in Oyo Yoruba Religion* (New York: Berghahn Books, 2005), 4, 140. See Ayodeji Ogunnaike, "Mamalawo: The Controversy over Women Practicing Ifa Divination," *Journal for the*

*Study of the Religions of Africa and Its Diaspora* 4, no. 1 (December 2018): 15–34, for a comprehensive overview of different perspectives on gender in Ifa.

30. The initiate's wife or mother provides the pots and or calabashes for the initiate's *ikin*, and dances with them on her head during a ritual known as *iyi Ifa*.

31. Nevertheless, many details of *itefa* ceremonies conducted in the 1990s in Ijẹbu can be found in the fifth chapter of Drewal's *Yoruba Ritual*.

32. Ibid.

33. Araba of Modakẹkẹ, interview with the author, conducted in Yoruba, November 18, 2013, Modakẹkẹ, Nigeria. The name of the Odu and "Cricket presses two" are homonyms. The opening lines liken the signature of the Odu to farming rows and the tracks of a cricket. "Opening [the way] wide" is a standard symbol for progress and prosperity.

34. Bascom, *Ifa Divination*, 88–89.

35. Professor Agboola, interview with the author, conducted in English and Yoruba, November 24, 2013, Ile-Ifẹ, Nigeria.

36. Professor Agboola, interview with the author, conducted in English and Yoruba, November 26, 2013, Ile-Ifẹ, Nigeria.

37. Awo Faniyi presented a dissenting perspective, arguing that Odu was not female but rather a male divinity or force, citing a verse of Ifa from Odu that seemed to describe Odu in these terms.

38. Drewal, *Yoruba Ritual*, 74.

39. Video recordings of this stage of the initiation are easily available online—for example, this ceremony conducted by the Babalawo Efuwape Olatunji, the Ejugbona of Isara Remo (a town in Ijẹbu), can be accessed at https://www.youtube.com/watch?v=4O_fOf9esiE; https://www.youtube.com/watch?v=fYnFU2tuZwE; https://www.youtube.com/watch?v=UukecDnnB7E.

40. A widely reported taboo says that if a noninitiate were to look at Odu, he would go blind, and that if a woman were to look at Odu, she would lose the ability to bear children.

41. See Bascom, *Ifa Divination*, 83. Another name for the Odu Oturupon Meji is Ọlọgbọn Meji, or "Two Possessors of Wisdom," probably in reference to this and other similarly themed myths in the Odu.

42. Araba of Modakẹkẹ, interview with the author, conducted in Yoruba, November 11, 2013, Modakẹkẹ, Nigeria.

43. Professor Agboola, interview with the author, conducted in English and Yoruba, November 24, 2013, Ile-Ifẹ, Nigeria. Just as the *ikin* are linked/imbued with the presence of Ọrunmila/Ifa and the initiate's *ori* during the rituals of initiation, other orisa (such as Odu) can be "made"—that is, their presence can be built up and concentrated in a tangible object, which then becomes a primary site of interaction between the orisa and its devotee. This object is usually kept hidden in multiple layers of cloth and/or in calabashes and pots, which are themselves ritually prepared and imbued with certain properties. For babalawo, the *ikin* he or she receives during initiation serve as the physical presence of Ifa, and are kept in a special porcelain bowl. The *ikin* used to divine for clients (which are sometimes separate) are kept in an elaborately carved wooden bowl called *agẹrẹ Ifa*.

44. Awo Faniyi, interview with the author, conducted in Yoruba, November 27, 2013, Ile-Ifẹ, Nigeria. Awo Faniyi then quoted a lengthy verse of Ifa from Odu Otura Iwori in which Ọrunmila is told to use Odu as the power (*aṣẹ*) of all his decisions (*ipin*) in life, even down to what he should eat and drink.

45. Ibid.

46. Drewal, *Yoruba Ritual*, 79.

47. Drewal quotes Awo Ọsitọla's explanation of this process of collecting more verses from one's own Odu:

When you are asking about your verses [i.e., from other diviners], you ask generally. When you ask generally, then you extract what it has to do with you—its relationship. At the same time, you don't eliminate or abandon whatever meaning may be related to you. But you have to go in your own particular direction. What Ọyẹku Meji has to say to one person is different from what Ọyẹku Meji has to say to another person. . . . When somebody recites for you, you just say, that's alright. Not all they will say will be to your own way of life, but different, different people may say what they like, and then you relate it to yourself. For instance, when I am asking from other diviners about my children's signs, I will just mention the sign. It is my own concern to collate, or relate whatever verse I like. (Ibid., 78)

48. Ibid., 77.

49. Professor Agboola, interview with the author, conducted in English and Yoruba, November 24, 2013, Ile-Ifẹ, Nigeria.

50. Araba of Modakẹkẹ, interview with the author, conducted in Yoruba, November 12, 2013, Modakẹkẹ, Nigeria. This attitude of embracing or "marrying" suffering embodied in this mythical narrative seemed to be characteristic of the most respected babalawo I encountered. This does not imply a passive acceptance or submission to the difficulties of life (the Araba of Modakẹkẹ once told me how "Ifa agreed to fight for him" in a dispute with the king of Modakẹkẹ that eventually ended in the king being driven from his palace), but rather an active process of engagement with the difficulty, born of the knowledge that difficulties bring

change, and change can bring new knowledge and good things. This is related to the babalawo's (and Ọrunmila's) close relationship to Eṣu, the mischief-making deity who tends to turn lives upside-down, as Femi Oṣofisan notes:

> If a knowledge needs to be carried forward, something must come and disturb the present stability. It is when the present stability is disturbed that we then move forward again, else we stagnate, and die. . . . Revolts must come in order to have progress, which is why questioning must continue. That's the principle that Eshu represents, constant questioning, constant challenge to authority, to orthodoxy. The restless iconoclastic spirit. But the resolution of that comes out of the Ifa principle. The synthesis, the gathering of everything together, then, that's resolved in the Ifa principle in the union of Eshu and Ọrunmila. (Femi Oṣofisan and Muyiwa Awodiya, eds., *Excursions in Drama and Literature: Interviews with Femi Oṣofisan* [Ibadan, Nigeria: Kraft Books 1993], 81)

51. Drewal, *Yoruba Ritual*, 80–81.
52. Ibid., 81.
53. Ibid., 174–85. The epigraph for this section is drawn from Rowland Abiodun, *Yoruba Art and Language: Seeking the African in African Art* (Cambridge: Cambridge University Press, 2014), 88.
54. See Ayodeji Ogunnaike, "Mamalawo? The Controversy over Women Practicing Ifa Divination" *Journal for the Study of the Religions of Africa and Its Diaspora* 4, no. 1 (December 2018): 15–34. For an example of one such debate, see the discussion on the blog post "Iyanifa, an Ode Remo perspective . . . ," *Ifa Yesterday, Ifa Today, Ifa Tomorrow*, January 14, 2009, available at http://ifalola.blogspot.com/2009/01/iyanifa-ode-remo-perspective.html, which highlights the diversity of perspectives and arguments in Nigeria itself, as well as in the diaspora.
55. For example, see M. A. Abimbola, "The Role of Women in the Ifa Priesthood: Inclusion versus Exclusion," in *Ifá Divination: Knowledge, Power, and Performance*, ed. Jacob Olupọna and Rowland Abiọdun (Bloomington: Indiana University Press, 2016), 246–59.
56. For example, Oyeronke Olajubu notes, "Female principles are generally regarded as symbols of coolness (*ero*) whereas male principles are construed as representing toughness (*lile*). This underlines the people's conception of female (*abo*) and male (*ako*). Hence the people say, 'k'odun yi y'abo fun wa o' meaning 'may this year be female for us' (bring us all that the female principle stands for). The converse implication of this is the avoidance of a male year, which by all indications may be tough and unpleasant." Olajubu, *Women in the Yoruba Religious Sphere* (Albany: SUNY Press, 2003), 9.

57. Ibid., 9–10.
58. Ibid., 116–17.
59. The Araba of Modakẹkẹ gave the same explanation, as did Wande Abimbola in his *Sixteen Great Poems of Ifa*, 8.
60. Olajubu, *Women in the Yoruba Religious Sphere*, 117.
61. Bernard Maupoil, *La géomancie à l'ancienne côte des esclaves* (Paris: Institut D'Ethnologie, 1988), 153.
62. It is worth noting that Fakẹmide was known as a "Babalawo," not an "iyanifa." In the words of a male former babalawo interviewed by Barber, "She learnt Ifa. If a woman goes to school she becomes an educated person; if she learns Ifa, she becomes a babalawo. Her father was a babalawo, so was her husband, so she picked it up little by little from them. There was never a time when the association of babalawo said she had no right to participate in their activities. She would go to the cult and participate in meetings just like the others. They would ask her about a certain verse of Ifa: if she answered correctly, they would accept that she was a babalawo. The verses she learnt were the same as those of the other babalawo. Once she learnt them, she was a babalawo. Then she also had the right to examine other people on their knowledge, just as they had examined her. Both men and women would come as clients to consult her." Karin Barber, *I Could Speak Until Tomorrow: Oriki, Women, and the Past in a Yoruba Town* (London: Edinburgh University Press for the International African Institute, 1991), 289.
63. Ibid., 289.
64. Ibid., 288.
65. As a part of the ceremony, a specially prepared bracelet (*idẹ*) is tied to the left wrist of the *apẹtẹbi*. Examples of this ceremony can be seen in the following YouTube videos: https://www.youtube.com/watch?v=3wIuMQTf69g; https://www.youtube.com/watch?v=rKLfJ433V78; and https://www.youtube.com/watch?v=fnfeWPJpD8A.
66. See Bascom, *Ifa Divination*, 82–115. For example, the royal babalawo of Ile-Ifẹ (Awọni) must all be Olodu, who are considered senior to all other babalawo. Neither I, nor any of the people I interviewed, had ever heard of a female Araba (i.e., chief priest of Ifa of a town).
67. Professor Agboola, interview with the author, conducted in English and Yoruba, November 24, 2013, Ile-Ifẹ, Nigeria.
68. It is quite common for the orisa to have different genders in different contexts. In fact, J. D. Y. Peel notes that "one would be hard put to insist that any deity's gender was unalterably fixed." J. D. Y. Peel, "Gender in Yoruba Religious Change," *Journal of Religion in Africa* 32, no. 2 (2002): 140.

69. Bascom, *Ifa Divination*, 115.

70. Abimbola, "Role of Women in the Ifa Priesthood," 255.

71. Professor Agboola, interview with the author, conducted in English and Yoruba, November 24, 2013, Ile-Ifẹ, Nigeria.

72. Drewal, *Yoruba Ritual*, 78.

73. Ibid., 66.

74. Araba of Modakẹkẹ, interview with the author, conducted in Yoruba, November 11, 2013, Modakẹkẹ, Nigeria.

75. Both Akọda and Aṣeda are titles in hierarchy of babalawo of a given town (especially Ile-Ifẹ), as well as legendary disciples of Ọrunmila. See Bascom, *Ifa Divination*, 91–102.

76. Professor Agboola, interview with the author, conducted in English and Yoruba, November 24, 2013, Ile-Ifẹ, Nigeria.

77. Epega and Neimark, *Sacred Ifa Oracle*, 522.

78. Babatunde Lawal, "Àwòrán: Representing the Self and Its Metaphysical Other in Yoruba Art," *Art Bulletin* 83, no. 3 (2001): 515.

79. Epega and Neimark, *Sacred Ifa Oracle*, 188–89.

80. Professor Agboola, interview with the author, conducted in English and Yoruba, November 24, 2013, Ile-Ifẹ, Nigeria.

81. Araba of Modakẹkẹ, interview with the author, conducted in Yoruba, November 20, 2013, Modakẹkẹ, Nigeria.

82. Verger, *Ewé*, 92.

83. The roots of which are famously known in hoodoo (and blues music) as "John the Conqueror Root."

84. Bascom, *Ifa Divination*, 130.

85. This is true of indigenous semiotics of the Yoruba language itself. In addition to the verses of Ifa, many proverbs, poems, and ritual songs of praise employ creative etymologies to highlight or explain how the name of an object provides insight into its nature. In his book on Yoruba poetry, Ulli Beier explains this polysemic feature of the language: "Not only are the Yoruba highly conscious of the meaning behind the names, they also like to interpret every word they use. They believe that every name is really a sentence that has been contracted through a series of elisions into a single word. Naturally, in the attempt to reconstruct the original sentence one may arrive at various meanings." Ulli Beier and Bakare Gbadamosi, eds., *Yoruba Poetry: Traditional Yoruba Poems* (Ibadan, Nigeria: Ministry of Education, 1959), 31. Knowing the name of a person, place, or thing gives you knowledge of its origin and destiny, and thus power in relation to it.

86. For example, see Drewal's *Yoruba Ritual* for a discussion of the significant role of improvisation and play in Yoruba rituals.

87. Verger, *Ewé*, 37–38. Cloth is a symbol of wealth and status in traditional Yoruba cultures. For this reason, maize is used in several sacrifices or preparations to attract fertility, wealth, and general good luck.

88. Araba of Modakẹkẹ, interview with the author, conducted in Yoruba, November 18, 2013, Modakẹkẹ, Nigeria.

89. Professor Agboola, interview with the author, conducted in English and Yoruba, November 26, 2013, Ile-Ifẹ, Nigeria.

90. Verger, *Ewé*, 23.

91. Professor Agboola, interview with the author, conducted in English and Yoruba, November 26, 2013, Ile-Ifẹ, Nigeria. The Araba also described several different kinds of incantatory "magic" practiced by ritual specialists, including some babalawo, all of which are distinct from *ẹbọ* (sacrifices prescribed by Ifa): *ọfọ*—incantations, which can be used to harm or help their intended target; *oogun*—charms or medicine, which can be used to harm or help their intended target; *epe*—invocatory curses intended to harm; *abilu*—a form of incantatory magic that employs the signatures of the Odu pressed into the camwood powder (*iyẹ irosun*) on the divining tray (*ọpọn Ifa*), intended to harm its target; and *igede*—a "very bad" form of curse that the Araba described as "Ọrunmila's wicked younger brother." Araba of Modakẹkẹ, interview with the author, conducted in Yoruba, November 20, 2013, Modakẹkẹ, Nigeria.

92. Bascom, *Ifa Divination*, 499.

93. Professor Agboola, interview with the author, conducted in English and Yoruba, November 26, 2013, Ile-Ifẹ, Nigeria.

94. Ibid. See also this from Peter Cole and Aminadav Dykman, eds., *The Poetry of Kabbalah: Mystical Verse from the Jewish Tradition* (New Haven: Yale University Press, 2012), 241:

> Toward the end of his *Major Trends in Jewish Mysticism*, Gershom Scholem relates a Hasidic tale that applies in uncanny [fashion to the story above]. . . . Whenever the Baal Shem Tov was faced with a grave task, the story has it, he would make his way to a certain place in the forest, light a fire in a special manner, say a particular set of prayers, and—miraculously—the task would be accomplished. When his disciple the Maggid of Mezeritch faced a similar challenge, he would go to the same place in the forest and say: "We no longer know how to light the fire, but we can still say the prayers." He would say them, and the deed would be done. In the next generation, Rabbi Moshe Leib of Sassov was

compelled to take up the challenge and perform the task in question. He went to the forest and said: "We can no longer light the fire, nor do we know the secret prayers, but we know the place in the forest—and that is enough."

95. Bascom, *Ifa Divination*, 76.
96. Beier, *Return of the Gods*, 45.
97. Ibid., 59.
98. Araba of Modakẹkẹ, interview with the author, conducted in Yoruba, October 25, 2013, Modakẹkẹ, Nigeria.
99. Professor Agboola, interview with the author, conducted in English and Yoruba, November 24, 2013, Ile-Ifẹ, Nigeria.
100. Araba of Modakẹkẹ, interview with the author, conducted in Yoruba, November 12, 2013, Modakẹkẹ, Nigeria. Similarly, describing Susanne Wenger's bout of tuberculosis that preceded her initiation, "Friend Ajani Adigun Davies says Mrs. Wenger believes the illness was a kind of sacrifice, in return for the knowledge she was receiving about the gods. 'The Yoruba beliefs all depend on sacrifice, that you must give something of value to get something of value, you must suffer pain to gain knowledge,' he says." Andrew Walker, "The White Priestess of 'Black Magic,'" *BBC News*, http://news.bbc.co.uk/2/hi/africa/7595841.stm.
101. Epega and Neimark, *Sacred Ifa Oracle*, 203.
102. Araba of Modakẹkẹ, interview with the author, conducted in Yoruba, November 12, 2013, Modakẹkẹ, Nigeria.
103. *Babalawo koṣe jẹ ọlọrọ ninu owo bikoṣe ninu ogbọn* (Epega and Neimark, *Sacred Ifa Oracle*, 62).
104. *Ẹni ṣe rere o ṣe e fun ara rẹ. Ẹni ṣe ika o ṣe e fun ara rẹ* (ibid., 230).
105. Ibid., 329.
106. Professor Agboola, interview with the author, conducted in English and Yoruba, November 24, 2013, Ile-Ifẹ, Nigeria.
107. Ibid.
108. Beier, *Return of the Gods*, 51.
109. Awo Faniyi, interview with the author, conducted in Yoruba, November 27, 2013, Ile-Ifẹ, Nigeria.
110. Professor Agboola, interview with the author, conducted in English and Yoruba, November 24, 2013, Ile-Ifẹ, Nigeria.
111. Professor Agboola and Awo Faniyi, interview with the author, conducted in Yoruba, November 28, 2013, Ile-Ifẹ, Nigeria.
112. Traditional Yoruba homes were often rectangular with a central courtyard (*ode*) surrounded by rooms that faced in on the courtyard. This structure resembles the shape of many divining trays, with Eṣu standing at the doorway.

113. Araba of Modakẹkẹ, interview with the author, conducted in Yoruba, November 19, 2013, Modakẹkẹ, Nigeria.
114. Epega and Neimark, *Sacred Ifa Oracle*, xvi.
115. This is the Ifẹ ordering of the Odu (compare with fig. 7) taken from Bascom, *Ifa Divination*, 4.
116. Epega and Neimark, *Sacred Ifa Oracle*, 234.
117. Araba of Modakẹkẹ, interview with the author, conducted in Yoruba, November 19, 2013, Modakẹkẹ, Nigeria.
118. Epega and Neimark, *Sacred Ifa Oracle*, 213.
119. Ibid., 269–70.
120. Beier, *Return of the Gods*, 56.
121. Ibid., 47.
122. Araba of Modakẹkẹ, interview with the author, conducted in Yoruba, November 12, 2013, Modakẹkẹ, Nigeria.
123. Lawal, "Àwòrán," 514–15.
124. Ibid., 513.
125. Professor Agboola, interview with the author, conducted in English and Yoruba, November 24, 2013, Ile-Ifẹ, Nigeria.
126. Epega and Neimark, *Sacred Ifa Oracle*, 321. This refusal to sacrifice is implicitly given as the reason most people fear death.
127. A different set of rituals is performed for those who die in childhood, especially for those suspected of being *abiku*, those children "born to die" who keep coming and going between heaven and earth, inflicting a great emotional toll on their mothers and family. The wicked may be refused a funeral and buried in the bush.
128. Drewal, *Yoruba Ritual*, 41.
129. Professor Agboola, interview with the author, conducted in English and Yoruba, November 26, 2013, Ile-Ifẹ, Nigeria.
130. Epega and Neimark, *Sacred Ifa Oracle*, 186.
131. Ibid., 192–94.
132. Araba of Modakẹkẹ, interview with the author, conducted in Yoruba, November 12, 2013, Modakẹkẹ, Nigeria; Awo Faniyi, interview with the author, conducted in Yoruba, November 27, 2013, Ile-Ifẹ, Nigeria.
133. Epega and Neimark, *Sacred Ifa Oracle*, 186–87.
134. This unique Yoruba genre of orature is derived from the combination of *ori* (source, head, destiny/self) and the verb *ki* (to greet, salute, or even provoke/evoke), and thus it means to salute one's origin or inner self. Nearly everything has *oriki*: deities, people, towns, instruments, plants, animals, et cetera. Karin Barber describes *oriki* as "collections or strings of name-like attributive epithets, 'praises' which are neither narrative nor descriptive, but vocative. They are addressed to their subject or 'owner,' and are felt to encapsulate, and evoke in some way that subject's essential powers and qualities" (*I Could Speak Until Tomorrow*, 1).

135. Epega and Neimark, *Sacred Ifa Oracle*, xi–xii.
136. Translation by the author.
137. Similarly, the Araba of Modakẹkẹ explained, "Ọrunmila is inside of everyone. He is what makes you study Ifa" (interview with the author, conducted in Yoruba, November 12, 2013, Modakẹkẹ, Nigeria).
138. Epega and Neimark, *Sacred Ifa Oracle*, 322.

CHAPTER 8

The epigraph for this chapter is a Yoruba proverb cited by babalawo to explain why they consult other babalawo for divination. See Bascom, *Ifa Divination*, 98.

1. See Plato's *Phaedrus* and Jacob Olupọna, *City of 201 Gods: Ile-Ifẹ in Time, Space, and the Imagination* (Berkeley: University of California Press, 2011), 179.
2. Emmanuel Chukwudi Eze, "The Problem of Knowledge in 'Divination': The Example of Ifa," in *African Philosophy: A Critical Reader*, ed. E. C. Eze (Oxford, UK: Blackwell, 1998), 174.
3. Abiodun, "Verbal and Visual Metaphors," 256.
4. Epega and Neimark, *Sacred Ifa Oracle*, 186–87.
5. The prayer recited by Jonah in this Qur'anic account (21:87) is one that is commonly recited by Muslims in times of distress and repentance.
6. Professor Agboola, interview with the author, conducted in English and Yoruba, November 26, 2013, Ile-Ifẹ, Nigeria.
7. Ibid.
8. Ibid.
9. Ibid.
10. Araba of Modakẹkẹ, interview with the author, conducted in Yoruba, October 20, 2013, Modakẹkẹ, Nigeria.
11. Names changed to protect privacy.
12. The "just-so" stories contained in many of the Ifa verses, which provide a mythological explanation of the properties and behavior of minerals, plants, animals, people, and so forth, also serve as a means of "verification" of the verses. Bascom writes, "In addition to their usual functions in myths and tales, these aetiological elements serve another purpose in the Ifa verses: by referring to the features of plants, animals, objects, or rituals which are common knowledge or which the client can verify for himself, they substantiate the truth of the verse, with its prediction and sacrifice, and the system of divination as a whole" (*Ifa Divination*, 128).
13. Ibid., 79–80.
14. Bade Ajayi, "Ifa Divination Process," *Essays in Honour of Professor Wande Abimbola: Research in Yoruba Language and Literature* 8 (1996): 33.
15. Bascom, *Ifa Divination*, 76–79. It is important to note, first, that the practice of reciting verses until the client determines one that is relevant is one that I have not observed. Second, most babalawo I have encountered said that there are far more fraudulent babalawo in operation today than there were in Bascom's time.
16. Barber, "How Man Makes God in West Africa," 737.
17. Peel, *Religious Encounter and the Making of the Yoruba*, 215–47.
18. Ogunnaike, "Myth of Purity." In the same vein, Olasope Oyelaran cites the following saying: "*Orişa ti a sin sin sin, ti ko gbe ni, a a pada le yin in rẹ ni*. The Orişa whom one serves, serves, and serves, and does not prosper one, we must turn back away from him" ("Eṣu: Rehabilitation the Basis of Ethical Living in the Yoruba worldview," paper presented at Línguas é culturas Afro-brasileiras E As Novas Tecnologicas [Salvador, Brazil, September 2014], 36).
19. Similarly, Bascom writes:
> Yet it would be wrong to conclude that the Yoruba were resigned to uncontrollable destinies, or that they were content to rely on divination and other religious practices to solve all their problems. Several Yoruba proverbs clearly convey the message that "God helps those who help themselves," and some show an almost skeptical attitude toward these religious beliefs: "Bravery by itself is as good as magic." "A Chief is calling you and you are casting Ifa; if Ifa speaks of blessing and the chief speaks of evil, what then?" "A charm for invisibility is no better than finding a big forest to hide in; a sacrifice is no better than many supporters; and a deity to lift me onto a platform is no better than having a horse to ride away on." (*Ifa Divination*, 119)

20. Susanne Wenger, *The Timeless Mind of the Sacred: Its New Manifestation in the Ọṣun Groves* (Ibadan, Nigeria: Institute of African Studies, University of Ibadan, 1977), 23.
21. Professor Agboola, interview with the author, conducted in English and Yoruba, November 26, 2013, Ile-Ifẹ, Nigeria.
22. The Araba also explained that many of these pastors and even a few Muslim leaders came to him privately for divination and other ritual help and "power" in establishing their ministries and handling their personal affairs, although these same people would often publicly denounce Ifa and traditional Yoruba religious practices.
23. Araba of Modakẹkẹ, interview with the author, conducted in Yoruba, November 24, 2013, Modakẹkẹ, Nigeria.
24. Noel Amherd, *Reciting Ifá: Difference, Heterogeneity, and Identity* (Trenton, N.J.: Africa World Press, 2010), 223.

25. And I have tried to follow suit methodologically in this chapter.

26. Ayọ Salami, "Interview with Chief Ayo Salami; and the Oba Oriate Accord," April 25, 2011, https://www.youtube.com/watch?v=lW-tHypvvxM.

27. Beier, *Return of the Gods*, 49.

28. Professor Agboola, interview with the author, conducted in English and Yoruba, November 26, 2013, Ile-Ifẹ, Nigeria.

29. Awo Faniyi, interview with the author, conducted in Yoruba, November 27, 2013, Ile-Ifẹ, Nigeria.

30. Epega and Neimark, *Sacred Ifa Oracle*, xii.

31. Beier, *Return of the Gods*, 45.

32. Ibid., 56.

33. Epega and Neimark, *Sacred Ifa Oracle*, 192–94.

CHAPTER 9

1. Kimberley C. Patton and Benjamin C. Ray, eds., *A Magic Still Dwells: Comparative Religion in the Postmodern Age* (Berkeley: University of California Press, 2000), 2.

2. J. Z. Smith, *Imagining Religion: From Babylon to Jonestown* (Chicago: University of Chicago Press, 1982), 21.

3. I use the parentheses instead of hyphens to suggest precisely these kinds of deep and abiding continuities between "colonial" and "postcolonial" structures of knowledge and power, and likewise between the "modern" and "postmodern," particularly when one considers the perspectives of traditions such as Ifa and Sufism.

4. Michel Foucault, *The Order of Things: An Archaeology of the Human Sciences* (New York: Vintage Books, 1994), 54–55.

5. In both traditions, from a certain perspective, the "level" at which things are the same, ultimately in Allah/Olodumare, is more real than the "level" at which things are different and distinct (manifestation / the world).

6. For example, despite the many strengths of J. D. Y. Peel's *Christianity, Islam, and Orişa Religion: Three Traditions in Comparison and Interaction* (Berkeley: University of California Press, 2016), the work suffers from the old, orientalist stereotypes and mistakes of *islam noir* and lack of knowledge of the Islamic tradition. To highlight but one example, Peel cites an account of people fighting each other to capture some of the water left over from Shaykh Ibrahim Niasse's ablutions before the Friday prayer at a mosque in Ibadan, Nigeria, writing, "The source of this demand lay much more in Yoruba than in Islamic culture. It recalls nothing so much as the power attributed to the water blessed by Prophet Babalola in the *Aladura* revival of 1930–31, known as *omi iye* (water of life)—or, going further back, to the water of the river Ogun at Abeokuta sanctified by the prophetess Akere in 1855–56" (179–80), completely ignoring the precedents for this occurrence in the biographies of the Prophet Muḥammad (and later Islamic spiritual leaders), whose companions are reported to have similarly fought over the water remaining from his ablutions.

7. Ibn al-'Arabi, *The Ringstones of Wisdom* (*Fuṣūṣ al-ḥikam*), trans. Caner Dagli (Chicago: Kazi, 2004), 115–16.

8. William Chittick, *The Sufi Path of Knowledge: Ibn Al-'Arabi's Metaphysics of Imagination* (Albany: SUNY Press, 1989), 110–11.

9. Quoted in William Chittick, *Imaginal Worlds: Ibn al-'Arabi and the Problem of Religious Diversity* (Albany: SUNY Press, 1994), 176.

10. There are distinct lineages of Ifa practice, often associated with ethno-linguistic regions and city-states such as Ijẹbu, Ọyọ, Ifẹ, and so forth, but these operate and are conceptualized very differently from the different Sufi orders or schools—for example, I have never heard of anyone "switching from" Ifẹ to Ijẹbu traditions of Ifa.

11. For example, some verses mock the Muslim practice of fasting, which in traditional Yoruba society was practiced as a rite of mourning, asking, "All Muslims, when did you hear of the death of the almighty God? You liars; Or what else makes you fast (for so long)?" (Wande Abimbola, *Ifa Divination Poetry* [New York: Nok, 1977], 131). Others ridicule Muslim clothes and prayer, describing them as "those who tied their mother's headwrap on their heads and bobbed up and down in the dirt" (Wande Abimbola, *Ijinlẹ Ohun Ẹnu Ifa Apa Kini* [Glasgow: Collins, 1968], 96).

12. For more on Ifa's interpretation of Islam, see Jacob Olupọna, "Odù Imole: Islamic Tradition in Ifá and the Yoruba Religious Imagination," in *Ifá Divination, Knowledge, Power, and Performance*, ed. Jacob Oluona and Rowland Abiodun (Bloomington: Indiana University Press, 2016), 169–78.

13. Araba of Modakẹkẹ, interview with the author, conducted in Yoruba, November 12, 2013, Modakẹkẹ, Nigeria.

14. See T. G. O. Gbadamosi, "Odu Imale: Islam in Ifa Divination and the Case of Predestined Muslims," *Journal of the Historical Society of Nigeria* 8, no. 4 (1977): 91–92; and T. G. O. Gbadamosi, *The Growth of Islam among the Yoruba, 1841–1908* (Ibadan, Nigeria: University of Ibadan, 1978), 68–69.

15. This Yoruba word, derived from the Arabic *walī*, meaning "friend of God" or "saint," is used in the parlance of babalawo almost interchangeably with the

Arabic *nabī* (Prophet—i.e., *wọli Sulayman* [the prophet Solomon] or *wọli Nūḥ* [the Prophet Noah]) and the Christian/English "prophet," as in one blessed with the gift of prophesying future events.

16. A form of the word alfa, the Yoruba term (of Songhai origin) for a Muslim religious specialist or shaykh. Here the Prophet of Islam is the original and archetypal alfa.

17. Note the wordplay between the name of the Odu (Otura-Yapin) and the end result of the narrative: the division (*ipin*) of Ifa and Islam. Araba of Modakẹkẹ, interview with the author, conducted in Yoruba, November 20, 2013, Modakẹkẹ, Nigeria. For a recording and full transcription and translation of this verse, see "13.2 Otura-Yapin [Oyẹku]," African Sources of Knowledge—Digital Library, Odu Ifa Collection, Harvard University, http://ask-dl.fas.harvard.edu/content/132-otura-yapin-oy-ku.

18. This somewhat parallels the Qur'anic description of previous prophets (Adam, Noah, Abraham, Moses, Jesus, etc.) as "Muslim," and the religious traditions they brought as "Islam."

19. For more on Ifa's various descriptions of Islam, see Jacob Olupọna, "The Slaves of Allah," in *Alternative Voices: A Plurality Approach for Religious Studies: Essays in Honor of Ulrich Berner*, ed. Afe Adogame, Magnus Echtler, and Oliver Freiberger (Göttingen: Vandenhoeck & Ruprecht, 2013), 75–85.

20. Ayodeji Ogunnaike, "God, Gods, and Prophets: The Cosmology of Muslim Babalawo." bachelor's thesis, Harvard University, 2012.

21. Araba of Modakẹkẹ, interview with the author, conducted in Yoruba, October 12, 2017, Williamsburg, Virginia.

22. Many babalawo have an intimate knowledge of Muslim ritual and practice. Olupọna records that the Araba of Ifẹ equated the climbing of Oke Itasẹ, the sacred hill of Ifa, during the annual Ifa festival to the climbing of the mount of 'Arafāt by Muslim pilgrims during the ḥajj. Jacob Olupọna, *City of 201 Gods: Ile-Ifẹ in Time, Space, and the Imagination* (Berkeley: University of California Press, 2011), 193.

23. This tendency to explain Ifa's doctrines, rites, and rituals through comparison to those of Islam and Christianity can also be understood as a comparative interpretive strategy used by babalawo to speak to an increasingly Muslim and Christian Nigerian public in terms they can understand and respect. However, these comparisons appear to be based on the babalawo's perception of these traditions and their practices as profoundly similar or even identical. They also may reflect the increasing influence of Christianity and Islam on the way babalawo themselves understand and interpret their own tradition.

24. Araba of Modakẹkẹ, interview with the author, conducted in Yoruba, November 12, 2013, Modakẹkẹ, Nigeria.

25. Susanne Wenger, *The Timeless Mind of the Sacred: Its New Manifestation in the Ọṣun Groves* (Ibadan, Nigeria: Institute of African Studies, University of Ibadan, 1977), 46.

26. Araba of Modakẹkẹ, interview with the author, conducted in Yoruba, November 12, 2013, Modakẹkẹ, Nigeria.

27. Incidentally, Ṣango is often described as being Muslim himself. See J. L. Matory, *Sex and the Empire That Is No More: Gender and the Politics of Metaphor in Oyo Yoruba Religion* (New York: Berghahn Books, 2005), 265.

28. Zachary Wright, *Living Knowledge in West African Islam: The Sufi Community of Ibrahim Niasse* (Leiden: Brill, 2015), 213.

29. Similarly, the Divine Names that are said to govern the lives of different Sufis or the Prophets from whom various Sufis inherit or are "upon the foot of," could also be seen as playing a similar role to the Odu that give birth to babalawo.

30. Karin Barber, *I Could Speak Until Tomorrow: Oriki, Women, and the Past in a Yoruba Town* (London: Edinburgh University Press for the International African Institute, 1991), 1.

31. Ifayemi Elebuibon, *Ìyẹ̀rẹ̀ Ifá: Tonal Poetry, the Voice of Ifá: An Exposition of Yorùbá Divinational Chants* (San Bernardino, Calif.: Ilé Ọ̀rúnmìlà Communications, 1999), 101.

32. However, it should be noted that many Tijani shaykhs and disciples are adepts in the talismanic arts, which often involve animal sacrifices and preparations involving animal parts, plant life, and certain metals and stones—much like the sacrifices prescribed by Ifa. Although not directly involved in the acquisition of *ma'rifa*, this talismanic tradition forms an integral part of daily life for many Tijanis in West Africa and the diaspora.

33. Araba of Modakẹkẹ, interview with Ayọdeji Ogunnaike, conducted in Yoruba, December 2, 2012, Modakẹkẹ, Nigeria.

34. Sunan of Abu-Dawūd Ḥadīth 4781: "The Prophet said: 'There is nothing heavier than good character put in the Scale of a believer on the Day of Resurrection.'"

35. Alfa Akurede, interview with Ayọdeji Ogunnaike, conducted in English and Yoruba. October 7, 2010, Ogbagba, Nigeria.

36. Ibid.

37. Ismaheel Bakare, personal communication, conducted in English, February 9, 2016.

38. Ibid.

39. Yusuf Jones, personal communication, November 13, 2018.

40. David Robinson, "Failed Islamic States in Senegambia: Al-Hajj Umar Tall," *Pluralism and Adaptation in the Islamic Practice of Senegal and Ghana*, n.d., http://aodl.org/islamicpluralism/failedislamicstates/essays/43-1A9-F/#jump.

41. Amadou Hampâté Bâ, *A Spirit of Tolerance: The Inspiring Life of Tierno Bokar*, trans. Jane Casewit (Bloomington, Ind.: World Wisdom, 2008), 126–27.

42. Ibid., 129.

43. Louis Brenner, *West African Sufi: The Religious Heritage and Spiritual Search of Cerno Bokar Saalif Taal* (Berkeley: University of California Press, 1984), 87, 122.

44. Amadou Hampâté Bâ, *Aspects de la Civilisation Africaine* (Paris: Présence Africaine, 1972), 137–40.

45. Ibrahim Niasse, *Pearls from the Divine Flood: Selected Discourses from Shaykh Al-Islam Ibrahim Niasse*, trans. Zachary Wright (Atlanta: African American Islamic Institute, 2006), 29–30.

46. Quoted in Fakhruddin Owaisi al-Madani al-Tijani, "Understanding the Fayḍah Tijaniyyah—Part 1," n.d., 4, http://www.tariqa-tijaniyya.es/archivos_documentos/Understanding%20the%20Faydah%20Tijaniyyah%20-%201.pdf.

47. Mallam Shittu Olanipekun, "The Biography of Shaykh Muḥammad Jami'u Bulala (Alfa Offa)," n.d., University of Ilorin, unpublished article, https://www.slideshare.net/shittu14/shaykh-bulalas-biography.

48. For more on Yoruba Muslim perspectives on Ifa and other Orișa traditions, see J. Patrick Ryan, *Imale: Yoruba Participation in the Muslim Tradition: A Study of Clerical Piety* (Missoula, Mont.: Scholars Press, 1977); and Gbadamosi, *Growth of Islam Among the Yoruba*.

49. Interestingly, this is remarkably similar to the role that the verses and narratives of the Odu play in Ifa.

50. Shaykh Ibrahim Niasse's commentary on this verse reads, "'Only purely sincere religion is for God, other than this is not befitting for Him. And those who take other than Him,' idols, 'as patrons' [*awliyā'*], and they are the disbelievers [*kuffār*] of Mecca, they say, 'We only worship them that they may bring us nearer unto God.' They say that they place these gods as intermediaries [*wasā'iṭ*] between them and God. 'God will judge between them' and between the Muslims 'concerning that wherein they differ' about the matter of religion, and so He will enter the believers into the garden and the disbelievers into the fire." Shaykh Ibrāhīm Inyās, *Fī Riyāḍ al-Tafsīr li'l-Qur'ān al-Karīm* (Tunis: al-Yamāma, 2010), 5:181. Another similar verse (7:30) is even more negative: "A party has He led aright, while error has just hold over [another] party, for lo! they choose the devils for protecting supporters instead of God and deem that they are rightly guided."

51. This practice is, however, described as being more akin to casting lots than to the kind of divination employed in Ifa. Moreover, another verse (3:44) describes how the prophet Zakariya and the other priests of the temple *threw their pens* [in casting lots] *(to know) which of them should be the guardian of Mary*. Implying that this practice, although now forbidden to Muslims, may have been allowed and even encouraged for the followers of other prophets, like the drinking of wine.

52. The ḥadīth literature sets the number of prophets (*al-anbiyā'*) at 124,000 and the number of messengers (*rusul*) at 313 or 315. See Ibn Ḥanbal, Musnad, 5, 169.

53. In another version of the ḥadīth (found in Mālik's *Muwaṭṭā'*), the Prophet asks the slave woman if she testifies that there is no God but God, that Muḥammad is His Messenger and believes in the resurrection after death. See Johnathan Brown, *Ḥadīth: Muḥammad's Legacy in the Medieval and Modern World* (Oxford: Oneworld, 2009), 181.

54. Adherents of "indigenous" Hausa religious traditions in northern Nigeria were (and are still) known as Maguzawa, a term deriving from the Arabic word for "Magian," members of a Zoroastrian tradition considered as People of the Book and granted *dhimmī* status by some Islamic scholars. By analogy and this act of naming, some West African scholars granted the same status to these Hausa communities; however, other scholars such as 'Uthman dan Fodio classified them as "idolaters," "disbelievers," and/or "sorcerers." David Robinson, *Muslim Societies in African History* (New York: Cambridge University Press, 2004), 141–46, 202.

55. See "A Myth of Origins," in Chittick, *Imaginal Worlds*, 129–32. This narrative of Ibn 'Arabi's bears a striking resemblance to the myths cited in chapter 5. The role played by the Divine Name "The Governor" in Ibn 'Arabi's mythical account is very similar to the role played by Ọrunmila in the myths of Ifa cited above.

56. Jalāl al-dīn Muḥammad Rūmī, *Mathnawi of Jalaluddin Rumi*, trans. R. A. Nicholson (London: Luzac, 1972), 1.1106.

57. Numerous other statements in the ḥadīth, Qur'an, as well as Sufi and Tijani literature extol the superiority of the Prophet as the "best of creation."

58. For Ibrahim Niasse's discussion of this issue, see Inyās, *Fī Riyāḍ al-Tafsīr*, 1:135 and 213–20, an English translation of which can be found in *In the Meadows of Tafsīr for the Noble Qur'an*, trans. Moctar Boubakar Ba (Atlanta: Fayda Books, 2014), 1:175 and 276–82. Shaykh Ibrahim concludes this long discussion by clearly affirming the superiority of the Prophet Muḥammad over all other prophets, saying, "Since the Qur'an has clearly affirmed that He has favored certain Prophets over others and since we have witnessed these favors

as well as these indisputable proofs of the fact that Muḥammad is the best of the Prophets, then no one doubts the superiority of Muḥammad, except one who does not believe in the Qurʾan and has, as a result, completely gone out of this matter."

59. Chittick, *Imaginal Worlds*, 125.

60. Ibn al-ʿArabi, *Ringstones of Wisdom*, 251. Or, as Rumi says more poetically, "When the colourless became enmeshed in colours / a Moses came into conflict with a Moses" *Mathnawī*, 1.2467.

CHAPTER 10

1. This distinction bears some resemblance to Russell's distinction between "knowledge by acquaintance" and "knowledge by description." However, both Ifa and Tijani Sufism posit that one can know truths or the Truth/Reality (*al-Ḥaqq/Otitọ*) through this kind of "knowledge by acquaintance," and not just ordinary "things," as Russell asserts.

2. Compare with this description of the Eleusian mysteries from the introduction to Pierre Hadot's *Philosophy as a Way of Life: Spiritual Exercises from Socrates to Foucault*, trans. Michael Chase (Oxford, UK: Blackwell, 1995): "Indeed, recalling the importance of the mysteries of Eleusis in the history of ancient thought, Hadot reminds us of the famous sentence attributed to Aristotle that the initiates of Eleusis do not *learn* anything, but they *experience* a certain impression or emotion. The initiate did not learn his other-worldly fate at Eleusis, but lived this supra-individual life of the other world. The 'true secret of Eleusis is therefore *this very experience*, this moment when one plunges into the completely other, this discovery of an unknown dimension of existence" (168).

3. Although in some traditions, babalawo are initiated as young children and many Tijani shuyūkh give *tarbiya* to people who have only a basic understanding of Islamic and Sufi doctrines, so this process is less gradual in these cases.

4. Inyās, *Fī Riyāḍ al-Tafsīr*, 1:272–74.

5. Ibrahim Niasse, *The Removal of Confusion Concerning the Flood of the Saintly Seal Aḥmad al-Tijānī*, trans. Zachary Wright, Muhtar Holland, and Abdullahi Okene (Louisville, Ky.: Fons Vitae, 2010), 47–48.

6. Ibn ʿArabi writes, "For when He is invoked, He is invoked through Him. And through Him, He is reflected upon and conceived of. He is the rational faculty of the rational thinkers, the reflection of the reflectors, the invocation of the invokers, the proof of the provers. Were He to come out of a thing, it would cease to be. And were He to be within a thing, it would cease to be." Chittick, *Sufi Path of Knowledge*, 381.

7. Shaykh Ibrāhīm Inyās, *al-Sirr al-Akbar wa'l Kibrīt al-Aḥmar*, ed. Maigari, in Muḥammad Maigari, *Shaykh Ibrāhīm Aniyās [sic] al-Sinighālī ḥayatuhu wa arāʾuhu wa taʿlīmuhu* (Beirut: Dar al-ʿArabiyya, 1981), 447–48.

8. Ibn al-ʿArabi, *Ringstones of Wisdom*, 133.

9. Chittick, *Sufi Path of Knowledge*, 299.

10. This is also known as the Most Holy Effusion (*al-fayḍ al-aqdas*) and the Self-disclosure of the invisible (*al-tajallī al-ghayb*) discussed in chapter 4.

11. Ibn al-ʿArabi, *Ringstones of Wisdom*, 63.

12. Barry Hallen *The Good, the Bad, and the Beautiful: Discourse About Values in Yoruba Culture* (Bloomington: Indiana University Press, 2000), 52.

13. Ibid., 52–53.

14. Ibn al-ʿArabi, *Ringstones of Wisdom*, 127–28.

15. Seyyed Hossein Nasr, *The Garden of Truth: The Vision and Promise of Sufism, Islam's Mystical Tradition* (New York: HarperOne, 2007), 40.

16. Wenger, *Timeless Mind of the Sacred*, 29.

17. K. S., Skype interview with the author, conducted in English, March, 26, 2014.

18. Ibn al-ʿArabi, *Ringstones of Wisdom*, 23.

19. Awo Faniyi, interview with the author, conducted in Yoruba, November 27, 2013, Ile-Ifẹ, Nigeria. Awo Faniyi then quoted a lengthy verse of Ifa from Odu Otura Iwori in which Ọrunmila is told to use Odu as the power (*aṣẹ*) behind all his decisions (*ipin*) in life, even what he should eat and drink.

20. Ibn al-ʿArabi, *Ringstones of Wisdom*, 33.

21. This concept of a "heavenly self"—which is at once destiny, guardian angel, muse, and source and goal of knowledge—is not limited to Ifa and Sufism, but has close counterparts in Greek (*daimon*), Roman (*genius*), Igbo, Akan, and Zoroastrian mythology and philosophy. See Oludamini Ogunanike, "Myth and the Secret of Destiny: Mircea Eliade's Creative Hermeneutics and the Yorùbá Concept of Ori," *Journal of Comparative Theology* 1, no. 3 (2012): 4–42.

22. T. S. Eliot, *The Four Quartets* (New York: Harcourt, 1943), 39.

23. Tidiane Ali Cissé, *What the Knowers of Allah Have Said About the Knowledge of Allah*, trans. Zachary Wright and Muḥammad Hassiem Abdullahi (Atlanta: Fayda Books, 2014), 20.

24. Ibid., 91.

25. Chittick, *Sufi Path of Knowledge*, 367–67.

26. Ibid., 377.

27. Niasse, *Pearls from the Divine Flood*, 97.

28. Diedre Badejo, "Ọrunmila," in *Encyclopedia of African Religion*, ed. Molefi Asante and Ama Mazama (Los Angeles: Sage, 2009), 508–10.

29. Teresa Washington, *Our Mothers, Our Powers, Our Texts: Manifestations of Aje in Africana Literature* (Bloomington: Indiana University Press, 2005), 42.

30. Araba of Modakẹkẹ, interview with the author, conducted in Yoruba, December 2, 2013, Modakẹkẹ, Nigeria. See also African Sources of Knowledge—Digital Library, Odu Ifa Collection, Harvard University, http://ask-dl.fas.harvard.edu/content/12-ogbe-y-ku.

31. Or leaving aside any notion of superiority, this story mirrors the relationship between the Transcendent Real (Orişanla), the cosmos in its infinite diversity (Olokun and her many cloths), and the Muḥammadan / Perfect Human (insān al-kāmil), the barzakh between them (agẹmọ), who can take on all of the forms of the cosmos; and in doing so, actually exhausts her. Similarly, the Perfect Human, in achieving this infinite flexibility, in a certain sense, exhausts and transcends the infinite play of manifest existence.

32. Afolabi Epega and Philip John Neimark, *The Sacred Ifa Oracle* (San Francisco: Harper, 1995), xi. Translation by the author.

33. Chittick, *Sufi Path of Knowledge*, 377–78.

34. As alluded to in the previously cited phrases: "If I want, I want to not want; for whatever the Willer [al-Murīd] wills, that is what I want" and "The incapacity to attain realization is itself realization"; the description of *ma'rifa* as the "utmost degree of ignorance"; and Shaykh Tijānī's statement that "the reality of oneness [tawḥīd] is not perceived, because as long as you continue to speak, you exist and God exists, and so there are two, and then where is the oneness [tawḥīd]? There is no oneness [tawḥīd] except when it is for God, by God, and to God. The servant has no entrance to this, and no exit from it."

35. Shaykh Ibrāhīm Inyās, *Jawāhir al-rasā'il wa-yaliyya ziyādat al-jawāhir al-ḥāwī ba'ḍ 'ulūm wasīlat al-wasā'il*, ed. Aḥmad Abū'l-Fatḥ (Borno: Aḥmad Abī'l-Fatḥ, n.d.), 1:6. Similarly, Shaykh Aḥmad al-Tijānī is recorded in Zachary Wright's *On the Path of the Prophet: Shaykh Ahmad Tijani and the Tariqa Muḥammadiyya* (Atlanta: African American Islamic Institute, 2005), 120, as saying:

> The disciple must strive towards these two goals: [First] to prefer God to everything else. God must be for him the principal and the end of his desires so that not one single instant of his life be dedicated to another, because to look to another is to find self-interest or squandering. [And second] to devote himself completely to God, free from all bonds, completely and mysteriously united to Him in body, soul, spirit, and heart, in such a manner that not one particle of the being is a stranger to God. The disciple will give himself over completely to this goal, detached from all passion. Like this, he will stand before God, in the total renunciation of his whole being, in order to accomplish an act of pure adoration and satisfaction of divine laws, without expecting the slightest advantage. He will not despair of God's mercy nor will he pridefully err in believing himself full of good qualities.

Note here that the two goals are really the same, and that is to abandon all of one's goals for God.

36. Inyās, *Jawāhir al-rasā'il*, 1:24.

37. Niasse, *Pearls from the Divine Flood*, 98. Similarly Ibn 'Arabi writes, "The knower is he who worships God for God, while other than the knower worships God for what he hopes for from God—the shares of his soul in the worship." William Chittick, *The Self-Disclosure of God: Principles of Ibn Al-'Arabī's Cosmology* (Albany: SUNY Press, 1998), 374.

38. Sidi Mohamed Kane, interview with the author, conducted in French, April 4, 2014, Dakar, Senegal.

39. See William Chittick and Peter Lamborn Wilson, *Fakhruddin 'Iraqi: Divine Flashes* (New York: Paulist Press, 1982), 116.

40. Ibn 'Arabi famously wrote, "So glory be to Him who veils Himself in His manifestation and becomes manifest in His veil! No eye witnesses anything other than He, and no veils are lifted from Him" (Chittick, *Sufi Path of Knowledge*, 129). Similarly, Ibn 'Aṭā' Allāh's aphorism no. 15 reads, "That which shows you the existence of His Omnipotence is that He veiled you from Himself by what has no existence alongside of Him." Victor Danner, *Ibn 'Aṭā'Illāh's Ṣūfī Aphorisms* (Leiden: Brill, 1973), 25.

41. Inyās, *Jawāhir al-rasā'il*, 1.56–69.

42. Ibid., 1.81.

43. See Annemarie Schimmel, *Mystical Dimensions of Islam* (Chapel Hill: University of North Carolina Press, 1975), 99.

44. Shaykh Ibrahim also comments on the verse of the Qurʾan "Worship your Lord until certainty comes to you" (15:99) as follows: "'Certainty' here is 'death,' not as some of the Sufis without a foot in the *sharī'a* say, that man worships his Lord until he finds certainty and then he leaves aside worship. Rather worship only stops with death. Certainty here means death, not only direct witnessing [mushāhadah]" (Inyās, *Fī Riyāḍ al-tafsīr*, 3:269).

45. Afolabi Epega and Philip John Neimark, *The Sacred Ifa Oracle* (San Francisco: Harper, 1995), 412.

46. Professor Agboola, interview with the author, conducted in English and Yoruba, November 24, 2013, Ile-Ifẹ, Nigeria.

47. Ibn 'Arabi and Ismail Haqqi Bursawī, *Kernel of the Kernel*, trans. Bulent Rauf (Sherborne, UK: Beshara Publications for the Beshara Trust, 1981), 2–3. From the perspective of Ifa, the role of these "servants" would be played by the orişa, especially Ọrunmila, the Odu of Ifa, and the elder babalawo.

48. Awo Faniyi, interview with the author, conducted in Yoruba, November 27, 2013, Ile-Ifẹ, Nigeria.

49. Inyās, *Fī Riyāḍ al-Tafsīr*, 5:250–51. See also Ibn ʿAṭāʾ Allāh's *Ḥikam* no. 246: "The cosmos is large in respect to your body, but it is not large in respect to your soul." Ibn ʿAṭā Allāh al-Iskandarī, *Kitāb al-ḥikam* (Cairo: Maktaba Madbūlī, n.d.), 41.

50. Niasse, *Pearls from the Divine Flood*, 114.

51. "*Awo j'awo lọ; awo le gbawo mi tori tori.*" Quoted in Andrew Apter, "'Que Faire?' Reconsidering Inventions of Africa," *Critical Inquiry* 19, no. 1 (1992): 100.

52. Niasse, *Pearls from the Divine Flood*, 82.

53. Araba of Modakẹkẹ, interview with the author, conducted in Yoruba, November 11, 2013, Modakẹkẹ, Nigeria.

54. As mentioned above, this implies a theory of language that differs markedly from structuralist and poststructuralist semiotics. This approach is not based on a logic of difference, of an arbitrary relationship between signifier and signified, but rather one of symbolism, of the ontological continuities that exist between the domains of metacosm, microcosm, macrocosm, and language. The ineffable Real reveals itself in and as these different domains, creating a vast network of symbolic correspondences that can be discovered by those who "have eyes to see."

55. For examples, see Wright, *Living Knowledge in West African Islam*, 42–50; and David Owusu-Ansah, *Islamic Talismanic Tradition in Nineteenth-Century Asante* (Lewiston, N.Y.: Edwin Mellen Press, 1991), 29–30.

56. Niasse, *Pearls from the Divine Flood*, 92.

57. Femi Makinde, "Many Pastors and Imams Secretly Come to Me to Consult Ifa—Ifayemi elebuibon, traditional priest," Punchng.com, October 26, 2013, https://www.modernghana.com/nollywood/25092/many-pastors-and-imams-secretly-come-to-me-to-cons.html.

58. Inyās, *Jawāhir al-rasāʾil*, 1.30.

59. The Qurʾanic verse "You are the best community that hath been raised up for mankind" (3:110) and the following ḥadīths are often cited in this regard: "The best of you are my generation, then those that follow them and then those that follow them"; "My community is like the rain, for it is not known whether the best is in its first part or its last," and "Verily God sends to this community at the head of every century, a renewer of its religion." Niasse, *Removal of Confusion*, 11–12, 62.

60. It should be noted that these perspectives on time and history differ markedly from the nearly ubiquitous assumptions of "the march of progress" and "development" that characterize so much of Western thought post-Hegel, and undergird contemporary parlance such as "the wrong/right side of history."

61. This and the general concept of the *fayḍa* come from the following saying of Shaykh Aḥmad al-Tijānī: "A *fayḍa* will come upon my companions, so people will enter our spiritual path group upon group. This *fayḍa* will come when people are in their utmost state of distress and hardship." Niasse, *Removal of Confusion*, 59.

62. M. D., interview with author, conducted in French, March 19, 2014, Dakar, Senegal.

63. Wright, *Living Knowledge in West African Islam*, 208.

64. Anonymous disciple, interview with the author, conducted in French, March, 26, 2014, Dakar, Senegal.

65. See J. Lorand Matory, "The English Professors of Brazil: On the Diasporic Roots of the Yorùbá Nation," *Comparative Studies in Society and History* 41, no. 1 (1999): 72–103; and J. D. Y. Peel, *Religious Encounter and the Making of the Yoruba* (Bloomington: Indiana University Press, 2003).

66. Anonymous shaykh, interview with the author, conducted in Arabic, March 6, 2014, Dakar, Senegal.

67. Ustadh Barham Diop, interview with the author, conducted in Arabic, January 10, 2012, Medina Baye, Senegal.

68. Cheikh Hamidou Kane, *Ambiguous Adventure* (London: Heinemann, 1972).

69. Muḥamamd al-Makkī, interview with the author, conducted in Arabic, April 14, 2012, Medina Baye, Senegal.

70. For a detailed discussion of these adaptations, see Wright, *Living Knowledge in West African Islam*, 192–210.

71. Araba of Modakẹkẹ interview with the author, conducted in Yoruba, November 22, 2014, Modakẹkẹ, Nigeria.

72. Ibid.

73. Araba of Modakẹkẹ, interview with the author, conducted in Yoruba, December 7, 2012, Modakẹkẹ, Nigeria.

74. Araba of Modakẹkẹ, interview with the author, conducted in Yoruba, April 11, 2014, Modakẹkẹ, Nigeria.

75. See "Eji Ogbe Oyinbo," African Sources of Knowledge—Digital Library, Odu Ifa Collection, Harvard University, http://ask-dl.fas.harvard.edu/content/10-eji-ogbe-oyinbo.

76. I owe this insight to Ayọdeji Ogunnaike.

77. As the previously cited verse from Odu Irẹtẹ Meji says, "The one who is the messenger of Ẹlẹdumare / The king's messenger does not go to the farm / The king's messenger does not go to the river / If I am the messenger of Ifa / I will be happy." Araba of Modakẹkẹ, interview with the author, conducted in Yoruba, November 18, 2013, Modakẹkẹ, Nigeria.

78. While there are numerous other important and interesting dimensions of comparison to be explored

between these two traditions (such as comparing the concepts of *iwa* and *adab/akhlāq*), these will have to await future studies. Furthermore, while the above discussion suggests possible influences of Islam on Ifa and of indigenous African traditions and worldviews on Tijani Sufism, such a discussion is outside the scope of this project. Still, I hope this work will be a useful resource to the intrepid scholars who take up this important work. In addition to the possible influences of Islam on Ifa mentioned above, several disciples in Senegal told me that they believed in reincarnation (a doctrine officially rejected by most schools of Sufi thought and Islamic theology), some told me that Shaykh Ibrahim was the reincarnation of the Prophet Muḥammad, and some even explained that they knew who they were in their former lives and that they had lived with Shaykh Aḥmad al-Tijānī and, before that, with the Prophet. Perhaps these statements are a different formulation of the transhistorical spiritual relationships and identities between the disciples, Sufi masters, and the Prophet discussed in the previous chapters, but I believe it is likely that these particular formulations were influenced by the traditional Wolof, Serër, and Fulani cosmologies in which reincarnation feature prominently, as it does in traditional Yoruba worldviews.

79. See chapter 1, note 259; and Niasse, *Removal of Confusion*, vi. Personally, I am more inclined to trust the estimates that put the following in the high tens of millions, which is still significant. For comparison with the population of another intellectual tradition, the U.S. 2016 census data suggests that around seventy-five million Americans hold bachelor's degrees or higher (U.S. Census Bureau. "Educational Attainment in the United States: 2016," n.d., https://www.census.gov/data/tables/2016/demo/education-attainment/cps-detailed-tables.html, while a study conducted by researchers at the Asian Development Bank and Harvard University estimated that around 470 million people in the world have college degrees (David Wilson, "College Graduates to Make Economy More Productive—Chart of the Day," *Bloomberg*, May 18, 2010).

80. For example, see E. E. Evans-Pritchard's and Robin Horton's work on African religions and the works of Fazlur Rahman and Hossein Ziai on the Islamic intellectual tradition.

81. For example, see Noel Amherd, *Reciting Ifá: Difference, Heterogeneity, and Identity* (Trenton, N.J.: Africa World Press, 2010); and Ebrahim Moosa, *Ghazali and the Poetics of Imagination* (Chapel Hill: University of North Carolina Press, 2005). Notable exceptions to these trends include the work of Rowland Abiọdun and Jacob Olupọna, and to a certain extent Helen Verran's *Science and an African Logic* (Chicago: University of Chicago Press, 2001). The latter's work compares Yoruba and contemporary Western mathematical-linguistic concepts.

82. Hadot, *Philosophy as a Way of Life*, 100. Even Aristotle, who is often portrayed as a thinker who separated theory from praxis, describes *theoria* as the highest and best activity of humankind, and its ultimate happiness. In his *Nicomachean Ethics*, *theoria* is described as the actualization of the Divine Intellect (*nous*) immanent in man, as a participation in the divine way of life, and as such requires inner transformation and personal *askesis*, and thus, a way of life producing a blissful contemplative vision of reality. Plotinus calls *theoria* "the goal and end of all action."

83. I believe this distinction is absent in Ifa because of the relatively recent encounter of Ifa with this perspective of "theory," whereas Sufis were more familiar with traditions of discursive thought divorced from *theoria*. It is also significant in this regard that the term for the modern, European version of Christianity / secular modernity that the babalawo encountered was called *igbagbọ*. I suspect that had the Yoruba first encountered the Christianity of St. Augustine or the Ethiopian Orthodox Church, it may not have been called *igbagbọ*.

84. Abimbola, *Ifa Divination Poetry*, 124–25.

85. William Chittick, *Kashf Al-asrar: The Unveiling of the Mysteries* (Louisville, Ky.: Fons Vitae, 2015), 295.

86. Although the first chapter of this book describes Ibn ʿArabi as a theorist, this is not quite accurate. Ibn ʿArabi's writings are far more concerned with provoking, inciting, and inspiring readers to *theoria* (which roughly corresponds to the Arabic *mushāhada* [direct witnessing of the Real]) than with constructing a particular theory or conceptual representation of reality. In other words, he is interested in "untying" the knots of theory, instead of tying a new, better knot.

87. Niasse, *Removal of Confusion*, 88.

88. Jay Garfield, *Empty Words: Buddhist Philosophy and Cross-Cultural Interpretation* (Oxford: Oxford University Press, 2001), 229.

89. Peter Coates, *Ibn ʿArabi and Modern Thought: The History of Taking Metaphysics Seriously* (Oxford, UK: Anqa, 2008), 118.

90. If the academy can accommodate Marxist revolutionaries and Freudian/Lacanian psychoanalysts writing and working as such, why not babalawo and *shuyūkh*?

91. While this is true of everyone to a certain extent—we all perform in a professional setting—it is much more true (and, one could argue, oppressive) for those people who have been profoundly formed by traditions that neither seriously form nor inform the structures and discourse of contemporary academia.

92. Hadot, *Philosophy as a Way of Life*, 108.

93. Quoted in Wright, *On the Path of the Prophet*, 121.

94. Incidentally, Plato concludes *The Republic* with a remarkably similar account of man's "choice of destiny" and forgetting of it after drinking from the river of forgetfulness (Lethe) on his way into the world. See "The Myth of Er" in George Grube and C. D. C. Reeve, *Plato's Republic* (Cambridge, Mass.: Hackett, 1992), 285–92.

95. This is very different from contemporary academic approaches to knowledge: one can be a total jerk and an accomplished physicist, sociologist, scholar of religion, or philosopher.

96. The first epigraph for this section comes from an interview with Shaykh Tijani 'Alī Cissé, conducted in Arabic, January 14, 2012, Medina Baye, Senegal. Versions of this saying have been attributed to the Egyptian scholar Jalāl al-Dīn Suyūṭī (d. 1505) and the Andalusian scholar al-Shāṭibī (d. 1388). Although there has been a great deal of recent scholarship, across a number of fields, on "embodiment," with certain exceptions, our academic productions (books, articles, lectures) and practices (classes, conferences, lectures, articles, and books) rarely apply such insights reflexively to these embodied practices. Moreover, most work on "embodiment" adopts materialist-reductionist and/or phenomenological approaches and assumptions, which differ markedly from the approaches to and assumptions about the body in many non-Western traditions, such as Sufism and Ifa.

97. This is why cremation of the dead (with the exception of certain kinds of people that families seek to be rid of, such as *abiku* among the Yoruba, children "born to die" who plague their families with misfortune) is widely considered an anathema among many, if not most Africans—not only Muslims, but also Christians and practitioners of traditional African religions.

98. Rudolph Ware, *The Walking Qur'an: Islamic Education, Embodied Knowledge, and History in Africa* (Chapel Hill: University of North Carolina Press, 2014).

99. *Al-Riḥla al-Kunākiriyya* (*Nafaḥat al-Malik al-Ghanī*), 4–5, quoted in Rüdiger Seesemann, *The Divine Flood: Ibrahim Niasse and the Roots of a Twentieth-Century Sufi Revival* (New York: Oxford University Press, 2011), 193.

100. This integration is believed to have given the Prophet's body certain qualities possessed by none other, which allows him to be present (if not physically) in many places at once, and to continue to provide direct spiritual guidance and initiation after his death, as in the case of the founding of the Tijāniyya.

101. Niasse, *Removal of Confusion*, 86.

102. Inyās, *Fī Riyāḍ al-Tafsīr*, 3:345. Similarly, the disciples I interviewed commonly recited the Prophet's *Du'ā Nūr* after prayers, which reads, "O God put light in my heart, and light in my tongue . . . and put light in my nerves, and light in my flesh, and light in my blood, and light in my hair, and light in my skin . . . and light in my bones." In the context of the hadith "Knowledge is light," this prayer is a request for the full embodiment of knowledge.

103. Ibid., 3:251–52.

104. Sīdī 'Alī Harāzim, *Kitāb Jawāhir al-Ma'ānī wa-bulūgh al-amānī fī fayḍ Sīdī Abī'l al-'Abbās al-Tijānī*, trans. Ravane Mbaye (Dakar: Dar Albouraq, 2011), 395–97.

105. Niasse, *Removal of Confusion*, 85.

106. Radtke and O'Kane, *Pure Gold*, 225.

107. Moreover, the Qur'an speaks of God's "hand," "leg," and so forth, implying that the highest level of reality of the body exists in the Divine Order. Again, this should not be confused with anthropomorphism; according to this perspective, the human's being, including its body, is theomorphic.

108. This should not be taken as implying some form of incarnation (*ḥulūl*) or unification (*ittiḥād*)—positions which are strongly rejected by Tijani *shuyūkh*. Ibn 'Arabi and al-Tijānī both explain that these perspectives are invalid because there is nothing other than the Real for Him to become unified with or incarnate in.

109. Because of this integration the bodies of saints are popularly believed to not decay. This integration is one of the theoretical rationales given to explain the extraordinary feats (*karamāt*) of the saints such as flying, walking on water, walking long distances in a short time, and the like.

110. Abu Hamid al-Ghazali, "Elaboration of the Marvels of the Heart," in *Knowledge of God in Classical Sufism*, trans. John Renard (New York: Paulist Press, 2004), 317.

111. Ibn 'Arabi even explains that there are specific forms of knowledge unique to parts of the body such as the feet, and that modes of bodily knowledges "complete" God's knowledge. Commenting on the verse "He is the Subtle, the Informed" (31:16), Ibn 'Arabi explains that God knows Himself absolutely in Himself, directly but then completes this perfect self-knowledge through the indirect "knowledge of taste," knowledge of Himself as other, through the faculties and bodies of his servants (see *Ringstones of Wisdom*, 241). Thus the body is, from a certain perspective, necessary for God's full knowledge of Himself. For a more detailed discussion of these and other points, see Seyyed Hossein Nasr, *Religion and the Order of Nature* (New York: Oxford University Press, 1996), 235–70.

112. Like many Muslims, the Tijani disciples and *shuyūkh* I interviewed preferred to face the *qibla* when

doing work—even students studying for their *bac* exams.

113. Yolanda Covington-Ward, *Gesture and Power: Religion, Nationalism, and Everyday Performance in Congo* (Durham: Duke University Press, 2016), 231.

114. Ulli Beier, *The Return of the Gods: The Sacred Art of Susanne Wenger* (Cambridge: Cambridge University Press, 1975), 49.

115. Paul Stoller and Cheryl Olkes, *In Sorcery's Shadow: A Memoir of Apprenticeship Among the Songhay of Niger* (Chicago: University of Chicago Press, 2013); Robert Rozehnal, *Islamic Sufism Unbound: Politics and Piety in Twenty-First-Century Pakistan* (New York: Macmillan, 2007).

116. Johann Wolfgang von Goethe, *Maxims and Reflections*, trans. Elisabeth Stopp (New York: Penguin, 1998), 12.

117. For example, Wael Hallaq's *Restating Orientalism: A Critique of Modern Knowledge* (New York: Columbia University Press, 2018) argues that "secular humanism, like liberalism, is not only anthropocentric, structurally intertwined with violence, and incapable of sympathy with the nonsecular Other, but it is also anchored, perforce, in a structure of thought wholly defined by modes of sovereign domination" (5); and "that while the greatest majority of scholars may entertain the noblest of intentions when they embark on the study of Islamic and other non-Occidental cultures, their intentions and, at times, their admirable work and erudition have little to do with how the aggregate literary production, as a cultural collectivity, percolates into a paradigm that ultimately partakes in domination and endless forms of violence" (407).

118. E. E. Evans-Pritchard, *Witchcraft, Oracles, and Magic Among the Azande* (Oxford, UK: Clarendon Press, 1976), 68.

119. Michel Foucault, *The Hermeneutics of the Subject: Lectures at the Collège de France, 1981–82*, trans. Graham Burchell (New York: Palgrave Macmillan, 2005), 19.

120. William Chittick, *The Sufi Path of Love: The Spiritual Teachings of Rumi* (Albany: SUNY Press, 1998), 273.

121. Araba of Modakẹkẹ, interview with the author, conducted in Yoruba, November 14, 2013, Modakẹkẹ, Nigeria.

122. Charles Taylor, *Sources of the Self: The Making of the Modern Identity* (Cambridge: Harvard University Press, 1989).

123. Steven Pinker, *The Better Angels of Our Nature: Why Violence Has Declined* (New York: Viking, 2011); Jared Diamond, *Guns, Germs, and Steel: The Fates of Human Societies* (New York: W. W. Norton, 1998).

124. Frithjof Schuon, "The Human Margin," *Studies in Comparative Religion* 5, no. 3 (1971), http://www.studiesincomparativereligion.com/Public/articles/The_Human_Margin_Part_1-by_Frithjof_Schuon.aspx.

125. Hadot, *Philosophy as a Way of Life*, 265.

126. 'Arabī and Bursawī, *Kernel of the Kernel*, 2.

# Index

Aafa. *See* Muḥammad
Abimbola, M. Ajisebo McElwaine, 277
Abimbola, Wande, 24, 213, 243, 259–60, 262
Abiodun, Rowland, 17, 234–37, 291, 307
*aborisa* (worshippers of orisa). *See olorisa*
abrogation, 337, 343–44, 348–49
    *See also* Ifa and Tijani Sufism, compared
Abū Bakr (al-Ṣiddīq), 125, 228
Abū Ḥanīfa al-Nuʿmān ibn Thābit, 124
Abū Lahab (uncle of Muḥammad), 154
Abū'l Khayr, Abū Saʿīd, 34
Abū Madyan al-Ghawth, 88
abundance, 395
    *See also* perspectivism
Abū Yazīd al-Bistāmī, 88–89, 105, 149–50, 152, 363
academia
    African traditions and Eurocentrism of, 13–15, 17
    embodiment as challenge to, 389
    Ifa and Tijani Sufism as theoretical challenge to, 22, 25–27, 326, 328, 378–80, 396
    (post)colonialism and (post)modernity in, 391–94, 396, 437n117
    rituals and community, need for recognition of, 390–91, 395
    theoretical and existential perspectives, need for both, 317, 325–26, 380–85
    *See also* philosophy, Western
acts of worship. *See* worship
*adab* (good manners)
    conformity with God's command and, 161–62
    Day of Judgment and, 338
    embodiment and, 384
    explanation of, 89
    and false thought, elimination of, 356
    gods created in belief and, 155
    and levels of reality, recognition of, 90, 128, 157–58
    *maʿrifa* and necessity of, 90–91
    of Niasse, 88
    stations of religion (*maqāmāt*) and, 135
    in Sufism, emphasis on, 43
    *See also iwa pęlę*
Adam, 39–40, 59, 140, 151, 348, 415n83
*adhkār*. *See dhikr, adhkār*

Aesop, 394
Africa, problematic definitions of, 11–12, 14–15
*African Philosophy* (Eze), 1–2, 4, 12
Afrocentrism, 14
afterlife. *See* death; *orun*
Afuwapę, 239–41
    *See also* orisa
Agbonbon of Ife, 265
Agboola (professor)
    on babalawo, spiritual and secular, 287
    on deep knowledge (*imo ijinlę*), 233–34
    on divination, processes of, 307–8
    on feminine energy, 276–77
    on funerary rites as transition to level of orisa, 299–300
    on good character (*iwa pęlę*), importance of, 289
    on herbal medicine (*ewe*), 282, 284–85
    on infants, ceremonies for, 253–54
    on initiation into Ifa (*igbodu*), 267, 268–69
    on Odu, 260–62, 266, 290, 293
    on Olodumare, good and bad actions of, 291
    on personal discernment, importance of, 296
    on predictions in Ifa, verification of, 308–9
    on proverbs of death and rebirth, 298
    on sacrifices, 285, 313
    on truth (*otito*) and character (*iwa*), 238, 251, 318
*agęmo* (chameleon), 365–66
    *See also* orisa
al-Aḥadiyya (Unicity), 141, 143, 145, 410n41
    *See also ḥaqīqa al-Muḥammadiyya*
Aḥmad al-Tijānī. *See* al-Tijānī, Aḥmad
Aḥmadi presence (*ḥaḍrat al-Aḥmadiyya*), 58, 137, 140–41, 143–45, 347–48, 350
    *See also ḥaḍarāt*
*aḥwāl* (states), 33, 82, 92, 115–16, 359, 385
    *See also baqāʾ; fanāʾ; ḥaḍarāt; sulūk*
*Aḥzāb wa Awrād* (al-Tijānī), 99
Ajagunmole (diviner of heaven), 261–62, 335–36
Ajala (mythical potter), 239–40
    *See also* orisa
Ajayi, Bade, 311
*aję* (those with power to curse or bless), 22, 211–12, 277, 313

ajogun, 211–12
    See also orișa
al-Akbar. See Ibn al-'Arabi, Muḥyī al-Dīn
akhbār (science of reports), 92
Akorede, Abdul-Hameed, 339
Akurede of Ogbagba, 338
alașẹ (possessors of așẹ), 210
    See also așẹ
al-'Alawī, 'Abd Allāh ould al-Ḥājj, 48
al-'Alāwī, Aḥmad, 45
"The Aleph" (Borges), 177, 414n63
Alfa. See Muḥammad.
Alfā Hāshim Muḥammad al-Hāshimī, 53
'Alī ibn Abī Ṭālib, 47, 144, 154, 157
Allah. See God (Allah)
Allāhumma 'alayka mu'awallī (prayer), 171–72
alphabets, 100, 164, 218, 371
al-Sabzawarī, al-Ḥājj Mullā Hādī, 6
Ambiguous Adventure (Kane), 375
Amherd, Noel, 315
Amo, Anton Wilhem, 11–12
anamnesis, 384
    See also self-knowledge
ancestors
    funerary rituals and initiation into group of, 299
    qualifications for, 212–13
    realm of, in Yoruba cosmology, 219–20, 420n95
    reincarnation of, 254, 300, 418n68
    symbolic arts (owe) and communication with, 236
    See also Egungun; ọrun
angels, 39, 110, 134, 148, 201, 345
angels, guardian, 213, 239, 358
    See also ori and ori inu
animism, 337, 342–43, 348
annihilation. See fanā'
anthropology
    ma'rifa and, 190–91
    ontology and, linking of, 26
    perspective of no perspective and, 369–71
    postmodernism and, 380
    spiritual, 39
    subject/object relationship and, 390–92
    See also personhood, Yoruba
anthropomorphism, 39, 436n107
apẹtẹbi (wife of babalawo), 260, 264, 275
apprentices. See disciples, Sufi; ọmọ awo
Apter, Andrew, 370
'aql (intellect or reason)
    analysis and discrimination, role of, 325–26
    conceptual thought, role in, 355–57
    in Islamic philosophy, 15
    levels of, 96–98
    ma'rifa and, 93–94, 103, 351, 386–87
    Muḥammadan reality and, 40, 140–41

world of spirit (Jabarūt) and, 139
ara (body or person), 247
    See also embodiment; personhood, Yoruba
Araba of Modakẹkẹ
    on babalawo, 286, 289, 298, 301
    on breath of life (ẹmi) as child of Olodumare, 239
    on children of babalawo, rules for, 255
    on complementarity of existence, 294
    consultation with other ritual specialists, 314
    on decline of history in contemporary time, 376
    on deep knowledge (imọ ijinlẹ), 233
    on destiny (ori) and effort (ẹsẹ), 244–45
    on divination, 308, 314
    on God, existence of only one, 336
    on good character (iwa pẹlẹ) and death, 238
    on herbal medicine (ewe) and sacrifices (ẹbọ), 284, 313–14
    on his predecessor, 288
    on incantatory magic, 426n91
    on initiation into Ifa (igbodu), 267
    on Muslims and Islam, 332, 340
    on Odu, 252, 260, 262–63, 293
    on Olodumare, unequivocal existence of, 249
    on Ọrunmila, 287, 319, 377, 392
    on personal discernment, importance of, 296
    on personhood, aspects of, 247
    postmodernism and, 325
    predictions of, efficacy of, 309–10
    on Tijani Sufism, 333
    training after initiation, 282
    on wisdom (ọgbọn), 237
Arabs, pre-Islamic, 337, 343, 345
'arafa. See ma'rifa
archetypes
    destiny (ori) and, 239, 361
    historical events as manifestations of, 221
    Muḥammad and Ọrunmila as, 72, 202, 331
    Odu and, 218, 293, 306–7
    orișa and, 202, 208–9, 298
'ārif and 'ārif biLlāh (knowers and Knowers by God)
    annihilation (fanā') and, 136–37, 147, 150, 152
    deep knowers (onimọ ijinlẹ) compared to, 352
    democratization of knowledge and, 375
    enlightenment (fatḥ) and, 82–83, 136
    highest mode of, 97–98, 362–64, 367–68
    invocation (dhikr) and, 163
    known and knowledge and, relationship of, 170, 384, 391–92
    and ma'rifa, verification of, 188
    ma'rifa and limitations of, 73–78, 85, 102–3, 171, 189
    as means of access (wasīla) to ma'rifa, 367–68
    mindfulness (taqwā) and, 134
    physical and spiritual body, linking of, 387–88
    qibla and, 161

sainthood and, 41
subsistence (*baqāʾ*) and, 35, 83–84, 90, 157–58, 349, 394
verification of, 182–83, 185
and wayfaring in rapture, state of, 123
See also *onimọ ijinlẹ*
Aristotle and Aristotelianism, 7, 349, 435n82
*Art and Risk in Ancient Yoruba* (Blier), 227
art forms. See *owe*
*asānīd* (initiatory lineages). See *silsila*
ascent and descent
in divination, 306–7
embodiment and, 386–87
meaning (*ọrọ*) and symbolic arts (*owe*) and, 234–37
orisa and myths of, 204
Ọrunmila and myths of, 223–27
See also *aye*, mending of; history, decline of; *igi igbagbe*
asceticism (*zuhd*), 47, 51, 116, 404n90
See also *iwọn*
*aṣẹ* (power or divine force)
of all aspects of creation, 209–10
babalawo's words and, 289
*baraka* compared to, 335
beauty and, 417n42
breath (*nafas*) and effusion (*fayḍ*) compared to, 360
definitions of, 197, 372
divining tray (*ọpọn Ifa*) and, 292
Eṣu as embodiment of, 198–99
governance and manipulation of, 372–73
herbal medicine (*ewe*) and, 284
initiation (*igbodu*) and destiny (*ori*) and, 354, 358, 394
of Odu, 266–68, 372
of orisa, rituals to fix in shrines, 388
*Aspects de la Civilisation Africaine* (Bâ), 342
*asrār* (mysteries or secrets)
in body not books, location of, 385
explanations of, 80–81, 92–93, 99–101
Ifa and Tijani Sufism, compared, 335, 345
*maʿrifa* and, 99, 103, 183
Muḥammadan reality and, 141
self-knowledge and, 83
taboos on revelation and use of, 55, 100–101, 373
atheists, 62
Atọwọda or Atunda, 207
See also *orisa*
Attributes, Divine. See God (Allah)
authenticity, 3, 10, 33, 314–15, 377
See also *imọ*, verification of; *maʿrifa*, verification of
authority, 32, 59–60, 69–73, 173–77, 196, 226–27
avatars, 204–5
Averroës (Ibn Rushd), 5–6

Avicenna (Ibn Sīnā), 5
awakeness, 86, 128, 137, 367
See also *maʿrifa*
al-ʿawām (the masses), 132–35
See also *tarbiya*
*awliyāʾ* (friends of God), 41–42, 92–93, 124, 149, 172, 185
See also *ʿārif* and *ʿārif biLlāh*; Muḥammadans; *quṭb*; *walāya*
*awrād* (litanies). See *wird, awrād*
axial saints (*quṭb*), 41, 46, 134, 143, 145, 185, 411n56
axis mundi, 226–27, 279
*aye* (world)
descent into, as loss of primordial knowledge, 213, 253, 268, 318, 358, 362, 384
earth (*ilẹ*) compared to, 214, 418n69
*imọ ijinlẹ* as knowledge of, 233
inner reality or self (*inu*) and, 245, 247
inner self (*inu*) as boundary of, 371
perspectives as distinct in, 350
and time, nature of, 219–21
in Yoruba cosmology, 213–14
*aye*, mending of
deep knowledge (*imọ ijinlẹ*) and, 231, 234, 248, 250, 318–20
human role in and goal of, 248, 250, 299–303, 395
Ifa and, 214, 224–27
Odu and, 218, 267, 371–72, 388
Ọrunmila and, 302–3, 307
See also history, decline of
*ʿayn thābit* (immutable entity or identity), 75, 76–77, 171, 352, 358–62, 413n37
See also *ori* and *ori inu*

Bâ, Amadou Hampâté, 3, 27, 53, 342–44
Ba ʿAlawī (Sufi order), 45
babalawo (priests of Ifa)
authority of, mythical precedent for, 224, 226–27, 240
character (*iwa*) and honesty of, 233, 248, 255–60, 286–91, 311–12, 315, 319–20
communal consultation of, 222, 313, 315
death, burial, and rebirth of, 296–301, 388
deep knowledge (*imọ ijinlẹ*) and power to mend the world, 248, 250, 301–3, 320
definition of, 196
in divination, process of, 215–18, 296, 307–8, 310
full-time careers of, 286, 377–78
influence of, in present day, 3, 229–30
and initiation, renewal of, 278–82
initiation and gender of, 272–78
initiation of, 248, 264–72, 354
interpretations of, creative, 201, 272, 284–86, 290–96, 416n17
on Islam and Tijani Sufism, 331–33, 339, 430n23

babalawo (*continued*)
   on literal and mythological truth, 223
   as midwives of knowledge, 384, 389
   on modernism and decline of history, 376–77
   Muḥammad and, 330–31
   on occult sciences, 373
   Odu and, 218, 317–18, 371
   Ọrunmila and, 206, 209, 253, 273, 297–99, 319, 334
   from perspective of Tijani Sufism, 345–46
   perspectives, ability to understand all, 365–66
   training of, 225, 232, 251, 253–55, 260–64, 282–86, 318
Baghdad, school of, 44
Bakare, Ismaheel, 339
Balyānī, Awḥad ad-Dīn, 37–38
*baqā'* (subsistence)
   after annihilation (*fanā'*), transition to, 80, 114–15, 122, 156–58, 163
   ethics and, 130
   explanations of, 35, 63, 110–11, 145–46
   Ifa and perspective of, 335
   levels of reality, perception of all in, 122, 157, 348–49, 394
   and *ma'rifa*, acquisition of, 81–83, 89–90, 98, 103, 106, 120
   as realization of one's inherent enlightenment, 368
   spiritual firmness and, 167
   in stations of religion (*maqāmāt*), 136
   See also *dhikr, adhkār; fanā'*
*baraka* (blessing or sacred presence), 172, 175, 335, 372–73, 388
   See also *aṣẹ*
Barber, Karin, 203–5, 275, 312, 335
*barzakh* (isthmus), 38, 144, 157, 161, 170–71, 433n31
   See also Ọrunmila
Bascom, William, 228–29, 265, 283–84, 285–86, 293, 310–12
Bashir, Shahzad, 176–77
al-Basri, Hasan, 388
*bāṭin* (inner reality)
   conceptual thought, role in, 355–57
   guide (*wasīla*) through, need for, 113
   and initiation, secrets of, 353
   invocation (*dhikr*) and, 163–64
   Muḥammad and mediation of, 40–41, 168
   outer reality (*ẓāhir*) and, 114
   of prophets, unity of, 347–48
   reality, correspondence to levels of, 370
   ritual practice and impact on, 161–62, 177–78, 368
   Sufism and emphasis on, 31
   See also *haqīqa al-Muḥammadiyya; inu; nafs;* reality
*bay'a* (pledge, taking by the hand), 44, 118, 123, 175
bearing witness, 162
   See also *khayāl*

Beattie, James, 9
Beier, Ulli
   on belief and security of worldview, 248–49
   on dynamic relaxation, 297, 319
   on elderly Yoruba men, power of, 296–97
   on Olodumare and oriṣa, 198
   on oriṣa priests, essential qualities of, 289
   on Yoruba and oriṣa, relationship of, 205–6
   on Yoruba ethics, 195, 318, 390
being, levels of. See *ḥaḍarāt;* reality
being, modes of. See *adab;* Ifa; *iwa pẹlẹ;* Muḥammad, following; Ọrunmila, emulation of; Tijani Sufism
Bektashī (Sufi order), 46
belief, translations of, 248–49
   See also perspectivism
Bello, Muḥammad, 52
Benin, 25, 196, 275, 415n4
Benjamin, Walter, 15
"Big English" (Ṣoyinka), 16
birth
   aspects of personhood and, 246–47
   of babalawo, Odu and, 218, 253, 268, 316, 318, 335
   initiation as, 267, 272–73, 281, 354
   Odu and, 277, 307, 316
   oriṣa and multiple stories of, 204, 263
   stepping into world ritual (*ikọse aye*) after, 253–55, 268, 277, 329
   See also *igi igbagbe;* reincarnation
al-Bisṭāmī, Abū Yazīd, 88–89, 105, 149–50, 152, 363
Blame, People of (Malāmiyya), 51
blessings. See *baraka; ṣalāt*
Blier, Suzanne, 227
bodies and embodiment, 385–89
   See also personhood, Yoruba
Bokar, Tierno, 3, 27, 31, 53, 341–42, 344
Borges, Jorge Luis, 177, 358, 414n63
botanical medicine. See *ewe Ifa*
Brazil, 201, 249, 416n11
breath of life. See *ẹmi; fayḍ; nafas, anfās*
Brenner, Louis, 228
bridges. See *barzakh;* Muḥammad; Ọrunmila
Buddah nature, docrine of, 40
Buddhism, 2, 367, 381–82, 394, 398n29, 400n60
*Bughyat al-mustafīd* (Ibn Sā'iḥ), 52
Bulala, Muḥammad Jami'u, 344
Burckhardt, Titus, 35, 41, 167
*burhan 'aqlī* (rational demonstration), 66, 93–94
   See also rationality; reason
burial (*isinku*), 299–300
Burkina Faso, 53, 342
al-Buṣīrī, Sharaf al-Dīn Muḥammad ibn Sa'īd, 170
butterflies, 252–53

calabashes, 207, 214, 256–57, 273, 320
calabash of wisdom (*igba iwa*), 213, 224–25, 237–38, 267, 371, 388
    *See also* Ọrunmila
calendar, ritual, 222–23
camwood powder (*iye irosun*), 215, 260, 292, 334, 372
    *See also* divination, Ifa
Candomblé, 201
    *See also* Ifa
capitalism, 393
    *See also* academia; colonialism
Cartesian subject, 389–90
Catholicism, 7, 16, 201–2
    *See also* Christianity; sainthood
ceremonies. *See* ritual or spiritual practice
certainty. *See ma'rifa; yaqīn*
chains of transmission (*sanad*). *See silsila*
chameleons (*agẹmọ*), 365–66
character. *See iwa; iwa pẹlẹ*
charms. *See oogun*
children, Yoruba, 252, 254–56, 423n5
Chishtiyya (Sufi order), 45
Chittick, William, 17–21, 38
Christianity
    African thought and philosophical traditions of, 16
    colonialism and, 342, 374
    comparative studies, roots in, 324
    Ifa and, 273, 332, 375–77, 379, 430n23
    Islam and, 22
    *ma'rifa* and concept of gnosis, 78
    Muḥammadan reality and, 140–41
    in philosophy, history of, 5, 6–7
    *tarbiya* and, 348
    Yoruba religions and, 203, 205, 338
cinema, metaphor of, 128, 157, 170
Cissé, Tijānī 'Alī, 54, 83–84, 87–88, 101, 120–21, 363
Cissé, Ḥasan, 54, 149
Cissé, Māḥī, 54, 172–73, 175, 182–83
civilization. *See* colonialism; modernity
*Classics of Philosophy* (Pojman), 2
Coates, Peter, 382
coherentism, 190
colonialism
    academia and, 391–94, 396, 437n117
    African authenticity and, 3
    African traditional religions and, 342
    comparative studies and heritage of, 324–26
    Ifa in Yorubaland and, 227–28, 374–75, 377, 420n110
    nationalism and, 14
    rationality and justification for, 9–10
    Tijani Sufism and, 53, 374
colors, symbolism of, 294–96
    *See also* rainbows
communal worship of Ifa (*itadoogun*), 263–64

comparative studies, 324–28, 350
"In Comparison a Magic Dwells" (Smith), 324
complementarity, 244, 247, 273–74, 292–94, 302, 306, 353
conceptual or discursive thought
    existential knowledge compared to, 31, 69, 191
    realization and role of, 32–34, 190, 355–58, 386
    ritual practice and, 26
    *theoria* compared to, 380–84
    *See also* academia; *igbagbọ*; reason; reason, limitations of
conduct. *See adab*
conscience (*ẹri ọkan*), 246
    *See also* personhood, Yoruba
consciousness. *See aḥwāl; baqāʾ; bāṭin; fanāʾ; ḥaḍarāt; ḥaqīqa al-Muḥammadiyya; inu; jadhb; ori* and *ori inu; sulūk*
contradictions
    babalawo's treatment of, 227, 306, 310, 416n17
    in goals of Ifa and Tijani Sufism, 362–67
    *ma'rifa* and transcendence of, 178, 184, 189
    in Muḥammadan reality, examination of, 347–48
    oral tradition and space for, 200–201
    postmodern celebration of, 382
Coomaraswamy, Ananda, 17
cosmos and cosmology, Yoruba
    Catholic sainthood and, 201–2
    divination and, 218, 292, 318
    doctrine of Ifa as map of, 355–56
    gender and, 273–77
    Greek mythology and, 199–201
    Hinduism and, 204–5
    Ifa rituals as structure and guide to, 210, 222, 355–56
    Islamic tradition and, 202–4
    pantheon of, 210–12
    realms of, 213–14, 220
    theology and symbolism in, 206–14, 320
    Tijani Sufism and, 370–72
    time and eternity in, 203, 210, 219–23, 224, 374
    *See also* Odu; oriṣa; personhood, Yoruba; reality
*Cosmos and History* (Eliade), 221–22
Covington-Ward, Yolanda, 389
creation
    attachment to, as veil over Knowledge, 116
    divine breath and words in process of, 165, 218, 307, 318–19, 359–60, 370, 409n32
    God's self-knowledge as purpose of, 19
    humans as micro- and macrocosm of, 39–40, 73–74, 214, 370
    love as necessary for, 160
    *ma'rifa* as reason for, 68, 84
    Muḥammadan reality as distributor of, 40, 48, 109, 140–41, 144–45, 156–57, 167–71
    ritual myth as giving meaning to, 210
    thought as, 289, 355

Index • 443

creation (*continued*)
   transformation vs., 59
   in Yoruba cosmology and Ifa, 222–23
   *See also aye*, mending of; humanity; reality
Cuba, 201, 249, 416n11
Cummings, E. E., 379
curses, 285, 289
   *See also ewe Ifa*

*Dalāʾil al-Khayrāt* (al-Jazūlī), 47
dance, 45, 236, 356
   *See also owe*; ritual or spiritual practice
Dante, 8
darkness, 9, 294–96
   *See also* light
al-Darqawī, Muḥammad, 45
death
   dynamic relaxation and, 297–99
   fear of, 296, 427n126
   good character (*iwa pẹlẹ*), importance before, 238–39
   knowledge and, 99, 106, 303, 388
   mature vs. premature, 212–13, 239, 298, 427n127
   *See also fanāʾ*; reincarnation
decline of history, 227, 374, 376–78, 393
   *See also igi igbagbe*
deep knowledge. *See imọ ijinlẹ*
*Deliverance from Error* (al-Ghazālī), 1–2
Delphi, 304, 305
demonstration, rational (*burhan ʿaqlī*), 66, 93–94
   *See also* rationality; reason
Derrida, Jacques, 325
dervishes, 33, 44, 45, 100
Descartes, René, 7, 391
descent and ascent. *See* ascent and descent; *igi igbagbe*
desert, nature of, 51–52
destiny. *See ori and ori inu*
development and progress, 9–10, 392–94, 434n60
   *See also* colonialism
al-dhāt (Divine Essence)
   annihilation (*fanāʾ*) and, 126–27, 142–52, 156–57
   Divine Names and, 411n65
   humans as encompassing, 39
   immutable entities (*ʿayn thābit*) and, 359–60, 362, 413n37
   independence from all relationships, 204
   *maʿrifa* and, 70, 189, 363
   Muḥammad and, 154, 167, 170
   Niasse and, 185–86
   physical world as manifestations (*tajallī*) of, 152, 177–78
   presences (*ḥaḍarāt*) and, 37–38, 139
   qibla and, 161–62
   reflection (*tafakkur*) and, 103–4
   sincerity (*ṣidq*) and, 135
   subsistence (*baqāʾ*) and, 122
   Sufism and subject matter of, 32
   transcendence of all forms of belief in, 348
   *See also ḥadrat al-Quds*
*dhawq* (tasting or experiential knowledge)
   in academic work, need for, 383–84
   direct knowledge (*imọ*) compared to, 351
   discursive knowledge and, 33–34, 352, 380–81, 386
   *maʿrifa* and, 49–50, 81–82, 89–90, 101, 103, 190
   states (*aḥwāl*) and, 92–93
   stations of religion (*maqāmāt*) and, 136
   *See also jijẹun Ifa*
*dhikr, adhkār* (invocation or remembrance)
   annihilation (*fanāʾ*) and, 127, 136
   embodiment and, 385–86
   explanation of, 43–44
   hierarchy of, 162–63, 172–73
   inner meanings of, 129–30, 166–73
   *maʿrifa* and, 79, 83
   meditation compared to, 176–77
   mindfulness and, 125–26
   occult sciences and efficacy of, 101, 165–66
   praise-prayer (*oriki*) compared to, 335–36
   reflection (*fikr*) and, 355
   sanctity and, 130, 368
   in spiritual training, importance of, 116–17
   Sufi rites and, 45, 50
   *tarbiya* and, 118–19, 121, 130, 162–64, 182
   *See also maʿrifa; wird, awrād*
diasporic traditions of Ifa, 196, 201, 205, 393
difference vs. resemblance, logics of, 324–27, 429n5
   *See also* perspectivism
Diop, Barham, 88–89, 166, 173, 375
*dirāya* (discursive knowledge), 352, 381, 383, 386
   *See also* conceptual or discursive thought; *igbagbọ; ʿilm*
direct vision, 34
   *See also maʿrifa*
direct witnessing (*mushāhada*), 83, 103, 132, 136, 167, 435n86
   *See also dhawq*
disciples, Sufi, 44–45, 50, 87, 90, 122–23, 125, 174–75
   *See also ọmọ awo; tarbiya*
discourse. *See* conceptual or discursive thought
discrimination, 325
   *See also* academia
diversity. *See* perspectivism
divination, Ifa
   for children and newborns, 253–54, 264–65, 275
   destiny (*ori inu*), knowledge of through, 213, 243–44, 247, 268, 303–4, 306, 308
   devotion to but not reliance on, 296, 428n19
   dynamic relaxation and, 297

good character and efficacy of, 290–91
history of, 227–29
human error and fraud in, 310–14
incantatory and mirroring explanations of, 307–8
myth and history, access through, 221
Ọrunmila and, 198, 206, 214, 217–18, 225, 249, 305–6, 365
from perspective of Tijani Sufism, 345
power of, to mend the world, 218, 227
predestined Muslims revealed through, 254, 329, 339–40, 344
process and structure of, 215–18, 292–93, 305–8
ritual precedent for, in myth, 223–27
symbolic logic of, 284
verification of, 308–10, 312, 314–16, 428n12
women and, 274–75
*See also* babalawo; Odu
divination, Islamic, 332, 340, 345
Divine. *See* al-dhāt; God (Allah); ḥadrat al-Quds; Olodumare; orisa; Ọrunmila
*Divine Flood* (Seesemann), 147
*Divine Openings* (Ibn ʿAjība), 167–68
divining tray (*ọpọn Ifa*), 214–15, 260, 292, 334, 365
divinity (quality of), 204, 207, 213, 239, 297, 360–61
doctrines. *See* conceptual or discursive thought; Ifa; taṣawwuf; Tijani Sufism
Dogen, 351, 367–68
dreams
  Ifa and, 333, 377
  *maʿrifa* and, 33, 89–90
  of Muḥammad, 169, 333, 336, 354
  presences (*ḥaḍarāt*) and, 139, 387
  of ultimate reality, cosmos as, 19–20, 39, 144–45
Drewal, Margaret Thompson, 214, 220, 266, 268, 270, 273, 299
drunkenness, 33, 74, 85, 122, 128, 192
  *See also maʿrifa*
dynamic relaxation, 297–99, 319
  *See also imọ ijinlẹ*

earth (*ilẹ*), 199, 208, 214, 418n69
  *See also aye*
eating Ifa (*jijẹun Ifa*), 225, 260, 334, 371, 388
  *See also* igba iwa; Odu
ẹbọ Ifa (sacrifices)
  efficacy of, sincerity and, 285–86
  environment, effect on, 308
  Ẹṣu as enforcer of, 198, 211–12, 224, 263
  individual nature of, 336
  interpretations of, individual, 285–86, 294–96
  malevolent forces and, 212
  menstruation and, 277
  orisa and specificity of, 208
  orisa not Olodumare as focus of, 197

precedent for, mythological, 224–26
symbolic logic in, 283–84, 286, 304
Tijani Sufism and, 336, 345, 430n32
training in, 262
verification of, 313–14
*See also* divination, Ifa
education, 44–45, 53, 87, 385, 393
  *See also* academia
eewọ (taboos)
  divination to determine, 253, 254, 268, 272
  for herbal medicine (*ewe*) and sacrifices (*ẹbọ*), 313
  individual nature of, 336
  initiation (*igbodu*) and continued observation of, 279–82
  on killing, 373
  Odu, association with, 253, 268, 388
  orisa, association with, 211, 213, 254
  of Ọrunmila, importance of respecting, 288–89
  from perspective of Tijani Sufism, 346
  on possession by deities, 297, 335
  on women witnessing Odu, 264, 274–78, 424n40
effacement (*al-maḥū*), 80, 106, 140, 175
  *See also fanāʾ*
effort (*ẹsẹ*), 244–45, 371
  *See also* ori and ori inu
effusion, divine. *See fayḍ*
ego. *See nafs*
Egungun, 197, 212–13, 222, 258–59
  *See also* ancestors
Egypt, 46, 393
Ẹla, 236–37, 307, 335, 365
  *See also* Ọrunmila
Ẹlẹbuibọn, Yẹmi, 261–62, 336, 373
electricity, 174, 209
  *See also* light
Eliade, Mircea, 209–10, 221–23
Eliot, T. S., 362
elite (*al-khāṣa*), 132–36, 163
  *See also* ʿārif and ʿārif biLlāh; tarbiya
emanations. *See fayḍ*
embodiment, 385–89, 436n96
  *See also* ritual or spiritual practice
ẹmi (self or breath of life), 238–39, 247, 300, 360
  *See also fayḍ; nafs, anfās*; personhood, Yoruba
*Empty Words* (Garfield), 382
eniyan (person or human), 247–48, 301
  *See also* humanity; personhood, Yoruba
enlightenment. *See fatḥ*
Enlightenment, age of, 8–9, 16, 375, 392, 395–96
Epega, Afolabi, 292–93
epistemologies. *See* Ifa; philosophy, Western; Tijani Sufism
ẹri ọkan (conscience), 246
  *See also* personhood, Yoruba

*ero* and *ironu* (thought and thinking), 246, 355–56
  *See also* personhood, Yoruba
*ẹṣẹ* (effort or struggle), 244–45, 371
  See also *ori* and *ori inu*
*ẹṣẹ Ifa* (verses of Ifa)
  authentication of, 314–16
  breadth and depth of, 196, 234
  fluid and emergent nature of, 336
  levels of reality, linking of, 208
  memorization of, 261
  power or divine force (*aṣẹ*) of, 307–8, 372
  Qurʾanic verses compared to, 334
  words of senior babalawo as, 297
  *See also* Odu
*ẹṣẹ n taye* (feet touching the world), 253–55, 268, 277, 329
  *See also* rituals (Ifa)
esoterism, Islamic. See *taṣawwuf*
Essence, Divine. See *al-dhāt*
Eṣu
  as divine mediator, 198–99, 271, 422n35
  myths, appearance in, 239, 258, 271–72, 311
  Odu Ọṣẹ-Otura and, 218, 263
  Ọrunmila as ally of, 212, 424n50
  sacrifices, enforcement of, 198, 211–12
eternity, 157, 219–24
  *See also* time
ethics and morality
  conscience (*ẹri ọkan*) as guide to, 246
  knowledge and convergence with, 129–30, 133–35, 138, 335–36
  oriṣa as guides for, 200, 202
  in Yoruba thought, 421n16
  *See also* adab; *iwa pẹlẹ*
Eurocentrism, 17
  *See also* academia; colonialism
Europe, 3, 6–10, 13, 52, 393
Evans-Pritchard, E. E., 391
*ewe Ifa* (herbal medicine), 232, 255, 282–86, 308, 313–14
  *See also* divination, Ifa
Excellence (*Iḥsān*), 131–33, 136–37
existence. *See* creation; humanity; reality
experiential knowledge. See *imọ ijinlẹ*; *maʿrifa*
exposition. *See* conceptual or discursive thought
Eze, Emmanuel, 1–2, 8, 12, 306

Faith (*Īmān*), 131–33, 134–36, 137
Fakẹmide of Okuku, 275, 425n62
Fāl, Mawlūd, 52
*falsafa* (Islamic philosophy), 5–7, 15, 98, 352, 380–81, 407n81
  *See also* philosophy, Western
*fanāʾ* (annihilation)
  as beginning not end to spiritual path, 184
  death, association with, 99

Divine Intellect and, 98
  gender in, lack of, 183
  in God (Allah), 34–38, 109–10, 126–30, 145–52, 156–57, 162–63, 180–81
  limitations of, 73
  *maʿrifa* and, 80–83, 89–91, 103, 106, 188
  in Muḥammad, 130, 134, 150, 152–58, 180–81, 371
  in Muḥammadan reality, 141
  possession by deities compared to, 335
  rapture (*jadhb*) and wayfaring (*sulūk*) and, 121–22
  shahāda in process of, 35–38, 166
  stages of, 85, 126–29, 146–47, 156–57, 162–63
  in stations of religion (*maqāmāt*), 136–37
  *tarbiya* and, 111, 120, 145–52, 174–76, 394
  thought (*khāṭir*) and, 104, 357
  transcendence of all forms of belief and, 348–49, 363
  verification of, 182–83
  *See also* baqāʾ
Faniyi (babalawo)
  on babalawo, 289–90, 301
  on deep knowledge (*imọ ijinlẹ*), 231, 234, 248, 318–19
  on man as small world, containing everything, 214, 370
  on Odu, 262, 267–68, 361–62
  on Olodumare, good and bad actions of, 291
  on personhood, aspects of, 246–47
*faqr* (spiritual poverty), 43–44, 121
  *See also* dhikr, adhkār
fate. *See* ori and ori inu
*fatḥ* (opening or enlightenment)
  accessibility of, Niasse's influence on, 160
  and gratitude, disinterested, 367
  initiation in Ifa (*igbodu*) compared to, 361–62
  *maʿrifa* and, 81–83, 136, 191
  process of, explanation, 95
  and Qurʾan, understanding of, 100
  rapture (*jadhb*) and, 121
  *tarbiya* and, 140, 141, 175, 361
  of al-Tijānī, 46
Fa tradition, 229, 275
*fayḍ* (divine effusion)
  explanations of, 48–50, 413n37
  immutable entities (*ʿayān al-thābita*) and, 359–60
  litanies (*awrād*) and conveyance of, 166–68, 171, 173–74, 354–55
  *maʿrifa* and, 81, 82
  Muḥammadan reality and, 40, 48, 166–68, 171
  *tarbiya* and, 93, 95, 160–61, 188, 354
  See also *aṣẹ*; *ẹmi*; *nafas, anfās*
*fayḍa*
  decline in history and, 374, 376, 378
  explanation of, 403n82, 434n61
  mass initiation into Tijani order and, 54

446 • Index

of Niasse, 173, 175
of al-Tijānī, 113, 117
*See also* Tijani Sufism
feminine energy, 276–77
*See also* gender
Fes, 46, 53
festivals, 330–32
*See also* rituals (Ifa)
*fikr, fikra* (reflection or meditation), 43–44, 70, 93, 104, 163, 351, 357–58
See also *dhikr, adhkār*
*fiqh* (jurisprudence), 5, 32, 65, 88–89, 352, 407n66
*Fī Riyaḍ al-Tafsīr lil-Qurʾān al-Karīm* (Niasse), 54
flood. See *fayḍ*
focus (*tawajjuh*), 159–62
See also *ṣidq*
Fon (language), 228–29
forgiveness (*istighfār*), 45, 51, 84, 129, 166, 346
Foucault, Michel, 325, 392
foundationalism, 190
friends (*awliyāʾ*) of God, 41–42, 92–93, 124, 149, 172, 185
See also *ʿārif* and *ʿārif biLlāh*; Muḥammadans; *quṭb*; *walāya*
Fukuyama, Francis, 393
fundamental knowledge. See *imọ ijinlẹ*
*Futūḥāt al-Ilāhiya* (Ibn ʿAjība), 167–68
*Futūḥāt al-Makkiya* (Ibn ʿArabi), 69, 152–53

Gabriel (angel), 86, 131, 201
*In the Gardens of Tafsir of the Noble Qurʾan* (Niasse), 54
Garfield, Jay, 10, 382
Gbadegesin, Segun, 246
gender
conceptions of, in Ifa tradition, 273–74, 275–77, 292, 425n56
initiation rites of babalawo and, 264, 272–78
lack of, in state of annihilation, 183
and oriṣa, traditions of, 423n29
gentle character. See *iwa pẹlẹ*
geomancy, Islamic, 228, 332, 345, 420n115
al-Ghālī, Muḥammad, 46, 52
al-Ghazālī, Abū Ḥāmid, 1, 6, 32–33, 381, 388
Giddens, Anthony, 382
gnosis, 14–15, 78–79
See also *maʿrifa*
*Goals of the Aspirant* (Ibn Baba), 52
God (Allah)
as active subject in revelation of knowledge, 19–20, 104, 391–92, 411n77
annihilation (*fanāʾ*) in, 34–38, 109–10, 126–30, 145–52, 156–57, 162–63, 180–81
Attributes of, 39, 43, 72–73, 80–81, 85–86, 104, 140, 143, 146–50, 164, 170, 346–47, 387
divine effusion (*fayḍ*) and, 48–50, 359–60
embodiment and, 386–87
Greatest Name of, 148–52, 166, 186, 381, 385, 413n35
human need for only, 367
intellect of, 15, 96–98, 351, 435n82
jealous nature of, 114
manifestations (*tajallī*) of, unique and varied, 74–77, 85, 102–3, 153–55, 189, 327, 360–61, 364–65, 372
mindfulness (*taqwā*) and love (*maḥabba*), 124–25
Names of, 37, 39, 80–81, 85–86, 116, 140, 143, 147–51, 346–47, 411n66, 430n29
Perfect Human and, 38–40
reality of, Divine, 42–43, 76–77, 148, 168, 369–70, 372–73, 394
self-knowledge and, 69–72, 77, 109, 368
Sufism and emphasized focus on, 31–32
undelimited nature of, 19, 21, 57–59, 77, 152–53, 155, 157, 327, 368
unity (*tawḥīd*) and, 19, 35–38, 41, 127, 133, 168, 341–42, 345–46, 394, 433n34
will and judgment of, 123, 408n14
See also *al-dhāt*; *ḥaḍrat al-Quds*; *maʿrifa*
God (Christian), 7–9
*See also* Christianity
gods created in belief, 19, 154–56, 204, 363
See also Ibn al-ʿArabi, Muḥyī al-Dīn; perspectivism
Goethe, Johann Wolfgang von, 391
good character. See *iwa pẹlẹ*
good manners. See *adab*
good position (*ipo rere*), 300–301, 319
grammar, 90, 126
See also *fanāʾ*
gratitude (*shukr*), 51, 367, 404n90
*The Greatest Secret* (Niasse), 54, 120–21, 139–40, 143, 148–49, 174–75
Greek mythology, 199–201
guardian angels, 213, 239, 358
See also *ori* and *ori inu*

*ḥaḍarāt* (presences or levels of being)
annihilation (*fanāʾ*) and subsistence (*baqāʾ*) as perception of all, 122, 130, 147, 157, 348–49
divine unity (*tawḥīd*) and, 37, 59, 347–48, 350
human body and, 387
secrets (*asrār*) and, 81
stations of religion (*maqāmāt*) and, 137
*tarbiya* and, 58–60, 139–45, 147
See also *aḥwāl*
al-Ḥaddād, Abū Ḥafṣ, 67, 405n12
ḥadīth, 32–33, 65, 67–68, 187, 336, 431n52
See also Qurʾan
ḥadīth (by theme or first line)
of Gabriel, 129, 131, 409n24
God created Adam in His image, 39, 109

ḥadīth (*continued*)
    He who knows himself, knows his Lord, 68, 71–72, 75, 85
    If not for you, O Muḥammad, I would not have brought forth creation, 48, 371
    I was a hidden treasure and I loved to be known, so I created the creatures that they might know me, 68, 117, 160, 168, 171, 413n22
    I was a prophet while Adam was betwixt water and clay, 40, 416n20
    My servant does not cease to draw near to me through supererogatory works until I love him, 42–44, 68, 96, 125, 180, 357, 386, 388
    Search for knowledge of me before you worship Me, 57, 91, 113, 405n1
    on the *sharīʿa*, *ṭarīqa*, and *ḥaqīqa*, 42, 43–44
    of the slave-woman (*ḥadīth jāriya*), 346, 431n53
    of transformations, 106, 155, 168–69, 408n96
Hadot, Pierre, 5, 7, 24, 55, 380, 384, 395
ḥaḍrat al-Aḥmadiyya (Aḥmadī presence), 58, 137, 140–41, 143–45, 347–48, 350
ḥaḍrat al-Muḥammadiyya (Muḥammadan presence), 58, 137, 140–41, 143, 145
    See also *ḥaḍarāt*
ḥaḍrat al-Quds (Divine Presence)
    Ifa and, 350
    intellect (*ʿaql*) and, 97
    invocation (*dhikr*) and, 119, 163–64
    Knowers by God (*ʿārif biLlāh*) and, 83, 133
    *maʿrifa* and, 85
    nocturnal ascent (*miʿrāj*) of Prophet and, 386
    secrets (*asrār*) and, 81
    *tarbiya* and, 58–59, 119, 140
    See also *al-dhāt*; God (Allah); *ḥaḍarāt*
al-Ḥāfiẓ, Muḥammad, 46, 52, 358
Ḥāfiẓiyya branch (Tijani Sufism), 52, 53
hagiology, Sufi, 41–42, 46
ḥajj, 46, 332, 354, 374, 430n22
al-Ḥallāj, Manṣūr, 34, 36, 203
Hallen, Barry, 22, 232, 360
Ḥamāhallāh (shaykh), 53
*Hama Ust* ("All is He"), 37
Ḥamawwiya branch (Tijani Sufism), 53
hand, pledge of (*bayʿa*), 44, 118, 123, 175
ḥaqīqa (Divine Reality), 42–43, 113, 179, 368
al-ḥaqīqa al-Muḥammadiyya (Muḥammadan reality)
    corpus of Islam as coming from and leading to, 370–72
    as distributor of creation, 40, 48, 109, 140–41, 144–45, 156–57, 167–71
    Divine Essence, manifestations (*tajallī*) of in, 143–44, 152–53
    divine unity (*tawḥīd*) and, 143–44, 348, 410n52
    Ifa and, 335, 347, 350

    *maʿrifa* and, 85
    Muḥammad as fullest embodiment of, 167, 347
    Perfect Human and, 370–71
    See also Muḥammad
al-Ḥaqq (the Real). See *al-dhāt*; God (Allah)
Harāzim al-Barrāda, ʿAlī, 47–48
    See also *Jawāhir al-Maʿānī*
Hausa, 228–29
head, inner. See *ori* and *ori inu*
heart. See *ọkàn*; *qalb*
heaven. See *ọrun*
heavenly ascent (*miʿrāj*), 33, 174, 386
Hegel, G. W. F., 9, 16, 203
herbal medicine (*ewe Ifá*), 232, 255, 282–86, 308, 313–14
    See also divination, Ifa
hermeneutics. See interpretation
Hesiod, 200
hierophanies, 209–10
Ḥikam (Ibn ʿAṭāʾ Allāh), 100, 357
ḥikma (occult sciences), 100, 164–65, 337, 345, 349, 372–73
    See also *falsafa*
Hill, Joseph, 79
himma (zeal), 160–61, 165–66, 174, 179
    See also *ṣidq*
Hinduism, 204–5
history, decline of, 227, 374, 376–78, 393
    See also *igi igbagbe*
Hoffman, Valerie, 18
Homer, 200
Houtondji, Paulin, 14
al-Hujwīrī, Abūʾl Ḥasan ʿAlī, 66–67
humanity
    diversity of tradition, relevance for, 17–18
    and divine beings, interdependency and connection of, 38–39, 40, 203–6, 209, 226–27, 370–72, 390, 391–92
    embodiment and perfection of, 386–88
    goals and purposes of, 18–19, 67–68, 139, 174, 319
    as incapable of not believing in something, 341
    invocation (*dhikr*) and, 164, 167, 176–77
    *maʿrifa*, unique and varied capacity for, 74–75, 85, 102, 153–55, 171, 184, 359–61
    *maʿrifa* and ignorance of, 187–88
    mending the world, role in, 248, 250, 299–303, 395
    as microcosm or macrocosm, 39, 73–74, 214, 370
    Muḥammad as inner reality of, 168
    orisa, ability to join ranks of, 199
    self-limiting nature of, 94
    as shaped by stories, 317–18
    station of no station and, 19–21, 363–64
    supremacy and variable nature of, 110
    as talking word, 165
    unity of, in Muḥammadan reality, 410n52

Western philosophical measures of, 7, 9, 10
worth of, as dependent on *ma'rifa*, 66
Yoruba worldview as centered on, 208
*See also* personhood, Yoruba
humanity, limitations of
   initiation as transcendence of, 354
   oriṣa worship and transcendence of, 237, 286, 297–300, 319
   true knowledge as recognition of, 19–21, 75–77, 95–96, 155–56, 178–79, 327, 341–42, 396, 412n81
hunter's chants (*Ijala*)
   *See also* Odu
*hyle* (Prime Matter), 21, 76, 155, 327

Ibn al-'Abbās, 'Abd Allāh, 68, 129
Ibn 'Ajība, Aḥmad ibn Muḥammad, 167–68
Ibn Anbūja, 'Ubayda ibn Muḥammad al-Ṣaghīr, 52, 118, 132
Ibn al-'Arabi, Muḥyī al-Dīn
   on annihilation (*fanā'*), 35
   on the body and perfect servanthood, 387
   on breaths (*anfās*), doctrine of, 165
   divine effusion (*fayḍ*) in cosmology of, 40
   on divine unity (*tawḥīd*), 36–37
   on gods created in belief, 19, 154–56, 204, 358
   on *ḥadīth* of the cloud, 170–71
   on humanity and God, relationship of, 38, 39, 204
   on imagination (*khayāl*), 161–62
   on immutable entities (*'ayān al-thābita*), 359, 360–62
   on inward recognition but outward denial of other traditions, 349
   on Islam as all inclusive religion, 348
   Islamic philosophy and, 6
   on levels of reality, 178
   on *ma'rifa*, acquisition of, 33, 70–73, 93, 369
   on *ma'rifa*, difficulty of conceiving of, 56
   on *ma'rifa* and *'ilm*, usage of, 67, 405n15
   on *ma'rifa* as creation as a mirage, 126
   on *ma'rifa* as self-knowledge, 68, 69–70, 71
   on *ma'rifa* of others, recognition of, 183
   on *ma'rifa* vs. other forms of knowledge, 88–89, 92, 105–6, 174
   on Muḥammadans, 366
   on Muḥammad as perfect manifestation (*tajallī*) of the Divine, 152–54
   Odu compared to mythical language of, 334
   People of Blame (Malāmiyya), use of, 51
   on Perfect Human, 39–40, 171
   perspectivism and, 19–21, 75–78, 83, 96, 102, 152–56, 327, 396
   on reason and imagination, need for both, 20, 325–26
   on sainthood (*walāya*), 41, 402n51
   on science of letters (*'ilm al-ḥurūf*), 101
   on station of no station, 19, 363–64
   theory vs. *theoria* and, 435n86
   Western methodologies and, 18
Ibn 'Aṭā Allāh al-Iskandarī, 100, 357
Ibn Baba, Aḥmad, 52
Ibn al-Fāriḍ, 'Umar, 134
Ibn al-Jarrāḥ, Wakī', 124
Ibn Mashīsh, 'Abd al-Salām, 149, 167
Ibn al-Mishrī, Muḥammad, 117
Ibn Rushd (Averroës), 5–6
Ibn Sab'īn, 'Abd al-Ḥaqq, 37
Ibn Sā'iḥ, Muḥammad al-'Arabī, 52
Ibn Sīnā (Avicenna), 5, 34
   *See also falsafa*
*ibo* (divination tool), 217–18, 263, 306, 310
*'ibra* (insight), 104, 163
   *See also fikr, fikra; oju inu*
Ibrahim, Abu, 60–64, 99, 145, 166, 168–69, 185
*Ibrīz* (al-Lamaṭī), 387
*I Ching*, 228, 294
*I Could Speak until Tomorrow* (Barber), 275
Idaw 'Alī tribe, 52
identification, existential. See *ma'rifa*
identity. See *'ayn thābit*; humanity; *ori* and *ori inu*
idol-worship, 323, 337, 339–40, 343–45, 349, 377
Idowu, Bolaji, 197, 206–7
Ifa
   the body, importance of in, 388–89
   character (*iwa*) as central to, 318
   colonialism and modernism, impact on, 227–28, 374–77, 420n110
   definitions of, 196, 210, 218, 415n2, 418n77
   diasporic traditions of, 201, 205
   dynamic and living nature of, 200–201, 208–9, 227, 230, 315–16, 319, 354
   and gender, conceptions of, 273–74, 292, 425n56
   goal of no goal in, 362–67, 396
   history of, mythological, 222–27, 228
   history of, nonmythological, 227–29, 420n115
   influence of, 3–4, 379, 393
   Islam as derivative of, 329–31, 332, 338
   knowledge, forms of in, 232–38
   personhood, Yoruba and, 238–48
   and practice and realization, unity of, 251, 316–17, 369–70
   in present day, 229–30, 287–88
   resemblance and difference in, 324–27, 429n5
   study and practice of, as lifelong process, 278–79, 282, 301, 319, 354
   symbolic language in, 283–84, 304
   as theoretical challenge to Western academia, 22, 25–27, 317, 326, 328, 380, 381–84, 389, 393, 396
   time, conceptions of, 219–23
   *See also* divination, Ifa; *imọri*; Odu

Ifa and Tijani Sufism, compared
  conceptual or discursive thought, 355–58
  divine force (aṣẹ) and blessing (baraka), 372–73
  eternal self (ori and 'ayn thābit), 358–62
  goal of no goal, 362–67
  God, humanity, and cosmos, relationship of, 370–72
  Ifa, as seen by Tijani Sufism, 337–50
  initiation (tarbiya and igbodu), 353–55
  knowledge, forms of, 351–53
  modernity and present time, challenges for, 374–78
  reasons for comparison, 324–28
  ritual practice and realization, unity of, 353, 367–70
  Tijani Sufism, as seen by Ifa, 328–36
Ifa and Tijani Sufism, Western academia compared to
  embodiment, 384–89
  (post)colonial (post)modernity and, 392–94
  the Real as active teacher, 391–92
  ritual practice and realization, 389–91
  theory vs. theoria, 380–84
igbagbọ (received knowledge), 232, 305, 318, 351–53, 362, 380–81, 435n83
  See also imọ; reason
igba iwa (calabash of wisdom), 213, 224–25, 237–38, 267, 371, 388
  See also Ọrunmila
igbodu (grove of mysteries)
  as beginning, not end, 278–79, 354
  destiny and inner self (ori inu), revelation of, 267–69, 271, 318, 354, 358, 361–62, 369, 394
  doctrine, transcendence of in, 355
  Ka'ba compared to, 332, 354
  memorization of Odu before, 264, 266, 352
  and Ọrunmila, becoming like, 371
  overview and explanation of, 264–67
  real thinking as beginning after, 356
  as rebirth, 267, 272–73, 354
  as source and verification of knowledge, 316
  as symbolic marriage, 273, 294
  tarbiya compared to, 25, 353–55
  women and, 276–78
igi igbagbe (tree of forgetfulness), 213, 253, 268, 318, 358, 362, 384
  See also history, decline of
Igilango Gẹẹsi (Ṣoyinka), 16
ignorance, 187–88, 191, 296, 368
  See also ma'rifa
igun (possession), 204, 297, 335–36, 356–57
Iḥsān (Excellence), 131–33, 136–37
Ijala (hunter's chants), 208
ikhlāṣ (pure devotion), 131, 135
  See also ṣidq
ikin (palm nuts)
  babalawo's relationship with, 266–68
  in divination, 209, 215–16, 292, 306
  divination chain (ọpẹlẹ) as less reliable than, 216, 310
  myth of man who throws away, 316–17
  mythological precedent for use of, 226–27
  Ọrunmila as speaking through, 249
  storage of, 273, 424n43
  training to use, 260, 423n16
  wives of babalawo (apẹtẹbi) and, 275
ikọse aye (stepping into the world), 253–55, 268, 277, 329
  See also rituals (Ifa)
ilẹ (earth), 199, 208, 214, 418n69
  See also aye
Ileya ('Eīd al-Kabīr), 328–29, 330
'ilm (knowledge)
  definitions of, 65, 170
  knowledge in Ifa compared to, 351–53
  ma'rifa and, 65, 67, 69, 73
  by representation (al-ḥuṣūlī) vs. by presence (al-ḥuḍūrī), 380–81
  scope of, 405n15
'ilm al-ḥurūf (science of letters), 67, 100–101, 164–66, 172
  See also ḥikma; ma'rifa
Imaginal Worlds (Chittick), 18
imagination (general concept), 14, 20–21, 156, 209, 317, 356, 383–84
imagination (khayāl), 161–62, 164, 172, 325–26
Īmān (Faith), 131–33, 134–36, 137
immutable entities ('ayān al-thābita), 75, 76–77, 171, 352, 358–62, 413n37
  See also ori and ori inu
imọ (realized or verified knowledge)
  contemporary conceptions of knowledge and, 380–81, 435n83
  deep knowledge (imọ ijinlẹ) compared to, 233, 250
  divine word (ọrọ) and, 234–37, 307, 319
  knowledge in Sufism compared to, 351–53
  levels of, as infinite, 370
  received knowledge (igbagbọ) compared to, 232–33, 250, 305, 318
  religious discrimination as destruction of, 333
  self-knowledge (imọri) and, 362
  wisdom (ọgbọn) and, 237
imọ ijinlẹ (deep knowledge)
  burial (isinku) and, 299
  contemporary conceptions of knowledge and, 380–81, 435n83
  definitions of, 233–34, 250, 319
  divine word (ọrọ) and, 234–36, 250
  dynamic relaxation and, 296–98
  interpretation as strengthened by, 290–91
  ma'rifa and, 352–53
  power of, to mend the world, 231, 234, 248, 250, 318–19

imọ ijinlẹ, acquisition of
   conceptual thought and, 355
   early training, 253–55
   good character (*iwa pẹlẹ*) and, 248, 255–60, 289–91, 318, 320
   herbal medicine (*ewe*) and, 282–86
   initiation (*igbodu*) and destiny (*ori*) and, 264–72, 278–81
   interpersonal relationships and, 390
   as lifelong process, 278–79, 282, 301, 319, 354, 394–95
   Odu, memorization of, 260–64, 371, 394
   overview, 301, 319
   personal sacrifice and, 288, 424n40
   reincarnation and, 300–301
   Tijani Sufism compared to, 353
imọ ijinlẹ, verification of
   consultation with other babalawo and Odu, 313–16
   direct and live experience in, 305, 316–17
   and divination, verification of, 305–10, 312
   human error and fraud and, 311–13
   in sacrifices (*ẹbọ*) and medicines, 313–14
   through practice of Ifa, 316–18
imọri (self-knowledge)
   ceremony for, after birth, 253, 277, 423n5
   deep knowledge (*imọ ijinlẹ*) as, 27, 232, 233, 248, 250, 301, 318–20, 352, 362
   as foundation of all other knowledge, 25, 362
   initiation (*igbodu*) and acquisition of, 25, 218, 268, 281, 318, 354, 394
   Odu and acquisition of, 218, 268, 281, 316–17, 370–71
   Ọrunmila and acquisition of, 303–4, 319, 353, 362–63, 369, 371
   stories and, 317
   theoretical knowledge (*igbagbọ*) compared to, 381
   virtue and, 384, 389–90
   See also *iwa pẹlẹ*; *ori* and *ori inu*; self-knowledge
imperialism. See colonialism
implantation (*talqīn*), 50, 119, 174–76, 354–55
   See also *jiiẹun Ifa*; *tarbiya*
incantations (*ọfọ*), 283–84, 285, 307–8, 345, 426n91
   See also divination, Ifa; *ewe Ifa*
incarnations, 38, 204–5
   See also *orişa*; reincarnation
indigenous theory, 17
   See also academia
indigenous traditions. See Ifa; religions, Yoruba
individualism, 176–77, 289
Indonesia, 52, 393
ingestion, ritual, 225, 260, 334, 371, 388
   See also *igba iwa*; rituals (Ifa)
initiation rites. See *igbodu*; *tarbiya*
initiatory lineages. See *silsila*
inner eye (*oju inu*), 246
   See also *'ibra*

inner reality or self. See *bāṭin*; *inu*; *ori* and *ori inu*; reality
Insa, Mamour, 111
*insān* (human being), 39–40
   See also humanity; Perfect Human
al-*Insān al-Kāmil* (al-Jīlī), 34
insight (*'ibra*), 104, 122, 163
   See also *fikr, fikra*; *oju inu*
inspiration (*wārid*), 81, 82
inspired descriptions, 370–72
   See also ḥadīth; Odu; Qur'an
integrity (*istiqāma*), 131, 133–34
intellect (*intellectus* or *nous*), 7–8
   See also reason
intellectual traditions, African, 15–18, 26–27
   See also Ifa; Tijani Sufism
intention, 161, 246, 285–86, 356, 367
   See also *ṣidq*
interpretation
   by babalawo, creative, 201, 272, 285–86, 290–96, 315, 416n17
   conceptual thought and, 355–56
   divination and Odu and, 272, 290–94, 306–8
   levels of reality and, 370
   of sacrifices (*ẹbọ*), 285–86, 294–96
   suspicion in Western academia and, 391
   See also Ifa and Tijani Sufism, compared; perspectivism
*inu* (inner dimension)
   bodies and objects as physical symbols of, 208, 214, 239, 243, 245, 247, 388
   as challenge to Western academia, 382
   conceptual thought, role in, 355–57
   explanation of, 245–46
   and language, symbolic relationship to, 284, 353, 370
   openness of, need for, 252
   rituals and doctrine as shaping, 247, 298, 355–56, 385
   self-knowledge and fluid conditions of, 362
   as site of struggle for wisdom, 371
   See also *bāṭin*; *ori* and *ori inu*; reality
*Invention of Africa* (Mudimbe), 14
invocation. See *dhikr*
the Inward. See God (Allah)
Inyās, Ibrāhīm. See Niasse, Ibrahim
*ipo rere* (good position), 300–301, 319
   See also *iwa pẹlẹ*
*ironu* and *ero* (thinking and thought), 246, 355–56
   See also personhood, Yoruba
irradiation. See *tajallī*
*isinku* (burial), 299–300
Islam
   African traditional religions and, 337, 340–43
   babalawo on, 331–33, 430n23
   Christianity and, 22

Islam (*continued*)
    as derivative of Ifa, 329–31, 332, 334, 338
    Divine Attributes in theology of, 146
    embodiment and pedagogy of, 385
    Ifa and influence of, 227–28, 273, 328–29, 434n78
    Muslim thinking on Ifa, 337–38, 376–77
    in Odu and Ifa divination, 254, 323, 329, 339–40, 344, 346
    and practice and realization, unity of, 367–68
    Sufism as most inner aspect of, 32
    three levels of tradition in, 131
    Tijani Sufism as perfection of, 48
    and time, conceptions of, 374
    as universal religion, containing all others, 343, 348
    Western academic legitimation of, 380
    See also *taṣawwuf*
*Islām* (Submission), 131–34, 137, 343
*islam noir*, 326, 429n6
isolated retreats (*khalwas*), 45, 47, 51, 106
isthmus (*barzakh*), 38, 144, 157, 161, 170–71, 433n31
    See also Ọrunmila
*istiʿdād* (preparedness), 75, 76–77, 85, 360–61
    See also *ori* and *ori inu*
*istighfār* (forgiveness), 45, 51, 84, 129, 166, 346
*istiqāma* (integrity), 131, 133–34
*itadoogun* (communal worship of Ifa), 263–64
*itan* (history or myth), 219–23, 419n92
    See also myths and mythology, Yoruba
*itẹfa* (initiation ceremony). See *igbodu*
*iwa* (character), 237–38, 246, 247, 251, 300–301, 318
*iwa pẹlẹ* (good character)
    acquisition of knowledge and, 248, 318, 320, 384, 394–95
    of babalawo, importance of, 232, 233, 255–59, 281, 288–91
    destiny (*ori*) and, 241
    embodied ritual actions and, 388
    false thought and, 356
    funerary rites and necessity of, 299
    importance of, for all Yoruba, 259–60
    money as spoiling, 287
    as only thing that matters on Judgment Day, 338
    Ọrunmila and Olodumare and, 237–38, 248, 259, 290–91, 318, 320, 395
    See also *adab*
*iwọn* (moderation), 281, 289
    See also *zuhd*
*iya* (suffering), 269–70, 424n50
iyanifa (female priests of Ifa)
    babalawo compared to, 264, 274, 276–78, 415n1
    description of, 275, 276
    herbal medicine (*ewe*) and, 282–86
    and initiation of, renewal, 279–82
    interpretation of Ifa and, 290
    Odu and destiny (*ori inu*) of, 317–18
    Ọrunmila, emulation of, 319
    from perspective of Tijani Sufism, 345
    See also babalawo
*iyawo* (wife), 269–70
*iye irosun* (camwood powder), 215, 260, 292, 334, 372
    See also divination, Ifa
Izutsu, Toshihiko, 17–18

*jadhb* (rapture), 44, 106, 120–23, 409n35, 411n65
Jakuta, 222, 420n10
    See also Ṣango
Jāmī (poet), 355
*Jawāhir al-Maʿānī* (Harāzim al-Barrāda)
    on annihilation (*fanāʾ*), 127
    influence of, 47
    on intellect (*ʿaql*), 96–98
    on *maʿrifa*, 79–82
    on Muḥammad, following and visualization of, 174, 179–80
    on spiritual training, requirements of, 115–17
    ʿUmar's *Rimāḥ* and, 52
    on Uways al-Qaranī, 154
*Jawāhir al-Rasāʾil* (Niasse), 54
*Jawharat al-Kamāl* (Pearl of Perfection), 51, 169–71, 335, 404n89
    See also *ṣalāt*
al-Jazūlī, Muḥammad, 47
Jesus, 41, 141, 151, 202
    See also Christianity
Jeyifo, Biọdun, 16
jihads, 52
*jijẹun Ifa* (eating Ifa), 225, 260, 334, 371, 388
    See also *igba iwa*; Odu
al-Jīlānī, ʿAbd al-Qādir, 45
al-Jīlī, ʿAbd al-Karīm, 34
jinn
    as created to worship God, 67, 113, 117–18, 129, 174
    humans as better than, 110
    Ifa as interactions with, 337
    Muḥammadan reality and, 143
    soothsaying (*al-kihāna*) and, 345
Jones, Yusuf, 339–40
Junayd, 44, 73–74, 76, 85, 157, 363
jurisprudence (*fiqh*), 5, 32, 65, 88–89, 352, 407n66

Kaʿba, 161, 267, 332, 342, 354
*kalām* (Islamic theology), 6, 352
    See also theology
*Kama Sutra*, 33
Kane, Ben Omar, 410n52
Kane, Cheikh Hamidou, 375
Kane, Mohamed, 74, 85, 87, 89
Kant, Immanuel, 8–9, 15–16, 390–91

*kashf* (unveiling)
   invocation (*dhikr*) and, 126
   knowledge in Ifa compared to, 351
   *maʿrifa* and, 80–82, 83, 93–94, 96, 103, 105
   rapture (*jadhb*) and, 122–23
   science of letters (ʿ*ilm al-ḥurūf*) and, 164
   spiritual training and, 115–17
   Sufism and, 33
   See also *dhawq*
*Kashf al-Mahjūb* (al-Hujwīrī), 66
*Kāshif al-Ilbās* (Niasse), 54, 105, 117, 173–74, 357, 372, 386–87
al-Kattānī, Abū ʿAbdallāh Muḥammad, 93–94
*khalwas* (spiritual retreats), 45, 47, 51, 106
Khalwatī (Sufi order), 46
*al-khāṣa* (elite), 132–36, 163
   See also ʿ*ārif* and ʿ*ārif biLlāh*; *tarbiya*
*khāṭir* (thought), 104, 144, 357
   See also *ero* and *ironu*; *fikr*, *fikra*
*khatm al-awliyāʾ* (seal of saints), 42, 48, 50, 151
   See also *fayḍ*; sainthood
*khayāl* (imagination), 161–62, 164, 172, 325–26
   See also reason
*al-kihāna* (soothsaying), 345, 420n115
   See also divination, Ifa
knots of reality, 19–21, 27, 363
   See also reality
knowers and Knowers by God. See ʿ*ārif* and ʿ*ārif biLlāh*
knowledge
   as active subject, not passive object, 391
   all, as self-knowledge, 362
   and being, in Ifa and Tijani Sufism, 384
   contemporary conceptions of, 380–81
   epistemology and nature of, 26
   *maʿrifa* compared to, 87–91, 105–6
   need for diverse institutional, 10, 392–94, 395–96
   ordinary, levels of, 92
   philosophy as search for, 11
   rationality and, 7
   resemblance and difference, relation to, 325
   socialization, impact on, 390
   as unity of diverse truths, 341–42
   Western discourse on Africa and, 14
   Western philosophical paradigms of, 190–91
   writing compared to, 3
   See also conceptual or discursive thought; ʿ*ilm*; *imọ*; *imọ ijinlẹ*; *imọri*; *maʿrifa*; perspectivism; self-knowledge
al-Kurdī, Maḥmūd, 46

*The Lances of the Party of the Compassionate* (ʿUmar Tal), 51, 52
language
   babalawo and Muḥammadans as fluent in every, 366
   Islam as repetition of Ifa in different, 334
   *maʿrifa*, inability to describe with, 65, 84, 101–2, 191–92
   Ọrunmila as fluent in every, 365
   power of words in different, 172–73, 338, 372
   Sufism and limitations of, 31–33
   symbolic, compared in Ifa and Tijani Sufism, 352–53, 356, 365, 370–72, 434n54
   symbolic, Tijani Sufism, 164–66
   symbolic, Yoruba, 208, 247, 283–84, 426n85
   of thought, need for diversification of, 391, 393
*laṭāʾif* (subtleties), 80, 82
   See also *maʿrifa*
Lavoisier, Antoine, 59
law, way, and reality. See *ḥaqīqa*; *sharīʿa*; *ṭarīqa*
Lawal, Babatunde, 17, 298
Layla, 101, 180
legs (*ẹsẹ*), 244–45, 371
letters, science of (ʿ*ilm al-ḥurūf*), 67, 100–101, 164–66, 172
   See also *ḥikma*; language; *maʿrifa*
levels of being. See *ḥaḍarāt*; reality
light
   darkness, complementarity of, 294–96
   diverse rainbow of, prophets and religions as, 341, 347–48, 349–50
   divine effusion (*fayḍ*) as, 48
   Ẹla as, 365
   in etymology of *itan* (history), 221
   following Muḥammad and, 179
   knowledge and, 97–98, 124
   *maʿrifa* and, 66, 80–82, 405n14
   Muḥammadan reality as prism of, 347–48
   in Pearl of Perfection (*Jawharat al-Kamāl*), 169–71
   Qurʾanic symbolism of, 36–37, 406n49
   *Ṣalāt al-Fātiḥ* and, 167–68
   spiritual bodies of, 387
   in Tijani mythology of creation, 157
lightning, 170–71, 413n37
limitations. See humanity, limitations of; reason, limitations of
lineages, spiritual. See *silsila*
litanies. See *wird*, *awrād*
*Litanies and Prayers* (al-Tijānī), 99
literacy, 12–13
   See also Odu
Logos, doctrine of, 40, 157, 234
love. See *maḥabba*

the Maghreb, 46, 54
Maghrebi Sufism, 149

magical preparations. See *oogun*
*A Magic Still Dwells* (Patton and Ray), 324
maḥabba (love)
    following the Prophet as sign of, 179–80
    human perfection as goalless, 363
    maʿrifa and, 68, 78, 82, 405n20
    oriṣa worship and, 286
    relationship with God and, 124–25, 180
    *tarbiya* and, 117–18, 135, 159–62
al-maḥū (effacement), 80, 106, 140, 175
    See also *fanāʾ*
Maigari, Muḥammad al-Ṭāhir, 121–22, 174–75
al-Makkī, Muḥammad, 376
Malāmiyya (People of Blame), 51
    See also *taṣawwuf*
Mali, 52, 53, 342
maʿnā (spirit), 31
    See also *ẹmi*; *ori* and *ori inu*; soul or spirit
Manichean dichotomy, 14
manifestations (Ifa)
    babalawo after death as, of oriṣa, 298
    divine word (ọrọ) and, 236–37, 291, 307
    of eternal realities, historical events as, 221
    of spiritual realities, things in world as, 208–10, 245, 247, 342
    See also *tajallī*
manners. See *adab*
*Maqāmāt al-dīn al-thalāth* (Niasse), 102, 131–38, 139, 145, 147, 188
maʿrifa
    and body, perfection of, 386–88
    certainty (*yaqīn*) and, 55, 84, 99
    definitions of, 56, 61, 65–66, 103, 106–7, 188–89, 371, 403n80
    democratizing nature of, 60, 102, 155, 190, 191, 375, 412n81
    divine effusion (*fayḍ*) and, 49–50, 81, 82
    dynamic and living nature of, 85, 88–89, 103, 189
    in early and classical Sufism, 65–68
    good manners (*adab*) and, 90–91
    Ibn ʿArabi's epistemology of, 69–73
    Ifa concepts compared to, 351–53
    ʿilm compared to, 65, 67, 69, 405n15
    ineffable quality of, 60, 65, 84, 101–2, 187–88, 191
    levels and limitations of, 73–78, 85–87, 184
    nonbelievers and access to, 61–62
    other knowledges and paradigms compared to, 63, 69, 87–103, 105–6, 190–92, 380–81
    as perception of all levels of reality, 75–77, 90, 122, 142, 181, 191, 364–65, 388
    reason, continuity with, 33–34, 89–90, 92–98, 103
    reflection (*fikra*) and, 103–4
    in stations of religion (*maqāmāt*), 136–37
    Sufism's focus on, 6, 31–33
    in Tijani texts and contemporary accounts, 79–84
    translations of, contemporary, 78–79
    as united with acquisition of itself, 368
    verification of, 63, 72, 181–88, 189
    See also *ʿārif* and *ʿārif biLlāh*; *tarbiya*
maʿrifa, acquisition of
    annihilation (*fanāʾ*) and subsistance (*baqāʾ*) and, 80–83, 89–91, 98, 103–4, 106, 126–30, 145–58, 188
    as beginning, not end, 184, 354, 394
    embodiment and, 388–89
    following Muḥammad and, 71–73, 115–16, 125, 130, 154, 156, 177–81, 189, 357
    Ifa tradition compared to, 353
    presences (*ḥaḍarāt*) and, 139–45
    purification of self and, 115–17, 138–39
    reason and conceptual thought in, 66–67, 68, 93–96, 355
    social nature of, 390
    spiritual practice, importance for, 69–71, 73, 116–17, 124–30, 139, 190, 389–90
    stations of religion (*maqāmāt*) and, 131–38, 139
    Sufi masters (*shuyūkh*), role in, 126, 185–86, 369, 388–89, 411n77
    *tarbiya* and, 56, 64, 108–15, 374–75, 394
    as united with *maʿrifa* itself, 368
    See also *maʿrifa*
marriage, symbolic, 273, 294
    See also babalawo; *igbodu*
Marxism, 87, 375
the masses (*al-ʿawām*), 132–35
    See also *tarbiya*
Massignon, Louis, 39
master-slave dialectic, 203
mathematics, 94–95
Matory, J. Lorand, 375
maturity, spiritual. See dynamic relaxation; *imọ ijinlẹ*; *maʿrifa*
Maupoil, Bernard, 229, 275
Mauritania, 47, 52, 53
Mauritanian sermon, 124–30, 139, 146–47, 156–58, 335–36
    See also Niasse, Ibrahim
Mawlāwī (Sufi order), 45
Mawlay Idrīs, 46
Mawlay Sulaymān (sultan), 46
maẓhar (place of manifestation). See *tajallī*
means of access (*wasīla*), 112, 125–26, 140, 180, 357
Mecca, 46, 52–53, 161, 228, 267, 374
*Meccan Openings* (Ibn ʿArabi), 69
medicine, 32, 91, 105, 282, 381
    See also *ewe Ifa*; *oogun*
medicine men (*oniṣegun*), 232, 285, 313
    See also babalawo
Medina, 46, 53, 175, 228

meditation, modern concept of, 176–77
    See also *fikr, fikra*
memorization, 260–64, 266, 290, 334, 352, 371, 394
memory, 124, 261–62, 335–36
men of the unseen (*rijāl al-ghayb*), 41
    See also *quṭb*
menstruation, 277
    See also *eewọ*
Messenger of God. See Muḥammad; Ọrunmila
metaphysics. See *bāṭin*; Ifa; *imọ ijinlẹ*; *inu*; knowledge; *maʿrifa*; reality; Tijani Sufism; time
methodology, 20, 22–25, 324
mindfulness (*taqwā*), 69, 124–26, 129, 133–34
    See also *tarbiya*
miracles, 201
    See also sainthood
*miʿrāj* (heavenly ascent), 33, 174, 386
mirrors
    gods created in belief and, 19, 154–55
    humans as Divine, 39, 43, 388
    Ifa divination as metaphysical, 307–8
    manifestation (*tajallī*) of Divine Essence and, 143–44, 153–54
    Muḥammadan reality as divine, 171
    of nonbeing, cosmos as, 19
    Odu as, of whole cosmos, 318
    opening (*fatḥ*) and, 83
    perfect souls as, 139
    in Rumi, 406n40
    of self-knowledge, 268, 303, 362
al-Miṣrī, Dhū'l-Nūn, 66, 358, 363
missionaries, 196, 227, 375
    See also colonialism
*Mizāb al-Raḥma al-Rabbāniyya* (Ibn Anbūja), 52, 118, 132
moderation (*iwọn*), 281, 289
    See also *zuhd*
modernity, 374–78, 382, 392–94
monasticism, 5, 397n6
    See also Christianity
money, 255, 258, 287–88
    See also *ẹbọ Ifa*; *iwa pẹlẹ*
morality. See *adab*; ethics and morality; *iwa pẹlẹ*
Moses, 36, 41, 127, 152
Mouride Sufism, 54
*Muʿawwaliyya* (prayer), 119
    See also *ṣalāt*
Mudimbe, Valentin, 14–15
Muḥammad (Prophet)
    as active subject in revelation of knowledge, 177, 391–92
    annihilation (*fanāʾ*) in, 130, 134, 150, 152–58, 180–81, 371
    as divine intermediary, 40–41, 49, 338

    on friends (*awliyāʾ*) of God, 124
    on gratitude (*shukr*), 51
    Greatest Name of God and, 148–49, 151
    heavenly ascent (*miʿrāj*) of, 174, 386, 436n100
    history of Sufism and, 32
    Ifa and, 202–3, 228, 328–31, 333–36, 338, 346, 366
    as inner reality of humanity, 168
    nature of cosmos and, 59
    as Perfect Human, 38–39, 153–54, 156, 171, 177–78, 386–87
    in spiritual lineage (*silsila*) of Tijani Sufism, 42, 47–48
    See also *ḥadīth*; *ḥaqīqa al-Muḥammadiyya*; *tarbiya*
Muḥammad, following
    as ideal mode of being, 177, 353, 369
    and Ifa, concepts of, 349
    integrity (*istiqāma*) and, 134
    limitations to, 184, 363
    and *maʿrifa*, acquisition of, 71–73, 115–17, 125, 130, 154, 156, 177–81, 189, 357
    See also *adab*; *iwa pẹlẹ*; Ọrunmila, emulation of
Muḥammadan presence (*ḥaḍrat al-Muḥammadiyya*), 58, 137, 140–41, 143, 145
    See also *ḥaḍarāt*
Muḥammadan reality. See *ḥaqīqa al-Muḥammadiyya*
Muḥammadans, 363–64, 366, 368, 433n31
    See also *ʿārif* and *ʿārif biLlāh*; *onimọ ijinlẹ*
Muḥammadan sainthood, 41–42
    See also *walāya*
Mullā Ṣadrā, 6
multiplicity. See perspectivism; unity
*Munyāt al-Murīd* (Ibn Baba), 52
*muqaddams*, 45, 46–47, 54, 58–59, 119
    See also *shuyūkh*
*murāqaba* (observing), 132, 136
Mūridiyya (Sufi order), 45
al-Mursī, Abū'l ʿAbbās, 167
*mushāhada* (direct witnessing), 83, 103, 132, 136, 167, 435n86
    See also *dhawq*
music, 45, 159, 164, 183, 208–9, 290
    See also *owe*; ritual or spiritual practice
Muslims, predestined, 254, 329, 339–40, 344, 346
Muslims, Yoruba, 337–38, 344
mysteries. See *asrār*
mysticism, 7–8, 10, 16, 31, 140, 191, 401n6
    See also Ifa; *taṣawwuf*
myths and mythology, Yoruba
    body parts as characters in, 388–89
    definitions of, 210, 223
    discovery of new, 209, 417n41
    on divination, 228
    on divine word (*ọrọ*), 234–36
    as giving meaning to existence, 210

myths and mythology, Yoruba (*continued*)
    Greek mythology compared to, 199–201
    history (*itan*) and time and, 219–21, 223, 420n97
    on Ifa, history of, 223–27
    on Islam, 328–31
    on king's diviner, 311
    on man who throws away *ikin*, 316–17
    on Odu, mystical wife of Ọrunmila, 276, 278
    on the Odu, personalities of, 262–63
    on *ori* (destiny or self), 213, 239–42, 253, 267–68, 358
    on oriṣa, 204–5, 207, 365–66
    on Ọrunmila, 213–14, 223–27, 239, 256–59, 269–70
    pantheon of, 210–11
    on plants and herbal medicine (*ewe*), 282–83
    realms in, 213
    on reincarnation, 220, 295, 300–301
    on ritual calendar, creation of, 222
    rituals and, 208, 221–22, 223–27, 417n48
    on the Sea Goddess, 312
    on the Sunrise and Eṣu, 271–72

*nafas, anfās* (breaths), 136, 165, 170, 359–60, 409n32, 413n37, 414n38
    See also *ẹmi; fayḍ*
*nafs* (carnal soul or ego)
    conceptual thought and, 357
    expectation of enlightenment and depravity of, 51, 367
    gods created in belief and, 155
    good manners (*adab*) and subdual of, 43
    invocation (*dhikr*) and freedom from, 119
    purification of, 138–39
    repentance (*tawba*) and slaying of, 133
    rituals as shaping, 355
    See also *bāṭin; ori* and *ori inu*
Names, Divine. See God (Allah)
Naqshbandī (Sufi order), 46
Nasr, Seyyed Hossein, 6, 17
nationalism, 14
    See also colonialism
N'Diaye, Babacar, 57
Ndiaye, Seyyida Diarra, 174
*négritude*, 14, 375
Neimark, Philip John, 292–93
neo-Platonism, 5, 7, 8–9, 15–16, 40, 98, 394
    See also philosophy, Greco-Roman
neo-Sufism, 47
    See also *taṣawwuf*
Niang, Inaya, 85, 87, 147, 159, 186–87
Niasse, ʿAbdallāh, 53
Niasse, Ibrahim
    on annihilation (*fanāʾ*), 126–29, 146–47, 156–57
    on bodily sensations of realization, 385–86
    on changes to daily prayers, 88–89
    discussion and debate, encouragement of, 186–87
    on divine effusion (*fayḍ*), 48–49
    on divine secrets, revelation of, 101
    on esoteric sciences, dangers of, 373
    experiential and discursive knowledge (*dhawq* and *dirāya*), unification of, 352
    *fayḍa* in, 175
    on following Muḥammad, 179, 180, 356–57
    on Greatest Name of God, 148–51
    on heavenly ascent (*miʿrāj*), 386, 387
    on his secret, conversation with, 172–73, 185–86
    on humanity as macrocosm, 73–74, 370
    on invocation (*dhikr*), hierarchy of, 162–63
    on Islam and other religions, relationship of, 343
    judge of Ibadan and, 173
    on Knowers by God (*ʿārif biLlāh*), 41, 83, 90, 147, 150, 157–58, 367
    on knowledge disciples must acquire, 90
    legacy of, 53–54, 107
    as manifestation (*tajallī*) of Divine Essence, 142–43
    on manifestations (*tajallī*) of God, 85, 143–44, 364–65, 372
    on *maʿrifa*, 67–68, 82–83, 102–4, 181, 184, 187–88, 386–87
    as means of access (*wasīla*) to *tarbiya*, 113
    on modern technologies and traditions, 374, 376
    on Muḥammadan reality, 48, 371
    on Pearl of Perfection (*Jawharat al-Kamāl*), 413n35
    postmodernism and, 325
    on practice and realization, unity of, 368
    on presences (*ḥaḍarāt*), 139–40, 143–45
    on *qibla*, importance of, 161–62
    Qurʾan as integral for, 138, 334
    on rapture (*jadhb*) and wayfaring (*sulūk*), 121–23
    on real ḥajj as journey to the heart, 354
    on reflection (*tafakkur*), 103–4
    as reincarnation of oriṣa, from perspective of Ifa, 333–34
    as renewer reversing decline of history, 374
    on saintly poles (*quṭb*), 411n56
    on science of Sufism, primacy of, 105
    on secrets as in the body, not books, 3, 385
    on shaykhs, importance of qualified, 175
    on stations of religion (*maqāmāt*), 131–38
    on *tarbiya*, 120, 121, 124–30, 160, 173, 348
    *tarbiya*, establishment of, 50, 51, 117–18
    on "There is no God but I," explanation, 36
    on wanting not to want, 186, 363
    on worship of God for His own sake, 51, 367
Niasse, Māḥī, 99, 117–19, 138–41, 160
Niasse, Maryam, 23, 87, 405n20
Nigeria

babalawo in, fraudulent, 311
hereditary oriṣa worship in, decrease, 255
Ifa and Tijani Sufism in, 25, 326, 393
Ifa in, 3, 229, 287, 375, 377–78
Ogunnaike's research in, 23
Ogun River, goddess of, 198
Tijani Sufism in, 52, 54, 173, 343
wicked medicine (*oogun ika*) and politicians of, 373
women and Ifa in, 264, 277
Yoruba mythology, diversity in, 201
Yoruba religions in, 196
Ni'matullahī (Sufi order), 46
noetic realms of reality, 7–8
  *See also* reality
no god but God. See *tawḥīd*
North America, 3, 52, 54, 393
nothing, creation as, 58–59, 83–84, 90, 121, 128, 158, 189
  *See also fanāʾ*; reality
noumenal vs. phenomenal, 15, 399n35
numbers, Yoruba, 207, 417n35
numerology, Arabic, 165, 413n22

Ọbatala
  alcohol taboo, 211, 213, 254
  bodies of people, formation of, 239, 300, 388, 422n20
  description of, 198
  and Funfun and Orişanla, as same deity, 204
observing (*murāqaba*), 132, 136
occult sciences (*ḥikma*), 100, 164–65, 337, 345, 349, 372–73
  *See also* philosophy, Islamic
oceans. *See* water, metaphors and symbolism of
*ode* (outer dimension), 245, 298, 353, 370
  *See also aye; inu; ẓāhir*
Odu
  as active subject in revelation of knowledge, 391–92
  authority of, mythical precedent for, 196, 314–15
  Christian scripture, similarity to, 375
  complementary relationships in, 292–94
  deep knowledge (*imọ ijinlẹ*) and, 233–34, 250, 316, 319
  in divination, process of, 213, 215–18, 243, 307, 314
  divine force (*aṣẹ*) and, 292, 372
  as divinities with personalities, 218, 262–63, 274
  dynamic and living nature of, 200–201, 209, 227
  dynamic relaxation and, 297
  history of, 227–29
  initiation (*igbodu*) and revelation of personal, 264, 266–68, 273, 280–81, 294, 316, 318, 354
  inspired concepts in, 356–58
  interpretation of, 272, 290, 292–93, 306, 315
  Islam in, 227, 328–31
  memorization and learning of, 232, 260–64, 266, 290, 318, 352, 370–71, 394
  names of diviners in, 298
  as only language babalawo understand after death, 299–300
  from perspective of Tijani Sufism, 345
  Qurʾan compared to, 334, 431n49
  ritual internalization of, 225, 260, 334, 371, 388
  structure of, 196, 216, 252, 260–61, 292–93
  Sufi orders compared to, 335
  symbolic language in, 247, 281, 283–84, 365
  transformative power of, 252–53
  as transmitter and summary of creation, 214, 218, 307, 318, 334, 370–71
  truth in, nature of, 399n43
Odu (deity)
  women, relationship to, 264, 272–78
  as mythical wife of Ọrunmila, 266, 273, 276, 278
Odu (by name)
  Eji-Ogbe, 199, 216, 225, 238, 246–47, 260–61, 263, 274, 279, 292, 371, 377, 388, 419n93, 419n94
  Irẹtẹ-Meji, 245, 252, 253–54, 264–65, 424n33, 434n77
  Irẹtẹ-Ogbe, 278, 293
  Irosun-Iwori, 247–48, 294, 300–301, 419n90
  Irosun-Ofun, 298–99
  Iru-ẹkun (too dangerous for its name), 263
  Iwori-Atẹ, 288, 427n104
  Iwori-Meji, 223, 225–27, 283–84
  Iwori-Odi, 300, 302, 307, 320
  Iwori-Ọsẹ, 294
  Ọbara-Iwori, 261, 287
  Ọbara-Meji, 282, 423n17
  Odi-Iwori, 282
  Ofun-Meji (Ọrangun Meji), 262–63, 276, 288, 392, 427n103
  Ofun-Otura, 290
  Ogbe-Alara (Otura), 256–59
  Ogbe-Atẹ, 269, 279–80, 282, 316–17, 369
  Ogbe-Ogunda (Ogbe-Yọnu), 239–41, 269–70, 298
  Ogunda-Meji, 219, 242–43, 314
  Ọkanran-Oturupọn, 251, 328–29, 369
  Ọkanran-Ọwọnrin, 233, 288–89
  Ọsa-Ogunda, 234–35, 307, 319
  Ọsa-Otura, 195
  Ọsẹ-Ogbe, 365
  Ọsẹ-Otura, 218, 233, 263, 272, 283, 416n9
  Otura-Irẹtẹ, 281
  Otura-Meji, 215–16, 227, 254, 291, 323, 329, 336, 339, 346
  Otura-Ogbe, 251
  Otura-Yapin (Otura-Oyẹku), 329–31, 332
  Oturupọn-Meji, 223–25, 237, 244–45, 267–68, 381

Odu (by name) (*continued*)
    Oturupọn-Odi, 295–96
    Ọwọnrin-Ọbara, 303–4
    Oyẹku-Meji, 242, 263, 271–72, 292, 302, 319, 424n47
*ọfọ* (incantations), 283–84, 285, 307–8, 345, 426n91
    See also divination, Ifa; ewe Ifa
*ọgbọn* (wisdom)
    brain or intelligence (*ọpọlọ*) and, 247
    character (*iwa*) and acquisition of, 248
    deep knowledge (*imọ ijinlẹ*) and, 233
    description of, 237
    divine word (*ọrọ*) and, 234–37, 291, 307, 319
    elderly men as embodiment of, 297
    funerary rites and necessity of, 299
    individual, importance of, 295–96
    reincarnation as perfecting of, 300–301
    See also *imọ ijinlẹ*
Ogun
    bones of people, formation of, 239, 388, 422n20
    burial rituals for devotees of, 243
    description of, 198
    iron as, 208
    moral enforcement of, 211
    motorized vehicles and, 209
    in myth of ritual calendar, 222
    orisa derivatives of, 204–5
    praise names of, 206
    son of, myth on, 239–40
    white people and idolization of, 377
    See also orisa
Ogunnaike, Ayọdeji, 23, 331
*oju inu* (inner eye or insight), 246
    See also *'ibra*
*ọkan* (heart/mind), 246, 247, 355–57
    See also *qalb*
Olajubu, Oyeronke, 273–74
*olodu* (possessors of Odu), 264, 276–77, 291, 425n66
Olodumare
    as active subject in revelation of knowledge, 391–92
    breath of life (*ẹmi*) as child of, 239, 247
    deep knowledge (*imọ ijinlẹ*) and, 231, 233–34, 248, 250, 318–19
    as definition and wisdom of Ifa, 196, 210
    description of, 197, 198
    destiny (*ori*) and, 213, 242–43, 267–68
    divine force (*aṣẹ*) and, 372
    divine word (*ọrọ*) and, 234–37, 250, 291, 319–20
    good and evil, transcendence of, 210–11, 212, 291
    good character (*iwa pẹlẹ*) and, 195, 237–38, 248, 259, 291, 318, 320, 395
    Greek pantheon compared to, 200
    human self-reliance and, 295–96
    Ifa as word from mouth of, 218, 415n2
    independence from humanity, 203–4

    Muḥammad, creation of, 329–31
    name of, 365
    in origin myths of Ifa, 223–25
    orisa, relationship to, 198–99, 205, 211–12
    Ọrunmila and, 198, 202, 205–6, 213–14, 222, 225, 242, 249
    ritual calendar, creation of, 222
    as source of all creation, 198, 209, 238
    unequivocal existence of, in Yoruba worldview, 249
    See also God (Allah)
*Olodumare, The Concept of God in Yoruba Belief* (Idowu), 206–7
Olokun, 198, 222, 227, 365–66
    See also orisa
*olorisa* (worshippers of orisa)
    acceptance of other traditions, 332–33, 422n47
    community consultation of, 313
    community support for, decline in, 377
    in contemporary academia, 383
    devotees of Catholic saints compared to, 201
    divination and decision making of, 202
    elderly, resemblance to orisa, 297–98
    inner wisdom and divine consultation, combination of, 296
    lifelong practice of, 286, 319
    moral responsibility of, 289, 355
    possession by orisa, 297, 356
    and ritual performance, importance of, 417n48
    translation and meaning of, 205–6
    verses of Ifa (*ẹsẹ Ifa*), importance for, 315
    See also babalawo; orisa
Ọlọrun. See Olodumare
Olupọna, Jacob, 17
*oluwo* (godfather or master of secrets), 254–55, 261, 263, 282
    See also babalawo
*ọmọ awo* (apprentices of babalawo), 254–56, 260–64, 264–72, 282–86, 314–15, 318, 388
    See also disciples, Sufi
Oneness of Being. See *tawḥīd*
*onimọ ijinlẹ* (deep knowers), 234, 318, 352
    See also *'ārif* and *'ārif biLlāh*; babalawo
*oniṣegun* (medicine men), 232, 285, 313
    See also babalawo
ontological hierarchy of humans, 162–64
    See also humanity; reality
ontology. See *bāṭin*; Ifa; *imọ ijinlẹ*; *inu*; knowledge; *ma'rifa*; reality; Tijani Sufism; time
*oogun* (charms or medicine)
    abuse of, 282, 373
    dishonest babalawo and use of, 311
    efficacy of, 284, 313
    Ifa as, from Yoruba Muslim perspective, 337
    Ifa compared to, 285–86, 308

secrets (*asrār*) of Tijani Sufism as, 335
  use to help or harm, 426n91
  See also *ewe Ifa*
ọpẹlẹ (divination chain), 215–18, 225, 249, 260, 310, 334, 423n16
  See also divination, Ifa; *ikin*
opening. See *fatḥ*
ọpọlọ (brain or intelligence), 246–47
  See also personhood, Yoruba
Oracle at Delphi, 304, 305
oral tradition. See Odu
orders of Sufism (*ṭarīqas* or *ṭuruq*), 44–47, 51–52, 54
  See also Tijani Sufism
*ori* and *ori inu* (head or destiny)
  babalawo and, 253, 266–67
  character (*iwa*) and, 241, 289–90
  divination and communication with, 213, 243–44, 247, 268, 303–4, 306, 308
  as a divinity, 242–43, 388
  effort (*ẹsẹ*) and, 244–45
  explanation of, 213, 239–41
  immutable entity (*'ayn thābit*) compared to, 358–62
  *imọ ijinlẹ* as knowledge of, 233, 248, 250, 301, 318–20
  initiation (*igbodu*) as revelation of, 266–68, 281, 316, 318, 369, 394
  orisa as governing, 203, 253–54, 268–69
  Ọrunmila as witness to choice of, 213, 267–68, 302–4
  reincarnation and, 300
  and time, conceptions of, 220–21
origins
  of beauties in the world, heaven (*ọrun*) as, 295–96
  of creation, each generation as further from, 374
  deep knowledge (*imọ ijinlẹ*) and sacred, 233, 250, 318–19
  of Divine Truth, inspired concepts as coming from and leading to, 356, 371
  divine unity (*tawḥīd*) and return to, 59
  end of knowledge as coming to, 358–59, 362, 368
  good character (*iwa pẹlẹ*) and human reintegration with, 238–39
  loss of, on descent into world, 384
  oral traditions and connection to primordial, 218, 222–23
  of problems, divination as addressing, 307, 308–9
  See also myths and mythology, Yoruba; *ori* and *ori inu*
*oriki* (praise-prayer), 206, 217, 298, 302, 319, 335–36, 427n134
  See also *dhikr, adhkār*
Orileemere, 239–40
  See also orisa
orisa
  Abrahamic prophets and, 202–3
  Catholic saints compared to, 201–2
  destiny (*ori*), governance of, 203, 253–54, 268–69
  destiny (*ori*), possession of, 213
  empirical attitude to worship of, 312–13
  etymology of, 206–7
  gender and worship of, 277, 425n68
  Greek pantheon compared to, 199–200
  Hindu pantheon compared to, 204–5
  human relationship to, 199, 203–6, 209, 214, 254–55, 286
  Ifa as corpus of all, 209, 210
  insight (*oju inu*) and recognition of, 246
  Islam as tradition of, 328–30, 333, 336
  making or building up a presence of, 273, 354, 388, 424n43
  mature babalawo and knowledge of, 248
  as moral exemplars, 200, 202–3
  Niasse and al-Tijānī as reincarnations of, 333
  origin myths and, 204, 207–8, 222, 223–24, 263
  Ọrunmila and babalawo compared to, 366
  from perspective of Tijani Sufism, 345, 346–47
  sacrifices (*ẹbọ*) as focused on, 197
  symbolic arts (*owe*) and communication with, 236–37
  transcendence of human limitations and worship of, 237, 286, 297–300, 319
  Yoruba pantheon, place in, 198–99, 205, 211–12
Orisanla, 199, 204, 207, 222, 239, 243, 365–66
  See also orisa
Orisẹẹku, 239–40
  See also orisa
ọrọ (divine word or speech)
  and creation, process of, 234–36, 250, 319
  danger of distorting, 233
  deep knowledge (*imọ ijinlẹ*) and, 231, 234, 250, 318–19, 370
  embodied ritual actions and, 388
  Muḥammadan reality compared to, 335
  symbolic arts (*owe*) as expression of, 236–37, 291, 307
  understanding divine reality through, 237, 291, 306–7, 319
  varied forms of, 356
Oro, cult of, 212
  See also Egungun
ọrun (heaven)
  all religions as united in, 350
  descent from, as loss of primordial knowledge, 213, 253, 268, 318, 358, 362, 384
  as goal of Ifa, 279
  inner self (*inu*) as boundary of, 371
  as origin of world's beauties, 295–96
  physical world as manifestations of, 245, 247
  and time, nature of, 219–21

Index • 459

ọrun (heaven) (continued)
  in Yoruba mythology, 199, 213–14
  See also aye, mending of
Ọrunmila
  as active subject in revelation of knowledge, 391–92
  babalawo and, 206, 209, 253, 273, 297–99, 319, 334
  calabash of wisdom (igwa iwa), acquisition of, 213, 224–25, 371, 388
  deep knowledge (imọ ijinlẹ) and power to mend world, 231, 234, 248, 250, 301–3, 307, 318–19, 320, 353
  destiny (ori), witnessing of, 213, 267–68, 302–4, 306
  divination and, 198, 206, 214, 217–18, 225, 249, 305–6, 365
  divine word (ọrọ) and, 236–37, 307
  in dreams, inability to encounter, 333
  Eṣu as ally of, 212, 424n50
  good character (iwa pẹlẹ) and, 237–38, 248, 259, 290–91, 320, 395
  herbal medicine (ewe) and, 282–83
  on human ability to become oriṣa, 199
  Idrīs or Luqmān, identification with, 337
  Ifa and, 196, 415n2
  levels of reality, connection to all, 264–65, 371
  mending the world, as work of, 301–3
  modernism and spiritual return of, 377–78
  as moral exemplar, 202, 211, 288–89
  Muḥammad and, 202, 228, 329–31, 335, 338, 366
  in myths of Ifa, 207, 213–14, 222–27, 239, 256–59, 269–70
  Odu and, 263, 266, 273, 276, 278
  Olodumare and, 198, 202, 205–6, 213–14, 222, 225, 242, 249
  as Perfect Human, 370
  from perspective of Tijani Sufism, 345–47, 350
  wisdom of, supremacy of, 237, 303, 365
Ọrunmila, emulation of
  as becoming more like oneself, 319
  initiation (igbodu) and, 371
  as ultimate but unattainable goal, 287–88, 362–63, 365
  and wisdom of, 248, 279, 291, 303, 319, 345, 369
Ọsanyin, 198, 282–83
  See also ewe Ifa; oriṣa
Ọṣitọla (awo), 271–72, 278–79
Ọṣumare, 365
  See also oriṣa
Ọṣun, 197–98, 208, 222, 254, 416n8
  See also oriṣa
othering, 8–10
  See also colonialism
otitọ (truth or honesty), 233, 238, 248, 251, 255, 318
outward form (ṣūra), 31
  See also ode; ori and ori inu; ẓāhir

overflowing, divine. See fayḍ
owe (proverbs or symbolic arts), 236–37, 291, 307
  See also proverbs, Yoruba
Ọya, 204–5
  See also oriṣa
oye (understanding), 233, 234–37, 306–7, 319

palm nuts. See ikin
Pannwitz, Rudolf, 15, 16
pantheons, 199–201, 204, 207, 210–12
Park, Peter K. J., 8
path, Sufi. See sharīʿa; tarbiya; ṭarīqa
patience (suuru), 248, 255–57, 259, 269–70, 298
  See also iwa pẹlẹ
Patton, Kimberley, 324
Pearl of Perfection (Jawharat al-Kamāl), 51, 169–71, 335, 404n89
  See also ṣalāt
Pearls of Letters (Niasse), 54
Peel, J. D. Y., 312, 375
People of Blame (Malāmiyya), 51
  See also taṣawwuf
Perfect Human
  Enlightenment thinkers and, 396
  as Greatest Name of God, 149
  manifest existence, transcendence of, 433n31
  methods to embody reality of, 42
  Muḥammad as, 38–39, 153–54, 156, 177–78, 386–87
  multidimensional reality, synthesis in, 38–40, 178–79, 370–71, 388
  Ọrunmila as, 370
  purification of soul and, 139
  as seal protecting creation, 171
personhood, Yoruba
  body and person (ara and eniyan), 247–48
  brain (ọpọlọ), 246–47
  breath of life (ẹmi), 238–39
  heart/mind (ọkan), 246
  inner dimension (inu), 245–46
  outer or inner head (ori), 213, 239–45, 253
  thought and thinking (ero and ironu), 246
  See also inu; ori
perspectivism
  babalawo's transcendence of, 365–66
  of humanity, 19–21, 102, 152–54, 178, 360–61
  Ogunnaike's methodology and, 18, 22, 24
  subsistence (baqāʾ) and transcendence of, 122, 157, 348–49
  in theory and institutions, need for, 17, 381, 390–95
  true knowledge as recognition of, 19–21, 75–77, 95–96, 155–56, 178–79, 327, 341–42, 396, 412n81
Phaedo (Plato), 12
pharmacology. See ewe Ifa
phenomenal vs. noumenal, 15, 399n35

Philo of Alexandria, 5
philosophy, African, 2–3, 4, 10–18, 25, 26–27
    See also Ifa; Tijani Sufism
philosophy, Greco-Roman
    definitions of, 11, 12
    history of, 4
    noetic faculties in, 7
    revisitation of, need for, 16, 394
    Tijani Sufism and, 60
    as way of life, 5, 6, 55, 395
    See also neo-Platonism
philosophy, Western
    African philosophy and, 11–12, 15–16
    expansion of, need for, 10, 16, 394
    history of, 4–5
    Ifa and Sufism as challenge to, 379–80, 382
    limitations of, 22, 328
    *ma'rifa* compared to, 58, 66, 91
    as marker civilized humanity, 9–10
    and rationality, rise of, 6–9, 13, 395–96
    reactionary movements to, 14
    Sufism compared to, 62, 189–92
    *tarbiya* and, 59, 111
    See also academia; *falsafa*
"Philosophy of Illumination" (Suhrawardī), 6
physiognomy, 298
piety, 32, 51, 202, 401n4
    See also *adab*; *iwa pẹlẹ*
plants, 282–84, 308
    See also *ewe Ifa*
Plato, 4, 12, 140–41, 178, 200, 305, 384
Platonic archetypes and forms, 8, 218
Plotinus, 7, 435n82
Pojman, Louis, 2
poles, saintly (*quṭb*), 41, 46, 134, 143, 145, 185, 411n56
polish, 39, 43, 83, 154, 406n40
    See also *dhikr*, *adhkār*; Muḥammad, following
polyvocality. *See* perspectivism
Porphyry, 380
possession (*igun*), 204, 297, 335–36, 356–57
postmodernism, 324–25, 380, 382
power, 14, 17, 222, 296–97, 373, 426n85
    See also *aṣẹ*
prayers. *See ṣalāt, ẹbọ Ifa, oogun, ọfọ*
predestined Muslims, 254, 329, 339–40, 344, 346
preparedness (*istiʿdād*), 75, 76–77, 85, 360–61
    See also *ori* and *ori inu*
presences. *See ḥaḍarāt*; *ḥaḍrat al-Quds*
Prime Matter (*hyle*), 21, 76, 155, 327
*Principles of Sufism* (Zarrūq), 159
prophecy of *fayḍa*, 54, 403n82, 434n61
    See also history, decline of
prophets
    Abrahamic, 202

    as guides to true religion, 343
    Muḥammadan reality as encompassing all, 347
    Muḥammad compared to, 366
    number of, in ḥadīth, 431n52
    sainthood (*walāya*) of, 41–42
    saints and messengers compared to, 41, 203
    See also Muḥammad; Ọrunmila
proverbs and sayings, Yoruba
    However sharp the knife, it cannot carve its own handle, 305, 316
    Like proverbs, like proverbs is how Ifa speaks, 291, 310, 421n11
    The oriṣa that doesn't hear you when you cry, or doesn't help you when you worship it, get rid of it, 201, 313
    Ọrọ moves around naked, 237, 307
    We met Ifa when we came to the world. We met Islam when we came to the world. It was at noon that Christianity arrived on the scene, 374, 379
    The world is a market, heaven is home, 214, 298
    See also *owe*
psychology, Yoruba. *See* personhood, Yoruba
*Punch* (Nigerian newspaper), 373
puns, 283–84
    See also language
pure devotion (*ikhlāṣ*), 131, 135
    See also *ṣidq*
pure substance (*hyle*), 21, 76, 155, 327
purification of the soul (*tazkiyat al-nafs*), 81–82, 117, 138–39
    See also *ma'rifa*, acquisition of
Pythagoras and Pythagoreanism, 4, 5, 11, 13, 16, 55, 394

Qādiriyya (Sufi order), 45, 46, 47, 339
*qalb* (heart)
    conceptual thought, role in, 355, 357
    flexibility and changing states of, 76–77, 362–63
    illumination of, in following Muḥammad, 179–81, 357
    invocation (*dhikr*) and, 43, 162–63
    preparedness (*istiʿdād*) of, appearance of God and, 360–61
    presence of *Malakūt* and, 139
    real *hajj* as journey to, 354
    and reason, need for both, 95
    receptivity to diverse manifestations (*tajallī*) of the Divine, 156, 178–79, 406n40
    reflection (*tafakkur*) and, 103–4
    subsistence (*baqāʾ*) and, 128
    See also *ọkan*
al-Qandūsī, Muḥammad ibn al-Qāsim, 149
*qibla*, 161–62, 178–79
Qualities, Divine. *See* God (Allah)

Qur'an
  as active subject in revelation of knowledge, 391–92
  anthropomorphic language of, 39
  doctrine of breaths (*anfās*) in, 165
  embodiment and, 385
  Greatest Name of God in, 148
  Ifa and, 330–31, 334, 336, 337, 345–47, 431n49
  invocation (*dhikr*) and, 43
  knowledge of all realities and, 370–72
  litanies (*awrād*) and, 45
  and *ma'rifa*, acquisition of, 72, 99–100
  and *ma'rifa*, verification of, 187
  *ma'rifa* in, 65, 67–68
  mindfulness (*taqwā*) in, 125–26
  Niasse, importance for, 138, 334
  religions other than Islam in, 343
  sacred presence (*baraka*), transmission of, 372
  Sufism and, 31–33, 35
  symbolism of light, 36–37
  Tijani Sufism and centrality of, 344
  truth in, nature of, 399n43
Qur'anic verses (by number)
  2:115, 76, 155–56, 161–62, 178–79, 327, 342, 402n27
  2:136, 347, 366
  2:255, 35, 83–84, 121, 127, 130, 368
  3:31, 117–18, 125, 143, 179–80, 356–57
  5:35, 125, 369
  6:91, 137, 155, 168–69, 412n79, 413n33
  8:17, 143, 413n31
  20:14, 36, 127, 152
  20:144, 68, 184
  21:27, 36, 84, 121, 127, 130, 368
  21:87, 35, 84, 121, 127, 130, 368, 428n5
  33:6, 40, 168
  33:21, 32, 401n11
  39:3, 345, 431n50
  39:67, 155, 168–69, 412n79
  41:53, 72, 73–74
  48:10, 143, 175–76, 403n63
  50:16, 40, 89
  51:56, 67–68, 113, 117–18, 129
  69:51, 34, 402n23
  81:29, 123, 368
  89:27, 136, 138
  102, 34, 402n23
  See also ḥadīth; Odu; shahāda, first
*quṭb* (poles or axial saints), 41, 46, 134, 143, 145, 185, 411n56

Rabelais, François, 87
racism, 9–10, 16
  See also colonialism
rainbows, 347–48, 349–50, 365
  See also perspectivism
rapture (*jadhb*), 44, 106, 120–23, 409n35, 411n65
rational demonstration (*burhan 'aqlī*), 66, 93–94
  See also reason
rationality, 7–10, 13, 16, 33–34, 324, 379–80, 395–96
  See also reason
Ray, Benjamin, 220, 324
al-Rāzī, Fakhr ad-Dīn, 105
the Real. See *al-dhāt*; God (Allah); ḥaḍrat al-Quds
reality
  as active subject, 384
  annihilation (*fanā'*) and subsistence (*baqā'*) as perception of all levels of, 122, 130, 147, 157, 348–49
  cyclical nature of, in Yoruba cosmology, 219–22
  discursive inability to represent, 14–15
  Divine (*ḥaqīqa*), 42–43, 113, 179, 368
  epistemologies, relationship to, 26
  humanity, Perfect Human, and Ọrunmila as connecting all levels of, 38–40, 72, 178–79, 364–65, 370–71, 386, 388
  human's partial perspectives of ultimate, 19–21, 75–77, 152–56, 178, 327, 360–61, 396
  *ma'rifa* as perception of all levels of, 75–77, 90, 122, 142, 181, 191, 364–65, 388
  morality and ultimate, 90, 128, 157–58, 238, 318
  Names of God and aspects of, 148
  nature of, as subject matter of Sufism, 32–34, 108–9
  Olodumare and, 198, 209, 238
  and ritual practice, impact of, 126, 161–62, 166–67, 177–79, 354–56, 369, 388–89
  theoretical vs. existential approaches to, 7–9, 26, 191, 380–82, 395
  unity (*tawḥīd*) and, 36–38, 59, 62, 90, 128, 129–30, 147, 157–58
  visible world as projection of spiritual, 171, 208–10, 245, 247, 342, 353, 387
  See also *bāṭin*; *ḥaḍarāt*; *haqīqa al-Muḥammadiyya*; *inu*
realization. See *imọ ijinlẹ*; *imọ ijinlẹ*, acquisition of; *ma'rifa*; *ma'rifa*, acquisition of
reason
  as blind imitation (*taqlid*), 69
  diversity of, in humans, 153
  Enlightenment identity and, 8–9
  examination of, need for, 16, 380
  and imagination, need for both, 20, 325–26
  intellect compared to, 7
  *ma'rifa*, continuity with, 33–34, 89–90, 92–98, 103, 386
  *ma'rifa* compared to, 63, 87, 91, 351
  as meaningless without myth, 210
  science of letters (*'ilm al-ḥurūf*) and, 164
  secrets (*asrār*) and, 81
  as spiritual exercise, 5
  See also conceptual or discursive thought

reason, limitations of
    blessings (ṣalāt) and, 167
    gods created in belief and, 156
    and maʿrifa, acquisition of, 38, 66–67, 68, 76–78, 83
    qibla and, 162
    ritual practice and transcendence of, 70–72, 94–96, 382–83
    study of Ifa and, 317
    received knowledge (igbagbọ), 232, 305, 318, 351–53, 362, 380–81, 435n83
        See also imọ; reason
recitation. See wird, awrād
recognition. See maʿrifa
reflection. See fikr, fikra; tafakkur
reflexivity, 225, 420n108
    See also myths and mythology, Yoruba
reincarnation
    of ancestors in children, 418n68
    babalawo and, 300–301
    breath of life (ẹmi) and, 239
    elderly Yoruba and, 297
    from heaven (ọrun), as desirable, 214
    Odu and, 295, 302
    Tijani Sufism and, 434n78
    and time, Yoruba conceptions of, 220–21
    See also birth
relationships, spiritual. See barzakh; ori and ori inu; silsila; web of relationships
relaxation, dynamic, 297–99, 319
    See also imọ ijinlẹ
religion
    category of, need to examine, 16
    comparative study of, 324–28, 350
    each as unique color in united rainbow, 341, 347
    goal of, 117
    Ibn ʿArabi on diversity of, 20–21, 76, 78, 155, 327, 412n81
    methodological approaches to, 18–19
    modern impulse to transcend, 178
    philosophy and separation from, 6–9
    remembrance of God as point of all, 43
    role of Islam in, 48
    Hampâté Bâ on diversity of, 341–42
    See also Christianity; Ifa; taṣawwuf; Tijani Sufism
religions, African, 337, 342–44, 380, 385, 431n54, 434n78
religions, Yoruba
    Catholic sainthood and, 201–2
    Christianity and, 205
    cosmology of, 197–99
    Greek mythology and, 199–201
    Hinduism and, 204–5
    history of Ifa in, 227
    as influential and studied, 196

    interpersonal relationships in, 209, 296
    Islam as derivative of, 329–31, 332, 338
    Islamic tradition compared to, 202–4
    pragmatic or skeptical attitudes in, 201, 312–13, 428n19
    theology and symbolism in, 206–14
    See also Ifa
*Religious Encounter and the Making of the Yoruba* (Peel), 312
remembrance. See dhikr, adhkār; igi igbagbe
*Removal of Confusion* (Niasse), 54, 105, 117, 173–74, 357, 372, 386–87
Renaissance, 7–8
repentance (ronupiwada), 246
repentance (tawba), 131, 133, 137, 138, 188
reports, science of (akhbār), 92
resemblance vs. difference, logics of, 324–27, 429n5
    See also perspectivism
retreats, spiritual, 45, 47, 51, 106
revelations, 6, 343–44, 397n8
    See also igbodu; tarbiya
rijāl al-ghayb (men of the unseen), 41
    See also quṭb
*Rimāḥ Ḥizb al-Raḥīm ʿalā Nuḥūr Ḥizb al-Rajīm* (ʿUmar Tal), 51, 52
*Ringstones of Wisdom* (Ibn ʿArabi), 76, 358, 359, 405n19
rites. See igbodu; tarbiya; wazīfa; wird, awrād
ritual calendar (Ifa), 222–23
ritual or spiritual practice
    divine word (ọrọ) and animating logic of, 237
    doctrine or conceptual thought and, 26, 32–33, 355–58
    embodiment and, 384, 385–89
    inner reality or self, impact on, 161–62, 177–78, 247, 298, 355, 368
    maʿrifa, acquisition through, 69–70, 73, 116–17, 124–30, 139, 190
    realization in Ifa and Tijani Sufism, unification with, 172, 353, 367–70, 371, 389–91
    reason, transcending limitations of through, 70–72, 94–96, 382–83
    self-knowledge, acquisition through, 25, 41, 71, 352–53, 389–90
    subjectivity, cultivation through, 318, 390
    unemployment and time for, 375
    See also igbodu; tarbiya
rituals (Ifa)
    complementarity in, 247, 273–74, 292–94, 302, 353
    discipline of, for babalawo, 289
    discovery of new, 209, 417n41
    divine word (ọrọ) and, 236–37
    eating Ifa (jijẹun Ifa), 225, 260, 334, 371, 388
    eternity, connection to, 220, 420n97

rituals (Ifa) (*continued*)
    funerary, of babalawo, 299–300, 388
    Islam, similarities with and shared participation in, 330–32, 430n22
    myths and, 208, 221–22, 223–27, 417n48
    for newborns, 253–54, 268, 275, 277, 329
    simplification of, 285–86
    as structure and guide to existence, 210, 221–22, 355–56
    symbolic language in, 208, 247, 283–84, 426n85
    verification of Ifa with, 316–18
    women's roles in, 275, 277
    *See also* divination, Ifa; *igbodu*; ritual or spiritual practice
rivers. *See* water, metaphors and symbolism of
Robinson, Cedric, 379
*ronupiwada* (repentance), 246
    *See also tawba*
Royal Islamic Strategic Studies Center of Jordan, 54
Rozehnal, Robert, 390
ruby, realized, 169–70
    *See also haqīqa al-Muḥammadiyya*
*Rūḥ al-Adab* (Niasse), 90, 111
Rūmī, Jalāl al-Dīn
    Greek and Chinese painters, story of, 406n40
    on intelligence, types of, 379
    *ma'rifa* in water metaphors, 406n37
    on the Qur'an, understanding truth of, 392
    on realization, nature of, 368
    on self-knowledge, science and, 358
    on soul and body, 385
    on Sufism, nature of, 33
    on unity of prophets, 348
    on windows between hearts, 323
Russell, Bertrand, 190

Sacred Grove of Oṣun, 11
    *See also igbodu*
*Sacred Ifa Oracle* (Epega and Neimark), 292–93
sacrifices. *See ẹbọ Ifa*
al-Ṣādiq, Jaʿfar, 65–66
Sahara, 47, 51–52
*al-ṣaḥū* (sobriety), 80, 152
    *See also baqāʾ*
al-Sāʾiḥ, al-ʿArabī, 173–74
sainthood
    doctrine of, 41–42
    mindfulness (*taqwā*) and, 124
    People of Blame (Malāmiyya) and, 51
    prophets and, 203
    sacred presence (*baraka*) and, 388, 436n109
    in Tijani Sufism, 48
    Yoruba *orişa* and Catholic, 201–2
Salafi, 376

*ṣalāt* (prayers or blessings)
    as connection to God, 129
    divine effusion (*fayḍ*) and, 48
    Pearl of Perfection (*Jawharat al-Kamāl*), 51, 169–71, 335, 404n89
    on the Prophet (*Ṣalāt ʿalāʾl-Nabī*), 166–71, 414n59
    science of letters (*ʿilm al-ḥurūf*) and efficacy of, 165
    *See also dhikr, adhkār*; shahāda, first
*Ṣalāt al-Fātiḥ*
    divine effusion (*fayḍ*) and, 48
    inner meanings of, 166–69
    Muḥammadan reality and, 372
    praise-prayer (*oriki*) compared to, 335
    science of letters (*ʿilm al-ḥurūf*) and efficacy of, 165
    in *tarbiya*, 112, 113, 119, 160
    Tijani Sufism and importance of, 50–51, 163, 403n78
    in translation, efficacy of, 172–73
salvation, 72, 125
    *See also* self-knowledge; *taqwā*
*sanad* (chains of transmission). *See silsila*
sanctity or sacredness, 130, 202, 203, 209–10, 227, 342, 368
    *See also walāya*
Şango
    children of, 254
    death of devotees of, 243
    description of, 198
    electricity, identification with, 209
    Jakuta, amalgamation with, 334, 420n102
    moral enforcement of, 211
    as Muslim, 328, 430n27
    in myths of Ifa, 222, 270
Santería, 201
    *See also* Ifa
al-Sanūsī, Muḥammad ibn Yūsuf, 6
science, Western, 391
    *See also* philosophy, Western
science of hearts. *See qalb; taṣawwuf*
science of letters (*ʿilm al-ḥurūf*), 67, 100–101, 164–66, 172
    *See also ḥikma*; language; *maʿrifa*
science of reports (*akhbār*), 92
sciences (*ʿulūm*), 80, 82, 115, 373
    *See also ḥikma*
*scienta* vs. *sapientia*, 380
    *See also* reason
Sea Goddess, 312
    *See also orişa*
seal of saints (*khatm al-awliyāʾ*), 42, 48, 50, 151
    *See also fayḍ*; sainthood
secrets. *See asrār*
Seesemann, Rüdiger, 79, 147
self-disclosures. *See tajallī*
self-knowledge
    deep knowledge (*imọ ijinlẹ*) as, 27, 232, 233, 248, 250, 301, 318–20, 352, 362

464 • Index

diversity and limitations of, 19, 74–75, 77, 84, 103, 153–54, 361
divine unity (*tawḥīd*) and, 38
Dogen on, 351
as foundation of all other knowledge, 25, 85, 362
as identical with knower and known, 25, 34, 83, 188, 353, 384, 392
interpersonal connections and, 355
knowledge of God as, 32, 68, 71–72, 111–12, 352, 362, 368, 384, 392
loss of, on descent into world, 213, 253, 384, 435n94
*maʿrifa* and, 27, 56, 60, 65, 68–69, 77, 83–85, 103, 106, 181, 188–89, 351, 362, 368
Muḥammadan reality and, 171
personal development and, 358
stories and, 317
Sufism and focus on, 32
virtue and, 384, 389–90
See also *adab; iwa pẹlẹ*
self-knowledge, acquisition of
cosmos and God's, 19–20, 39
doctrine of Islam and, 69–70, 72, 355–56, 370
as impossible through reason, 68, 69, 83, 317
initiation in Ifa (*igbodu*) and, 25, 218, 268, 281, 318, 354, 394
invocation (*dhikr*) and, 119–21, 164
and Muḥammad, following, 40–41, 69–71, 72–73, 181, 353, 362–63, 369
and Odu, learning of, 218, 268, 281, 316–17, 370–71
and Ọrunmila, emulation of, 303–4, 319, 353, 362–63, 369, 371
*quibla* and, 162
*Ṣalāt al-Fātiḥ* and, 168–69
spiritual or ritual practice and, 25, 41, 71, 352–53, 389–90
*tarbiya* and, 25, 56, 60, 108–9, 111–12, 114, 121, 158, 354, 394
self-portraits of the Real, 19–21, 327, 363
See also Ibn al-ʿArabī, Muḥyī al-Dīn; perspectivism
*sema* (Sufi ritual), 45
semiotics, symbolic. *See* language
Senegal, 3, 23, 45, 52–55, 87, 375
senses, 7, 92, 162, 198
See also reason
separation, illusion of, 38, 43, 166
See also *fanāʾ; tawḥīd*
serenity (*al-ṭumaʾnīna*), 131, 135–36, 138
servanthood (*ʿubūdiyya*), 387
See also *ʿārif* and *ʿārif biLlāh*; Muḥammad
Setiu, 228, 365, 415n4
See also *orisa*
Shabistarī, Maḥmūd, 36, 323, 381
Shādhilī (Sufi order), 45

al-Shādhilī, Abūʾl-Ḥasan, 46, 149–50
al-Shāfiʿī, Muḥammad ibn Idrīs, 124, 335–36
shahāda, first
divine unity (*tawḥīd*) and, 35–38
efficacy of, 165
as invocation (*dhikr*), 43, 116, 119, 121
as litany (*wird*) of Tijani Sufism, 45, 50
meanings of, 129–30, 166, 338
stations of religion (*maqāmāt*) and, 132–33, 137
See also *fanāʾ*
shahāda, second, 35, 38–41
See also Muḥammad; Perfect Human
*sharīʿa* (path or way)
ability to follow only one, 178, 336
explanation of, 42, 179
litanies (*awrād*) and, 112
maintenance of, 142
practice and realization, unity of and, 368
in Tijani Sufism, 47, 50
See also *tarbiya*
Shaykh al-Akbar. *See* Ibn al-ʿArabī, Muḥyī al-Dīn
Shaykh Ibrahim. *See* Niasse, Ibrahim
shaykhs. *See shuyūkh*
al-Shīrāzī, Quṭb al-Dīn, 6
Shiva, 205, 416n30
shrines, 199, 202, 204–5, 273, 277, 297, 388
See also *orisa*
*shuhūd* (witnessing), 105, 185, 327
See also *kashf; mushāhada*
*shukr* (gratitude), 51, 367, 404n90
al-Shushtarī, Abūʾl-Ḥasan, 37
*shuyūkh* (Sufi masters)
and *maʿrifa*, acquisition of, 126, 185–86, 369, 388–89, 411n77
as midwives of knowledge, 384, 389
professions of, 378
qualified, importance of, 175
in Sufi orders, role of, 44–45
*tarbiya*, guidance through, 59–60, 113, 118–19, 140, 173–77
See also al-Tijānī, Aḥmad; babalawo; Niasse, Ibrahim
al-Ṣiddīq (Abū Bakr), 125, 144
*ṣidq* (sincerity)
annihilation (*fanāʾ*) and, 130
Greatest Name of God and, 148
in stations of religion (*maqāmāt*), 131, 134–35
Sufism as, 159
*tarbiya* and, 120, 160–61, 188–89
in worship, need for, 128–29, 176
signatures. *See* Odu
signifier and signified, 283–84, 434n54
See also language

*silsila* (initiatory lineages), 42, 44–45, 47–48, 52–53, 173–74, 174–76, 185–86
　See also *tarbiya*
similarity vs. difference, logics of, 324–27, 429n5
sincerity. See *ṣidq*
*al-Sirr al-Akbar* (Niasse), 54, 120–21, 139–40, 143, 148–49, 174–75
Skīraj, Aḥmad, 53, 169
Smith, J. Z., 324
sobriety (*al-ṣaḥū*), 80, 152
　See also *baqāʾ*
socialization, 254–55, 390
　See also academia; babalawo
Socrates, 11, 12, 200
soothsaying (*al-kihāna*), 345, 420n115
　See also divination, Ifa
Ṣopido, J. Olubi, 232
soul or spirit
　body, unity with, 385, 386–88
　conceptual thought and, 357
　divine effusion (*fayḍ*) and, 50
　Divine Intellect and, 96, 98
　expectation of enlightenment and deprivity of, 51, 367
　following Muḥammad and illumination of, 179
　gods created in belief and, 155
　good manners (*adab*) and subdual of, 43
　initiation rites and heightened subjectivity of, 354
　invocation (*dhikr*) and freedom from, 119
　knowledge of God and book of, 99
　*maʿrifa* and faults of, 90, 104
　purification of (*tazkiyat al-nafs*), 81–82, 117, 138–39
　*qibla* and training of, 161–62
　repentance (*tawba*) and slaying of, 133
　rituals as shaping, 355
　Sufism and study of, 32
　See also *bāṭin*; *ẹmí*; *orí* and *orí inú*
*Source of Proofs* (Sanūsī), 6
sources, 23–24
South Africa, 52, 54, 393
Sowande, Fela, 199
Ṣoyinka, Wọle, 16, 200, 203, 208, 219–21, 248–49
speculation. See conceptual or discursive thought
speech. See *ẹmí*; *fayḍ*; *nafas, anfās*; *ọrọ*
spells. See *ọfọ*
spirit. See soul or spirit
*Spirit of Good Manners* (Niasse), 90, 111
spiritual exercises. See *dhikr, adhkār*; *tarbiya*; *wird, awrād*
spoken word. See *ẹmí*; *fayḍ*; language; *nafas, anfās*; *ọrọ*
states (*aḥwāl*), 33, 82, 92, 115–16, 359, 385
　See also *baqāʾ*; *fanāʾ*; *ḥaḍarāt*; *sulūk*
station of no station, 19, 169, 363–64, 368, 369–70, 396

stations of religion (*maqāmāt*), 102, 131–38, 147, 163, 188, 363
　See also *ḥaḍarāt*
St. Augustine, 380, 435n83
Strauss, Leo, 349
stepping into the world (*ikọse aye*), 253–55, 268, 277, 329
　See also rituals (Ifa)
Stoller, Paul, 390
stone, paradox of, 58, 91
struggle (*ẹṣẹ*), 244–45, 371
　See also legs, *orí* and *orí inú*
subjectivity. See *ʿayn thābit*; humanity; *orí* and *orí inú*
subject/object relationship
　initiation rites and, 354–55
　knowledge of God and collapse of, 32, 68, 71–72, 111–12, 352, 362, 368, 384, 392
　*maʿrifa* and collapse of, 189, 191
　Muḥammadan reality and, 170
　self-knowledge and, 25, 34, 83, 188, 353, 384, 391–92
　See also *fanāʾ*
Submission (*Islām*), 131–34, 137, 343
subsistence. See *baqāʾ*
subtleties (*laṭāʾif*), 80, 82
　See also *maʿrifa*
Sudan, 52, 54
suffering (*iya*), 269–70, 424n50
Sufi centers (*zāwiyas*), 45–46, 52, 53, 54, 60, 390
Sufism. See *taṣawwuf*; Tijani Sufism
*Sufism, Mystics, and Saints in Modern Egypt* (Hoffman), 18
*Sufism and Taoism* (Izutsu), 18
al-Suhrawardī, Shihāb al-Dīn, 6
*sulūk* (wayfaring), 44, 69, 120–23, 160–61, 368, 409n35, 411n65
Sunna, 31–32, 72, 180, 368, 389
　See also Muḥammad, following; Qurʾan
supererogatory acts of worship. See worship
suprarationality, 33–34
　See also rationality; reason
*ṣūra* (outward form), 31
　See also *orí* and *orí inú*; *ẓāhir*
*suuru* (patience), 248, 255–57, 259, 269–70, 298
　See also *iwa pẹlẹ*
Sy, al-Ḥājj Malik, 53
Sylla, Yacouba, 53
symbolism. See language

Ṭabāṭabāʾī, Sayyid Muḥammad Ḥusayn, 6
taboos. See *eewọ*
*tafakkur* (reflection), 103–4
　See also *fikr*
*tajallī* (manifestations or self-disclosures of God)
　annihilation (*fanāʾ*) and, 122, 156
　bodies and all existence as, 75, 152, 177–78, 387

diversity of religions and, 21, 327, 347
and divine creation, process of, 359–60
embodiment, importance for, 385
evolving nature of, 364–65, 372
lightning as symbol of, 170
litanies (*awrād*) and, 176
*maʿrifa* and, 77, 80–81, 93, 189
Muḥammadan reality and, 141, 144, 147–48, 171, 347
Muḥammad as most perfect, 147–48, 152–54, 167
Ọrunmila as, of Muḥammadan reality, 347
perfect knowers and, 142, 349, 363, 394
prayer on the Prophet (*Ṣalāt al-Fātiḥ*) and, 166–68
preparedness (*istiʿdād*) and, 360–61
presences (*ḥaḍarāt*) and, 139, 142–44
as specific to each human, 74–77, 85, 102–3, 153–55
veils of ignorance as, 368
See also *fayḍ*
Tal, al-Ḥājj ʿUmar, 51–53, 340–41
Tal, Seydou Nourou, 53
*talqīn* (implantation or initiation), 50, 119, 174–76, 354–55
See also *jijẹun Ifa*; *tarbiya*
Tamāsīnī, ʿAlī, 53
*taqwā* (mindfulness), 69, 124–26, 129, 133–34
See also *tarbiya*
tarbiya
accessibility of, 61, 107, 160, 375
activities to avoid during, 119–20
annihilation (*fanāʾ*) in process of, 109–11, 114–15, 120, 126–29, 145–52, 174–76, 394
completion of, as beginning, not end, 64, 184, 354, 394
as consolidation of faith, 108, 111–12
definitions of, 56, 158, 188–89, 394, 404n87
divine effusion (*fayḍ*) and, 93, 95, 160–61, 188, 354
and doctrine, verification and transcendence of, 355
embodiment and, 385–86
experiential nature of, 60–61, 62–64, 112–13, 146, 176
focus (*tawajjuh*) and love (*maḥabba*) and, 117–18, 135, 159–62
following Muḥammad in, 117, 177–81
guidance and transmission, need for, 59–60, 112, 113, 118–19, 140, 173–77, 185–86
Ifa initiation (*igbodu*) compared to, 25, 353–55, 361
invocation (*dhikr*) and, 118–19, 121, 129–30, 162–64, 166–73, 182
knowing like Muḥammad after, 371
litanies (*awrād*) and, 50, 112–14, 119, 121, 176
mindfulness (*taqwa*) and, 124–26, 129
opening (*fatḥ*) and, 140, 141, 175, 361
presences (*ḥaḍarāt*) and, 58–60, 119, 139–45, 147
purpose of, 114, 117, 189
qualifications and knowledge needed for, 113–14, 115–17

rapture (*jadhb*) and wayfaring (*sulūk*) and, 120–23
real thinking as beginning after, 113, 356–57
science of letters (*ʿilm al-ḥurūf*) and language and, 164–66
secret nature of, 55
stations of religion (*maqāmāt*) and, 131–38
success and influence of, widespread, 51, 54, 64
time commitment of, 59, 114, 120, 160, 374
as transformation of consciousness, 56, 60–61, 84, 87, 91, 115, 157–58, 160, 189, 394
uniformity of, from perspective of Ifa, 336
unity of all religions and, 348
See also self-knowledge
*ṭarīqa* (path or way to God), 42–44, 112, 122–23, 175–76, 179, 368, 378
See also *tarbiya*
*ṭarīqas* or *ṭuruq* (Sufi orders), 44–47, 51–52, 54
See also Tijani Sufism
*taṣawwuf* (Sufism)
definitions and subject matter of, 6, 31–34, 159
divine unity (*tawḥīd*) and, 35
doctrines of, 34–42, 48
embodiment and, 385
Ifa and, 326–31
intellect (*ʿaql*) in, 15
knowledge, approaches to, 351, 380–82
*maʿrifa* in early and classical, 33, 65–68
Muḥammadan reality in, 347
orders of, 44–46
philosophy (*falsafa*) compared to, 33–34, 62, 407n81
primacy of, Niasse on, 105
and prophets, atemporal existence of, 202
and resemblance, symbolic logic of, 324–27, 429n5
sainthood in, 203
and surahs, attributes or personalities of, 334
techniques and practices of, 42–44
theology (*kalām*) and philosophy (*falsafa*) and, 6
and time, nature of, 111, 157
Western academia, challenge to, 382–84
Western philosophy compared to, 62, 189–92
See also *maʿrifa*; Tijani Sufism
"Task of the Translator" (Benjamin), 15
tasting. See *dhawq*; *jijẹun Ifa*
*tawajjuh* (focus), 159–62
See also *ṣidq*
*tawba* (repentance), 131, 133, 137, 138, 188
*tawḥīd* (unity or oneness)
doctrine of, 35–38, 433n34
invocation (*dhikr*) and, 127, 129–30
*maʿrifa* and recognition of, 62, 90, 128, 147, 157–58, 189, 394
Muḥammad and mediation of, 40–41, 168
Muḥammadan reality and, 143–44, 348, 410n52

Index • 467

*tawḥīd* (unity or oneness) (*continued*)
    Ọrunmila and, 345
    presences (*ḥaḍarāt*) and, 37, 59, 347–48, 350
    stations of religion (*maqāmāt*) and, 133
    *tarbiya* and recognition of, 159
    Ultimate Reality and, 19
*tazkiyat al-nafs* (purification of the soul), 81–82, 117, 138–39
    See also *ma'rifa*, acquisition of
technology, 374, 376, 389
temperament, balancing of, 115–17
    See also *adab; iwa pẹlẹ*
testimonies of faith (*shahādatayn*). See shahāda, first; shahāda, second
Thatcher, Margaret, 393
theoanthropocosmic perspectives, 40, 370
    See also Perfect Human
theology
    Divine Attributes in Islamic, 127, 146
    *ma'rifa* and, 66, 68, 91
    philosophy and Sufism, convergence with, 6, 352
    philosophy's separation from, 7–8, 16
    Yoruba, 197
    See also religions, Yoruba
theomorphism, 39, 388, 436n107
    See also oriṣa; Perfect Human
theory vs. *theoria*, 380–84, 435n82, 435n86
    See also reason
"There is no god but God." See *tawḥīd*
thought (*khāṭir*), 104, 144, 357
    See also conceptual or discursive thought; *ero* and *ironu; fikr, fikra*
*Three Stations of Religion* (Niasse), 102, 131–38, 139, 145, 147, 188
al-Tijānī, Aḥmad
    annihilation (*fanā'*) in, 130, 146, 147, 150, 174–75
    on divine secrets, revealing of as forbidden, 101
    on divine unity (*tawḥīd*), 36, 127
    on esoteric sciences as evil, 373
    on following Muḥammad, 179–80
    on his words, efficacy of, 42
    on humans and reflection of Divinity, 39
    on ignorance as perfection of *ma'rifa*, 187–88
    on initiation, rules of, 48
    on intellect (*'aql*), levels of, 96–98
    life and Sufi order of, 46, 52
    on litanies (*awrād*), his role in efficacy of, 173
    as manifestation (*tajallī*) of Divine Essence, 142–45, 147, 148, 152
    on *ma'rifa*, 79–83, 83, 91
    on Muḥammadan reality, 40
    in parable of *fayḍ*, 49
    Pearl of Perfection (*Jawharat al-Kamāl*) and, 169
    as reincarnation of oriṣa, 333–34
    as renewer, reversing decline of history, 374
    on repentance (*tawba*), his state of, 137
    sainthood of, 42, 151
    on soul's loss of original knowledge, 384
    on spiritual training, requirements for, 115–17
    on *theoria* vs. theory, 381
Tijani Sufism
    as challenge to Western academia, 22, 25–27, 326, 328, 378–80, 396
    babalawo on, 331–33
    contemporary period, conceptions of, 374–76
    definitions of, 31
    divine word and realization in, 370–72
    doctrines of, 47–50
    embodiment and, 384–89
    goal of no goal in, 362–67, 433n35
    history of, 46–47, 51–53
    Ifa, reasons to compare with, 326
    Ifa, Tijani Sufis on, 337–44
    Ifa from perspective of, 344–50
    influence of, 3–4, 31, 379, 393, 435n79
    methods of, 50–51
    Ogunnaike's study of, 54–55
    from perspective of Ifa, 333–36
    and practice and realization, unity of, 367–68
    reincarnation and, 434n78
    sacrifices and, 336, 345, 430n32
    as theoretical perspective, 25, 326–27, 350, 380–84
    Western traditions and, 189–92, 375–76
    See also Ifa and Tijani Sufism, compared; *tarbiya; taṣawwuf*
Tijāniyya-Ibrāhīmiyya. See Tijani Sufism
time
    Abrahamic prophets and, 202
    as descent from perfection of creation, 374, 384
    heaven (*ọrun*) and world (*aye*) and meaning of, 227
    history of concept, 419n88
    invocation (*dhikr*) and, 163
    physical body as aspect of being that emerges in, 387
    and predictions of Ifa, verification of, 309–10
    self-knowledge as mode of being in, 362
    Sufism and nature of, 110, 157
    in Yoruba cosmology, 203, 210, 219–23, 224, 374
al-Tirmidhī, Ḥakīm, 41
Tosh, Peter, 159
"Transcendent Philosophy" (Mullā Ṣadrā), 6
transformation. See *fanā'; igbodu;* Muḥammad, following; Ọrunmila, emulation of; *tarbiya*
translation, 14–16, 18, 22
    See also language
transmission, chains of. See *silsila*
*Treatise of Oneness* (Balyānī), 37–38

tree of forgetfulness (*igi igbagbe*), 213, 253, 268, 318, 358, 362, 384
   *See also* history, decline of
trickster. *See* Eṣu
truth. *See* ma'rifa; otitọ; unity
al-ṭuma'nīna (serenity), 131, 135–36, 138
al-Ṭūsī, Naṣīr al-Dīn, 6

'ubūdiyya (servanthood), 387
   *See also* 'ārif and 'ārif biLlāh; Muḥammad
'ulūm (sciences), 80, 82, 115, 373
   *See also* ḥikma
'Umar ibn al-Khaṭṭāb, 125, 131, 154
'Umar Tal, al-Ḥājj, 51–53, 340–41
*Umm al-Barāhīn* (Sanūsī), 6
unborn, realm of. *See* ọrun
uncertainty. *See* yaqīn
*Uncovering of the Veiled* (al-Hujwīrī), 66
understanding (*oye*), 233, 234–37, 306–7, 319
   *See also* ọrọ
unemployment, 375
UNESCO, 11
Unicity (*al-Aḥadiyya*), 141, 143, 145, 410n41
   *See also* haqīqa al-Muḥammadiyya
unity
   of all divinity, in Yoruba religion, 207
   of body and spirit, 385, 386–88
   of diverse religions, 20–21, 76, 155, 331, 341–42, 345–46, 347
   divination and, 218, 306
   doctrine of, 35–38, 433n34
   invocation (*dhikr*) and, 117, 129–30
   ma'rifa as recognition of multiplicity and, 62, 90, 128, 147, 157–58, 189, 394
   Muḥammad and mediation of divine, 40–41, 168
   Muḥammadan reality and, 143–44, 348, 410n52
   Ọrunmila and, 345
   presences (*ḥaḍarāt*) and, 37, 59, 347–48, 350
   of realization and practice, 368
   stations of religion (*maqāmāt*) and, 133
   tarbiya and recognition of multiplicity and, 159
   Ultimate Reality and, 19
   *See also* Perfect Human
Unity (*al-Waḥidiyya*), 141, 143, 410n41
   *See also* haqīqa al-Muḥammadiyya; tawḥīd
Universal Human. *See* Perfect Human
*Universal Human* (al-Jīlī), 34
unlettered traditions, 12–13
   *See also* Odu
unveiling. *See* kashf
Uways al-Qaranī, 154

validity, 332

   *See also* Ifa and Tijani Sufism, compared; perspectivism
Vauvenargues (Luc de Clapiers), 384
Verger, Pierre, 283–84
verification. *See* imọ ijinlẹ, verification of; ma'rifa, verification of
virtue, 43, 384, 389–90
   *See also* adab; iwa pẹlẹ
Vishnu, 205, 416n30
visions, 33, 89–90, 139, 169, 334, 336, 354
   *See also* divination, Ifa; ma'rifa

Wach, Joachim, 215
*waḥdat al-wujūd* (Oneness of Being). *See* tawḥīd
al-Waḥidiyya (Unity), 141, 143, 410n41
   *See also* haqīqa al-Muḥammadiyya; tawḥīd
walāya (power of sainthood), 41–42, 176, 354
   *See also* fayḍ; sanctity or sacredness
*Walking Qur'an* (Ware), 385
Ware, Rudolph, 385
wārid (inspiration), 81, 82
wasīla (means of access), 112, 125–26, 140, 180, 357
Wāsiṭī, Abu Bakr, 381
water, metaphors and symbolism of
   annihilation (*fanā'*) and, 181
   ma'rifa and, 68, 73–76, 85, 182
   occultation in unseen realm and, 227
   in parable of *fayḍ*, 49–50
   in Pearl of Perfection (*Jawharat al-Kamāl*), 169–70, 171
   tarbiya and, 108–9, 156
   time in Yoruba cosmos and, 221
   transcendence of belief and, 363
way, Sufi. *See* sharī'a; tarbiya; ṭarīqa
wayfaring (*sulūk*), 44, 69, 120–23, 160–61, 368, 409n35, 411n65
ways of knowing, definition, 3
   *See also* Ifa; Tijani Sufism
ways of life. *See* adab; iwa pẹlẹ; Muḥammad, following; Ọrunmila, emulation of; philosophy, Greco-Roman
wazīfa (Tijani daily office), 50, 119, 165, 413n22
   *See also* wird, awrād
web of relationships
   in acquisition of knowledge, 296–97, 301, 354–55, 390
   divine beings and humanity in, 203–6, 209, 370–72, 391–92
   heaven (ọrun) and world (aye) in, 226–27
   *See also* barzakh; ori and ori inu; oriṣa; silsila
Wenger, Susanne
   on "to believe" in Yoruba worldview, 249
   on destiny (*ori*), 244, 360, 361
   on dynamic repose, 297–98, 319

Wenger, Susanne (*continued*)
   life and spiritual practice of, 11–12
   on Olodumare and oriṣa, 198
   on *oloriṣa*'s acceptance of varied traditions, 332–33
   on oriṣa, worship of, 286
   on Ọṣun, 198
   on thought as creation, 355
Western traditions. *See* academia; philosophy, Western
"What Occurred Between Me and My Secret from my Lord" (Niasse), 172–73, 185–86
Whirling Dervishes, 33, 45
wife (*iyawo*), 269–70
*wilāya*. *See* sanctity or sacredness; *walāya*
Willett, Frank, 298
Williamson, Timothy, 191
*wird, awrād* (litanies)
   divine effusion (*fayḍ*), conveyance of, 173–74
   effect of reciting, 159–60
   explanation of, 45
   science of letters (*'ilm al-ḥurūf*) and efficacy of, 164–66, 354–55
   *tarbiya* and, 112–14, 119, 121, 176
   in Tijani method, 46, 50
   See also *dhikr, adhkār*
wisdom. *See imọ ijinlẹ; ma'rifa; ọgbọn*
*Witchcraft, Oracles, and Magic Among the Azande* (Evans-Pritchard), 391
witnessing (*shuhūd*), 105, 185, 327
   See also *kashf; mushāhada*
witnessing or bearing witness, 162
wives of babalawo (*apẹtẹbi*), 260, 264, 275
   See also babalawo
women in Ifa. *See* iyanifa
*Women in the Yoruba Religious Sphere* (Olajubu), 273–74
world. *See aye*
worldview, Yoruba, 208, 210, 221, 248–49, 296–97, 426n85
   See also cosmos and cosmology, Yoruba
worship
   communal, in Ifa (*itadoogun*), 263–64
   disinterested gratitude (*shukr*) in, 51, 367, 404n90
   immutable entities (*'ayān al-thābita*) and, 360

   knowledge as precondition of, 113
   of oriṣa and transcendence of human limits, 237, 286, 297–300, 319
   as part of human nature, 118
   pragmatic reasons for, 312–13
   reflection (*tafakkur*) and, 103–4
   sincere, 128, 130
   supererogatory acts of, 42–44, 68, 120, 180, 357, 367
Wright, Zachary, 79

Yacob, Zera, 2, 12
al-Yadālī, Muḥammad, 163–64
*yaqīn* (certainty)
   annihilation (*fanā'*), dependence on, 81–82
   invocation (*dhikr*) in path to, 182
   levels of, 34, 85, 99
   *ma'rifa* as essence of, 55, 84
   serenity (*al-ṭuma'nīna*) and, 135–36
   Sufism as search for, 33
   in verification of knowledge, 185
   See also *fanā'*
Yemọja, 198, 201
   See also oriṣa
Yorubaland, 226–27, 227–29, 252, 328, 337, 420n110
   See also cosmos and cosmology, Yoruba

*ẓāhir* (outer reality)
   Divine Name as interior of, 147
   dominance of, in contemporary time, 376
   inner reality (*bāṭin*) and, 113, 114, 161, 353
   levels of reality and, 370
   as projection of spiritual reality, 171
   See also *ode*; reality
Zarrūq, Aḥmad, 47, 100, 118, 159, 165
*zāwiyas* (Sufi centers or mosques), 45–46, 52, 53, 54, 60, 390
zeal (*himma*), 160–61, 165–66, 174, 179
   See also *ṣidq*
Zeus, 200
   See also Olodumare
*zuhd* (asceticism), 47, 51, 116, 404n90
   See also *iwọn*

Printed in the USA
CPSIA information can be obtained
at www.ICGtesting.com
CBHW060357080824
12641CB00004B/11

9 780271 086910